CORE STATUTES ON FAMILY LAW

The palgrave core statutes series:

Core EU Legislation	Rhona Smith
Core Statutes on Commercial & Consumer Law	Graham Stephenson
Core Statutes on Company Law	Cowan Ervine
Core Statutes on Contract, Tort & Restitution	Graham Stephenson
Core Statutes on Criminal Justice & Sentencing	Martin Wasik
Core Statutes on Criminal Law	Kate Cook, Mark James & Richard Lee
Core Statutes on Employment Law	Dominique Lauterburg
Core Statutes on Evidence	Christina McAlhone
Core Statutes on Family Law	Frances Burton
Core Statutes on Intellectual Property	Margaret Dowie-Whybrow
Core Statutes on Property Law	Peter Luther & Alan Moran
Core Statutes on Public Law & Civil Liberties	Rhona Smith, Eimear Spain & Richard Glancey
Core Documents on International Law	Karen Hulme
Core Documents on European/International Human Rights	Rhona Smith

CORE STATUTES ON FAMILY LAW

Frances Burton

macmillan education palgrave

First published 2015 by
PALGRAVE

Palgrave in the UK is an imprint of Macmillan Publishers Limited, registered in England, company number 785998, of 4 Crinan Street, London N1 9XW.

Palgrave Macmillan in the US is a division of St Martin's Press LLC, 175 Fifth Avenue, New York, NY 10010.

Palgrave is a global imprint of the above companies and is represented throughout the world.

Palgrave® and Macmillan® are registered trademarks in the United States, the United Kingdom, Europe and other countries.

ISBN 978–1–137–54509-1 paperback

This book is printed on paper suitable for recycling and made from fully managed and sustained forest sources. Logging, pulping and manufacturing processes are expected to conform to the environmental regulations of the country of origin.

A catalogue record for this book is available from the British Library.

Printed and bound by CPI Group UK Ltd, Croydon, CR0 4YY

PREFACE

The core materials provided in this collection aim to cover the primary sources most likely to be required for undergraduate study of family law in each of the law schools whose courses were included in the survey for my UKCLE jointly-authored manual on *Teaching Family Law* in 1999; they also take account of subsequent annual feedback from users, including newer institutions and changes to courses in the last 15 years. The collection has been updated to include materials on topics which have since jostled for space in an already bulging syllabus, whether in respect of child law, the study of adult relationships or some mix of these subject areas, and in particular in relation to the creation of the new Family Court and the introduction of the CMS.

However, family law was already so oversized, with so many 'kissing cousins' in peripheral subject areas, that inevitably some students and tutors may still find items missing which ideally they would have liked included. For these (and the full text of all statutes and statutory instruments) there is always The National Archives (which provides full text in various formats at www.legislation.gov.uk) or the electronic databases to which university libraries usually provide ample access. Unfortunately, it is just not possible to include 'everything' in a 'core' statutes collection, sold at a student friendly price.

For example, only some of the detailed amendments to s 25 of the Matrimonial Causes Act 1973 in relation to pension compensation have been included, but the full text (and text of associated regulations) can be obtained from The National Archives where required for any course. The same applies to provisions of other statutes which are likely to be too detailed for general undergraduate use, such as in the Human Fertilisation and Embryology Acts, the Child Support Acts (and their voluminous regulations, especially in relation to the appeal structures to the First Tier and Upper Tribunals and on process and enforcement), the Pensions Act 2008 and the detailed provisions of registration of buildings for same sex marriages in the Marriage Act 1949. The text of the Welfare Reform Acts 2009 and 2012, as amended, and similar statutes are not included in this collection as few courses include extensive provision on benefits; their impact on other statutes included is reflected in amendments to those statutes.

Amendments made by the Crime and Courts Act 2013 have been included as far as possible. But this is a huge statute, creating the new unified Family Court from April 2014 and fundamentally changing how family justice is delivered, with as much significance as the far-reaching LASPO 2012, and the same goes for some more detailed provisions of the Children and Families Act 2014 and the impact on the Marriage Act 1949 and the Marriage (Registrar General's Licence) Act 1970 of the Marriage (Same Sex Couples) Act 2013. The result is such an impact on previous established (and familiar) legislation that, for any in-depth academic study of the complete reforms, readers will need to obtain the full texts from The National Archives, especially when as yet unmade further amendments are made to the Family Procedure Rules 2010.

By special request of readers, the latest edition of the IFLA Family Law Arbitration Scheme Rules is included (for which also see www.familyarbitrator.com, where the full text of the Arbitration Act 1996 is also included, in versions with and without commentary and where further amendments always appear promptly). Unfortunately, space precludes adding within the collection even the few sections of the Arbitration Act which are referenced in the Rules of the IFLA Scheme. However, there is a certain benefit in not doing so, since users will find the additional materials available with the www.familyarbitrator.com text of some assistance in early study of this innovative ADR method, which (like much modernisation of family justice) is as yet not entirely familiar to many family lawyers.

Any particular requests to be considered for inclusion in the 2016/17 edition should be sent to me at frb@frburton.com or to the publishers. If I receive such requests early in 2016, there is a better chance of making space available while maintaining a convenient length of the collection, especially as the continued modernisation of family justice in the Family Court, now still under way, is likely to lead to a good deal of amendments before the changes are fully realised by 2016.

I have endeavoured to edit the materials to reflect the law as at 1 June 2015.

Frances Burton
International Centre for Family Law, Policy and Practice
www.famlawandpractice.com
and Buckinghamshire New University

CONTENTS

ALPHABETICAL LIST OF CONTENTS

WILLS ACT 1837
(7 Will. 4 & 1 Vict., c. 26)

18. Wills to be revoked by marriage, except in certain cases

(1) Subject to subsections (2) to (4) below, a will shall be revoked by the testator's marriage.

(2) A disposition in a will in exercise of a power of appointment shall take effect notwithstanding the testator's subsequent marriage unless the property so appointed would in default of appointment pass to his personal representatives.

(3) Where it appears from a will that at the time it was made the testator was expecting to be married to a particular person and that he intended that the will should not be revoked by the marriage, the will shall not be revoked by his marriage to that person.

(4) Where it appears from a will that at the time it was made the testator was expecting to be married to a particular person and that he intended that a disposition in the will should not be revoked by his marriage to that person,—

(a) that disposition shall take effect notwithstanding the marriage; and

(b) any other disposition in the will shall take effect also, unless it appears from the will that the testator intended the disposition to be revoked by the marriage.

18A. Effect of dissolution or annulment of marriage on wills

(1) Where, after a testator has made a will, a decree of a court of civil jurisdiction in England and Wales dissolves or annuls his marriage or his marriage is dissolved or annulled and the divorce or annulment is entitled to recognition in England and Wales by virtue of Part II of the Family Law Act 1986,—

(a) provisions of the will appointing executors or trustees or conferring a power of appointment, if they appoint or confer the power on the former spouse, shall take effect as if the former spouse had died on the date on which the marriage is dissolved or annulled, and

(b) any property which, or an interest in which, is devised or bequeathed to the former spouse shall pass as if the former spouse had died on that date,

except in so far as a contrary intention appears by the will.

(2) Subsection (1)(b) above is without prejudice to any right of the former spouse to apply for financial provision under the Inheritance (Provision for Family and Dependants) Act 1975.

18B. Will to be revoked by civil partnership

(1) Subject to subsections (2) to (6), a will is revoked by the formation of a civil partnership between the testator and another person.

(2) A disposition in a will in exercise of a power of appointment takes effect despite the formation of a subsequent civil partnership between the testator and another person unless the property so appointed would in default of appointment pass to the testator's personal representatives.

(3) If it appears from a will—

(a) that at the time it was made the testator was expecting to form a civil partnership with a particular person, and

(b) that he intended that the will should not be revoked by the formation of the civil partnership,

the will is not revoked by its formation.

(4) Subsections (5) and (6) apply if it appears from a will—

(a) that at the time it was made the testator was expecting to form a civil partnership with a particular person, and

(b) that he intended that a disposition in the will should not be revoked by the formation of the civil partnership.

(5) The disposition takes effect despite the formation of the civil partnership.

(6) Any other disposition in the will also takes effect, unless it appears from the will that the testator intended the disposition to be revoked by the formation of the civil partnership.

18C. Effect of dissolution or annulment of civil partnership on wills

(1) This section applies if, after a testator has made a will—

(a) a court of civil jurisdiction in England and Wales dissolves his civil partnership or makes a nullity order in respect of it, or

(b) his civil partnership is dissolved or annulled and the dissolution or annulment is entitled to recognition in England and Wales by virtue of Chapter 3 of Part 5 of the Civil Partnership Act 2004.

(2) Except in so far as a contrary intention appears by the will—
  (a) provisions of the will appointing executors or trustees or conferring a power of appointment, if they appoint or confer the power on the former civil partner, take effect as if the former civil partner had died on the date on which the civil partnership is dissolved or annulled, and
  (b) any property which, or an interest in which, is devised or bequeathed to the former civil partner shall pass as if the former civil partner had died on that date.

(3) Section (2)(b) does not affect any right of the former civil partner to apply for financial provision under the Inheritance (Provision for Family and Dependants) Act 1975.

MARRIED WOMEN'S PROPERTY ACT 1882
(45 & 46 Vict., c. 75)

11. Moneys payable under policy of assurance not to form part of estate of the insured

A married woman may effect a policy upon her own life or the life of her husband for her own benefit; and the same and all benefit thereof shall enure accordingly.

A policy of assurance effected by any man on his own life, and expressed to be for the benefit of his wife, or of his children, or of his wife and children, or any of them, or by any woman on her own life, and expressed to be for the benefit of her husband, or of her children, or of her husband and children, or any of them, shall create a trust in favour of the objects therein named, and the moneys payable under any such policy shall not, so long as any object of the trust remains unperformed, form part of the estate of the insured, or be subject to his or her debts: Provided, that if it shall be proved that the policy was effected and the premiums paid with intent to defraud the creditors of the insured, they shall be entitled to receive, out of the moneys payable under the policy, a sum equal to the premiums so paid. …

17. Questions between husband and wife as to property to be decided in a summary way

In any question between husband and wife as to the title to or possession of property, either party may apply by summons or otherwise in a summary way to the High Court or the family court and the court may, on such an application (which may be heard in private), make such order with respect to the property as it thinks fit.

In this section 'prescribed' means prescribed by rules of court.

LAW OF PROPERTY ACT 1925
(15 & 16 Geo. 5, c. 20)

37. Rights of husband and wife

A husband and wife shall, for all purposes of acquisition of any interest in property, under a disposition made or coming into operation after the commencement of this Act, be treated as two persons.

53. Instruments required to be in writing

(1) Subject to the provision hereinafter contained with respect to the creation of interests in land by parol—
  (a) no interest in land can be created or disposed of except by writing signed by the person creating or conveying the same, or by his agent thereunto lawfully authorised in writing, or by will, or by operation of law;
  (b) a declaration of trust respecting any land or any interest therein must be manifested and proved by some writing signed by some person who is able to declare such trust or by his will;
  (c) a disposition of an equitable interest or trust subsisting at the time of the disposition, must be in writing signed by the person disposing of the same, or by his agent thereunto lawfully authorised in writing or by will.

(2) This section does not affect the creation or operation of resulting, implied or constructive trusts.

MARRIAGE ACT 1949
(12 & 13 Geo. 6, c. 76)

PART I
RESTRICTIONS ON MARRIAGE

1. Marriages within prohibited degrees

(1) A marriage solemnized between a person and any person mentioned in the list in Part 2 of Schedule 1 shall be void.

(2) Subject to subsection (3) of this section, a marriage solemnized between a person and any person mentioned in the list in Part 2 of Schedule 1 shall be void.

(3) Any such marriage as is mentioned in subsection (2) of this section shall not be void by reason only of affinity if both the parties to the marriage have attained the age of twenty-one at the time of the marriage and the younger party has not at any time before attaining the age of eighteen been a child of the family in relation to the other party.

(4)–(8) ...

2. Marriages of persons under sixteen

A marriage solemnized between persons either of whom is under the age of sixteen shall be void.

3. Marriages of persons under eighteen

(1) Where the marriage of a child, not being a widower or widow, is intended to be solemnized on the authority of certificates issued by a superintendent registrar under Part III of this Act, the consent of the appropriate persons shall be required.

Provided that—

(a) if the superintendent registrar is satisfied that the consent of any person whose consent is so required cannot be obtained by reason of absence or inaccessibility or by reason of his being under any disability, the necessity for the consent of that person shall be dispensed with, if there is any other person whose consent is also required; and if the consent of no other person is required, the Registrar General may dispense with the necessity of obtaining any consent, or the court may, on application being made, consent to the marriage, and the consent of the court so given shall have the same effect as if it had been given by the person whose consent cannot be so obtained;

(b) if any person whose consent is required refuses his consent, the court may, on application being made, consent to the marriage, and the consent of the court so given shall have the same effect as if it had been given by the person whose consent is refused.

(1A) The appropriate persons are—

(a) if none of paragraphs (b) to (h) apply, each of the following—
  (i) any parent of the child who has parental responsibility for him; and
  (ii) any guardian of the child;

(b) where a special guardianship is in force with respect to the child, each of the child's special guardians, unless any of paragraphs (c) to (g) applies;

(c) where a care order has effect with respect to the child, the local authority designated in the order, and each parent, guardian or special guardian (in so far as their parental responsibility has not been restricted under section 33(3) of the Children Act 1989), unless paragraph (e) applies;

(d) where a child arrangements order to which subsection (1C) applies has effect with respect to the child, the persons with whom the child lives, or is to live, as a result of the order, unless paragraph (e) applies;

(e) where an adoption agency is authorised to place a child for adoption under section 19 of the Adoption and Children Act 2002, that agency, or, where a care order has effect with respect to the child, the local authority designated in the order;

(f) where a placement order is in force with respect to a child, the appropriate local authority;

(g) where a child has been placed for adoption with prospective adopters, the prospective adopters (in so far as their parental responsibility has not been restricted under section 25(4) of the Adoption and Children Act 2002), in addition to the persons specified in paragraph (e) or (f);

(h) where none of paragraphs (b) to (g) apply but a child arrangements order to which subsection (1C) applies was in force with respect to the child immediately before he reached the age of sixteen, the persons with whom he lived, or was to live, as a result of the order.

(1B) In this section—
'guardian of the child', 'parental responsibility', 'child arrangements order', 'special guardian', 'special guardianship order' and 'care order' have the same meaning as in the Children Act 1989;
'adoption agency', 'placed for adoption, 'placements order' and 'local authority' have the same meaning as in the Adoption and Children Act 2002;
'appropriate local authority' means the local authority authorised by the placement order to place the child for adoption.

(1C) A child arrangements order is one to which this subsection applies if the order regulates arrangements that consist of, or include, arrangements which relate to either or both of the following—
(a) with whom the child is to live, and
(b) when the child is to live with any person.

(2) Subsection (1) shall apply to marriages intended to be solemnized on the authority of a common licence, with the substitution of references to the ecclesiastical authority by whom the licence was granted for references to the superintendent registrar, and with the substitution of a reference to the Master of the Faculties for the reference to the Registrar General.

(3) Where the marriage of a child not being a widower or widow, is intended to be solemnized after the publication of banns of matrimony then, if any person whose consent to the marriage would have been required under this section in the case of a marriage intended to be solemnized otherwise than after the publication of the banns, openly and publicly declares or causes to be declared, in the church or chapel in which the banns are published, at the time of the publication, his dissent from the intended marriage, the publication of banns shall be void.

(4) A clergyman shall not be liable to ecclesiastical censure for solemnizing the marriage of a child after the publication of banns without the consent of the parents or guardians of the child unless he had notice of the dissent of any person who is entitled to give notice of dissent under the last foregoing subsection.

(5) For the purposes of this section, 'the court' means the High Court or the family court, and rules of court may be made for enabling applications under this section—
(a) if made to the High Court, to be heard in chambers;
(b) ...
(c) if made to the family court, to be heard and determined otherwise than in open court,
and shall provide that, where an application is made in consequence of a refusal to give consent, notice of the application shall be served on the person who has refused consent.

(6) Nothing in this section shall dispense with the necessity of obtaining the consent of the High Court to the marriage of a ward of court.

PART II
MARRIAGE ACCORDING TO RITES OF THE CHURCH OF ENGLAND

Preliminary

5. Methods of authorising marriages

A marriage according to the rites of the Church of England may be solemnized—
(a) after the publication of banns of matrimony;
(b) on the authority of a special licence of marriage granted by the Archbishop of Canterbury or any other person by virtue of the Ecclesiastical Licences Act 1533 (in this Act referred to as a 'special licence');
(c) on the authority of a licence of marriage (other than a special licence) granted by an ecclesiastical authority having power to grant such a licence (in this Act referred to as a 'common licence'); or
(d) on the authority of certificates issued by a superintendent registrar under Part III of this Act,
except that paragraph (a) of this section shall not apply in relation to the solemnization of any marriage mentioned in subsection (2) of section 1 of this Act.

5A. Marriages between certain persons related by affinity

No clergyman shall be obliged—
(a) to solemnize a marriage which, apart from the Marriage (Prohibited Degrees of Relationship) Act 1986, or the Marriage Act 1949 (Remediel Order) 2007, would have been void by reason of the relationship of the persons to be married; or
(b) to permit such a marriage to be solemnized in the church or chapel of which he is the minister.

5B. Marriages involving person of acquired gender

(1) A clergyman is not obliged to solemnize the marriage of a person if the clergyman reasonably believes that the person's gender has become the acquired gender under the Gender Recognition Act 2004.

(2) A clerk in Holy Orders of the Church of Wales is not obliged to permit the marriage of a person to be solemnized in the church or chapel of which the clerk is minister if the clerk reasonably believes that the person's gender has become the acquired gender under that Act.

Marriage by banns

6. Place of publication of banns

(1) Subject to the provisions of this Act, where a marriage is intended to be solemnized after the publication of banns of matrimony, the banns shall be published—

(a) if the persons to be married reside in the same parish, in the parish church of that parish;

(b) if the persons to be married do not reside in the same parish, in the parish church of each parish in which one of them resides:

Provided that if either of the persons to be married resides in a chapelry or in a district specified in a licence granted under section twenty of this Act, the banns may be published in an authorised chapel of that chapelry or district instead of in the parish church of the parish in which that person resides.

...

(4) Banns of matrimony may be published in any parish church or authorised chapel which is the usual place of worship of the persons to be married or of one of them although neither of those persons resides in the parish or chapelry to which the church or chapel belongs;

Provided that the publication of the banns by virtue of this subsection shall be in addition to and not in substitution for the publication of banns required by subsection (1) of this section.

8. Notice to clergyman before publication of banns

No clergyman shall be obliged to publish banns of matrimony unless the persons to be married, at least seven days before the date on which they wish the banns to be published for the first time, deliver or cause to be delivered to him a notice in writing, dated on the day on which it is so delivered, stating the christian name and surname and the place of residence of each of them, and the period during which each of them has resided at his or her place of residence.

10. Publication of banns commenced in one church and completed in another

(1) Where the publication of banns of matrimony has been duly commenced in any church, the publication may be completed in the same church or in any other church which, by virtue of the Union of Benefices Measure 1923 or the New Parishes Measure 1943, has at the time of the completion taken the place of the first-mentioned church for the purpose of publication of banns of matrimony either generally or in relation to the parties to the intended marriage.

...

11. Certificates of publication of banns

(1) Where a marriage is intended to be solemnized after the publication of banns of matrimony and the persons to be married do not reside in the same parish or other ecclesiastical district, a clergyman shall not solemnize the marriage in the parish or district in which one of those persons resides unless there is produced to him a certificate that the banns have been published in accordance with the provisions of this Part of this Act in the parish or other ecclesiastical district in which the other person resides.

(2) Where a marriage is intended to be solemnized in a church or chapel of a parish or other ecclesiatical district in which neither of the persons to be married resides, after the publication of banns therein by virtue of subsection (4) of section six of this Act, a clergyman shall not solemnize the marriage unless there is produced to him—

(a) if the persons to be married reside in the same parish or other ecclesiastical district, a certificate that the banns have been published in accordance with the provisions of this Part of this Act in that parish or district; or

(b) if the persons to be married do not reside in the same parish or other ecclesiastical district, certificates that the banns have been published as aforesaid in each parish or district in which one of them resides.

...
(4) Any certificate required under this section shall be signed by the incumbent or minister in charge of the building in which the banns were published or by a clergyman nominated in that behalf by the bishop of the diocese.

12. Solemnization of marriage after publication of banns

(1) Subject to the provisions of this Part of this Act, where banns of matrimony have been published, the marriage shall be solemnized in the church or chapel or, as the case may be, one of the churches or chapels in which the banns have been published.
(2) Where a marriage is not solemnized within three months after the completion of the publication of the banns, that publication shall be void and no clergyman shall solemnize the marriage on the authority thereof.

Marriage by common licence

15. Places in which marriages may be solemnized by common licence

(1) Subject to the provisions of this Part of this Act, a common licence shall not be granted for the solemnization of a marriage in any church or chapel other than—
  (a) the parish church of the parish, or an authorised chapel of the ecclesiastical district, in which one of the persons to be married has had his or her usual place of residence for fifteen days immediately before the grant of the licence; or
  (b) a parish church or authorised chapel which is the usual place of worship of the persons to be married or of one of them.
(2) For the purposes of this section, any parish in which there is no parish church or chapel belonging thereto or no church or chapel in which divine service is usually solemnized every Sunday, and any extra-parochial place which has no authorised chapel, shall be deemed to belong to any adjoining parish or chapelry.

16. Provisions as to common licences

(1) A common licence shall not be granted unless one of the persons to be married has sworn before a person having authority to grant such a licence—
  (a) that he or she believes that there is no impediment of kindred or alliance or any other lawful cause, nor any suit commenced in any court, to bar or hinder the solemnizing of the marriage in accordance with the licence:
  (b) that one of the persons to be married has had his or her usual place of residence in the parish or other ecclesiastical district in which the marriage is to be solemnized for fifteen days immediately before the grant of the licence or that the parish church or authorised chapel in which the marriage is to be solemnized is the usual place of worship of those persons or of one of them;
  (c) where one of the persons to be married is a child and is not a widower or widow, that the consent of the person or persons whose consent to the marriage is required under section three of this Act has been obtained, that the necessity of obtaining any such consent has been dispensed with under that section, that the court has consented to the marriage under that section, or that there is no person whose consent to the marriage is so required.
(1A) A common licence shall not be granted for the solemnization of a marriage mentioned in subsection (2) of section 1 of this Act unless—
  (a) the person having authority to grant the licence is satisfied by the production of evidence that both the persons to be married have attained the age of twenty-one; and
  (b) he has received a declaration in writing made by each of those persons specifying their affinal relationship and declaring that the younger of those persons has not at any time before attaining the age of eighteen been a child of the family in relation to the other.
(1B) . . .
(2) Subject to subsection (2A) of this section, if any caveat is entered against the grant of a common licence, the caveat having been duly signed by or on behalf of the person by whom it is entered and stating his place of residence and the ground of objection on which the caveat is founded, no licence shall be granted until the caveat or a copy thereof is transmitted to the ecclesiastical judge out of whose office the licence is to issue, and the judge has certified to the registrar of the diocese that he has examined into the matter of the caveat and is satisfied that it ought not to obstruct the grant of the licence, or until the caveat is withdrawn by the person who entered it.
(2A) Where in the case of a marriage mentioned in subsection (2) of section 1 of this Act a caveat is entered under subsection (2) of this section on the ground that the persons to be married have not both attained the age of twenty-one or that one of those persons has at any time before attaining the age of eighteen been a child of the family in relation

to the other, then, notwithstanding that the caveat is withdrawn by the person who entered it, no licence shall be issued unless the judge has certified that he has examined into that ground of objection and is satisfied that the ground ought not to obstruct the grant of the licence.

(2B) In the case of a marriage mentioned in subsection (2) of section 1 of this Act, one of the persons to be married may apply to the ecclesiastical judge out of whose office the licence is to issue for a declaration that, both those persons having attained the age of twenty-one and the younger of those persons not having at any time before attaining the age of eighteen been a child of the family in relation to the other, there is no impediment of affinity to the solemnization of the marriage; and where any such declaration is obtained the common licence may be granted notwithstanding that no declaration has been made under the said subsection (1A).

(3) Where a marriage is not solemnized within three months after the grant of a common licence, the licence shall be void and no clergyman shall solemnize the marriage on the authority thereof.

. . .

Marriage under superintendent registrar's certificate

17. Marriage under superintendent registrar's certificate

A marriage according to the rites of the Church of England may be solemnized on the authority of certificates of a superintendent registrar in force under Part III of this Act in any church or chapel in which banns of matrimony may be published or in the case of a marriage in pursuance of section 26(1)(dd) of this Act the place specified in the notices of marriage and certificates as the place where the marriage is to be solemnized.

Provided that a marriage shall not be solemnized as aforesaid in any such church or chapel without the consent of the minister thereof or wherever the marriage is solemnized by any person other than a clergyman.

. . .

Miscellaneous provisions

22. Witnesses

All marriages solemnized according to the rites of the Church of England shall be solemnized in the presence of two or more witnesses in addition to the clergyman by whom the marriage is solemnized.

24. Proof of residence not necessary to validity of marriage by banns or common licence

(1) Where any marriage has been solemnized after the publication of banns of matrimony, it shall not be necessary in support of the marriage to give any proof of the residence of the parties or either of them in any parish or other ecclesiastical district in which the banns were published, and no evidence shall be given to prove the contrary in any proceedings touching the validity of the marriage.

(2) Where any marriage has been solemnized on the authority of a common licence, it shall not be necessary in support of the marriage to give any proof that the usual place of residence of one of the parties was for fifteen days immediately before the grant of the licence in the parish or other ecclesiastical district in which the marriage was solemnized, and no evidence shall be given to prove the contrary in any proceedings touching the validity of the marriage.

25. Void marriages

(1) A marriage shall be void in any of the following cases.

(2) Case A is where any persons knowingly and wilfully intermarry according to the rites of the Church of England (otherwise than by special licence)—

(a) except in the case of a marriage in pursuance of section 26(1)(dd) of this Act, in any place other than a church or other building in which banns may be published;

(b) without banns having been duly published, a common licence having been obtained, or certificates having been duly issued under Part III of this Act by a superintendent registrar to whom due notice of marriage has been given; or

(c) on the authority of a publication of banns which is void by virtue of subsection (3) of section three or subsection (2) of section twelve of this Act, on the authority of a common licence which is void by virtue of subsection (3) of section sixteen of this Act, or on the authority of certificates of a superintendent registrar which are void by virtue of subsection (2) of section thirty-three of this Act;

(d) in the case of a marriage on the authority of certificates of a superintendent registrar, in any place other than the church building or other place specified in the notices of marriage and certificates as the place where the marriage is to be solemnized;

(3) Case B is where any persons knowingly and wilfully consent to or acquiesce in the solemnization of a Church of England marriage between them by a person who is not in Holy Orders.

(4) Case C is where any persons of the same sex consent to or acquiesce in the solemnization of a Church of England marriage between them.

(5) In subsection (3) and (4) 'Church of England marriage' means a marriage according to the rites of the Church of England.

PART III

MARRIAGE UNDER SUPERINTENDENT REGISTRAR'S CERTIFICATE

Issue of certificates

26. Marriage of a man and a woman: marriage of same sex couples for which no opt-in is necessary

(1) The following marriages may be solemnized on the authority of two certificates of a superintendant registrar—

(a) a marriage of a man and a woman in a registered building under section 4 according to such form and ceremony as the persons to be married see fit to adopt;

(b) a marriage of any couple in the office of a superintendant register;

(bb) a marriage of any couple on approved premises;

(c) a marriage of a man and a woman according to the usages of the Society of Friends (commonly called Quakers);

(d) a marriage between a man and a woman professing the Jewish religion according to the usages of the Jews;

(dd) a qualifying residential marriage;

(e) a marriage of a man and a woman according to the rites of the Church of England in any church or chapel in which banns of matrimony may be published.

26A. Opt-in to marriage of same sex couples: places of worship

(1) A marriage of a same sex couple in an appropriately registered building according to such form and ceremony as the persons to be married may see fit to adopt may be solemnized on the authority of two certificates of a superintendant registrar.

(2) For the purposes of this section 'appropriately registered building' means a building which has been registered under section 43A.

(3) An application for registration of a building under section 43A may not be made unless the relevant governing authority has given written consent to marriages of same sex couples.

26B. Opt-in marriages of same sex couples: other religious ceremonies

(1) A marriage may, in any of the following cases, be solemnized on the authority of two certificates of a superintendant registrar.

(2) Case A is where—

(a) the marriage is of a same sex couple according to the usages of the Society of Friends (commonly called Quakers), and

(b) the relevant governing authority has given written consent to such marriages of same sex couples.

...

(4) Case B is where—

(a) the marriage is of a same sex couple professing the Jewish religion according to the usages of the Jews, and

(b) the relevant governing authority has given written consent to marriages of same sex couples.

...

(6) Case C is where—

(a) the marriage is of a same sex couple according to religious rites or usages (other than the rites of the Church of England),

(b) the marriage is at the usual place of residence of the housebound or detained person or persons, and

...

(d) the relevant governing authority has given written consent to marriages of same sex couples according to those religious rites or usages.

27. Notice of marriage

(1) Where a marriage is intended to be solemnized on the authority of certificates of a superintendent registrar, notice of marriage in the prescribed form shall be given—

(a) if the persons to be married have resided in the same registration district for the period of seven days immediately before the giving of the notice, by each of those persons to the superintendent registrar of that district;

(b) if the persons to be married have not resided in the same registration district for the said period of seven days as aforesaid, by either of those persons to the superintendent registrar of the registration district in which he or she resided for that period.

(3) A notice of marriage shall state the name and surname, marital status, occupation, place of residence and nationality of each of the persons to be married, whether either of them has previously been married or formed a civil partnership and, if so, how the marriage or civil partnership ended, and in the case of a marriage intended to be solemnized at a person's residence in pursuance of section 26(1)(dd) of this Act, which residence is to be the place of solemnization of the marriage and, in any other case, the church or other building or premises in or on which the marriage is to be solemnized and—

(a) shall state the period, not being less than seven days, during which each of the persons to be married has resided in his or her place of residence;

(4) The superintendent registrar shall file all notices of marriage and keep them with the records of his office, and shall subject to section 27A of this Act also forthwith enter the particulars given in every such notice, together with the date of the notice and the name of the person by whom the notice was given, in a book (in this Act referred to as 'the marriage notice book') furnished to him for that purpose by the Registrar General, and the marriage notice book shall be open for inspection free of charge at all reasonable hours.

(4A) The duty imposed by subsection (4) to enter information in the marriage notice book may be discharged by entering the information in an approved electronic form; and information so entered must be made available for inspection free of charge at all reasonable hours

(5) If the persons to be married wish to be married in the presence of a registrar in a registered building for which an authorised person has been appointed, they shall, at the time when notice of marriage is given to the superintendent registrar under this section, give notice to him that they require a registrar to be present at the marriage.

. . .

27A. Additional information required in certain cases

(1) This section applies in relation to any marriage intended to be solemnized at a person's residence in pursuance of section 26(1)(dd) of this Act, and in the following provisions of this section that person is referred to as 'the relevant person'.

(2) Where the relevant person is not a detained person, each notice of marriage required by section 27 of this Act shall be accompanied by a medical statement relating to that person made not more than fourteen days before the date on which the notice is given.

(3) Where the relevant person is a detained person, each notice of marriage required by section 27 of this Act shall be accompanied by a statement made in the prescribed form by the responsible authority not more than twenty-one days before the date on which notice of the marriage is given under section 27—

(a) identifying the establishment where the person is detained; and

(b) stating that the responsible authority has no objection to that establishment being specified in the notice of marriage as the place where that marriage is to be solemnized.

(4) Each person who gives notice of the marriage to the superintendent registrar in accordance with section 27 of this Act shall give the superintendent registrar the prescribed particulars, in the prescribed form, of the person by or before whom the marriage is intended to be solemnized.

(5) The superintendent registrar shall not enter the particulars given in the marriage notice book, or in an approved electronic form by virtue of section 27(4A), until he has received the statement and the particulars required by subsections (2) or (3) and (4) of this section.

(6) The fact that a superintendent registrar has received a statement under subsection (2) or (as the case may be) (3) of this section shall be entered in the marriage notice book together with the particulars given in the notice of marriage and any such statement together with the form received under subsection (4) of this section shall be filed and kept with the records of the office of the superintendent registrar or, where notice of marriage is required to be given to two superintendent registrars, of each of them.

(6A) Where the particulars given in the notice of marriage are to be entered in an approved electronic form by virtue of section 27(4A), the duty imposed by subsection (6) to enter the statement in the marriage notice book is to be discharged by entering the statement in an approved electronic form.

(7) In this section—

'medical statement', in relation to any person, means a statement made in the prescribed form by a registered medical practitioner that in his opinion at the time the statement is made—

(a) by reason of illness or disability, he or she ought not to move or be moved from the place where he or she is at the time, and

(b) it is likely that it will be the case for at least the following three months that by reason of the illness or disability he or she ought not to move or be moved from that place; and

'registered medical practitioner' has the meaning given by Schedule 1 to the Interpretation Act 1978; and

'responsible authority' means—

(a) if the person is detained in a hospital (within the meaning of Part II of section 145(1) of that Act); or

(b) if the person is detained in a prison or other place to which the Prison Act 1952 applies, the governor or other officer for the time being in charge of that prison or other place.

27B. Provisions relating to section 1(3) marriages

(1) This section applies in relation to any marriage mentioned in subsection (2) of section 1 of this Act which is intended to be solemnized on the authority of certificates of a superintendent registrar.

(2) The superintendent registrar shall not enter notice of the marriage in the marriage notice book, or in an approved electronic form by virtue of section 27(4A), unless—

(a) he is satisfied by the production of evidence that both the persons to be married have attained the age of twenty-one; and

(b) he has received a declaration made in the prescribed form by each of those persons, each declaration having been signed and attested in the prescribed manner, specifying their affinal relationship and declaring that the younger of those persons has not at any time before attaining the age of eighteen been a child of the family in relation to the other.

(3) The fact that a superintendent registrar has received a declaration under subsection (2) of this section shall be entered in the marriage notice book together with the particulars given in the notice of marriage and any such declaration shall be filed and kept with the records of the office of the superintendent registrar or, where notice of marriage is required to be given to two superintendent registrars, of each of them.

(4) Where the superintendent registrar receives from some person other than the persons to be married a written statement signed by that person which alleges that the declaration made under subsection (2) of this section is false in a material particular, the superintendent registrar shall not issue a certificate unless a declaration is obtained under subsection (5) of this section.

(5) Either of the persons to be married may, whether or not any statement has been received by the superintendent registrar under subsection (4) of this section, apply to the High Court for a declaration that, both those persons having attained the age of twenty-one and the younger of those persons not having at any time before attaining the age of eighteen been a child of the family in relation to the other, there is no impediment of affinity to the solemnization of the marriage; and where such a declaration is obtained the superintendent registrar may enter notice of the marriage in the marriage notice book, or in an approved electronic form by virtue of section 27(4A), and may issue a certificate whether or not any declaration has been made under subsection (2) of this section.

(6) Section 29 of this Act shall not apply in relation to a marriage to which this section applies, except so far as a caveat against the issue of a certificate for the marriage is entered under that section on a ground other than the relationship of the persons to be married.

31. Marriage under certificate without licence

(1) Where a marriage is intended to be solemnized on the authority of certificates of a superintendent registrar, the superintendent registrar to whom notice of marriage has been given shall suspend or affix in some conspicuous place in his office, for 15 successive days next after the day on which the notice was entered in the marriage book, the notice of marriage, or an exact copy signed by him of the particulars thereof as entered in the marriage notice book.

...

(4) No marriage shall be solemnized on the production of certificates of a superintendent registrar until after the expiration of the waiting period in relation to each notice of marriage.

(4A) 'The waiting period', in relation to a notice of marriage, means—
(a) the period of 15 days, or
(b) such shorter period as may be determined by the Registrar General under subsection (5A) or by a superintendent registrar under any provision of regulations made under subsection (5D),

after the day on which the notice of marriage was entered in the marriage notice book, or in an approved electronic form by virtue of section 27(4A).

...

(5A) If, on an application made to the Registrar General, he is satisfied that there are compelling reasons for reducing the 15 day period because of the exceptional circumstances of the case, he may reduce that period to such shorter period as he considers appropriate.

35. Marriages in registration districts in which neither party resides

...

(3A) A superintendant registrar may issue a certificate for the solemnization of a marriage in any parish church or authorised chapel which is the usual place of worship of the persons to be married, or one of them, notwithstanding that the church or chapel is not within a registration district where either of those persons resides.

...

39A. Marriage of former civil partners one of whom has changed sex

(1) This section applies if—
(a) a court—
(i) makes final a nullity order which annuls a civil partnership on the ground that an interim gender recognition certificate has been issued to one of the civil partners, ...

and, on doing so, issues a full gender recognition certificate (under section 5A(1) of the Gender Recognition Act 2004(c)) to that civil partner, and
(b) the former civil partners wish to marry each other in England or Wales in accordance with this Part without being delayed by the waiting period.

(2) For the purposes of this section the relevant period is the period—
(a) beginning with the issue of the full gender recognition certificate, and
(b) ending at the end of 1 month from the day on which it is issued.

(3) If either of the former civil partners—
(a) gives notice of marriage in accordance with this Part during the relevant period; and
(b) on doing so, makes an election under this section,

this Act applies with the modifications set out in subsections (4) to (6).

(4) In section 31 (marriage under certificates)—
(a) omit subsections (1), (4), (4A) and (5A) to (5I), and
(b) in subsection (2), for 'At the expiration of the said period of 15 days', substitute 'As soon as notice of marriage has been given,'.

Marriages in registered buildings

41. Registration of buildings: a marriage of a man and a women

(1) Any proprietor or trustee of a building, which has been certified by law as a place of religious worship may apply to the superintendent registrar of the registration district in which the building is situated for the building to be registered for the solemnization of marriages therein.

(1A) A reference in this section to the solemnization of marriage is a reference to the solemnization of marriage of a man and a women.

(2) Any person making such an application as aforesaid shall deliver to the superintendent registrar a certificate, signed in duplicate by at least twenty householders and dated not earlier than one month before the making of the application, stating that the building is being used by them as their usual place of public religious worship and that they desire that the building should be registered as aforesaid, and both certificates shall be countersigned by the proprietor or trustee by whom they are delivered.

(3) The superintendent registrar shall send both certificates delivered to him under the last foregoing subsection to the Registrar General who shall register the building in a book to be kept for that purpose in the General Register Office.

(3A) The duty imposed by subsection (3) to register the building in a book may be discharged by registering the building in an approved electronic form.

...

43. Appointment of authorised persons

(1) For the purpose of enabling marriages to be solemnized in a registered building without the presence of a registrar, the trustees or governing body of that building may authorise

a person to be present at the solemnization of marriages in that building and, where a person is so authorised in respect of any building, registered under section 41 the trustees or governing body of that building shall within the prescribed time and in the prescribed manner, certify the name and address of the person so authorised to the Registrar General and to the superintendent registrar of the registration district in which the building is situated.

. . .

. . .

43A. Registration of buildings: marriage of same sex couples

(1) A building that has been certified by law as a place of religious worship may be registered under this section for the solemnization of marriages of same sex couples.

. . .

44. Solemnization of marriage in registered building

(1) Subject to the provisions of this section, where the notices of marriage and certificates issued by a superintendent registrar state that a marriage between the persons named therein is intended to be solemnized in a registered building, the marriage may be solemnized in that building according to such form and ceremony as those persons may see fit to adopt:

Provided that no marriage shall be solemnized in any registered building without the consent of the minister or of one of the trustees, owners, deacons, or managers thereof, or in the case of a registered building of the Roman Catholic Church, without the consent of the officiating minister thereof.

(2) Subject to the provisions of this section, a marriage solemnized in a registered building shall be solemnized with open doors in the presence of two or more witnesses and in the presence of either—

(a) a registrar of the registration district in which the registered building is situated, or

(b) an authorised person whose name and address have been certified in accordance with the last foregoing section by the trustees or governing body of that registered building or of some other registered building in the same registration district.

(3) Where a marriage is solemnized in a registered building each of the persons contracting the marriage shall, in some part of the ceremony and in the presence of the witnesses and the registrar or authorised person, make the following declaration:—

'I do solemnly declare that I know not of any lawful impediment why I, *AB,* may not be joined in matrimony to *CD*'

and each of them shall say to the other:—

'I call upon these persons here present to witness that I, *AB*, do take thee, *CD,* to be my lawful wedded wife [*or* husband]':

(3A) As an alternative to the declaration set out in subsection (3) of this section the persons contracting the marriage may make the requisite declaration either—

(a) by saying 'I declare that I know of no legal reason why I [*name*] may not be joined in marriage to [*name*]'; or

(b) by replying 'I am' to the question put to them successively 'Are you [*name*] free lawfully to marry [*name*]?';

and as an alternative to the words of contract set out in that subsection the persons to be married may say to each other 'I [*name*] take you [*or* thee] [*name*] to be my wedded wife [*or* husband]'.

. . .

Marriages in register offices

45. Solemnization of marriage in register office

(1) Where a marriage is intended to be solemnized on the authority of certificates of a superintendent registrar, the persons to be married may state in the notices of marriage that they wish to be married in the office of the superintendent registrar or one of the superintendent registrars, as the case may be, to whom notice of marriage is given, and where any such notices have been given and the certificates have been issued accordingly, the marriage may be solemnized in the said office, with open doors in the presence of the superintendent registrar and a registrar of the registration district of that superintendent registrar and in the presence of two witnesses, and the persons to be married shall make the declarations and use the form of words set out in subsection (3) or (3A) of the last foregoing section in the case of marriages in registered buildings.

(2) No religious service shall be used at any marriage solemnized in the office of a superintendent registrar.

45A. Solemnization of certain marriages

(1) This section applies to marriages solemnized, otherwise than according to the rites of the Church of England, in pursuance of section 26(1)(dd) of this Act at the place where a person usually resides.

(2) The marriage may be solemnized according to a relevant form, rite or ceremony in the presence of a registrar of the registration district in which the place where the marriage is solemnized is situated and of two witnesses and each of the persons contracting the marriage shall make the declaration and use the form of words set out in subsection (3) or (3A) of section 44 of this Act in the case of marriages in registered buildings.

(3) Where the marriage is not solemnized in pursuance of subsection (2) of this section it shall be solemnized in the presence of the superintendent registrar and a registrar of the registration district in which the place where the marriage is solemnized is situated and in the presence of two witnesses, and the persons to be married shall make the declarations and use the form of words set out in subsection (3) or (3A) of section 44 of this Act in the case of marriages in registered buildings.

(4) No religious service shall be used at any marriage solemnized in the presence of a superintendent registrar.

(5) In subsection (2) of this section a 'relevant form, rite or ceremony' means a form, rite or ceremony of a body of persons who meet for religious worship in any registered building being a form, rite or ceremony in accordance with which members of that body are married in any such registered building.

46. Register office marriage followed by religious ceremony

(1) If the parties to a marriage solemnized in the presence of a superintendent registrar desire to add the religious ceremony ordained or used by the church or persuasion of which they are members, they may present themselves, after giving notice of their intention so to do, to the clergyman or minister of the church or persuasion of which they are members, and the clergyman or minister, upon the production of a certificate of their marriage before the superintendent registrar and upon the payment of the customary fees (if any), may, if he sees fit, read or celebrate in the church or chapel of which he is the regular minister the marriage service of the church or persuasion to which he belongs or nominate some other minister to do so.

(1A) In this section 'relevant marriage' means—

- (a) the marriage of a man and a woman solemnized in the presence of a superintendant registrar,
- (b) the marriage of a same sex couple solemnized in the presence of a superintendant registrar, and
- (c) a marriage which arises from the conversion of a same sex partnership under section 9 of the Marriage (Same Sex Couples) Act 2013.

(1B) This section does not authorise the marriage service of the Church of England to be read or celebrated in the case of a relevant marriage of a same sex couple.

(1C) This section does not authorise any other marriage service to be read or celebrated in the case of a relevant marriage of a same sex couple unless the relevant governing authority has given written consent to such reading or celebration of that service in the case of such marriages.

(2) Nothing in the reading or celebration of a marriage service under this section shall supersede or invalidate any marriage previously solemnized in the presence of a superintendent registrar, and the reading or celebration shall not be entered as a marriage in any marriage register book kept under Part IV of this Act.

(3) No person who is not entitled to solemnize marriages according to the rites of the Church of England shall by virtue of this section be entitled to read or celebrate the marriage service in any church or chapel of the Church of England.

Marriages on approved premises

46A. Approval of premises

(1) The Chancellor of the Exchequer may by regulations make provision for and in connection with the approval by local authorities of premises for the solemnization of marriages in pursuance of section 26(1)(bb) of this Act.

. . .

46B. Solemnization of marriage on approved premises

(1) Any marriage on approved premises in pursuance of section 26(1)(bb) of this Act shall be solemnized in the presence of—

- (a) two witnesses, and

(b) the superintendent registrar and a registrar of the registration district in which the premises are situated.

(2) Without prejudice to the width of section 46A(2)(e) of this Act, the Secretary of State shall exercise his power to provide for the imposition of conditions as there mentioned so as to secure that members of the public are permitted to attend any marriage solemnized on approved premises in pursuance of section 26(1)(bb) of this Act.

(3) Each of the persons contracting such a marriage shall make the declaration and use the form of words set out in section 44(3) or (3A) of this Act in the case of marriages in registered buildings.

(4) No religious service shall be used at a marriage on approved premises in pursuance of section 26(1)(bb) of this Act.

Marriages according to usages of Society of Friends

47. Marriages according to usages of Society of Friends

(1) No person who is not a member of the Society of Friends shall be married according to the usages of that Society unless he or she is authorised to be so married under or in pursuance of a general rule of the said Society in England.

(2) A marriage solemnized according to the said usages shall not be valid unless either—

(a) each person giving notice of marriage declares, either verbally or, if so required, in writing, that each of the parties to the marriage is either a member of the Society of Friends or is in profession with or of the persuasion of that Society; or

(b) there is produced to the superintendent registrar, at the time when notice of marriage is given, a certificate purporting to be signed by a registering officer of the Society of Friends in England to the effect that any party to the marriage who is not a member of the Society of Friends or in profession with or of the persuasion of that Society, is authorised to be married according to the said usages under or in pursuance of a general rule of the said Society in England.

(3) Any such certificate as aforesaid shall be for all purposes conclusive evidence that any person to whom it relates is authorised to be married according to the usages of the said Society, and the entry of the marriage in a marriage register book under Part IV of this Act, or a certified copy thereof made under the said Part IV, shall be conclusive evidence of the production of such a certificate.

. . .

Miscellaneous provisions

48. Proof of certain matters not necessary to validity of marriages

(1) Where any marriage has been solemnized under the provisions of this Part of this Act, it shall not be necessary in support of the marriage to give any proof—

(a) that before the marriage either of the parties thereto resided, or resided for any period, in the registration district stated in the notices of marriage to be that of his or her place of residence;

(b) that any person whose consent to the marriage was required by section three of this Act had given his consent;

(c) that the registered building in which the marriage was solemnized had been certified as required by law as a place of religious worship;

(d) that that building was the usual place of worship of either of the parties to the marriage;

(da) that in the case of a marriage under section 26B(2), (4) or (6) the relevant governing authority had given written consent as mentioned in section 26B(2)(b), 4(b) or 6(b);

(e) that the facts stated in a declaration made under subsection (1) of section thirty-five of this Act were correct; or

(ea) that in the case of a marriage under section 26A the relevant governing authority had given consent as mentioned in section 26A(3).

nor shall any evidence be given to prove the contrary in any proceedings touching the validity of the marriage.

(2) A marriage solemnized in accordance with the provisions of this Part of this Act in a registered building which has not been certified as required by law as a place of religious worship shall be as valid as if the building had been so certified.

49. Void marriages

If any persons knowingly and wilfully intermarry under the provisions of this Part of this Act—

(a) without having given due notice of marriage to the superintendent registrar;

(b) without a certificate for marriage having been duly issued, in respect of each of the persons to be married, by the superintendent registrar to whom notice of marriage was given;

(d) on the authority of certificates which are void by virtue of subsection (2) of section thirty-three of this Act;

(e) in any place other than the church, chapel, registered building, office or other place specified in the notices of marriage and certificates of the superintendent registrar;

(ee) in the case of a marriage purporting to be in pursuance of section 26(1)(bb) of this Act, on any premises that at the time the marriage is solemnized are not approved premises;

(f) in the case of a marriage in a registered building (not being a marriage in the presence of an authorised person), in the absence of a registrar of the registration district in which the registered building is situated;

(g) in the case of a marriage in the office of a superintendent registrar, in the absence of the superintendent registrar or of a registrar of the registration district of that superintendent registrar;

(gg) in the case of a marriage on approved premises, in the absence of the superintendent registrar of the registration district in which the premises are situated or in the absence of a registrar of that district; or

(h) in the case of a marriage to which section 45A of this Act applies, in the absence of any superintendent registrar or registrar whose presence at that marriage is required by that section;

the marriage shall be void.

49A. Void marriages: additional provisions about same sex marriages

(1) If a same sex couple knowingly and wilfully intermarries under the provisions of this Part of this Act in the absence of the required consent, the marriage shall be void.

. . .

55. Manner of registration of marriages

(1) Every person who is required under this Part of this Act to register a marriage shall immediately after solemnization of the marriage, or, in the case of a marriage according to the usages of the Society of Friends, as soon as conveniently may be after the solemnization of the marriage, register in duplicate in two marriage books the particulars of the marriage in the prescribed form.

. . .

PART VI
GENERAL

72. Supplementary provisions as to marriages in usual places of worship

(1) For the purposes of the following provisions of this Act, that is to say, subsection (4) of section six, paragraph (b) of subsection (1) of section fifteen and subsection (3) of section thirty-five, no parish church or authorised chapel shall be deemed to be the usual place of worship of any person unless he is enrolled on the church electoral roll of the area in which that church or chapel is situated, and where any person is enrolled on the church electoral roll of an area in which he does not reside that enrolment shall be sufficient evidence that his usual place of worship is a parish church or authorised chapel in that area.

(2) Persons intending to be married shall have the like but no greater right of having their banns published and marriage solemnized by virtue of the said provisions in a parish church or authorised chapel which is the usual place of worship of one or both of them as they have of having their banns published and marriage solemnized in the parish church or public chapel of the parish or chapelry in which they or one of them resides.

(3) Where any marriage has been solemnized by virtue of the said provisions it shall not be necessary in support of the marriage to give any proof of the actual enrolment of the parties or of one of them on the church electoral roll of the area in which the parish church or authorised chapel in which the marriage was solemnized was situated, nor shall any evidence be given to prove the contrary in any proceedings touching the validity of the marriage.

. . .

75. Offences relating to solemnization of marriages

(1) Any person who knowingly and wilfully—

(a) . . .

(b) solemnizes a marriage according to the rites of the Church of England without banns of matrimony having been duly published (not being a marriage solemnized on the authority of a special licence, a common licence, or certificates of a superintendent registrar);

(c) solemnizes a marriage according to the said rites (not being a marriage by special licence or a marriage in pursuance of section 26(1)(dd) of this Act) in any place other than a church or other building in which banns may be published;

(d) solemnizes a marriage according to the said rites falsely pretending to be in Holy Orders;

shall be guilty of felony and shall be liable to imprisonment for a term not exceeding fourteen years.

(2) Any person who knowingly and wilfully—

(a) solemnizes a marriage (not being a marriage by special licence, a marriage according to the usages of the Society of Friends or a marriage between two persons professing the Jewish religion according to the usages of the Jews) in any place other than—

(i) a church or other building in which marriages may be solemnized according to the rites of the Church of England, or

(ii) the registered building, office, approved premises or person's residence specified as the place where the marriage was to be solemnized in the notices of marriage and certificates required under Part III of this Act;

(aa) solemnizes a marriage purporting to be in pursuance of section 26(1)(bb) of this Act on premises that are not approved premises;

(b) solemnizes a marriage in any such registered building as aforesaid (not being a marriage in the presence of an authorised person) in the absence of a registrar of the district in which the registered building is situated;

(bb) solemnizes a marriage in pursuance of section 26(1)(dd) of this Act, otherwise than according to the rites of the Church of England, in the absence of a registrar of the registration district in which the place where the marriage is solemnized is situated;

(c) solemnizes a marriage in the office of a superintendent registrar in the absence of a registrar of the district in which the office is situated;

(cc) solemnizes a marriage on approved premises in pursuance of section 26(1)(bb) of this Act in the absence of a registrar of the district in which the premises are situated;

(d) solemnizes a marriage on the authority of certificates of a superintendent registrar before the expiry of the waiting period in relation to each notice of marriage; or

(e) solemnizes a marriage on the authority of certificates of a superintendent registrar after the expiration of the period which is, in relation to that marriage, the applicable period for the purposes of section 33 of this Act;

shall be guilty of felony and shall be liable to imprisonment for a term not exceeding five years.

(2A) In subsection (2)(d) 'the waiting period' has the same meaning as in section 31(4A).

(3) A superintendent registrar who knowingly and wilfully—

(a) issues any certificate for marriage before the expiry of 15 days from the day on which the notice of marriage was entered in the marriage notice book;

(b) issues any certificate for marriage after the expiration of the period which is, in relation to that marriage, the applicable period for the purposes of section 33 of this Act;

(c) issues any certificate the issue of which has been forbidden under section thirty of this Act by any person entitled to forbid the issue of such a certificate; or

(d) solemnizes or permits to be solemnized in his office or, in the case of a marriage in pursuance of section 26(1)(bb) or (dd) of this Act, in any other place, any marriage which is void by virtue of any of the provisions of Part III of this Act;

shall be guilty of felony and shall be liable to imprisonment for a term not exceeding five years.

(4) No prosecution under this section shall be commenced after the expiration of three years from the commission of the offence.

. . .

76. Offences relating to registration of marriages

(1) Any person who refuses or without reasonable cause omits to register any marriage which he is required by this Act to register, and any person having the custody of a marriage register book or a certified copy of a marriage register book or part thereof who carelessly allows the said book or copy to be injured while in his keeping, shall be liable on summary conviction to a fine not exceeding level 3 on the standard scale.

SCHEDULE 1
KINDRED AND AFFINITY

PART 1
PROHIBITED DEGREES: KINDRED

1. (1) The list referred to in section 1(1) is—

Adoptive child
Adoptive parent
Child
Former adoptive child
Former adoptive parent
Grandparent
Grandchild
Parent
Parent's sibling
Sibling
Sibling's child

(2) In the list 'sibling' means a brother, sister, half-brother or half-sister.

PART 2
DEGREES OF AFFINITY REFERRED TO IN SECTION 1(2) AND (3)

2. The list referred to in section 1(2) is as follows—

Child of former civil partner
Child of former spouse
Former civil partner of grandparent
Former civil partner of parent
Former spouse of grandparent
Former spouse of parent
Grandchild of former civil partner
Grandchild of former spouse

MAINTENANCE ORDERS ACT 1950
(14 Geo. 6, c. 37)

PART II
ENFORCEMENT

16. Application of Part II

(1) Any order to which this section applies (in this Part of this Act referred to as a maintenance order) made by a court in any part of the United Kingdom may, if registered in accordance with the provisions of this Part of this Act in a court in another part of the United Kingdom, be enforced in accordance with those provisions in that other part of the United Kingdom.

(2) This section applies to the following orders, that is to say—

(a) an order for alimony, maintenance or other payments made or deemed to be made by a court in England under any of the following enactments:—

(i) sections 15 to 17, 19 to 22, 30, 34 and 35 of the Matrimonial Causes Act 1965, and sections 22, 22A, 23 and 27 of the Matrimonial Causes Act 1973 (as that Act had effect immediately before the passing of the Family Law Act 1996), and section 14 or 17 of the Matrimonial and Family Proceedings Act 1984;

(ii) Part I of the Domestic Proceedings and Magistrates' Courts Act 1978;

(iii) Schedule 1 to the Children Act 1989;

(v) paragraph 23 of Schedule 2 to the Children Act 1989 or section forty-three of the National Assistance Act 1948;

(vi) section 18 of the Supplementary Benefits Act 1976;

(viii) section 106 of the Social Security Administration Act 1992;

(ix) Part 1, 8 or 9 of Schedule 5 to the Civil Partnership Act 2004, Schedule 6 of that Act or paragraph 5 or 9 of Schedule 7 to that Act.

17. Procedure for registration of maintenance orders

(1) An application for the registration of a maintenance order under this Part of this Act shall be made in the prescribed manner to the appropriate authority, that is to say—

(a) . . .

(b) where the maintenance order was made by a court of summary jurisdiction in Northern Ireland, a resident magistrate acting for the same petty sessions district as the court which made the order;

(c) in every other case, the prescribed officer of the court which made the order.

(2) If upon application made as aforesaid by or on behalf of the person entitled to payments under a maintenance order it appears that the person liable to make those payments resides in another part of the United Kingdom, and that it is convenient that the order should be enforceable there, the appropriate authority shall cause a certified copy of the order to be sent to the prescribed officer of a court in that part of the United Kingdom in accordance with the provisions of the next following subsection.

(3) The court to whose officer the certified copy of a maintenance order is sent under this section shall be—

(a) where the maintenance order was made by a superior court, the Senior Courts, the Court of Session or the Court of Judicature of Northern Ireland, as the case may be;

(b) in any other case—

(i) where the defendant appears to be in England and Wales, the family court;

(ii) where the defendant appears to be in Northern Ireland, a court of summary jurisdiction acting for the place in which the defendant appears to be;

(iii) where the defendant appears to be in Scotland, the sheriff court within the jurisdiction of which the defendant appears to be.

(4) Where the prescribed officer of any court receives a certified copy of a maintenance order sent to him under this section, he shall cause the order to be registered in that court in the prescribed manner, and shall give notice of the registration in the prescribed manner to the prescribed officer of the court which made the order.

(5) The officer to whom any notice is given under the last foregoing subsection shall cause particulars of the notice to be registered in his court in the prescribed manner.

(6) Where the sums payable under a maintenance order, being an order made by a court of summary jurisdiction in England or Northern Ireland, are payable to or through an officer of any court, that officer shall, if the person entitled to the payments so requests, make an application on behalf of that person for the registration of the order under this Part of this Act; but the person at whose request the application is made shall have the same liability for costs properly incurred in or about the application as if the application had been made by him.

(7) An order which is for the time being registered under this Part of this Act in any court shall not be registered thereunder in any other court.

18. Enforcement of registered orders

(1) Subject to the provisions of this section, a maintenance order registered under this Part of this Act in the family court or a court in any part of the United Kingdom may be enforced in that part of the United Kingdom in all respects as if it had been made by that court and as if that court had had jurisdiction to make it; and proceedings for or with respect to the enforcement of any such order may be taken accordingly.

(1A) A maintenance order registered under this Part of this Act in a court of summary jurisdiction in Northern Ireland shall not carry interest; but where a maintenance order so registered is registered in the High Court under section 36 of the Civil Jurisdiction and Judgments Act 1982, this subsection shall not prevent any sum for whose payment the order provides from carrying interest in accordance with section 11A of the Maintenance and Affiliation Orders Act (Northern Ireland) 1966.

. . .

21. Discharge and variation of maintenance orders registered in superior courts

(1) The registration of a maintenance order in a superior court under this Part of this Act shall not confer on that court any power to vary or discharge the order, or affect any jurisdiction of the court in which the order was made to vary or discharge the order.

. . .

22. Discharge and variation of maintenance orders registered in summary or sheriff courts

(1) Subject to subsection (1ZA), where a maintenance order is for the time being registered under this Part of this Act in the family court, a court of summary jurisdiction or sheriff court, that court may, upon application made in the prescribed manner by or on behalf of the person liable to make periodical payments under the order or the person entitled to those payments, by order make such variation as the court thinks fit in the rate of the payments under the maintenance order; but no such variation shall impose on the person liable to make payments under the maintenance order a liability to make payments in excess of the maximum rate (if any) authorised by the law for the time being in force in the part of the United Kingdom in which the maintenance order was made.

(1ZA)The power under subsection (1) to vary the rate of payments may not be exercised where paragraph 9(2) of Schedule 6 to the Civil Jurisdiction and Judgments (Maintenance) Regulations 2011 applies (restriction on modifying maintenance decision where creditor remains habitually resident in the part of the United Kingdom in which the decision was made).

(1A) The family court may exercise the same powers in relation to an order registered in the family court under this Part of this Act as are exercisable by the family court under section 1 of the Maintenance Enforcement Act 1991 in relation to a qualifying periodical maintenance order (within the meaning of that section) which has been made by the family court, including the power under subsection (7) of that section to revoke, suspend, revive or vary any means of payment order (within the meaning of that subsection) made by virtue of this subsection.

INTESTATES' ESTATES ACT 1952
(15 & 16 Geo. 6 & 1 Eliz. 2, c. 64)

PART I

AMENDMENTS OF LAW OF INTESTATE SUCCESSION

5. Rights of surviving spouse or civil partner as respects the matrimonial or civil partnership home

The Second Schedule to this Act shall have effect for enabling the surviving spouse or civil partner of a person dying intestate after the commencement of this Act to acquire the matrimonial home or civil partnership home.

SCHEDULES

Section 5 SECOND SCHEDULE

Rights of Surviving Spouse or Civil Partner as respects the Matrimonial Home

1.— (1) Subject to the provisions of this Schedule, where the residuary estate of the intestate comprises an interest in a dwelling-house in which the surviving spouse or civil partner was resident at the time of the intestate's death, the surviving spouse or civil partner may require the personal representative, in exercise of the power conferred by section forty-one of the principal Act (and with due regard to the requirements of that section as to valuation) to appropriate the said interest in the dwelling-house in or towards satisfaction of any absolute interest of the surviving spouse or civil partner in the real and personal estate of the intestate.

(2) The right conferred by this paragraph shall not be exercisable where the interest is—

(a) a tenancy which at the date of the death of the intestate was a tenancy which would determine within the period of two years from that date; or

(b) a tenancy which the landlord by notice given after that date could determine within the remainder of that period.

(3) Nothing in subsection (5) of section forty-one of the principal Act (which requires the personal representative, in making an appropriation to any person under that section, to have regard to the rights of others) shall prevent the personal representative from giving effect to the right conferred by this paragraph.

(4) The reference in this paragraph to an absolute interest in the real and personal estate of the intestate includes a reference to the capital value of a life interest which the surviving spouse or civil partner has under this Act elected to have redeemed.

(5) Where part of a building was, at the date of the death of the intestate, occupied as a separate dwelling, that dwelling shall for the purposes of this Schedule be treated as a dwelling-house.

2. Where—

(a) the dwelling-house forms part of a building and an interest in the whole of the building is comprised in the residuary estate; or

(b) the dwelling-house is held with agricultural land and an interest in the agricultural land is comprised in the residuary estate; or

(c) the whole or part of the dwelling-house was at the time of the intestate's death used as a hotel or lodging house; or

(d) a part of the dwelling-house was at the time of the intestate's death used for purposes other than domestic purposes, the right conferred by paragraph 1 of this Schedule shall not be exercisable unless the court, on being satisfied that the exercise of that right is not likely to diminish the value of assets in the residuary estate (other than the said interest in the dwelling-house) or make them more difficult to dispose of, so orders.

3.— (1) The right conferred by paragraph 1 of this Schedule—

(a) shall not be exercisable after the expiration of twelve months from the first taking out of representation with respect to the intestate's estate;

(b) shall not be exercisable after the death of the surviving spouse or civil partner;

(c) shall be exercisable, except where the surviving spouse or civil partner is the sole personal representative, by notifying the personal representative (or, where there are two or more personal representatives of whom one is the surviving spouse or civil partner, all of them except the surviving spouse or civil partner) in writing.

(2) A notification in writing under paragraph (c) of the foregoing sub-paragraph shall not be revocable except with the consent of the personal representative; but the surviving spouse or civil partner may require the personal representative to have the said interest in the dwelling-house valued in accordance with section forty-one of the principal Act and to inform him or her of the result of that valuation before he or she decides whether to exercise the right.

(3) Subsection (9) of the section forty-seven A added to the principal Act by section two of this Act shall apply for the purposes of the construction of the reference in this paragraph to the first taking out of representation, and the proviso to subsection (5) of that section shall apply for the purpose of enabling the surviving spouse or civil partner to apply for an extension of the period of twelve months mentioned in this paragraph.

4.— (1) During the period of twelve months mentioned in paragraph 3 of this Schedule the personal representative shall not without the written consent of the surviving spouse or civil partner sell or otherwise dispose of the said interest in the dwelling-house except in the course of administration owing to want of other assets.

(2) An application to the court under paragraph 2 of this Schedule may be made by the personal representative as well as by the surviving spouse or civil partner, and if, on an application under that paragraph, the court does not order that the right conferred by paragraph 1 of this Schedule shall be exercisable by the surviving spouse or civil partner, the court may authorise the personal representative to dispose of the said interest in the dwelling-house within the said period of twelve months.

(3) Where the court under sub-paragraph (3) of paragraph 3 of this Schedule extends the said period of twelve months, the court may direct that this paragraph shall apply in relation to the extended period as it applied in relation to the original period of twelve months.

(4) This paragraph shall not apply where the surviving spouse or civil partner is the sole personal representative or one of two or more personal representatives.

(5) Nothing in this paragraph shall confer any right on the surviving spouse or civil partner as against a purchaser from the personal representative.

5.— (1) Where the surviving spouse or civil partner is one of two or more personal representatives, the rule that a trustee may not be a purchaser of trust property shall not prevent the surviving spouse or civil partner from purchasing out of the estate of the intestate an interest in a dwelling-house in which the surviving spouse or civil partner was resident at the time of the intestate's death.

(2) The power of appropriation under section forty-one of the principal Act shall include power to appropriate an interest in a dwelling-house in which the surviving spouse or civil partner was resident at the time of the intestate's death partly in satisfaction of an interest of the surviving spouse or civil partner in the real and personal estate of the intestate and partly in return for a payment of money by the surviving spouse or civil partner to the personal representative.

6.— (1) Where the surviving spouse or civil partner is a person of unsound mind or a defective, a requirement or consent under this Schedule may be made or given on his or her behalf by the committee or receiver, if any, or, where there is no committee or receiver, by the court.

(2) A requirement or consent made or given under this Schedule by a surviving spouse or civil partner who is an infant shall be as valid and binding as it would be if he or she were of age; and, as respects an appropriation in pursuance of paragraph 1 of this Schedule, the provisions of section forty-one of the principal Act as to obtaining the consent of the infant's parent or guardian, or of the court on behalf of the infant, shall not apply.

7.— (1) Except where the context otherwise requires, references in this Schedule to a dwelling-house include references to any garden or portion of ground attached to and usually occupied with the dwelling-house or otherwise required for the amenity or convenience of the dwelling-house.

(2) This Schedule shall be construed as one with Part IV of the principal Act.

BIRTHS AND DEATHS REGISTRATION ACT 1953
(1953, c. 20)

1. Particulars of births to be registered

...

(2) The following persons shall be qualified to give information concerning a birth, that is to say—
- (a) the mother of the child;
- (aa) the father of the child where—
  - (i) the child is one whose father and mother were married to each other at the time of the child's birth, or
  - (ii) the father is a qualified informant by virtue of subsection (2)(a) of section 10 (registration of father where parents not married or of second female parent where parents not civil partners) or by virtue of regulations under subsection (6)(b) of section 2E (scientific tests);
- (b) the occupier of the house in which the child to the knowledge of that occupier was born;
- (c) any person present at the birth;
- (d) any person having charge of the child;
- (e) in the case of a still-born child found exposed the person who found the child.

(3) In subsection (2)(aa)—
- (a) the first reference to the father is, in the case of a child who has a parent by virtue of section 42 or 43 of the Human Fertilisation and Embryology Act 2008, to be read as a reference to the woman who is a parent by virtue of that section;
- (b) the reference in sub-paragraph (ii) to the father being a qualified informant by virtue of section 10(2)(a) is, in the case of a child who has a parent by virtue of section 43 of that Act, to be read as a reference to that parent being a qualified informant by virtue of section 10(2A)(a).

(4) In this Part, references to a child whose father and mother were, or were not, married to each other at the time of the child's birth are to be read in accordance with section 1 of the Family Law Reform Act 1987 (which extends the cases in which a person is treated as being a person whose father and mother were married to each other at the time of the person's birth).

2A. Information concerning birth of child whose parents are not married

(1) In the case of the birth of a child whose parents were not married to each other at the time of the birth, it shall be the duty—
- (a) of the mother of the child, and
- (b) in the case of the death or inability of the mother, of each qualified informant falling within section 1(2) to give the registrar, before the expiration of 42 days of the date of the birth, information of the particulars required to be registered concerning the birth, together with any other information required by section 2(1) and in the presence of the registrar to sign the register.

2B. Duties of unmarried mother when acting alone

(1) Where no request for the entry of a person's name as the father of the child is made by virtue of any of paragraphs (a) to (g) of section 10(1) (registration of father where parents are not married) or by virtue of regulations under section 2E (scientific tests), the information to be given under section 2A(1) by the mother includes such information relating to the father as may be prescribed for the purposes of this subsection by regulations made by the Minister, which may include information that is not intended to be entered on the register.

...

(3) Subsection (1) does not require the mother to provide information relating to the father if she makes in the presence of the registrar a declaration in the prescribed form stating that one or more of the following conditions is met.

(4) Those conditions are—
- (a) that by virtue of section 41 of the Human Fertilisation and Embryology Act 2008 the child has no father,
- (b) that the father has died,
- (c) that the mother does not know the father's identity,
- (d) that the mother does not know the father's whereabouts,
- (e) that the father lacks capacity (within the meaning of the Mental Capacity Act 2005) in relation to decisions under this Part,

(f) that the mother has reason to fear for her safety or that of the child if the father is contacted in relation to the registration of the birth, and
(g) any other conditions prescribed by regulations made by the Minister.

2C. Confirmation of parentage information given by mother

(1) The Minister may by regulations provide for a procedure under which a person may be registered as the father of a child in a case where information relating to that person is given by virtue of section 2B(1) by the mother of the child and is subsequently confirmed by that person.

...

2E. Use of scientific tests with consent of parties

(1) The Minister may by regulations make provision enabling a report of a qualifying scientific test to be used in connection with the registration or re-registration under this Act of the birth of a child in cases where—
(a) the birth has not been registered under this Act, or
(b) the birth has been registered but no person has been registered as the father of the child (or as a parent of the child by virtue of section 42, 43 or 46(1) or (2) of the Human Fertilisation and Embryology Act 2008).

...

10. Registration of father where parents not married or of second female parent where parents not civil partners

...

(1B) In the case of a child to whom section 1(3) of the Family Law Reform Act 1987 does not apply, no woman shall as a parent of the child by virtue of section 43 of the Human Fertilisation and Embryology Act 2008 be required to give information concerning the birth of the child except by virtue of regulations under section 2C, and the registrar shall not enter in the register the name of any woman as a parent of the child by virtue of that section except—
(a) at the joint request of the mother and the person stating herself to be the other parent of the child (in which case that person shall sign the register together with the mother);

...

10ZA. Registration of father or second female parent by virtue of certain provisions of Human Fertilisation and Embryology Act 2008

(1) Notwithstanding anything in the foregoing provisions of this Act, the registrar shall not enter in the register—
(a) as the father of a child, the name of a man who is to be treated for that purpose as the father of the child by virtue of section 39(1) or 40(1) or (2) of the Human Fertilisation and Embryology Act 2008 (circumstances in which man to be treated as father of child for purposes of registration of birth where fertility treatment undertaken after his death); or
(b) as a parent of the child, the name of a woman who is to be treated for that purpose as a parent of the child by virtue of section 46(1) or (2) of that Act (circumstances in which woman to be treated as parent of child for purposes of registration of birth where fertility treatment undertaken after her death),

unless the condition in subsection (2) below is satisfied.

(2) The condition in this subsection is satisfied if—
(a) the mother requests the registrar to make such an entry in the register and produces the relevant documents;

...

(3) In this section 'the relevant documents' means—
(a) the consent in writing and election mentioned in section 39(1), 40(1) or (2) or 46(1) or (2) (as the case requires) of the Human Fertilisation and Embryology Act 2008;
(b) a certificate of a registered medical practitioner as to the medical facts concerned; and
(c) such other documentary evidence (if any) as the registrar considers appropriate.

MATRIMONIAL CAUSES (PROPERTY AND MAINTENANCE) ACT 1958
(6 & 7 Eliz. 2, c. 35)

7. Extension of s. 17 of Married Women's Property Act 1882

(1) Any right of a wife, under section seventeen of the Married Women's Property Act 1882 to apply to a judge of the High Court or of the family court in any question between

husband and wife as to the title to or possession of property, shall include the right to make such an application where it is claimed by the wife that her husband has had in his possession or under his control—

(a) money to which, or to a share of which, she was beneficially entitled (whether by reason that it represented the proceeds of property to which, or to an interest in which, she was beneficially entitled, or for any other reason), or

(b) property (other than money) to which, or to an interest in which, she was beneficially entitled,

and that either that money or other property has ceased to be in his possession or under his control or that she does not know whether it is still in his possession or under his control.

(2) Where, on an application made to a judge of the High Court or of the family court under the said section seventeen, as extended by the preceding subsection, the judge is satisfied—

(a) that the husband has had in his possession or under his control money or other property as mentioned in paragraph (a) or paragraph (b) of the preceding subsection, and

(b) that he has not made to the wife, in respect of that money or other property, such payment or disposition as would have been appropriate in the circumstances,

the power to make orders under that section shall be extended in accordance with the next following subsection.

(3) Where the last preceding subsection applies, the power to make orders under the said section seventeen shall include power for the judge to order the husband to pay to the wife—

(a) in a case falling within paragraph (a) of subsection (1) of this section, such sum in respect of the money to which the application relates, or the wife's share thereof, as the case may be, or

(b) in a case falling within paragraph (b) of the said subsection (1), such sum in respect of the value of the property to which the application relates, or the wife's interest therein, as the case may be,

as the judge may consider appropriate.

(4) Where on an application under the said section seventeen as extended by this section it appears to the judge that there is any property which—

(a) represents the whole or part of the money or property in question, and

(b) is property in respect of which an order could have been made under that section if an application had been made by the wife thereunder in a question as to the title to or possession of that property,

the judge (either in substitution for or in addition to the making of an order in accordance with the last preceding subsection) may make any order under that section in respect of that property which he could have made on such an application as is mentioned in paragraph (b) of this subsection.

(5) The preceding provisions of this section shall have effect in relation to a husband as they have effect in relation to a wife, as if any reference to the husband were a reference to the wife and any reference to the wife were a reference to the husband.

(6) Any power of a judge which is exercisable on an application under the said section seventeen shall be exercisable in relation to an application made under that section as extended by this section.

(7) For the avoidance of doubt it is hereby declared that any power conferred by the said section seventeen to make orders with respect to any property includes power to order a sale of the property.

MAINTENANCE ORDERS ACT 1958
(6 & 7 Eliz. 2, c. 39)

PART I

REGISTRATION, ENFORCEMENT AND VARIATION OF CERTAIN MAINTENANCE ORDERS

1. Application of Part I

(1) The provisions of this Part of this Act shall have effect for the purpose of enabling maintenance orders to which this Part of this Act applies to be registered in the family court and, subject to those provisions, while so registered to be enforced in like manner as an order made by the family court and to be varied by that court.

(1A) In the following provisions of the Act 'maintenance order' means any order specified in Schedule 8 to the Administration of Justice Act 1970.

1. (2) For the purposes of subsection (1) above, a maintenance order made by a court in Scotland or Northern Ireland and registered in the High Court under Part II of the Maintenance Orders Act 1950 shall be deemed to have been made by the High Court.

(2A) This Part of this Act applies—

(a) to maintenance orders made by the High Court, other than orders registered in Scotland or Northern Ireland under Part II of the Maintenance Orders Act 1950, and

(b) to maintenance orders made by a court in Scotland or Northern Ireland and registered in the High Court under Part II of the Maintenance Orders Act 1950.

. . .

MARRIAGE (ENABLING) ACT 1960
(8 & 9 Eliz., c. 29)

1. Certain marriages not to be void

(1) No marriage hereafter contracted (whether in or out of Great Britain) between a man and a woman who is the sister, aunt or niece of a former wife of his (whether living or not), or was formerly the wife of his brother, uncle or nephew (whether living or not), shall by reason of that relationship be void or voidable under any enactment or rule of law applying in Great Britain as a marriage between persons within the prohibited degrees of affinity.

(2) In the foregoing subsection words of kinship apply equally to kin of the whole and of the half blood.

(3) This section does not validate a marriage, if either party to it is at the time of the marriage domiciled in a country outside Great Britain, and under the law of that country there cannot be a valid marriage between the parties.

LAW REFORM (HUSBAND AND WIFE) ACT 1962
(10 & 11 Eliz. 2, c. 48)

1. Actions in tort between husband and wife

(1) Subject to the provisions of this section, each of the parties to a marriage shall have the like right of action in tort against the other as if they were not married.

(2) Where an action in tort is brought by one of the parties to a marriage against the other during the subsistence of the marriage, the court may stay the action if it appears—

(a) that no substantial benefit would accrue to either party from the continuation of the proceedings; or

(b) that the question or questions in issue could more conveniently be disposed of on an application made under section seventeen of the Married Women's Property Act 1882 (determination of questions between husband and wife as to the title to or possession of property);

and without prejudice to paragraph (b) of this section the court may, in such an action, either exercise any power which could be exercised on an application under the said section seventeen, or give such directions as it thinks fit for the disposal under that section of any question arising in the proceedings.

MATRIMONIAL PROPERTY ACT 1964
(1964 c. 19)

1. Money and property derived from housekeeping allowance

If any question arises as to the right of a husband or wife to money derived from any allowance made by either of them for the expenses of the matrimonial home or for similar purposes, or to any property acquired out of such money, the money or property shall, in the absence of any agreement between them to the contrary, be treated as belonging to them in equal shares.

ABORTION ACT 1967
(1967 c. 87)

1. Medical termination of pregnancy

(1) Subject to the provisions of this section, a person shall not be guilty of an offence under the law relating to abortion when a pregnancy is terminated by a registered medical practitioner if two registered medical practitioners are of the opinion, formed in good faith—
  (a) that the pregnancy has not exceeded its twenty-fourth week and that the continuance of the pregnancy would involve risk, greater than if the pregnancy were terminated, of injury to the physical or mental health of the pregnant woman or any existing children of her family; or
  (b) that the termination is necessary to prevent grave permanent injury to the physical or mental health of the pregnant woman; or
  (c) that the continuance of the pregnancy would involve risk to the life of the pregnant woman, greater than if the pregnancy were terminated; or
  (d) that there is a substantial risk that if the child were born it would suffer from such physical or mental abnormalities as to be seriously handicapped.

(2) In determining whether the continuance of a pregnancy would involve such risk of injury to health as is mentioned in paragraph (a) or (b) of subsection (1) of this section, account may be taken of the pregnant woman's actual or reasonably foreseeable environment.

(3) Except as provided by subsection (4) of this section, any treatment for the termination of pregnancy must be carried out in a hospital vested in the Secretary of State for the purposes of his functions under the National Health Service Act 2006 or the National Health Service (Scotland) Act 1978 or in a hospital vested in a Primary Care Trust or a National Health Service trust or an NHS foundation trust or in a place approved for the purposes of this section by the Secretary of State.

(3A) The power under subsection (3) of this section to approve a place includes power, in relation to treatment consisting primarily in the use of such medicines as may be specified in the approval and carried out in such manner as may be so specified, to approve a class of places.

(4) Subsection (3) of this section, and so much of subsection (1) as relates to the opinion of two registered medical practitioners, shall not apply to the termination of a pregnancy by a registered medical practitioner in a case where he is of the opinion, formed in good faith, that the termination is immediately necessary to save the life or to prevent grave permanent injury to the physical or mental health of the pregnant woman.

2. Notification

(1) The Minister of Health in respect of England and Wales, and the Secretary of State in respect of Scotland, shall by statutory instrument make regulations to provide—
  (a) for requiring any such opinion as is referred to in section 1 of this Act to be certified by the practitioners or practitioner concerned in such form and at such time as may be prescribed by the regulations, and for requiring the preservation and disposal of certificates made for the purposes of the regulations;
  (b) for requiring any registered medical practitioner who terminates a pregnancy to give notice of the termination and such other information relating to the termination as may be so prescribed;
  (c) for prohibiting the disclosure, except to such persons or for such purposes as may be so prescribed, of notices given or information furnished pursuant to the regulations.

(2) The information furnished in pursuance of regulations made by virtue of paragraph (b) of subsection (1) of this section shall be notified solely to the Chief Medical Officers of the Department of Health, or of the Welsh Office, or of the Scottish Administration.

(3) Any person who wilfully contravenes or wilfully fails to comply with the requirements of regulations under subsection (1) of this section shall be liable on summary conviction to a fine not exceeding level 5 on the standard scale.

(4) Any statutory instrument made by virtue of this section shall be subject to annulment in pursuance of a resolution of either House of Parliament.

CIVIL EVIDENCE ACT 1968
(1968 c. 64)

PART II

MISCELLANEOUS AND GENERAL

12. Findings of adultery and paternity as evidence in civil proceedings

(1) In any civil proceedings—

(a) the fact that a person has been found guilty of adultery in any matrimonial proceedings; and

(b) the fact that a person has been found to be the father of a child in relevant proceedings before any court in England or Wales or Northern Ireland or has been adjudged to be the father of a child in affiliation proceedings before any court in the United Kingdom;

shall (subject to subsection (3) below) be admissible in evidence for the purpose of proving, where to do so is relevant to any issue in those civil proceedings, that he committed the adultery to which the finding relates, or, as the case may be, is (or was) the father of that child, whether or not he offered any defence to the allegation of adultery or paternity and whether or not he is a party to the civil proceedings; but no finding or adjudication other than a subsisting one shall be admissible in evidence by virtue of this section.

(2) In any civil proceedings in which by virtue of this section a person is proved to have been found guilty of adultery as mentioned in subsection (1)(a) above or to have been found or adjudged to be the father of a child as mentioned in subsection (1)(b) above—

(a) he shall he taken to have committed the adultery to which the finding relates, or as the case may be, to be (or have been) the father of that child, unless the contrary is proved; and

(b) without prejudice to the reception of any other admissible evidence for the purpose of identifying the facts on which the finding or adjudication was based, the contents of any document which was before the court, or which contains any pronouncement of the court in the other proceedings in question shall be admissible in evidence for that purpose.

(3) Nothing in this section shall prejudice the operation of any enactment whereby a finding of fact in any matrimonial or affiliation proceedings is for the purposes of any other proceedings made conclusive evidence of any fact.

(4) Subsection (4) of section 11 of this Act shall apply for the purposes of this section as if the references to subsection (2) were a reference to subsection (2) of this section.

(5) In this section—

'matrimonial proceedings' means any matrimonial cause in the High Court or a county court in England and Wales or any appeal arising out of any such cause or action;

'relevant proceedings' means—

(a) proceedings on a complaint under section 42 of the National Assistance Act 1948 or section 26 of the Social Security Act 1986;

(b) proceedings under the Children Act 1989;

. . .

FAMILY LAW REFORM ACT 1969
(1969 c. 46)

PART I

REDUCTION OF AGE OF MAJORITY AND RELATED PROVISIONS

1. Reduction of age of majority from 21 to 18

(1) As from the date on which this section comes into force a person shall attain full age on attaining the age of eighteen instead of on attaining the age of twenty-one; and a person shall attain full age on that date if he has then already attained the age of eighteen but not the age of twenty-one.

(2) The foregoing subsection applies for the purposes of any rule of law, and, in the absence of a definition or of any indication of a contrary intention, for the construction of 'full age,' 'infant,' 'infancy,' 'minor,' 'minority' and similar expressions in—

(a) any statutory provision, whether passed or made before, on or after the date on which this section comes into force; and

(b) any deed, will or other instrument of whatever nature (not being a statutory provision) made on or after that date.

. . .

(7) Notwithstanding any rule of law, a will or codicil executed before the date on which this section comes into force shall not be treated for the purposes of this section as made on or after that date by reason only that the will or codicil is confirmed by a codicil executed on or after that date.

8. Consent by persons over 16 to surgical, medical and dental treatment

(1) The consent of a minor who has attained the age of sixteen years to any surgical, medical or dental treatment which, in the absence of consent, would constitute a trespass to his person, shall be as effective as it would be if he were of full age; and where a minor has by virtue of this section given an effective consent to any treatment it shall not be necessary to obtain any consent for it from his parent or guardian.

(2) In this section 'surgical, medical or dental treatment' includes any procedure undertaken for the purposes of diagnosis, and this section applies to any procedure (including, in particular, the administration of an anaesthetic) which is ancillary to any treatment as it applies to that treatment.

(3) Nothing in this section shall be construed as making ineffective any consent which would have been effective if this section had not been enacted.

9. Time at which a person attains a particular age

(1) The time at which a person attains a particular age expressed in years shall be the commencement of the relevant anniversary of the date of his birth.

(2) This section applies only where the relevant anniversary falls on a date after that on which this section comes into force, and, in relation to any enactment, deed, will or other instrument, has effect subject to any provision therein.

12. Persons under full age may be described as minors instead of infants

A person who is not of full age may be described as a minor instead of as an infant, and accordingly in this Act 'minor' means such a person as aforesaid.

PART II

PROPERTY RIGHTS OF ILLEGITIMATE CHILDREN

19. Policies of assurance and property in industrial and provident societies

(1) In section 11 of the Married Women's Property Act 1882 (policies of assurance effected for the benefit of children) the expression 'children' shall include illegitimate children.

. . .

PART III

PROVISIONS FOR USE OF SCIENTIFIC TESTS IN DETERMINING PARENTAGE

20. Power of court to require use of scientific tests

(1) In any civil proceedings in which the parentage of any person falls to be determined, the court may, either of its own motion or on an application by any party to the proceedings, give a direction—

(a) for the use of scientific tests to ascertain whether such tests show that a party to the proceedings is or is not the father or mother of that person; and

(b) for the taking, within a period specified in the direction, of bodily samples from all or any of the following, namely, that person, any party who is alleged to be the father or mother of that person and any other party to the proceedings;

and the court may at any time revoke or vary a direction previously given by it under this subsection.

(1A) Tests required by a direction under this section may only be carried out by a body which has been accredited for the purposes of this section by—

(a) the Lord Chancellor, or

(b) a body appointed by him for the purpose.

(2) The individual carrying out scientific tests in pursuance of a direction under subsection (1) above shall make to the court a report in which he shall state—

(a) the results of the tests;

(b) whether any party to whom the report relates is or is not excluded by the results from being the father or mother of the person whose parentage is to be determined; and

(c) in relation to any party who is not so excluded, the value, if any, of the results in determining whether that party is the father or mother of that person;

and the report shall be received by the court as evidence in the proceedings of the matters stated in it.

(2A) Where the proceedings in which the parentage of any person falls to be determined are proceedings on an application under section 55A or 56 of the Family Law Act 1986, any reference in subsection (1) or (2) of this section to any party to the proceedings shall include a reference to any person named in the application.

(3) A report under subsection (2) of this section shall be in the form prescribed by regulations made under section 22 of this Act.

(4) Where a report has been made to a court under subsection (2) of this section, any party may, with the leave of the court, or shall, if the court so directs, obtain from the tester a written statement explaining or amplifying any statement made in the report, and that statement shall be deemed for the purposes of this section (except subsection (3) thereof) to form part of the report made to the court.

. . .

21. Consents, etc., required for taking of bodily samples

(1) Subject to the provisions of subsections (3) and (4) of this section, a bodily sample which is required to be taken from any person for the purpose of giving effect to a direction under section 20 of this Act shall not be taken from that person except with his consent.

(2) The consent of a minor who has attained the age of sixteen years to the taking from himself of a bodily sample shall be as effective as it would be if he were of full age; and where a minor has by virtue of this subsection given an effective consent to the taking of a bodily sample it shall not be necessary to obtain any consent for it from any other person.

(3) A bodily sample may be taken from a person under the age of sixteen years, not being a person as is referred to in subsection (4) of this section,

(a) if the person who has the care and control of him consents; or

(b) where that person does not consent, if the court considers that it would be in his best interests for the sample to be taken.

(4) A bodily sample may be taken from a person who lacks capacity (within the meaning of the Mental Capacity Act 2005) to give his consent, if consent is given by the court giving the direction under section 20 or by—

(a) a donee of an enduring power of attorney or lasting power of attorney (within the meaning of that Act), or

(b) a deputy appointed, or any other person authorised, by the Court of Protection, with power in that respect.

(5) The foregoing provisions of this section are without prejudice to the provisions of section 23 of this Act.

. . .

23. Failure to comply with direction for taking bodily samples

(1) Where a court gives a direction under section 20 of this Act and any person fails to take any step required of him for the purpose of giving effect to the direction, the court may draw such inferences, if any, from that fact as appear proper in the circumstances.

(2) Where in any proceedings in which the parentage of any person falls to be determined by the court hearing the proceedings there is a presumption of law that that person is legitimate, then if—

(a) a direction is given under section 20 of this Act in those proceedings, and

(b) any party who is claiming any relief in the proceedings and who for the purpose of obtaining that relief is entitled to rely on the presumption fails to take any step required of him for the purpose of giving effect to the direction,

the court may adjourn the hearing for such period as it thinks fit to enable that party to take that step, and if at the end of that period he has failed without reasonable cause to take it the court may, without prejudice to subsection (1) of this section, dismiss his claim for relief notwithstanding the absence of evidence to rebut the presumption.

(3) Where any person named in a direction under section 20 of this Act fails to consent to the taking of a bodily sample from himself or from any person named in the direction of whom he has the care and control, he shall be deemed for the purposes of this section to have failed to take a step required of him for the purpose of giving effect to the direction.

24. Penalty for personating another, etc., for purposes of providing bodily sample

If for the purpose of providing a bodily sample for a test required to give effect to a direction under section 20 of this Act any person personates another, or proffers a child knowing that it is not the child named in the direction, he shall be liable—

(a) on conviction on indictment, to imprisonment for a term not exceeding two years, or
(b) on summary conviction, to a fine not exceeding the prescribed sum.

25. Interpretation of Part III

In this Part of this Act the following expressions have the meanings hereby respectively assigned to them, that is to say—

'bodily sample' means a sample of bodily fluid or bodily tissue taken for the purpose of scientific tests;

'excluded' means excluded subject to the occurrence of mutation, to section 27 of the Family Law Reform Act 1987, to sections 27 to 29 of the Human Fertilisation and Embryology Act 1990 and to sections 33 to 47 of the Human Fertilisation and Embryology Act 2008;

'scientific tests' means scientific tests carried out under this Part of this Act and made with the object of ascertaining the inheritable characteristics of bodily fluids or bodily tissue.

PART IV
MISCELLANEOUS AND GENERAL

26. Rebuttal of presumption as to legitimacy and illegitimacy

Any presumption of law as to the legitimacy or illegitimacy of any person may in any civil proceedings be rebutted by evidence which shows that it is more probable than not that that person is illegitimate or legitimate, as the case may be, and it shall not be necessary to prove that fact beyond reasonable doubt in order to rebut the presumption.

LAW REFORM (MISCELLANEOUS PROVISIONS) ACT 1970
(1970 c. 33)

Legal consequences of termination of contract to marry

1. Engagements to marry not enforceable at law

(1) An agreement between two persons to marry one another shall not under the law of England and Wales have effect as a contract giving rise to legal rights and no action shall lie in England and Wales for breach of such an agreement, whatever the law applicable to the agreement.

(2) This section shall have effect in relation to agreements entered into before it comes into force, except that it shall not affect any action commenced before it comes into force.

2. Property of engaged couples

(1) Where an agreement to marry is terminated, any rule of law relating to the rights of husbands and wives in relation to property in which either or both has or have a beneficial interest, including any such rule as explained by section 37 of the Matrimonial Proceedings and Property Act 1970, shall apply, in relation to any property in which either or both of the parties to the agreement had a beneficial interest while the agreement was in force, as it applies in relation to property in which a husband or wife has a beneficial interest.

(2) Where an agreement to marry is terminated, section 17 of the Married Women's Property Act 1882 and section 7 of the Matrimonial Causes (Property and Maintenance) Act 1958 (which sections confer power on a judge of the High Court or the family court to settle disputes between husband and wife about property) shall apply, as if the parties were married, to any dispute between, or claim by, one of them in relation to property in which either or both had a beneficial interest while the agreement was in force; but an application made by virtue of this section to the judge under the said section 17, as originally enacted or as extended by the said section 7, shall be made within three years of the termination of the agreement.

3. Gifts between engaged couples

(1) A party to an agreement to marry who makes a gift of property to the other party to the agreement on the condition (express or implied) that it shall be returned if the agreement is terminated shall not be prevented from recovering the property by reason only of his having terminated the agreement.

(2) The gift of an engagement ring shall be presumed to be an absolute gift; this presumption may be rebutted by proving that the ring was given on the condition, express or implied, that it should be returned if the marriage did not take place for any reason.

MARRIAGE (REGISTRAR GENERAL'S LICENCE) ACT 1970
(1970 c. 34)

1. Marriages which may be solemnised by Registrar General's licence

(1) Subject to the provisions of subsection (2) below, any marriage which may be solemnised on the authority of certificates of a superintendent registrar may be solemnised on the authority of the Registrar General's licence elsewhere than at a registered building, the office of a superintendent registrar, or approved premises.

Provided that any such marriage shall not be solemnised according to the rites of the Church of England or the Church in Wales.

(2) The Registrar General shall not issue any licence for the solemnisation of a marriage as is mentioned in subsection (1) above unless he is satisfied that one of the persons to be married is seriously ill and is not expected to recover and cannot be moved to a place at which under the provisions of the Marriage Act 1949 (hereinafter called the 'principal Act') the marriage could be solemnised (disregarding for this purpose the provisions of that Act relating to marriages in pursuance of section 26(1)(dd) or section 26B(6) of that Act).

(3) A marriage of a same sex couple according to religious rites or usages may not be solemnized in accordance with this Act unless the relevant governing authority has given written consent to marriages of same sex couples according to those religious rites or usages.

. . .

2. Notice of marriage

(1) Where a marriage is intended to be solemnised on the authority of the Registrar General's licence, notice shall be given in the prescribed form by either of the persons to be married to the superintendent registrar of the registration district in which it is intended that the marriage shall be solemnised, and the notice shall state by or before whom it is intended that the marriage shall be solemnised.

(2) The provisions of section 27(4) of the principal Act (which relate to entries in the marriage notice book) shall apply to notices of marriage on the authority of the Registrar General's licence.

(3) The provisions of section 28 of the principal Act (declaration to accompany notice of marriage) shall apply to the giving of notice under this Act with the exception of paragraph (b) of subsection (1) of that section and with the modification that in section 28(2) references to the registrar of births and deaths or of marriages and deputy registrar shall be omitted.

3. Evidence of capacity, consent etc., to be produced

The person giving notice to the superintendent registrar under the provisions of the foregoing section shall produce to the superintendent registrar such evidence as the Registrar General may require to satisfy him—

(a) that there is no lawful impediment to the marriage;
(b) that the consent of any person whose consent to the marriage is required under section 3 of the principal Act has been duly given; and
(c) that there is sufficient reason why a licence should be granted;
(d) that the conditions contained in section 1(2) of this Act are satisfied and that the person in respect of whom such conditions are satisfied is able to and does understand the nature and purport of the marriage ceremony:

Provided that the certificate of a registered medical practitioner shall be sufficient evidence of any or all of the matters in subsection (1)(d) of this section referred to.

4. Application to be reported to Registrar General

Upon receipt of any notice and evidence as mentioned in sections 2 and 3 above respectively the superintendent registrar shall inform the Registrar General and shall comply with any directions he may give for verifying the evidence given.

5. Caveat against issue of Registrar General's licence

The provisions of section 29 of the principal Act (caveat against issue of certificate) shall apply to the issue of a licence by the Registrar General with the modification that caveat may be entered with either the superintendent registrar or the Registrar General and in either case it shall be for the Registrar General to examine into the matter of the caveat and to decide whether or not the licence should be granted and his decision shall be final, and with a further modification that the references to the superintendent registrar in that section shall refer to the superintendent registrar of the registration district in which the marriage is intended to be solemnised.

6. Marriage of persons under eighteen

The provisions of section 3 of the principal Act (marriage of persons under 18) shall apply for the purposes of this Act to a marriage intended to be solemnised by Registrar General's licence as they apply to a marriage intended to be solemnised on the authority of certificates of a superintendent registrar under Part III of the principal Act with the modification that if the consent of any person whose consent is required under that Act cannot be obtained by reason of absence or inaccessibility or by reason of his being under any disability, the superintendent registrar shall not be required to dispense with the necessity for the consent of that person and the Registrar General may dispense with the necessity of obtaining the consent of that person, whether or not there is any other person whose consent is also required.

7. Issue of licence by Registrar General

Where the marriage is intended to be solemnised on the authority of the Registrar General and he is satisfied that sufficient grounds exist why a licence should be granted he shall issue in the prescribed form unless—

(a) any lawful impediment to the issue of the licence has been shown to his satisfaction to exist; or

(b) the issue of the licence has been forbidden under section 30 of the principal Act.

8. Period of validity of licence

(1) A marriage may be solemnised on the authority of the Registrar General's licence at any time within one month from the day on which the notice of marriage was entered in the marriage notice book.

(2) If the marriage is not solemnised within the said period of one month, the notice of marriage and the licence shall be void, and no person shall solemnise the marriage on the authority thereof.

9. Place of solemnisation

A marriage on the authority of the Registrar General's licence shall be solemnised in the place stated in the notice of marriage.

10. Manner of solemnisation

(1) Any marriage to be solemnised on the authority of the Registrar General's licence shall be solemnised at the wish of the persons to be married either—

  (a) according to such form or ceremony, not being the rites or ceremonies of the Church of England or the Church in Wales, as the persons to be married shall see fit to adopt, or

  (b) by civil ceremony.

(2) Except where the marriage is solemnised according to the usages of the Society of Friends or is a marriage between two persons professing the Jewish religion according to the usages of the Jews, it shall be solemnised in the presence of a registrar:

Provided that where the marriage is to be by civil ceremony it shall be solemnised in the presence of the superintendent registrar as well as the registrar.

(3) Except where the marriage is solemnised according to the usages of the Society of Friends or is a marriage between two persons professing the Jewish religion according to the usages of the Jews, the persons to be married shall in some part of the ceremony in the presence of two or more witnesses and the registrar and, where appropriate, the superintendent registrar, make the declaration and say to one another the words prescribed by section 44(3) or (3A) of the principal Act.

(4) No person who is a clergyman within the meaning of section 78 of the principal Act shall solemnise any marriage which is solemnised on the authority of the Registrar General.

11. Civil marriage followed by religious ceremony

(1) If the parties to a marriage solemnised on the authority of the Registrar General's licence before a superintendent registrar desire to add the religious ceremony ordained or used by the church or persuasion of which they are members and have given notice of their desire so to do a clergyman or minister of that church or persuasion upon the production of a certificate of their marriage before the superintendent registrar and upon

the payment of the customary fees (if any), may, if he sees fit, read or celebrate in the presence of the parties to the marriage the marriage service of the church or persuasion to which he belongs or nominate some other minister to do so.

(2) The provisions of section 46(2) and (3) of the principal Act shall apply to such a reading or celebration as they apply to the reading or celebration of a marriage service following a marriage solemnised in the office of a superintendent registrar.

12. Proof of certain matters not necessary to validity of marriages

The provisions of section 48 of the principal Act (proof of certain matters not necessary to validity of marriages) shall apply with the appropriate modifications to a marriage solemnised under the authority of the Registrar General's licence as they apply to a marriage solemnised under the authority of a certificate of a superintendent registrar.

13. Void marriages

The provisions of section 49 of the principal Act (void marriages) shall apply to a marriage under the authority of the Registrar General's licence:—

(a) with the substitution in paragraph (b) for the words from 'certificates for marriage' onwards of the words 'a Registrar General's licence';

(c) with the substitution for paragraph (d) of the words 'on the authority of a licence which is void by virtue of section 8(2) of the Marriage (Registrar General's Licence) Act 1970';

(d) with the substitution for paragraph (e) of the words 'in any place other than the place specified in the notice of marriage and the Registrar General's licence';

(e) with the substitution for paragraphs (f) and (g) of the words 'in the absence of a registrar or, where the marriage is by civil ceremony, of a superintendent registrar, except where the marriage is solemnised according to the usages of the Society of Friends or is a marriage between two persons professing the Jewish religion according to the usages of the Jews'.

13A. Void marriages: additional provision about same sex couples

(1) If a same sex couple knowingly and wilfully intermarries under the provisions of this Act in the absence of the required consent, the marriage shall be void.

(2) In this section 'required consent' means consent under section 1(3).

15. Registration of marriages

A marriage solemnised on the authority of the Registrar General's licence shall be registered in accordance with the provisions of the principal Act which apply to the registration of marriages solemnised in the presence of a registrar or according to the usages of the Society of Friends or of persons professing the Jewish religion.

16. Offences

(1) It shall be an offence knowingly and wilfully—

(a) to solemnise a marriage by Registrar General's licence in any place other than the place specified in the licence;

(b) to solemnise a marriage by Registrar General's licence without the presence of a registrar except in the case of a marriage according to the usages of the Society of Friends or a marriage between two persons professing the Jewish religion according to the usages of the Jews;

(c) to solemnise a marriage by Registrar General's licence after the expiration of one month from the date of entry of the notice of marriage in the marriage notice book;

(d) to give false information by way of evidence as required by section 3 of this Act;

(e) to give a false certificate as provided for in section 3(1)(d) of this Act;

and any person found guilty of any of the above-mentioned offences shall be liable on summary conviction to a fine not exceeding the prescribed sum or on indictment to a fine or to imprisonment not exceeding three years or to both such fine and such imprisonment.

(2) A superintendent registrar who knowingly and wilfully solemnises or permits to be solemnised in his presence, or a registrar who knowingly and wilfully registers a marriage by Registrar General's licence which is void by virtue of Part III of the principal Act as amended by this Act shall be guilty of an offence and shall be liable on summary conviction to a fine not exceeding the prescribed sum or on indictment to a fine or to imprisonment not exceeding three years or to both such fine and such imprisonment.

(3) No prosecution under this section shall be commenced after the expiration of three years from the commission of the offence.

(4) The provisions of sections 75(1)(a) and 75(2)(a) of the principal Act shall not apply to a marriage solemnised on the authority of the Registrar General's licence.

MATRIMONIAL PROCEEDINGS AND PROPERTY ACT 1970
(1970 c. 45)

Provisions relating to property of married persons

37. Contributions by spouse in money or money's worth to the improvement of property

It is hereby declared that where a husband or wife contributes in money or money's worth to the improvement of real or personal property in which or in the proceeds of sale of which either or both of them has or have a beneficial interest, the husband or wife so contributing shall, if the contribution is of a substantial nature and subject to any agreement between them to the contrary express or implied, be treated as having then acquired by virtue of his or her contribution a share or an enlarged share, as the case may be, in that beneficial interest of such an extent as may have been then agreed or, in default of such agreement, as may seem in all the circumstances just to any court before which the question of the existence or extent of the beneficial interest of the husband or wife arises (whether in proceedings between them or in other proceedings).

39. Extension of s. 17 of Married Women's Property Act 1882

An application may be made to the High Court or the family court under section 17 of the Married Women's Property Act 1882 (powers of the court in disputes between husband and wife about property) (including that section as extended by section 7 of the Matrimonial Causes (Property and Maintenance) Act 1958) by either of the parties to a marriage notwithstanding that their marriage has been dissolved or annulled so long as the application is made within the period of three years beginning with the date on which the marriage was dissolved or annulled; and references in the said section 17 and the said section 7 to a husband or a wife shall be construed accordingly.

LAND CHARGES ACT 1972
(1972 c. 61)

2. The register of land charges

(1) If a charge on or obligation affecting land falls into one of the classes described in this section, it may be registered in the register of land charges as a land charge of that class.

. . .

(7) A Class F land charge is a charge affecting any land by virtue of Part IV of the Family Law Act 1996.

MATRIMONIAL CAUSES ACT 1973
(1973 c. 18)

PART I

DIVORCE, NULLITY AND OTHER MATRIMONIAL SUITS

Divorce

1. Divorce on breakdown of marriage

(1) Subject to section 3 below, a petition for divorce may be presented to the court by either party to a marriage on the ground that the marriage has broken down irretrievably.

(2) The court hearing a petition for divorce shall not hold the marriage to have broken down irretrievably unless the petitioner satisfies the court of one or more of the following facts, that is to say—

- (a) that the respondent has committed adultery and the petitioner finds it intolerable to live with the respondent;
- (b) that the respondent has behaved in such a way that the petitioner cannot reasonably be expected to live with the respondent;
- (c) that the respondent has deserted the petitioner for a continuous period of at least two years immediately preceding the presentation of the petition;

(d) that the parties to the marriage have lived apart for a continuous period of at least two years immediately preceding the presentation of the petition (hereafter in this Act referred to as 'two years' separation') and the respondent consents to a decree being granted;

(e) that the parties to the marriage have lived apart for a continuous period of at least five years immediately preceding the presentation of the petition (hereafter in this Act referred to as 'five years' separation').

(3) On a petition for divorce it shall be the duty of the court to enquire, so far as it reasonably can, into the facts alleged by the petitioner and into any facts alleged by the respondent.

(4) If the court is satisfied on the evidence of any such fact as is mentioned in subsection (2) above, then, unless it is satisfied on all the evidence that the marriage has not broken down irretrievably, it shall, subject to section 5 below, grant a decree of divorce.

(5) Every decree of divorce shall in the first instance be a decree nisi and shall not be made absolute before the expiration of six months from its grant unless the High Court by general order from time to time fixes a shorter period, or unless in any particular case the court in which the proceedings are for the time being pending from time to time by special order fixes a shorter period than the period otherwise applicable for the time being by virtue of this subsection.

2. Supplemental provision as to facts raising presumption of breakdown

(1) One party to a marriage shall not be entitled to rely for the purposes of section 1(2)(a) above on adultery committed by the other if, after it became known to him that the other had committed that adultery, the parties have lived with each other for a period exceeding, or periods together exceeding, six months.

(2) Where the parties to a marriage have lived with each other after it became known to one party that the other had committed adultery, but subsection (1) above does not apply, in any proceedings for divorce in which the petitioner relies on that adultery the fact that the parties have lived with each other after that time shall be disregarded in determining for the purposes of section 1(2)(a) above whether the petitioner finds it intolerable to live with the respondent.

(3) Where in any proceedings for divorce the petitioner alleges that the respondent has behaved in such a way that the petitioner cannot reasonably be expected to live with him, but the parties to the marriage have lived with each other for a period or periods after the date of the occurrence of the final incident relied on by the petitioner and held by the court to support his allegation, that fact shall be disregarded in determining for the purposes of section 1(2)(b) above whether the petitioner cannot reasonably be expected to live with the respondent if the length of that period or of those periods together was six months or less.

(4) For the purposes of section 1(2)(c) above the court may treat a period of desertion as having continued at a time when the deserting party was incapable of continuing the necessary intention if the evidence before the court is such that, had that party not been so incapable, the court would have inferred that his desertion continued at that time.

(5) In considering for the purposes of section 1(2) above whether the period for which the respondent has deserted the petitioner or the period for which the parties to a marriage have lived apart has been continuous, no account shall be taken of any one period (not exceeding six months) or of any two or more periods (not exceeding six months in all) during which the parties resumed living with each other, but no period during which the parties lived with each other shall count as part of the period of desertion, or of the period for which the parties to the marriage lived apart, as the case may be.

(6) For the purposes of section 1(2)(d) and (e) above and this section a husband and wife shall be treated as living apart unless they are living with each other in the same household, and references in this section to the parties to a marriage living with each other shall be construed as references to their living with each other in the same household.

(7) Provision shall be made by rules of court for the purpose of ensuring that where in pursuance of section 1(2)(d) above the petitioner alleges that the respondent consents to a decree being granted the respondent has been given such information as will enable him to understand the consequences to him of his consenting to a decree being granted and the steps which he must take to indicate that he consents to the grant of a decree.

3. Bar on petitions for divorce within one year of marriage

(1) No petition for divorce shall be presented to the court before the expiration of the period of one year from the date of the marriage.

(2) Nothing in this section shall prohibit the presentation of a petition based on matters which occurred before the expiration of that period.

4. Divorce not precluded by previous judicial separation

(1) A person shall not be prevented from presenting a petition for divorce, or the court from granting a decree of divorce, by reason only that the petitioner or respondent has at any time, on the same facts or substantially the same facts as those proved in support of the petition, been granted a decree of judicial separation or an order under, or having effect as if made under, the Matrimonial Proceedings (Magistrates' Courts) Act 1960 or Part I of the Domestic Proceedings and Magistrates' Courts Act 1978 or any corresponding enactments in force in Northern Ireland, the Isle of Man or any of the Channel Islands.

(2) On a petition for divorce in such a case as is mentioned in subsection (1) above, the court may treat the decree or order as sufficient proof of any adultery, desertion or other fact by reference to which it was granted, but shall not grant a decree of divorce without receiving evidence from the petitioner.

(3) Where a petition for divorce in such a case follows a decree of judicial separation or (subject to subsection (5) below) an order containing a provision exempting one party to the marriage from the obligation to cohabit with the other, for the purposes of that petition a period of desertion immediately preceding the institution of the proceedings for the decree or order shall, if the parties have not resumed cohabitation and the decree or order has been continuously in force since it was granted, be deemed immediately to precede the presentation of the petition.

(4) For the purposes of section 1(2)(c) above the court may treat as a period during which the respondent has deserted the petitioner any of the following periods, that is to say—
- (a) any period during which there is in force an injunction granted by the High Court, the family court which excludes the respondent from the matrimonial home;
- (b) any period during which there is in force an order made by the High Court or a county court under section 1 or 9 of the Matrimonial Homes Act 1983 which prohibits the exercise by the respondent of the right to occupy a dwelling-house in which the applicant and the respondent have or at any time have had a matrimonial home;
- (c) any period during which there is in force an order made by a magistrates' court under section 16(3) of the Domestic Proceedings and Magistrates' Courts Act 1978 which requires the respondent to leave the matrimonial home or prohibits the respondent from entering the matrimonial home.

(5) Where—
- (a) a petition for divorce is presented after the date on which Part I of the Domestic Proceedings and Magistrates' Courts Act 1978 comes into force, and
- (b) an order made under the Matrimonial Proceedings (Magistrates' Courts) Act 1960 containing a provision exempting the petitioner from the obligation to cohabit with the respondent is in force on that date,

then, for the purposes of section 1(2)(c) above, the court may treat a period during which such a provision was included in that order (whether before or after that date) as a period during which the respondent has deserted the petitioner.

5. Refusal of decree in five year separation cases on ground of grave hardship to respondent

(1) The respondent to a petition for divorce in which the petitioner alleges five years' separation may oppose the grant of a decree on the ground that the dissolution of the marriage will result in grave financial or other hardship to him and that it would in all the circumstances be wrong to dissolve the marriage.

(2) Where the grant of a decree is opposed by virtue of this section, then—
- (a) if the court finds that the petitioner is entitled to rely in support of his petition on the fact of five years' separation and makes no such finding as to any other fact mentioned in section 1(2) above, and
- (b) if apart from this section the court would grant a decree on the petition,

the court shall consider all the circumstances, including the conduct of the parties to the marriage and the interests of those parties and of any children or other persons concerned, and if of opinion that the dissolution of the marriage will result in grave financial or other hardship to the respondent and that it would in all the circumstances be wrong to dissolve the marriage it shall dismiss the petition.

(3) For the purposes of this section hardship shall include the loss of the chance of acquiring any benefit which the respondent might acquire if the marriage were not dissolved.

6. Attempts at reconciliation of parties to marriage

(1) Provision shall be made by rules of court for requiring the solicitor acting for a petitioner for divorce to certify whether he has discussed with the petitioner the possibility of a reconciliation and given him the names and addresses of persons qualified to help effect a reconciliation between parties to a marriage who have become estranged.

(2) If at any stage of proceedings for divorce it appears to the court that there is a reasonable possibility of a reconciliation between the parties to the marriage, the court may adjourn the proceedings for such period as it thinks fit to enable attempts to be made to effect such a reconciliation.

The power conferred by the foregoing provision is additional to any other power of the court to adjourn proceedings.

7. Consideration by the court of certain agreements or arrangements

Provision may be made by rules of court for enabling the parties to a marriage, or either of them, in application made either before or after the presentation of a petition for divorce, to refer to the court any agreement or arrangement made or proposed to be made between them, being an agreement or arrangement which relates to, arises out of, or is connected with, the proceedings for divorce which are contemplated or, as the case may be, have begun, for enabling the court to express an opinion, should it think it desirable to do so, as to the reasonableness of the agreement or arrangement and to give such directions, if any, in the matter as it thinks fit.

8. Intervention of Queen's Proctor

(1) In the case of a petition for divorce—

(a) the court may, if it thinks fit, direct all necessary papers in the matter to be sent to the Queen's Proctor, who shall under the directions of the Attorney-General instruct counsel to argue before the court any question in relation to the matter which the court considers it necessary or expedient to have fully argued;

(b) any person may at any time during the progress of the proceedings or before the decree nisi is made absolute give information to the Queen's Proctor on any matter material to the due decision of the case, and the Queen's Proctor may thereupon take such steps as the Attorney General considers necessary or expedient.

(2) Where the Queen's Proctor intervenes or shows cause against a decree nisi in any proceedings for divorce, the court may make such order as may be just as to the payment by other parties to the proceedings of the costs incurred by any of those parties by reason of his so doing.

. . .

9. Proceedings after decree nisi: general powers of court

(1) Where a decree of divorce has been granted but not made absolute, then, without prejudice to section 8 above, any person (excluding a party to the proceedings other than the Queen's Proctor) may show cause why the decree should not be made absolute by reason of material facts not having been brought before the court; and in such a case the court may—

(a) notwithstanding anything in section 1(5) above (but subject to sections 10(2) to (4) below) make the decree absolute; or

(b) rescind the decree; or

(c) require further inquiry; or

(d) otherwise deal with the case as it thinks fit.

(2) Where a decree of divorce has been granted and no application for it to be made absolute has been made by the party to whom it was granted, then, at any time after the expiration of three months from the earliest date on which that party could have made such an application, the party against whom it was granted may make an application to the court, and on that application the court may exercise any of the powers mentioned in paragraphs (a) to (d) of subsection (1) above.

10. Proceedings after decree nisi: special protection for respondent in separation cases

(1) Where in any case the court has granted a decree of divorce on the basis of a finding that the petitioner was entitled to rely in support of his petition on the fact of two years' separation coupled with the respondent's consent to a decree being granted and has made no such finding as to any other fact mentioned in section 1(2) above, the court may, on an application made by the respondent at any time before the decree is made absolute, rescind the decree if it is satisfied that the petitioner misled the respondent (whether intentionally or unintentionally) about any matter which the respondent took into account in deciding to give his consent.

(2) The following provisions of this section apply where—

(a) the respondent to a petition for divorce in which the petitioner alleged two years' or five years' separation coupled, in the former case, with the respondent's consent to a decree being granted, has applied to the court for consideration under subsection (3) below of his financial position after the divorce; and

(b) the court has granted a decree on the petition on the basis of a finding that the petitioner was entitled to rely in support of his petition on the fact of two years' or five years' separation (as the case may be) and has made no such finding as to any other fact mentioned in section 1(2) above.

(3) The court hearing an application by the respondent under subsection (2) above shall consider all the circumstances including the age, health, conduct, earning capacity, financial resources, and financial obligations of each of the parties, and the financial position of the respondent as, having regard to the divorce, it is likely to be after the death of the petitioner should the petitioner die first; and, subject to subsection (4) below, the court shall not make the decree absolute unless it is satisfied—

(a) that the petitioner should not be required to make any financial provision for the respondent, or

(b) that the financial provision made by the petitioner for the respondent is reasonable and fair or the best that can be made in the circumstances.

(4) The court may if it thinks fit make the decree absolute notwithstanding the requirements of subsection (3) above if—

(a) it appears that there are circumstances making it desirable that the decree should be made absolute without delay, and

(b) the court has obtained a satisfactory undertaking from the petitioner that he will make such financial provision for the respondent as the court may approve.

10A. Proceedings after decree nisi: religious marriage

(1) This section applies if a decree of divorce has been granted but not made absolute and the parties to the marriage concerned—

(a) were married in accordance with—

(i) the usages of the Jews, or

(ii) any other prescribed religious usages; and

(b) must co-operate if the marriage is to be dissolved in accordance with those usages.

(2) On the application of either party, the court may order that a decree of divorce is not to be made absolute until a declaration made by both parties that they have taken such steps as are required to dissolve the marriage in accordance with those usages is produced to the court.

(3) An order under subsection (2)—

(a) may be made only if the court is satisfied that in all the circumstances of the case it is just and reasoanble to do so; and

(b) may be revoked at any time.

. . .

Nullity

11. Grounds on which a marriage is void

A marriage celebrated after 31st July 1971 shall be void on the following grounds only, that is to say—

(a) that it is not a valid marriage under the provisions of the Marriages Acts 1949 to 1986 (that is to say where—

(i) the parties are within the prohibited degrees of relationship;

(ii) either party is under the age of sixteen; or

(iii) the parties have intermarried in disregard of certain requirements as to the formation of marriage);

(b) that at the time of the marriage either party was already lawfully married;

(c) that the parties are not respectively male and female;

(d) in the case of a polygamous marriage entered into outside England and Wales, that either party was at the time of the marriage domiciled in England and Wales.

For the purposes of paragraph (d) of this subsection a marriage is not polygamous if at its inception neither party has any spouse additional to the other.

12. Grounds on which a marriage is voidable

A marriage celebrated after 31st July 1971 shall be voidable on the following grounds only, that is to say—

(a) that the marriage has not been consummated owing to the incapacity of either party to consummate it;

(b) that the marriage has not been consummated owing to the wilful refusal of the respondent to consummate it;

(c) that either party to the marriage did not validly consent to it, whether in consequence of duress, mistake, unsoundness of mind or otherwise;

(d) that at the time of the marriage either party, though capable of giving a valid consent, was suffering (whether continuously or intermittently) from mental disorder within the meaning of the Mental Health Act 1983 of such a kind or to such an extent as to be unfitted for marriage;
(e) that at the time of the marriage the respondent was suffering from venereal disease in a communicable form;
(f) that at the time of the marriage the respondent was pregnant by some person other than the petitioner;
(g) that an interim gender recognition certificate under the Gender Recognition Act 2004 has, after the time of the marriage, been issued to either party to the marriage;
(h) that the respondent is a person whose gender at the time of the marriage had become the acquired gender under the Gender Recognition Act 2004.

13. Bars to relief where marriage is voidable

(1) The court shall not, in proceedings instituted after 31st July 1971, grant a decree of nullity on the ground that a marriage is voidable if the respondent satisfies the court—
(a) that the petitioner, with knowledge that it was open to him to have the marriage avoided, so conducted himself in relation to the respondent as to lead the respondent reasonably to believe that he would not seek to do so; and
(b) that it would be unjust to the respondent to grant the decree.

(2) Without prejudice to subsection (1) above, the court shall not grant a decree of nullity by virtue of section 12 above on the grounds mentioned in paragraph (c), (d), (e) or (f) of that section unless—
(a) it is satisfied that proceedings were instituted within the period of three years from the date of the marriage, or
(b) leave for the institution of proceedings after the expiration of that period has been granted under subsection (4) below.

(2A) Without prejudice to subsection (1) above, the court shall not grant a decree of nullity by virtue of section 12 above on the ground mentioned in paragraph (g) of that section unless it is satisfied that proceedings were instituted within the period of six months from the date of issue of the interim gender recognition certificate.

(3) Without prejudice to subsections (1) and (2) above, the court shall not grant a decree of nullity by virtue of section 12 above on the grounds mentioned in paragraph (e) (f) or (h) of that section unless it is satisfied that the petitioner was at the time of the marriage ignorant of the facts alleged.

(4) In the case of proceedings for the grant of a decree of nullity by virtue of section 12 above on the grounds mentioned in paragraph (c), (d), (e) (f) or (h) of that section, a judge of the court may, on an application made to him, grant leave for the institution of proceedings after the expiration of the period of three years from the date of the marriage if—
(a) he is satisfied that the petitioner has at some time during that period suffered from mental disorder within the meaning of the Mental Health Act 1983, and
(b) he considers that in all the circumstances of the case it would be just to grant leave for the institution of proceedings.

(5) An application for leave under subsection (4) above may be made after the expiration of the period of three years from the date of the marriage.

14. Marriages governed by foreign law or celebrated abroad under English law

(1) Subject to subsection (3) where, apart from this Act, any matter affecting the validity of a marriage would fall to be determined (in accordance with the rules of private international law) by reference to the law of the country outside England and Wales, nothing in section 11, 12 or 13(1) above shall—
(a) preclude the determination of that matter as aforesaid; or
(b) require the application to the marriage of the grounds or bar there mentioned except so far as applicable in accordance with those rules.

(2) In the case of a marriage which purports to have been celebrated under the Foreign Marriages Acts 1892 to 1947 or has taken place outside England and Wales and purports to be a marriage under common law, section 11 above is without prejudice to any ground on which the marriage may be void under those Acts or, as the case may be, by virtue of the rules governing the celebration of marriages outside England and Wales under common law.

(3) No marriage is to be treated as valid by virtue of subsection (1) if, at the time when it purports to be celebrated, either party was already a civil partner.

16. Effect of decree of nullity in case of voidable marriage

A decree of nullity granted after 31st July 1971 in respect of a voidable marriage shall operate to annul the marriage only as respects any time after the decree has been made absolute, and the marriage shall, notwithstanding the decree, be treated as if it had existed up to that time.

Other matrimonial suits

17. Judicial separation

(1) A petition for judicial separation may be presented to the court by either party to a marriage on the ground that any such fact as is mentioned in section 1(2) above exists, and the provisions of section 2 above shall apply accordingly for the purposes of a petition for judicial separation alleging any such fact, as they apply in relation to a petition for divorce alleging that fact.

(2) On a petition for judicial separation it shall be the duty of the court to inquire, so far as it reasonably can, into the facts alleged by the petitioner and into any facts alleged by the respondent, but the court shall not be concerned to consider whether the marriage has broken down irretrievably, and if it is satisfied on the evidence of any such fact as is mentioned in section 1(2) above it shall, subject to section 41 below, grant a decree of judicial separation.

(3) Sections 6 and 7 above shall apply for the purpose of encouraging the reconciliation of parties to proceedings for judicial separation and of enabling the parties to a marriage to refer to the court for its opinion an agreement or arrangement relevant to actual or contemplated proceedings for judicial separation, as they apply in relation to proceedings for divorce.

18. Effects of judicial separation

(1) Where the court grants a decree of judicial separation it shall no longer be obligatory for the petitioner to cohabit with the respondent.

(2) If while a decree of judicial separation is in force and the separation is continuing either of the parties to the marriage dies intestate as respects all or any of his or her real or personal property, the property as respects which he or she died intestate shall devolve as if the other party to the marriage had then been dead.

(3) Notwithstanding anything in section 2(1)(a) of the Matrimonial Proceedings (Magistrates' Courts) Act 1960, a provision in force under an order made, or having effect as if made, under that section exempting one party to a marriage from the obligation to cohabit with the other shall not have effect as a decree of judicial separation for the purposes of subsection (2) above.

19. Presumption of death and dissolution of marriage

(1) Any married person who alleges that reasonable grounds exist for supposing that the other party to the marriage is dead may present a petition to the court to have it presumed that the other party is dead and to have the marriage dissolved, and the court may, if satisfied that such reasonable grounds exist, grant a decree of presumption of death and dissolution of marriage.

(3) In any proceedings under this section the fact that for a period of seven years or more the other party to the marriage has been continually absent from the petitioner and the petitioner has no reason to believe that the other party has been living within that time shall be evidence that the other party is dead until the contrary is proved.

(4) Sections 1(5), 8 and 9 shall apply to a petition and a decree under this section as they apply to a petition for divorce and a decree of divorce respectively.

(6) It is hereby declared that neither collusion nor any other conduct on the part of the petitioner which has at any time been a bar to relief in matrimonial proceedings constitutes a bar to the grant of a decree under this section.

General

20. Relief for respondent in divorce proceedings

If in any proceedings for divorce the respondent alleges and proves any such fact as is mentioned in subsection (2) of section 1 above (treating the respondent as the petitioner and the petitioner as the respondent for the purposes of that subsection) the court may give to the respondent the relief to which he would have been entitled if he had presented a petition seeking that relief.

PART II
FINANCIAL RELIEF FOR PARTIES TO MARRIAGE AND CHILDREN OF FAMILY

Financial provision and property adjustment orders

21. Financial provision and property adjustment orders

(1) The financial provision orders for the purposes of this Act are the orders for periodical or lump sum provision available (subject to the provisions of this Act) under section 23 below for the purpose of adjusting the financial position of the parties to a marriage and any children of the family in connection with proceedings for divorce, nullity of marriage or judicial separation and under section 27(6) below on proof of neglect by one party to a marriage to provide, or to make a proper contribution towards, reasonable maintenance for the other or a child of the family, that is to say—

(a) any order for periodical payments in favour of a party to a marriage under section 23(1)(a) or 27(6)(a) or in favour of a child of the family under section 23(1)(d), (2) or (4) or 27(6)(d);

(b) any order for secured periodical payments in favour of a party to a marriage under section 23(1)(b) or 27(6)(b) or in favour of a child of the family under section 23(1)(e), (2) or (4) or 27(6)(e); and

(c) any order for lump sum provision in favour of a party to a marriage under section 23(1)(c) or 27(6)(c) or in favour of a child of the family under section 23(1)(f), (2) or (4) or 27(6)(f);

and references in this Act (except in paragraphs 17(1) and 23 of Schedule 1 below) to periodical payments orders, secured periodical payments orders, and orders for the payment of a lump sum are references to all or some of the financial provision orders requiring the sort of financial provision in question according as the context of each reference may require.

(2) The property adjustment orders for the purposes of this Act are the orders dealing with property rights available (subject to the provisions of this Act) under section 24 below for the purpose of adjusting the financial position of the parties to a marriage and any children of the family on or after the grant of a decree of divorce, nullity of marriage or judicial separation, that is to say—

(a) any order under subsection (1)(a) of that section for a transfer of property;

(b) any order under subsection (1)(b) of that section for a settlement of property; and

(c) any order under subsection (1)(c) or (d) of that section for a variation of settlement.

21A. Pension sharing orders

(1) For the purposes of this Act, a pension sharing order is an order which—

(a) provides that one party's—

(i) shareable rights under a specified pension arrangement, or

(ii) shareable state scheme rights,

be subject to pension sharing for the benefit of the other party, and

(b) specifies the percentage value to be transferred.

(2) In subsection (1) above—

(a) the reference to shareable rights under a pension arrangement is to rights in relation to which pension sharing is available under Chapter I of Part IV of the Welfare Reform and Pensions Act 1999, or under corresponding Northern Ireland legislation,

(b) the reference to shareable state scheme rights is to rights in relation to which pension sharing is available under Chapter II of Part IV of the Welfare Reform and Pensions Act 1999, or under corresponding Northern Ireland legislation, and

(c) 'party' means a party to a marriage.

21B. Pension compensation sharing orders

(1) For the purposes of this Act, a pension compensation sharing order is an order which—

(a) provides that one party's shareable rights to PPF compensation that derive from rights under a specified pension scheme are to be subject to pension compensation sharing for the benefit of the other party, and

(b) specifies the percentage value to be transferred.

(2) In subsection (1)—

(a) the reference to shareable rights to PPF compensation is to rights in relation to which pension compensation sharing is available under Chapter 1 of Part 3 of the Pensions Act 2008 or under corresponding Northern Ireland legislation;

(b) 'party' means a party to a marriage;

(c) 'specified' means specified in the order.

21C. Pension compensation: interpretation

In this Part—

'PPF compensation' means compensation payable under the pension compensation provisions;

'the pension compensation provisions' means—

(a) Chapter 3 of Part 2 of the Pensions Act 2004 (pension protection) and any regulations or order made under it,

(b) Chapter 1 of Part 3 of the Pensions Act 2008 (pension compensation on divorce etc) and any regulations or order made under it, and

. . .

Ancillary relief in connection with divorce proceedings, etc.

22. Maintenance pending suit

(1) On a petition for divorce, nullity of marriage or judicial separation, the court may make an order for maintenance pending suit, that is to say, an order requiring either party to the marriage to make to the other such periodical payments for his or her maintenance and for such term, being a term beginning not earlier than the date of the presentation of the petition and ending with the date of the determination of the suit, as the court thinks reasonable.

(2) An order under this section may not require a party to a marriage to pay to the other party any amount in respect of legal services for the purposes of the proceedings.

(3) In subsection (2) 'legal services' has the same meaning as in section 22ZA.

22ZA. Orders for payment in respect of legal services

(1) In proceedings for divorce, nullity of marriage or judicial separation, the court may make an order or orders requiring one party to the marriage to pay to the other ('the applicant') an amount for the purpose of enabling the applicant to obtain legal services for the purposes of the proceedings.

(2) The court may also make such an order or orders in proceedings under this Part for financial relief in connection with proceedings for divorce, nullity of marriage or judicial separation.

(3) The court must not make an order under this section unless it is satisfied that, without the amount, the applicant would not reasonably be able to obtain appropriate legal services for the purposes of the proceedings or any part of the proceedings.

(4) For the purposes of subsection (3), the court must be satisfied, in particular, that—

(a) the applicant is not reasonably able to secure a loan to pay for the services, and

(b) the applicant is unlikely to be able to obtain the services by granting a charge over any assets recovered in the proceedings.

(5) An order under this section may be made for the purpose of enabling the applicant to obtain legal services of a specified part of the proceedings.

(6) An order under this section may—

(a) provide for the payment of all or part of the amount by instalments of specified amounts, and

(b) require the instalments to be secured to the satisfaction of the court.

(7) An order under this section may direct that payment of all or part of the amount is to be deferred.

(8) The court may at any time in the proceedings vary an order made under this section if it considers that there has been a material change of circumstances since the order was made.

(9) For the purposes of the assessment of costs in the proceedings, the applicant's costs are to be treated as reduced by any amount paid to the applicant pursuant to an order under this section for the purposes of those proceedings.

(10) In this section 'legal services', in relation to proceedings, means the following types of services—

(a) providing advice as to how the law applies in the particular circumstances,

(b) providing advice and assistance in relation to the proceedings,

(c) providing other advice and assistance in relation to the settlement or other resolution of the dispute that is the subject of the proceedings, and

(d) providing advice and assistance in relation to the enforcement of decisions in the proceedings or as part of the settlement or resolution of the dispute, and they include, in particular, advice and assistance in the form of representation and any form of dispute resolution, including mediation.

(11) In subsections (5) and (6) 'specified' means specified in the order concerned.

22ZB. Matters to which court is to have regard in deciding how to exercise power under section 22ZA

(1) When considering whether to make or vary an order under section 22ZA, the court must have regard to—

(a) the income, earning capacity, property and other financial resources which each of the applicant and the paying party has or is likely to have in the foreseeable future,

(b) the financial needs, obligations and responsibilities which each of the applicant and the paying party has or is likely to have in the foreseeable future,

(c) the subject matter of the proceedings, including the matters in issue in them,

(d) whether the paying party is legally represented in the proceedings,

(e) any steps taken by the applicant to avoid all or part of the proceedings, whether by proposing or considering mediation or otherwise,

(f) the applicant's conduct in relation to the proceedings,

(g) any amount owed by the applicant to the paying party in respect of costs in the proceedings or other proceedings to which both the applicant and the paying party are or were party, and

(h) the effect of the order or variation on the paying party.

(2) In subsection (1)(a) 'earning capacity', in relation to the applicant or the paying party, includes any increase in earning capacity which, in the opinion of the court, it would be reasonable to expect the applicant or the paying party to take steps to acquire.

(3) For the purposes of subsection (1)(h), the court must have regard, in particular, to whether the making or variation of the order is likely to—

(a) cause undue hardship to the paying party, or

(b) prevent the paying party from obtaining legal services for the purposes of the proceedings.

(4) The Lord Chancellor may by order amend this section by adding to, omitting or varying the matters mentioned in subsections (1) to (3).

(5) An order under subsection (4) must be made by statutory instrument.

(6) A statutory instrument containing an order under subsection (4) may not be made unless a draft of the instrument has been laid before, and approved by a resolution of, each House of Parliament.

(7) In this section 'legal services' has the same meaning as in section 22ZA.

23. Financial provision orders in connection with divorce proceedings, etc.

(1) On granting a decree of divorce, a decree of nullity of marriage or a decree of judicial separation or at any time thereafter (whether, in the case of a decree of divorce or of nullity of marriage, before or after the decree is made absolute), the court may make any one or more of the following orders, that is to say—

(a) an order that either party to the marriage shall make to the other such periodical payments, for such term, as may be specified in the order;

(b) an order that either party to the marriage shall secure to the other to the satisfaction of the court such periodical payments, for such term, as may be so specified;

(c) an order that either party to the marriage shall pay to the other such lump sum or sums as may be so specified;

(d) an order that a party to the marriage shall make to such person as may be specified in the order for the benefit of a child of the family, or to such a child, such periodical payments, for such term, as may be so specified;

(e) an order that a party to the marriage shall secure to such person as may be so specified for the benefit of such a child, or to such a child, to the satisfaction of the court, such periodical payments, for such term, as may be so specified;

(f) an order that a party to the marriage shall pay to such person as may be so specified for the benefit of such a child, or to such a child, such lump sum as may be so specified;

subject however, in the case of an order under paragraph (d), (e) or (f) above, to the restrictions imposed by section 29(1) and (3) below on the making of financial provision orders in favour of children who have attained the age of eighteen.

(2) The court may also, subject to those restrictions, make any one or more of the orders mentioned in subsection (1)(d), (e) and (f) above—

(a) in any proceedings for divorce, nullity of marriage or judicial separation, before granting a decree; and

(b) where any such proceedings are dismissed after the beginning of the trial, either forthwith or within a reasonable period after the dismissal.

(3) Without prejudice to the generality of subsection (1)(c) or (f) above—

(a) an order under this section that a party to a marriage shall pay a lump sum to the other party may be made for the purpose of enabling that other party to meet any liabilities or expenses reasonably incurred by him or her in maintaining himself or herself or any child of the family before making an application for an order under this section in his or her favour;

(b) an order under this section for the payment of a lump sum to or for the benefit of a child of the family may be made for the purpose of enabling any liabilities or expenses reasonably incurred by or for the benefit of that child before the making of an application for an order under this section in his favour to be met; and

(c) an order under this section for the payment of a lump sum may provide for the payment of that sum by instalments of such amount as may be specified in the order and may require the payment of the instalments to be secured to the satisfaction of the court.

(4) The power of the court under subsection (1) or (2)(a) above to make an order in favour of a child of the family shall be exercisable from time to time; and where the court makes an order in favour of a child under subsection (2)(b) above, it may from time to time, subject to the restrictions mentioned in subsection (1) above, make a further order in his favour of any of the kinds mentioned in subsection (1)(d), (e) or (f) above.

(5) Without prejudice to the power to give a direction under section 30 below for the settlement of an instrument by conveyancing counsel, where an order is made under subsection (1)(a), (b) or (c) above on or after granting a decree of divorce or nullity of marriage, neither the order nor any settlement made in pursuance of the order shall take effect unless the decree has been made absolute.

(6) Where the court—

(a) makes an order under this section for the payment of a lump sum; and

(b) directs—

(i) that payment of that sum or any part of it shall be deferred; or

(ii) that that sum or any part of it shall be paid by instalments,

the court may order that the amount deferred or the instalments shall carry interest at such rate as may be specified by the order from such date, not earlier than the date of the order, as may be so specified, until the date when payment of it is due.

24. Property adjustment orders in connection with divorce proceedings, etc.

(1) On granting a decree of divorce, a decree of nullity of marriage or a decree of judicial separation or at any time thereafter (whether, in the case of a decree of divorce, or of nullity of marriage, before or after the decree is made absolute), the court may make any one or more of the following orders, that is to say—

(a) an order that a party to the marriage shall transfer to the other party, to any child of the family or to such person as may be specified in the order for the benefit of such a child such property as may be so specified, being property to which the first-mentioned party is entitled, either in possession or reversion;

(b) an order that a settlement of such property as may be so specified, being property to which a party to the marriage is so entitled, be made to the satisfaction of the court for the benefit of the other party to the marriage and of the children of the family or either or any of them;

(c) an order varying for the benefit of the parties to the marriage and of the children of the family or either or any of them any ante-nuptial or post-nuptial settlement (including such a settlement made by will or codicil) made on the parties to the marriage, other than one in the form of a pension arrangement (within the meaning of section 25D below);

(d) an order extinguishing or reducing the interest of either of the parties to the marriage under any such settlement, other than one in the form of a pension arrangement (within the meaning of section 25D below);

subject, however, in the case of an order under paragraph (a) above, to the restrictions imposed by section 29(1) and (3) below on the making of orders for a transfer of property in favour of children who have attained the age of eighteen.

(2) The court may make an order under subsection (1)(c) above notwithstanding that there are no children of the family.

(3) Without prejudice to the power to give a direction under section 30 below for the settlement of an instrument by conveyancing counsel, where an order is made under this section on or after granting a decree of divorce or nullity of marriage, neither the order nor any settlement made in pursuance of the order shall take effect unless the decree has been made absolute.

24A. Orders for sale of property

(1) Where the court makes under section 23 or 24 of this Act a secured periodical payments order, an order for the payment of a lump sum or a property adjustment order, then, on making that order or at any time thereafter, the court may make a further order for the

sale of such property as may be specified in the order, being property in which or in the proceeds of sale of which either or both of the parties to the marriage has or have a beneficial interest, either in possession or reversion.

(2) Any order made under subsection (1) above may contain such consequential or supplementary provisions as the court thinks fit and, without prejudice to the generality of the foregoing provision, may include—

(a) provision requiring the making of a payment out of the proceeds of sale of the property to which the order relates, and

(b) provision requiring any such property to be offered for sale to a person, or class of persons, specified in the order.

(3) Where an order is made under subsection (1) above on or after the grant of a decree of divorce or nullity of marriage, the order shall not take effect unless the decree has been made absolute.

(4) Where an order is made under subsection (1) above, the court may direct that the order, or such provision thereof as the court may specify, shall not take effect until the occurrence of an event specified by the court or the expiration of a period so specified.

(5) Where an order under subsection (1) above contains a provision requiring the proceeds of sale of the property to which the order relates to be used to secure periodical payments to a party to the marriage, the order shall cease to have effect on the death or re-marriage of that person.

(6) Where a party to a marriage has a beneficial interest in any property, or in the proceeds of sale thereof, and some other person who is not a party to the marriage also has a beneficial interest in that property or in the proceeds of sale thereof, then, before deciding whether to make an order under this section in relation to that property, it shall be the duty of the court to give that other person an opportunity to make representations with respect to the order; and any representations made by that other person shall be included among the circumstances to which the court is required to have regard under section 25(1) below.

24B. Pension sharing orders in connection with divorce proceedings, etc.

(1) On granting a decree of divorce or a decree of nullity of marriage or at any time thereafter (whether before or after the decree is made absolute), the court may, on an application made under this section, make one or more pension sharing orders in relation to the marriage.

(2) A pension sharing order under this section is not to take effect unless the decree on or after which it is made has been made absolute.

(3) A pension sharing order under this section may not be made in relation to a pension arrangement which—

(a) is the subject of a pension sharing order in relation to the marriage, or

(b) has been the subject of pension sharing between the parties to the marriage.

(4) A pension sharing order under this section may not be made in relation to shareable state scheme rights if—

(a) such rights are the subject of a pension sharing order in relation to the marriage, or

(b) such rights have been the subject of pension sharing between the parties to the marriage.

(5) A pension sharing order under this section may not be made in relation to the rights of a person under a pension arrangement if there is in force a requirement imposed by virtue of section 25B or 25C below which relates to benefits or future benefits to which he is entitled under the pension arrangement.

24C. Pension sharing orders: duty to stay

(1) No pension sharing order may be made so as to take effect before the end of such period after the making of the order as may be prescribed by regulations made by the Lord Chancellor.

(2) The power to make regulations under this section shall be exercisable by statutory instrument which shall be subject to annulment in pursuance of a resolution of either House of Parliament.

24D. Pension sharing orders: apportionment of charges

If a pension sharing order relates to rights under a pension arrangement, the court may include in the order provision about the apportionment between the parties of any charge under section 41 of the Welfare Reform and Pensions Act 1999 (charges in respect of pension sharing costs), or under corresponding Northern Ireland legislation.

24E. Pension compensation sharing orders in connection with divorce proceedings

(1) On granting a decree of divorce or a decree of nullity of marriage or at any time thereafter (whether before or after the decree is made absolute), the court may, on an application made under this section, make a pension compensation sharing order in relation to the marriage.

(2) A pension compensation sharing order under this section is not to take effect unless the decree on or after which it is made has been made absolute.

(3) A pension compensation sharing order under this section may not be made in relation to rights to PPF compensation that—

(a) are the subject of pension attachment,

(b) derive from rights under a pension scheme that were the subject of pension sharing between the parties to the marriage,

(c) are the subject of pension compensation attachment, or

(d) are or have been the subject of pension compensation sharing between the parties to the marriage.

...

24F. Pension compensation sharing orders: duty to stay

(1) No pension compensation sharing order may be made so as to take effect before the end of such period after the making of the order as may be prescribed by regulations made by the Lord Chancellor.

(2) The power to make regulations under this section shall be exercisable by statutory instrument which shall be subject to annulment in pursuance of a resolution of either House of Parliament.

24G. Pension compensation sharing orders: apportionment of charges

The court may include in a pension compensation sharing order provision about the apportionment between the parties of any charge under section 117 of the Pensions Act 2008 (charges in respect of pension compensation sharing costs) ...

25. Matters to which court is to have regard in deciding how to exercise its powers under sections 23, 24, 24A, 24B and 24E

(1) It shall be the duty of the court in deciding whether to exercise its powers under sections 23, 24, 24A, 24B or 24E above and, if so, in what manner, to have regard to all the circumstances of the case, first consideration being given to the welfare while a minor of any child of the family who has not attained the age of eighteen.

(2) As regards the exercise of the powers of the court under section 23(1)(a), (b) or (c), 24, 24A, 24B or 24E above in relation to a party to the marriage, the court shall in particular have regard to the following matters—

(a) the income, earning capacity, property and other financial resources which each of the parties to the marriage has or is likely to have in the foreseeable future, including in the case of earning capacity any increase in that capacity which it would in the opinion of the court be reasonable to expect a party to the marriage to take steps to acquire;

(b) the financial needs, obligations and responsibilities which each of the parties to the marriage has or is likely to have in the foreseeable future;

(c) the standard of living enjoyed by the family before the breakdown of the marriage;

(d) the age of each party to the marriage and the duration of the marriage;

(e) any physical or mental disability of either of the parties to the marriage;

(f) the contributions which each of the parties has made or is likely in the foreseeable future to make to the welfare of the family, including any contribution by looking after the home or caring for the family;

(g) the conduct of each of the parties, if that conduct is such that it would in the opinion of the court be inequitable to disregard it;

(h) in the case of proceedings for divorce or nullity of marriage, the value to each of the parties to the marriage of any benefit which, by reason of the dissolution or annulment of the marriage, that party will lose the chance of acquiring.

(3) As regards the exercise of the powers of the court under section 23(1)(d), (e) or (f), (2) or (4), 24 or 24A above in relation to a child of the family, the court shall in particular have regard to the following matters—

(a) the financial needs of the child;

(b) the income, earning capacity (if any), property and other financial resources of the child;

(c) any physical or mental disability of the child;

(d) the manner in which he was being and in which the parties to the marriage expected him to be educated or trained;

(e) the considerations mentioned in relation to the parties to the marriage in paragraphs (a), (b), (c) and (e) of subsection (2) above.

(4) As regards the exercise of the powers of the court under section 23(1)(d), (e) or (f), (2) or (4), 24 or 24A above against a party to a marriage in favour of a child of the family who is not the child of that party, the court shall also have regard—

(a) to whether that party assumed any responsibility for the child's maintenance, and, if so, to the extent to which, and the basis upon which, that party assumed such responsibility and to the length of time for which that party discharged such responsibility;

(b) to whether in assuming and discharging such responsibility that party did so knowing that the child was not his or her own;

(c) to the liability of any other person to maintain the child.

25A. Exercise of court's powers in favour of party to marriage on decree of divorce or nullity of marriage

(1) Where on or after the grant of a degree of divorce or nullity of marriage the court decides to exercise its powers under section 23(1)(a), (b) or (c), 24, 24A, 24B or 24E above in favour of a party to the marriage, it shall be the duty of the court to consider whether it would be appropriate so to exercise those powers that the financial obligations of each party towards the other will be terminated as soon after the grant of the decree as the court considers just and reasonable.

(2) Where the court decides in such a case to make a periodical payments or secured periodical payments order in favour of a party to the marriage, the court shall in particular consider whether it would be appropriate to require those payments to be made or secured only for such term as would in the opinion of the court be sufficient to enable the party in whose favour the order is made to adjust without undue hardship to the termination of his or her financial dependence on the other party.

(3) Where on or after the grant of a decree of divorce or nullity of marriage an application is made by a party to the marriage for a periodical payments order in his or her favour, then, if the court considers that no continuing obligation should be imposed on either party to make or secure periodical payments in favour of the other, the court may dismiss the application with a direction that the applicant shall not be entitled to make any further application in relation to that marriage for an order under section 23(1)(a) or (b) above.

25B. Pensions

(1) The matters to which the court is to have regard under section 25(2) above include—

(a) in the case of paragraph (a), any benefits under a pension arrangement which a party to the marriage has or is likely to have, and

(b) in the case of paragraph (h), any benefits under a pension arrangement which, by reason of the dissolution or annulment of the marriage, a party to the marriage will lose the chance of acquiring,

and, accordingly, in relation to benefits under a pension arrangement, section 25(2)(a) above shall have effect as if 'in the foreseeable future' were omitted.

(3) The following provisions apply where, having regard to any benefits under a pension arrangement, the court determines to make an order under section 23 above.

(4) To the extent to which the order is made having regard to any benefits under a pension arrangement, the order may require the person responsible for the pension arrangement in question, if at any time any payment in respect of any benefits under the arrangement becomes due to the party with pension rights, to make a payment for the benefit of the other party.

(5) The order must express the amount of any payment required to be made by virtue of subsection (4) above as a percentage of the payment which becomes due to the party with pension rights.

(6) Any such payment by the person responsible for the arrangement—

(a) shall discharge so much of his liability to the party with pension rights as corresponds to the amount of the payment, and

(b) shall be treated for all purposes as a payment made by the party with pension rights in or towards the discharge of his liability under the order.

(7) Where the party with pension rights has a right of commutation under the arrangement, the order may require him to exercise it to any extent; and this section applies to any payment due in consequence of commutation in pursuance of the order as it applies to other payments in respect of benefits under the arrangement.

(7A) The power conferred by subsection (7) above may not be exercised for the purpose of commuting a benefit payable to the party with pension rights to a benefit payable to the other party.

(7B) The power conferred by subsection (4) or (7) above may not be exercised in relation to a pension arrangement which—

(a) is the subject of a pension sharing order in relation to the marriage, or
(b) has been the subject of pension sharing between the parties to the marriage.

(7C) In subsection (1) above, references to benefits under a pension arrangement include any benefits by way of pension, whether under a pension arrangement or not.

25C. Pensions: lump sums

(1) The power of the court under section 23 above to order a party to a marriage to pay a lump sum to the other party includes, where the benefits which the party with pension rights has or is likely to have under a pension arrangement include any lump sum payable in respect of his death, power to make any of the following provision by the order.

(2) The court may—
(a) if the person responsible for the pension arrangement in question has power to determine the person to whom the sum, or any part of it, is to be paid, require him to pay the whole or part of that sum, when it becomes due, to the other party,
(b) if the party with pension rights has power to nominate the person to whom the sum, or any part of it, is to be paid, require the party with pension rights to nominate the other party in respect of the whole or part of that sum,
(c) in any other case, require the person responsible for the pension arrangement in question to pay the whole or part of that sum, when it becomes due, for the benefit of the other party instead of to the person to whom, apart from the order, it would be paid.

(3) Any payment by the person responsible for the arrangement under an order made under section 23 above by virtue of this section shall discharge so much of his liability in respect of the party with pension rights as corresponds to the amount of the payment.

(4) The powers conferred by this section may not be exercised in relation to a pension arrangement which—
(a) is the subject of a pension sharing order in relation to the marriage, or
(b) has been the subject of pension sharing between the parties to the marriage.

25D. Pensions: supplementary

(1) Where—
(a) an order made under section 23 above by virtue of section 25B or 25C above imposes any requirement on the person responsible for a pension arrangement ('the first arrangement') and the party with pension rights acquires rights under another pension arrangement ('the new arrangement') which are derived (directly or indirectly) from the whole of his rights under the first arrangement, and
(b) the person responsible for the new arrangement has been given notice in accordance with regulations made by the Lord Chancellor,

the order shall have effect as if it had been made instead in respect of the person responsible for the new arrangement.

(2) The Lord Chancellor may by regulations—
(a) in relation to any provision of sections 25B or 25C above which authorises the court making an order under section 23 above to require the person responsible for a pension arrangement to make a payment for the benefit of the other party, make provision as to the person to whom, and the terms on which, the payment is to be made,
(ab) make, in relation to payment under a mistaken belief as to the continuation in force of a provision included by virtue of section 25B or 25C above in an order under section 23 above, provision about the rights or liabilities of the payer, the payee or the person to whom the payment was due.
(b) require notices to be given in respect of changes of circumstances relevant to such orders which include provision made by virtue of sections 25B and 25C above,
(ba) make provision for the person responsible for a pension arrangement to be discharged in prescribed circumstances from a requirement imposed by virtue of section 25B or 25C above,
(e) make provision about calculation and verification in relation to the valuation of—
(i) benefits under a pension arrangement, or
(ii) shareable state scheme rights,

for the purposes of the court's functions in connection with the exercise of any of its powers under this Part of this Act.

(2A) Regulations under subsection (2)(e) above may include—
(a) provision for calculation or verification in accordance with guidance from time to time prepared by a prescribed person, and

(b) provision by reference to regulations under section 30 or 49(4) of the Welfare Reform and Pensions Act 1999.

(2B) Regulations under subsection (2) above may make different provision for different cases.

(2C) Power to make regulations under this section shall be exercisable by statutory instrument which shall be subject to annulment in pursuance of a resolution of either House of Parliament.

(3) In this section and sections 25B and 25C above—

'occupational pension scheme' has the same meaning as in the Pension Schemes Act 1993;

'the party with pension rights' means the party to the marriage who has or is likely to have benefits under a pension arrangement and 'the other party' means the other party to the marriage;

'pension arrangement' means—

(a) an occupational pension scheme,
(b) a personal pension scheme,
(c) a retirement annuity contract,
(d) an annuity or insurance policy purchased, or transferred, for the purpose of giving effect to rights under an occupational pension scheme or a personal pension scheme, and
(e) an annuity purchased, or entered into, for the purpose of discharging liability in respect of a pension credit under section 29(1)(b) of the Welfare Reform and Pensions Act 1999 or under corresponding Northern Ireland legislation;

'personal pension scheme' has the same meaning as in the Pension Schemes Act 1993;

'prescribed' means prescribed by regulations;

'retirement annuity contract' means a contract or scheme approved under Chapter III of Part XIV of the Income and Corporation Taxes Act 1988;

'shareable state scheme rights' has the same meaning as in section 21A(1) above; and

'trustees or managers', in relation to an occupational pension scheme, means—

(a) in the case of a scheme established under a trust, the trustees of the scheme, and
(b) in any other case, the managers of the scheme.

(4) In this section and sections 25B and 25C above, references to the person responsible for a pension arrangement are—

(a) in the case of an occupational pension scheme or a personal pension scheme, to the trustees or managers of the scheme,
(b) in the case of a retirement annuity contract or an annuity falling within paragraph (d) or (e) of the definition of 'pension arrangement' above, the provider of the annuity, and
(c) in the case of an insurance policy falling within paragraph (d) of the definition of that expression, the insurer.

25E. The Pension Protection Fund

(1) The matters to which the court is to have regard under section 25(2) include—

(a) in the case of paragraph (a), any PPF compensation to which a party to the marriage is or is likely to be entitled, and
(b) in the case of paragraph (h), any PPF compensation which, by reason of the dissolution or annulment of the marriage, a party to the marriage will lose the chance of acquiring entitlement to,

and, accordingly, in relation to PPF compensation, section 25(2)(a) shall have effect as if 'in the foreseeable future' were omitted.

(2) Subsection (3) applies in relation to an order under section 23 so far as it includes provision made by virtue of section 25B(4) which—

(a) imposed requirements on the trustees or managers of an occupational pension scheme for which the Board has assumed responsibility in accordance with Chapter 3 of Part 2 of the Pensions Act 2004 (pension protection) or any provision in force in Northern Ireland corresponding to that Chapter, and
(b) was made before the trustees or managers of the scheme received the transfer notice in relation to the scheme.

(3) The order is to have effect from the time when the trustees or managers of the scheme receive the transfer notice—

(a) as if, except in prescribed descriptions of case—
    (i) references in the order to the trustees or managers of the scheme were references to the Board, and
    (ii) references in the order to any pension or lump sum to which the party with pension rights is or may become entitled under the scheme were references to any PPF compensation to which that person is or may become entitled in respect of the pension or lump sum, and
(b) subject to such other modifications as may be prescribed.

(4) Subsection (5) applies to an order under section 23 if—
(a) it includes provision made by virtue of section 25B(7) which requires the party with pension rights to exercise his right of commutation under an occupational pension scheme to any extent, and
(b) before the requirement is complied with the Board has assumed responsibility for the scheme as mentioned in subsection (2)(a).

(5) From the time the trustees or managers of the scheme receive the transfer notice, the order is to have effect with such modifications as may be prescribed.

(6) Regulations may modify section 25C as it applies in relation to an occupational pension scheme at any time when there is an assessment period in relation to the scheme.

(7) Where the court makes a pension sharing order in respect of a person's shareable rights under an occupational pension scheme, or an order which includes provision made by virtue of section 25B(4) or (7) in relation to such a scheme, the Board subsequently assuming responsibility for the scheme as mentioned in subsection (2)(a) does not affect—
(a) the powers of the court under section 31 to vary or discharge the order or to suspend or revive any provision of it, or
(b) on an appeal, the powers of the appeal court to affirm, reinstate, set aside or vary the order.

(8) . . .

(9) In this section—
'assessment period' means an assessment period within the meaning of Part 2 of the Pensions Act 2004 (pension protection) (see sections 132 and 159 of that Act) or an equivalent period under any provision in force in Northern Ireland corresponding to that Part;
'the Board' means the Board of the Pension Protection Fund;
'occupational pension scheme' has the same meaning as in the Pension Schemes Act 1993;
'prescribed' means prescribed by regulations;
'PPF compensation' means compensation payable under Chapter 3 of Part 2 of the Pensions Act 2004 (pension protection) or any provision in force in Northern Ireland corresponding to that Chapter;
'regulations' means regulations made by the Lord Chancellor;
'shareable rights' are rights in relation to which pension sharing is available under Chapter 1 of Part 4 of the Welfare Reform and Pensions Act 1999 or any provision in force in Northern Ireland corresponding to that Chapter;
'transfer notice' has the same meaning as in section 160 of the Pensions Act 2004 ...

(10) . . .

26. Commencement of proceedings for ancillary relief, etc.

(1) Where a petition for divorce, nullity of marriage or judicial separation has been presented, then, subject to subsection (2) below, proceedings for maintenance pending suit under section 22 above, for a financial provision order under section 23 above, or for a property adjustment order may be begun, subject to and in accordance with rules of court, at any time after the presentation of the petition.

(2) Rules of court may provide, in such cases as may be prescribed by the rules—
(a) that applications for any such relief as is mentioned in subsection (1) above shall be made in the petition or answer; and
(b) that applications for any such relief which are not so made, or are not made until after the expiration of such period following the presentation of the petition or filing of the answer as may be so prescribed, shall be made only with the leave of the court.

Financial provision in case of neglect to maintain

27. Financial provision orders, etc., in case of neglect by party to marriage to maintain other party or child of the family

(1) Either party to a marriage may apply to the court for an order under this section on the ground that the other party to the marriage (in this section referred to as the respondent)—
(a) has failed to provide reasonable maintenance for the applicant, or
(b) has failed to provide, or to make a proper contribution towards, reasonable maintenance for any child of the family.

(2) The court may not entertain an application under this section unless it has jurisdiction to do so by virtue of the Maintenance Regulation and Schedule 6 to the Civil Jurisdiction and Judgments (Maintenance) Regulations 2011.

(3) Where an application under this section is made on the ground mentioned in subsection (1)(a) above, then, in deciding—
(a) whether the respondent has failed to provide reasonable maintenance for the applicant, and
(b) what order, if any, to make under this section in favour of the applicant,
the court shall have regard to all the circumstances of the case including the matters mentioned in section 25(2) above, and where an application is also made under this section in respect of a child of the family who has not attained the age of eighteen, first consideration shall be given to the welfare of the child while a minor.

(3A) Where an application under this section is made on the ground mentioned in subsection (1)(b) above then, in deciding—
(a) whether the respondent has failed to provide, or to make a proper contribution towards, reasonable maintenance for the child of the family to whom the application relates, and
(b) what order, if any, to make under this section in favour of the child,
the court shall have regard to all the circumstances of the case including the matters mentioned in section 25(3)(a) to (e) above, and where the child of the family to whom the application relates is not the child of the respondent, including also the matters mentioned in section 25(4) above.

(3B) In relation to an application under this section on the ground mentioned in subsection (1)(a) above, section 25(2)(c) above shall have effect as if for the reference therein to the breakdown of the marriage there were substituted a reference to the failure to provide reasonable maintenance for the applicant, and in relation to an application under this section on the ground mentioned in subsection (1)(b) above, section 25(2)(c) above (as it applies by virtue of section 25(3)(e) above) shall have effect as if for the reference therein to the breakdown of the marriage there were substituted a reference to the failure to provide, or to make a proper contribution towards, reasonable maintenance for the child of the family to whom the application relates.

(5) Where on an application under this section it appears to the court that the applicant or any child of the family to whom the application relates is in immediate need of financial assistance, but it is not yet possible to determine what order, if any, should be made on the application, the court may make an interim order for maintenance, that is to say, an order requiring the respondent to make to the applicant until the determination of the application such periodical payments as the court thinks reasonable.

(6) Where on an application under this section the applicant satisfies the court of any ground mentioned in subsection (1) above, the court may make any one or more of the following orders, that is to say—
(a) an order that the respondent shall make to the applicant such periodical payments, for such term, as may be specified in the order;
(b) an order that the respondent shall secure to the applicant, to the satisfaction of the court, such periodical payments, for such term, as may be so specified;
(c) an order that the respondent shall pay to the applicant such lump sum as may be so specified;
(d) an order that the respondent shall make to such person as may be specified in the order for the benefit of the child to whom the application relates, or to that child, such periodical payments, for such term, as may be so specified;
(e) an order that the respondent shall secure to such person as may be so specified for the benefit of that child, or to that child, to the satisfaction of the court, such periodical payments, for such term, as may be so specified;
(f) an order that the respondent shall pay to such person as may be so specified for the benefit of that child, or to that child, such lump sum as may be so specified;
subject, however, in the case of an order under paragraph (d), (e) or (f) above, to the restrictions imposed by section 29(1) and (3) below on the making of financial provision orders in favour of children who have attained the age of eighteen.

(6A) An application for the variation under section 31 of this Act of a periodical payments order or secured periodical payments order made under this section in favour of a child may, if the child has attained the age of sixteen, be made by the child himself.

(6B) Where a periodical payments order made in favour of a child under this section ceases to have effect on the date on which the child attains the age of sixteen or at any time after that date but before or on the date on which he attains the age of eighteen, then if, on an application made to the court for an order under this subsection, it appears to the court that—
(a) the child is, will be or (if an order were made under this subsection) would be receiving instruction at an educational establishment or undergoing training for a trade, profession or vocation, whether or not he also is, will be or would be in gainful employment; or

(b) there are special circumstances which justify the making of an order under this subsection,

the court shall have power by order to revive the first mentioned order from such date as the court may specify, not being earlier than the date of the making of the application, and to exercise its power under section 31 of this Act in relation to any order so revived.

(7) Without prejudice to the generality of subsection (6)(c) or (f) above, an order under this section for the payment of a lump sum—

(a) may be made for the purpose of enabling any liabilities or expenses reasonably incurred in maintaining the applicant or any child of the family to whom the application relates before the making of the application to be met;

(b) may provide for the payment of that sum by instalments of such amount as may be specified in the order and may require the payment of the instalments to be secured to the satisfaction of the court.

Additional provisions with respect to financial provision and property adjustment orders

28. Duration of continuing financial provision orders in favour of party to marriage, and effect of remarriage or formation of civil partnership

(1) Subject in the case of an order made on or after the grant of a decree of divorce or nullity of marriage to the provisions of sections 25A(2) above and 31(7) below, the term to be specified in a periodical payments or secured periodical payments order in favour of a party to a marriage shall be such term as the court thinks fit, except that the term shall not begin before or extend beyond the following limits, that is to say—

(a) in the case of a periodical payments order, the term shall begin not earlier than the date of the making of an application for the order, and shall be so defined as not to extend beyond the death of either of the parties to the marriage or, where the order is made on or after the grant of a decree of divorce or nullity of marriage, the remarriage of the party in whose favour the order is made; and

(b) in the case of a secured periodical payments order, the term shall begin not earlier than the date of the making of an application for the order, and shall be so defined as not to extend beyond the death or, where the order is made on or after the grant of such a decree, the remarriage of the party in whose favour the order is made.

(1A) Where a periodical payments or secured periodical payments order in favour of a party to a marriage is made on or after the grant of a decree of divorce or nullity of marriage, the court may direct that that party shall not be entitled to apply under section 31 below for the extension of the term specified in the order.

(2) Where a periodical payments or secured periodical payments order in favour of a party to a marriage is made otherwise than on or after the grant of a decree of divorce or nullity of marriage, and the marriage in question is subsequently dissolved or annulled but the order continues in force, the order shall, notwithstanding anything in it, cease to have effect on the remarriage of that party, except in relation to any arrears due under or on the date of the remarriage.

(3) If after the grant of a decree dissolving or annulling a marriage either party to that marriage remarries, whether at any time before or after the commencement of this Act, that party shall not be entitled to apply, by reference to the grant of that decree, for a financial provision order in his or her favour, or for a property adjustment order, against the other party to that marriage.

29. Duration of continuing financial provision orders in favour of children, and age limit on making certain orders in their favour

(1) Subject to subsection (3) below, no financial provision order and no order for a transfer of property under section 24(1)(a) above shall be made in favour of a child who has attained the age of eighteen.

(2) The term to be specified in a periodical payments or secured periodical payments order in favour of a child may begin with the date of the making of an application for the order in question or any later date or a date ascertained in accordance with subsection (5) or (6) below but—

(a) shall not in the first instance extend beyond the date of the birthday of the child next following his attaining the upper limit of the compulsory school age (construed in accordance with section 8 of the Education Act 1996) unless the court considers that in the circumstances of the case the welfare of the child requires that it should extend to a later date; and

(b) shall not in any event, subject to subsection (3) below, extend beyond the date of the child's eighteenth birthday.

(3) Subsection (1) above, and paragraph (b) of subsection (2), shall not apply in the case of a child, if it appears to the court that—

(a) the child is, or will be, or if an order were made without complying with either or both of those provisions would be, receiving instruction at an educational establishment or undergoing training for a trade, profession or vocation, whether or not he is also or will also be, in gainful employment; or

(b) there are special circumstances which justify the making of an order without complying with either or both of those provisions.

(4) Any periodical payments order in favour of a child shall, notwithstanding anything in the order, cease to have effect on the death of the person liable to make payments under the order, except in relation to any arrears due under the order on the date of the death.

(5) Where—

(a) a maintenance calculation ('the current calculation') is in force with respect to a child; and

(b) an application is made under Part II of this Act for a periodical payments or secured periodical payments order in favour of that child—

(i) in accordance with section 8 of the Child Support Act 1991; and

(ii) before the end of the period of 6 months beginning with the making of the current calculation

the term to be specified in any such order made on that application may be expressed to begin on, or at any time after, the earliest permitted date.

(6) For the purposes of subsection (5) above, 'the earliest permitted date' is whichever is the later of—

(a) the date 6 months before the application is made; or

(b) the date on which the current calculation took effect or, where successive maintenance calculations have been continuously in force with respect to a child, on which the first of those calculations took effect.

(7) Where—

(a) a maintenance calculation ceases to have effect by or under a provision of the Child Support Act 1991; and

(b) an application is made before the end of the period of 6 months beginning with the relevant date, for a periodical payments or secured periodical payments order in favour of a child with respect to whom that maintenance calculation was in force immediately before it ceased to have effect,

the term to be specified in any such order made on that application may begin with the date on which that maintenance calculation ceased to have effect, or any later date.

(8) In subsection (7)(b) above—

(a) where the maintenance calculation ceased to have effect, the relevant date is the date on which it so ceased.

30. Direction for settlement of instrument for securing payments or effecting property adjustment

Where the court decides to make a financial provision order requiring any payments to be secured or a property adjustment order—

(a) it may direct that the matter be referred to one of the conveyancing counsel of the court for him to settle a proper instrument to be executed by all necessary parties; and

(b) where the order is to be made in proceedings for divorce, nullity of marriage or judicial separation it may, if it thinks fit, defer the grant of the decree in question until the instrument has been duly executed.

Variation, discharge and enforcement of certain orders, etc.

31. Variation, discharge, etc., of certain orders for financial relief

(1) Where the court has made an order to which this section applies, then, subject to the provisions of this section and of section 28(1A) above, the court shall have power to vary or discharge the order or to suspend any provision thereof temporarily and to revive the operation of any provision so suspended.

(2) This section applies to the following orders, that is to say—

(a) any order for maintenance pending suit and any interim order for maintenance;

(b) any periodical payments order;

(c) any secured periodical payments order;

(d) any order made by virtue of section 23(3)(c) or 27(7)(b) above (provision for payment of a lump sum by instalments);

(dd) any deferred order made by virtue of section 23(1)(c) (lump sums) which includes provision made by virtue of—
(i) section 25B(4) or
(ii) section 25C,

(provision in respect of pension rights);

(e) any order for a settlement of property under section 24(1)(b) or for a variation of settlement under section 24(1)(c) or (d) above, being an order made on or after the grant of a decree of judicial separation;

(f) any order made under section 24A(1) above for the sale of property;

(g) a pension sharing order under section 24B above which is made at a time before the decree has been made absolute.

(2A) Where the court has made an order referred to in subsection (2)(a), (b) or (c) above, then, subject to the provisions of this section, the court shall have power to remit the payment of any arrears due under the order or of any part thereof.

(2B) Where the court has made an order referred to in subsection (2)(dd)(ii) above, this section shall cease to apply to the order on the death of either of the parties to the marriage.

(3) The powers exercisable by the court under this section in relation to an order shall be exercisable also in relation to any instrument executed in pursuance of the order.

(4) The court shall not exercise the powers conferred by this section in relation to an order for a settlement under section 24(1)(b) or for a variation of settlement under section 24(1)(c) or (d) above except on an application made in proceedings—

(a) for the rescission of the decree of judicial separation by reference to which the order was made, or

(b) for the dissolution of the marriage in question.

(4A) In relation to an order which falls within paragraph (g) of subsection (2) above ('the subsection (2) order')—

(a) the powers conferred by this section may be exercised—
(i) only on an application made before the subsection (2) order has or, but for paragraph (b) below, would have taken effect; and
(ii) only if, at the time when the application is made, the decree has not been made absolute; and

(b) an application made in accordance with paragraph (a) above prevents the subsection (2) order from taking effect before the application has been dealt with.

(4B) No variation of a pension sharing order shall be made so as to take effect before the decree is made absolute.

(4C) The variation of a pension sharing order prevents the order taking effect before the end of such period after the making of the variation as may be prescribed by regulations made by the Lord Chancellor.

(5) Subject to subsections (7A) to (7G) below and without prejudice to any power exercisable by virtue of subsection (2)(d), (dd), (e) or (g) above or otherwise than by virtue of this section, no property adjustment order or pension sharing order shall be made on an application for the variation of a periodical payments or secured periodical payments order made (whether in favour of a party to a marriage or in favour of a child of the family) under section 23 above, and no order for the payment of a lump sum shall be made on an application for the variation of a periodical payments or secured periodical payments order in favour of a party to a marriage (whether made under section 23 or under section 27 above).

(6) Where the person liable to make payments under a secured periodical payments order has died, an application under this section relating to that order (and to any order made under section 24A(1) above which requires the proceeds of sale of property to be used for securing those payments) may be made by the person entitled to payments under the periodical payments order or by the personal representatives of the deceased person, but no such application shall, except with the permission of the court, be made after the end of the period of six months from the date on which representation in regard to the estate of that person is first taken out.

(7) In exercising the powers conferred by this section the court shall have regard to all the circumstances of the case, first consideration being given to the welfare while a minor of any child of the family who has not attained the age of eighteen, and the circumstances of the case shall include any change in any of the matters to which the court was required to have regard when making the order to which the application relates, and—

(a) in the case of a periodical payments or secured periodical payments order made on or after the grant of a decree of divorce or nullity of marriage, the court shall consider whether in all the circumstances and after having regard to any such change it would be appropriate to vary the order so that payments under the order are required to be made or secured only for such further period as will in the opinion of the court be sufficient (in the light of any proposed exercise by the court, where the marriage has been dissolved of its powers under subsection (7B) below) to enable the party in whose favour the order was made to adjust without undue hardship to the termination of those payments;

(b) in a case where the party against whom the order was made has died, the circumstances of the case shall also include the changed circumstances resulting from his or her death.

(7A) Subsection (7B) below applies where, after the dissolution of a marriage, the court—

(a) discharges a periodical payments order or secured periodical payments order made in favour of a party to the marriage; or

(b) varies such an order so that payments under the order are required to be made or secured only for such further period as is determined by the court.

(7B) The court has power, in addition to any power it has apart from this subsection, to make supplemental provision consisting of any of—

(a) an order for the payment of a lump sum in favour of a party to the marriage;

(b) one or more property adjustment orders in favour of a party to the marriage;

(ba) one or more pension sharing orders;

(c) a direction that the party in whose favour the original order discharged or varied was made is not entitled to make any further application for—

(i) a periodical payments or secured periodical payments order, or

(ii) an extension of the period to which the original order is limited by any variation made by the court.

(7C) An order for the payment of a lump sum made under subsection (7B) above may—

(a) provide for the payment of that sum by instalments of such amount as may be specified in the order; and

(b) require the payment of the instalments to be secured to the satisfaction of the court.

(7D) Section 23(6) above apply where the court makes an order for the payment of a lump sum under subsection (7B) above as they apply where it makes such an order under section 23 above.

(7E) If under subsection (7B) above the court makes more than one property adjustment order in favour of the same party to the marriage, each of those orders must fall within a different paragraph of section 21(2) above.

(7F) Sections 24A and 30 above apply where the court makes a property adjustment order under subsection (7B) above as they apply where it makes such an order under section 24 above.

(7G) Subsections (3) to (5) of section 24B above apply in relation to a pension sharing order under subsection (7B) above as they apply in relation to a pension sharing order under that section.

(7H) Subsections (3) to (10) of section 24E above apply in relation to a pension compensation sharing order under subsection (7B) above as they apply in relation to a pension compensation order under that section.

(8) The personal representatives of a deceased person against whom a secured periodical payments order was made shall not be liable for having distributed any part of the estate of the deceased after the expiration of the period of six months referred to in subsection (6) above on the ground that they ought to have taken into account the possibility that the court might permit an application under this section to be made after that period by the person entitled to payments under the order; but this subsection shall not prejudice any power to recover any part of the estate so distributed arising by virtue of the making of an order in pursuance of this section.

(9) In considering for the purposes of subsection (6) above the question when representation was first taken out, a grant limited to settled land or to trust property shall be left out of account and a grant limited to real estate or to personal estate shall be left out of account unless a grant limited to the remainder of the estate has previously been made or is made at the same time.

(10) Where the court, in exercise of its powers under this section, decides to vary or discharge a periodical payments or secured periodical payments order, then, subject to section 28(1) and (2) above, the court shall have power to direct that the variation or discharge shall not take effect until the expiration of such period as may be specified in the order.

(11) Where—

(a) a periodical payments or secured periodical payments order in favour of more than one child ('the order') is in force;

(b) the order requires payments specified in it to be made to or for the benefit of more than one child without apportioning those payments between them;

(c) a maintenance calculation ('the calculation') is made with respect to one or more, but not all, of the children with respect to whom those payments are to be made; and

(d) an application is made, before the end of the period of 6 months beginning with the date on which the assessment was made, for the variation or discharge of the order,

the court may, in exercise of its powers under this section to vary or discharge the order, direct that the variation or discharge shall take effect from the date on which the assessment took effect or any later date.

(12) Where—

(a) an order ('the child order') of a kind prescribed for the purposes of section 10(1) of the Child Support Act 1991 is affected by a maintenance calculation;

(b) on the date on which the child order became so affected there was in force a periodical payments or secured periodical payments order ('the spousal order') in favour of a party to a marriage having the care of the child in whose favour the child order was made; and

(c) an application is made, before the end of the period of 6 months beginning with the date on which the maintenance calculation was made, for the spousal order to be varied or discharged,

the court may, in exercise of its powers under this section to vary or discharge the spousal order, direct that the variation or discharge shall take effect from the date on which the child order became so affected or any later date.

(13) For the purposes of subsection (12) above, an order is affected if it ceases to have effect or is modified by or under section 10 of the Child Support Act 1991.

(14) Subsections (11) and (12) above are without prejudice to any other power of the court to direct that the variation or discharge of an order under this section shall take effect from a date earlier than that on which the order for variation or discharge was made.

(15) The power to make regulations under subsection (4C) above shall be exercisable by statutory instrument which shall be subject to annulment in pursuance of a resolution of either House of Parliament.

32. Payment of certain arrears unenforceable without the leave of the court

(1) A person shall not be entitled to enforce through the High Court or any county court the payment of any arrears due under an order for maintenance pending suit, an interim order for maintenance or any financial provision order without the leave of that court if those arrears became due more than twelve months before proceedings to enforce the payment of them are begun.

(2) The court hearing an application for the grant of leave under this section may refuse leave, or may grant leave subject to such restrictions and conditions (including conditions as to the allowing of time for payment or the making of payments by instalments) as that court thinks proper, or may remit the payment of the arrears or any part thereof.

(3) An application for the grant of leave under this section shall be made in such manner as may be prescribed by rules of court.

33. Orders for repayment in certain cases of sums paid under certain orders

(1) Where on an application made under this section in relation to an order to which this section applies it appears to the court that by reason of—

(a) a change in the circumstances of the person entitled to, or liable to make, payments under the order since the order was made, or

(b) the changed circumstances resulting from the death of the person so liable,

the amount received by the person entitled to payments under the order in respect of a period after those circumstances changed or after the death of the person liable to make payments under the order, as the case may be, exceeds the amount which the person so liable or his or her personal representatives should have been required to pay, the court may order the respondent to the application to pay to the applicant such sum, not exceeding the amount of the excess, as the court thinks just.

(2) This section applies to the following orders, that is to say—

(a) any order for maintenance pending suit and any interim order for maintenance;

(b) any periodical payments order; and

(c) any secured periodical payments order.

(3) An application under this section may be made by the person liable to make payments under an order to which this section applies or his or her personal representatives and may be made against the person entitled to payments under the order or her or his personal representatives.

(4) An application under this section may be made in proceedings in the High Court or a county court for—

(a) the variation or discharge of the order to which this section applies, or

(b) leave to enforce, or the enforcement of, the payment of arrears under that order;

but when not made in such proceedings shall be made to a county court, and accordingly references in this section to the court are references to the High Court or a county court, as the circumstances require.

(5) ...

(6) An order under this section for the payment of any sum may provide for the payment of that sum by instalments of such amount as may be specified in the order.

Consent orders

33A. Consent orders for financial provision or property adjustment

(1) Notwithstanding anything in the preceding provisions of this Part of this Act, on an application for a consent order for financial relief the court may, unless it has reason to think that there are other circumstances into which it ought to inquire, make an order in the terms agreed on the basis only of the prescribed information furnished with the application.

(2) Subsection (1) above applies to an application for a consent order varying or discharging an order for financial relief as it applies to an application for an order for financial relief.

(3) In this section—

'consent order,' in relation to an application for an order, means an order in the terms applied for to which the respondent agrees;

'order for financial relief' means an order under any of sections 23, 24, 24A, 24B or 27 above; and

prescribed' means prescribed by rules of court.

Maintenance agreements

34. Validity of maintenance agreements

(1) If a maintenance agreement includes a provision purporting to restrict any right to apply to a court for an order containing financial arrangements, then—

(a) that provision shall be void; but

(b) any other financial arrangements contained in the agreement shall not thereby be rendered void or unenforceable and shall, unless they are void or unenforceable for any other reason (and subject to sections 35 and 36 below), be binding on the parties to the agreement.

(2) In this section and in section 35 below—

'maintenance agreement' means any agreement in writing made, whether before or after the commencement of this Act, between the parties to a marriage, being—

(a) an agreement containing financial arrangements, whether made during the continuance or after the dissolution or annulment of the marriage; or

(b) a separation agreement which contains no financial arrangements in a case where no other agreement in writing between the same parties contains such arrangements;

'financial arrangements' means provisions governing the rights and liabilities towards one another when living separately of the parties to a marriage (including a marriage which has been dissolved or annulled) in respect of the making or securing of payments or the disposition or use of any property, including such rights and liabilities with respect to the maintenance or education of any child, whether or not a child of the family.

35. Alteration of agreements by court during lives of parties

(1) Where a maintenance agreement is for the time being subsisting and each of the parties to the agreement is for the time being either domiciled or resident in England and Wales, then, subject to subsection (3) below, either party may apply to the court or to a magistrates' court for an order under this section.

(2) If the court to which the application is made is satisfied either—

(a) that by reason of a change in the circumstances in the light of which any financial arrangements contained in the agreement were made or, as the case may be, financial arrangements were omitted from it (including a change foreseen by the parties when making the agreement), the agreement should be altered so as to make different, or, as the case may be, so as to contain, financial arrangements, or

(b) that the agreement does not contain proper financial arrangements with respect to any child of the family,

then subject to subsections (3), (4) and (5) below, that court may by order make such alterations in the agreement—

(i) by varying or revoking any financial arrangements contained in it, or
(ii) by inserting in it financial arrangements for the benefit of one of the parties to the agreement or of a child of the family,

as may appear to that court to be just having regard to all the circumstances, including, if relevant, the matters mentioned in section 25(4) above; and the agreement shall have effect thereafter as if any alteration made by the order had been made by agreement between the parties and for valuable consideration.

(3) ...

(4) Where a court decides to alter, by order under this section, an agreement by inserting provision for the making or securing by one of the parties to the agreement of periodical payments for the maintenance of the other party or by increasing the rate of the periodical payments which the agreement provides shall be made by one of the parties for the maintenance of the other, the term for which the payments or, as the case may be, the additional payments attributable to the increase are to be made under the agreement as altered by the order shall be such term as the court may specify, subject to the following limits, that is to say—

(a) where the payments will not be secured, the term shall be so defined as not to extend beyond the death of either of the parties to the agreement or the remarriage of the party to whom the payments are to be made;
(b) where the payments will be secured, the term shall be so defined as not to extend beyond the death or remarriage of that party.

(5) Where a court decides to alter, by order under this section, an agreement by inserting provision for the making or securing by one of the parties to the agreement of periodical payments for the maintenance of a child of the family or by increasing the rate of the periodical payments which the agreement provides shall be made or secured by one of the parties for the maintenance of such a child, then, in deciding the term for which under the agreement as altered by the order the payments, or as the case may be, the additional payments attributable to the increase are to be made or secured for the benefit of the child, the court shall apply the provisions of section 29(2) and (3) above as to age limits as if the order in question were a periodical payments or secured periodical payments order in favour of the child.

(6) For the avoidance of doubt it is hereby declared that nothing in this section or in section 34 above affects any power of a court before which any proceedings between the parties to a maintenance agreement are brought under any other enactment (including a provision of this Act) to make an order containing financial arrangements or any right of either party to apply for such an order in such proceedings.

Miscellaneous and supplemental

37. Avoidance of transactions intended to prevent or reduce financial relief

(1) For the purposes of this section 'financial relief' means relief under any of the provisions of sections 22, 23, 24, 24B, 27, 31 (except subsection (6)) and 35 above, and any reference in this section to defeating a person's claim for financial relief is a reference to preventing financial relief from being granted to that person, or to that person for the benefit of a child of the family, or reducing the amount of any financial relief which might be so granted, or frustrating or impeding the enforcement of any order which might be or has been made at his instance under any of those provisions.

(2) Where proceedings for financial relief are brought by one person against another, the court may, on the application of the first-mentioned person—

(a) if it is satisfied that the other party to the proceedings is, with the intention of defeating the claim for financial relief, about to make any disposition or to transfer out of the jurisdiction or otherwise deal with any property, make such order as it thinks fit for restraining the other party from so doing or otherwise for protecting the claim;
(b) if it is satisfied that the other party has, with that intention, made a reviewable disposition and that if the disposition were set aside financial relief or different financial relief would be granted to the applicant, make an order setting aside the disposition;
(c) if it is satisfied, in a case where an order has been obtained under any of the provisions mentioned in subsection (1) above by the applicant against the other party, that the other party has, with that intention, made a reviewable disposition, make an order setting aside the disposition;

and an application for the purposes of paragraph (b) above shall be made in the proceedings for the financial relief in question.

(3) Where the court makes an order under subsection (2)(b) or (c) above setting aside a disposition it shall give such consequential directions as it thinks fit for giving effect to the order (including directions requiring the making of any payments or the disposal of any property).

(4) Any disposition made by the other party to the proceedings for financial relief in question (whether before or after the commencement of those proceedings) is a reviewable disposition for the purposes of subsection (2)(b) and (c) above unless it was made for valuable consideration (other than marriage) to a person who, at the time of the disposition, acted in relation to it in good faith and without notice of any intention on the part of the other party to defeat the applicant's claim for financial relief.

(5) Where an application is made under this section with respect to a disposition which took place less than three years before the date of the application or with respect to a disposition or other dealing with property which is about to take place and the court is satisfied—

(a) in a case falling within subsection (2)(a) or (b) above, that the disposition or other dealing would (apart from this section) have the consequence, or

(b) in a case falling within subsection (2)(c) above, that the disposition has had the consequence,

of defeating the applicant's claim for financial relief, it shall be presumed, unless the contrary is shown, that the person who disposed of or is about to dispose of or deal with the property did so or, as the case may be, is about to do so, with the intention of defeating the applicant's claim for financial relief.

(6) In this section 'disposition'does not include any provision contained in a will or codicil but, with that exception, includes any conveyance, assurance or gift of property of any description, whether made by an instrument or otherwise.

(7) This section does not apply to a disposition made before 1st January 1968.

38. Order for repayment in certain cases of sums paid after cessation of order by reason of remarriage or formation of civil partnership

(1) Where—

(a) a periodical payments or secured periodical payments order in favour of a party to a marriage (hereafter in this section referred to as 'a payments order') has ceased to have effect by reason of the remarriage of, or formation of a civil partnership by, that party, and

(b) the person liable to make payments under the order or his or her personal representatives made payments in accordance with it in respect of a period after the date of the remarriage or formation of the civil partnership in the mistaken belief that the order was still subsisting,

the person so liable or his or her personal representatives shall not be entitled to bring proceedings in respect of a cause of action arising out of the circumstances mentioned in paragraphs (a) and (b) above against the person entitled to payments under the order or her or his personal representatives, but may instead make an application against that person or her or his personal representatives under this section.

. . .

39. Settlement, etc., made in compliance with a property adjustment order may be avoided on bankruptcy of settlor

The fact that a settlement or transfer of property had to be made in order to comply with a property adjustment order shall not prevent that settlement or transfer from being a transaction in respect of which an order may be made under section 339 or 340 of the Insolvency Act 1986 (transactions at an undervalue and preferences).

40. Payments etc under order made in favour of a person suffering mental disorder

(1) Where the court makes an order under this Part of this Act requiring payments (including a lump sum payment) to be made, or property to be transferred, to a party to a marriage and the court is satisfied that the person in whose favour the order is made ('P') lacks capacity (within the meaning of the Mental Capacity Act 2005) in relation to the provisions of the order then, subject to any order, direction or authority made or given in relation to P under that Act, the court may order the payments to be made, or as the case may be, the property to be transferred, to such person ('D') as it may direct.

(2) In carrying out any functions of his in relation to an order made under subsection (1), D must act in P's best interests (within the meaning of that Act).

40A. Appeals relating to pension sharing orders which have taken effect

(1) Subsections (2) and (3) below apply where an appeal against a pension sharing order is begun on or after the day on which the order takes effect.

(2) If the pension sharing order relates to a person's rights under a pension arrangement, the appeal court may not set aside or vary the order if the person responsible for the pension arrangement has acted to his detriment in reliance on the taking effect of the order.
(3) If the pension sharing order relates to a person's shareable state scheme rights, the appeal court may not set aside or vary the order if the Secretary of State has acted to his detriment in reliance on the taking effect of the order.
(4) In determining for the purposes of subsection (2) or (3) above whether a person has acted to his detriment in reliance on the taking effect of the order, the appeal court may disregard any detriment which in its opinion is insignificant.
(5) Where subsection (2) or (3) above applies, the appeal court may make such further orders (including one or more pension sharing orders) as it thinks fit for the purpose of putting the parties in the position it considers appropriate.
(6) Section 24C above only applies to a pension sharing order under this section if the decision of the appeal court can itself be the subject of an appeal.
(7) In subsection (2) above, the reference to the person responsible for the pension arrangement is to be read in accordance with section 25D(4) above.

PART IV
MISCELLANEOUS AND SUPPLEMENTAL

48. Evidence

(1) The evidence of a husband or wife shall be admissible in any proceedings to prove that marital intercourse did or did not take place between them during any period.
(2) In any proceedings for nullity of marriage, evidence on the question of sexual capacity shall be heard in camera unless in any case the judge is satisfied that in the interests of justice any such evidence ought to be heard in open court.

49. Parties to proceedings under this Act

(1) Where in a petition for divorce or judicial separation, or in any other pleading praying for either form of relief, one party to a marriage alleges that the other has committed adultery, he or she shall make the person alleged to have committed adultery with the other party to the marriage a party to the proceedings unless excused by the court on special grounds from doing so.
(2) Rules of court may, either generally or in such case as may be prescribed by the rules, exclude the application of subsection (1) above where the person alleged to have committed adultery with the other party to the marriage is not named in the petition or other pleading.
(3) Where in pursuance of subsection (1) above a person is made a party to proceedings for divorce or judicial separation, the court may, if after the close of the evidence on the part of the person making the allegation of adultery it is of opinion that there is not sufficient evidence against the person so made a party, dismiss him or her from the suit.
(4) Rules of court may make provision, in cases not failing within subsection (1) above, with respect to the joinder as parties to proceedings under this Act of persons involved in allegations of adultery or other improper conduct made in those proceedings, and with respect to the dismissal from such proceedings of any parties so joined, and rules of court made by virtue of this subsection may make different provision for different cases.
(5) In every case in which adultery with any party to a suit is alleged against any person not made a party to the suit or in which the court considers, in the interest of any person not already a party to the suit, that that person should be made a party to the suit, the court may if it thinks fit allow that person to intervene upon such terms, if any, as the court thinks just.

52. Interpretation

(1) In this Act—
'child', in relation to one or both of the parties to a marriage, includes an illegitimate child of that party or, as the case may be, of both parties;
'child of the family,' in relation to the parties to a marriage, means—
(a) a child of both of those parties; and
(b) any other child, not being a child who is placed with those parties as foster parents by a local authority or voluntary organisation, who has been treated by both of those parties as a child of their family;
'the court' (except where the context otherwise requires) means the High Court or, where a county court has jurisdiction by virtue of Part V of the Matrimonial and Family

Proceedings Act 1984, a county court;
'education' includes training;
'maintenance calculation' has the same meaning as it has in the Child Support Act 1991 by virtue of section 54 of that Act as read with any regulations in force under that section;

(2) In this Act—
(a) references to financial provision orders, periodical payments and secured periodical payments orders and orders for the payment of a lump sum, and references to property adjustment orders, shall be construed in accordance with section 21 above;
(aa) references to pension sharing orders shall be construed in accordance with section 21A above; and
(b) references to orders for maintenance pending suit and to interim orders for maintenance shall be construed respectively in accordance with section 22 and section 27(5) above.

(3) For the avoidance of doubt it is hereby declared that references in this Act to remarriage include references to a marriage which is by law void or voidable.

(3A) References in this Act to the formation of a civil partnership by a person include references to a civil partnership which is by law void or voidable.

(4) Except where the contrary intention is indicated, references in this Act to any enactment include references to that enactment as amended, extended or applied by or under any subsequent enactment, including this Act.

DOMICILE AND MATRIMONIAL PROCEEDINGS ACT 1973
(1973 c. 45)

PART I
DOMICILE

Husband and wife

1. Abolition of wife's dependent domicile

(1) Subject to subsection (2) below, the domicile of a married woman as at any time after the coming into force of this section shall, instead of being the same as her husband's by virtue only of marriage, be ascertained by reference to the same factors as in the case of any other individual capable of having an independent domicile.

(2) Where immediately before this section came into force a woman was married and then had her husband's domicile by dependence, she is to be treated as retaining that domicile (as a domicile of choice, if it is not also her domicile of origin) unless and until it is changed by acquisition or revival of another domicile either on or after the coming into force of this section.

(3) This section extends to England and Wales, Scotland and Northern Ireland.

Minors and pupils

3. Age at which independent domicile can be acquired

(1) The time at which a person first becomes capable of having an independent domicile shall be when he attains the age of sixteen or marries under that age; and in the case of a person who immediately before 1 January 1974 was incapable of having an independent domicile, but had then attained the age of sixteen or been married, it shall be that date.

(2) This section extends to England and Wales and Northern Ireland (but not to Scotland).

4. Dependent domicile of child not living with his father

(1) Subsection (2) of this section shall have effect with respect to the dependent domicile of a child as at any time after the coming into force of this section when his father and mother are alive but living apart.

(2) The child's domicile as at that time shall be that of his mother if—
(a) he then has his home with her and has no home with his father; or
(b) he has at any time had her domicile by virtue of paragraph (a) above and has not since had a home with his father.

(3) As at any time after the coming into force of this section, the domicile of a child whose mother is dead shall be that which she last had before she died if at her death he had her domicile by virtue of subsection (2) above and he has not since had a home with his father.

(4) Nothing in this section prejudices any existing rule of law as to cases in which a child's domicile is regarded as being, by dependence, that of his mother.

. . .

PART II
JURISDICTION IN MATRIMONIAL PROCEEDINGS (ENGLAND AND WALES)

5. Jurisdiction of High Court and family court

(1) Subsections (2) to (5) below shall have effect, subject to section 6(3) and (4) of this Act, with respect to the jurisdiction of the court to entertain—
   (a) proceedings for divorce, judicial separation or nullity of marriage; and
   (b) proceedings for death to be presumed and a marriage to be dissolved in pursuance of section 19 of the Matrimonial Causes Act 1973;

. . .

(4) The court shall have jurisdiction to entertain proceedings for death to be presumed and a marriage to be dissolved if (and only if) the petitioner—
   (a) is domiciled in England and Wales on the date when the proceedings are begun; or
   (b) was habitually resident in England and Wales throughout the period of one year ending with that date.

. . .

INHERITANCE (PROVISION FOR FAMILY AND DEPENDANTS) ACT 1975
(1975 c. 63)

1. Application for financial provision from deceased's estate

(1) Where after the commencement of this Act a person dies domiciled in England and Wales and is survived by any of the following persons:—
   (a) the spouse or civil partner of the deceased;
   (b) a former spouse or former civil partner of the deceased, but not one who has formed a subsequent marriage or civil partnership;
   (ba) any person (not being a person included in paragraph (a) or (b) above) to whom subsection (1A) or (1B) below applies;
   (c) a child of the deceased;
   (d) any person (not being a child of the deceased) who, in the case of any marriage or civil partnership to which the deceased was at any time a party, was treated by the deceased as a child of the family in relation to that marriage or civil partnership;
   (e) any person (not being a person included in the foregoing paragraphs of this subsection) who immediately before the death of the deceased was being maintained, either wholly or partly, by the deceased;

that person may apply to the court for an order under section 2 of this Act on the ground that the disposition of the deceased's estate effected by his will or the law relating to intestacy, or the combination of his will and that law, is not such as to make reasonable financial provision for the applicant.

(1A) This subsection applies to a person if the deceased died on or after 1st January 1996 and, during the whole of the period of two years ending immediately before the date when the deceased died, the person was living—
   (a) in the same household as the deceased, and
   (b) as the husband or wife of the deceased.

(1B) This subsection applies to a person if for the whole of the period of two years ending immediately before the date when the deceased died the person was living—
   (a) in the same household as the deceased, and
   (b) as the civil partner of the deceased.

(2) In this Act 'reasonable financial provision'—
   (a) in the case of an application made by virtue of subsection (1)(a) above by the husband or wife of the deceased (except where the marriage with the deceased was the subject of a decree of judicial separation and at the date of death the

decree was in force and the separation was continuing), means such financial provision as it would be reasonable in all the circumstances of the case for a husband or wife to receive, whether or not that provision is required for his or her maintenance;

(aa) in the case of an application made by virtue of subsection (1)(a) above by the civil partner of the deceased (except where, at the date of death, a separation order under Chapter 2 of Part 2 of the Civil Partnership Act 2004 was in force in relation to the civil partnership and the separation was continuing), means such financial provision as would be reasonable in all the circumstances of the case for a civil partner to receive, whether or not that provision is required for his or her maintenance;

(b) in the case of any other application made by virtue of subsection (1) above, means such financial provision as it would be reasonable in all the circumstances of the case for the applicant to receive for his maintenance.

(2A) The reference in subsection (1)(d) above to a family in which the deceased stood in the role of a parent includes a family of which the deceased was the only member (apart from the applicant).

(3) For the purposes of subsection (1)(e) above, a person shall be treated as being maintained by the deceased, either wholly or partly, as the case may be, if the deceased, otherwise than for full valuable consideration, was making a substantial contribution in money or money's worth towards the reasonable needs of that person.

2. Powers of court to make orders

(1) Subject to the provisions of this Act, where an application is made for an order under this section, the court may, if it is satisfied that the disposition of the deceased's estate effected by his will or the law relating to intestacy, or the combination of his will and that law, is not such as to make reasonable financial provision for the applicant, make any one or more of the following orders:—

(a) an order for the making to the applicant out of the net estate of the deceased of such periodical payments and for such term as may be specified in the order;

(b) an order for the payment to the applicant out of that estate of a lump sum of such amount as may be so specified;

(c) an order for the transfer to the applicant of such property comprised in that estate as may be so specified;

(d) an order for the settlement for the benefit of the applicant of such property comprised in that estate as may be so specified;

(e) an order for the acquisition out of property comprised in that estate of such property as may be so specified and for the transfer of the property so acquired to the applicant or for the settlement thereof for his benefit;

(f) an order varying any ante-nuptial or post-nuptial settlement (including such a settlement made by will) made on the parties to a marriage to which the deceased was one of the parties, the variation being for the benefit of the surviving party to that marriage, or any child of that marriage, or any person who was treated by the deceased as a child of the family in relation to that marriage;

(g) an order varying any settlement made—

(i) during the subsistence of a civil partnership formed by the deceased, or

(ii) in anticipation of the formation of a civil partnership by the deceased, on the civil partners (including such a settlement made by will), the variation being for the benefit of the surviving civil partner, or any person who was treated by the deceased as a child of the family in relation to the civil partnership.

(2) An order under subsection (1)(a) above providing for the making out of the net estate of the deceased of periodical payments may provide for—

(a) payments of such amount as may be specified in the order,

(b) payments equal to the whole of the income of the net estate or of such portion thereof as may be so specified,

(c) payments equal to the whole of the income of such part of the net estate as the court may direct to be set aside or appropriated for the making out of the income thereof of payments under this section,

or may provide for the amount of the payments or any of them to be determined in any other way the court thinks fit.

(3) Where an order under subsection (1)(a) above provides for the making of payments of an amount specified in the order, the order may direct that such part of the net estate as may be so specified shall be set aside or appropriated for the making out of the income thereof of those payments; but no larger part of the net estate shall be so set aside or appropriated than is sufficient, at the date of the order, to produce by the income thereof the amount required for the making of those payments.

(3A) In assessing for the purpose of an order under this section the extent (if any) to which the net estate is reduced by any debts or liabilities (including any inheritance tax paid or payable out of the estate) the court may assume that the order has already been made.

(4) An order under this section may contain such consequential and supplemental provisions as the court thinks necessary or expedient for the purpose of giving effect to the order or for the purpose of securing that the order operates fairly as between one beneficiary of the estate of the deceased and another and may, in particular, but without prejudice to the generality of this subsection—

(a) order any person who holds any property which forms part of the net estate of the deceased to make such payment or transfer such property as may be specified in the order;

(b) vary the disposition of the deceased's estate effected by the will or the law relating to intestacy, or by both the will and the law relating to intestacy, in such manner as the court thinks fair and reasonable having regard to the provisions of the order and all the circumstances of the case;

(c) confer on the trustees of any property which is the subject of an order under this section such powers as appear to the court to be necessary or expedient.

3. Matters to which court is to have regard in exercising powers under s. 2

(1) Where an application is made for an order under section 2 of this Act, the court shall, in determining whether the disposition of the deceased's estate effected by his will or the law relating to intestacy, or the combination of his will and that law, is such as to make reasonable financial provision for the applicant and, if the court considers that reasonable financial provision has not been made, in determining whether and in what manner it shall exercise its powers under that section, have regard to the following matters, that is to say—

(a) the financial resources and financial needs which the applicant has or is likely to have in the foreseeable future;

(b) the financial resources and financial needs which any other applicant for an order under section 2 of this Act has or is likely to have in the foreseeable future;

(c) the financial resources and financial needs which any beneficiary of the estate of the deceased has or is likely to have in the foreseeable future;

(d) any obligations and responsibilities which the deceased had towards any applicant for an order under the said section 2 or towards any beneficiary of the estate of the deceased;

(e) the size and nature of the net estate of the deceased;

(f) any physical or mental disability of any applicant for an order under the said section 2 or any beneficiary of the estate of the deceased;

(g) any other matter, including the conduct of the applicant or any other person, which in the circumstances of the case the court may consider relevant.

(2) This subsection applies, without prejudice to the generality of paragraph (g) of subsection (1) above, where an application for an order under section 2 of this Act is made by virtue of section 1(1)(a) or (b) of this Act. The court shall, in addition to the matters specifically mentioned in paragraphs (a) to (f) of that subsection, have regard to—

(a) the age of the applicant and the duration of the marriage or civil partnership;

(b) the contribution made by the applicant to the welfare of the family of the deceased, including any contribution made by looking after the home or caring for the family.

In the case of an application by the wife or husband of the deceased, the court shall also, unless at the date of death a decree of judicial separation was in force and the separation was continuing, have regard to the provision which the applicant might reasonably have expected to receive if on the day on which the deceased died the marriage, instead of being terminated by the death, had been terminated by a decree of divorce. In the case of an application by the civil partner of the deceased, the court shall also, unless at the date of the death a separation order under Chapter 2 of Part 2 of the Civil Partnership Act 2004 was in force and the separation was continuing, have regard to the provision which the applicant might reasonably have expected to receive if on the day on which the deceased died the civil partnership, instead of being terminated by death, had been terminated by a dissolution order.

(2A) Without prejudice to the generality of paragraph (g) of subsection (1) above, where an application for an order under section 2 of this Act is made by virtue of section 1(1)(ba) of this Act, the court shall, in addition to the matters specifically mentioned in paragraphs (a) to (f) of that subsection, have regard to—

(a) the age of the applicant and the length of the period during which the applicant lived as the husband or wife of the deceased and in the same household as the deceased;

(b) the contribution made by the applicant to the welfare of the family of the deceased, including any contribution made by looking after the home or caring for the family.

(3) Without prejudice to the generality of paragraph (g) of subsection (1) above, where an application for an order under section 2 of this Act is made by virtue of section 1(1)(c) or 1(1)(d) of this Act, the court shall, in addition to the matters specifically mentioned in paragraphs (a) to (f) of that subsection, have regard to the manner in which the applicant was being or in which he might be expected to be educated or trained, and where the application is made by virtue of section 1(1)(d) the court shall also have regard—

(a) to whether the deceased had assumed any responsibility for the applicant's maintenance and, if so, to the extent to which and the basis upon which the deceased assumed that responsibility and to the length of time for which the deceased discharged that responsibility;

(b) to whether in assuming and discharging that responsibility the deceased did so knowing that the applicant was not his own child;

(c) to the liability of any other person to maintain the applicant.

(4) Without prejudice to the generality of paragraph (g) of subsection (1) above, where an application for an order under section 2 of this Act is made by virtue of section 1(1)(e) of this Act, the court shall, in addition to the matters specifically mentioned in paragraphs (a) to (f) of that subsection, have regard to the extent to which and the basis upon which the deceased assumed responsibility for the maintenance of the applicant and to the length of time for which the deceased discharged that responsibility.

(5) In considering the matters to which the court is required to have regard under this section, the court shall take into account the facts as known to the court at the date of the hearing.

. . .

4. Time-limit for application

An application for an order under section 2 of this Act shall not, except with the permission of the court, be made after the end of the period of six months from the date on which representation with respect to the estate of the deceased is first taken out.

Special provisions relating to cases of divorce, separation etc.

14. Provision as to cases where no financial relief was granted in divorce proceedings etc.

(1) Where, within twelve months from the date on which a decree of divorce or nullity of marriage has been made absolute or a decree of judicial separation has been granted, a party to the marriage dies and—

(a) an application for a financial provision order under section 23 of the Matrimonial Causes Act 1973 or a property adjustment order under section 24 of that Act has not been made by the other party to that marriage, or

(b) such an application has been made but the proceedings thereon have not been determined at the time of the death of the deceased,

then, if an application for an order under section 2 of this Act is made by that other party, the court shall, notwithstanding anything in section 1 or section 3 of this Act, have power, if it thinks it just to do so, to treat that party for the purposes of that application as if the decree of divorce or nullity of marriage had not been made absolute or the decree of judicial separation had not been granted, as the case may be.

(2) This section shall not apply in relation to a decree of judicial separation unless at the date of the death of the deceased the decree was in force and the separation was continuing.

14A. Provision as to cases where no financial relief was granted in proceedings for dissolution etc. of a civil partnership

(1) Subsection (2) below applies where—

(a) a dissolution order, nullity order, separation order or presumption of death order has been made under Chapter 2 of Part 2 of the Civil Partnership Act 2004 in relation to a civil partnership,

(b) one of the civil partners dies within twelve months from the date on which the order is made, and

(c) either—

(i) an application for a financial provision order under Part 1 of Schedule 5 to that Act or a property adjustment order under Part 2 of that Schedule has not been made by the other civil partner, or

(ii) such an application has been made but the proceedings on the application have not been determined at the time of the death of the deceased.

(2) If an application for an order under section 2 of this Act is made by the surviving civil partner, the court shall, notwithstanding anything in section 1 or section 3 of this Act, have power if it thinks it just to do so, to treat the surviving civil partner as if the order mentioned in subsection (1)(a) had not been made.

(3) This section shall not apply in relation to a separation order unless at the date of the death of the deceased the separation order was in force and the separation was continuing.

15. Restriction imposed in divorce proceedings etc. on application under this Act

(1) On the grant of a decree of divorce, a decree of nullity of marriage or a decree of judicial separation or at any time thereafter the court, if it considers it just to do so, may, on the application of either party to the marriage, order that the other party to the marriage shall not on the death of the applicant be entitled to apply for an order under section 2 of this Act.

In this subsection 'the court' means the High Court or the family court.

(2) In the case of a decree of divorce or nullity of marriage an order may be made under subsection (1) above before or after the decree is made absolute, but if it is made before the decree is made absolute it shall not take effect unless the decree is made absolute.

(3) Where an order made under subsection (1) above on the grant of a decree of divorce or nullity of marriage has come into force with respect to a party to a marriage, then, on the death of the other party to that marriage, the court shall not entertain any application for an order under section 2 of this Act made by the first-mentioned party.

(4) Where an order made under subsection (1) above on the grant of a decree of judicial separation has come into force with respect to any party to a marriage, then, if, the other party to that marriage dies while the decree is in force and the separation is continuing, the court does not entertain any application for an order under section 2 of this Act made by the first-mentioned party.

15ZA. Restriction imposed in proceedings for the dissolution etc. of a civil partnership on application under this Act

(1) On making a dissolution order, nullity order, separation order or presumption of death order under Chapter 2 of Part 2 of the Civil Partnership Act 2004, or at any time after making such an order, the court if it considers it just to do so, may, on the application of either of the civil partners, order that the other civil partner shall not on the death of the applicant be entitled to apply for an order under section 2 of this Act.

(2) In subsection (1) above 'the court' means the High Court, or where a county court has jurisdiction by virtue of Part 5 of the Matrimonial and Family Proceedings Act 1984, a county court.

(3) In the case of a dissolution order, nullity order or presumption of death order ('the main order') an order may be made under subsection (1) above before (as well as after) the main order is made final, but if made before the main order is made final it shall not take effect unless the main order is made final.

(4) Where an order under subsection (1) above made in connection with a dissolution order, nullity order or presumption of death order has come into force with respect to a civil partner, then, on the death of the other civil partner, the court shall not entertain any application for an order under section 2 of the Act made by the surviving civil partner.

(5) Where an order under subsection (1) above made in connection with a separation order has come into force with respect to a civil partner, then, if the other civil partner dies while the separation order is in force and the separation is continuing, the court shall not entertain any application for an order under section 2 of this Act made by the surviving civil partner.

15A. Restriction imposed in proceedings under Matrimonial and Family Proceedings Act 1984 on application under this Act

(1) On making an order under section 17 of the Matrimonial and Family Proceedings Act 1984 (orders for financial provision and property adjustment following overseas divorces, etc.) the court, if it considers it just to do so, may, on the application of either

party to the marriage, order that the other party to the marriage shall not on the death of the applicant be entitled to apply for an order under section 2 of this Act.

In this subsection 'the court' means the High Court or the family court.

(2) Where an order under subsection (1) above has been made with respect to a party to a marriage which has been dissolved or annulled, then, on the death of the other party to that marriage, the court shall not entertain an application under section 2 of this Act made by the first-mentioned party.

(3) Where an order under subsection (1) above has been made with respect to a party to a marriage the parties to which have been legally separated, then, if the other party to the marriage dies while the legal separation is in force, the court shall not entertain an application under section 2 of this Act made by the first-mentioned party.

15B. Restriction imposed in proceedings under Schedule 7 to the Civil Partnership Act 2004 on application under this Act

(1) On making an order under paragraph 9 of Schedule 7 to the Civil Partnership Act 2004 (orders for financial provision, property adjustment and pension-sharing following overseas dissolution etc of civil partnership) the court, if it considers it just to do so, may, on the application of either of the civil partners, order that the other civil partner shall not on the death of the applicant be entitled to apply for an order under section 2 of this Act.

(2) In subsection (1) above 'the court' means the High Court or the family court.

(3) Where an order under subsection (1) above has been made with respect to one of the civil partners in a case where a civil partnership has been dissolved or annulled, then, on the death of the other civil partner, the court shall not entertain an application under section of this Act made by the surviving civil partner.

(4) Where an order under subsection (1) above has been made with respect to one of the civil partners in a case where civil partners have been legally separated, then, if the other civil partner dies while the legal separation is in force, the court shall not entertain an application under section 2 of this Act made by the surviving civil partner.

16. Variation and discharge of secured periodical payments orders made under Matrimonial Causes Act 1973

(1) Where an application for an order under section 2 of this Act is made to the court by any person who was at the time of the death of the deceased entitled to payments from the deceased under a secured periodical payments order made under the Matrimonial Causes Act 1973 or Schedule 5 to the Civil Partnership Act 2004, then, in the proceedings on that application, the court shall have power, if an application is made under this section by that person or by the personal representative of the deceased, to vary or discharge that periodical payments order or to revive the operation of any provision thereof which has been suspended under section 31 of that Act of 1973 or Part 11 of that Schedule.

(2) In exercising the powers conferred by this section the court shall have regard to all the circumstances of the case, including any order which the court proposes to make under section 2 or section 5 of this Act and any change (whether resulting from the death of the deceased or otherwise) in any of the matters to which the court was required to have regard when making the secured periodical payments order.

(3) The powers exercisable by the court under this section in relation to an order shall be exercisable also in relation to any instrument executed in pursuance of the order.

17. Variation and revocation of maintenance agreements

(1) Where an application for an order under section 2 of this Act is made to the court by any person who was at the time of the death of the deceased entitled to payments from the deceased under a maintenance agreement which provided for the continuation of payments under the agreement after the death of the deceased, then, in the proceedings on that application, the court shall have power, if an application is made under this section by that person or by the personal representative of the deceased, to vary or revoke that agreement.

(2) In exercising the powers conferred by this section the court shall have regard to all the circumstances of the case, including any order which the court proposes to make under section 2 or section 5 of this Act and any change (whether resulting from the death of the deceased or otherwise) in any of the circumstances in the light of which the agreement was made.

(3) If a maintenance agreement is varied by the court under this section the like consequences shall ensue as if the variation had been made immediately before the death of the deceased by agreement between the parties and for valuable consideration.

(4) In this section 'maintenance agreement,' in relation to a deceased person, means any agreement made, whether in writing or not and whether before or after the commencement of this Act, by the deceased with any person with whom he formed a marriage or civil partnership, being an agreement which contained provisions governing the rights and liabilities towards one another when living separately of the parties to that marriage or of the civil partners (whether or not the marriage or civil partnership has been dissolved or annulled) in respect of the making or securing of payments or the disposition or use of any property, including such rights and liabilities with respect to the maintenance or education of any child, whether or not a child of the deceased or a person who was treated by the deceased as a child of the family in relation to that marriage or civil partnership.

18. Availability of court's powers under this Act in applications under ss. 31 and 36 of the Matrimonial Causes Act 1973

(1) Where—

(a) a person against whom a secured periodical payments order was made under the Matrimonial Causes Act 1973 has died and an application is made under section 31(6) of that Act for the variation or discharge of that order or for the revival of the operation of any provision thereof which has been suspended, or

(b) a party to a maintenance agreement within the meaning of section 34 of that Act has died, the agreement being one which provides for the continuation of payments thereunder after the death of one of the parties, and an application is made under section 36(1) of that Act, for the alteration of the agreement under section 35 thereof,

the court shall have power to direct that the application made under the said section 31(6) or 36(1) shall be deemed to have been accompanied by an application for an order under section 2 of this Act.

(2) Where the court gives a direction under subsection (1) above it shall have power, in the proceedings on the application under the said section 31(6) or 36(1), to make any order which the court would have had power to make under the provisions of this Act if the application under the said section 31(6) or 36(1), as the case may be, had been made jointly with an application for an order under the said section 2; and the court shall have power to give such consequential directions as may be necessary for enabling the court to exercise any of the powers available to the court under this Act in the case of an application for an order under section 2.

(3) Where an order made under section 15(1) of this Act is in force with respect to a party to a marriage, the court shall not give a direction under subsection (1) above with respect to any application made under the said section 31(6) or 36(1) by that party on the death of the other party.

18A. Availability of court's powers under this Act in applications under paragraphs 60 and 73 of Schedule 5 to the Civil Partnership Act 2004

(1) Where—

(a) a person against whom a secured periodical payments order was made under Schedule 5 to the Civil Partnership Act 2004 has died and an application is made under paragraph 60 of that Schedule for the variation or discharge of that order or for the revival of the operation of any suspended provision of the order, or

(b) a party to a maintenance agreement within the meaning of Part 13 of that Schedule has died, the agreement being one which provides for the continuation of payments under the agreement after the death of one of the parties, and an application is made under paragraph 73 of that Schedule for the alteration of the agreement under paragraph 69 of that Schedule,

the court shall have power to direct that the application made under paragraph 60 or 73 of that Schedule shall be deemed to have been accompanied by an application for an order under section 2 of this Act.

(2) Where the court gives a direction under subsection (1) above it shall have power, in the proceedings on the application under paragraph 60 or 73 of that Schedule, to make an order which the court would have had the power to make under the provisions of this Act if the application under that paragraph had been made jointly with an application for an order under section 2 of this Act; and the court shall have power to give such consequential directions as may be necessary for enabling the court to exercise any of the powers available to the court under this Act in the case of an application for an order under section 2.

(3) Where an order made under section 15ZA(1) of this Act is in force with respect to a civil partner, the court shall not give a direction under subsection (1) above with respect to any application made under paragraph 60 or 73 of that Schedule by that civil partner on the death of the other civil partner.

LEGITIMACY ACT 1976
(1976 c. 31)

1. Legitimacy of children of certain void marriages

(1) The child of a void marriage, whenever born, shall, subject to subsection (2) below and Schedule 1 to this Act, be treated as the legitimate child of his parents if at the time of the insemination resulting in the birth, or where there was no such insemination, the child's conception (or at the time of the celebration of the marriage if later) both or either of the parties reasonably believed that the marriage was valid.

(2) This section applies where the father of the child was domiciled in England and Wales at the time of the birth or, if he died before the birth, was so domiciled immediately before his death.

(3) It is hereby declared for the avoidance of doubt that subsection (1) above applies notwithstanding that the belief that the marriage was valid was due to a mistake as to law.

(4) In relation to a child born after the coming into force of section 28 of the Family Law Reform Act 1987, it shall be presumed for the purposes of subsection (1) above, unless the contrary is shown, that one of the parties to the void marriage reasonably believed at the time of the insemination resulting in the birth or, where there was no such insemination, the child's conception (or at the time of the celebration of the marriage if later) that the marriage was valid.

2. Legitimation by subsequent marriage of parents

Subject to the following provisions of this Act, where the parents of an illegitimate person marry one another, the marriage shall, if the father of the illegitimate person is at the date of marriage domiciled in England and Wales, render that person, if living, legitimate from the date of the marriage.

2A. Legitimation by subsequent civil partnership of parents

Subject to the following provisions of this Act, where—

(a) a person ('the child') has a parent ('the female parent') by virtue of section 43 of the Human Fertilisation and Embryology Act 2008 (treatment provided to woman who agrees that second woman to be parent),

(b) at the time of the child's birth, the female parent and the child's mother are not civil partners of each other,

(c) the female parent and the child's mother subsequently enter into a civil partnership, and

(d) the female parent is at the date of the formation of the civil partnership domiciled in England and Wales,

the civil partnership shall render the child, if living, legitimate from the date of the formation of the civil partnership.

3. Legitimation by extraneous law

(1) Subject to the following provisions of this Act, where the parents of an illegitimate person marry one another and the father of the illegitimate person is not at the time of the marriage domiciled in England and Wales but is domiciled in a country by the law of which the illegitimate person became legitimated by virtue of such subsequent marriage, that person, if living, shall in England and Wales be recognised as having been so legitimated from the date of the marriage notwithstanding that, at the time of his birth, his father was domiciled in a country the law of which did not permit legitimation by subsequent marriage.

(2) Subject to the following provisions of this Act, where—

   (a) a person ('the child') has a parent ('the female parent') by virtue of section 43 of the Human Fertilisation and Embryology Act 2008 (treatment provided to woman who agrees that second woman to be parent),

   (b) at the time of the child's birth, the female parent and the child's mother are not civil partners of each other,

   (c) the female parent and the child's mother subsequently enter into a civil partnership, and

(d) the female parent is not at the time of the formation of the civil partnership domiciled in England and Wales but is domiciled in a country by the law of which the child became legitimated by virtue of the civil partnership,

the child, if living, shall in England and Wales be recognised as having been so legitimated from the date of the formation of the civil partnership notwithstanding that, at the time of the child's birth, the female parent was domiciled in a country the law of which did not permit legitimation by subsequent civil partnership.

4. Legitimation of adopted child

(1) Section 39 of the Adoption Act 1976 or section 67 of the Adoption and Children Act 2002 does not prevent an adopted child being legitimated under section 2 or 3 above if either natural parent is the sole adoptive parent.

(2) Where an adoptive child (with a sole adoptive parent) is legitimated—

(a) subsection (2) of the said section 39 or subsection (3)(b) of the said section 67 shall not apply after the legitimation to the natural relationship with the other natural parent, and

(b) revocation of the adoption order in consequence of the legitimation shall not affect section 39, 41 or 42 of the Adoption Act 1976 or section 67, 68 or 60 of the Adoption and Children Act 2002 as it applies to any instrument made before the date of legitimation.

ADOPTION ACT 1976
(1976 c. 36)

PART IV

STATUS OF ADOPTED CHILDREN

39. Status conferred by adoption

(1) An adopted child shall be treated in law—

(a) where the adopters are a married couple, as if he had been born as a child of the marriage (whether or not he was in fact born after the marriage was solemnized);

(b) in any other case, as if he had been born to the adopter in wedlock (but not as a child of any actual marriage of the adopter).

(2) An adopted child shall, subject to subsections (3) and (3A), be treated in law as if he were not the child of any person other than the adopters or adopter.

(3) In the case of a child adopted by one of its natural parents as sole adoptive parent, subsection (2) has no effect as respects entitlement to property depending on relationship to that parent, or as respects anything else depending on that relationship.

. . .

(4) It is hereby declared that this section prevents an adopted child from being illegitimate.

(5) This section has effect—

(a) in the case of an adoption before 1st January 1976, from that date, and

(b) in the case of any other adoption, from the date of the adoption.

(6) Subject to the provisions of this Part, this section—

(a) applies to the construction of enactments or instruments passed or made before the adoption or later, and so applies subject to any contrary indication; and

(b) has effect as respects things done, or events occurring, after the adoption, or after 31st December 1975, whichever is the later.

41. Adoptive relatives

A relationship existing by virtue of section 39 may be referred to as an adoptive relationship, and—

(a) a male adopter may be referred to as the adoptive father;

(b) a female adopter may be referred to as the adoptive mother;

(c) any other relative of any degree under an adoptive relationship may be referred to as an adoptive relative of that degree,

but this section does not prevent the term 'parent,' or any other term not qualified by the word 'adoptive' being treated as including an adoptive relative.

44. Property devolving with peerages etc.

(1) An adoption does not affect the descent of any peerage or dignity or title of honour.

. . .

DOMESTIC PROCEEDINGS AND MAGISTRATES' COURTS ACT 1978
(1978 c. 22)

PART I
MATRIMONIAL PROCEEDINGS IN MAGISTRATES' COURTS

Powers of court to make orders for financial provision for parties to a marriage and children of the family

1. Grounds of application for financial provision

Either party to a marriage may apply to a magistrates' court for an order under section 2 of this Act on the ground that the other party to the marriage—
(a) has failed to provide reasonable maintenance for the applicant; or
(b) has failed to provide, or to make a proper contribution towards, reasonable maintenance for any child of the family; or
(c) has behaved in such a way that the applicant cannot reasonably be expected to live with the respondent; or
(d) has deserted the applicant.

2. Powers of court to make orders for financial provision

(1) Where on an application for an order under this section the applicant satisfies the court of any ground mentioned in section 1 of this Act, the court may, subject to the provisions of this Part of this Act, make any one or more of the following orders, that is to say—
(a) an order that the respondent shall make to the applicant such periodical payments, and for such term, as may be specified in the order;
(b) an order that the respondent shall pay to the applicant such lump sum as may be so specified;
(c) an order that the respondent shall make to the applicant for the benefit of a child of the family to whom the application relates, or to such a child, such periodical payments, and for such term, as may be so specified;
(d) an order that the respondent shall pay to the applicant for the benefit of a child of the family to whom the application relates, or to such a child, such lump sum as may be so specified.

(2) Without prejudice to the generality of subsection (1)(b) or (d) above, an order under this section for the payment of a lump sum may be made for the purpose of enabling any liability or expenses reasonably incurred in maintaining the applicant, or any child of the family to whom the application relates, before the making of the order to be met.

(3) The amount of any lump sum required to be paid by such an order under this section shall not exceed £1,000 or such larger amount as the Lord Chancellor may from time to time by order fix for the purposes of this subsection.

3. Matters to which court is to have regard in exercising its powers under s. 2

(1) Where an application is made for an order under section 2 of this Act, it shall be the duty of the court, in deciding whether to exercise its powers under that section and, if so, in what manner, to have regard to all the circumstances of the case, first consideration being given to the welfare while a minor of any child of the family who has not attained the age of eighteen.

(2) As regards the exercise of its powers under subsection (1)(a) or (b) of section 2, the court shall in particular have regard to the following matters—
(a) the income, earning capacity, property and other financial resources which each of the parties to the marriage has or is likely to have in the foreseeable future, including in the case of earning capacity any increase in that capacity which it would in the opinion of the court be reasonable to expect a party to the marriage to take steps to acquire;
(b) the financial needs, obligations and responsibilities which each of the parties to the marriage has or is likely to have in the foreseeable future;
(c) the standard of living enjoyed by the parties to the marriage before the occurrence of the conduct which is alleged as the ground of the application;
(d) the age of each party to the marriage and the duration of the marriage;
(e) any physical or mental disability of either of the parties to the marriage;
(f) the contributions which each of the parties has made or is likely in the foreseeable future to make to the welfare of the family, including any contribution by looking after the home or caring for the family;
(g) the conduct of each of the parties, if that conduct is such that it would in the opinion of the court be inequitable to disregard it.

(3) As regards the exercise of its powers under subsection (1)(c) or (d) of section 2, the court shall in particular have regard to the following matters—
(a) the financial needs of the child;
(b) the income, earning capacity (if any), property and other financial resources of the child;
(c) any physical or mental disability of the child;
(d) the standard of living enjoyed by the family before the occurrence of the conduct which is alleged as the ground of the application;
(e) the manner in which the child was being and in which the parties to the marriage expected him to be educated or trained;
(f) the matters mentioned in relation to the parties to the marriage in paragraphs (a) and (b) of subsection (2) above.

(4) As regards the exercise of its powers under section 2 in favour of a child of the family who is not the child of the respondent, the court shall also have regard—
(a) to whether the respondent has assumed any responsibility for the child's maintenance and, if he did, to the extent to which, and the basis on which, he assumed that responsibility and to the length of time during which he discharged that responsibility;
(b) to whether in assuming and discharging that responsibility the respondent did so knowing that the child was not his own child;
(c) to the liability of any other person to maintain the child.

6. Orders for payments which have been agreed by the parties

(1) Either party to a marriage may apply to a magistrates' court for an order under this section on the ground that either the party making the application or the other party to the marriage has agreed to make such financial provision as may be specified in the application and, subject to subsection (3) below, the court on such an application may, if—
(a) it is satisfied that the applicant or the respondent, as the case may be, has agreed to make that provision, and
(b) it has no reason to think that it would be contrary to the interests of justice to exercise its powers hereunder,

order that the applicant or the respondent, as the case may be, shall make the financial provision specified in the application.

(2) In this section 'financial provision' means the provision mentioned in any one or more of the following paragraphs, that is to say—
(a) the making of periodical payments by one party to the other,
(b) the payment of a lump sum by one party to the other,
(c) the making of periodical payments by one party to a child of the family or to the other party for the benefit of such a child,
(d) the payment by one party of a lump sum to a child of the family or to the other party for the benefit of such a child,

and any reference in this section to the financial provision specified in an application made under subsection (1) above or specified by the court under subsection (5) below is a reference to the type of provision specified in the application or by the court, as the case may be, to the amount so specified as the amount of any payment to be made thereunder and, in the case of periodical payments, to the term so specified as the term for which the payments are to be made.

(3) Where the financial provision specified in an application under subsection (1) above includes or consists of provision in respect of a child of the family, the court shall not make an order under that subsection unless it considers that the provision which the applicant or the respondent, as the case may be, has agreed to make in respect of that child provides for, or makes a proper contribution towards, the financial needs of the child.

(4) A party to a marriage who has applied for an order under section 2 of this Act shall not be precluded at any time before the determination of that application from applying for an order under this section; but if an order is made under this section on the application of either party and either of them has also made an application for an order under section 2 of this Act, the application made for the order under section 2 shall be treated as if it had been withdrawn.

(5) Where on an application under subsection (1) above the court decides—
(a) that it would be contrary to the interests of justice to make an order for the making of the financial provision specified in the application, or
(b) that any financial provision which the applicant or the respondent, as the case may be, has agreed to make in respect of a child of the family does not provide for, or make a proper contribution towards, the financial needs of that child,

but is of the opinion—
(i) that it would not be contrary to the interests of justice to make an order for the making of some other financial provision specified by the court, and

(ii) that, in so far as that other financial provision contains any provision for a child of the family, it provides for, or makes a proper contribution towards, the financial needs of that child,

then if both the parties agree, the court may order that the applicant or the respondent, as the case may be, shall make that other financial provision.

(6) Subject to subsection (8) below, the provisions of section 4 of this Act shall apply in relation to an order under this section which requires periodical payments to be made to a party to a marriage for his own benefit as they apply in relation to an order under section 2(1)(a) of this Act.

(7) Subject to subsection (8) below, the provisions of section 5 of this Act shall apply in relation to an order under this section for the making of financial provision in respect of a child of the family as they apply in relation to an order under section 2(1)(c) or (d) of this Act.

(8) Where the court makes an order under this section which contains provision for the making of periodical payments and, by virtue of subsection (4) above, an application for an order under section 2 of this Act is treated as if it had been withdrawn, then the term which may be specified as the term for which the payments are to be made may begin with the date of the making of the application for the order under section 2 or any later date.

(9) Where the respondent is not present or respresented by counsel or solicitor at the hearing of an application for an order under subsection (1) above, the court shall not make an order under this section unless there is produced to the court such evidence as may be prescribed by rules of—

(a) the consent of the respondent to the making of the order,

(b) the financial resources of the respondent, and

(c) in a case where the financial provision specified in the application includes or consists of provision in respect of a child of the family to be made by the applicant to the respondent for the benefit of the child or to the child, the financial resources of the child.

7. Powers of court where parties are living apart by agreement

(1) Where the parties to a marriage have been living apart for a continuous period exceeding three months, neither party having deserted the other, and one of the parties has been making periodical payments for the benefit of the other party or of a child of the family, that other party may apply to a magistrates' court for an order under this section, and any application made under this subsection shall specify the aggregate amount of the payments so made during the period of three months immediately preceding the date of the making of the application.

(2) Where on an application for an order under this section the court is satisfied that the respondent has made the payments specified in the application, the court may, subject to the provisions of this Part of this Act, make one or both of the following orders, that is to say—

(a) an order that the respondent shall make to the applicant such periodical payments, and for such term, as may be specified in the order;

(b) an order that the respondent shall make to the applicant for the benefit of a child of the family to whom the application relates, or to such a child, such periodical payments, and for such term, as may be so specified.

(3) The court in the exercise of its powers under this section—

(a) shall not require the respondent to make payments which exceed in aggregate during any period of three months the aggregate amount paid by him for the benefit of the applicant or a child of the family during the period of three months immediately preceding the date of the making of the application;

(b) shall not require the respondent to make payments to or for the benefit of any person which exceed in amount the payments which the court considers that it would have required the respondent to make to or for the benefit of that person on an application under section 1 of this Act;

(c) shall not require payments to be made to or for the benefit of a child of the family who is not a child of the respondent unless the court considers that it would have made an order in favour of that child on an application under section 1 of this Act.

(4) Where on an application under this section the court considers that the orders which it has the power to make under this section—

(a) would not provide reasonable maintenance for the applicant, or

(b) if the application relates to a child of the family, would not provide, or make a proper contribution towards reasonable maintenance for that child,

the court shall refuse to make an order under this section, but the court may treat the application as if it were an application for an order under section 2 of this Act.

(5) The provisions of section 3 of this Act shall apply in relation to an application for an order under this section as they apply in relation to an application for an order under section 2 of this Act subject to the modification that for the reference in subsection 2(c) of the said section 3 to the occurrence of the conduct which is alleged as the ground of the application there shall be substituted a reference to the living apart of the parties to the marriage.

(6) The provisions of section 4 of this Act shall apply in relation to an order under this section which requires periodical payments to be made to the applicant for his own benefit as they apply in relation to an order made under section 2(1)(a) of this Act.

(7) The provisions of section 5 of this Act shall apply in relation to an order under this section for the making of periodical payments in respect of a child of the family as they apply in relation to an order under section 2(1)(c) of this Act.

Powers of court as to the custody etc. of children

8. Restrictions on making of orders under this Act: welfare of children

Where an application is made by a party to a marriage for an order under section 2, 6 or 7 of this Act, then, if there is a child of the family who is under the age of eighteen, the court shall not dismiss or make a final order on the application until it has decided whether to exercise any of its powers under the Children Act 1989 with respect to the child.

Interim orders

19. Interim orders

(1) Where an application is made for an order under section 2, 6 or 7 of this Act—

(a) the family court at any time before making a final order on, or dismissing, the application,

(b), (c) ... ,

shall, subject to the provisions of this Part of this Act, have the

(i) power to make an order (in this Part of this Act referred to as an 'interim maintenance order') which requires the respondent to make to the applicant or to any child of the family who is under the age of eighteen, or to the applicant for the benefit of such a child, such periodical payments as the court thinks reasonable.

(ii) ...

(2) ...

(3) An interim maintenance order may provide for payments to be made from such date as the court may specify, except that, subject to section 5(5) and (6) of this Act, the date shall not be earlier than the date of the making of the application for an order under section 2, 6 or 7 of this Act.

(3A) Where an application is made for an order under section 6 of this Act by the party to the marriage who has agreed to make the financial provision specified in the application—

(a) subsection (1) shall apply as if the reference in paragraph (i) to the respondent were a reference to the applicant and the references to the applicant were references to the respondent; and

(b) subsection (3) shall apply accordingly.

(5) Subject to subsection (6) below, an interim order made on an application for an order under section 2, 6 or 7 of this Act shall cease to have effect on whichever of the following dates occurs first, that is to say—

(a) the date, if any, specified for the purpose of the interim order;

(b) the date of the expiration of the period of three months beginning with the date of the making of the interim order;

(c) the date on which a magistrates' court either makes a final order on or dismisses the application.

(6) Where an interim order made under subsection (1) above would, but for this subsection, cease to have effect by virtue of subsection (5)(a) or (b) above, the magistrates' court which made the order or, in the case of an interim order made by the High Court, the magistrates' court by which the application for an order under section 2, 6 or 7 of this Act is to be reheard, shall have power by order to provide that the interim order shall continue in force for a further period, and any order continued in force under this subsection shall cease to have effect on whichever of the following dates occurs first, that is to say—

(a) the date, if any, specified for the purpose in the order made under this subsection;

(b) the date of the expiration of the period of three months beginning with the date of the making of the order under this subsection or, if more than one order has been made under this subsection with respect to the application, beginning with the date of the making of the first of those orders;

(c) the date on which the court either makes a final order on, or dismisses, the application.

(7) Not more than one interim maintenance order may be made with respect to any application for an order under section 2, 6 or 7 of this Act, but without prejudice to the powers of a court under this section on any further such application.

(8) No appeal shall lie from the making of or refusal to make, the variation of or refusal to vary, or the revocation of or refusal to revoke, an interim maintenance order.

(9) ...

Variation, revocation and cessation of orders etc.

20. Variation, revival and revocation of orders for periodical payments

(1) Where the family court has made an order under section 2(1)(a) or (c) of this Act for the making of periodical payments, the court shall have power, on an application made under this section, to vary or revoke that order and also to make an order under section 2(1)(b) or (d) of this Act.

(2) Where the family court has made an order under section 6 of this Act for the making of periodical payments by a party to a marriage the court shall have power, on an application made under this section, to vary or revoke that order and also to make an order for the payment of a lump sum by that party either—

(a) to the other party to the marriage, or

(b) to a child of the family or to that other party for the benefit of that child.

(3) Where the family court has made an order under section 7 of this Act for the making of periodical payments, the court shall have power, on an application made under this section, to vary or revoke that order.

(5) Where the family court has made an interim maintenance order under section 19 of this Act, the court, on an application made under this section, shall have power to vary or revoke that order, except that the court shall not by virtue of this subsection extend the period for which the order is in force.

(6) The power of the court under this section to vary an order for the making of periodical payments shall include power to suspend any provision thereof temporarily and to revive any provision so suspended.

(7) Where the court has power by virtue of this section to make an order for the payment of a lump sum, the amount of the lump sum shall not exceed the maximum amount that may at that time be required to be paid under section 2(3) of this Act, but the court may make an order for the payment of a lump sum not exceeding that amount notwithstanding that the person required to pay the lump sum was required to pay a lump sum by a previous order under this Part of this Act.

(8) Where the court has power by virtue of subsection (2) above to make an order for the payment of a lump sum and the respondent or the applicant, as the case may be, has agreed to pay a lump sum of an amount exceeding the maximum amount that may at that time be required to be paid under section 2(3) of this Act, the court may, notwithstanding anything in subsection (7) above, make an order for the payment of a lump sum of that amount.

(9) An order by virtue of this section which varies an order for the making of periodical payments may provide that the payments as so varied shall be made from such date as the court may specify, except that, subject to subsections (9A) and (9B) below, the date shall not be earlier than the date of the making of the application under this section.

(9A) Where—

(a) there is in force an order ('the order')—

(i) under section 2(1)(c) of this Act,

(ii) under section 6(1) of this Act making provision of a kind mentioned in paragraph (c) of section 6(2) of this Act (regardless of whether it makes provision of any other kind mentioned in that paragraph),

(iii) under section 7(2)(b) of this Act, or

(iv) which is an interim maintenance order under which the payments are to be made to a child or to the applicant for the benefit of a child;

(b) the order requires payments specified in it to be made to or for the benefit of more than one child without apportioning those payments between them;

(c) a maintenance calculation ('the calculation') is made with respect to one or more, but not all, of the children with respect to whom those payments are to be made; and

(d) an application is made, before the end of the period of 6 months beginning with the date on which the calculation was made, for the variation or revocation of the order,

the court may, in exercise of its powers under this section to vary or revoke the order, direct that the variation or revocation shall take effect from the date on which the calculation took effect or any later date.

(9B) Where—
(a) an order ('the child order') of a kind prescribed for the purposes of section 10(1) of the Child Support Act 1991 is affected by a maintenance calculation;
(b) on the date on which the child order became so affected there was in force an order ('the spousal order')—
(i) under section 2(1)(a) of this Act,
(ii) under section 6(1) of this Act making provision of a kind mentioned in section 6(2)(a) of this Act (regardless of whether it makes provision of any other kind mentioned in that paragraph),
(iii) under section 7(2)(a) of this Act, or
(iv) which is an interim maintenance order under which the payments are to be made to the applicant (otherwise than for the benefit of a child); and
(c) an application is made, before the end of the period of 6 months beginning with the date on which the maintenance calculation was made, for the spousal order to be varied or revoked,

the court may, in exercise of its powers under this section to vary or revoke the spousal order, direct that the variation or revocation shall take effect from the date on which the child order became so affected or any later date.

(9C) For the purposes of subsection (9B) above, an order is affected if it ceases to have effect or is modified by or under section 10 of the Child Support Act 1991.

...

(11) In exercising the powers conferred by this section, the court shall, so far as it appears to the court just to do so, give effect to any agreement which has been reached between the parties in relation to the application and, if there is no such agreement or if the court decides not to give effect to the agreement, the court shall have regard to all the circumstances of the case, first consideration being given to the welfare while a minor of any child of the family who has not attained the age of eighteen, and the circumstances of the case shall include any change in any of the matters to which the court was required to have regard when making the order to which the application relates or, in the case of an application for the variation or revocation of an order made under section 6 of this Act or on an appeal under section 29 of this Act, to which the court would have been required to have regard if that order had been made under section 2 of this Act.

(12) An application under this section may be made—
(a) where it is for the variation or revocation of an order under section 2, 6, 7 or 19 of this Act for periodical payments, by either party to the marriage in question; and
(b) where it is for the variation of an order under section 2(1)(c), 6 or 7 of this Act for periodical payments to or in respect of a child, also by the child himself, if he has attained the age of sixteen.

...

20ZA. Variation of orders for periodical payments: further provisions

(1) Subject to subsections (7) and (8) below, the power of the court under section 20 of this Act to vary an order for the making of periodical payments shall include power, if the court is satisfied that payment has not been made in accordance with the order, to exercise one of its powers under subsection (6) of section 1 of the Maintenance Enforcement Act 1991.

(2) ...

(3) Subject to subsection (5) below, where an application is made under subsection (2) above, the clerk, after giving written notice (by post or otherwise) of the application to the respondent and allowing the respondent, within the period of 14 days beginning with the date of the giving of that notice, an opportunity to make written representations, may vary the order to provide that payments under the order shall be made to the justices' chief executive for the court.

(4) The clerk may proceed with an application under subsection (2) above notwithstanding that the respondent has not received written notice of the application.

(5) ...

(6) Subsection (6) of section 1 of the Maintenance Enforcement Act 1991 (power of court to order that account be opened) shall apply for the purposes of subsection (1) above as it applies for the purposes of that section.

(7) Before varying the order by exercising one of its powers under subsection (6) of section 1 of the Maintenance Enforcement Act 1991, the court shall have regard to any representations made by the parties to the application.

(8), (9) ...

(10) None of the powers of the court conferred by this section shall be exercisable in relation to an order under this Part of this Act for the making of periodical payments unless, at the time when the order was made, the person required to make the payments was ordinarily resident in England and Wales.

20A. Revival of orders for periodical payments

(1) Where an order made by a magistrates' court under this Part of this Act for the making of periodical payments to or in respect of a child (other than an interim maintenance order) ceases to have effect—

(a) on the date on which the child attains the age of sixteen, or

(b) at any time after that date but before or on the date on which he attains the age of eighteen,

the child may apply to the family court.

(2) If on such an application it appears to the court that—

(a) the child is, will be or (if an order were made under this subsection) would be receiving instruction at an educational establishment or undergoing training for a trade, profession or vocation, whether or not while in gainful employment, or

(b) there are special circumstances which justify the making of an order under this subsection,

the court shall have power by order to revive the order from such date as the court may specify, not being earlier than the date of the making of the application.

(3) Any order revived under this section may be varied or revoked under section 20 in the same way as it could have been varied or revoked had it continued in being.

25. Effect on certain orders of parties living together

(1) Where—

(a) periodical payments are required to be made to one of the parties to a marriage (whether for his own benefit or for the benefit of a child of the family) by an order made under section 2 or 6 of this Act or by an interim maintenance order made under section 19 of this Act (otherwise than on an application under section 7 of this Act),

the order shall be enforceable notwithstanding that the parties to the marriage are living with each other at the date of the making of the order or that, although they are not living with each other at that date, they subsequently resume living with each other; but the order shall cease to have effect if after that date the parties continue to live with each other, or resume living with each other, for a continuous period exceeding six months.

(2) Where any of the following orders is made under this Part of this Act, that is to say—

(a) an order under section 2 or 6 of this Act which requires periodical payments to be made to a child of the family, or

(b) an interim maintenance order under section 19 of this Act (otherwise than on an application under section 7 of this Act) which requires periodical payments to be made to a child of the family,

then, unless the court otherwise directs, the order shall continue to have effect and be enforceable notwithstanding that the parties to the marriage in question are living with each other at the date of the making of the order or that, although they are not living with each other at that date, they subsequently resume living with each other.

(3) Any order made under section 7 of this Act, and any interim maintenance order made on an application for an order under that section, shall cease to have effect if the parties to the marriage resume living with each other.

(4) Where an order made under this Part of this Act ceases to have effect by virtue of subsection (1) or (3) above or by virtue of a direction given under subsection (2) above, a magistrates' court may, on an application made by either party to the marriage, make an order declaring that the first mentioned order ceased to have effect from such date as the court may specify.

Reconciliation

26. Reconciliation

(1) Where an application is made for an order under section 2 of this Act the court, before deciding whether to exercise its powers under that section, shall consider whether there is any possibility of reconciliation between the parties to the marriage in question: and if at any stage of the proceedings on that application it appears to the court that there is a reasonable possibility of such a reconciliation, the court may adjourn the proceedings for such period as it thinks fit to enable attempts to be made to effect a reconciliation.

(2) Where the court adjourns any proceedings under subsection (1) above, it may request an officer of the Service (within the meaning of the Criminal Justice and Court Services Act 2000) or any other person to attempt to effect a reconciliation between the parties to the marriage, and where any such request is made, that officer or other person shall report in writing to the court whether the attempt has been successful or not, but shall not include in that report any other information.

35. Orders for repayment in certain cases of sums paid after cessation of order by reason of remarriage or formation of a civil partnership

(1) Where—

(a) an order made under section 2(1)(a), 6 or 7 of this Act has, by virtue of section 4(2) of this Act, ceased to have effect by reason of the remarriage of, or formation of a civil partnership by, the party in whose favour it was made, and

(b) the person liable to make payments under the order made payments in accordance with it in respect of a period after the date of that remarriage in the mistaken belief that the order was still subsisting,

no proceedings in respect of a cause of action arising out of the circumstances mentioned in paragraphs (a) and (b) above shall be maintainable by the person so liable or his personal representatives against the person so entitled or his personal representatives, but on an application made under this section the court may exercise the powers conferred on it by subsection (2) below.

(2) The court may order the respondent to an application made under this section to pay to the applicant a sum equal to the amount of the payments made in respect of the period mentioned in subsection (1)(b) above or, if it appears to the court that it would be unjust to make that order, it may either order the respondent to pay to the applicant such lesser sum as it thinks fit or dismiss the application.

. . .

PART V
SUPPLEMENTARY PROVISIONS

88. Interpretation

(1) In this Act—

'child,' in relation to one or both of the parties to a marriage, includes a child whose father and mother were not married to each other at the time of his birth;

'child of the family,' in relation to the parties to a marriage, means—

(a) a child of both of those parties; and

(b) any other child, not being a child who is placed with those parties as foster parents by a local authority or voluntary organisation, who has been treated by both of those parties as a child of their family;

'local authority' means the council of a county (other than a metropolitan county), of a metropolitan district or of a London borough, or the Common Council of the City of London;

'maintenance calculation' has the same meaning as it has in the Child Support Act 1991 by virtue of section 54 of that Act as read with any regulations in force under that section;

'rules' means rules made under section 144 of the Magistrates' Courts Act 1980.

(2) References in this Act to the parties to a marriage living with each other shall be construed as references to their living with each other in the same house-hold.

(3) For the avoidance of doubt it is hereby declared that references in this Act to remarriage include references to a marriage which is by law void or voidable.

. . .

MAGISTRATES' COURTS ACT 1980
(1980 c. 43)

PART II

Orders for periodical payment

59. Orders for periodical payment: means of payment

(1) In any case where a magistrates' court orders money to be paid periodically by one person (in this section referred to as 'the debtor') to another (in this section referred to as 'the creditor'), the court shall at the same time exercise one of its powers under paragraphs (a) and (b) of subsection (3) below.

(2) ...

(3) The powers of the court are—

(a) the power to order that payments under the order be made directly by the debtor to the creditor;

(b) the power to order that payments under the order be made to a justices' chief executive;

(c) the power to order that payments under the order be made by the debtor to the creditor by such method of payment falling within subsection (6) below as may be specified;

(cc) ...

(d) the power to make an attachment of earnings order under the Attachment of Earnings Act 1971 to secure payments under the order.

(3A) ...

(4) In any case where—

(a) the court proposes to exercise its power under paragraph (c) of subsection (3) above, and

(b) having given the debtor an opportunity of opening an account from which payments under the order may be made in accordance with the method of payment proposed to be ordered under that paragraph, the court is satisfied that the debtor has failed, without reasonable excuse, to open such an account,

the court in exercising its power under that paragraph may order that the debtor open such an account.

(5) ...

(6) The methods of payment referred to in subsection (3)(c) above are the following, that is to say—

(a) payment by standing order; or

(b) payment by any other method which requires one person to give his authority for payments of a specific amount to be made from an account of his to an account of another's on specific dates during the period for which the authority is in force and without the need for any further authority from him.

(7)–(12) ...

SENIOR COURTS ACT 1981
(1981 c. 54)

PART II
JURISDICTION: THE HIGH COURT

Powers

41. Wards of court

(1) Subject to the provisions of this section, no minor shall be made a ward of court except by virtue of an order to that effect made by the High Court.

(2) Where an application is made for such an order in respect of a minor, the minor shall become a ward of court on the making of the application, but shall cease to be a ward of court at the end of such period as may be prescribed unless within that period an order has been made in accordance with the application.

(2A) Subsection (2) does not apply with respect to a child who is the subject of a care order (as defined by section 105 of the Children Act 1989).

(3) The High Court may, either upon an application in that behalf or without such an application, order that any minor who is for the time being a ward of court shall cease to be a ward of court.

PART III
PRACTICE AND PROCEDURE

THE HIGH COURT

Distribution of business

61. Distribution of business among Divisions

(1) Subject to any provision made by or under this or any other Act (and in particular to any rules of court made in pursuance of subsection (2) and any order under subsection (3)), business in the High Court of any description mentioned in Schedule 1, as for the time being in force, shall be distributed among the Divisions in accordance with that Schedule.

...

Section 61(1), (3)

SCHEDULE 1
DISTRIBUTION OF BUSINESS IN HIGH COURT

Family Division

3. To the Family Division are assigned—
   (a) all matrimonial causes and matters (whether at first instance or on appeal);
   (b) all causes and matters (whether at first instance or on appeal) relating to—
      (i) legitimacy;
      (ii) the exercise of the inherent jurisdiction of the High Court with respect to minors, the maintenance of minors and any proceedings under the Children Act 1989, except proceedings solely for the appointment of a guardian of a minor's estate;
      (iii) adoption;
      (iv) non-contentious or common form probate business;
   (c) applications for consent to the marriage of a minor or for a declaration under section 27B(5) of the Marriage Act 1949;
   (d) proceedings on appeal under section 13 of the Administration of Justice Act 1960 from an order or decision made under section 63(3) of the Magistrates' Courts Act 1980 to enforce an order of a magistrates' court made in matrimonial proceedings or proceedings under Part IV of the Family Law Act 1996 or with respect to the guardianship of a minor.
   (e) applications under Part III of the Family Law Act 1986.
   (ea) proceedings under section 79 of the Childcare Act 2006.
   (f) all proceedings under:—
      (i) Part IV or 4A of the Family Law Act 1996;
      (ii) the Child Abduction and Custody Act 1985
      (iii) the Family Law Act 1986;
      (iv) section 54 of the Human Fertilisation and Embryology Act 2008;
   (fa) all proceedings relating to a debit or credit under section 29(1) or 49(1) of the Welfare Reform and Pensions Act 1999;
   (g) all proceedings for the purpose of enforcing an order made in any proceedings of a type described in this paragraph;
   (h) all proceedings under the Child Support Act 1991;
   (i) all proceedings under sections 6 and 8 of the Gender Recognition Act 2004;
   (j) all civil partnership causes and matters (whether at first instance or on appeal);
   (k) applications for consent to the formation of a civil partnership by a minor or for a declaration under paragraph 7 of Schedule 1 of the Civil Partnership Act 2004;
   (l) applications under section 58 of that Act (declarations relating to civil partnerships).

MARRIAGE ACT 1983
(1983 c. 32)

Marriages in England and Wales

1. Marriages of house-bound and detained persons in England and Wales

(1) Subject to the provisions of this Act and the Marriage Act 1949, the marriage of a person who is house-bound or is a detained person may be solemnized in England and Wales, on the authority of certificates of a superintendent registrar issued under Part III of the Marriage Act 1949, at the place where that person usually resides.

(2) For the purposes of this section a person is house-bound if—
   (a) each notice of his or her marriage given in accordance with section 27 of the Marriage Act 1949 is accompanied by a statement, made in a form prescribed under that Act by a registered medical practitioner not more than fourteen days before that notice is given, that, in his opinion—
      (i) by reason of illness or disability, he or she ought not to move or be moved from his or her home or the other place where he or she is at that time, and
      (ii) it is likely that it will be the case for at least the three months following the date on which the statement is made that by reason of the illness or disability he or she ought not to move or be moved from that place; and
   (b) he or she is not a detained person.

(3) For the purposes of this section, a person is a detained person if he or she is for the time being detained—
   (a) otherwise than by virtue of section 2, 4, 5, 35, 36 or 136 of the Mental Health Act 1983 (short term detentions), as a patient in a hospital; or
   (b) in a prison or other place to which the Prison Act 1952 applies.

...

CHILD ABDUCTION ACT 1984
(1984 c. 37)

PART I
OFFENCES UNDER LAW OF ENGLAND AND WALES

1. Offence of abduction of child by parent, etc.

(1) Subject to subsections (5) and (8) below, a person connected with a child under the age of sixteen commits an offence if he takes or sends the child out of the United Kingdom without the appropriate consent.

(2) A person is connected with a child for the purposes of this section if—
- (a) he is a parent of the child; or
- (b) in the case of a child whose parents were not married to each other at the time of his birth, there are reasonable grounds for believing that he is the father of the child; or
- (c) he is a guardian of the child; or
- (ca) he is a special guardian of the child; or
- (d) he is a person named in a child arrangements order as a person with whom the child is to live; or
- (e) he has custody of the child.

(3) In this section 'the appropriate consent', in relation to a child, means—
- (a) the consent of each of the following—
  - (i) the child's mother;
  - (ii) the child's father, if he has parental responsibility for him;
  - (iii) any guardian of the child;
  - (iiia) any special guardian of the child;
  - (iv) any person named in a child arrangements order as a person with whom the child is to live;
  - (v) any person who has custody of the child; or
- (b) the leave of the court granted under or by virtue of any provision of Part II of the Children Act 1989; or
- (c) if any person has custody of the child, the leave of the court which awarded custody to him.

(4) A person does not commit an offence under this section by taking or sending a child out of the United Kingdom without obtaining the appropriate consent if—
- (a) he is a person named in a child arrangements order as a person with whom the child is to live and he takes or sends him out of the United Kingdom for a period of less than one month; or
- (b) he is a special guardian of the child and he takes or sends the child out of the United Kingdom for a period of less than three months.

(4A) Subsection (4) above does not apply if the person taking or sending the child out of the United Kingdom does so in breach of an order under Part II of the Children Act 1989.

(5) A person does not commit an offence under this section by doing anything without the consent of another person whose consent is required under the foregoing provisions if—
- (a) he does it in the belief that the other person—
  - (i) has consented; or
  - (ii) would consent if he was aware of all the relevant circumstances; or
- (b) he has taken all reasonable steps to communicate with the other person but has been unable to communicate with him; or
- (c) the other person has unreasonably refused to consent.

(5A) Subsection (5)(c) above does not apply if—
- (a) the person who refused to consent is a person—
  - (i) named in a child arrangements order as a person with whom the child is to live;
  - (ia) who is a special guardian of the child; or
  - (ii) who has custody of the child; or
- (b) the person taking or sending the child out of the United Kingdom is, by so acting, in breach of an order made by a court in the United Kingdom.

(6) Where, in proceedings for an offence under this section, there is sufficient evidence to raise an issue as to the application of subsection (5) above, it shall be for the prosecution to prove that that subsection does not apply.

(7) For the purposes of this section—
- (a) 'guardian of a child', 'special guardian', 'child arrangements order' and 'parental responsibility' have the same meaning as in the Children Act 1989; and

(b) a person shall be treated as having custody of a child if there is in force an order of a court in the United Kingdom awarding him (whether solely or jointly with another person) custody, legal custody or care and control of the child.

(8) This section shall have effect subject to the provisions of the Schedule to this Act in relation to a child who is in the care of a local authority, detained in a place of safety, remanded to a local authority accommodation or the subject of proceedings or an order relating to adoption.

2. Offence of abduction of child by other persons

(1) Subject to subsection (3) below, a person, other than one mentioned in subsection (2) below commits an offence if, without lawful authority or reasonable excuse, he takes or detains a child under the age of sixteen—

(a) so as to remove him from the lawful control of any person having lawful control of the child; or

(b) so as to keep him out of the lawful control of any person entitled to lawful control of the child.

(2) The persons are—

(a) where the father and mother of the child in question were married to each other at the time of his birth, the child's father and mother;

(b) where the father and mother of the child in question were not married to each other at the time of his birth, the child's mother; and

(c) any other person mentioned in section 1(2)(c) to (e) above.

(3) In proceedings against any person for an offence under this section, it shall be a defence for that person to prove—

(a) where the father and mother of the child in question were not married to each other at the time of his birth—

(i) that he is the child's father; or

(ii) that, at the time of the alleged offence, he believed, on reasonable grounds, that he was the child's father; or

(b) that, at the time of the alleged offence, he believed that the child had attained the age of sixteen.

3. Construction of references to taking, sending and detaining

For the purposes of this Part of this Act—

(a) a person shall be regarded as taking a child if he causes or induces the child to accompany him or any other person or causes the child to be taken;

(b) a person shall be regarded as sending a child if he causes the child to be sent;

(c) a person shall be regarded as detaining a child if he causes the child to be detained or induces the child to remain with him or any other person; and

(d) references to a child's parents and to a child whose parents were (or were not) married to each other at the time of his birth shall be construed in accordance with section 1 of the Family Law Reform Act 1987 (which extends their meaning).

MATRIMONIAL AND FAMILY PROCEEDINGS ACT 1984
(1984 c. 42)

PART 4A

THE FAMILY COURT

31A. Establishment of the family court

(1) There is to be a court in England and Wales, called the family court, for the purpose of exercising the jurisdiction and powers conferred on it—

(a) by or under this or any other Act, or

(b) by or under any Act, or Measure, of the National Assembly for Wales.

(2) The family court is to be a court of record and have a seal

31B. Sittings

(1) Sittings of the family court may be held, and any other business of the family court may be conducted, at any place in England and Wales.

(2) Sittings of the family court at any place may be continuous or intermittent or occasional.

(3) Sittings of the family court may be held simultaneously to take any number of different cases in the same place or different places, and the court may adjourn cases from place to place at any time.

(4) The places at which the family court sits, and the days and times at which it sits in any place, are to be determined in accordance with directions given by the Lord Chancellor after consulting the Lord Chief Justice.

(5) The Lord Chief Justice may nominate a judicial office holder (as defined in section 109(4) of the Constitutional Reform Act 2005) to exercise functions of the Lord Chief Justice under this section.

31C. Judges

(1) A person is a judge of the family court if the person—
 (a) is the Lord Chief Justice,
 (b) is the Master of the Rolls,
 (c) is the President of the Queen's Bench Division,
 (d) is the President of the Family Division,
 (e) is the Chancellor of the High Court,
 (f) is an ordinary judge of the Court of Appeal (including the vice-president, if any, of either division of that court),
 (g) is the Senior President of Tribunals,
 (h) is a puisne judge of the High Court,
 (i) is a deputy judge of the High Court,
 (j) is a Circuit judge,
 (k) is the Judge Advocate General,
 (l) is a Recorder,
 (m) holds an office listed—
  (i) in the first column of the table in section 89(3C) of the Senior Courts Act 1981 (senior High Court Masters etc), or
  (ii) in column 1 of Part 2 of Schedule 2 to that Act (High Court Masters etc),
 (n) is a district judge (which, by virtue of section 8(1C) of the County Courts Act 1984, here includes a deputy district judge appointed under section 8 of that Act),
 (o) is a deputy district judge appointed under section 102 of the Senior Courts Act 1981,
 (p) is a Chamber President, or a Deputy Chamber President, of a chamber of the Upper Tribunal or of a chamber of the First-tier Tribunal,
 (q) is a judge of the Upper Tribunal by virtue of appointment under paragraph 1(1) of Schedule 3 to the Tribunals, Courts and Enforcement Act 2007, (r) is a transferred-in judge of the Upper Tribunal (see section 31(2) of that Act),
 (s) is a deputy judge of the Upper Tribunal (whether under paragraph 7 of Schedule 3 to, or section 31(2) of, that Act),
 (t) is a judge of the First-tier Tribunal by virtue of appointment under paragraph 1(1) of Schedule 2 to that Act,
 (u) is a transferred-in judge of the First-tier Tribunal (see section 31(2) of that Act),
 (v) is a member of a panel of Employment Judges established for England and Wales or for Scotland,
 (w) is a person appointed under section 30(1)(a) or (b) of the Courts-Martial (Appeals) Act 1951 (assistants to the Judge Advocate General),
 (x) is a District Judge (Magistrates' Courts), or
 (y) is a justice of the peace who is not a District Judge (Magistrates' Courts),

but see also section 9 of the Senior Courts Act 1981 (certain ex-judges may act as judges of the family court).

(2) A decision of the family court, if made by or by persons who include—
 (a) a judge within subsection (1)(a) to (i),
 (b) a person who has been a judge of the Court of Appeal, or
 (c) a person who has been a puisne judge of the High Court,

is (so far as relevant) to be followed by a judge within subsection (1)(j) to (y), and by a justices' clerk or an assistant to a justices' clerk, when carrying out functions of the family court unless doing so with a person within paragraphs (a) to (c) of this subsection.

(3) A fee-paid, or unsalaried, part-time judge of the family court may not act as a judge of the court in relation to any proceedings in the court in which the judge, or a partner or employer of the judge, or a body of which the judge is a member or officer, or a body of whose governing body the judge is a member, is directly or indirectly engaged as legal representative or agent for any party.

(4) In this section 'legal representative' means a person who, for the purposes of the Legal Services Act 2007, is an authorised person in relation to an activity which constitutes the exercise of a right of audience or the conduct of litigation (within the meaning of that Act).

31D. Composition of the court and distribution of its business

(1) Rules may be made in accordance with Part 1 of Schedule 1 to the Constitutional Reform Act 2005 (process for making designated rules) about—
(a) the composition of the family court, and
(b) the distribution of business of the family court among judges of the court.
(2) Rules about the composition of the family court may in particular—
(a) provide for the court to be constituted differently for the purpose of deciding different matters;
(b) make provision about who is to preside where the court is composed of more than one judge.
(3) Rules about the distribution of business of the family court may in particular—
(a) prohibit specified judges from conducting specified business;
(b) prohibit judges from conducting specified business unless authorised to do so by a specified judicial office holder;
(c) prohibit specified judges from conducting business, or specified business, unless authorised to do so by a specified judicial office holder;
(d) prohibit specified judges from exercising specified powers of the court.
(4) In subsection (3)—
'judge' does not include a judge within section 31C(1)(a) to (i); 'specified' means specified in, or of a description specified in, rules under this section.
(5) Rules under this section—
(a) may confer powers on the Lord Chief Justice or on a judicial office holder;
(b) may be made only after consultation with the Family Procedure Rule Committee.
(6) Family Procedure Rules are subject to rules under this section.
(7) The Lord Chief Justice's power under paragraph 2(2)(b) of Schedule 1 to the Constitutional Reform Act 2005 to nominate a judicial office holder to make rules under this section includes power to nominate different judicial office holders to make rules under this section for different purposes.
(8) Paragraph 5 of that Schedule (duty to make rules to achieve purpose specified by Lord Chancellor) does not apply in relation to rules under this section.
(9) In this section 'judicial office holder' has the meaning given by section 109(4) of that Act.
(10) No proceedings in the family court are to be with a jury.

31E. Family court has High Court and county court powers

(1) In any proceedings in the family court, the court may make any order—
(a) which could be made by the High Court if the proceedings were in the High Court, or
(b) which could be made by the county court if the proceedings were in the county court.
(2) In its application to a power of the High Court to issue a writ directed to an enforcement officer, subsection (1)(a) gives the family court power to issue a warrant, directed to an officer of the family court, containing provision corresponding to any that might be contained in the writ.
(3) Subsection (1) is subject to section 38(3) of the County Courts Act 1984.
(4) Subsection (1) is without prejudice to, and not limited by, any other powers of the family court.
(5) The Lord Chancellor may by regulations make provision, about or in connection with the effect or execution of warrants issued by the family court for enforcing any order or judgment enforceable by the court, that corresponds to any provision applying in relation to the effect or execution of writs issued by the High Court, or warrants issued by the county court, for the purpose of enforcing any order or judgment enforceable by that court.

31I. Powers of the High Court in respect of family court proceedings

(1) If the High Court, at any stage in proceedings in the family court, thinks it desirable that the proceedings, or any part of them, should be transferred to the High Court, it may order the transfer to the High Court of the proceedings or part.
(2) The power given by subsection (1) is without prejudice to section 29 of the Senior Courts Act 1981, and is to be exercised—
(a) in accordance with any directions given as to the distribution or transfer of proceedings, and
(b) subject to any provision made under section 1 of the Courts and Legal Services Act 1990 or made by or under any other enactment.

31O. Justices' clerks and assistants: functions

(1) The Lord Chancellor may by rules made with the agreement of the Lord Chief Justice and after consulting the Family Procedure Rule Committee—

(a) make provision enabling functions of the family court, or of a judge of the court, to be carried out by a justices' clerk;
(b) make provision enabling functions of a justices' clerk given under paragraph (a), or specified in subsection (2), to be carried out by an assistant to a justices' clerk.

(2) The functions of a justices' clerk include—
(a) giving advice to lay judges of the family court about matters of law (including procedure and practice) on questions arising in connection with the discharge by them of functions conferred on them or the court, including questions arising when the clerk is not personally attending on them, and
(b) power, at any time when the clerk thinks that the clerk should do so, to bring to the attention of lay judges of the family court any point of law (including procedure and practice) that is or may be involved in any question so arising;
and in this subsection 'lay judge of the family court' means a judge of the court who is within section 31C(1)(y).

(3) Subsection (2) does not limit—
(a) the functions of a justices' clerk, or
(b) the matters on which any judge of the family court may obtain assistance from a justices' clerk.

(4) A justices' clerk is not subject to the direction of the Lord Chancellor or any other person when carrying out—
(a) a function of the family court or of a judge of the court, or
(b) a function specified in subsection (2);
and an assistant to a justices' clerk when carrying out any such function is not subject to the direction of any person other than a justices' clerk.

(5) No action lies against a person in respect of anything done or not done in carrying out functions of the family court or of a judge of the court—
(a) in execution of the person's duties as a justices' clerk or an assistant to a justices' clerk, and
(b) in relation to matters within the person's jurisdiction.

(6) An action lies against a person in respect of anything done or not done in carrying out functions of the family court or of a judge of the court—
(a) in purported execution of the person's duties as a justices' clerk or an assistant to a justices' clerk, and
(b) in relation to a matter not within the person's jurisdiction,
if, but only if, it is proved that the person acted in bad faith.

(7) If an action is brought in circumstances in which subsection (5) or (6) provides that no action lies, the court in which the action is brought—
(a) may, on the application of the defendant, strike out the proceedings in the action, and
(b) if it does so, may if it thinks fit order the person bringing the action to pay costs.

(8) The Lord Chief Justice may nominate a judicial office holder (as defined in section 109(4) of the Constitutional Reform Act 2005) to exercise functions of the Lord Chief Justice under this section.

31P. Orders, regulations and rules under Part 4A

(1) Any power of the Lord Chancellor to make an order, regulations or rules under this Part—
(a) is exercisable by statutory instrument,
(b) includes power to make different provision for different purposes, and
(c) includes power to make supplementary, incidental, consequential, transitional, transitory or saving provision.

(2) The Lord Chancellor may not make the first rules under section 31O(1) unless a draft of the statutory instrument containing the rules (whether alone or with other provisions) has been laid before, and approved by a resolution of, each House of Parliament.

(3) A statutory instrument that—
(a) contains an order, regulations or rules made under this Part by the Lord Chancellor other than regulations under section 31M, and
(b) is not subject to any requirement that a draft of the instrument be laid before, and approved by a resolution of, each House of Parliament,
is subject to annulment in pursuance of a resolution of either House of Parliament.

PART V
FAMILY BUSINESS: DISTRIBUTION AND TRANSFER

Preliminary

32. What is family business

In this Part of this Act—

'family business' means business of any description which in the High Court is for the time being assigned to the Family Division and to no other Division by or under section 61 of (and Schedule 1 to) the Supreme Court Act 1981;

'family proceedings' means proceedings which are family business;

'matrimonial cause' means an action for divorce, nullity or marriage, or judicial separation;

...

Distribution and transfer of family business and proceedings

37. Directions as to distribution and transfer of family business and proceedings

The President of the Family Division may, with the concurrence of the Lord Chancellor, give directions with respect to the distribution and transfer between the High Court and county courts of family business and family proceedings.

38. Transfer of family proceedings from High Court

(1) At any stage of any family proceedings in the High Court, the High Court may, if the proceedings are transferable under this section, either of its own motion or on the application of any party to the proceedings, order the transfer of the whole or any part of the proceedings to the family court.

(2) The following family proceedings are transferable to the family court under this section, namely—

(a) all family proceedings commenced in the High Court which are within the jurisdiction of the family court;

(b) wardship proceedings, except applications for an order that a minor be made a ward of court, or any other proceedings which relate to the exercise of the inherent jurisdiction of the High Court with respect to minors.

39. Transfer of family proceedings to the High Court

(1) At any stage in any proceedings in the family court, the family court may, if the proceedings are transferable under this section, either of its own motion or on the application of any party to the proceedings, order the transfer of the whole or any part of the proceedings to the High Court.

(2) The following are transferable under this section namely –

(a) all family proceedings commenced in the family court which are within the jurisdiction of the High Court, and

(b) all family proceedings transferred from the High Court under section 38 above.

SURROGACY ARRANGEMENTS ACT 1985
(1985 c. 49)

1. Meaning of 'surrogate mother,' 'surrogacy arrangement' and other terms

(1) The following provisions shall have effect for the interpretation of this Act.

(2) 'Surrogate mother' means a woman who carries a child in pursuance of an arrangement—

(a) made before she began to carry the child, and

(b) made with a view to any child carried in pursuance of it being handed over to, and parental responsibility being met (so far as practicable) by, another person or other persons.

(3) An arrangement is a surrogacy arrangement if, were a woman to whom the arrangement relates to carry a child in pursuance of it, she would be a surrogate mother.

(4) In determining whether an arrangement is made with such a view as is mentioned in subsection (2) above regard may be had to the circumstances as a whole (and, in

particular, where there is a promise or understanding that any payment will or may be made to the woman or for her benefit in respect of the carrying of any child in pursuance of the arrangement, to that promise or understanding).

(5) An arrangement may be regarded as made with such a view though subject to conditions relating to the handing over of any child.

(6) A woman who carries a child is to be treated for the purposes of subsection (2)(a) above as beginning to carry it at the time of the insemination or of the placing in her of an embryo, of an egg in the process of fertilisation or of sperm and eggs, as the case may be, that results in her carrying the child.

(7) 'Body of persons' means a body of persons corporate or unincorporate.

(7A) 'Non-profit making body' means a body of persons whose activities are not carried on for profit.

(8) 'Payment' means payment in money or money's worth.

(9) This Act applies to arrangements whether or not they are lawful.

1A. Surrogacy arrangements unenforceable

No surrogacy arrangement is enforceable by or against any of the persons making it.

2. Negotiating surrogacy arrangements on a commercial basis, etc.

(1) No person shall on a commercial basis do any of the following acts in the United Kingdom, that is—

- (a) initiate . . . any negotiations with a view to the making of a surrogacy arrangement,
- (aa) take part in any negotiations with a view to the making of a surrogacy arrangement,
- (b) offer or agree to negotiate the making of a surrogacy arrangement, or
- (c) compile any information with a view to its use in making, or negotiating the making of, surrogacy arrangements;

and no person shall in the United Kingdom knowingly cause another to do any of those acts on a commercial basis.

(2) A person who contravenes subsection (1) above is guilty of an offence; but it is not a contravention of that subsection—

- (a) for a woman, with a view to becoming a surrogate mother herself, to do any act mentioned in that subsection or to cause such an act to be done, or
- (b) for any person, with a view to a surrogate mother carrying a child for him, to do such an act or to cause such an act to be done.

(2A) A non-profit making body does not contravene subsection (1) merely because—

- (a) the body does an act falling within subsection (1)(a) or (c) in respect of which any reasonable payment is at any time received by it or another, or
- (b) it does an act falling within subsection (1)(a) or (c) with a view to any reasonable payment being received by it or another in respect of facilitating the making of any surrogacy arrangement.

(2B) A person who knowingly causes a non-profit making body to do an act falling within subsection (1)(a) or (c) does not contravene subsection (1) merely because—

- (a) any reasonable payment is at any time received by the body or another in respect of the body doing the act, or
- (b) the body does the act with a view to any reasonable payment being received by it or another person in respect of the body facilitating the making of any surrogacy arrangement.

(2C) Any reference in subsection (2A) or (2B) to a reasonable payment in respect of the doing of an act by a non-profit making body is a reference to a payment not exceeding the body's costs reasonably attributable to the doing of the act.

(3) For the purposes of this section, a person does an act on a commercial basis (subject to subsection (4) below) if—

- (a) any payment is at any time received by himself or another in respect of it, or
- (b) he does it with a view to any payment being received by himself or another in respect of making, or negotiating or facilitating the making of, any surrogacy arrangement.

In this subsection 'payment' does not include payment to or for the benefit of a surrogate mother or prospective surrogate mother.

(4) In proceedings against a person for an offence under subsection (1) above, he is not to be treated as doing an act on a commercial basis by reason of any payment received by another in respect of that act if it is proved that—

- (a) in a case where the payment was received before he did the act, he did not do the act knowing or having reasonable cause to suspect that any payment had been received in respect of the act; and
- (b) in any other case, he did not do the act with a view to any payment being received in respect of it.

(5) Where—

- (a) a person acting on behalf of a body of persons takes any part in negotiating or facilitating the making of a surrogacy arrangement in the United Kingdom, and

(b) negotiating or facilitating the making of surrogacy arrangements is an activity of the body,

then, if the body at any time receives any payment made by or on behalf of—

(i) a woman who carries a child in pursuance of the arrangement,

(ii) the person or persons for whom she carries it, or

(iii) any person connected with the woman or with that person or those persons,

the body is guilty of an offence.

For the purposes of this subsection, a payment received by a person connected with a body is to be treated as received by the body.

(5A) A non-profit making body is not guilty of an offence under subsection (5), in respect of the receipt of any payment described in that subsection, merely because a person acting on behalf of the body takes part in facilitating the making of a surrogacy arrangement.

(6) In proceedings against a body for an offence under subsection (5) above, it is a defence to prove that the payment concerned was not made in respect of the arrangement mentioned in paragraph (a) of that subsection.

(7) A person who in the United Kingdom takes part in the management or control—

(a) of any body of persons, or

(b) of any of the activities of any body of persons,

is guilty of an offence if the activity described in subsection (8) below is an activity of the body concerned.

(8) The activity referred to in subsection (7) above is negotiating or facilitating the making of surrogacy arrangements in the United Kingdom, being—

(a) arrangements the making of which is negotiated or facilitated on a commercial basis, or

(b) arrangements in the case of which payments are received (or treated for the purposes of subsection (5) above as received) by the body concerned in contravention of subsection (5) above.

(8A) A person is not guilty of an offence under subsection (7) if—

(a) the body of persons referred to in that subsection is a non-profit making body, and

(b) the only activity of that body which falls within subsection (8) is facilitating the making of surrogacy arrangements in the United Kingdom.

(8B) In subsection (8A)(b) 'facilitating the making of surrogacy arrangements' is to be construed in accordance with subsection (8).

(9) In proceedings against a person for an offence under subsection (7) above, it is a defence to prove that he neither knew nor had reasonable cause to suspect that the activity described in subsection (8) above was an activity of the body concerned; and for the purposes of such proceedings any arrangement falling within subsection (8)(b) above shall be disregarded if it is proved that the payment concerned was not made in respect of the arrangement.

3. Advertisements about surrogacy

(1) This section applies to any advertisement containing an indication (however expressed)—

(a) that any person is or may be willing to enter into a surrogacy arrangement or to negotiate or facilitate the making of a surrogacy arrangement, or

(b) that any person is looking for a woman willing to become a surrogate mother or for persons wanting a woman to carry a child as a surrogate mother.

(1A) This section does not apply to any advertisement placed by, or on behalf of, a non-profit making body if the advertisement relates only to the doing by the body of acts that would not contravene section 2(1) even if done on a commercial basis (within the meaning of section 2).

(2) Where a newspaper or periodical containing an advertisement to which this section applies is published in the United Kingdom, any proprietor, editor or publisher of the newspaper or periodical is guilty of an offence.

(3) Where an advertisement to which this section applies is conveyed by means of an electronic communications network so as to be seen or heard (or both) in the United Kingdom, any person who in the United Kingdom causes it to be so conveyed knowing it to contain such an indication as is mentioned in subsection (1) above is guilty of an offence.

(4) A person who publishes or causes to be published in the United Kingdom an advertisement to which this section applies (not being an advertisement contained in a newspaper or periodical or conveyed by means of an electronic communications network) is guilty of an offence.

(5) A person who distributes or causes to be distributed in the United Kingdom an advertisement to which this section applies (not being an advertisement contained in a newspaper or periodical published outside the United Kingdom or an advertisement conveyed by means of an electronic communications network) knowing it to contain such an indication as is mentioned in subsection (1) above is guilty of an offence.

. . .

4. Offences

(1) A person guilty of an offence under this Act shall be liable on summary conviction—
 (a) in the case of an offence under section 2 to a fine not exceeding level 5 on the standard scale or to imprisonment for a term not exceeding 3 months or both,
 (b) in the case of an offence under section 3 to a fine not exceeding level 5 on the standard scale.

(2) No proceedings for an offence under this Act shall be instituted—
 (a) in England and Wales, except by or with the consent of the Director of Public Prosecutions; and
 (b) in Northern Ireland, except by or with the consent of the Director of Public Prosecutions for Northern Ireland.

(3) Where an offence under this Act committed by a body corporate is proved to have been committed with the consent or connivance of, or to be attributable to any neglect on the part of, any director, manager, secretary or other similar officer of the body corporate or any person who was purporting to act in any such capacity, he as well as the body corporate is guilty of the offence and is liable to be proceeded against and punished accordingly.

(4) Where the affairs of a body corporate are managed by its members, subsection (3) above shall apply in relation to the acts and defaults of a member in connection with his functions of management as if he were a director of the body corporate.

(5) In any proceedings for an offence under section 2 of this Act, proof of things done or of words written, spoken or published (whether or not in the presence of any party to the proceedings) by any person taking part in the management or control of a body of persons or of any of the activities of the body, or by any person doing any of the acts mentioned in subsection (1)(a) to (c) of that section on behalf of the body, shall be admissible as evidence of the activities of the body.

(6) In relation to an offence under this Act, section 127(1) of the Magistrates' Courts Act 1980 (information must be laid within six months of commission of offence), . . . shall have effect as if for the reference to six months there were substituted a reference to two years.

CHILD ABDUCTION AND CUSTODY ACT 1985

(1985 c. 60)

12. The European Convention

(1) In this Part of this Act 'the Convention' means the European Convention on Recognition and Enforcement of Decisions concerning Custody of Children and on the Restoration of Custody of Children which was signed in Luxembourg on 20th May 1980.

(2) Subject to the provisions of this Part of this Act, the provisions of that Convention set out in Schedule 2 to this Act (which include Articles 9 and 10 as they have effect in consequence of a reservation made by the United Kingdom under Article 17) shall have the force of law in the United Kingdom.

...

HOUSING ACT 1985

(1985 c. 68)

PART IV

SECURE TENANCIES AND RIGHTS OF SECURE TENANTS

Succession on death of tenant

86A. Persons qualified to succeed tenant: England

(1) A person ('P') is qualified to succeed the tenant under a secure tenancy of a dwellinghouse in England if—
 (a) P occupies the dwelling-house as P's only or principal home at the time of the tenant's death, and
 (b) P is the tenant's spouse or civil partner.

(2) A person ('P') is qualified to succeed the tenant under a secure tenancy of a dwellinghouse in England if—
(a) at the time of the tenant's death the dwelling-house is not occupied by a spouse or civil partner of the tenant as his or her only or principal home,
(b) an express term of the tenancy makes provision for a person other than such a spouse or civil partner of the tenant to succeed to the tenancy, and
(c) P's succession is in accordance with that term.

...

87. Persons qualified to succeed tenant: Wales

A person is qualified to succeed the tenant under a secure tenancy if he occupies the dwelling-house as his only or principal home at the time of the tenant's death and either—
(a) he is the tenant's spouse or civil partner, or
(b) he is another member of the tenant's family and has resided with the tenant throughout the period of twelve months ending with the tenant's death;
unless, in either case, the tenant was himself a successor, as defined in section 88.

113. Members of a person's family

(1) A person is a member of another's family within the meaning of this Part if—
(a) he is the spouse or civil partner of that person, or he and that person live together as husband and wife or as if they were civil partners, or
(b) he is that person's parent, grandparent, child, grandchild, brother, sister, uncle, aunt, nephew or niece.
(2) For the purpose of subsection (1)(b)—
(a) a relationship by marriage shall be treated as a relationship by blood,
(b) a relationship of the half-blood shall be treated as a relationship of the whole blood,
(c) the stepchild of a person shall be treated as his child, and
(d) an illegitimate child shall be treated as the legitimate child of his mother and reputed father.

MARRIAGE (PROHIBITED DEGREES OF RELATIONSHIP) ACT 1986
(1986 c. 16)

1. Marriage between certain persons related by affinity not to be void

(1) A marriage solemnized after the commencement of this Act between a man and a woman who is the daughter or grand-daughter of a former spouse of his (whether the former spouse is living or not) or who is the former spouse of his father or grandfather (whether his father or grandfather is living or not) shall not be void by reason only of that relationship if both the parties have attained the age of twenty-one at the time of the marriage and the younger party has not at any time before attaining the age of eighteen been a child of the family in relation to the other party.
(2) A marriage solemnized after the commencement of this Act between a man and a woman who is the grandmother of a former spouse of his (whether the former spouse is living or not) or is a former spouse of his grandson (whether his grandson is living or not) shall not be void by reason only of that relationship.

...

(5) In this section 'child of the family' in relation to any person, means a child who has lived in the same household as that person and been treated by that person as a child of his family.
(6) The Marriage Act 1949 shall have effect subject to the amendments specified in the Schedule to this Act, being amendments consequential on the preceding provisions of this section.
(7) Where, apart from this Act, any matter affecting the validity of a marriage would fall to be determined (in accordance with the rules of private international law) by reference to the law of a country outside England and Wales nothing in this Act shall preclude the determination of that matter in accordance with that law.
(8) Nothing in this section shall affect any marriage solemnized before the commencement of this Act.

INSOLVENCY ACT 1986
(1986 c. 45)

PART IX
BANKRUPTCY

CHAPTER V
EFFECT OF BANKRUPTCY ON CERTAIN RIGHTS, TRANSACTIONS, ETC.

Rights under trusts of land

335A. Rights under trusts of land

(1) Any application by a trustee of a bankrupt's estate under section 14 of the Trusts of Land and Appointment of Trustees Act 1996 (powers of court in relation to trusts of land) for an order under that section for the sale of land shall be made to the court having jurisdiction in relation to the bankruptcy.

(2) On such an application the court shall make such order as it thinks just and reasonable having regard to—
- (a) the interests of the bankrupt's creditors;
- (b) where the application is made in respect of land which includes a dwelling house which is or has been the home of the bankrupt or the bankrupt's spouse or civil partner or former spouse or former civil partner—
  - (i) the conduct of the spouse, civil partner, former spouse or former civil partner, so far as contributing to the bankruptcy,
  - (ii) the needs and financial resources of the spouse, civil partner, former spouse or former civil partner, and
  - (iii) the needs of any children; and
- (c) all the circumstances of the case other than the needs of the bankrupt.

(3) Where such an application is made after the end of the period of one year beginning with the first vesting under Chapter IV of this Part of the bankrupt's estate in a trustee, the court shall assume, unless the circumstances of the case are exceptional, that the interests of the bankrupt's creditors outweigh all other considerations.

(4) The powers conferred on the court by this section are exercisable on an application whether it is made before or after the commencement of this section.

Rights of occupation

336. Rights of occupation etc. of bankrupt's spouse or civil partner

(1) Nothing occurring in the initial period of the bankruptcy (that is to say, the period beginning with the day of the presentation of the petition for the bankruptcy order and ending with the vesting of the bankrupt's estate in a trustee) is to be taken as having given rise to any home rights under Part IV of the Family Law Act 1996 in relation to a dwelling house comprised in the bankrupt's estate.

(2) Where a spouse's or civil partner's home rights under the Act of 1996 are a charge on the estate or interest of the other spouse or civil partner, or of trustees for the other spouse or civil partner, and the other spouse or civil partner is adjudged bankrupt—
- (a) the charge continues to subsist notwithstanding the bankruptcy and, subject to the provisions of that Act, binds the trustee of the bankrupt's estate and persons deriving title under that trustee, and
- (b) any application for an order under section 33 of that Act shall be made to the court having jurisdiction in relation to the bankruptcy.

(4) On such an application as is mentioned in subsection (2) the court shall make such order under section 33 of the Act of 1996 as it thinks just and reasonable having regard to—
- (a) the interests of the bankrupt's creditors,
- (b) the conduct of the spouse or former spouse or civil partner or former civil partner, so far as contributing to the bankruptcy,
- (c) the needs and financial resources of the spouse or former spouse or civil partner,
- (d) the needs of any children, and
- (e) all the circumstances of the case other than the needs of the bankrupt.

(5) Where such an application is made after the end of the period of one year beginning with the first vesting under Chapter IV of this Part of the bankrupt's estate in a trustee, the court shall assume, unless the circumstances of the case are exceptional, that the interests of the bankrupt's creditors outweigh all other considerations.

337. Rights of occupation of bankrupt

(1) This section applies where—
   (a) a person who is entitled to occupy a dwelling house by virtue of a beneficial estate or interest is adjudged bankrupt, and
   (b) any persons under the age of 18 with whom that person had at some time occupied that dwelling house had their home with that person at the time when the bankruptcy petition was presented and at the commencement of the bankpruptcy.

(2) Whether or not the bankrupt's spouse or civil partner (if any) has home rights under Part IV of the Family Law Act 1996—
   (a) the bankrupt has the following rights as against the trustee of his estate—
      (i) if in occupation, a right not to be evicted or excluded from the dwelling house or any part of it, except with the leave of the court,
      (ii) if not in occupation, a right with the leave of the court to enter into and occupy the dwelling house, and
   (b) the bankrupt's rights are a charge, having the like priority as an equitable interest created immediately before the commencement of the bankruptcy, on so much of his estate or interest in the dwelling house as vests in the trustee.

(3) The Act of 1996 has effect, with the necessary modifications, as if—
   (a) the rights conferred by paragraph (a) of subsection (2) were home rights under that Act,
   (b) any application for such leave as is mentioned in that paragraph were an application for an order under section 33 of that Act, and
   (c) any charge under paragraph (b) of that subsection on the estate or interest of the trustee were a charge under that Act on the estate or interest of a spouse or civil partner.

(4) Any application for leave such as is mentioned in subsection (2)(a) or otherwise by virtue of this section for an order under section 33 of the Act of 1996 shall be made to the court having jurisdiction in relation to the bankruptcy.

(5) On such an application the court shall make such order under section 33 of the Act of 1996 as it thinks just and reasonable having regard to the interests of the creditors, to the bankrupt's financial resources, to the needs of the children and to all the circumstances of the case other than the needs of the bankrupt.

(6) Where such an application is made after the end of the period of one year beginning with the first vesting (under Chapter IV of this Part) of the bankrupt's estate in a trustee, the court shall assume, unless the circumstances of the case are exceptional, that the interests of the bankrupt's creditors outweigh all other considerations.

Adjustment of prior transactions, etc.

339. Transactions at an undervalue

(1) Subject as follows in this section and sections 341 and 342, where an individual is adjudged bankrupt and he has at a relevant time (defined in section 341) entered into a transaction with any person at an undervalue, the trustee of the bankrupt's estate may apply to the court for an order under this section.

(2) The court shall, on such an application, make such order as it thinks fit for restoring the position to what it would have been if that individual had not entered into that transaction.

(3) For the purposes of this section and sections 341 and 342, an individual enters into a transaction with a person at an undervalue if—
   (a) he makes a gift to that person or he otherwise enters into a transaction with that person on terms that provide for him to receive no consideration,
   (b) he enters into a transaction with that person in consideration of marriage, or the formation of a civil partnership, or
   (c) he enters into a transaction with that person for a consideration the value of which, in money or money's worth, is significantly less than the value, in money or money's worth, of the consideration provided by the individual.

FAMILY LAW ACT 1986
(1986 c. 55)

PART II
RECOGNITION OF DIVORCES, ANNULMENTS AND LEGAL SEPARATIONS

Divorces, annulments and judicial separations granted in the British Islands

44. Recognition in United Kingdom of divorces, annulments and judicial separations granted in the British Islands

(1) Subject to section 52(4) and (5)(a) of this Act, no divorce or annulment obtained in any part of the British Islands shall be regarded as effective in any part of the United Kingdom unless granted by a court of civil jurisdiction.

(2) Subject to section 51 of this Act, the validity of any divorce, annulment or judicial separation granted by a court of civil jurisdiction in any part of the British Islands shall be recognised throughout the United Kingdom.

Overseas divorces, annulments and legal separations

45. Recognition in the United Kingdom of overseas divorces, annulments and legal separations

(1) Subject to subsection (2) of this section and to sections 51 and 52 of this Act, the validity of a divorce, annulment or legal separation obtained in a country outside the British Islands (in this Part referred to as an overseas divorce, annulment or legal separation) shall be recognised in the United Kingdom if, and only if, it is entitled to recognition—
- (a) by virtue of sections 46 to 49 of this Act, or
- (b) by virtue of any enactment other than this Part.

(2) Subsection (1) and the following provisions of this Part do not apply to an overseas divorce, annulment or legal separation as regards which provision as to recognition is made by Articles 14 to 20 of the Council Regulation.

46. Grounds for recognition

(1) The validity of an overseas divorce, annulment or legal separation obtained by means of proceedings shall be recognised if—
- (a) the divorce, annulment or legal separation is effective under the law of the country in which it was obtained; and
- (b) at the relevant date either party to the marriage—
  - (i) was habitually resident in the country in which the divorce, annulment or legal separation was obtained; or
  - (ii) was domiciled in that country; or
  - (iii) was a national of that country.

(2) The validity of an overseas divorce, annulment or legal separation obtained otherwise than by means of proceedings shall be recognised if—
- (a) the divorce, annulment or legal separation is effective under the law of the country in which it was obtained;
- (b) at the relevant date—
  - (i) each party to the marriage was domiciled in that country; or
  - (ii) either party to the marriage was domiciled in that country and the other party was domiciled in a country under whose law the divorce, annulment or legal separation is recognised as valid; and
- (c) neither party to the marriage was habitually resident in the United Kingdom throughout the period of one year immediately preceding that date.

(3) In this section 'the relevant date' means—
- (a) in the case of an overseas divorce, annulment or legal separation obtained by means of proceedings, the date of the commencement of the proceedings;
- (b) in the case of an overseas divorce, annulment or legal separation obtained otherwise than by means of proceedings, the date on which it was obtained.

(4) Where in the case of an overseas annulment, the relevant date fell after the death of either party to the marriage, any reference in subsection (1) or (2) above to that date shall be construed in relation to that party as a reference to the date of death.

(5) For the purpose of this section, a party to a marriage shall be treated as domiciled in a country if he was domiciled in that country either according to the law of that country in family matters or according to the law of the part of the United Kingdom in which the question of recognition arises.

Supplemental

51. Refusal of recognition

(1) Subject to section 52 of this Act, recognition of the validity of—

(a) a divorce, annulment or judicial separation granted by a court of civil jurisdiction in any part of the British Islands, or

(b) an overseas divorce, annulment or legal separation,

may be refused in any part of the United Kingdom if the divorce, annulment or separation was granted or obtained at a time when it was irreconcilable with a decision determining the question of the subsistence or validity of the marriage of the parties previously given (whether before or after the commencement of this Part) by a court of civil jurisdiction in that part of the United Kingdom or by a court elsewhere and recognised or entitled to be recognised in that part of the United Kingdom.

(2) Subject to section 52 of this Act, recognition of the validity of—

(a) a divorce or judicial separation granted by a court of civil jurisdiction in any part of the British Islands, or

(b) an overseas divorce or legal separation,

may be refused in any part of the United Kingdom if the divorce or separation was granted or obtained at a time when, according to the law of that part of the United Kingdom (including its rules of private international law and the provisions of this Part), there was no subsisting marriage between the parties.

(3) Subject to section 52 of this Act, recognition by virtue of section 45 of this Act of the validity of an overseas divorce, annulment or legal separation may be refused if—

(a) in the case of a divorce, annulment or legal separation obtained by means of proceedings, it was obtained—

(i) without such steps having been taken for giving notice of the proceedings to a party to the marriage as, having regard to the nature of the proceedings and all the circumstances, should reasonably have been taken; or

(ii) without a party to the marriage having been given (for any reason other than lack of notice) such opportunity to take part in the proceedings as, having regard to those matters, he should reasonably have been given; or

(b) in the case of a divorce, annulment or legal separation obtained otherwise than by means of proceedings—

(i) there is no official document certifying that the divorce, annulment or legal separation is effective under the law of the country in which it was obtained; or

(ii) where either party to the marriage was domiciled in another country at the relevant date, there is no official document certifying that the divorce, annulment or legal separation is recognised as valid under the law of that other country; or

(c) in either case, recognition of the divorce, annulment or legal separation would be manifestly contrary to public policy.

(4) In this section—

'official', in relation to a document certifying that a divorce, annulment or legal separation is effective, or is recognised as valid, under the law of any country, means issued by a person or body appointed or recognised for the purpose under that law;

'the relevant date' has the same meaning as in section 46 of this Act;

and subsection (5) of that section shall apply for the purposes of this section as it applies for the purposes of that section.

(5) Nothing in this Part shall be construed as requiring the recognition of any finding of fault made in any proceedings for divorce, annulment or separation or of any maintenance, custody or other ancillary order made in any such proceedings.

PART III
DECLARATIONS OF STATUS

55. Declarations as to marital status

(1) Subject to the following provisions of this section, any person may apply to the High Court or a county court for one or more of the following declarations in relation to a marriage specified in the application, that is to say—

(a) a declaration that the marriage was at its inception a valid marriage;

(b) a declaration that the marriage subsisted on a date specified in the application;

(c) a declaration that the marriage did not subsist on a date so specified;

(d) a declaration that the validity of a divorce, annulment or legal separation obtained in any country outside England and Wales in respect of the marriage is entitled to recognition in England and Wales;

(e) a declaration that the validity of a divorce, annulment or legal separation so obtained in respect of the marriage is not entitled to recognition in England and Wales.

(2) A court shall have jurisdiction to entertain an application under subsection (1) above if, and only if, either of the parties to the marriage to which the application relates—
(a) is domiciled in England and Wales on the date of the application, or
(b) has been habitually resident in England and Wales throughout the period of one year ending with that date, or
(c) died before that date and either—
(i) was at death domiciled in England and Wales, or
(ii) had been habitually resident in England and Wales throughout the period of one year ending with the date of death.

(3) Where an application under subsection (1) above is made to a court by any person other than a party to the marriage to which the application relates, the court shall refuse to hear the application if it considers that the applicant does not have a sufficient interest in the determination of that application.

55A. Declarations of parentage

(1) Subject to the following provisions of this section, any person may apply to the High Court, a county court or a magistrates' court for a declaration as to whether or not a person named in the application is or was the parent of another person so named.

(2) A court shall have jurisdiction to entertain an application under subsection (1) above if, and only if, either of the persons named in it for the purposes of that subsection—
(a) is domiciled in England and Wales on the date of the application, or
(b) has been habitually resident in England and Wales throughout the period of one year ending with that date, or
(c) died before that date and either—
(i) was at death domiciled in England and Wales, or
(ii) had been habitually resident in England and Wales throughout the period of one year ending with the date of death.

(3) Except in a case falling within subsection (4) below, the court shall refuse to hear an application under subsection (1) above unless it considers that the applicant has a sufficient personal interest in the determination of the application (but this is subject to section 27 of the Child Support Act 1991).

(4) The excepted cases are where the declaration sought is as to whether or not—
(a) the applicant is the parent of a named person;
(b) a named person is the parent of the applicant; or
(c) a named person is the other parent of a named child of the applicant.

(5) Where an application under subsection (1) above is made and one of the persons named in it for the purposes of that subsection is a child, the court may refuse to hear the application if it considers that the determination of the application would not be in the best interests of the child.

(6) Where a court refuses to hear an application under subsection (1) above it may order that the applicant may not apply again for the same declaration without leave of the court.

(7) Where a declaration is made by a court on an application under subsection (1) above, the prescribed officer of the court shall notify the Registrar General, in such a manner and within such period as may be prescribed, of the making of that declaration.

56. Declarations of parentage, legitimacy or legitimation

(1) Any person may apply to the High Court or a county court for a declaration—
(b) that he is the legitimate child of his parents.

(2) Any person may apply to the High Court or a county court for one (or for one or, in the alternative, the other) of the following declarations, that is to say—
(a) a declaration that he has become a legitimated person;
(b) a declaration that he has not become a legitimated person.

(3) The Family court shall have jurisdiction to entertain an application under this section if, and only if, the applicant—
(a) is domiciled in England and Wales on the date of the application; or
(b) has been habitually resident in England and Wales throughout the period of one year ending with that date.

(4) Where a declaration is made by a court on an application under subsection (1) above, the prescribed officer of the court shall notify the Registrar General, in such manner and within such period as may be prescribed, of the making of that declaration.

(5) In this section 'legitimated person' means a person legitimated or recognised as legitimated—

(a) under section 2, 2A or 3 of the Legitimacy Act 1976;
(b) under section 1 or 8 of the Legitimacy Act 1926; or
(c) by a legitimation (whether or not by virtue of the subsequent marriage of his parents) recognised by the law of England and Wales and effected under the law of another country.

58. General provisions as to the making and effect of declarations

(1) Where on an application to a court for a declaration under this Part the truth of the proposition to be declared is proved to the satisfaction of the court, the court shall make that declaration unless to do so would manifestly be contrary to public policy.
(2) Any declaration made under this Part shall be binding on Her Majesty and all other persons.
(3) A court, on the dismissal of an application for a declaration under this Part, shall not have power to make any declaration for which the application has not been made.
(4) No declaration which may be applied for under this Part may be made otherwise than under this Part by any court.
(5) No declaration may be made by any court, whether under this Part or otherwise—
(a) that a marriage was at its inception void.
(6) Nothing in this section shall affect the powers of any court to grant a decree of nullity of marriage.

61. Abolition of right to petition for jactitation of marriage

No person shall after the commencement of this Part be entitled to petition the High Court or a county court for jactitation of marriage.

. . .

FAMILY LAW REFORM ACT 1987
(1987 c. 42)

PART I
GENERAL PRINCIPLE

1. General principle

(1) In this Act and enactments passed and instruments made after the coming into force of this section, references (however expressed) to any relationship between two persons shall, unless the contrary intention appears, be construed without regard to whether or not the father and mother of either of them, or the father and mother of any person through whom the relationship is deduced, have or had been married to each other at any time.
(2) In this Act and enactments passed after the coming into force of this section, unless the contrary intention appears—
(a) references to a person whose father and mother were married to each other at the time of his birth include; and
(b) references to a person whose father and mother were not married to each other at the time of his birth do not include,
references to any person to whom subsection (3) below applies, and cognate references shall be construed accordingly.
(3) This subsection applies to any person who—
(a) is treated as legitimate by virtue of section 1 of the Legitimacy Act 1976;
(b) is a legitimated person within the meaning of section 10 of that Act;
(ba) has a parent by virtue of section 42 of the Human Fertilisation and Embryology Act 2008 (which relates to treatment provided to a woman who is at the time of treatment a party to a civil partnership or, in certain circumstances, a void civil partnership);
(bb) has a parent by virtue of section 43 of that Act (which relates to treatment provided to woman who agrees that second woman to be parent) who—
(i) is the civil partner of the child's mother at the time of the child's birth, or
(ii) was the civil partner of the child's mother at any time during the period beginning with the time mentioned in section 43(b) of that Act and ending with the child's birth;
(c) is an adopted child within the meaning of chapter 4 of Part I of the Adoption and Children Act 2002; or
(d) is otherwise treated in law as legitimate.

(4) For the purpose of construing references falling within subsection (2) above, the time of a person's birth shall be taken to include any time during the period beginning with—
(a) the insemination resulting in his birth; or
(b) where there was no such insemination, his conception,
and (in either case) ending with his birth.

(5) A child whose parents are parties to a void civil partnership shall, subject to subsection (6), be treated as falling within subsection (3)(bb) if at the time when the parties registered as civil partners of each other both or either of the parties reasonably believed that the civil partnership was valid.

(6) Subsection (5) applies only where the woman who is a parent by virtue of section 43 was domiciled in England and Wales at the time of the birth or, if she died before the birth, was so domiciled immediately before her death.

(7) Subsection (5) applies even though the belief that the civil partnership was valid was due to a mistake as to law.

(8) It shall be presumed for the purposes of subsection (5), unless the contrary is shown, that one of the parties to a void civil partnership reasonably believed at the time of the formation of the civil partnership that the civil partnership was valid.

PART II
RIGHTS AND DUTIES OF PARENTS ETC.

Parental rights and duties: general

2. Construction of enactments relating to parental rights and duties

(1) In the following enactments, namely—
. . .
(b) section 6 of the Family Law Reform Act 1969;
(c) the Guardianship of Minors Act 1971 (in this Act referred to as 'the 1971 Act');
(d) Part I of the Guardianship Act 1973 (in this Act referred to as 'the 1973 Act');
(e) Part II of the Children Act 1975;
(f) the Child Care Act 1980 except Part I and sections 13, 24, 64 and 65;
references (however expressed) to any relationship between two persons shall be construed in accordance with section 1 above.

PART III
PROPERTY RIGHTS

18. Succession on intestacy

(1) In Part IV of the Administration of Estates Act 1925 (which deals with the distribution of the estate of an intestate), references (however expressed) to any relationship between two persons shall be construed in accordance with section 1 above.

(2) For the purposes of subsection (1) above and that Part of that Act, a person whose father and mother were not married to each other at the time of his birth shall be presumed not to have been survived by his father, or by any person related to him only through his father, unless the contrary is shown.

(2A) In the case of a person who has a parent by virtue of section 43 of the Human Fertilisation and Embryology Act 2008 (treatment provided to woman who agrees that second woman to be parent), the second and third references in subsection (2) to the person's father are to be read as references to the woman who is a parent of the person by virtue of that section.

(3) In section 50(1) of the Administration of Estates Act 1925 (which relates to the construction of documents), the reference to Part IV of that Act, or to the foregoing provisions of that Part, shall in relation to an instrument inter vivos made, or a will or codicil coming into operation, after the coming into force of this section (but not in relation to instruments inter vivos made or wills or codicils coming into operation earlier) be construed as including references to this section.

(4) This section does not affect any rights under the intestacy of a person dying before the coming into force of this section.

PART VI
MISCELLANEOUS AND SUPPLEMENTAL

Miscellaneous

27. Artificial insemination

(1) Where after the coming into force of this section a child is born in England and Wales as the result of the artificial insemination of a woman who—
   (a) was at the time of the insemination a party to a marriage (being a marriage which had not at that time been dissolved or annulled); and
   (b) was artificially inseminated with the semen of some person other than the other party to that marriage,

then, unless it is proved to the satisfaction of any court by which the matter has to be determined that the other party to that marriage did not consent to the insemination, the child shall be treated in law as the child of the parties to that marriage and shall not be treated as the child of any person other than the parties to that marriage.

(2) Any reference in this section to a marriage includes a reference to a void marriage if at the time of the insemination resulting in the birth of the child both or either of the parties reasonably believed that the marriage was valid; and for the purposes of this section it shall be presumed, unless the contrary is shown, that one of the parties so believed at that time that the marriage was valid.

(3) Nothing in this section shall affect the succession to any dignity or title of honour or render any person capable of succeeding to or transmitting a right to succeed to any such dignity or title.

Supplemental

30. Orders applying section 1 to other enactments

(1) The Lord Chancellor may by order make provision for the construction in accordance with section 1 above of such enactments passed before the coming into force of that section as may be specified in the order.

. . .

HOUSING ACT 1988
(1988 c. 50)

PART I
RENTED ACCOMMODATION

CHAPTER I
ASSURED TENANCIES

Miscellaneous

17. Succession to assured tenancy

(1) Subject to subsection (1D), in any case where—
   (a) the sole tenant under an assured periodic tenancy dies, and
   (b) immediately before the death, the tenant's spouse or civil partner was occupying the dwelling-house as his or her only or principal home,

then, on the death, the tenancy vests by virtue of this section in the spouse or civil partner (and, accordingly, does not devolve under the tenant's will or intestacy).

...

(1D) Subsection (1), (1A), (1B) or (1C) does not apply if the tenant was himself a successor as defined in subsection (2) or subsection (3).

(1E) In such a case, on the death, the tenancy vests by virtue of this section in a person ('P') (and, accordingly, does not devolve under the tenant's will or intestacy) if and only if—
   (a) (in a case within subsection (1)) the tenancy is of a dwelling house in England under which the landlord is a private registered provider of social housing,
   (b) an express term of the tenancy makes provision for a person to succeed as successor to the tenancy, and
   (c) P's succession is in accordance with that term.

(2) For the purposes of this section, a tenant is a successor in relation to a tenancy if—
(a) the tenancy became vested in him either by virtue of this section or under the will or intestacy of a previous tenant; or
(b) at some time before the tenant's death the tenancy was a joint tenancy held by himself and one or more other persons and, prior to his death, he became the sole tenant by survivorship; or
(c) he became entitled to the tenancy as mentioned in section 39(5) below.
(3) For the purposes of this section, a tenant is also a successor in relation to a tenancy (in this subsection referred to as 'the new tenancy') which was granted to him (alone or jointly with others) if—
(a) at some time before the grant of the new tenancy, he was, by virtue of subsection (2) above, a successor in relation to an earlier tenancy of the same or substantially the same dwelling-house as is let under the new tenancy; and
(b) at all times since he became such a successor he has been a tenant (alone or jointly with others) of the dwelling-house which is let under the new tenancy or of a dwelling-house which is substantially the same as that dwelling-house.
(4) For the purposes of this section—
(a) a person who was living with the tenant as his or her wife or husband shall be treated as the tenant's spouse, and
(b) a person who was living with the tenant as if they were civil partners shall be treated as the tenant's civil partner.
(5) If, on the death of the tenant, there is, by virtue of subsection (4) above, more than one person who fulfils the condition in subsection (1)(b) above, such one of them as may be decided by agreement or, in default of agreement, by the county court shall for the purposes of this section be treated (according to whether that one of them is of the opposite sex to, or of the same sex as, the tenant) as the tenant's spouse or the tenant's civil partner.
(6) If, on the death of the tenant, there is more than one person in whom the tenancy would otherwise vest by virtue of subsection (1A), (1C) or (1E), the tenancy vests in such one of them as may be agreed between them or, in default of agreement, as is determined by the county court.

...

CHILDREN ACT 1989
(1989 c. 41)

PART I
INTRODUCTORY

1. Welfare of the child

(1) When a court determines any question with respect to—
(a) the upbringing of a child; or
(b) the administration of a child's property or the application of any income arising from it,

the child's welfare shall be the court's paramount consideration.
(2) In any proceedings in which any question with respect to the upbringing of a child arises, the court shall have regard to the general principle that any delay in determining the question is likely to prejudice the welfare of the child.
(2A) A court, in the circumstances mentioned in subsection (4)(a) or (7), is as respects each parent within subsection (6)(a) to presume, unless the contrary is shown, that involvement of that parent in the life of the child concerned will further the child's welfare.
(2B) In subsection (2A) 'involvement' means involvement of some kind, either direct or indirect, but not any particular division of a child's time.
(3) In the circumstances mentioned in subsection (4), a court shall have regard in particular to—
(a) the ascertainable wishes and feelings of the child concerned (considered in the light of his age and understanding);
(b) his physical, emotional and educational needs;
(c) the likely effect on him of any change in his circumstances;
(d) his age, sex, background and any characteristics of his which the court considers relevant;
(e) any harm which he has suffered or is at risk of suffering;
(f) how capable each of his parents, and any other person in relation to whom the court considers the question to be relevant, is of meeting his needs;

(g) the range of powers available to the court under this Act in the proceedings in question.

(4) The circumstances are that—

(a) the court is considering whether to make, vary or discharge a section 8 order, and the making, variation or discharge of the order is opposed by any party to the proceedings; or

(b) the court is considering whether to make, vary or discharge a special guardianship order or an order under Part IV.

(5) Where a court is considering whether or not to make one or more orders under this Act with respect to a child, it shall not make the order or any of the orders unless it considers that doing so would be better for the child than making no order at all.

(6) In subsection (2A) 'parent' means parent of the child concerned; and for the purposes of that subsection, a parent of the child concerned—

(a) is within this paragraph if that parent can be involved in the child's life in a way that does not put the child at risk of suffering harm; and

(b) is to be treated as within paragraph (a) unless there is some evidence before the court in the particular proceedings to suggest that involvement of that parent in the child's life would put the child at risk of suffering harm whatever the form of the involvement.

(7) The circumstances referred to are that the court is considering whether to make an order under section 4(1)(c) or (2A) or 4ZA(1)(c) or (5) (parental responsibility other than mother).

2. Parental responsibility for children

(1) Where a child's father and mother were married to each other at the time of his birth, they shall each have parental responsibility for the child.

(1A) Where a child—

(a) has a parent by virtue of section 42 of the Human Fertilisation and Embryology Act 2008; or

(b) has a parent by virtue of section 43 of that Act and is a person to whom section 1(3) of the Family Law Reform Act 1987 applies,

the child's mother and the other parent shall each have parental responsibility for the child.

(2) Where a child's father and mother were not married to each other at the time of his birth—

(a) the mother shall have parental responsibility for the child;

(b) the father shall have parental responsibility for the child if he has acquired it (and has not ceased to have it) in accordance with the provisions of this Act.

(2A) Where a child has a parent by virtue of section 43 of the Human Fertilisation and Embryology Act 2008 and is not a person to whom section 1(3) of the Family Law Reform Act 1987 applies—

(a) the mother shall have parental responsibility for the child;

(b) the other parent shall have parental responsibility for the child if she has acquired it (and has not ceased to have it) in accordance with the provisions of this Act.

(3) References in this Act to a child whose father and mother were, or (as the case may be) were not, married to each other at the time of his birth must be read with section 1 of the Family Law Reform Act 1987 (which extends their meaning).

(4) The rule of law that a father is the natural guardian of his legitimate child is abolished.

(5) More than one person may have parental responsibility for the same child at the same time.

(6) A person who has parental responsibility for a child at any time shall not cease to have that responsibility solely because some other person subsequently acquires parental responsibility for the child.

(7) Where more than one person has parental responsibility for a child, each of them may act alone and without the other (or others) in meeting that responsibility; but nothing in this Part shall be taken to affect the operation of any enactment which requires the consent of more than one person in a matter affecting the child.

(8) The fact that a person has parental responsibility for a child shall not entitle him to act in any way which would be incompatible with any order made with respect to the child under this Act.

(9) A person who has parental responsibility for a child may not surrender or transfer any part of that responsibility to another but may arrange for some or all of it to be met by one or more persons acting on his behalf.

(10) The person with whom any such arrangement is made may himself be a person who already has parental responsibility for the child concerned.

(11) The making of any such arrangement shall not affect any liability of the person making it which may arise from any failure to meet any part of his parental responsibility for the child concerned.

3. Meaning of 'parental responsibility'

(1) In this Act 'parental responsibility' means all the rights, duties, powers, responsibilities and authority which by law a parent of a child has in relation to the child and his property.

(2) It also includes the rights, powers and duties which a guardian of the child's estate (appointed, before the commencement of section 5, to act generally) would have had in relation to the child and his property.

(3) The rights referred to in subsection (2) include, in particular, the right of the guardian to receive or recover in his own name, for the benefit of the child, property of whatever description and wherever situated which the child is entitled to receive or recover.

(4) The fact that a person has, or does not have, parental responsibility for a child shall not affect—

(a) any obligation which he may have in relation to the child (such as a statutory duty to maintain the child); or

(b) any rights which, in the event of the child's death, he (or any other person) may have in relation to the child's property.

(5) A person who—

(a) does not have parental responsibility for a particular child; but

(b) has care of the child,

may (subject to the provisions of this Act) do what is reasonable in all the circumstances of the case for the purpose of safeguarding or promoting the child's welfare.

4. Acquisition of parental responsibility by father

(1) Where a child's father and mother were not married to each other at the time of his birth, the father shall acquire parental responsibility for the child if—

(a) except where subsection (1C) applies, he becomes registered as the child's father under any of the enactments specified in subsection (1A);

(b) he and the child's mother make an agreement (a 'parental responsibility agreement') providing for him to have parental responsibility for the child; or

(c) the court, on his application, orders that he shall have parental responsibility for the child.

(1A) The enactments referred to in subsection (1)(a) are—

(a) paragraphs (a), (b) and (c) of section 10(1) and of section 10A(1) of the Births and Deaths Registration Act 1953;

(aa) regulations under section 2C, 2D, 2E, 10B or 10C of the Births and Deaths Registration Act 1953;

. . .

(1B) The Secretary of State may by order amend subsection (1A) so as to add further enactments to the list in that subsection.

(1C) The father of a child does not acquire parental responsibility by virtue of subsection (1)(a) if, before he became registered as the child's father under the enactment in question—

(a) the court considered an application by him for an order under subsection (1)(c) in relation to the child but did not make such an order, or—

(b) in a case where he had previously acquired parental responsibility for the child, the court ordered that he was to cease to have that responsibility.

(2) No parental responsibility agreement shall have effect for the purposes of this Act unless—

(a) it is made in the form prescribed by regulations made by the Lord Chancellor; and

(b) where regulations are made by the Lord Chancellor prescribing the manner in which such agreements must be recorded, it is recorded in the prescribed manner.

(2A) A person who has acquired parental responsibility under subsection (1) shall cease to have that responsibility only if the court so orders.

(3) The court may make an order under subsection (2A) on the application—

(a) of any person who has parental responsibility for the child; or

(b) with the leave of the court, of the child himself,

subject, in the case of parental responsibility acquired under subsection (1)(c), to section 12(4).

(4) The court may only grant leave under subsection (3)(b) if it is satisfied that the child has sufficient understanding to make the proposed application.

4ZA. Acquisition of parental responsibility by second female parent

(1) Where a child has a parent by virtue of section 43 of the Human Fertilisation and Embryology Act 2008 and is not a person to whom section 1(3) of the Family Law Reform Act 1987 applies, that parent shall acquire parental responsibility for the child if—

(a) except where subsection (3A) applies, she becomes registered as a parent of the child under any of the enactments specified in subsection (2);

(b) she and the child's mother make an agreement providing for her to have parental responsibility for the child; or

(c) the court, on her application, orders that she shall have parental responsibility for the child.

(2) The enactments referred to in subsection (1)(a) are—
(a) paragraphs (a), (b) and (c) of section 10(1B) and of section 10A(1B) of the Births and Deaths Registration Act 1953;
(aa) regulations under section 2C, 2D, 10B or 10C of the Births and Deaths Registration Act 1953;
(b) paragraphs (a), (b) and (d) of section 18B(1) and sections 18B(3)(a) and 20(1)(a) of the Registration of Births, Deaths and Marriages (Scotland) Act 1965; and
(c) sub-paragraphs (a), (b) and (c) of Article 14ZA(3) of the Births and Deaths Registration (Northern Ireland) Order 1976.

(3) The Secretary of State may by order amend subsection (2) so as to add further enactments to the list in that subsection.

(3A) A person who is a parent of a child by virtue of section 43 of the Human Fertilisation and Embryology Act 2008 does not acquire parental responsibility by virtue of subsection (1)(a) if, before she became registered as a parent of the child under the enactment in question—
(a) the court considered an application by her for an order under subsection (1)(c) in relation to the child but did not make such an order, or
(b) in a case where she had previously acquired parental responsibility for the child, the court ordered that she was to cease to have that responsibility.

(4) An agreement under subsection (1)(b) is also a 'parental responsibility agreement', and section 4(2) applies in relation to such an agreement as it applies in relation to parental responsibility agreements under section 4.

(5) A person who has acquired parental responsibility under subsection (1) shall cease to have that responsibility only if the court so orders.

(6) The court may make an order under subsection (5) on the application—
(a) of any person who has parental responsibility for the child; or
(b) with the leave of the court, of the child himself,
subject, in the case of parental responsibility acquired under subsection (1)(c), to section 12(4).

(7) The court may only grant leave under subsection (6)(b) if it is satisfied that the child has sufficient understanding to make the proposed application.

4A. Acquisition of parental responsibility by step-parent

(1) Where a child's parent ('parent A') who has parental responsibility for the child is married to, or a civil partner of a person who is not the child's parent ('the step-parent')—
(a) parent A, or if the other parent of the child also has parental responsibility for the child, both parents may by agreement with the step-parent provide for the step-parent to have parental responsibility for the child; or
(b) the court may, on the application of the step-parent, order that the step-parent shall have parental responsibility for the child.

(2) An agreement under subsection (1)(a) is also a 'parental responsibility agreement', and section 4(2) applies in relation to such agreements as it applies in relation to parental responsibility agreements under section 4.

(3) A parental responsibility agreement under subsection (1)(a), or an order under subsection (1)(b), may only be brought to an end by an order of the court made on the application—
(a) of any person has parental responsibility for the child; or
(b) with the leave of the court, of the child himself.

(4) The court may only grant leave under subsection (3)(b) if it is satisfied that the child has sufficient understanding to make the proposed application.

5. Appointment of guardians

(1) Where an application with respect to a child is made to the court by any individual, the court may by order appoint that individual to be the child's guardian if—
(a) the child has no parent with parental responsibility for him; or
(b) parent, guardian or special guardian of the child's was named in a child arrangements order as a person with whom the child was to live and has died while the order was in force; or
(c) paragraph (b) does not apply, and the child's only or last surviving special guardian dies.

(2) The power conferred by subsection (1) may also be exercised in any family proceedings if the court considers that the order should be made even though no application has been made for it.

(3) A parent who has parental responsibility for his child may appoint another individual to be the child's guardian in the event of his death.

(4) A guardian of a child may appoint another individual to take his place as the child's guardian in the event of his death; and a special guardian of a child may appoint another individual to be the child's guardian in the event of his death.

(5) An appointment under subsection (3) or (4) shall not have effect unless it is made in writing, is dated and is signed by the person making the appointment or—
  (a) in the case of an appointment made by a will which is not signed by the testator, is signed at the direction of the testator in accordance with the requirements of section 9 of the Wills Act 1837; or
  (b) in any other case, is signed at the direction of the person making the appointment, in his presence and in the presence of two witnesses who each attest the signature.

(6) A person appointed as a child's guardian under this section shall have parental responsibility for the child concerned.

(7) Where—
  (a) on the death of any person making an appointment under subsection (3) or (4), the child concerned has no parent with parental responsibility for him; or
  (b) immediately before the death of any person making such an appointment, a child arrangements order was in force in which the person was named as a person with whom the child was to live or the person was the child's only (or last surviving) special guardian,

the appointment shall take effect on the death of that person.

(8) Where, on the death of any person making an appointment under subsection (3) or (4)—
  (a) the child concerned has a parent with parental responsibility for him; and
  (b) subsection (7)(b) does not apply,

the appointment shall take effect when the child no longer has a parent who has parental responsibility for him.

(9) Subsections (1) and (7) do not apply if the child arrangements order referred to in paragraph (b) of those subsections also named a surviving parent of the child as a person with whom the child was to live.

(10) Nothing in this section shall be taken to prevent an appointment under subsection (3) or (4) being made by two or more persons acting jointly.

(11) Subject to any provision made by rules of court, no court shall exercise the High Court's inherent jurisdiction to appoint a guardian of the estate of any child.

(12) Where rules of court are made under subsection (11) they may prescribe the circumstances in which, and conditions subject to which, an appointment of such a guardian may be made.

(13) A guardian of a child may only be appointed in accordance with the provisions of this section.

6. Guardians: revocation and disclaimer

(1) An appointment under section 5(3) or (4) revokes an earlier such appointment (including one made in an unrevoked will or codicil) made by the same person in respect of the same child, unless it is clear (whether as the result of an express provision in the later appointment or by any necessary implication) that the purpose of the later appointment is to appoint an additional guardian.

(2) An appointment under section 5(3) or (4) (including one made in an unrevoked will or codicil) is revoked if the person who made the appointment revokes it by a written and dated instrument which is signed—
  (a) by him; or
  (b) at his direction, in his presence and in the presence of two witnesses who each attest the signature.

(3) An appointment under section 5(3) or (4) (other than one made in a will or codicil) is revoked if, with the intention of revoking the appointment, the person who made it—
  (a) destroys the instrument by which it was made; or
  (b) has some other person destroy that instrument in his presence.

(3A) An appointment under section 5(3) or (4) (including one made in an unrevoked will or codicil) is revoked if the person appointed is the spouse of the person who made the appointment and either—
  (a) a decree of a court of civil jurisdiction in England and Wales dissolves or annuls the marriage, or
  (b) the marriage is dissolved or annulled and the divorce or annulment is entitled to recognition in England and Wales by virtue of Part II of the Family Law Act 1986,

unless a contrary intention appears by the appointment.

(3B) An appointment under section 5(3) or (4) (including one made in an unrevoked will or codicil) is revoked if the person appointed is the civil partner of the person who made the appointment and either—
  (a) an order of a court of civil jurisdiction in England and Wales dissolves or annuls the civil partnership, or
  (b) the civil partnership is dissolved or annulled and the dissolution or annulment is entitled to recognition in England and Wales by virtue of Chapter 3 of Part 5 of the Civil Partnership Act 2004, unless a contrary intention appears by the appointment.

(4) For the avoidance of doubt, an appointment under section 5(3) or (4) made in a will or codicil is revoked if the will or codicil is revoked.

(5) A person who is appointed as a guardian under section 5(3) or (4) may disclaim his appointment by an instrument in writing signed by him and made within a reasonable time of his first knowing that the appointment has taken effect.

(6) Where regulations are made by the Lord Chancellor prescribing the manner in which such disclaimers must be recorded, no such disclaimer shall have effect unless it is recorded in the prescribed manner.

(7) Any appointment of a guardian under section 5 may be brought to an end at any time by order of the court—
   (a) on the application of any person who has parental responsibility for the child;
   (b) on the application of the child concerned, with leave of the court; or
   (c) in any family proceedings, if the court considers that it should be brought to an end even though no application has been made.

7. Welfare reports

(1) A court considering any question with respect to a child under this Act may—
   (a) ask an officer of the Service; or
   (b) ask a local authority to arrange for—
      (i) an officer of the authority; or
      (ii) such other person (other than an officer of the Service) as the authority considers appropriate,

   to report to the court on such matters relating to the welfare of that child as are required to be dealt with in the report.

(2) The Lord Chancellor may make regulations specifying matters which, unless the court orders otherwise, must be dealt with in any report under this section.

(3) The report may be made in writing, or orally, as the court requires.

(4) Regardless of any enactment or rule of law which would otherwise prevent it from doing so, the court may take account of—
   (a) any statement contained in the report; and
   (b) any evidence given in respect of the matters referred to in the report,

   in so far as the statement or evidence is, in the opinion of the court, relevant to the question which it is considering.

(5) It shall be the duty of the authority or officer of the Service or a Welsh family proceedings officer to comply with any request for a report under this section.

...

PART II

ORDERS WITH RESPECT TO CHILDREN IN FAMILY PROCEEDINGS

General

8. Child arrangements orders and other orders with respect to children

(1) In this Act—

   'a child arrangements order' means an order regulating arrangements relating to any of the following –
   (a) with whom a child is to live, spend time or otherwise have contact, and
   (b) when a child is to live, spend time or otherwise have contact with any person;

   'a prohibited steps order' means an order that no step which could be taken by a parent in meeting his parental responsibility for a child, and which is of a kind specified in the order, shall be taken by any person without the consent of the court;

   'a specific issue order' means an order giving directions for the purpose of determining a specific question which has arisen, or which may arise, in connection with any aspect of parental responsibility for a child.

(2) In this Act 'a section 8 order' means any of the orders mentioned in subsection (1) and any order varying or discharging such an order.

(3) For the purposes of this Act 'family proceedings' means any proceedings—
   (a) under the inherent jurisdiction of the High Court in relation to children; and
   (b) under the enactments mentioned in subsection (4),

   but does not include proceedings on an application for leave under section 100(3).

(4) The enactments are—
   (a) Parts I, II and IV of this Act;
   (b) the Matrimonial Causes Act 1973;
   (ba) Schedule 5 to the Civil Partnership Act 2004;
   (c) ...
   (d) the Adoption and Children Act 2002;

(e) the Domestic Proceedings and Magistrates' Courts Act 1978;
(ea) Schedule 6 to the Civil Partnership Act 2004;
(f) . . .
(g) Part III of the Matrimonial and Family Proceedings Act 1984;
(h) the Family Law Act 1996;
(i) sections 11 and 12 of the Crime and Disorder Act 1998.

9. Restrictions on making section 8 orders

(1) No court shall make any section 8 order, other than a child arrangements order to which subsection (6B) applies, with respect to a child who is in the care of a local authority.
(2) No application may be made by a local authority for a child arrangements order and no court shall make such an order in favour of a local authority.
(3) A person who is, or was at any time within the last six months, a local authority foster parent of a child may not apply for leave to apply for a section 8 order with respect to the child unless—
(a) he has the consent of the authority;
(b) he is a relative of the child; or
(c) the child has lived with him for at least one year preceding the application.
(4) . . .
(5) No court shall exercise its powers to make a specific issue order or prohibited steps order—
(a) with a view to achieving a result which could be achieved by making a child arrangements order or an order under section 51A of the Adoption and Children Act 2002 (post-adoption contact): or
(b) in any way which is denied to the High Court (by section 100(2)) in the exercise of its inherent jurisdiction with respect to children.
(6) No court shall make any section 8 order which is to have effect for a period which will end after the child has reached the age of sixteen unless it is satisfied that the circumstances of the case are exceptional.
(6A) Subsection 6 does not apply to a child arrangements order to which subsection (6B) applies.
(6B) This subsection applies to a child arrangements order if the arrangements regulated by the order relate only to either or both of the following—
(a) with whom the child concerned is to live, and
(b) when the child is to live with any person.
(7) No court shall make any section 8 order, other than one varying or discharging such an order, with respect to a child who has reached the age of sixteen unless it is satisfied that the circumstances of the case are exceptional.

10. Power of court to make section 8 orders

(1) In any family proceedings in which a question arises with respect to the welfare of any child, the court may make a section 8 order with respect to the child if—
(a) an application for the order has been made by a person who—
(i) is entitled to apply for a section 8 order with respect to the child; or
(ii) has obtained the leave of the court to make the application; or
(b) the court considers that the order should be made even though no such application has been made.
(2) The court may also make a section 8 order with respect to any child on the application of a person who—
(a) is entitled to apply for a section 8 order with respect to the child; or
(b) has obtained the leave of the court to make the application.
(3) This section is subject to the restrictions imposed by section 9.
(4) The following persons are entitled to apply to the court for any section 8 order with respect to a child—
(a) any parent, guardian or special guardian of the child;
(aa) any person who by virtue of section 4A has parental responsibility for the child;
(b) any person who is named, in a child arrangements order that is in force with respect to the child, as a person with whom the child is to live.
(5) The following persons are entitled to apply for a residence or contact order with respect to a child—
(a) any party to a marriage (whether or not subsisting) in relation to whom the child is a child of the family;
(aa) any civil partner in a civil partnership (whether or not subsisting) in relation to whom the child is a child of the family;
(b) any person with whom the child has lived for a period of at least three years;
(c) any person who—
(i) in any case where a child arrangements order in force with respect to the child regulates arrangements relating to with whom the child is to live or

when the child is to live with any person, has the consent of each of the persons named in the order as a person with whom the child is to live;

(ii) in any case where the child is in the care of a local authority, has the consent of that authority; or

(iii) in any other case, has the consent of each of those (if any) who have parental responsibility for the child;

(d) any person who has parental responsibility for the child by virtue of provision made under section 12(2A).

(5A) A local authority foster parent is entitled to apply for a child arrangements order to which subsection (5C) applies with respect to a child if the child has lived with him for a period of at least one year immediately preceding the application.

(5B) A relative of a child is entitled to apply for a child arrangements order to which subsection (5C) applies with respect to the child if the child has lived with the relative for a period of at least one year immediately preceding the application.

(5C) This subsection applies to a child arrangements order if the arrangements regulated by the order relate only to either or both of the following—

(a) with whom the child concerned is to live, and

(b) when the child is to live with any person.

(6) A person who would not otherwise be entitled (under the previous provisions of this section) to apply for the variation or discharge of a section 8 order shall be entitled to do so if—

(a) the order was made on his application; or

(b) in the case of a child arrangements order, he is named in provisions of the order regulating arrangements relating to—

(i) with whom the child concerned is to spend time or otherwise have contact, or

(ii) when the child is to spend time or otherwise have contact with any person.

(7) Any person who falls within a category of person prescribed by rules of court is entitled to apply for any such section 8 order as may be prescribed in relation to that category of person.

(7A) If a special guardianship order is in force with respect to a child, an application for a child arrangements order to which subsection (7B) applies may only be made with respect to him, if apart from this subsection the leave of the court is not required, with such leave.

(7B) This subsection applies to a child arrangements order if the arrangements regulated by the order consist of, or include, arrangements which relate to either or both of the following—

(a) with whom the child concerned is to live, and

(b) when the child is to live with any person.

(8) Where the person applying for leave to make an application for a section 8 order is the child concerned, the court may only grant leave if it is satisfied that he has sufficient understanding to make the proposed application for the section 8 order.

(9) Where the person applying for leave to make an application for a section 8 order is not the child concerned, the court shall, in deciding whether or not to grant leave, have particular regard to—

(a) the nature of the proposed application for the section 8 order;

(b) the applicant's connection with the child;

(c) any risk there might be of that proposed application disrupting the child's life to such an extent that he would be harmed by it; and

(d) where the child is being looked after by a local authority—

(i) the authority's plans for the child's future; and

(ii) the wishes and feelings of the child's parents.

(10) The period of three years mentioned in subsection (5)(b) need not be continuous but must not have begun more than five years before, or ended more than three months before, the making of the application.

11. General principles and supplementary provisions

(1) In proceedings in which any question of making a section 8 order, or any other question with respect to such an order arises, the court shall (in the light of any rules made by virtue of subsection (2))—

(a) draw up a timetable with a view to determining the question without delay; and

(b) give such directions as it considers appropriate for the purpose of ensuring, so far as is reasonably practicable, that that timetable is adhered to.

(2) Rules of court may—

(a) specify periods within which specified steps must be taken in relation to proceedings in which such questions arise; and

(b) make other provision with respect to such proceedings for the purpose of ensuring, so far as is reasonably practicable, that such questions are determined without delay.

(3) Where a court has power to make a section 8 order, it may do so at any time during the course of the proceedings in question even though it is not in a position to dispose finally of those proceedings.
(4) ...
(5) Where—
(a) a child arrangements order has been made with respect to a child; and
(b) the child has two parents who each have parental responsibility for him,
the order, so far as it has the result that there are times when the child lives or is to live with one of the parents, shall cease to have effect if the parents live together for a continuous period of more than six months.
(6) A child arrangements order made with respect to a child, so far as it provides for the child to spend time or otherwise have contact with one of the child's parents at times when the child is living with the child's other parent shall cease to have effect if the parents live together for a continuous period of more than six months.
(7) A section 8 order may—
(a) contain directions about how it is to be carried into effect;
(b) impose conditions which must be complied with by any person—
(i) who is named in the order as a person with whom the child concerned is to live, spend time or otherwise have contact;
(ii) who is a parent of the child
(iii) who is not a parent of his but who has parental responsibility for him; or
(iv) with whom the child is living,
and to whom the conditions are expressed to apply;
(c) be made to have effect for a specified period, or contain provisions which are to have effect for a specified period;
(d) make such incidental, supplemental or consequential provision as the court thinks fit.

11A. Activity directions

(1) Subsection (2) applies in proceedings in which the court is considering whether to make provision about one or more of the matters mentioned in subsection (1A) by making—
(a) a child arrangements order with respect to the child concerned, or
(b) an order varying or discharging a child arrangements order with respect to the child concerned.
(1A) The matters mentioned in this subsection are—
(a) with whom a child is to live,
(b) when a child is to live with any person,
(c) with whom a child is to spend time or otherwise have contact, and
(d) when a child is to spend time or otherwise have contact with any person.
(2) The court may make an activity direction in connection with the provision that the court is considering whether to make.
(2A) Subsection (2B) applies in proceedings in which subsection (2) does not apply and in which the court is considering—
(a) whether a person has failed to comply with a provision of a child arrangements order, or
(b) what steps to take in consequence of a person's failure to comply with a provision of a child arrangements order.
(2B) The court may make an activity direction in connection with that provision of a child arrangements order.
(3) An activity direction is a direction requiring an individual who is a party to the proceedings to take part in an activity that would, in the court's opinion, help to establish, maintain or improve the involvement in the life of the child concerned of—
(a) that individual, or
(b) another individual who is a party to the proceedings.
(4) The direction is to specify the activity and the person providing the activity.
(5) The activities that may be so required include, in particular—
(a) programmes, classes and counselling or guidance sessions of a kind that—
(i) may assist a person as regards establishing, maintaining or improving involvement in a child's life;
(ii) may, by addressing a person's violent behaviour, enable or facilitate involvement in a child's life;
(b) sessions in which information or advice is given as regards making or operating arrangements for involvement in a child's life, including making arrangements by means of mediation.
(6) No individual may be required by an activity direction—
(a) to undergo medical or psychiatric examination, assessment or treatment;
(b) to take part in mediation.
(7) A court may not on the same occasion—
(a) make an activity direction under subsection (2B) 9.p. 231, at 12 (5)(a).

. . .

(b) dispose finally of the proceedings as they relate to the matters mentioned in subsection (1A) in connection with which the activity direction is made.

(7A) A court may not on the same occasion—

(a) make an activity direction under subsection (2B), and

(b) dispose finally of the proceedings as they relate to failure to comply with the provision in connection with which the activity direction is made.

(8) Each of subsections (2) and (2B) has effect subject to the restrictions in sections 11B and 11E.

(9) In considering whether to make an activity direction, the welfare of the child concerned is to be the court's paramount consideration.

11B. Activity directions: further provision

(1) A court may not make an activity direction under section 11A(2) in connection with any matter mentioned in section 11A (1A) unless there is a dispute as regards the provision about that matter that the court is considering whether to make in the proceedings.

(2) A court may not make an activity direction requiring an individual who is a child to take part in an activity unless the individual is a parent of the child in relation to whom the court is considering provision about a matter mentioned in section 11A (1A).

(3) A court may not make an activity direction in connection with the making, variation or discharge of a child arrangements order, if the child arrangements order is, or would if made be, an excepted order.

(4) A child arrangements order with respect to a child is an excepted order if—

(a) it is made in proceedings that include proceedings on an application for a relevant adoption order in respect of the child; or

(b) it makes provision as regards contact between the child and a person who would be a parent or relative of the child but for the child's adoption by an order falling within subsection (5).

(5) An order falls within this subsection if it is—

(a) a relevant adoption order;

(b) an adoption order, within the meaning of section 72(1) of the Adoption Act 1976, other than an order made by virtue of section 14 of that Act on the application of a married couple one of whom is the mother or the father of the child;

. . .

(6) A relevant adoption order is an adoption order, within the meaning of section 46(1) of the Adoption and Children Act 2002, other than an order made—

(a) on an application under section 50 of that Act by a couple (within the meaning of that Act) one of whom is the mother or the father of the person to be adopted, or

(b) on an application under section 51(2) of that Act.

(7) A court may not make an activity direction in relation to an individual unless the individual is habitually resident in England and Wales; and a direction ceases to have effect if the individual subject to the direction ceases to be habitually resident in England and Wales.

11C. Activity conditions

(1) This section applies if in any family proceedings the court makes—

(a) a child arrangements order containing—

(i) provision for a child to live with different persons at different times,

(ii) provision regulating arrangements relating to with whom a child is to spend time or otherwise have contact, or

(iii) provision regulating arrangements relating to when a child is to spend time or otherwise have contact with any person; or

(b) an order varying a child arrangements order so as to add, vary or omit provision of a kind mentioned in paragraph (a) (i) (ii) or (iii).

(2) The child arrangements order may impose, or the order may be varied so as to impose, a condition (an 'activity condition') requiring an individual falling within subsection (3) to take part in an activity that would, in the court's opinion, help to establish, maintain or improve the involvement in the life of the child concerned of—

(a) that individual, or

(b) another individual who is a party to the proceedings.

(3) An individual falls within this subsection if he is—

(a) for the purposes of the child arrangements order so made or varied, a person with whom the child concerned lives or is to live;

(b) a person whose contact with the child concerned is provided for in that order; or

(c) a person upon whom that order imposes a condition under section 11(7)(b).

(4) The condition is to specify the activity and the person providing the activity.

(5) Subsections (5) and (6) of section 11A have effect as regards the activities that may be required by an activity condition as they have effect as regards the activities that may be required by an activity direction.

(6) Subsection (2) has effect subject to the restrictions in sections 11D and 11E.

11D. Activity conditions: further provision

(1) A child arrangements order may not impose an activity condition on an individual who is a child unless the individual is a parent of the child concerned.

(2) If a child arrangement order is an excepted order (within the meaning given by section 11B(4)), it may not impose (and it may not be varied so as to impose) an activity condition.

(3) A child arrangements order may not impose an activity condition on an individual unless the individual is habitually resident in England and Wales; and a condition ceases to have effect if the individual subject to the condition ceases to be habitually resident in England and Wales.

11E. Activity directions and conditions: making

(1) Before making an activity direction (or imposing an activity condition by means of a child arrangements order), the court must satisfy itself as to the matters falling within subsections (2) to (4).

(2) The first matter is that the activity proposed to be specified is appropriate in the circumstances of the case.

(3) The second matter is that the person proposed to be specified as the provider of the activity is suitable to provide the activity.

(4) The third matter is that the activity proposed to be specified is provided in a place to which the individual who would be subject to the direction (or the condition) can reasonably be expected to travel.

(5) Before making such a direction (or such an order), the court must obtain and consider information about the individual who would be subject to the direction (or the condition) and the likely effect of the direction (or the condition) on him.

(6) Information about the likely effect of the direction (or the condition) may, in particular, include information as to—

(a) any conflict with the individual's religious beliefs;

(b) any interference with the times (if any) at which he normally works or attends an educational establishment.

(7) The court may ask an officer of the Service or a Welsh family proceedings officer to provide the court with information as to the matters in subsections (2) to (5); and it shall be the duty of the officer of the Service or Welsh family proceedings officer to comply with any such request.

(8) In this section 'specified' means specified in an activity direction (or in an activity condition).

11F. Activity directions and conditions: financial assistance

(1) The Secretary of State may by regulations make provision authorising him to make payments to assist individuals falling within subsection (2) in paying relevant charges or fees.

(2) An individual falls within this subsection if he is required by an activity direction or condition to take part in an activity that is expected to help to establish, maintain or improve the involvement of that individual in the life of a child, not being a child ordinarily resident in Wales.

(3) The National Assembly for Wales may by regulations make provision authorising it to make payments to assist individuals falling within subsection (4) in paying relevant charges or fees.

(4) An individual falls within this subsection if he is required by an activity direction or condition to take part in an activity that is expected to help to establish, maintain or improve the involvement of that or another individual in the life of a child who is ordinarily resident in Wales.

(5) A relevant charge or fee, in relation to an activity required by an activity direction or condition, is a charge or fee in respect of the activity payable to the person providing the activity.

(6) Regulations under this section may provide that no assistance is available to an individual unless—

(a) the individual satisfies such conditions as regards his financial resources as may be set out in the regulations;

(b) the activity in which the individual is required by an activity direction or condition to take part is provided to him in England or Wales;

(c) where the activity in which the individual is required to take part is provided to him in England, it is provided by a person who is for the time being approved by the Secretary of State as a provider of activities required by an activity direction or condition;

(d) where the activity in which the individual is required to take part is provided to him in Wales, it is provided by a person who is for the time being approved by the National Assembly for Wales as a provider of activities required by an activity direction or condition.

(7) Regulations under this section may make provision—
(a) as to the maximum amount of assistance that may be paid to or in respect of an individual as regards an activity in which he is required by an activity direction or condition to take part;
(b) where the amount may vary according to an individual's financial resources, as to the method by which the amount is to be determined;
(c) authorising payments by way of assistance to be made directly to persons providing activities required by an activity direction or condition.

11G. Activity directions and conditions: monitoring

(1) This section applies if in any family proceedings the court—
(a) makes an activity direction in relation to an individual, or
(b) makes a child arrangements order that imposes, or varies a child arrangements order so as to impose, an activity condition on an individual.

(2) The court may on making the direction (or imposing the condition by means of a child arrangements order) ask an officer of the Service or a Welsh family proceedings officer—
(a) to monitor, or arrange for the monitoring of, the individual's compliance with the direction (or the condition);
(b) to report to the court on any failure by the individual to comply with the direction (or the condition).

(3) It shall be the duty of the officer of the Service or Welsh family proceedings officer to comply with any request under subsection (2).

11H. Monitoring contact and shared residence

(1) This section applies if in any family proceedings the court makes—
(a) a child arrangements order containing a provision of a kind mentioned in section 11C(1)(a) (i), (ii) or (iii), or
(b) an order varying a child arrangements order so as to add, vary or omit any of those kinds.

(2) The court may ask an officer of the Service or a Welsh family proceedings officer—
(a) to monitor whether an individual falling within subsection (3) complies with each provision of any of those kinds that is contained in the child arrangements order (or in the child arrangements order as varied);
(b) to report to the court on such matters relating to the individual's compliance as the court may specify in the request.

(3) An individual falls within this subsection if the child arrangements order so made (or the child arrangements order as so varied)—
(za) provides for the child concerned to live with different persons at different times and names the individual as one of those persons;
(a) imposes requirements on the individual with regard to the child concerned spending time or otherwise having contact with some other person;
(b) names the individual as a person with whom the child concerned is to spend time or otherwise have contact; or
(c) imposes a condition under section 11(7)(b) on the individual.

(4) If the child arrangements order (or the child arrangements order as varied) includes an activity condition, a request under subsection (2) is to be treated as relating to the provisions of the order other than the activity condition.

(5) The court may make a request under subsection (2)—
(a) on making the child arrangements order (or the order varying the child arrangements order), or
(b) at any time during the subsequent course of the proceedings as they relate to contact with the child concerned or to the child's living arrangements.

(6) In making a request under subsection (2), the court is to specify the period for which the officer of the Service or Welsh family proceedings officer is to monitor compliance with the order; and the period specified may not exceed twelve months.

(7) It shall be the duty of the officer of the Service or Welsh family proceedings officer to comply with any request under subsection (2).

(8) The court may order any individual falling within subsection (3) to take such steps as may be specified in the order with a view to enabling the officer of the Service or Welsh family proceedings officer to comply with the court's request under subsection (2).

(9) But the court may not make an order under subsection (8) with respect to an individual who is a child unless he is a parent of the child with respect to whom the order falling within subsection (1) was made.

(10) A court may not make a request under subsection (2) in relation to a child arrangements order that is an excepted order (within the meaning given by section 11B(4)).

11I. Child arrangements orders: warning notices

Where the court makes (or varies) a child arrangements order, it is to attach to the child arrangements order (or the order varying the child arrangements order) a notice warning of the consequences of failing to comply with the child arrangements order.

11J. Enforcement orders

(1) This section applies if a child arrangements order with respect to a child has been made.

(2) If the court is satisfied beyond reasonable doubt that a person has failed to comply with a provision of the child arrangements order, it may make an order (an 'enforcement order') imposing on the person an unpaid work requirement.

(3) But the court may not make an enforcement order if it is satisfied that the person had a reasonable excuse for failing to comply with the provision.

(4) The burden of proof as to the matter mentioned in subsection (3) lies on the person claiming to have had a reasonable excuse, and the standard of proof is the balance of probabilities.

(5) The court may make an enforcement order in relation to the child arrangements order only on the application of—

- (a) a person who is, for the purposes of the child arrangements order, the person with whom the child concerned lives or is to live;
- (b) a person whose contact with the child concerned is provided for in the child arrangements order;
- (c) any individual subject to a condition under section 11(7)(b) or an activity condition imposed by the contact order; or
- (d) the child concerned.

(6) Where the person proposing to apply for an enforcement order in relation to a child arrangements order is the child concerned, the child must obtain the leave of the court before making such an application.

(7) The court may grant leave to the child concerned only if it is satisfied that he has sufficient understanding to make the proposed application.

(8) Subsection (2) has effect subject to the restrictions in sections 11K and 11L.

(9) The court may suspend an enforcement order for such period as it thinks fit.

(10) Nothing in this section prevents a court from making more than one enforcement order in relation to the same person on the same occasion.

(11) Proceedings in which any question of making an enforcement order, or any other question with respect to such an order, arises are to be regarded for the purposes of section 11(1) and (2) as proceedings in which a question arises with respect to a section 8 order.

(12) In Schedule A1—

- (a) Part 1 makes provision as regards an unpaid work requirement;
- (b) Part 2 makes provision in relation to the revocation and amendment of enforcement orders and failure to comply with such orders.

(13) …

11K. Enforcement orders: further provision

(1) A court may not make an enforcement order against a person in respect of a failure to comply with a provision of a child arrangements order unless it is satisfied that before the failure occurred the person had been given (in accordance with rules of court) a copy of, or otherwise informed of the terms of—

- (a) in the case of a failure to comply with a provision of a child arrangements order where the order was varied before the failure occurred, a notice under section 11I relating to the order varying the child arrangements order or, where more than one such order has been made, the last order preceding the failure in question;
- (b) in any other case, a notice under section 11I relating to the child arrangements order.

(2) A court may not make an enforcement order against a person in respect of any failure to comply with a provision of a child arrangements order occurring before the person attained the age of 18.

(3) A court may not make an enforcement order against a person in respect of a failure to comply with a provision of a child arrangements order where the child arrangements order is an excepted order (within the meaning given by section 11B(4)).

(4) A court may not make an enforcement order against a person unless the person is habitually resident in England and Wales; and an enforcement order ceases to have effect if the person subject to the order ceases to be habitually resident in England and Wales.

11L. Enforcement orders: making

(1) Before making an enforcement order as regards a person in breach of a provision of a child arrangements order, the court must be satisfied that—

(a) making the enforcement order proposed is necessary to secure the person's compliance with the child arrangements order or any child arrangements order that has effect in its place;
(b) the likely effect on the person of the enforcement order proposed to be made is proportionate to the seriousness of the breach.

(2) Before making an enforcement order, the court must satisfy itself that provision for the person to work under an unpaid work requirement imposed by an enforcement order can be made in the local justice area in which the person in breach resides or will reside.

(3) Before making an enforcement order as regards a person in breach of a provision of a child arrangements order, the court must obtain and consider information about the person and the likely effect of the enforcement order on him.

(4) Information about the likely effect of the enforcement order may, in particular, include information as to—
(a) any conflict with the person's religious beliefs;
(b) any interference with the times (if any) at which he normally works or attends an educational establishment.

(5) A court that proposes to make an enforcement order may ask an officer of the Service or a Welsh family proceedings officer to provide the court with information as to the matters in subsections (2) and (3).

(6) It shall be the duty of the officer of the Service or Welsh family proceedings officer to comply with any request under this section.

(7) In making an enforcement order in relation to a child arrangements order, a court must take into account the welfare of the child who is the subject of the child arrangements order.

11M. Enforcement orders: monitoring

(1) On making an enforcement order in relation to a person, the court is to ask an officer of the Service or a Welsh family proceedings officer—
(a) to monitor, or arrange for the monitoring of, the person's compliance with the unpaid work requirement imposed by the order;
(b) to report to the court if a report under paragraph 8 of Schedule A1 is made in relation to the person;
(c) to report to the court on such other matters relating to the person's compliance as may be specified in the request;
(d) to report to the court if the person is, or becomes, unsuitable to perform work under the requirement.

(2) It shall be the duty of the officer of the Service or Welsh family proceedings officer to comply with any request under this section.

11N. Enforcement orders: warning notices

Where the court makes an enforcement order, it is to attach to the order a notice warning of the consequences of failing to comply with the order.

11O. Compensation for financial loss

(1) This section applies if a child arrangements order with respect to a child has been made.

(2) If the court is satisfied that—
(a) an individual has failed to comply with a provision of the child arrangements order, and
(b) a person falling within subsection (6) has suffered financial loss by reason of the breach,

it may make an order requiring the individual in breach to pay the person compensation in respect of his financial loss.

(3) But the court may not make an order under subsection (2) if it is satisfied that the individual in breach had a reasonable excuse for failing to comply with the particular provision of the child arrangements order.

(4) The burden of proof as to the matter mentioned in subsection (3) lies on the individual claiming to have had a reasonable excuse.

(5) An order under subsection (2) may be made only on an application by the person who claims to have suffered financial loss.

(6) A person falls within this subsection if he is—
(a) a person who is, for the purposes of the child arrangements order, the person with whom the child concerned lives or is to live;
(b) a person whose contact with the child concerned is provided for in the child arrangements order;
(c) an individual subject to a condition under section 11(7)(b) or an activity condition imposed by the child arrangements order; or
(d) the child concerned.

(7) Where the person proposing to apply for an order under subsection (2) is the child concerned, the child must obtain the leave of the court before making such an application.
(8) The court may grant leave to the child concerned only if it is satisfied that he has sufficient understanding to make the proposed application.
(9) The amount of compensation is to be determined by the court, but may not exceed the amount of the applicant's financial loss.
(10) In determining the amount of compensation payable by the individual in breach, the court must take into account the individual's financial circumstances.
(11) An amount ordered to be paid as compensation may be recovered by the applicant as a civil debt due to him.
(12) Subsection (2) has effect subject to the restrictions in section 11P.
(13) Proceedings in which any question of making an order under subsection (2) arises are to be regarded for the purposes of section 11(1) and (2) as proceedings in which a question arises with respect to a section 8 order.
(14) In exercising its powers under this section, a court is to take into account the welfare of the child concerned.

11P. Orders under section 11O(2): further provision

(1) A court may not make an order under section 11O(2) requiring an individual to pay compensation in respect of a failure by him to comply with a provision of a child arrangements order unless it is satisfied that before the failure occurred the individual had been given (in accordance with rules of court) a copy of, or otherwise informed of the terms of—
(a) in the case of a failure to comply with a provision of a child arrangements order where the order was varied before the failure occurred, a notice under section 11I relating to the order varying the child arrangements order or, where more than one such order has been made, the last order preceding the failure in question;
(b) in any other case, a notice under section 11I relating to the child arrangements order.
(2) A court may not make an order under section 11O(2) requiring an individual to pay compensation in respect of a failure by him to comply with a provision of a child arrangements order where the failure occurred before the individual attained the age of 18.
(3) A court may not make an order under section 11O(2) requiring an individual to pay compensation in respect of a failure by him to comply with a provision of a child arrangements order where the child arrangements order is an excepted order (within the meaning given by section 11B(4)).

12. Child arrangements orders and parental responsibility

(1) Where—
(a) the court makes a child arrangements order with respect to a child,
(b) the father of the child, or a woman who is a parent of the child by virtue of section 43 of the Human Fertilisation and Embryology Act 2008, is named in the order as a person with whom the child is to live, and
(c) the father, or the woman, would not otherwise have parental responsibility for the child,
the court must also make an order under section 4 giving the father, or under section 4ZA giving the woman, that responsibility.'
(1A) Where—
(a) the court makes a child arrangements order with respect to a child,
(b) the father of the child, or a woman who is a parent by virtue of section 43 of the Human Fertilisation and Embryology Act 2008, is named in the order as a person with whom the child is to spend time or otherwise have contact but is not named in the order as a person with whom the child is to live, and
(c) the father, or the woman, would not otherwise have parental responsibility for the child,
the court must decide whether it would be appropriate, in view of the provision made in the order with respect to the father or the woman, for him or her to have parental responsibility for the child and, if it decides that it would be appropriate for the father or the woman to have that responsibility, must also make an order under section 4 giving him, or under section 4ZA giving her, that responsibility.
(2) Where the court makes a child arrangements order and a person who is not a parent or guardian of the child concerned is named in the order as a person with whom the child is to live, that person shall have parental responsibility for the child while the order remains in force so far as providing for the child to live with that person.

(2A) Where the court makes a child arrangements order and—
(a) a person who is not a parent or guardian of the child concerned is named in the order as a person with whom the child is to spend time or otherwise have contact, but
(b) the person is not named in the order as a person with whom the child is to live,
the court may provide in the order for the person to have parental responsibility for the child while paragraphs (a) and (b) continue to be met in the person's case.
(3) Where a person has parental responsibility for a child as a result of subsection (2) or (2A), he shall not have the right—
(a) . . .
(b) to agree, or refuse to agree, to the making of an adoption order, or an order under section 84 of the Adoption and Children Act 2002, with respect to the child; or
(c) to appoint a guardian for the child.
(4) Where subsection (1) requires the court to make an order under section 4 or 4ZA in respect of a parent of a child, the court shall not bring that order to an end at any time while the child arrangements order concerned remains in force so far as providing for the child to live with that parent.
(5), (6) ...

13. Change of child's name or removal from jurisdiction

(1) Where a child arrangements order to which subsection (4) applies is in force with respect to a child, no person may—
(a) cause the child to be known by a new surname; or
(b) remove him from the United Kingdom;
without either the written consent of every person who has parental responsibility for the child or the leave of the court.
(2) Subsection (1)(b) does not prevent the removal of a child, for a period of less than one month, by a person named in the child arrangements order as a person with whom the child is to live.
(3) In making a child arrangements order to which subsection (4) applies, the court may grant the leave required by subsection (1)(b), either generally or for specified purposes.
(4) This subsection applies to a child arrangements order if the arrangements regulated by the order consist of, or include, arrangements which relate to either or both of the following—
(a) with whom the child concerned is to live, and
(b) when the child is to live with any person.

Special guardianship

14A. Special guardianship orders

(1) A 'special guardianship order' is an order appointing one or more individuals to be a child's 'special guardian' (or special guardians).
(2) A special guardian—
(a) must be aged eighteen or over; and
(b) must not be a parent of the child in question,
and subsections (3) to (6) are to be read in that light.
(3) The court may make a special guardianship order with respect to any child on the application of an individual who—
(a) is entitled to make such an application with respect to the child; or
(b) has obtained the leave of the court to make the application,
or on the joint application of more than one such individual.
(4) Section 9(3) applies in relation to an application for leave to apply for a special guardianship order as it applies in relation to an application for leave to apply for a section 8 order.
(5) The individuals who are entitled to apply for a special guardianship order with respect to a child are—
(a) any guardian of the child;
(b) any individual who is named in a child arrangements order as a person with whom the child is to live;
(c) any individual listed in subsection (5)(b) or (c) of section 10 (as read with subsection (10) of that section);
(d) a local authority foster parent with whom the child has lived for a period of at least one year immediately preceding the application.
(e) a relative with (e) whom the child has lived for a period of at least one year preceding the application.
(6) The court may also make a special guardianship order with respect to a child in any family proceedings in which a question arises with respect to the welfare of the child if—

(a) an application for the order has been made by an individual who falls within subsection (3)(a) or (b) (or more than one such individual jointly); or
(b) the court considers that a special guardianship order should be made even though no such application has been made.

(7) No individual may make an application under subsection (3) or (6)(a) unless, before the beginning of the period of three months ending with the date of the application, he has given written notice of his intention to make the application—
(a) if the child in question is being looked after by a local authority, to that local authority, or
(b) otherwise, to the local authority in whose area the individual is ordinarily resident.

(8) On receipt of such a notice, the local authority must investigate the matter and prepare a report for the court dealing with—
(a) the suitability of the applicant to be a special guardian;
(b) such matters (if any) as may be prescribed by the Secretary of State; and
(c) any other matter which the local authority consider to be relevant.

(9) The court may itself ask a local authority to conduct such an investigation and prepare such a report, and the local authority must do so.

(10) The local authority may make such arrangements as they see fit for any person to act on their behalf in connection with conducting an investigation or preparing a report referred to in subsection (8) or (9).

(11) The court may not make a special guardianship order unless it has received a report dealing with the matters referred to in subsection (8).

(12) Subsections (8) and (9) of section 10 apply in relation to special guardianship orders as they apply in relation to section 8 orders.

(13) This section is subject to section 29(5) and (6) of the Adoption and Children Act 2002.

14B. Special guardianship orders: making

(1) Before making a special guardianship order, the court must consider whether, if the order were made—
(a) a child arrangements order containing contact provision should also be made with respect to the child,
(b) any section 8 order in force with respect to the child should be varied or discharged,
(c) where provision contained in a child arrangements order made with respect to the child is not discharged, any enforcement order relating to that provision should be revoked, and
(d) where an activity direction has been made—
(i) in proceedings for the making, variation or discharge of a child arrangements order with respect to the child, or
(ii) in other proceedings that relate to such an order.
that direction should be discharged.

(1A) In subsection (1) 'contact provision' means provision which regulates arrangements relating to—
(a) with whom a child is to spend time or otherwise have contact, or
(b) when a child is to spend time or otherwise have contact with any person;
but in paragraphs (a) and (b) a reference to spending time or otherwise having contact with a person is to doing that otherwise than as a result of living with the person.

(2) On making a special guardianship order, the court may also—
(a) give leave for the child to be known by a new surname;
(b) grant the leave required by section 14C(3)(b), either generally or for specified purposes.

14C. Special guardianship orders: effect

(1) The effect of a special guardianship order is that while the order remains in force—
(a) a special guardian appointed by the order has parental responsibility for the child in respect of whom it is made; and
(b) subject to any other order in force with respect to the child under this Act, a special guardian is entitled to exercise parental responsibility to the exclusion of any other person with parental responsibility for the child (apart from another special guardian).

(2) Subsection (1) does not affect—
(a) the operation of any enactment or rule of law which requires the consent of more than one person with parental responsibility in a matter affecting the child; or
(b) any rights which a parent of the child has in relation to the child's adoption or placement for adoption.

(3) While a special guardianship order is in force with respect to a child, no person may—
(a) cause the child to be known by a new surname; or
(b) remove him from the United Kingdom,
without either the written consent of every person who has parental responsibility for the child or the leave of the court.

(4) Subsection (3)(b) does not prevent the removal of a child, for a period of less than three months, by a special guardian of his.

(5) If the child with respect to whom a special guardianship order is in force dies, his special guardian must take reasonable steps to give notice of that fact to—
(a) each parent of the child with parental responsibility; and
(b) each guardian of the child,
but if the child has more than one special guardian, and one of them has taken such steps in relation to a particular parent or guardian, any other special guardian need not do so as respects that parent or guardian.

(6) This section is subject to section 29(7) of the Adoption and Children Act 2002.

14D. Special guardianship orders: variation and discharge

(1) The court may vary or discharge a special guardianship order on the application of—
(a) the special guardian (or any of them, if there are more than one);
(b) any parent or guardian of the child concerned;
(c) any individual in whose favour a residence order is in force with respect to the child;
(d) any individual not falling within any of paragraphs (a) to (c) who has, or immediately before the making of the special guardianship order had, parental responsibility for the child;
(e) the child himself; or
(f) a local authority designated in a care order with respect to the child.

(2) In any family proceedings in which a question arises with respect to the welfare of a child with respect to whom a special guardianship order is in force, the court may also vary or discharge the special guardianship order if it considers that the order should be varied or discharged, even though no application has been made under subsection (1).

(3) The following must obtain the leave of the court before making an application under subsection (1)—
(a) the child;
(b) any parent or guardian of his;
(c) any step-parent of his who has acquired, and has not lost, parental responsibility for him by virtue of section 4A;
(d) any individual falling within subsection (1)(d) who immediately before the making of the special guardianship order had, but no longer has, parental responsibility for him.

(4) Where the person applying for leave to make an application under subsection (1) is the child, the court may only grant leave if it is satisfied that he has sufficient understanding to make the proposed application under subsection (1).

(5) The court may not grant leave to a person falling within subsection (3)(b)(c) or (d) unless it is satisfied that there has been a significant change in circumstances since the making of the special guardianship order.

14E. Special guardianship orders: supplementary

(1) In proceedings in which any question of making, varying or discharging a special guardianship order arises, the court shall (in the light of any rules made by virtue of subsection (3))—
(a) draw up a timetable with a view to determining the question without delay; and
(b) give such directions as it considers appropriate for the purpose of ensuring, so far as is reasonably practicable, that the timetable is adhered to.

(2) Subsection (1) applies also in relation to proceedings in which any other question with respect to a special guardianship order arises.

(3) The power to make rules in subsection (2) of section 11 applies for the purposes of this section as it applies for the purposes of that.

(4) A special guardianship order, or an order varying one, may contain provisions which are to have effect for a specified period.

(5) Section 11(7) (apart from paragraph (c)) applies in relation to special guardianship orders and orders varying them as it applies in relation to section 8 orders.

14F. Special guardianship support services

(1) Each local authority must make arrangements for the provision within their area of special guardianship support services, which means—
(a) counselling, advice and information; and
(b) such other services as are prescribed,
in relation to special guardianship.

(2) The power to make regulations under subsection (1)(b) is to be exercised so as to secure that local authorities provide financial support.

(3) At the request of any of the following persons—
(a) a child with respect to whom a special guardianship order is in force;
(b) a special guardian;

(c) a parent;
(d) any other person who falls within a prescribed description,
a local authority may carry out an assessment of that person's needs for special guardianship support services (but, if the Secretary of State so provides in regulations, they must do so if he is a person of a prescribed description, or if his case falls within a prescribed description, or if both he and his case fall within prescribed descriptions).

(4) A local authority may, at the request of any other person, carry out an assessment of that person's needs for special guardianship support services.

(5) Where, as a result of an assessment, a local authority decide that a person has needs for special guardianship support services, they must then decide whether to provide any such services to that person.

(6) If—
(a) a local authority decide to provide any special guardianship support services to a person, and
(b) the circumstances fall within a prescribed description,
the local authority must prepare a plan in accordance with which special guardianship support services are to be provided to him, and keep the plan under review.

(7) The Secretary of State may by regulations make provision about assessments, preparing and reviewing plans, the provision of special guardianship support services in accordance with plans and reviewing the provision of special guardianship support services.

(8) The regulations may in particular make provision—
(a) about the type of assessment which is to be carried out, or the way in which an assessment is to be carried out;
(b) about the way in which a plan is to be prepared;
(c) about the way in which, and the time at which, a plan or the provision of special guardianship support services is to be reviewed;
(d) about the considerations to which a local authority are to have regard in carrying out an assessment or review or preparing a plan;
(e) as to the circumstances in which a local authority may provide special guardianship support services subject to conditions (including conditions as to payment for the support or the repayment of financial support);
(f) as to the consequences of conditions imposed by virtue of paragraph (e) not being met (including the recovery of any financial support provided);
(g) as to the circumstances in which this section may apply to a local authority in respect of persons who are outside that local authority's area;
(h) as to the circumstances in which a local authority may recover from another local authority the expenses of providing special guardianship support services to any person.

(9) A local authority may provide special guardianship support services (or any part of them) by securing their provision by—
(a) another local authority; or
(b) a person within a description prescribed in regulations of persons who may provide special guardianship support services,
and may also arrange with any such authority or person for that other authority or that person to carry out the local authority's functions in relation to assessments under this section.

(10) A local authority may carry out an assessment of the needs of any person for the purposes of this section at the same time as an assessment of his needs is made under any other provision of this Act or under any other enactment.

(11) Section 27 (co-operation between authorities) applies in relation to the exercise of functions of a local authority under this section as it applies in relation to the exercise of functions of a local authority under Part 3.

14G. Special guardianship support services: representations

(1) Every local authority shall establish a procedure for considering representations (including complaints) made to them by any person to whom they may provide special guardianship support services about the discharge of their functions under section 14F in relation to him.

(2) Regulations may be made by the Secretary of State imposing time limits on the making of representations under subsection (1).

(3) In considering representations under subsection (1), a local authority shall comply with regulations (if any) made by the Secretary of State for the purposes of this subsection.

Financial relief

15. Orders for financial relief with respect to children

(1) Schedule 1 (which consists primarily of the re-enactment, with consequential amendments and minor modifications, of provisions of section 6 of the Family Law Reform Act 1969, the Guardianship of Minors Acts 1971 and 1973, the Children Act 1975 and of sections 15 and 16 of the Family Law Reform Act 1987) makes provision in relation to financial relief for children.

...

Family assistance orders

16. Family assistance orders

(1) Where, in any family proceedings, the court has power to make an order under this Part with respect to any child, it may (whether or not it makes such an order) make an order requiring—
 (a) an officer of the Service to be made available; or
 (b) a local authority to make an officer of the authority available,
 to advise, assist and (where appropriate) befriend any person named in the order.

(2) The persons who may be named in an order under this section ('a family assistance order') are—
 (a) any parent, guardian or special guardian of the child;
 (b) any person with whom the child is living or who is named in a child arrangements order as a person with whom the child is to live, spend time or otherwise have contact;
 (c) the child himself.

(3) No court may make a family assistance order unless—
 (a) ...
 (b) it has obtained the consent of every person to be named in the order other than the child.

(4) A family assistance order may direct—
 (a) the person named in the order; or
 (b) such of the persons named in the order as may be specified in the order,
 to take such steps as may be so specified with a view to enabling the officer concerned to be kept informed of the address of any person named in the order and to be allowed to visit any such person.

(4A) If the court makes a family assistance order with respect to a child and the order is to be in force at the same time as contact provision contained in a child arrangements order made with respect to the child, the family assistance order may direct the officer concerned to give advice and assistance as regards establishing, improving and maintaining contact to such of the persons named in the order as may be specified in the order.

(4B) In subsection (4A) 'contact provision' means provision which regulates arrangements relating to—
 (a) with whom a child is to spend time or otherwise have contact, or
 (b) when a child is to spend time or otherwise have contact with any person.

(5) Unless it specifies a shorter period, a family assistance order shall have effect for a period of twelve months beginning with the day on which it is made.

(6) If the court makes a family assistance order with respect to a child and the order is to be in force at the same time as a section 8 order made with respect to the child, the family assistance order may direct the officer concerned to report to the court on such matters relating to the section 8 order as the court may require (including the question whether the section 8 order ought to be varied or discharged).

(7) A family assistance order shall not be made so as to require a local authority to make an officer of theirs available unless—
 (a) the authority agree; or
 (b) the child concerned lives or will live within their area.

16A Risk assessments

(1) This section applies to the following functions of officers of the Service or Welsh family proceedings officers—
 (a) any function in connection with family proceedings in which the court has power to make an order under this Part with respect to a child or in which a question with respect to such an order arises;
 (b) any function in connection with an order made by the court in such proceedings.

(2) If, in carrying out any function to which this section applies, an officer of the Service or a Welsh family proceedings officer is given cause to suspect that the child concerned is at risk of harm, he must—
(a) make a risk assessment in relation to the child, and
(b) provide the risk assessment to the court.
(3) A risk assessment, in relation to a child who is at risk of suffering harm of a particular sort, is an assessment of the risk of that harm being suffered by the child.

PART III
LOCAL AUTHORITY SUPPORT FOR CHILDREN AND FAMILIES

Provision of services for children and their families

17. Provision of services for children in need, their families and others

(1) It shall be the general duty of every local authority (in addition to the other duties imposed on them by this Part)—
(a) to safeguard and promote the welfare of children within their area who are in need; and
(b) so far as is consistent with that duty, to promote the upbringing of such children by their families,
by providing a range and level of services appropriate to those children's needs.
(2) For the purpose principally of facilitating the discharge of their general duty under this section, every local authority shall have the specific duties and powers set out in Part 1 of Schedule 2.
(3) Any service provided by an authority in the exercise of functions conferred on them by this section may be provided for the family of a particular child in need or for any member of his family, if it is provided with a view to safeguarding or promoting the child's welfare.
(4) The Secretary of State may by order amend any provision of Part I of Schedule 2 or add any further duty or power to those for the time being mentioned there.
(4A) Before determining what (if any) services to provide for a particular child in need in the exercise of functions conferred on them by this section, a local authority shall, so far as is reasonably practicable and consistent with the child's welfare—
(a) ascertain the child's wishes and feelings regarding the provision of those services; and
(b) give due consideration (having regard to his age and understanding) to such wishes and feelings of the child as they have been able to ascertain.
(5) Every local authority—
(a) shall facilitate the provision by others (including in particular voluntary organisations) of services which the authority have power to provide by virtue of this section, or section 18, 20, 23, 23B to 23D, 24A or 24B; and
(b) may make such arrangements as they see fit for any person to act on their behalf in the provision of any such service.
(6) The services provided by a local authority in the exercise of functions conferred on them by this section may include providing accommodation and giving assistance in kind or, in exceptional circumstances, in cash.
(7) Assistance may be unconditional or subject to conditions as to the repayment of the assistance or of its value (in whole or in part).
(8) Before giving any assistance or imposing any conditions, a local authority shall have regard to the means of the child concerned and of each of his parents.
(9) No person shall be liable to make any repayment of assistance or of its value at any time when he is in receipt of any element of child tax credit other than the family element, of working tax credit or of an income-based jobseeker's allowance.
(10) For the purposes of this Part a child shall be taken to be in need if—
(a) he is unlikely to achieve or maintain, or to have the opportunity of achieving or maintaining, a reasonable standard of health or development without the provision for him of services by a local authority under this Part;
(b) his health or development is likely to be significantly impaired, or further impaired, without the provision for him of such services; or
(c) he is disabled,
and 'family', in relation to such a child, includes any person who has parental responsibility for the child and any other person with whom he has been living.
(11) For the purposes of this Part, a child is disabled if he is blind, deaf or dumb or suffers from mental disorder of any kind or is substantially and permanently handicapped by illness, injury or congenital deformity or such other disability as may be prescribed; and in this Part—

'development' means physical, intellectual, emotional, social or behavioural development; and
'health' means physical or mental health.

. . .

Provision of accommodation for children

20. Provision of accommodation for children: general

(1) Every local authority shall provide accommodation for any child in need within their area who appears to them to require accommodation as a result of—
(a) there being no person who has parental responsibility for him;
(b) his being lost or having been abandoned; or
(c) the person who has been caring for him being prevented (whether or not permanently, and for whatever reason) from providing him with suitable accommodation or care.

(2) Where a local authority provide accommodation under subsection (1) for a child who is ordinarily resident in the area of another local authority, that other local authority may take over the provision of accommodation for the child within—
(a) three months of being notified in writing that the child is being provided with accommodation; or
(b) such other longer period as may be prescribed.

(3) Every local authority shall provide accommodation for any child in need within their area who has reached the age of sixteen and whose welfare the authority consider is likely to be seriously prejudiced if they do not provide him with accommodation.

(4) A local authority may provide accommodation for any child within their area (even though a person who has parental responsibility for him is able to provide himwith accommodation) if they consider that to do so would safeguard or promote the child's welfare.

(5) A local authority may provide accommodation for any person who has reached the age of sixteen but is under twenty-one in any community home which takes children who have reached the age of sixteen if they consider that to do so would safeguard or promote his welfare.

(6) Before providing accommodation under this section, a local authority shall, so far as is reasonably practicable and consistent with the child's welfare—
(a) ascertain the child's wishes regarding the provision of accommodation; and
(b) give due consideration (having regard to his age and understanding) to such wishes of the child as they have been able to ascertain.

(7) A local authority may not provide accommodation under this section for any child if any person who—
(a) has parental responsibility for him;
(b) is willing and able to—
(i) provide accommodation for him; or
(ii) arrange for accommodation to be provided for him,
objects.

(8) Any person who has parental responsibility for a child may at any time remove the child from accommodation provided by or on behalf of the local authority under this section.

(9) Subsections (7) and (8) do not apply while any person—
(a) who is named in a child arrangements order as a person with whom the child is to live;
(aa) who is a special guardian of the child; or
(b) who has care of the child by virtue of an order made in the exercise of the High Court's inherent jurisdiction with respect to children,
agrees to the child being looked after in accommodation provided by or on behalf of the local authority.

(10) Where there is more than one such person as is mentioned in subsection (9), all of them must agree.

(11) Subsections (7) and (8) do not apply where a child who has reached the age of sixteen agrees to being provided with accommodation under this section.

Duties of local authorities in relation to children looked after by them

22. General duty of local authority in relation to children looked after by them

(1) In this Act, any reference to a child who is looked after by a local authority is a reference to a child who is—
(a) in their care; or

(b) provided with accommodation by the authority in the exercise of any functions (in particular those under this Act) which are social services functions within the meaning of the Local Authority Social Services Act 1970, apart from functions under sections 17, 23B and 24B.

(2) In subsection (1) 'accommodation' means accommodation which is provided for a continuous period of more than 24 hours.

(3) It shall be the duty of a local authority looking after any child—
(a) to safeguard and promote his welfare; and
(b) to make such use of services available for children cared for by their own parents as appears to the authority reasonable in his case.

(3A) The duty of a local authority under subsection (3)(a) to safeguard and promote the welfare of a child looked after by them includes in particular a duty to promote the child's educational achievement.

(3B) A local authority in England must appoint at least one person for the purpose of discharging the duty imposed by virtue of subsection (3A).

(3C) A person appointed by a local authority under subsection (3B) must be an officer employed by that authority or another local authority in England.

(4) Before making any decision with respect to a child whom they are looking after, or proposing to look after, a local authority shall, so far as is reasonably practicable, ascertain the wishes and feelings of—
(a) the child;
(b) his parents;
(c) any person who is not a parent of his but who has parental responsibility for him; and
(d) any other person whose wishes and feelings the authority consider to be relevant,
regarding the matter to be decided.

(5) In making any such decision a local authority shall give due consideration—
(a) having regard to his age and understanding, to such wishes and feelings of the child as they have been able to ascertain;
(b) to such wishes and feelings of any person mentioned in subsection (4)(b) to (d) as they have been able to ascertain; and
(c) to the child's religious persuasion, racial origin and cultural and linguistic background.

(6) If it appears to a local authority that it is necessary, for the purpose of protecting members of the public from serious injury, to exercise their powers with respect to a child whom they are looking after in a manner which may not be consistent with their duties under this section, they may do so.

(7) If the Secretary of State considers it necessary, for the purpose of protecting members of the public from serious injury, to give directions to a local authority with respect to the exercise of their powers with respect to a child whom they are looking after, he may give such directions to the authority.

(8) Where any such directions are given to an authority they shall comply with them even though doing so is inconsistent with their duties under this section.

22A. Provision of accommodation for children in care

When a child is in the care of a local authority, it is their duty to provide the child with accommodation.

22B. Maintenance of looked after children

It is the duty of a local authority to maintain a child they are looking after in other respects apart from the provision of accommodation.

22C. Ways in which looked after children are to be accommodated and maintained

(1) This section applies where a local authority are looking after a child ('C').

(2) The local authority must make arrangements for C to live with a person who falls within subsection (3) (but subject to subsection (4)).

(3) A person ('P')falls within this subsection if—
(a) P is a parent of C;
(b) P is not a parent of C but has parental responsibility for C; or
(c) in a case where C is in the care of the local authority and there was a child arrangements order in force with respect to C immediately before the care order was made, P was a person named in the child arrangements order as a person with whom C was to live.

(4) Subsection (2) does not require the local authority to make arrangements of the kind mentioned in that subsection if doing so—
(a) would not be consistent with C's welfare; or
(b) would not be reasonably practicable.

(5) If the local authority are unable to make arrangements under subsection (2), they must place C in the placement which is, in their opinion, the most appropriate placement available.

(6) In subsection (5) 'placement' means—
(a) placement with an individual who is a relative, friend or other person connected with C and who is also a local authority foster parent;
(b) placement with a local authority foster parent who does not fall within paragraph (a);
(c) placement in a children's home in respect of which a person is registered under Part 2 of the Care Standards Act 2000; or
(d) subject to section 22D, placement in accordance with other arrangements which comply with any regulations made for the purposes of this section.

(7) In determining the most appropriate placement for C, the local authority must, subject to the other provisions of this Part (in particular, to their duties under section 22)—
(a) give preference to a placement falling within paragraph (a) of subsection (6) over placements falling within the other paragraphs of that subsection;
(b) comply, so far as is reasonably practicable in all the circumstances of C's case, with the requirements of subsection (8); and
(c) comply with subsection (9) unless that is not reasonably practicable.

(8) The local authority must ensure that the placement is such that—
(a) it allows C to live near C's home;
(b) it does not disrupt C's education or training;
(c) if C has a sibling for whom the local authority are also providing accommodation, it enables C and the sibling to live together;
(d) if C is disabled, the accommodation provided is suitable to C's particular needs.

(9) The placement must be such that C is provided with accommodation within the local authority's area.

(9A) Subsection (9B) applies subject to subsection (9C) where the local authority are a local authority in England and—
(a) are considering adoption for C, or
(b) are satisfied that C ought to be placed for adoption but are not authorised under section 19 of the Adoption and Children Act 2002 (placement with parental consent) or by virtue of section 21 of that Act (placement orders) to place C for adoption.

(9B) Where this subsection applies—
(a) subsections (7) to (9) do not apply to the local authority,
(b) the local authority must consider placing C with an individual within subsection (6)(a), and
(c) where the local authority decide that a placement with such an individual is not the most appropriate placement for C, the local authority must consider placing C with a local authority foster parent who has been approved as a prospective adopter.

(9C) Subsection (9B) does not apply where the local authority have applied for a placement order under section 21 of the Adoption and Children Act 2002 in respect of C and the application has been refused.

(10) The local authority may determine—
(a) the terms of any arrangements they make under subsection (2) in relation to C (including terms as to payment); and
(b) the terms on which they place C with a local authority foster parent (including terms as to payment but subject to any order made under section 49 of the Children Act 2004).

(11) The appropriate national authority may make regulations for, and in connection with, the purposes of this section.

(12) In this Act 'local authority foster parent' means a person who is approved as a local authority foster parent in accordance with regulations made by virtue of paragraph 12F of Schedule 2.

22F. Regulations as to children looked after by local authorities

Part 2 of Schedule 2 has effect for the purposes of making further provision as to children looked after by local authorities and in particular as to the regulations which may be made under section 22C(11).

22G. General duty of local authority to secure sufficient accommodation for looked after children

(1) It is the general duty of a local authority to take steps that secure, so far as reasonably practicable, the outcome in subsection (2).

(2) The outcome is that the local authority are able to provide the children mentioned in subsection (3) with accommodation that—
(a) is within the authority's area; and
(b) meets the needs of those children.

(3) The children referred to in subsection (2) are those—
(a) that the local authority are looking after,
(b) in respect of whom the authority are unable to make arrangements under section 22C(2), and
(c) whose circumstances are such that it would be consistent with their welfare for them to be provided with accommodation that is in the authority's area.

(4) In taking steps to secure the outcome in subsection (2), the local authority must have regard to the benefit of having—
(a) a number of accommodation providers in their area that is, in their opinion, sufficient to secure that outcome; and
(b) a range of accommodation in their area capable of meeting different needs that is, in their opinion, sufficient to secure that outcome.

(5) In this section 'accommodation providers' means— local authority foster parents; and children's homes in respect of which a person is registered under Part 2 of the Care Standards Act 2000.

23ZA. Duty of local authority to ensure visits to, and contact with, looked after children and others

(1) This section applies to—
(a) a child looked after by a local authority;
(b) a child who was looked after by a local authority but who has ceased to be looked after by them as a result of prescribed circumstances.

(2) It is the duty of the local authority—
(a) to ensure that a person to whom this section applies is visited by a representative of the authority ('a representative');
(b) to arrange for appropriate advice, support and assistance to be available to a person to whom this section applies who seeks it from them.

(3) The duties imposed by subsection (2)—
(a) are to be discharged in accordance with any regulations made for the purposes of this section by the appropriate national authority;
(b) are subject to any requirement imposed by or under an enactment applicable to the place in which the person to whom this section applies is accommodated.

(4) Regulations under this section for the purposes of subsection (3)(a) may make provision about—
(a) the frequency of visits;
(b) circumstances in which a person to whom this section applies must be visited by a representative; and
(c) the functions of a representative.

(5) In choosing a representative a local authority must satisfy themselves that the person chosen has the necessary skills and experience to perform the functions of a representative.

Advice and assistance for certain children and young persons

23A. The responsible authority and relevant children

(1) The responsible local authority shall have the functions set out in section 23B in respect of a relevant child.

(2) In subsection (1) 'relevant child' means (subject to subsection (3)) a child who—
(a) is not being looked after by any local authority;
(b) was, before last ceasing to be looked after, an eligible child for the purposes of paragraph 19B of Schedule 2; and
(c) is aged sixteen or seventeen.

(3) The appropriate national authority may prescribe—
(a) additional categories of relevant children; and
(b) categories of children who are not to be relevant children despite falling within subsection (2).

(4) In subsection (1) the 'responsible local authority' is the one which last looked after the child.

(5) If under subsection (3)(a) the appropriate national authority prescribes a category of relevant children which includes children who do not fall within subsection (2)(b) (for example, because they were being looked after by a local authority in Scotland), the appropriate national authority may in the regulations also provide for which local authority is to be the responsible local authority for those children.

23B. Additional functions of the responsible authority in respect of relevant children

(1) It is the duty of each local authority to take reasonable steps to keep in touch with a relevant child for whom they are the responsible authority, whether he is within their area or not.

(2) It is the duty of each local authority to appoint a personal adviser for each relevant child (if they have not already done so under paragraph 19C of Schedule 2).

(3) It is the duty of each local authority, in relation to any relevant child who does not already have a pathway plan prepared for the purposes of paragraph 19B of Schedule 2—

(a) to carry out an assessment of his needs with a view to determining what advice, assistance and support it would be appropriate for them to provide him under this Part; and

(b) to prepare a pathway plan for him.

(4)–(7) ...

(8) The responsible local authority shall safeguard and promote the child's welfare and, unless they are satisfied that his welfare does not require it, support him by—

(a) maintaining him;

(b) providing him with or maintaining him in suitable accommodation; and

(c) providing support of such other descriptions as may be prescribed.

(9) Support under subsection (8) may be in cash.

(10) The appropriate national authority may by regulations make provision about the meaning of 'suitable accommodation' and in particular about the suitability of landlords or other providers of accommodation.

(11) If the local authority have lost touch with a relevant child, despite taking reasonable steps to keep in touch, they must without delay—

(a) consider how to re-establish contact; and

(b) take reasonable steps to do so,

and while the child is still a relevant child must continue to take such steps until they succeed.

(12) Subsections (7) to (9) of section 17 apply in relation to support given under this section as they apply in relation to assistance given under that section.

(13) Subsections (4) and (5) of section 22 apply in relation to any decision by a local authority for the purposes of this section as they apply in relation to the decisions referred to in that section.

23C. Continuing functions in respect of former relevant children

(1) Each local authority shall have the duties provided for in this section towards—

(a) a person who has been a relevant child for the purposes of section 23A (and would be one if he were under eighteen), and in relation to whom they were the last responsible authority; and

(b) a person who was being looked after by them when he attained the age of eighteen, and immediately before ceasing to be looked after was an eligible child,

and in this section such a person is referred to as a 'former relevant child'.

(2) It is the duty of the local authority to take reasonable steps—

(a) to keep in touch with a former relevant child whether he is within their area or not; and

(b) if they lose touch with him, to re-establish contact.

(3) It is the duty of the local authority—

(a) to continue the appointment of a personal adviser for a former relevant child; and

(b) to continue to keep his pathway plan under regular review.

(4) It is the duty of the local authority to give a former relevant child—

(a) assistance of the kind referred to in section 24B(1), to the extent that his welfare requires it;

(b) assistance of the kind referred to in section 24B(2), to the extent that his welfare and his educational or training needs require it;

(c) other assistance, to the extent that his welfare requires it.

(5) The assistance given under subsection (4)(c) may be in kind or, in exceptional circumstances, in cash.

(5A) It is the duty of the local authority to pay the relevant amount to a former relevant child who pursues higher education in accordance with a pathway plan prepared for that person.

(5B) The appropriate national authority may by regulations—

(a) prescribe the relevant amount for the purposes of subsection (5A);

(b) prescribe the meaning of 'higher education' for those purposes;

(c) make provision as to the payment of the relevant amount;

(d) make provision as to the circumstances in which the relevant amount (or any part of it) may be recovered by the local authority from a former relevant child to whom a payment has been made.

(5C) The duty set out in subsection (5A) is without prejudice to that set out in subsection (4)(b).

(6) Subject to subsection (7), the duties set out in subsections (2), (3) and (4) subsist until the former relevant child reaches the age of twenty-one.

(7) If the former relevant child's pathway plan sets out a programme of education or training which extends beyond his twenty-first birthday—

(a) the duty set out in subsection (4)(b) continues to subsist for so long as the former relevant child continues to pursue that programme; and

(b) the duties set out in subsections (2) and (3) continue to subsist concurrently with that duty.

(8) For the purposes of subsection (7)(a) there shall be disregarded any interruption in a former relevant child's pursuance of a programme of education or training if the local authority are satisfied that he will resume it as soon as is reasonably practicable.

(9) Section 24B(5) applies in relation to a person being given assistance under subsection (4)(b) or who is in receipt of a payment under subsection (5A) as it applies in relation to a person to whom section 24B(3) applies.

(10) Subsections (7) to (9) of section 17 apply in relation to assistance given under this section as they apply in relation to assistance given under that section.

23CZA. Arrangements for certain former relevant children to continue to live with former foster parents

(1) Each local authority in England have the duties provided for in subsection (3) in relation to staying put arrangements.

(2) A 'staying put arrangement' is an arrangement under which—

(a) a person who is a former relevant child by virtue of section 23(1)(b), and

(b) a person ('a former foster parent') who was the relevant child's former local authority foster parent immediately before the former relevant child ceased to be looked after by the local authority,

continue to live together after the former relevant child ceases to be looked after.

(3) It is the duty of the local authority (in discharging the duties in section 23C(3) and by other means)—

(a) to monitor the staying put arrangement, and

(b) to provide advice, assistance and support to the former relevant child and the former foster parent with a view to maintaining the staying put arrangement.

(4) Support provided to the former foster parent under subsection (3)(b) must include financial support.

(5) Subsection (3)(b) does not apply if the local authority consider that the staying put arrangement is not consistent with the welfare of the former relevant child.

(6) The duties set out in subsection (3) subsist until the former relevant child reaches the age of 21.

23CA. Further assistance to pursue education or training

(1) This section applies to a person if—

(a) he is under the age of twenty-five or of such lesser age as may be prescribed by the appropriate national authority;

(b) he is a former relevant child (within the meaning of section 23C) towards whom the duties imposed by subsections (2), (3) and (4) of that section no longer subsist; and

(c) he has informed the responsible local authority that he is pursuing, or wishes to pursue, a programme of education or training.

(2) It is the duty of the responsible local authority to appoint a personal adviser for a person to whom this section applies.

(3) It is the duty of the responsible local authority—

(a) to carry out an assessment of the needs of a person to whom this section applies with a view to determining what assistance (if any) it would be appropriate for them to provide to him under this section; and

(b) to prepare a pathway plan for him.

(4) It is the duty of the responsible local authority to give assistance of a kind referred to subsection (5) to a person to whom this section applies to the extent that his educational or training needs require it.

(5) The kinds of assistance are—

(a) contributing to expenses incurred by him in living near the place where he is, or will be, receiving education or training; or

(b) making a grant to enable him to meet expenses connected with his education and training.

(6) If a person to whom this section applies pursues a programme of education or training in accordance with the pathway plan prepared for him, the duties of the local authority

under this section (and under any provision applicable to the pathway plan prepared under this section for that person) subsist for as long as he continues to pursue that programme.

(7) For the purposes of subsection (6), the local authority may disregard any interruption in the person's pursuance of a programme of education or training if they are satisfied that he will resume it as soon as is reasonably practicable.

(8) Subsections (7) to (9) of section 17 apply to assistance given to a person under this section as they apply to assistance given to or in respect of a child under that section, but with the omission in subsection (8) of the words 'and of each of his parents'.

(9) Subsection (5) of section 24B applies to a person to whom this section applies as it applies to a person to whom subsection (3) of that section applies.

(10) Nothing in this section affects the duty imposed by subsection (5A) of section 23C to the extent that it subsists in relation to a person to whom this section applies; but the duty to make a payment under that subsection may be taken into account in the assessment of the person's needs under subsection (3)(a).

(11) In this section 'the responsible local authority' means, in relation to a person to whom this section applies, the local authority which had the duties provided for in section 23C towards him.

Personal advisers and pathway plans

23D. Personal advisers

(1) The appropriate national authority may by regulations require local authorities to appoint a personal adviser for children or young persons of a prescribed description who have reached the age of sixteen but not the age of twenty-five who are not—

(a) children who are relevant children for the purposes of section 23A;

(b) the young persons referred to in section 23C; or

(c) the children referred to in paragraph 19C of Schedule 2; or

(d) persons to whom section 23CA applies.

(2) Personal advisers appointed under or by virtue of this Part shall (in addition to any other functions) have such functions as the appropriate national authority prescribes.

23E. Pathway plans

(1) In this Part, a reference to a 'pathway plan' is to a plan setting out—

(a) in the case of a plan prepared under paragraph 19B of Schedule 2—

(i) the advice, assistance and support which the local authority intend to provide a child under this Part, both while they are looking after him and later; and

(ii) when they might cease to look after him; and

(b) in the case of a plan prepared under section 23B, the advice, assistance and support which the local authority intend to provide under this Part,

and dealing with such other matters (if any) as may be prescribed.

(1A) A local authority may carry out an assessment under section 23B(3) or 23CA(3) of a person's needs at the same time as any assessment of his needs is made under—

(a) the Chronically Sick and Disabled Persons Act 1970;

(b) Part 4 of the Education Act 1996 (in the case of an assessment under section 23B(3));

(c) the Disabled Persons (Services, Consultation and Representation) Act 1986; or

(d) any other enactment.

(IB) The appropriate national authority may by regulations make provision as to assessments for the purposes of section 23B(3) or 23CA.

(IC) Regulations under subsection (1B) may in particular make provision about—

(a) who is to be consulted in relation to an assessment;

(b) the way in which an assessment is to be carried out, by whom and when;

(c) the recording of the results of an assessment;

(d) the considerations to which a local authority are to have regard in carrying out an assessment.

(ID) A local authority shall keep each pathway plan prepared by them under section 23B or 23CA under review.

(2) The appropriate national authority may by regulations make provision about pathway plans and their review.

Secure accomodation

27. Co-operation between authorities

(1) Where it appears to a local authority that any authority ... mentioned in subsection (3) could, by taking any specified action, help in the exercise of any of their functions under this Part, they may request the help of that other authority ... specifying the action in question.

(2) An authority whose help is so requested shall comply with the request if it is compatible with their own statutory or other duties and obligations and does not unduly prejudice the discharge of any of their functions.

(3) The authorities are—
  (a) any local authority;
  (b) any local education authority;
  (c) any local housing authority;
  (d) any Local Health Board, Special Health Authority, Primary Care Trust, National Health Service trust or NHS foundation trust; and
  (e) any person authorised by the Secretary of State for the purposes of this section.

PART IV
CARE AND SUPERVISION

General

31. Care and supervision orders

(1) On the application of any local authority or authorised person, the court may make an order—
  (a) placing the child with respect to whom the application is made in the care of a designated local authority; or
  (b) putting him under the supervision of a designated local authority.

(2) A court may only make a care order or supervision order if it is satisfied—
  (a) that the child concerned is suffering, or is likely to suffer, significant harm; and
  (b) that the harm, or likelihood of harm, is attributable to—
    (i) the care given to the child, or likely to be given to him if the order were not made, not being what it would be reasonable to expect a parent to give to him; or
    (ii) the child's being beyond parental control.

(3) No care order or supervision order may be made with respect to a child who has reached the age of seventeen (or sixteen, in the case of a child who is married).

(3A) No care order made by made with respect to a child until the court has considered a section 31A care plan.

(3B) For the purposes of subsection (3A), the permanence provisions of the section 31A plan are such of the plan's provision setting out the long term plan for the upbringing of the child concerned as provide for any of the following—
  (a) the child to live with any parent of the child's or with any other member, or with any friend of, the child's family;
  (b) adoption;
  (c) long term care not within paragraph (a) or (b).

(3C) The Secretary of State may by regulations amend this section for the purpose of altering what for the purposes of subsection (3A) are the performance provisions of a section 31A plan.

(4) An application under this section may be made on its own or in any other family proceedings.

(5) The court may—
  (a) on an application for a care order, make a supervision order;
  (b) on an application for a supervision order, make a care order.

(6) Where an authorised person proposes to make an application under this section he shall—
  (a) if it is reasonably practicable to do so; and
  (b) before making the application,

consult the local authority appearing to him to be the authority in whose area the child concerned is ordinarily resident.

(7) An application made by an authorised person shall not be entertained by the court if, at the time when it is made, the child concerned is—
  (a) the subject of an earlier application for a care order, or supervision order, which has not been disposed of; or
  (b) subject to—

(i) a care order or supervision order;
(ii) an order under section 63(1) of the Powers of Criminal Courts (Sentencing) Act 2000; . . .

(8) The local authority designated in a care order must be—
(a) the authority within whose area the child is ordinarily resident; or
(b) where the child does not reside in the area of a local authority, the authority within whose area any circumstances arose in consequence of which the order is being made.

(9) In this section—
'authorised person' means—
(a) the National Society for the Prevention of Cruelty to Children and any of its officers; and
(b) any person authorised by order of the Secretary of State to bring proceedings under this section and any officer of a body which is so authorised.

'harm' means ill-treatment or the impairment of health or development including, for example, impairment suffered from seeing or hearing the ill-treatment of another;
'development' means physical, intellectual, emotional, social or behavioural development;
'health' means physical or mental health; and
'ill-treatment' includes sexual abuse and forms of ill-treatment which are not physical.

(10) Where the question of whether harm suffered by a child is significant turns on the child's health or development, his health or development shall be compared with that which could reasonably be expected of a similar child.

(11) In this Act—
'a care order' means (subject to section 105(1)) an order under subsection (1)(a) and (except where express provision to the contrary is made) includes an interim care order made under section 38; and
'a supervision order' means an order under subsection (1)(b) and (except where express provision to the contrary is made) includes an interim supervision order made under section 38.

31A. Care orders: care plans

(1) Where an application is made on which a care order might be made with respect to a child, the appropriate local authority must, within such time as the court may direct, prepare a plan ('a care plan') for the future care of the child.
(2) While the application is pending, the authority must keep any care plan prepared by them under review and, if they are of the opinion some change is required, revise the plan, or make a new plan, accordingly.
(3) A care plan must give any prescribed information and do so in the prescribed manner.
(4) For the purposes of this section, the appropriate local authority, in relation to a child in respect of whom a care order might be made, is the local authority proposed to be designated in the order.
(4A) In this section 'prescribed'—
(a) in relation to a care plan whose preparation is the responsibility of a local authority for an area in England, means prescribed by the Secretary of State; and
(b) in relation to a care plan whose preparation is the responsibility of a local authority in Wales, means prescribed by the Welsh Ministers.
(5) In section 31(3A) and this section, references to a care order do not include an interim care order.
(6) A plan prepared, or treated as prepared, under this section is referred to in this Act as a 'section 31A care plan'.

32. Period within which application for order under this Part must be disposed of

(1) A court in which an application for an order under this Part is proceeding shall (in the light of any provision in rules of court that is of a kind mentioned in subsection (2)(a) or (b)—
(a) draw up a timetable with a view to disposing of the application—
(i) without delay; and
(ii) in any event within twenty-six weeks beginning with the day on which the application was issued; and
(b) give such directions as it considers appropriate for the purpose of ensuring, so far as is reasonably practicable, that that timetable is adhered to.
(2) Rules of court may—
(a) specify periods within which specified steps must be taken in relation to such proceedings; and

(b) make other provision with respect to such proceedings for the purpose of ensuring, so far as is reasonably practicable, that they are disposed of without delay.

. . .

Care orders

33. Effect of care order

(1) Where a care order is made with respect to a child it shall be the duty of the local authority designated by the order to receive the child into their care and to keep him in their care while the order remains in force.

(2) Where—

(a) a care order has been made with respect to a child on the application of an authorised person; but

(b) the local authority designated by the order was not informed that that person proposed to make the application,

the child may be kept in the care of that person until received into the care of the authority.

(3) While a care order is in force with respect to a child, the local authority designated by the order shall—

(a) have parental responsibility for the child; and

(b) have the power (subject to the following provisions of this section) to determine the extent to which—

(i) a parent, guardian or special guardian of the child; or

(ii) a person who by virtue of section 4A has parental responsibility for the child,

may meet his parental responsibility for him.

(4) The authority may not exercise the power in subsection (3)(b) unless they are satisfied that it is necessary to do so in order to safeguard or promote the child's welfare.

(5) Nothing in subsection (3)(b) shall prevent a person mentioned in that provision who has care of the child from doing what is reasonable in all the circumstances of the case for the purpose of safeguarding or promoting his welfare.

(6) While a care order is in force with respect to a child, the local authority designated by the order shall not—

(a) cause the child to be brought up in any religious persuasion other than that in which he would have been brought up if the order had not been made; or

(b) have the right—

(i) . . .

(ii) to agree or refuse to agree to the making of an adoption order, or an order under section 84 of the Adoption and Children Act 2002 with respect to the child; or

(iii) to appoint a guardian for the child.

(7) While a care order is in force with respect to a child, no person may—

(a) cause the child to be known by a new surname; or

(b) remove him from the United Kingdom,

without either the written consent of every person who has parental responsibility for the child or the leave of the court.

(8) Subsection (7)(b) does not—

(a) prevent the removal of such a child, for a period of less than one month, by the authority in whose care he is; or

(b) apply to arrangements for such a child to live outside England and Wales (which are governed by paragraph 19 of Schedule 2).

(9) The power in subsection (3)(b) is subject (in addition to being subject to the provisions of this section) to any right, duty, power, responsibility or authority which a person mentioned in that provision has in relation to the child and his property by virtue of any other enactment.

34. Parental contact etc. with children in care

(1) Where a child is in the care of a local authority, the authority shall (subject to the provisions of this section) allow the child reasonable contact with—

(a) his parents;

(b) any guardian or special guardian of his;

(ba) any person who by virtue of section 4A has parental responsibility for him;

(c) where there was a child arrangements order in force with respect to the child immediately before the care order was made, any person named in the child arrangements order as a person with whom the child was to live; and

(d) where, immediately before the care order was made, a person had care of the child by virtue of an order made in the exercise of the High Court's inherent jurisdiction with respect to children, that person.

(2) On the application made by the authority or the child, the court may make such order as it considers appropriate with respect to the contact which is to be allowed between the child and any named person.

(3) On an application made by—

(a) any person mentioned in paragraphs (a) to (d) of subsection (1); or

(b) any person who has obtained the leave of the court to make the application,

the court may make such order as it considers appropriate with respect to the contact which is to be allowed between the child and that person.

(4) On an application made by the authority or the child, the court may make an order authorising the authority to refuse to allow contact between the child and any person who is mentioned in paragraphs (a) to (d) of subsection (1) and named in the order.

(5) When making a care order with respect to a child, or in any family proceedings in connection with a child who is in the care of a local authority, the court may make an order under this section, even though no application for such an order has been made with respect to the child, if it considers that the order should be made.

(6) An authority may refuse to allow the contact that would otherwise be required by virtue of subsection (1) or an order under this section if—

(a) they are satisfied that it is necessary to do so in order to safeguard or promote the child's welfare; and

(b) the refusal—

(i) is decided upon as a matter of urgency; and

(ii) does not last for more than seven days.

(6A) Where (by virtue of an order under this section, or because subsection (6) applies) a local authority in England are authorised to refuse to allow contact between the child and a person mentioned in any of paragraphs (a) to (c) of paragraph 15(1) of Schedule 2, paragraph 15(1) of that Schedule does not require the local authority to endeavour to promote contact between the child and that person.

(7) An order under this section may impose such conditions as the court considers appropriate.

(8) The Secretary of State may by regulations make provision as to—

(a) the steps to be taken by a local authority who have exercised their powers under subsection (6);

(b) the circumstances in which, and conditions subject to which, the terms of any order made under this section may be departed from by agreement between the local authority and the person in relation to whom this order is made;

(c) notification by a local authority of any variation or suspension of arrangements made (otherwise than under an order under this section) with a view to affording any person contact with a child to whom this section applies.

(9) The court may vary or discharge any order made under this section on the application of the authority, the child concerned or the person named in the order.

(10) An order under this section may be made either at the same time as the care order itself or later.

(11) Before making a care order with respect to any child the court shall—

(a) consider the arrangements which the authority have made, or propose to make, for affording any person contact with a child to whom this section applies; and

(b) invite the parties to the proceedings to comment on those arrangements.

Supervision orders

35. Supervision orders

(1) While a supervision order is in force it shall be the duty of the supervisor—

(a) to advise, assist and befriend the supervised child;

(b) to take such steps as are reasonably necessary to give effect to the order; and

(c) where—

(i) the order is not wholly complied with; or

(ii) the supervisor considers that the order may no longer be necessary,

to consider whether or not to apply to the court for its variation or discharge.

(2) Parts I and II of Schedule 3 make further provision with respect to supervision orders.

36. Education supervision orders

(1) On the application of any local education authority, the court may make an order putting the child with respect to whom the application is made under the supervision of a designated local education authority.

(2) In this Act 'an education supervision order' means an order under subsection (1).

(3) A court may only make an education supervision order if it is satisfied that the child concerned is of compulsory school age and is not being properly educated.

(4) For the purposes of this section, a child is being properly educated only if he is receiving efficient full-time education suitable to his age, ability and aptitude and any special educational needs he may have.

(5) Where a child is—
(a) the subject of a school attendance order which is in force under section 437 of the Education Act 1996 and which has not been complied with; or
(b) a registered pupil at a school which he is not attending regularly within the meaning of section 444 of that Act—
(i) the school at which he is a registered pupil.
(ii) any place at which education is provided for him in circumstances mentioned in subsection (1) or (1A) of section 444ZA of that Act, or
(iii) any place which he is required to attend in the circumstances mentioned in subsection (1B) or (2) of that section.

then, unless it is proved that he is being properly educated, it shall be assumed that he is not.

(6) An education supervision order may not be made with respect to a child who is in the care of a local authority.

(7) The local education authority designated in an education supervision order must be—
(a) the authority within whose area the child concerned is living or will live; or
(b) where—
(i) the child is a registered pupil at a school; and
(ii) the authority mentioned in paragraph (a) and the authority within whose area the school is situated agree,

the latter authority.

(8) Where a local education authority propose to make an application for an education supervision order they shall, before making the application, consult the appropriate local authority.

(9) The appropriate local authority is—
(a) in the case of a child who is being provided with accommodation by, or on behalf of, a local authority, that authority; and
(b) in any other case, the local authority within whose area the child concerned lives, or will live.

(10) Part III of Schedule 3 makes further provision with respect to education supervision orders.

Powers of court

37. Powers of court in certain family proceedings

(1) Where, in any family proceedings in which a question arises with respect to the welfare of any child, it appears to the court that it may be appropriate for a care or supervision order to be made with respect to him, the court may direct the appropriate authority to undertake an investigation of the child's circumstances.

(2) Where the court gives a direction under this section the local authority concerned shall, when undertaking the investigation, consider whether they should—
(a) apply for a care order or for a supervision order with respect to the child;
(b) provide services or assistance for the child or his family; or
(c) take any other action with respect to the child.

(3) Where a local authority undertake an investigation under this section, and decide not to apply for a care order or supervision order with respect to the child concerned, they shall inform the court of—
(a) their reasons for so deciding;
(b) any service or assistance which they have provided, or intend to provide, for the child and his family; and
(c) any other action which they have taken, or propose to take, with respect to the child.

(4) The information shall be given to the court before the end of the period of eight weeks beginning with the date of the direction, unless the court otherwise directs.

(5) The local authority named in a direction under subsection (1) must be—
(a) the authority in whose area the child is ordinarily resident; or
(b) where the child is not ordinarily resident in the area of a local authority, the authority within whose area any circumstances arose in consequence of which the direction is being given.

(6) If, on the conclusion of any investigation or review under this section, the authority decide not to apply for a care order or supervision order with respect to the child—
(a) they shall consider whether it would be appropriate to review the case at a later date; and
(b) if they decide that it would be, they shall determine the date on which that review is to begin.

38. Interim orders

(1) Where—
  (a) in any proceedings on an application for a care order or supervision order, the proceedings are adjourned; or
  (b) the court gives a direction under section 37(1),
the court may make an interim care order or an interim supervision order with respect to the child concerned.

(2) A court shall not make an interim care order or interim supervision order under this section unless it is satisfied that there are reasonable grounds for believing that the circumstances with respect to the child are as mentioned in section 31(2).

(3) Where, in any proceedings on an application for a care order or supervision order, a court makes a child arrangements order with respect to the living arrangements of the child concerned, it shall also make an interim supervision order with respect to him unless satisfied that his welfare will be satisfactorily safeguarded without an interim order being made.

(3A) For the purposes of subsection (3), a child arrangements order is one made with respect to the living arrangements of the child concerned if the arrangements regulated by the order consist of, or include, arrangements which relate to either or both of the following –
  (a) with whom the child is to live, and
  (b) when the child is to live with any person.

(4) An interim order made under or by virtue of this section shall have effect for such period as may be specified in the order, but shall in any event cease to have effect on whichever of the following events first occurs—
  ...
  (c) in a case which falls within subsection (1)(a), the disposal of the application;
  (d) in a case which falls within subsection (1)(b), the disposal of an application for a care order or supervision order made by the authority with respect to the child;
  (da) in a case which falls within subsection (1)(b) and in which –
    (i) no direction has been given under section 37(4), and
    (ii) no application for a care order or supervision order has been made with respect to the child,
  the expiry of eight weeks beginning with the date on which the order is made.
  (e) in a case which falls within subsection (1)(b) and in which—
    (i) the court has given a direction under section 37(4), but
    (ii) no application for a care order or supervision order has been made with respect to the child,
  the expiry of the period fixed by that direction.

...

(6) Where the court makes an interim care order, or interim supervision order, it may give such directions (if any) as it considers appropriate with regard to the medical or psychiatric examination or other assessment of the child; but if the child is of sufficient understanding to make an informed decision he may refuse to submit to the examination or other assessment.

(7) A direction under subsection (6) may be to the effect that there is to be—
  (a) no such examination or assessment; or
  (b) no such examination or assessment unless the court directs otherwise.

(8) A direction under subsection (6) may be—
  (a) given when the interim order is made or at any time while it is in force; and
  (b) varied at any time on the application of any person falling within any class of person prescribed by rules of court for the purposes of this subsection.

(9) Paragraphs 4 and 5 of Schedule 3 shall not apply in relation to an interim supervision order.

(10) Where a court makes an order under or by virtue of this section it shall, in determining the period for which the order is to be in force, consider whether any party who was, or might have been, opposed to the making of the order was in a position to argue his case against the order in full.

38A. Power to include exclusion requirement in interim care order

(1) Where—
  (a) on being satisfied that there are reasonable grounds for believing that the circumstances with respect to a child are as mentioned in section 31(2)(a) and (b)(i), the court makes an interim care order with respect to a child, and
  (b) the conditions mentioned in subsection (2) are satisfied,
the court may include an exclusion requirement in the interim care order.

(2) The conditions are—
  (a) that there is reasonable cause to believe that, if a person ('the relevant person') is excluded from a dwelling-house in which the child lives, the child will cease to suffer, or cease to be likely to suffer, significant harm, and

(b) that another person living in the dwelling-house (whether a parent of the child or some other person)—
(i) is able and willing to give to the child the care which it would be reasonable to expect a parent to give him, and
(ii) consents to the inclusion of the exclusion requirement.

(3) For the purposes of this section an exclusion requirement is any one or more of the following—
(a) a provision requiring the relevant person to leave a dwelling-house in which he is living with the child,
(b) a provision prohibiting the relevant person from entering a dwelling-house in which the child lives, and
(c) a provision excluding the relevant person from a defined area in which a dwelling-house in which the child lives is situated.

(4) The court may provide that the exclusion requirement is to have effect for a shorter period than the other provisions of the interim care order.

(5) Where the court makes an interim care order containing an exclusion requirement, the court may attach a power of arrest to the exclusion requirement.

(6) Where the court attaches a power of arrest to an exclusion requirement of an interim care order, it may provide that the power of arrest is to have effect for a shorter period than the exclusion requirement.

(7) Any period specified for the purposes of subsection (4) or (6) may be extended by the court (on one or more occasions) on an application to vary or discharge the interim care order.

(8) Where a power of arrest is attached to an exclusion requirement of an interim care order by virtue of subsection (5), a constable may arrest without warrant any person whom he has reasonable cause to believe to be in breach of the requirement.

(9) Sections 47(7), (11) and (12) and 48 of, and Schedule 5 to, the Family Law Act 1996 shall have effect in relation to a person arrested under subsection (8) of this section as they have effect in relation to a person arrested under section 47(6) of that Act.

(10) If, while an interim care order containing an exclusion requirement is in force, the local authority have removed the child from the dwelling-house from which the relevant person is excluded to other accommodation for a continuous period of more than 24 hours, the interim care order shall cease to have effect in so far as it imposes the exclusion requirement.

38B. Undertakings relating to interim care orders

(1) In any case where the court has power to include an exclusion requirement in an interim care order, the court may accept an undertaking from the relevant person.

(2) No power of arrest may be attached to any undertaking given under subsection (1).

(3) An undertaking given to a court under subsection (1)—
(a) shall be enforceable as if it were an order of the court, and
(b) shall cease to have effect if, while it is in force, the local authority have removed the child from the dwelling-house from which the relevant person is excluded to other accommodation for a continuous period of more than 24 hours.

(4) This section has effect without prejudice to the powers of the High Court and county court apart from this section.

(5) In this section 'exclusion requirement' and 'relevant person' have the same meaning as in section 38A.

39. Discharge and variation etc. of care orders and supervision orders

(1) A care order may be discharged by the court on the application of—
(a) any person who has parental responsibility for the child;
(b) the child himself; or
(c) the local authority designated by the order.

(2) A supervision order may be varied or discharged by the court on the application of—
(a) any person who has parental responsibility for the child;
(b) the child himself; or
(c) the supervisor.

(3) On the application of a person who is not entitled to apply for the order to be discharged, but who is a person with whom the child is living, a supervision order may be varied by the court in so far as it imposes a requirement which affects that person.

(3A) On the application of a person who is not entitled to apply for the order to be discharged, but who is a person to whom an exclusion requirement contained in the order applies, an interim care order may be varied or discharged by the court in so far as it imposes the exclusion requirement.

(3B) Where a power of arrest has been attached to an exclusion requirement of an interim care order, the court may, on the application of any person entitled to apply for the discharge of the order so far as it imposes the exclusion requirement, vary or discharge the order in so far as it confers a power of arrest (whether or not any application has been made to vary or discharge any other provision of the order).

(4) Where a care order is in force with respect to a child the court may, on the application of any person entitled to apply for the order to be discharged, substitute a supervision order for the care order.

(5) When a court is considering whether to substitute one order for another under subsection (4) any provision of this Act which would otherwise require section 31(2) to be satisfied at the time when the proposed order is substituted or made shall be disregarded.

40. Orders pending appeals in cases about care or supervision orders

(1) Where—

(a) a court dismisses an application for a care order; and

(b) at the time when the court dismisses the application, the child concerned is the subject of an interim care order,

the court may make a care order with respect to the child to have effect subject to such directions (if any) as the court may see fit to include in the order.

(2) Where—

(a) a court dismisses an application for a care order, or an application for a supervision order; and

(b) at the time when the court dismisses the application, the child concerned is the subject of an interim supervision order,

the court may make a supervision order with respect to the child to have effect subject to such directions (if any) as the court may see fit to include in the order.

(3) Where a court grants an application to discharge a care order or supervision order, it may order that—

(a) its decision is not to have effect; or

(b) the care order, or supervision order, is to continue to have effect but subject to such directions as the court sees fit to include in the order.

(4) An order made under this section shall only have effect for such period, not exceeding the appeal period, as may be specified in the order.

(5) Where—

(a) an appeal is made against any decision of a court under this section; or

(b) any application is made to the appellate court in connection with a proposed appeal against that decision,

the appellate court may extend the period for which the order in question is to have effect, but not so as to extend it beyond the end of the appeal period.

(6) In this section 'the appeal period' means—

(a) where an appeal is made against the decision in question, the period between the making of that decision and the determination of the appeal; and

(b) otherwise, the period during which an appeal may be made against the decision.

Representation of child

41. Representation of child and of his interests in certain proceedings

(1) For the purpose of any specified proceedings, the court shall appoint an officer of the Service for the child concerned unless satisfied that it is not necessary to do so in order to safeguard his interests.

(2) The officer of the Service shall—

(a) be appointed in accordance with rules of court; and

(b) be under a duty to safeguard the interests of the child in the manner prescribed by such rules.

(3) Where—

(a) the child concerned is not represented by a solicitor; and

(b) any of the conditions mentioned in subsection (4) is satisfied,

the court may appoint a solicitor to represent him.

(4) The conditions are that—

(a) no officer of the Service has been appointed for the child;

(b) the child has sufficient understanding to instruct a solicitor and wishes to do so;

(c) it appears to the court that it would be in the child's best interests for him to be represented by a solicitor.

(5) Any solicitor appointed under or by virtue of this section shall be appointed, and shall represent the child, in accordance with rules of court.

(6) In this section 'specified proceedings' means any proceedings—

(a) on an application for a care order or supervision order;

(b) in which the court has given a direction under section 37(1) and has made, or is considering whether to make, an interim care order;

(c) on an application for the discharge of a care order or the variation or discharge of a supervision order;
(d) on an application under section 39(4);
(e) in which the court is considering whether to make a child arrangements order with respect to the living arrangements of a child who is the subject of a care order;
(f) with respect to contact between a child who is the subject of a care order and any other person;
(g) under Part V;
(h) on an appeal against—
(i) the making of, or refusal to make, a care order, supervision order or any order under section 34;
(ii) the making of, or refusal to make, child arrangements order with respect to the living arrangements of a child who is the subject of a care order; or
(iii) the variation or discharge, or refusal of an application to vary or discharge, an order of a kind mentioned in subparagraph (i) or (ii);
(iv) the refusal of an application under section 39(4); or
(v) the making of, or refusal to make, an order under Part V; or
(hh) on an application for the making or revocation of a placement order (within the meaning of section 21 of the Adoption and Children Act 2002);
(i) which are specified for the time being, for the purposes of this section, by rules of court.

(6A) The proceedings which may be specified under subsection (6)(i) include (for example) proceedings for the making, varying or discharging of a section 8 order.

(6B) For the purposes of subsection (6), a child arrangements order is one made with respect to the living arrangements of a child if the arrangements regulated by the order consist of, or include, arrangements which relate to either or both of the following—
(a) with whom the child is to live, and
(b) when the child is to live with any person.

. . .

(11) Regardless of any enactment or rule of law which would otherwise prevent it from doing so, the court may take account of—
(a) any statement contained in a report made by an officer of the Service who is appointed under this section for the purpose of the proceedings in question; and
(b) any evidence given in respect of the matters referred to in the report,

in so far as the statement or evidence is, in the opinion of the court, relevant to the question which the court is considering.

PART V
PROTECTION OF CHILDREN

43. Child assessment orders

(1) On the application of a local authority or authorised person for an order to be made under this section with respect to a child, the court may make the order if, but only if, it is satisfied that—
(a) the applicant has reasonable cause to suspect that the child is suffering, or is likely to suffer, significant harm;
(b) an assessment of the state of the child's health or development, or of the way in which he has been treated, is required to enable the applicant to determine whether or not the child is suffering, or is likely to suffer, significant harm; and
(c) it is unlikely that such an assessment will be made, or be satisfactory, in the absence of an order under this section.

(2) In this Act 'a child assessment order' means an order under this section.

(3) A court may treat an application under this section as an application for an emergency protection order.

(4) No court shall make a child assessment order if it is satisfied—
(a) that there are grounds for making an emergency protection order with respect to the child; and
(b) that it ought to make such an order rather than a child assessment order.

(5) A child assessment order shall—
(a) specify the date by which the assessment is to begin; and
(b) have effect for such period, not exceeding 7 days beginning with that date, as may be specified in the order.

(6) Where a child assessment order is in force with respect to a child it shall be the duty of any person who is in a position to produce the child—

(a) to produce him to such person as may be named in the order; and
(b) to comply with such directions relating to the assessment of the child as the court thinks fit to specify in the order.

(7) A child assessment order authorises any person carrying out the assessment, or any part of the assessment, to do so in accordance with the terms of the order.

(8) Regardless of subsection (7), if the child is of sufficient understanding to make an informed decision he may refuse to submit to a medical or psychiatric examination or other assessment.

(9) The child may only be kept away from home—
(a) in accordance with directions specified in the order;
(b) if it is necessary for the purposes of the assessment; and
(c) for such period or periods as may be specified in the order.

(10) Where the child is to be kept away from home, the order shall contain such directions as the court thinks fit with regard to the contact that he must be allowed to have with other persons while away from home.

(11) Any person making an application for a child assessment order shall take such steps as are reasonably practicable to ensure that notice of the application is given to—
(a) the child's parents;
(b) any person who is not a parent of his but who has parental responsibility for him;
(c) any other person caring for the child;
(d) any person named in a child arrangements order as a person with whom the child is to spend time or otherwise have contact;
(e) any person who is allowed to have contact with the child by virtue of an order under section 34; and
(f) the child, before the hearing of the application.

(12) Rules of court may make provision as to the circumstances in which—
(a) any of the persons mentioned in subsection (11); or
(b) such other person as may be specified in the rules,

may apply to the court for a child assessment order to be varied or discharged.

(13) In this section 'authorised person' means a person who is an authorised person for the purposes of section 31.

44. Orders for emergency protection of children

(1) Where any person ('the applicant') applies to the court for an order to be made under this section with respect to a child, the court may make the order if, but only if, it is satisfied that—
(a) there is reasonable cause to believe that the child is likely to suffer significant harm if—
(i) he is not removed to accommodation provided by or on behalf of the applicant; or
(ii) he does not remain in the place in which he is then being accommodated;
(b) in the case of an application made by a local authority—
(i) enquiries are being made with respect to the child under section 47(1)(b); and
(ii) those enquiries are being frustrated by access to the child being unreasonably refused to a person authorised to seek access and that the applicant has reasonable cause to believe that access to the child is required as a matter of urgency; or
(c) in the case of an application made by an authorised person—
(i) the applicant has reasonable cause to suspect that a child is suffering, or is likely to suffer, significant harm;
(ii) the applicant is making enquiries with respect to the child's welfare; and
(iii) those enquiries are being frustrated by access to the child being unreasonably refused to a person authorised to seek access and the applicant has reasonable cause to believe that access to the child is required as a matter of urgency.

(2) In this section—
(a) 'authorised person' means a person who is an authorised person for the purposes of section 31; and
(b) 'a person authorised to seek access' means—
(i) in the case of an application by a local authority, an officer of the local authority or a person authorised by the authority to act on their behalf in connection with the enquiries; or
(ii) in the case of an application by an authorised person, that person.

(3) Any person—
(a) seeking access to a child in connection with enquiries of a kind mentioned in subsection (1); and

(b) purporting to be a person authorised to do so,

shall, on being asked to do so, produce some duly authenticated document as evidence that he is such a person.

(4) While an order under this section ('an emergency protection order') is in force it—

(a) operates as a direction to any person who is in a position to do so to comply with any request to produce the child to the applicant;

(b) authorises—

(i) the removal of the child at any time to accommodation provided by or on behalf of the applicant and his being kept there; or

(ii) the prevention of the child's removal from any hospital, or other place, in which he was being accommodated immediately before the making of the order; and

(c) gives the applicant parental responsibility for the child.

(5) Where an emergency protection order is in force with respect to a child, the applicant—

(a) shall only exercise the power given by virtue of subsection (4)(b) in order to safeguard the welfare of the child;

(b) shall take, and shall only take, such action in meeting his parental responsibility for the child as is reasonably required to safeguard or promote the welfare of the child (having regard in particular to the duration of the order); and

(c) shall comply with the requirements of any regulations made by the Secretary of State for the purposes of this subsection.

(6) Where the court makes an emergency protection order, it may give such directions (if any) as it considers appropriate with respect to—

(a) the contact which is, or is not, to be allowed between the child and any named person;

(b) the medical or psychiatric examination or other assessment of the child.

(7) Where any direction is given under subsection (6)(b), the child may, if he is of sufficient understanding to make an informed decision, refuse to submit to the examination or other assessment.

(8) A direction under subsection (6)(a) may impose conditions and one under subsection (6)(b) may be to the effect that there is to be—

(a) no such examination or other assessment; or

(b) no such examination or assessment unless the court directs otherwise.

(9) A direction under subsection (6) may be—

(a) given when the emergency protection order is made or at any time while it is in force; and

(b) varied at any time on the application of any person falling within any class of person prescribed by rules of court for the puposes of this subsection.

(10) Where an emergency protection order is in force with respect to a child and—

(a) the applicant has exercised the power given by subsection (4)(b)(i) but it appears to him that it is safe for the child to be returned; or

(b) the applicant has exercised the power given by subsection (4)(b)(ii) but it appears to him that it is safe for the child to be allowed to be removed from the place in question,

he shall return the child or (as the case may be) allow him to be removed.

(11) Where he is required by subsection (10) to return the child the applicant shall—

(a) return him to the care of the person from whose care he was removed; or

(b) if that is not reasonably practicable, return him to the care of—

(i) a parent of his;

(ii) any person who is not a parent of his but who has parental responsibility for him; or

(iii) such other person as the applicant (with the agreement of the court) considers appropriate.

(12) Where the applicant has been required by subsection (10) to return the child, or to allow him to be removed, he may again exercise his powers with respect to the child (at any time while the emergency protection order remains in force) if it appears to him that a change in the circumstances of the case makes it necessary for him to do so.

(13) Where an emergency protection order has been made with respect to a child, the applicant shall, subject to any direction given under subsection (6), allow the child reasonable contact with—

(a) his parents;

(b) any person who is not a parent of his but who has parental responsibility for him;

(c) any person with whom he was living immediately before the making of the order;

(d) any person named in a child arrangements order as a person with whom the child is to spend time or otherwise have contact;

(e) any person who is allowed to have contact with the child by virtue of an order under section 34; and

(f) any person acting on behalf of any of those persons.

(14) Wherever it is reasonably practicable to do so, an emergency protection order shall name the child; and where it does not name him it shall describe him as clearly as possible.

(15) A person shall be guilty of an offence if he intentionally obstructs any person exercising the power under subsection (4)(b) to remove, or prevent the removal of, a child.

(16) A person guilty of an offence under subsection (15) shall be liable on summary conviction to a fine not exceeding level 3 on the standard scale.

44A. Power to include exclusion requirement in emergency protection order

(1) Where—

(a) on being satisfied as mentioned in section 44(1)(a), (b) or (c), the court makes an emergency protection order with respect to a child, and

(b) the conditions mentioned in subsection (2) are satisfied,

the court may include an exclusion requirement in the emergency protection order.

(2) The conditions are—

(a) that there is reasonable cause to believe that, if a person ('the relevant person') is excluded from a dwelling-house in which the child lives, then—

(i) in the case of an order made on the ground mentioned in section 44(1)(a), the child will not be likely to suffer significant harm, even though the child is not removed as mentioned in section 44(1)(a)(i) or does not remain as mentioned in section 44(1)(a)(ii), or

(ii) in the case of an order made on the ground mentioned in paragraph (b) or (c) of section 44(1), the enquiries referred to in that paragraph will cease to be frustrated, and

(b) that another person living in the dwelling-house (whether a parent of the child or some other person)—

(i) is able and willing to give to the child the care which it would be reasonable to expect a parent to give him, and

(ii) consents to the inclusion of the exclusion requirement.

(3) For the purposes of this section an exclusion requirement is any one or more of the following—

(a) a provision requiring the relevant person to leave a dwelling-house in which he is living with the child,

(b) a provision prohibiting the relevant person from entering a dwelling-house in which the child lives, and

(c) a provision excluding the relevant person from a defined area in which a dwelling-house in which the child lives is situated.

(4) The court may provide that the exclusion requirement is to have effect for a shorter period than the other provisions of the order.

(5) Where the court makes an emergency protection order containing an exclusion requirement, the court may attach a power of arrest to the exclusion requirement.

(6) Where the court attaches a power of arrest to an exclusion requirement of an emergency protection order, it may provide that the power of arrest is to have effect for a shorter period than the exclusion requirement.

(7) Any period specified for the purposes of subsection (4) or (6) may be extended by the court (on one or more occasions) on an application to vary or discharge the emergency protection order.

(8) Where a power of arrest is attached to an exclusion requirement of an emergency protection order by virtue of subsection (5), a constable may arrest without warrant any person whom he has reasonable cause to believe to be in breach of the requirement.

(9) Sections 47(7), (11) and (12) and 48 of, and Schedule 5 to, the Family Law Act 1996 shall have effect in relation to a person arrested under subsection (8) of this section as they have effect in relation to a person arrested under section 47(6) of that Act.

(10) If, while an emergency protection order containing an exclusion requirement is in force, the applicant has removed the child from the dwelling-house from which the relevant person is excluded to other accommodation for a continuous period of more than 24 hours, the order shall cease to have effect in so far as it imposes the exclusion requirement.

44B. Undertakings relating to emergency protection orders

(1) In any case where the court has power to include an exclusion requirement in an emergency protection order, the court may accept an undertaking from the relevant person.

(2) No power of arrest may be attached to any undertaking given under subsection (1).

(3) An undertaking given to a court under subsection (1)—

(a) shall be enforceable as if it were an order of the court, and
(b) shall cease to have effect if, while it is in force, the applicant has removed the child from the dwelling-house from which the relevant person is excluded to other accommodation for a continuous period of more than 24 hours.

(4) This section has effect without prejudice to the powers of the High Court and county court apart from this section.

(5) In this section 'exclusion requirement' and 'relevant person' have the same meaning as in section 44A.

45. Duration of emergency protection orders and other supplemental provisions

(1) An emergency protection order shall have effect for such period, not exceeding eight days, as may be specified in the order.

(2) Where—
(a) the court making an emergency protection order would, but for this subsection, specify a period of eight days as the period for which the order is to have effect; but
(b) the last of those eight days is a public holiday (that is to say, Christmas Day, Good Friday, a bank holiday or a Sunday),

the court may specify a period which ends at noon on the first later day which is not such a holiday.

(3) Where an emergency protection order is made on an application under section 46(7), the period of eight days mentioned in subsection (1) shall begin with the first day on which the child was taken into police protection under section 46.

(4) Any person who—
(a) has parental responsibility for a child as the result of an emergency protection order; and
(b) is entitled to apply for a care order with respect to the child,

may apply to the court for the period during which the emergency protection order is to have effect to be extended.

(5) On an application under subsection (4) the court may extend the period during which the order is to have effect by such period, not exceeding seven days, as it thinks fit, but may do so only if it has reasonable cause to believe that the child concerned is likely to suffer significant harm if the order is not extended.

(6) An emergency protection order may only be extended once.

(7) Regardless of any enactment or rule of law which would otherwise prevent it from doing so, a court hearing an application for, or with respect to, an emergency protection order may take account of—
(a) any statement contained in any report made to the court in the course of, or in connection with, the hearing; or
(b) any evidence given during the hearing,

which is, in the opinion of the court, relevant to the application.

(8) Any of the following may apply to the court for an emergency protection order to be discharged—
(a) the child;
(b) a parent of his;
(c) any person who is not a parent of his but who has parental responsibility for him; or
(d) any person with whom he was living immediately before the making of the order.

(8A) On the application of a person who is not entitled to apply for the order to be discharged, but who is a person to whom an exclusion requirement contained in the order applies, an emergency protection order may be varied or discharged by the court in so far as it imposes the exclusion requirement.

(8B) Where a power of arrest has been attached to an exclusion requirement of an emergency protection order, the court may, on the application of any person entitled to apply for the discharge of the order so far as it imposes the exclusion requirement, vary or discharge the order in so far as it confers a power of arrest (whether or not any application has been made to vary or discharge any other provision of the order).

(9) No application for the discharge of an emergency protection order shall be heard by the court before the expiry of the period of 72 hours beginning with the making of the order.

(10) No appeal may be made against—
(a) the making of, or refusal to make, an emergency protection order;
(b) the extension of, or refusal to extend, the period during which such an order is to have effect;
(c) the discharge of, or refusal to discharge, such an order; or
(d) the giving of, or refusal to give, any direction in connection with such an order.

(11) Subsection (8) does not apply—

(a) where the person who would otherwise be entitled to apply for the emergency protection order to be discharged—
(i) was given notice (in accordance with rules of court) of the hearing at which the order was made; and
(ii) was present at that hearing; or
(b) to any emergency protection order the effective period of which has been extended under subsection (5).

(12) A court making an emergency protection order may direct that the applicant may, in exercising any powers which he has by virtue of the order, be accompanied by a registered medical practitioner, registered nurse or registered midwife, if he so chooses.

46. Removal and accommodation of children by police in cases of emergency

(1) Where a constable has reasonable cause to believe that a child would otherwise be likely to suffer significant harm, he may—
(a) remove the child to suitable accommodation and keep him there; or
(b) take such steps as are reasonable to ensure that the child's removal from any hospital, or other place, in which he is then being accommodated is prevented.

(2) For the purposes of this Act, a child with respect to whom a constable has exercised his powers under this section is referred to as having been taken into police protection.

(3) As soon as is reasonably practicable after taking a child into police protection, the constable concerned shall—
(a) inform the local authority within whose area the child was found of the steps that have been, and are proposed to be, taken with respect to the child under this section and the reasons for taking them;
(b) give details to the authority within whose area the child is ordinarily resident ('the appropriate authority') of the place at which the child is being accommodated;
(c) inform the child (if he appears capable of understanding)—
(i) of the steps that have been taken with respect to him under this section and of the reasons for taking them; and
(ii) of the further steps that may be taken with respect to him under this section;
(d) take such steps as are reasonably practicable to discover the wishes and feelings of the child;
(e) secure that the case is inquired into by an officer designated for the purposes of this section by the chief officer of the police area concerned; and
(f) where the child was taken into police protection by being removed to accommodation which is not provided—
(i) by or on behalf of a local authority; or
(ii) as a refuge, in compliance with the requirements of section 51,
secure that he is moved to accommodation which is so provided.

(4) As soon as is reasonably practicable after taking a child into police protection, the constable concerned shall take such steps as are reasonably practicable to inform—
(a) the child's parents;
(b) every person who is not a parent of his but who has parental responsibility for him; and
(c) any other person with whom the child was living immediately before being taken into police protection,
of the steps that he has taken under this section with respect to the child, the reasons for taking them and the further steps that may be taken with respect to him under this section.

(5) On completing any inquiry under subsection (3)(e), the officer conducting it shall release the child from police protection unless he considers that there is still reasonable cause for believing that the child would be likely to suffer significant harm if released.

(6) No child may be kept in police protection for more than 72 hours.

(7) While a child is being kept in police protection, the designated officer may apply on behalf of the appropriate authority for an emergency protection order to be made under section 44 with respect to the child.

(8) An application may be made under subsection (7) whether or not the authority know of it or agree to its being made.

(9) While a child is being kept in police protection—
(a) neither the constable concerned nor the designated officer shall have parental responsibility for him; but
(b) the designated officer shall do what is reasonable in all the circumstances of the case for the purpose of safeguarding or promoting the child's welfare (having regard in particular to the length of the period during which the child will be so protected).

(10) Where a child has been taken into police protection, the designated officer shall allow—
(a) the child's parents;
(b) any person who is not a parent of the child but who has parental responsibility for him;
(c) any person with whom the child was living immediately before he was taken into police protection;
(d) any person named in a child arrangements order as a person with whom the child is to spend time or otherwise have contact;
(e) any person who is allowed to have contact with the child by virtue of an order under section 34; and
(f) any person acting on behalf of any of those persons,
to have such contact (if any) with the child as, in the opinion of the designated officer, is both reasonable and in the child's best interests.

(11) Where a child who has been taken into police protection is in accommodation provided by, or on behalf of, the appropriate authority, subsection (10) shall have effect as if it referred to the authority rather than to the designated officer.

47. Local authority's duty to investigate

(1) Where a local authority—
(a) are informed that a child who lives, or is found, in their area—
(i) is the subject of an emergency protection order; or
(ii) is in police protection; or
(iii) has contravened a ban imposed by a curfew notice within the meaning of Chapter I of Part I of the Crime and Disorder Act 1998; or
(b) have reasonable cause to suspect that a child who lives, or is found, in their area is suffering, or is likely to suffer, significant harm,
the authority shall make, or cause to be made, such enquiries as they consider necessary to enable them to decide whether they should take any action to safeguard or promote the child's welfare.

(2) Where a local authority have obtained an emergency protection order with respect to a child, they shall make, or cause to be made, such enquiries as they consider necessary to enable them to decide what action they should take to safeguard or promote the child's welfare.

(3) The enquiries shall, in particular, be directed towards establishing—
(a) whether the authority should make any application to the court, or exercise any of their other powers under this Act or section 11 of the Crime and Disorder Act 1998 (child safety orders), with respect to the child;
(b) whether, in the case of a child—
(i) with respect to whom an emergency protection order has been made; and
(ii) who is not in accommodation provided by or on behalf of the authority,
it would be in the child's best interests (while an emergency protection order remains in force) for him to be in such accommodation; and
(c) whether, in the case of a child who has been taken into police protection, it would be in the child's best interests for the authority to ask for an application to be made under section 46(7).

(4) Where enquiries are being made under subsection (1) with respect to a child, the local authority concerned shall (with a view to enabling them to determine what action, if any, to take with respect to him) take such steps as are reasonably practicable—
(a) to obtain access to him; or
(b) to ensure that access to him is obtained, on their behalf, by a person authorised by them for the purpose,
unless they are satisfied that they already have sufficient information with respect to him.

(5) Where, as a result of any such enquiries, it appears to the authority that there are matters connected with the child's education which should be investigated, they shall consult the local authority (as defined in section 579(1) of the Education 1996), if different, specified in subsection (5ZA).

(5ZA) The local authority referred to in subsection (5) is—
(a) the local authority who —
(i) maintain any school at which the child is a pupil, or
(ii) make arrangements for the provision of education for the child otherwise than at school pursuant to section 19 of the Education Act 1996, or
(b) in a case where the child is a pupil at a school which is not maintained by a local authority, the local authority in whose area the school is situated.

(5A) For the purposes of making a determination under this section as to the action to be taken with respect to a child, a local authority shall, so far as is reasonably practicable and consistent with the child's welfare—
(a) ascertain the child's wishes and feelings regarding the action to be taken with respect to him; and

(b) give due consideration (having regard to his age and understanding) to such wishes and feelings of the child as they have been able to ascertain.

(6) Where, in the course of enquiries made under this section—
(a) any officer of the local authority concerned; or
(b) any person authorised by the authority to act on their behalf in connection with those enquiries—
(i) is refused access to the child concerned; or
(ii) is denied information as to his whereabouts,

the authority shall apply for an emergency protection order, a child assessment order, a care order or a supervision order with respect to the child unless they are satisfied that his welfare can be satisfactorily safeguarded without their doing so.

(7) If, on the conclusion of any enquiries or review made under this section, the authority decide not to apply for an emergency protection order, a child assessment order, a care order or a supervision order they shall—
(a) consider whether it would be appropriate to review the case at a later date; and
(b) if they decide that it would be, determine the date on which that review is to begin.

(8) Where, as a result of complying with this section, a local authority conclude that they should take action to safeguard or promote the child's welfare they shall take that action (so far as it is both within their power and reasonably practicable for them to do so).

(9) Where a local authority are conducting enquiries under this section, it shall be the duty of any person mentioned in subsection (11) to assist them with those enquiries (in particular by providing relevant information and advice) if called upon by the authority to do so.

(10) Subsection (9) does not oblige any person to assist a local authority where doing so would be unreasonable in all the circumstances of the case.

(11) The persons are—
(a) any local authority;
(b) …
(c) any local housing authority;
(d) any Local Health Board, Special Health Authority, Primary Care Trust, National Health Service trust or NHS foundation trust; and
(e) any person authorised by the Secretary of State for the purposes of this section.

(12) Where a local authority are making enquiries under this section with respect to a child who appears to them to be ordinarily resident within the area of another authority, they shall consult that other authority, who may undertake the necessary enquiries in their place.

48. Powers to assist in discovery of children who may be in need of emergency protection

(1) Where it appears to a court making an emergency protection order that adequate information as to the child's whereabouts—
(a) is not available to the applicant for the order; but
(b) is available to another person,

it may include in the order a provision requiring that other person to disclose, if asked to do so by the applicant, any information that he may have as to the child's whereabouts.

(2) No person shall be excused from complying with such a requirement on the ground that complying might incriminate him or his spouse of an offence; but a statement or admission made in complying shall not be admissible in evidence against either of them in proceedings for any offence other than perjury.

(3) An emergency protection order may authorise the appliant to enter premises specified by the order and search for the child with respect to whom the order is made.

(4) Where the court is satisfied that there is reasonable cause to believe that there may be another child on those premises with respect to whom an emergency protection order ought to be made, it may make an order authorising the applicant to search for that other child on those premises.

(5) Where—
(a) an order has been made under subsection (4);
(b) the child concerned has been found on the premises; and
(c) the applicant is satisfied that the grounds for making an emergency protection order exist with respect to him,

the order shall have effect as if it were an emergency protection order.

(6) Where an order has been made under subsection (4), the applicant shall notify the court of its effect.

(7) A person shall be guilty of an offence if he intentionally obstructs any person exercising the power of entry and search under subsection (3) or (4).

(8) A person guilty of an offence under subsection (7) shall be liable on summary conviction to a fine not exceeding level 3 on the standard scale.

(9) Where, on an application made by any person for a warrant under this section, it appears to the court—
(a) that a person attempting to exercise powers under an emergency protection order has been prevented from doing so by being refused entry to the premises concerned or access to the child concerned; or
(b) that any such person is likely to be so prevented from exercising any such powers,
it may issue a warrant authorising any constable to assist the person mentioned in paragraph (a) or (b) in the exercise of those powers using reasonable force if necessary.
(10) Every warrant issued under this section shall be addressed to, and executed by, a constable who shall be accompanied by the person applying for the warrant if—
(a) that person so desires; and
(b) the court by whom the warrant is issued does not direct otherwise.
(11) A court granting an application for a warrant under this section may direct that the constable conerned may, in executing the warrant, be accompanied by a registered medical practitioner, registered nurse or registered midwife if he so chooses.
(12) An application for a warrant under this section shall be made in the manner and form prescribed by rules of court.
(13) Wherever it is reasonably practicable to do so, an order under subsection (4), an application for a warrant under this section and any such warrant shall name the child; and where it does not name him it shall describe him as clearly as possible.

49. Abduction of children in care etc.

(1) A person shall be guilty of an offence if, knowingly and without lawful authority or reasonable excuse, he—
(a) takes a child to whom this section applies away from the responsible person;
(b) keeps such a child away from the responsible person; or
(c) induces, assists or incites such a child to run away or stay away from the responsible person.
(2) This section applies in relation to a child who is—
(a) in care;
(b) the subject of an emergency protection order; or
(c) in police protection,
and in this section 'the responsible person' means any person who for the time being has care of him by virtue of the care order, the emergency protection order, or section 46, as the case may be.
(3) A person guilty of an offence under this section shall be liable on summary conviction to imprisonment for a term not exceeding six months, or to a fine not exceeding level 5 on the standard scale, or to both.

50. Recovery of abducted children etc.

(1) Where it appears to the court that there is reason to believe that a child to whom this section applies—
(a) has been unlawfully taken away or is being unlawfully kept away from the responsible person;
(b) has run away or is staying away from the responsible person; or
(c) is missing,
the court may make an order under this section ('a recovery order').
(2) This section applies to the same children to whom section 49 applies and in this section 'the responsible person' has the same meaning as in section 49.
(3) A recovery order—
(a) operates as a direction to any person who is in a position to do so to produce the child on request to any authorised person;
(b) authorises the removal of the child by any authorised person;
(c) requires any person who has information as to the child's whereabouts to disclose that information, if asked to do so, to a constable or an officer of the court;
(d) authorises a constable to enter any premises specified in the order and search for the child, using reasonable force if necessary.
(4) The court may make a recovery order only on the application of—
(a) any person who has parental responsibility for the child by virtue of a care order or emergency protection order; or
(b) where the child is in police protection, the designated officer.
(5) A recovery order shall name the child and—
(a) any person who has parental responsibility for the child by virtue of a care order or emergency protection order; or
(b) where the child is in police protection, the designated officer.
(6) Premises may only be specified under subsection (3)(d) if it appears to the court that there are reasonable grounds for believing the child to be on them.

(7) In this section—
'an authorised person' means—
(a) any person specified by the court;
(b) any constable;
(c) any person who is authorised—
(i) after the recovery order is made; and
(ii) by a person who has parental responsibility for the child by virtue of a care order or an emergency protection order,
to exercise any power under a recovery order; and
'the designated officer' means the officer designated for the purposes of section 46.
(8) Where a person is authorised as mentioned in subsection (7)(c)—
(a) the authorisation shall identify the recovery order; and
(b) any person claiming to be so authorised shall, if asked to do so, produce some duly authenticated document showing that he is so authorised.
(9) A person shall be guilty of an offence if he intentionally obstructs an authorised person exercising the power under subsection (3)(b) to remove a child.
(10) A person guilty of an offence under this section shall be liable on summary conviction to a fine not exceeding level 3 on the standard scale.
(11) No person shall be excused from complying with any request made under subsection (3)(c) on the ground that complying with it might incriminate him or his spouse of an offence; but a statement or admission made in complying shall not be admissible in evidence against either of them in proceedings for an offence other than perjury.
(12) Where a child is made the subject of a recovery order whilst being looked after by a local authority, any reasonable expenses incurred by an authorised person in giving effect to the order shall be recoverable from the authority.

Effect and duration of orders etc.

91. Effect and duration of orders etc.

(1) The making of a child arrangements order with respect to the living arrangements of a child who is the subject of a care order discharges the care order.
(1A) For the purposes of subsection (1), a child arrangements order is one made with respect to the living arrangements of a child if the arrangements regulated by the order consist of, or include, arrangements which relate to either or both of the following—
(a) with whom the child is to live, and
(b) when the child is to live with any person.
(2) The making of a care order with respect to a child who is the subject of any section 8 order discharges that order.
(2A) Where an activity direction has been made with respect to a child, the making of a care order with respect to the child discharges the direction.
(3) The making of a care order with respect to a child who is the subject of a supervision order discharges that other order.
(4) The making of a care order with respect to a child who is a ward of court brings that wardship to an end.
(5) The making of a care order with respect to a child who is the subject of a school attendance order made under section 437 of the Education Act 1996 discharges the school attendance order.
(5A) The making of a special guardianship order with respect to a child who is the subject of—
(a) a care order; or
(b) an order under section 34,
discharges that order.
(6) Where an emergency protection order is made with respect to a child who is in care, the care order shall have effect subject to the emergency protection order.
(7) Any order made under section 4(1), 4ZA(1), 4A(1) or 5(1) shall continue in force until the child reaches the age of eighteen, unless it is brought to an end earlier.
(8) Any—
(a) agreement under section 4, 4ZA or 4A; or
(b) appointment under section 5(3) or (4),
shall continue in force until the child reaches the age of eighteen, unless it is brought to an end earlier.
(9) An order under Schedule 1 has effect as specified in that Schedule.
(10) A section 8 order shall, if it would otherwise still be in force, cease to have effect when the child reaches the age of sixteen, unless it is to have effect beyond that age by virtue of section 9(6).

(10A) Subsection 10 does not apply to provision in a child arrangements order which regulates arrangements relating to—
(a) with whom a child is to live, or
(b) when a child is to live with any person.
(11) Where a section 8 order has effect with respect to a child who has reached the age of sixteen, it shall, if it would otherwise still be in force, cease to have effect when he reaches the age of eighteen.
(12) Any care order, other than an interim care order, shall continue in force until the child reaches the age of eighteen, unless it is brought to an end earlier.
(13) Any order made under any other provision of this Act in relation to a child shall, if it would otherwise still be in force, cease to have effect when he reaches the age of eighteen.
(14) On disposing of any application for an order under this Act, the court may (whether or not it makes any other order in response to the application) order that no application for an order under this Act of any specified kind may be made with respect to the child concerned by any person named in the order without leave of the court.
(15) Where an application ('the previous application') has been made for—
(a) the discharge of a care order;
(b) the discharge of a supervision order;
(c) the discharge of an education supervision order;
(d) the substitution of a supervision order for a care order; or
(e) a child assessment order,
no further application of a kind mentioned in paragraphs (a) to (e) may be made with respect to the child concerned, without leave of the court, unless the period between the disposal of the previous application and the making of the further application exceeds six months.
(16) Subsection (15) does not apply to applications made in relation to interim orders.
(17) Where—
(a) a person has made an application for an order under section 34;
(b) the application has been refused; and
(c) a period of less than six months has elapsed since the refusal,
that person may not make a further application for such an order with respect to the same child, unless he has obtained the leave of the court.

Jurisdiction and procedure etc.

92. Jurisdiction of courts

(1)—(6)...
(7) For the purposes of this Act 'the court' means the High Court, a county court or a magistrates' court.
(8) Subsection (7) is subject to the provision made by or under Part I of Schedule 11 and to any express provision as to the jurisdiction of any court made by any other provision of this Act.
(9)—(10A)...
(11) Part II of Schedule 11 makes amendments consequential on this section.

95. Attendance of child at hearing under Part IV or V

(1) In any proceedings in which a court is hearing an application for an order under Part IV or V, or is considering whether to make any such order, the court may order the child concerned to attend such stage or stages of the proceedings as may be specified in the order.
(2) The power conferred by subsection (1) shall be exercised in accordance with rules of court.
(3) Subsections (4) to (6) apply where—
(a) an order under subsection (1) has not been complied with; or
(b) the court has reasonable cause to believe that it will not be complied with.
(4) The court may make an order authorising a constable, or such person as may be specified in the order—
(a) to take charge of the child and to bring him to the court; and
(b) to enter and search any premises specified in the order if he has reasonable cause to believe that the child may be found on the premises.
(5) The court may order any person who is in a position to do so to bring the child to the court.
(6) Where the court has reason to believe that a person has information about the whereabouts of the child it may order him to disclose it to the court.

96. Evidence given by, or with respect to, children

(1) Subsection (2) applies where a child who is called as a witness in any civil proceedings does not, in the opinion of the court, understand the nature of an oath.

(2) The child's evidence may be heard by the court if, in its opinion—
   (a) he understands that it is his duty to speak the truth; and
   (b) he has sufficient understanding to justify his evidence being heard.

(3) The Lord Chancellor may by order make provision for the admissibility of evidence which would otherwise be inadmissible under any rule of law relating to hearsay.

(4) An order under subsection (3) may only be made with respect to—
   (a) civil proceedings in general or such civil proceedings, or class of civil proceedings, as may be prescribed; and
   (b) evidence in connection with the upbringing, maintenance or welfare of a child.

(5) An order under subsection (3)—
   (a) may, in particular, provide for the admissibility of statements which are made orally or in a prescribed form or which are recorded by any prescribed method of recording;
   (b) may make different provision for different purposes and in relation to different descriptions of court; and
   (c) may make such amendments and repeals in any enactment relating to evidence (other than in this Act) as the Lord Chancellor considers necessary or expedient in consequence of the provision made by the order.

(6) Subsection (5)(b) is without prejudice to section 104(4):

(7) In this section—
'civil proceedings' means civil proceedings, before any tribunal, in relation to which the strict rules of evidence apply, whether as a matter of law or by agreement of the parties, and references to 'the court' shall be construed accordingly; and
'prescribed' means prescribed by an order under subsection (3).

100. Restrictions on use of wardship jurisdiction

(1) Section 7 of the Family Law Reform Act 1969 (which gives the High Court power to place a ward of court in the care, or under the supervision, of a local authority) shall cease to have effect.

(2) No court shall exercise the High Court's inherent jurisdiction with respect to children—
   (a) so as to require a child to be placed in the care, or put under the supervision, of a local authority;
   (b) so as to require a child to be accommodated by or on behalf of a local authority; or
   (c) so as to make a child who is the subject of a care order a ward of court; or
   (d) for the purpose of conferring on any local authority power to determine any question which has arisen, or which may arise, in connection with any aspect of parental responsibility for a child.

(3) No application for any exercise of the court's inherent jurisdiction with respect to children may be made by a local authority unless the authority have obtained the leave of the court.

(4) The court may only grant leave if it is satisfied that—
   (a) the result which the authority wish to achieve could not be achieved through the making of any order of a kind to which subsection (5) applies; and
   (b) there is reasonable cause to believe that if the court's inherent jurisdiction is not exercised with respect to the child he is likely to suffer significant harm.

(5) This subsection applies to any order—
   (a) made otherwise than in the exercise of the court's inherent jurisdiction; and
   (b) which the local authority is entitled to apply for (assuming, in the case of any application which may only be made with leave, that leave is granted).

105. Interpretation

(1) In this Act—
'activity condition' has the meaning given by section 11C;
'activity direction' has the meaning given by section 11A;
'adoption agency' means a body which may be referred to as an adoption agency by virtue of section 2 of the Adoption and Children Act 2002;
'appropriate children's home' has the meaning given by section 23;
'bank holiday' means a day which is a bank holiday under the Banking and Financial Dealings Act 1971;
'care home' has the same meaning as in the Care Standards Act 2000;
'care order' has the meaning given by section 31(11) and also includes any order which by or under any enactment has the effect of, or is deemed to be, a care order for the

purposes of this Act; and any reference to a child who is in the care of an authority is a reference to a child who is in their care by virtue of a care order;
'child arrangements order' has the meaning given by section 8(1);
'child' means, subject to paragraph 16 of Schedule 1, a person under the age of eighteen;
'child assessment order' has the meaning given by section 8(1);
'child assessment order' has the meaning given by section 43(2);
'child of the family', in relation to the parties to a marriage or to two people who are civil partners of each other, means—
(a) a child of both of them;
(b) any other child, other than a child placed with them as foster parents by a local authority or voluntary organisation, who has been treated by both of them as a child of their family;
'children's home' has the same meaning as it has for the purposes of the Care Standards Act 2000 (see section 1 of that Act);
'clinical commissioning group' means a body established under section 14D of the National Health Service Act 2006;
'community home' has the meaning given by section 53;
'day care' has the meaning given by section 18;
'disabled', in relation to a child, has the same meaning as in section 17(11);
'domestic premises' has the meaning given by section 71(12);
'dwelling-house' includes—
(a) any building or part of a building which is occupied as a dwelling;
(b) any caravan, house-boat or structure which is occupied as a dwelling;
and any yard, garden, garage or outhouse belonging to it and occupied with it;
'education functions' has the meaning given by section 579(1) of the Education Act 1996;
'education supervision order' has the meaning given in section 36;
'education supervision order' has the meaning given in section 36;
'emergency protection order' means an order under section 44;
'enforcement order' has the meaning given by section 11J;
'family assistance order' has the meaning given in section 16(2);
'family proceedings' has the meaning given by section 8(3);
'functions' includes powers and duties;
'guardian of a child' means a guardian (other than a guardian of the estate of a child) appointed in accordance with the provisions of section 5;
'harm' has the same meaning as in section 31(9) and the question of whether harm is significant shall be determined in accordance with section 31(10);
'Health Authority' means a Health Authority established under section 8 of the National Health Service Act 1977;
'health service hospital' means a health service hospital within the meaning given by the National Health Service Act 2006 or the National Health Service (Wales) Act 2006;
'hospital' (except in Schedule 9A) has the same meaning as in the Mental Health Act 1983, except that it does not include a hospital at which high security psychiatric services within the meaning of that Act are provided;
'ill-treatment' has the same meaning as in section 31(9);
'independent hospital'—
(a) in relation to England, means a hospital as defined by section 275 of the National Health Service Act 2006 that is not a health service hospital as defined by that Act;
(b) in relation to Wales, has the same meaning as in the Care Standards Act 2000;
'independent school' has the same meaning as in the Education Act 1996;
'local authority' means, in relation to England, the council of a county, a metropolitan district, a London Borough or the Common Council of the City of London, in relation to Wales, the council of a county or a county borough and, in relation to Scotland, a local authority within the meaning of section 1(2) of the Social Work (Scotland) Act 1968;
'local authority foster parent' has the same meaning as in section 22C(12);
'Local Health Board' means a Local Health Board established under section 11 of the National Health Service (Wales) Act 2006;
'local housing authority' has the same meaning as in the Housing Act 1985;
'officer of the Service' has the same meaning as in the Criminal Justice and Court Services Act 2000;
'parental responsibility' has the meaning given in section 3;
'parental responsibility agreement' has the meaning given in sections 4(1), (4ZA(4) and 4A(2);
'prescribed' means prescribed by regulations made under this Act;
'Primary Care Trust' means a Primary Care Trust established under section 18 of the National Health Service Act 2006;

'private children's home' means a children's home in respect of which a person is registered under Part II of the Care Standards Act 2000 which is not a community home or a voluntary home;
'privately fostered child' and 'to foster a child privately' have the same meaning as in section 66;
'prohibited steps order' has the meaning given by section 8(1);
'registered pupil' has the same meaning as in the Education Act 1996;
'relative', in relation to a child, means a grandparent, brother, sister, uncle or aunt (whether of the full blood or half blood or by marriage or civil partnership) or step-parent;
'responsible person', in relation to a child who is the subject of a supervision order, has the meaning given in paragraph 1 of Schedule 3;
'school' has the same meaning as in the Education Act 1996 or, in relation to Scotland, in the Education (Scotland) Act 1980;
'section 31A plan' has the meaning given by section 31A(6);
'service', in relation to any provision, made under Part III, includes any facility;
'signed', in relation to any person, includes the making by that person of his mark;
'special educational needs' has the same meaning as in the Education Act 1996;
'special guardian' and 'special guardianship order' have the meaning given by section 14A;
'Special Health Authority' means a Special Health Authority established under section 28 of the National Health Service Act 2006 or section 22 of the National Health Service (Wales) Act 2006;
'specific issue order' has the meaning given by section 8(1);
'supervision order' has the meaning given by section 31(11);
'supervised child' and 'supervisor', in relation to a supervision order or an education supervision order, mean respectively the child who is (or is to be) under supervision and the person under whose supervision he is (or is to be) by virtue of the order;
'upbringing', in relation to any child, includes the care of the child but not his maintenance;
'voluntary home' has the meaning given by section 60;
'voluntary organisation' means a body (other than a public or local authority) whose activities are not carried on for profit.
'Welsh family proceedings officer' has the meaning given by section 35 of the Children Act 2004.

(2) References in this Act to a child whose father and mother were, or (as the case may be) were not, married to each other at the time of his birth must be read with section 1 of the Family Law Reform Act 1987 (which extends the meaning of such references).

(3) ...

(4) References in this Act to a child who is looked after by a local authority have the same meaning as they have (by virtue of section 22) in Part III.

(5) References in this Act to accommodation provided by or on behalf of a local authority are references to accommodation so provided in the exercise of functions of that or any other local authority which are social services functions within the meaning of the Local Authority Social Services Act 1970.

(6) In determining the 'ordinary residence' of a child for any purpose of this Act, there shall be disregarded any period in which he lives in any place—
   (a) which is a school or other institution;
   (b) in accordance with the requirements of a supervision order under this Act;
   (ba) in accordance with the requirements of a youth rehabilitation order under Part 1 of the Criminal Justice and Immigration Act 2008; or
   (c) while he is being provided with accommodation by or on behalf of a local authority.

(7) References in this Act to children who are in need shall be construed in accordance with section 17.

(7A) References in this Act to a hospital or accommodation made available or provided pursuant to arrangements made by the Secretary of State under the National Health Service Act 2006 are references to a hospital or accommodation made available or provided pursuant to arrangements so made in the exercise of the public health functions of the Secretary of State (within the meaning of that Act).

(7B) References in this Act to arrangements made by the National Health Service Commissioning Board or a clinical commissioning group under the National Health Service Act 2006 include references to arrangements so made by virtue of section 7A of that Act.

(8) Any notice or other document required under this Act to be served on any person may be served on him by being delivered personally to him, or being sent by post to him in a registered letter or by the recorded delivery service at his proper address.

(9) Any such notice or other document required to be served on a body corporate or a firm shall be duly served if it is served on the secretary or clerk of that body or a partner of that firm.

(10) For the purposes of this section, and of section 7 of the Interpretation Act 1978 in its application to this section, the proper address of a person—
(a) in the case of a secretary or clerk of a body corporate, shall be that of the registered or principal office of that body;
(b) in the case of a partner of a firm, shall be that of the principal office of the firm; and
(c) in any other case, shall be last known address of the person to be served.

SCHEDULES

SCHEDULE A1
ENFORCEMENT ORDERS

PART 1
UNPAID WORK REQUIREMENT

General

1. Subject to the modifications in paragraphs 2 and 3, Chapter 4 of Part 12 of the Criminal Justice Act 2003 has effect in relation to an enforcement order as it has effect in relation to a community order (within the meaning of Part 12 of that Act).

References to an offender

2. Subject to paragraph 3, references in Chapter 4 of Part 12 of the Criminal Justice Act 2003 to an offender are to be treated as including references to a person subject to an enforcement order.

Specific modifications

3.— (1) The power of the Secretary of State by order under section 197(3) to amend the definition of 'responsible officer' and to make consequential amendments includes power to make any amendments of this Part (including further modifications of Chapter 4 of Part 12 of the Criminal Justice Act 2003) that appear to the Secretary of State to be necessary or expedient in consequence of any amendment made by virtue of section 197(3)(a) or (b).

...

PART 2
REVOCATION, AMENDMENT OR BREACH OF ENFORCEMENT ORDER

Power to revoke

4.— (1) This paragraph applies where a court has made an enforcement order in respect of a person's failure to comply with a provision of a child arrangements order and the enforcement order is in force.
(2) The court may revoke the enforcement order if it appears to the court that—
(a) in all the circumstances no enforcement order should have been made,
(b) having regard to circumstances which have arisen since the enforcement order was made, it would be appropriate for the enforcement order to be revoked, or
(c) having regard to the person's satisfactory compliance with the child arrangements order or any child arrangements order that has effect in its place, it would be appropriate for the enforcement order to be revoked.
(3) The enforcement order may be revoked by the court under sub-paragraph (2) of its own motion or on an application by the person subject to the enforcement order.
(4) In deciding whether to revoke the enforcement order under sub-paragraph (2)(b), the court is to take into account—
(a) the extent to which the person subject to the enforcement order has complied with it, and
(b) the likelihood that the person will comply with the child arrangements order or any child arrangements order that has effect in its place in the absence of an enforcement order.
(5) In deciding whether to revoke the enforcement order under sub-paragraph (2)(c), the court is to take into account the likelihood that the person will comply with the child arrangements order or any child arrangements order that has effect in its place in the absence of an enforcement order.

Amendment by reason of change of residence

5.— (1) This paragraph applies where a court has made an enforcement order in respect of a person's failure to comply with a provision of a child arrangements order and the enforcement order is in force.

(2) If the court is satisfied that the person has changed, or proposes to change, his residence from the local justice area specified in the order to another local justice area, the court may amend the order by substituting the other area for the area specified.

(3) The enforcement order may be amended by the court under sub-paragraph (2) of its own motion or on an application by the person subject to the enforcement order.

Amendment of hours specified under unpaid work requirement

6.— (1) This paragraph applies where a court has made an enforcement order in respect of a person's failure to comply with a provision of a child arrangements order and the enforcement order is in force.

(2) If it appears to the court that, having regard to circumstances that have arisen since the enforcement order was made, it would be appropriate to do so, the court may reduce the number of hours specified in the order (but not below the minimum specified in section 199(2)(a) of the Criminal Justice Act 2003).

(3) In amending the enforcement order under sub-paragraph (2), the court must be satisfied that the effect on the person of the enforcement order as proposed to be amended is no more than is required to secure his compliance with the child arrangements order or any child arrangements order that has effect in its place.

(4) The enforcement order may be amended by the court under sub-paragraph (2) of its own motion or on an application by the person subject to the enforcement order.

Amendment to extend unpaid work requirement

7.— (1) This paragraph applies where a court has made an enforcement order in respect of a person's failure to comply with a provision of a child arrangements order and the enforcement order is in force.

(2) If it appears to the court that, having regard to circumstances that have arisen since the enforcement order was made, it would be appropriate to do so, the court may, in relation to the order, extend the period of twelve months specified in section 200(2) of the Criminal Justice Act 2003 (as substituted by paragraph 3).

(3) The period may be extended by the court under sub-paragraph (2) of its own motion or on an application by the person subject to the enforcement order.

Warning and report following breach

8.— (1) This paragraph applies where a court has made an enforcement order in respect of a person's failure to comply with a provision of a child arrangements order.

(2) If the responsible officer is of the opinion that the person has failed without reasonable excuse to comply with the unpaid work requirement imposed by the enforcement order, the officer must give the person a warning under this paragraph unless—

(a) the person has within the previous twelve months been given a warning under this paragraph in relation to a failure to comply with the unpaid work requirement, or

(b) the responsible officer reports the failure to the appropriate person.

(3) A warning under this paragraph must—

(a) describe the circumstances of the failure,

(b) state that the failure is unacceptable, and

(c) inform the person that, if within the next twelve months he again fails to comply with the unpaid work requirement, the warning and the subsequent failure will be reported to the appropriate person.

(4) The responsible officer must, as soon as practicable after the warning has been given, record that fact.

(5) If—

(a) the responsible officer has given a warning under this paragraph to a person subject to an enforcement order, and

(b) at any time within the twelve months beginning with the date on which the warning was given, the responsible officer is of the opinion that the person has since that date failed without reasonable excuse to comply with the unpaid work requirement imposed by the enforcement order,

the officer must report the failure to the appropriate person.

(6) A report under sub-paragraph (5) must include a report of the warning given to the person subject to the enforcement order.

(7) The appropriate person, in relation to an enforcement order, is the officer of the Service or the Welsh family proceedings officer who is required under section 11M to report on matters relating to the enforcement order.

(8) 'Responsible officer', in relation to a person subject to an enforcement order, has the same meaning as in section 197 of the Criminal Justice Act 2003 (as modified by paragraph 2).

Breach of an enforcement order

9.— (1) This paragraph applies where a court has made an enforcement order ('the first order') in respect of a person's failure to comply with a provision of a child arrangements order.

(2) If the court is satisfied beyond reasonable doubt that the person has failed to comply with the unpaid work requirement imposed by the first order, the court may—

(a) amend the first order so as to make the requirement more onerous, or

(b) make an enforcement order ('the second order') in relation to the person and (if the first order is still in force) provide for the second order to have effect either in addition to or in substitution for the first order.

(3) But the court may not exercise its powers under sub-paragraph (2) if it is satisfied that the person had a reasonable excuse for failing to comply with the unpaid work requirement imposed by the first order.

(4) The burden of proof as to the matter mentioned in sub-paragraph (3) lies on the person claiming to have had a reasonable excuse, and the standard of proof is the balance of probabilities.

(5) The court may exercise its powers under sub-paragraph (2) in relation to the first order only on the application of a person who would be able to apply under section 11J for an enforcement order if the failure to comply with the first order were a failure to comply with a provision of the child arrangements order to which the first order relates.

(6) Where the person proposing to apply to the court is the child with respect to whom the child arrangements order was made, subsections (6) and (7) of section 11J have effect in relation to the application as they have effect in relation to an application for an enforcement order.

(7) An application to the court to exercise its powers under sub-paragraph (2) may only be made while the first order is in force.

(8) The court may not exercise its powers under sub-paragraph (2) in respect of a failure by the person to comply with the unpaid work requirement imposed by the first order unless it is satisfied that before the failure occurred the person had been given (in accordance with rules of court) a copy of, or otherwise informed of the terms of, a notice under section 11N relating to the first order.

(9) In dealing with the person under sub-paragraph (2)(a), the court may—

(a) increase the number of hours specified in the first order (but not above the maximum specified in section 199(2)(b) of the Criminal Justice Act 2003, as substituted by paragraph 3);

(b) in relation to the order, extend the period of twelve months specified in section 200(2) of the Criminal Justice Act 2003 (as substituted by paragraph 3).

(10) In exercising its powers under sub-paragraph (2), the court must be satisfied that, taking into account the extent to which the person has complied with the unpaid work requirement imposed by the first order, the effect on the person of the proposed exercise of those powers—

(a) is no more than is required to secure his compliance with the child arrangements order or any child arrangements order that has effect in its place, and

(b) is no more than is proportionate to the seriousness of his failures to comply with the provision of the child arrangements order and with and the first order.

(11) Where the court exercises its powers under sub-paragraph (2) by making an enforcement order in relation to a person who has failed to comply with another enforcement order—

(a) sections 11K(4), 11L(2) to (7), 11M and 11N have effect as regards the making of the order in relation to the person as they have effect as regards the making of an enforcement order in relation to a person who has failed to comply with a provision of a child arrangements order;

(b) this Part of this Schedule has effect in relation to the order so made as if it were an enforcement order made in respect of the failure for which the other order was made.

(12) Sub-paragraph (2) is without prejudice to section 63(3) of the Magistrates' Courts Act 1980 as it applies in relation to enforcement orders.

Provision relating to amendment of enforcement orders

10. Sections 11L(2) to (7) and 11M have effect in relation to the making of an order under paragraph 6(2), 7(2) or 9(2)(a) amending an enforcement order as they have effect in relation to the making of an enforcement order; and references in sections 11L(2) to (7) and 11M to an enforcement order are to be read accordingly.

Section 15(1)

SCHEDULE 1
FINANCIAL PROVISION FOR CHILDREN

Orders for financial relief against parents

1.— (1) On an application made by a parent, guardian or special guardian of a child, or by any person who is named in a child arrangements order as a person with whom a child is to live, the court may make one or more of the orders mentioned in sub-paragraph (2).—

(2) The orders referred to in sub-paragraph (1) are—

(a) an order requiring either or both parents of a child—

(i) to make to the applicant for the benefit of the child; or

(ii) to make to the child himself,

such periodical payments, for such term, as may be specified in the order;

(b) an order requiring either or both parents of a child—

(i) to secure to the applicant for the benefit of the child; or

(ii) to secure to the child himself,

such periodical payments, for such term, as may be so specified;

(c) an order requiring either or both parents of a child—

(i) to pay to the applicant for the benefit of the child; or

(ii) to pay to the child himself,

such lump sum as may be so specified;

(d) an order requiring a settlement to be made for the benefit of the child, and to the satisfaction of the court, of property—

(i) to which either parent is entitled (either in possession or in reversion); and

(ii) which is specified in the order;

(e) an order requiring either or both parents of a child—

(i) to transfer to the applicant, for the benefit of the child; or

(ii) to transfer to the child himself,

such property to which the parent is, or the parents are, entitled (either in possession or in reversion) as may be specified in the order.

(3) The powers conferred by this paragraph may be exercised at any time.

(4) An order under sub-paragraph (2)(a) or (b) may be varied or discharged by a subsequent order made on the application of any person by or to whom payments were required to be made under the previous order.

(5) Where a court makes an order under this paragraph—

(a) it may at any time make a further such order under sub-paragraph (2)(a), (b) or (c) with respect to the child concerned if he has not reached the age of eighteen;

(b) it may not make more than one order under sub-paragraph (2)(d) or (e) against the same person in respect of the same child.

(6) On making, varying or discharging a special guardianship order, or on making, varying or discharging provision in a child arrangements order with respect to the living arrangements of a child, the court may exercise any of its powers under this Schedule even though no application has been made to it under this Schedule.

(6A) For the purposes of sub-paragraph (6) provision in a child arrangements order is with respect to the living arrangements of a child if it regulates arrangements relating to—

(a) with whom the child is to live, or

(b) when the child is to live with any person.

(7) Where a child is a ward of court, the court may exercise any of its powers under this Schedule even though no application has been made to it.

Orders for financial relief for persons over eighteen

2.— (1) If, on an application by a person who has reached the age of eighteen, it appears to the court—

(a) that the applicant is, will be or (if an order were made under this paragraph) would be receiving instruction at an educational establishment or undergoing training for a trade, profession or vocation, whether or not while in gainful employment; or

(b) that there are special circumstances which justify the making of an order under this paragraph,

the court may make one or both of the orders mentioned in sub-paragraph (2).

(2) The orders are—

(a) an order requiring either or both of the applicant's parents to pay to the applicant such periodical payments, for such term, as may be specified in the order;

(b) an order requiring either or both of the applicant's parents to pay to the applicant such lump sum as may be so specified.

(3) An application may not be made under this paragraph by any person if, immediately before he reached the age of sixteen, a periodical payments order was in force with respect to him.

(4) No order shall be made under this paragraph at a time when the parents of the applicant are living with each other in the same household.

(5) An order under sub-paragraph (2)(a) may be varied or discharged by a subsequent order made on the application of any person by or to whom payments were required to be made under the previous order.

(6) In sub-paragraph (3) 'periodical payments order' means an order made under—
(a) this Schedule;
(b) ...
(c) section 23 or 27 of the Matrimonial Causes Act 1973;
(d) Part I of the Domestic Proceedings and Magistrates' Courts Act 1978;
(e) Part 1 or 9 of Schedule 5 to the Civil Partnership Act 2004 (financial relief in the High Court or county court);
(f) Schedule 6 to the 2004 Act (financial relief in the magistrates' courts),
for the making or securing of periodical payments.

(7) The powers conferred by this paragraph shall be exercisable at any time.

(8) Where the court makes an order under this paragraph it may from time to time while that order remains in force make a further such order.

Duration of orders for financial relief

3.— (1) The term to be specified in an order for periodical payments made under paragraph 1(2)(a) or (b) in favour of a child may begin with the date of the making of an application for the order in question or any later date or a date ascertained in accordance with sub-paragraph (5) or (6) but—
(a) shall not in the first instance extend beyond the child's seventeenth birthday unless the court thinks it right in the circumstances of the case to specify a later date; and
(b) shall not in any event extend beyond the child's eighteenth birthday.

(2) Paragraph (b) of sub-paragraph (1) shall not apply in the case of a child if it appears to the court that—
(a) the child is, or will be or (if an order were made without complying with that paragraph) would be receiving instruction at an educational establishment or undergoing training for a trade, profession or vocation, whether or not while in gainful employment; or
(b) there are special circumstances which justify the making of an order without complying with that paragraph.

(3) An order for periodical payments made under paragraph 1(2)(a) or 2(2)(a) shall, notwithstanding anything in the order, cease to have effect on the death of the person liable to make payments under the order.

(4) Where an order is made under paragraph 1(2)(a) or (b) requiring periodical payments to be made or secured to the parent of a child, the order shall cease to have effect if—
(a) any parent making or securing the payments; and
(b) any parent to whom the payments are made or secured, live together for a period of more than six months.

(5) Where—
(a) a maintenance calculation ('the current calculation') is in force with respect to a child; and
(b) an application is made for an order under paragraph 1(2)(a) or (b) of this Schedule for periodical payments in favour of that child—
(i) in accordance with section 8 of the Child Support Act 1991; and
(ii) before the end of the period of 6 months beginning with the making of the current calculation,
the term to be specified in any such order made on that application may be expressed to begin on, or at any time after, the earliest permitted date.

(6) For the purposes of subsection (5) above, 'the earliest permitted date' is which-ever is the later of—
(a) the date 6 months before the application is made; or
(b) the date on which the current calculation took effect or, where successive maintenance calculations have been continuously in force with respect to a child, on which the first of those calculations took effect.

(7) Where—
(a) a maintenance calculation ceases to have effect by or under any provision of the Child Support Act 1991, and
(b) an application is made, before the end of the period of 6 months beginning with the relevant date, for an order for periodical payments under paragraph 1(2)(a) or

(b) in favour of a child with respect to whom that maintenance calculation was in force immediately before it ceased to have effect,

the term to be specified in any such order, or in any interim order under paragraph 9, made on that application may begin with the date on which that maintenance calculation ceased to have effect, or any later date.

(8) In subsection (7)(b)—

(a) where the maintenance calculation ceased to have effect, the relevant date is the date on which it so ceased.

Matters to which court is to have regard in making orders for financial relief

4.— (1) In deciding whether to exercise its powers under paragraph 1 or 2, and if so in what manner, the court shall have regard to all the circumstances including—

(a) the income, earning capacity, property and other financial resources which each person mentioned in sub-paragraph (3) has or is likely to have in the foreseeable future;

(b) the financial needs, obligations and responsibilities which each person mentioned in sub-paragraph (3) has or is likely to have in the foreseeable future;

(c) the financial needs of the child;

(d) the income, earning capacity (if any), property and other financial resources of the child;

(e) any physical or mental disability of the child;

(f) the manner in which the child was being, or was expected to be, educated or trained.

(2) In deciding whether to exercise its powers under paragraph 1 against a person who is not the mother or father of the child, and if so in what manner, the court shall in addition have regard to—

(a) whether that person had assumed responsibility for the maintenance of the child and, if so, the extent to which and basis on which he assumed that responsibility and the length of the period during which he met that responsibility;

(b) whether he did so knowing that the child was not his child;

(c) the liability of any other person to maintain the child.

(3) Where the court makes an order under paragraph 1 against a person who is not the father of the child, it shall record in the order that the order is made on the basis that the person against whom the order is made is not the child's father.

(4) The persons mentioned in sub-paragraph (1) are—

(a) in relation to a decision whether to exercise its powers under paragraph 1, any parent of the child;

(b) in relation to a decision whether to exercise its powers under paragraph 2, the mother and father of the child;

(c) the applicant for the order;

(d) any other person in whose favour the court proposes to make the order.

(5) In the case of a child who has a parent by virtue of section 42 or 43 of the Human Fertilisation and Embryology Act 2008, any reference in sub-paragraph (2), (3) or (4) to the child's father is a reference to the woman who is a parent of the child by virtue of that section.

Provisions relating to lump sums

5.— (1) Without prejudice to the generality of paragraph 1, an order under that paragraph for the payment of a lump sum may be made for the purpose of enabling any liabilities or expenses—

(a) incurred in connection with the birth of the child or in maintaining the child; and

(b) reasonably incurred before the making of the order,

to be met.

(2) ...

(3) The power of the court under paragraph 1 or 2 to vary or discharge an order for the making or securing of periodical payments by a parent shall include power to make an order under that provision for the payment of a lump sum by that parent.

(4) ...

(5) An order made under paragraph 1 or 2 for the payment of a lump sum may provide for the payment of that sum by instalments.

(6) Where the court provides for the payment of a lump sum by instalments the court, on an application made either by the person liable to pay or the person entitled to receive that sum, shall have power to vary that order by varying—

(a) the number of instalments payable;

(b) the amount of any instalment payable;

(c) the date on which any instalment becomes payable.

Variation etc. of orders for periodical payments

6.— (1) In exercising its powers under paragraph 1 or 2 to vary or discharge an order for the making or securing of periodical payments the court shall have regard to all the circumstances of the case, including any change in any of the matters to which the court was required to have regard when making the order.

(2) The power of the court under paragraph 1 or 2 to vary an order for the making or securing of periodical payments shall include power to suspend any provision of the order temporarily and to revive any provision so suspended.

(3) Where on an application under paragraph 1 or 2 for the variation or discharge of an order for the making or securing of periodical payments the court varies the payments required to be made under that order, the court may provide that the payments as so varied shall be made from such date as the court may specify, except that, subject to sub-paragraph (9), the date shall not be earlier than the date of the making of the application.

(4) An application for the variation of an order made under paragraph 1 for the making or securing of periodical payments to or for the benefit of a child may, if the child has reached the age of sixteen, be made by the child himself.

(5) Where an order for the making or securing of periodical payments made under paragraph 1 ceases to have effect on the date on which the child reaches the age of sixteen, or at any time after that date but before or on the date on which he reaches the age of eighteen, the child may apply to the court which made the order for an order for its revival.

(6) If on such an application it appears to the court that—

(a) the child is, will be or (if an order were made under this sub-paragraph) would be receiving instruction at an educational establishment or undergoing training for a trade, profession or vocation, whether or not while in gainful employment; or

(b) there are special circumstances which justify the making of an order under this paragraph,

the court shall have power by order to revive the order from such date as the court may specify, not being earlier than the date of the making of the application.

(7) Any order which is revived by an order under sub-paragraph (5) may be varied or discharged under that provision, on the application of any person by whom or to whom payments are required to be made under the revived order.

(8) An order for the making or securing of periodical payments made under paragraph 1 or 2 may be varied or discharged, after the death of either parent, on the application of a guardian or special guardian of the child concerned.

(9) Where—

(a) an order under paragraph 1(2)(a) or (b) for the making or securing of periodical payments in favour of more than one child ('the order') is in force;

(b) the order requires payments specified in it to be made to or for the benefit of more than one child without apportioning those payments between them;

(c) a maintenance calculation ('the calculation') is made with respect to one or more, but not all, of the children with respect to whom those payments are to be made; and

(d) an application is made, before the end of the period of 6 months beginning with the date on which the calculation was made, for the variation or discharge of the order,

the court may, in exercise of its powers under paragraph 1 to vary or discharge the order, direct that the variation or discharge shall take effect from the date on which the calculation took effect or any later date.

...

Interpretation

16.— (1) In this Schedule 'child' includes, in any case where an application is made under paragraph 2 or 6 in relation to a person who has reached the age of eighteen, that person.

(2) In this Schedule, except paragraphs 2 and 15, 'parent' includes—

(a) any party to the marriage (whether or not subsisting) in relation to whom the child concerned is a child of the family, and

(b) any civil partner in a civil partnership (whether or not subsisting) in relation to whom the child concerned is a child of the family;

and for this purpose any reference to either parent or both parents shall be read as a reference to any parent of his and to all of his parents.

(3) In this Schedule, 'maintenance calculation' has the same meaning as it has in the Child Support Act 1991 by virtue of section 54 of that Act as read with any regulations in force under that section.

HUMAN FERTILISATION AND EMBRYOLOGY ACT 1990
(1990 c. 37)

Principal terms used

1. Meaning of 'embryo', 'gamete' and associated expressions

(1) In this Act (except in section 4A or in the term 'human admixed embryo')—
 (a) embryo means a live human embryo and does not include a human admixed embryo (as defined by section 4A(6)), and
 (b) references to an embryo include an egg that is in the process of fertilisation or is undergoing any other process capable of resulting in an embryo.

(2) This Act, so far as it governs bringing about the creation of an embryo, applies only to bringing about the creation of an embryo outside the human body; and in this Act—
 (a) references to embryos the creation of which was brought about *in vitro* (in their application to those where fertilisation or any other process by which an embryo is created is complete) are to those where fertilisation or any other process by which the embryo was created began outside the human body whether or not it was completed there, and
 (b) references to embryos taken from a woman do not include embryos whose creation was brought about *in vitro.*

(3) This Act, so far as it governs the keeping or use of an embryo, applies only to keeping or using an embryo outside the human body.

(4) In this Act (except in section 4A)—
 (a) references to eggs are to live human eggs, including cells of the female germ line at any stage of maturity, but (except in subsection (1)(b)) not including eggs that are in the process of fertilisation or are undergoing any other process capable of resulting in an embryo,
 (b) references to sperm are to live human sperm, including cells of the male germ line at any stage of maturity, and
 (c) references to gametes are to be read accordingly.

(5) For the purposes of this Act, sperm is to be treated as partner donated sperm if the donor of the sperm and the recipient of the sperm declare that they have an intimate physical relationship.

(6) If it appears to the Secretary of State necessary or desirable to do so in the light of developments in science or medicine, regulations may provide that in this Act (except in section 4A) 'embryo', 'eggs', 'sperm' or 'gametes' includes things specified in the regulations which would not otherwise fall within the definition.

(7) Regulations made by virtue of subsection (6) may not provide for anything containing any nuclear or mitochondrial DNA that is not human to be treated as an embryo or as eggs, sperm or gametes.

2. Other terms

(1) In this Act—
'the Authority' means the Human Fertilisation and Embryology Authority established under section 5 of this Act,
'basic partner treatment services' means treatment services that are provided for a woman and a man together without using—
 (a) the gametes of any other person, or
 (b) embryos created outside the woman's body,
'directions' means directions under section 23 of this Act,
'licence' means a licence under Schedule 2 to this Act and, in relation to a licence, 'the person responsible' has the meaning given by section 17 of this Act,
'non-medical fertility services' means any services that are provided, in the course of a business, for the purpose of assisting women to carry children, but are not medical, surgical or obstetric services,
'nuclear DNA', in relation to an embryo, includes DNA in the pronucleus of the embryo,
'treatment services' means medical, surgical or obstetric services provided to the public or a section of the public for the purpose of assisting women to carry children.

. . .

(3) For the purposes of this Act, a woman is not to be treated as carrying a child until the embryo has become implanted.

Licence conditions

13. Conditions of licences for treatment

...

(5) A woman shall not be provided with treatment services unless account has been taken of the welfare of any child who may be born as a result of the treatment (including the need of that child for supportive parenting), and of any other child who may be affected by the birth.

(6) A woman shall not be provided with treatment services of a kind specified in Part 1 of Schedule 3ZA unless she and any man or woman who is to be treated together with her have been given a suitable opportunity to receive proper counselling about the implications of her being provided with treatment services of that kind, and have been provided with such relevant information as is proper.

(6A) A woman shall not be provided with treatment services after the happening of any event falling within any paragraph of Part 2 of Schedule 3ZA unless (before or after the event) she and the intended second parent have been given a suitable opportunity to receive proper counselling about the implications of the woman being provided with treatment services after the happening of that event, and have been provided with such relevant information as is proper.

(6B) The reference in subsection (6A) to the intended second parent is a reference to—

(a) any man as respects whom the agreed fatherhood conditions in section 37 of the Human Fertilisation and Embryology Act 2008 ('the 2008 Act') are for the time being satisfied in relation to treatment provided to the woman mentioned in subsection (6A), and

(b) any woman as respects whom the agreed female parenthood conditions in section 44 of the 2008 Act are for the time being satisfied in relation to treatment provided to the woman mentioned in subsection (6A).

(6C) In the case of treatment services falling within paragraph 1 of Schedule 3ZA (use of gametes of a person not receiving those services) or paragraph 3 of that Schedule (use of embryo taken from a woman not receiving those services), the information provided by virtue of subsection (6) or (6A) must include such information as is proper about—

(a) the importance of informing any resulting child at an early age that the child results from the gametes of a person who is not a parent of the child, and

(b) suitable methods of informing such a child of that fact.

(6D) Where the person responsible receives from a person ('X') notice under section 37(1)(c) or 44(1)(c) of the 2008 Act of X's withdrawal of consent to X being treated as the parent of any child resulting from the provision of treatment services to a woman ('W'), the person responsible—

(a) must notify W in writing of the receipt of the notice from X, and

(b) no person to whom the licence applies may place an embryo or sperm and eggs in W, or artificially inseminate W, until W has been so notified.

(6E) Where the person responsible receives from a woman ('W') who has previously given notice under section 37(1)(b) or 44(1)(b) of the 2008 Act that she consents to another person ('X') being treated as a parent of any child resulting from the provision of treatment services to W—

(a) notice under section 37(1)(c) or 44(1)(c) of the 2008 Act of the withdrawal of W's consent, or

(b) a notice under section 37(1)(b) or 44(1)(b) of the 2008 Act in respect of a person other than X,

the person responsible must take reasonable steps to notify X in writing of the receipt of the notice mentioned in paragraph (a) or (b).

Information

31. Register of information

(1) The Authority shall keep a register which is to contain any information which falls within subsection (2) and which—

(a) immediately before the coming into force of section 24 of the Human Fertilisation and Embryology Act 2008, was contained in the register kept under this section by the Authority, or

(b) is obtained by the Authority.

(2) Subject to subsection (3), information falls within this subsection if it relates to—

(a) the provision for any identifiable individual of treatment services other than basic partner treatment services,

(b) the procurement or distribution of any sperm, other than sperm which is partner-donated sperm and has not been stored, in the course of providing non-medical fertility services for any identifiable individual,

(c) the keeping of the gametes of any identifiable individual or of an embryo taken from any identifiable woman,
(d) the use of the gametes of any identifiable individual other than their use for the purpose of basic partner treatment services, or
(e) the use of an embryo taken from any identifiable woman,
or if it shows that any identifiable individual is a relevant individual.
(3) Information does not fall within subsection (2) if it is provided to the Authority for the purposes of any voluntary contact register as defined by section 31ZF(1).
(4) In this section 'relevant individual' means an individual who was or may have been born in consequence of—
(a) treatment services, other than basic partner treatment services, or
(b) the procurement or distribution of any sperm (other than partner-donated sperm which has not been stored) in the course of providing non-medical fertility services.

31ZA. Request for information as to genetic parentage etc.

(1) A person who has attained the age of 16 ("the applicant") may by notice to the Authority require the Authority to comply with a request under subsection (2).
(2) The applicant may request the Authority to give the applicant notice stating whether or not the information contained in the register shows that a person ("the donor") other than a parent of the applicant would or might, but for the relevant statutory provisions, be the parent of the applicant, and if it does show that—
(a) giving the applicant so much of that information as relates to the donor as the Authority is required by regulations to give (but no other information), or
(b) stating whether or not that information shows that there are other persons of whom the donor is not the parent but would or might, but for the relevant statutory provisions, be the parent and if so—
(i) the number of those other persons,
(ii) the sex of each of them, and
(iii) the year of birth of each of them.
(3) The Authority shall comply with a request under subsection (2) if—
(a) the information contained in the register shows that the applicant is a relevant individual, and
(b) the applicant has been given a suitable opportunity to receive proper counselling about the implications of compliance with the request.
(4) Where a request is made under subsection (2)(a) and the applicant has not attained the age of 18 when the applicant gives notice to the Authority under subsection (1), regulations cannot require the Authority to give the applicant any information which identifies the donor.
(5) Regulations cannot require the Authority to give any information as to the identity of a person whose gametes have been used or from whom an embryo has been taken if a person to whom a licence applied was provided with the information at a time when the Authority could not have been required to give information of the kind in question.
(6) The Authority need not comply with a request made under subsection (2)(b) by any applicant if it considers that special circumstances exist which increase the likelihood that compliance with the request would enable the applicant—
(a) to identify the donor, in a case where the Authority is not required by regulations under subsection (2)(a) to give the applicant information which identifies the donor, or
(b) to identify any person about whom information is given under subsection (2)(b).
(7) In this section—
"relevant individual" has the same meaning as in section 31;
"the relevant statutory provisions" means sections 27 to 29 of this Act and sections 33 to 47 of the Human Fertilisation and Embryology Act 2008.

31ZB. Request for information as to intended spouse etc.

(1) Subject to subsection (4), a person ('the applicant') may by notice to the Authority require the Authority to comply with a request under subsection (2).
(2) The applicant may request the Authority to give the applicant notice stating whether or not information contained in the register shows that, but for the relevant statutory provisions, the applicant would or might be related to a person specified in the request ("the specified person") as—
(a) a person whom the applicant proposes to marry,
(b) a person with whom the applicant proposes to enter into a civil partnership, or
(c) a person with whom the applicant is in an intimate physical relationship or with whom the applicant proposes to enter into an intimate physical relationship.
(3) Subject to subsection (5), the Authority shall comply with a request under subsection (2) if—

(a) the information contained in the register shows that the applicant is a relevant individual,
(b) the Authority receives notice in writing from the specified person consenting to the request being made and that notice has not been withdrawn, and
(c) the applicant and the specified person have each been given a suitable opportunity to receive proper counselling about the implications of compliance with the request.

(4) A request may not be made under subsection (2)(c) by a person who has not attained the age of 16.

(5) Where a request is made under subsection (2)(c) and the specified person has not attained the age of 16 when the applicant gives notice to the Authority under subsection (1), the Authority must not comply with the request.

(6) Where the Authority is required under subsection (3) to comply with a request under subsection (2), the Authority must take all reasonable steps to give the applicant and the specified person notice stating whether or not the information contained in the register shows that, but for the relevant statutory provisions, the applicant and the specified person would or might be related.

(7) In this section—
'relevant individual' has the same meaning as in section 31;
'the relevant statutory provisions' has the same meaning as in section 31ZA.

31ZC. Power of Authority to inform donor of request for information

(1) Where—
(a) the Authority has received from a person ('the applicant') a notice containing a request under subsection (2)(a) of section 31ZA, and
(b) compliance by the Authority with its duty under that section has involved or will involve giving the applicant information relating to a person other than the parent of the applicant who would or might, but for the relevant statutory provisions, be a parent of the applicant ('the donor'),

the Authority may notify the donor that a request under section 31ZA(2)(a) has been made, but may not disclose the identity of the applicant or any information relating to the applicant.

(2) In this section 'the relevant statutory provisions' has the same meaning as in section 31ZA.

31ZD. Provision to donor of information about resulting children

(1) This section applies where a person ('the donor') has consented under Schedule 3 (whether before or after the coming into force of this section) to—
(a) the use of the donor's gametes, or an embryo the creation of which was brought about using the donor's gametes, for the purposes of treatment services provided under a licence, or
(b) the use of the donor's gametes for the purposes of non-medical fertility services provided under a licence.

(2) In subsection (1)—
(a) 'treatment services' do not include treatment services provided to the donor, or to the donor and another person together, and
(b) 'non-medical fertility services' do not include any services involving partner-donated sperm.

(3) The donor may by notice request the appropriate person to give the donor notice stating—
(a) the number of persons of whom the donor is not a parent but would or might, but for the relevant statutory provisions, be a parent by virtue of the use of the gametes or embryos to which the consent relates,
(b) the sex of each of those persons, and
(c) the year of birth of each of those persons.

(4) Subject to subsections (5) to (7), the appropriate person shall notify the donor whether the appropriate person holds the information mentioned in subsection (3) and, if the appropriate person does so, shall comply with the request.

(5) The appropriate person need not comply with a request under subsection (3) if the appropriate person considers that special circumstances exist which increase the likelihood that compliance with the request would enable the donor to identify any of the persons falling within paragraphs (a) to (c) of subsection (3).

(6) In the case of a donor who consented as described in subsection (1)(a), the Authority need not comply with a request made to it under subsection (3) where the person who held the licence referred to in subsection (1)(a) continues to hold a licence under paragraph 1 of Schedule 2, unless the donor has previously made a request under subsection (3) to the person responsible and the person responsible—

(a) has notified the donor that the information concerned is not held, or
(b) has failed to comply with the request within a reasonable period.

(7) In the case of a donor who consented as described in subsection (1)(b), the Authority need not comply with a request made to it under subsection (3) where the person who held the licence referred to in subsection (1)(b) continues to hold a licence under paragraph 1A of Schedule 2, unless the donor has previously made a request under subsection (3) to the person responsible and the person responsible—
(a) has notified the donor that the information concerned is not held, or
(b) has failed to comply with the request within a reasonable period.

(8) In this section 'the appropriate person' means—
(a) in the case of a donor who consented as described in paragraph (a) of subsection (1)—
(i) where the person who held the licence referred to in that paragraph continues to hold a licence under paragraph 1 of Schedule 2, the person responsible, or
(ii) the Authority, and
(b) in the case of a donor who consented as described in paragraph (b) of subsection (1)—
(i) where the person who held the licence referred to in that paragraph continues to hold a licence under paragraph 1A of Schedule 2, the person responsible, or
(ii) the Authority.

(9) In this section 'the relevant statutory provisions' has the same meaning as in section 31ZA.

31ZE. Provision of information about donor-conceived genetic siblings

(1) For the purposes of this section two relevant individuals are donor-conceived genetic siblings of each other if a person ('the donor') who is not the parent of either of them would or might, but for the relevant statutory provisions, be the parent of both of them.

(2) Where—
(a) the information on the register shows that a relevant individual ('A') is the donor-conceived genetic sibling of another relevant individual ('B'),
(b) A has provided information to the Authority ('the agreed information') which consists of or includes information which enables A to be identified with the request that it should be disclosed to—
(i) any donor-conceived genetic sibling of A, or
(ii) such siblings of A of a specified description which includes B, and
(c) the conditions in subsection (3) are satisfied,

then, subject to subsection (4), the Authority shall disclose the agreed information to B.

(3) The conditions referred to in subsection (2)(c) are—
(a) that each of A and B has attained the age of 18,
(b) that B has requested the disclosure to B of information about any donor-conceived genetic sibling of B, and
(c) that each of A and B has been given a suitable opportunity to receive proper counselling about the implications of disclosure under subsection (2).

(4) The Authority need not disclose any information under subsection (2) if it considers that the disclosure of information will lead to A or B identifying the donor unless—
(a) the donor has consented to the donor's identity being disclosed to A or B, or
(b) were A or B to make a request under section 31ZA(2)(a), the Authority would be required by regulations under that provision to give A or B information which would identify the donor.

(5) In this section—
'relevant individual' has the same meaning as in section 31;
'the relevant statutory provisions' has the same meaning as in section 31ZA.

31ZF. Power of Authority to keep voluntary contact register

(1) In this section and section 31ZG, a 'voluntary contact register' means a register of persons who have expressed their wish to receive information about any person to whom they are genetically related as a consequence of the provision to any person of treatment services in the United Kingdom before 1 August 1991.

(2) The Authority may—
(a) set up a voluntary contact register in such manner as it thinks fit,
(b) keep a voluntary contact register in such manner as it thinks fit,
(c) determine criteria for eligibility for inclusion on the register and the particulars that may be included,
(d) charge a fee to persons who wish their particulars to be entered on the register,

(e) arrange for samples of the DNA of such persons to be analysed at their request,
(f) make such arrangements as it thinks fit for the disclosure of information on the register between persons who appear to the Authority to be genetically related, and
(g) impose such conditions as it thinks fit to prevent a person ("A") from disclosing information to a person to whom A is genetically related ("B") where that information would identify any person who is genetically related to both A and B.

(3) The Authority may make arrangements with any person by whom a voluntary contact register is kept before the commencement of this section for the supply by that person to the Authority of the information contained in the register maintained by that person.

31ZG. Financial assistance for person setting up or keeping voluntary contact register

(1) The Authority may, instead of keeping a voluntary contact register, give financial assistance to any person who sets up or keeps a voluntary contact register.
(2) Financial assistance under subsection (1) may be given in any form, and in particular, may be given by way of—
(a) grants,
(b) loans,
(c) guarantees, or
(d) incurring expenditure for the person assisted.
(3) Financial assistance under subsection (1) may be given on such terms and conditions as the Authority considers appropriate.
(4) A person receiving assistance under subsection (1) must comply with the terms and conditions on which it is given, and compliance may be enforced by the Authority.

32. Information to be provided to Registrar General

(1) This section applies where a claim is made before the Registrar General that a person is or is not the parent of a child and it is necessary or desirable for the purpose of any function of the Registrar General to determine whether the claim is or may be well-founded.
(2) The Authority shall comply with any request made by the Registrar General by notice to the Authority to disclose whether any information on the register kept in pursuance of section 31 of this Act tends to show that the person may be a parent of the child by virtue of any of the relevant statutory provisions and, if it does, disclose that information.
(2A) In subsection (2) 'the relevant statutory provisions' means—
(a) section 28 of this Act, and
(b) sections 35 to 47 of the Human Fertilisation and Embryology Act 2008.

...

33A. Disclosure of information

(1) No person shall disclose any information falling within section 31(2) which the person obtained (whether before or after the coming into force of section 24 of the Human Fertilisation and Embryology Act 2008) in the person's capacity as—
(a) a member or employee of the Authority,
(b) any person exercising functions of the Authority by virtue of section 8B or 8C of this Act (including a person exercising such functions by virtue of either of those sections as a member of staff or as an employee),
(c) any person engaged by the Authority to provide services to the Authority,
(d) any person employed by, or engaged to provide services to, a person mentioned in paragraph (c),
(e) a person to whom a licence applies,
(f) a person to whom a third party agreement applies, or
(g) a person to whom directions have been given.
(2) Subsection (1) does not apply where—
(a) the disclosure is made to a person as a member or employee of the Authority or as a person exercising functions of the Authority as mentioned in subsection (1)(b),
(b) the disclosure is made to or by a person falling within subsection (1)(c) for the purpose of the provision of services which that person is engaged to provide to the Authority,
(c) the disclosure is made by a person mentioned in subsection (1)(d) for the purpose of enabling a person falling within subsection (1)(c) to provide services which that person is engaged to provide to the Authority,
(d) the disclosure is made to a person to whom a licence applies for the purpose of that person's functions as such,

(e) the disclosure is made to a person to whom a third party agreement applies for the purpose of that person's functions under that agreement,
(f) the disclosure is made in pursuance of directions given by virtue of section 24,
(g) the disclosure is made so that no individual can be identified from the information,
(h) the disclosure is of information other than identifying donor information and is made with the consent required by section 33B, the disclosure—
(i) is made by a person who is satisfied that it is necessary to make the disclosure to avert an imminent danger to the health of an individual ('P'),
(ii) is of information falling within section 31(2)(a) which could be disclosed by virtue of paragraph (h) with P's consent or could be disclosed to P by virtue of subsection (5), and
(iii) is made in circumstances where it is not reasonably practicable to obtain P's consent,
(j) the disclosure is of information which has been lawfully made available to the public before the disclosure is made,
(k) the disclosure is made in accordance with sections 31ZA to 31ZE,
(l) the disclosure is required or authorised to be made—
(i) under regulations made under section 33D, or
(ii) in relation to any time before the coming into force of the first regulations under that section, under regulations made under section 251 of the National Health Service Act 2006,
(m) the disclosure is made by a person acting in the capacity mentioned in subsection (1)(a) or (b) for the purpose of carrying out the Authority's duties under section 8A,
(n) the disclosure is made by a person acting in the capacity mentioned in subsection (1)(a) or (b) in pursuance of an order of a court under section 34 or 35,
(o) the disclosure is made by a person acting in the capacity mentioned in subsection (1)(a) or (b) to the Registrar General in pursuance of a request under section 32,
(p) the disclosure is made by a person acting in the capacity mentioned in subsection (1)(a) or (b) to any body or person discharging a regulatory function for the purpose of assisting that body or person to carry out that function,
(q) the disclosure is made for the purpose of establishing in any proceedings relating to an application for an order under subsection (1) of section 54 of the Human Fertilisation and Embryology Act 2008 whether the condition specified in paragraph (a) or (b) of that subsection is met,
(r) the disclosure is made under section 3 of the Access to Health Records Act 1990,
(s) ...
(t) the disclosure is made necessarily for—
(i) the purpose of the investigation of any offence (or suspected offence), or
(ii) any purpose preliminary to proceedings, or for the purposes of, or in connection with, any proceedings.

(3) Subsection (1) does not apply to the disclosure of information in so far as—
(a) the information identifies a person who, but for sections 27 to 29 of this Act or sections 33 to 47 of the Human Fertilisation and Embryology Act 2008, would or might be a parent of a person who instituted proceedings under section 1A of the Congenital Disabilities (Civil Liability) Act 1976, and
(b) the disclosure is made for the purpose of defending such proceedings, or instituting connected proceedings for compensation against that parent.

(4) Paragraph (t) of subsection (2), so far as relating to disclosure for the purpose of the investigation of an offence or suspected offence, or for any purpose preliminary to, or in connection with proceedings, does not apply—
(a) to disclosure of identifying donor information, or
(b) to disclosure, in circumstances in which subsection (1) of section 34 of this Act applies, of information relevant to the determination of the question mentioned in that subsection, made by any person acting in a capacity mentioned in any of paragraphs (c) to (g) of subsection (1).

(5) Subsection (1) does not apply to the disclosure to any individual of information which—
(a) falls within subsection (2) of section 31 of this Act by virtue of any of paragraphs (a) to (e) of that subsection, and
(b) relates only to that individual or, in the case of an individual who is treated together with, or gives a notice under section 37 or 44 of the Human Fertilisation and Embryology Act 2008 in respect of, another, only to that individual and that other.

(6) In subsection (2)—
(a) in paragraph (p) 'regulatory function' has the same meaning as in section 32 of the Legislative and Regulatory Reform Act 2006, and
(b) in paragraph (t) references to 'proceedings' include any formal procedure for dealing with a complaint.

(7) In this section 'identifying donor information' means information enabling a person to be identified as a person whose gametes were used in accordance with consent given under paragraph 5 of Schedule 3 for the purposes of treatment services or non-medical fertility services in consequence of which an identifiable individual was, or may have been, born.

33B. Consent required to authorise certain disclosures

(1) This section has effect for the purposes of section 33A(2)(h).
(2) Subject to subsection (5), the consent required by this section is the consent of each individual who can be identified from the information.
(3) Consent in respect of a person who has not attained the age of 18 years ("C") may be given—
 (a) by C, in a case where C is competent to deal with the issue of consent, or
 (b) by a person having parental responsibility for C, in any other case.
(4) Consent to disclosure given at the request of another shall be disregarded unless, before it is given, the person requesting it takes reasonable steps to explain to the individual from whom it is requested the implications of compliance with the request.
(5) In the case of information which shows that any identifiable individual ("A") was, or may have been, born in consequence of treatment services, the consent required by this section does not include A's consent if the disclosure is necessarily incidental to the disclosure of information falling within section 31(2)(a).
(6) The reference in subsection (3) to parental responsibility is—
 (a) in relation to England and Wales, to be read in accordance with the Children Act 1989;

...

33C. Power to provide for additional exceptions from section 33A(1)

(1) Regulations may provide for additional exceptions from section 33A(1).
(2) No exception may be made under this section for—
 (a) disclosure of a kind mentioned in paragraph (a) or (b) of subsection (4) of section 33A, or
 (b) disclosure in circumstances in which section 32 of this Act applies of information having the tendency mentioned in subsection (2) of that section, made by any person acting in a capacity mentioned in any of paragraphs (c) to (g) of subsection (1) of section 33A.

34. Disclosure in interests of justice

(1) Where in any proceedings before a court the question whether a person is or is not the parent of a child by virtue of sections 27 to 29 of this Act or sections 33 to 47 of the Human Fertilisation and Embryology Act 2008 falls to be determined, the court may on the application of any party to the proceedings make an order requiring the Authority—
 (a) to disclose whether or not any information relevant to that question is contained in the register kept in pursuance of section 31 of this Act, and
 (b) if it is, to disclose so much of it as is specified in the order,

but such an order may not require the Authority to disclose any information falling within section 31(2)(b) of this Act.
(2) The court must not make an order under subsection (1) above unless it is satisfied that the interests of justice require it to do so, taking into account—
 (a) any representations made by any individual who may be affected by the disclosure, and
 (b) the welfare of the child, if under 18 years old, and of any other person under that age who may be affected by the disclosure.
(3) If the proceedings before the court are civil proceedings, it—
 (a) may direct that the whole or any part of the proceedings on the application for an order under subsection (2) above shall be heard in camera, and
 (b) if it makes such an order, may then or later direct that the whole or any part of any later stage of the proceedings shall be heard in camera.
(4) An application for a direction under subsection (3) above shall be heard in camera unless the court otherwise directs.

Offences

41. Offences

...

(5) A person who discloses any information in contravention of section 33A of this Act is guilty of an offence and liable—

(a) on conviction on indictment, to imprisonment for a term not exceeding two years or a fine or both, and
(b) on summary conviction, to imprisonment for a term not exceeding six months or a fine not exceeding the statutory maximum or both.

...

(11) It is a defence for a person charged with an offence under this Act to prove—
(a) that at the material time he was a person to whom a licence applied or to whom directions had been given, and
(b) that he took all such steps as were reasonable and exercised all due diligence to avoid committing the offence.

42. Consent to prosecution

No proceedings for an offence under this Act shall be instituted—
(a) in England and Wales, except by or with the consent of the Director of Public Prosecutions, and

...

49. Short title, commencement, etc.

...

(4) Section 27 of the Family Law Reform Act 1987 (artificial insemination) does not have effect in relation to children carried by women as the result of their artificial insemination after the commencement of sections 27 to 29 of this Act.

Section 1.

SCHEDULE 3

CONSENTS TO USE OR STORAGE OF GAMETES, EMBRYOS OR HUMAN ADMIXED EMBRYOS ETC.

Consent

1.— (1) A consent under this Schedule, and any notice under paragraph 4 varying or withdrawing a consent under this Schedule, must be in writing and, subject to sub-paragraph (2), must be signed by the person giving it.
(2) A consent under this Schedule by a person who is unable to sign because of illness, injury or physical disability (a 'person unable to sign'), and any notice under paragraph 4 by a person unable to sign varying or withdrawing a consent under this Schedule, is to be taken to comply with the requirement of sub-paragraph (1) as to signature if it is signed at the direction of the person unable to sign, in the presence of the person unable to sign and in the presence of at least one witness who attests the signature.
(3) In this Schedule 'effective consent' means a consent under this Schedule which has not been withdrawn.

2.— (1) A consent to the use of any embryo must specify one or more of the following purposes—
(a) use in providing treatment services to the person giving consent, or that person and another specified person together,
(b) use in providing treatment services to persons not including the person giving consent, or
(ba) use for the purpose of training persons in embryo biopsy, embryo storage or other embryological techniques, or
(c) use for the purposes of any project of research,
and may specify conditions subject to which the embryo may be so used.

...

(2) A consent to the storage of any gametes, any embryo or any human admixed embryo must—
(a) specify the maximum period of storage (if less than the statutory storage period),
(b) except in a case falling within paragraph (c), state what is to be done with the gametes, embryo or human admixed embryo if the person who gave the consent dies or is unable, because the person lacks capacity to do so, to vary the terms of the consent or to withdraw it, and
(c) where the consent is given by virtue of paragraph 8(2A) or 13(2), state what is to be done with the embryo or human admixed embryo if the person to whom the consent relates dies,
and may (in any case) specify conditions subject to which the gametes, embryo or human admixed embryo may remain in storage.

(2A) A consent to the use of a person's human cells to bring about the creation *in vitro* of an embryo or human admixed embryo is to be taken unless otherwise stated to include consent to the use of the cells after the person's death.

...

(3) A consent under this Schedule must provide for such other matters as the Authority may specify in directions.

...

Procedure for giving consent

3.— (1) Before a person gives consent under this Schedule—
(a) he must be given a suitable opportunity to receive proper counselling about the implications of taking the proposed steps, and
(b) he must be provided with such relevant information as is proper.
(2) Before a person gives consent under this Schedule he must be informed of the effect of paragraph 4 below and, if relevant, paragraph 4A.

Variation and withdrawal of consent

4.— (1) The terms of any consent under this Schedule may from time to time be varied, and the consent may be withdrawn, by notice given by the person who gave the consent to the person keeping the gametes, human cells, embryo or human admixed embryo to which the consent is relevant.
(2) Subject to sub-paragraph (3), the terms of any consent to the use of any embryo cannot be varied, and such consent cannot be withdrawn, once the embryo has been used—
(a) in providing treatment services, or
(aa) in training persons in embryo biopsy, embryo storage or other embryological techniques, or
(b) for the purposes of any project of research.
(3) Where the terms of any consent to the use of an embryo ('embryo A') include consent to the use of an embryo or human admixed embryo whose creation may be brought about *in vitro* using embryo A, that consent to the use of that subsequent embryo or human admixed embryo cannot be varied or withdrawn once embryo A has been used for one or more of the purposes mentioned in sub-paragraph (2)(a) or (b).

...

4A.— (1) This paragraph applies where—
(a) a permitted embryo, the creation of which was brought about *in vitro*, is in storage,
(b) it was created for use in providing treatment services,
(c) before it is used in providing treatment services, one of the persons whose gametes were used to bring about its creation ('P') gives the person keeping the embryo notice withdrawing P's consent to the storage of the embryo, and
(d) the embryo was not to be used in providing treatment services to P alone.
(2) The person keeping the embryo must as soon as possible take all reasonable steps to notify each interested person in relation to the embryo of P's withdrawal of consent.
(3) For the purposes of sub-paragraph (2), a person is an interested person in relation to an embryo if the embryo was to be used in providing treatment services to that person.
(4) Storage of the embryo remains lawful until—
(a) the end of the period of 12 months beginning with the day on which the notice mentioned in sub-paragraph (1) was received from P, or
(b) if, before the end of that period, the person keeping the embryo receives a notice from each person notified of P's withdrawal under sub-paragraph (2) stating that the person consents to the destruction of the embryo, the time at which the last of those notices is received.
(5) The reference in sub-paragraph (1)(a) to a permitted embryo is to be read in accordance with section 3ZA.

Use of gametes for treatment of others

5.— (1) A person's gametes must not be used for the purposes of treatment services or non-medical fertility services unless there is an effective consent by that person to their being so used and they are used in accordance with the terms of the consent.
(2) A person's gametes must not be received for use for those purposes unless there is an effective consent by that person to their being so used.
(3) This paragraph does not apply to the use of a person's gametes for the purpose of that person, or that person and another together, receiving treatment services.

In vitro fertilisation and subsequent use of embryo

6.— (1) A person's gametes or human cells must not be used to bring about the creation of any embryo *in vitro* unless there is an effective consent by that person to any embryo, the creation of which may be brought about with the use of those gametes or human cells being used for one or more of the purposes mentioned in paragraph 2(1)(a), (b) and (c) above.

(2) An embryo the creation of which was brought about *in vitro* must not be received by any person unless there is an effective consent by each relevant person in relation to the embryo to the use for one or more of the purposes mentioned in paragraph 2(1)(a), (b), (ba) and (c) above of the embryo.

(3) An embryo the creation of which was brought about *in vitro* must not be used for any purpose unless there is an effective consent by each relevant person in relation to the embryo to the use for that purpose of the embryo and the embryo is used in accordance with those consents.

(3A) If the Authority is satisfied that the parental consent conditions in paragraph 15 are met in relation to the proposed use under a licence of the human cells of a person who has not attained the age of 18 years ('C'), the Authority may in the licence authorise the application of sub-paragraph (3B) in relation to C.

(3B) Where the licence authorises the application of this sub-paragraph, the effective consent of a person having parental responsibility for C—

(a) to the use of C's human cells to bring about the creation of an embryo *in vitro* for use for the purposes of a project of research, or

(b) to the use for those purposes of an embryo in relation to which C is a relevant person by reason only of the use of C's human cells,

is to be treated for the purposes of sub-paragraphs (1) to (3) as the effective consent of C.

(3C) If C attains the age of 18 years or the condition in paragraph 15(3) ceases to be met in relation to C, paragraph 4 has effect in relation to C as if any effective consent previously given under sub-paragraphs (1) to (3) by a person having parental responsibility for C had been given by C but, subject to that, sub-paragraph (3B) ceases to apply in relation to C.

(3D) Sub-paragraphs (1) to (3) have effect subject to paragraphs 16 and 20.

(3E) For the purposes of sub-paragraphs (2), (3) and (3B), each of the following is a relevant person in relation to an embryo the creation of which was brought about *in vitro* ('embryo A')—

(a) each person whose gametes or human cells were used to bring about the creation of embryo A,

(b) each person whose gametes or human cells were used to bring about the creation of any other embryo, the creation of which was brought about *in vitro*, which was used to bring about the creation of embryo A, and

(c) each person whose gametes or human cells were used to bring about the creation of any human admixed embryo, the creation of which was brought about *in vitro*, which was used to bring about the creation of embryo A.

(4) Any consent required by this paragraph is in addition to any consent that may be required by paragraph 5 above.

Embryos obtained by lavage, etc.

7.— (1) An embryo taken from a woman must not be used for any purpose unless there is an effective consent by her to the use of the embryo for that purpose and it is used in accordance with the consent.

(2) An embryo taken from a woman must not be received by any person for use for any purpose unless there is an effective consent by her to the use of the embryo for that purpose.

(3) Sub-paragraphs (1) and (2) do not apply to the use, for the purpose of providing a woman with treatment services, of an embryo taken from her.

(4) An embryo taken from a woman must not be used to bring about the creation of any embryo *in vitro* or any human admixed embryo *in vitro*.

Storage of gametes and embryos

8.— (1) A person's gametes must not be kept in storage unless there is an effective consent by that person to their storage and they are stored in accordance with the consent.

(2) An embryo the creation of which was brought about *in vitro* must not be kept in storage unless there is an effective consent, by each relevant person in relation to the embryo, to the storage of the embryo and the embryo is stored in accordance with those consents.

(2A) Where a licence authorises the application of paragraph 6(3B) in relation to a person who has not attained the age of 18 years ('C'), the effective consent of a person having parental responsibility for C to the storage of an embryo in relation to which C is a relevant person by reason only of the use of C's human cells is to be treated for the purposes of sub-paragraph (2) as the effective consent of C.

(2B) If C attains the age of 18 years or the condition in paragraph 15(3) ceases to be met in relation to C, paragraph 4 has effect in relation to C as if any effective consent previously given under sub-paragraph (2) by a person having parental responsibility for C had been given by C but, subject to that, sub-paragraph (2A) ceases to apply in relation to C.

(2C) For the purposes of sub-paragraphs (2) and (2A), each of the following is a relevant person in relation to an embryo the creation of which was brought about *in vitro* ('embryo A')—

(a) each person whose gametes or human cells were used to bring about the creation of embryo A,

(b) each person whose gametes or human cells were used to bring about the creation of any other embryo, the creation of which was brought about *in vitro*, which was used to bring about the creation of embryo A, and

(c) each person whose gametes or human cells were used to bring about the creation of any human admixed embryo, the creation of which was brought about *in vitro*, which was used to bring about the creation of embryo A.

(3) An embryo taken from a woman must not be kept in storage unless there is an effective consent by her to its storage and it is stored in accordance with the consent.

(4) Sub-paragraph (1) has effect subject to paragraphs 9 and 10; and sub-paragraph (2) has effect subject to paragraphs 4A(4), 16 and 20.

Cases where consent not required for storage

9.— (1) The gametes of a person ('C') may be kept in storage without C's consent if the following conditions are met.

(2) Condition A is that the gametes are lawfully taken from or provided by C before C attains the age of 18 years.

(3) Condition B is that, before the gametes are first stored, a registered medical practitioner certifies in writing that C is expected to undergo medical treatment and that in the opinion of the registered medical practitioner—

(a) the treatment is likely to cause a significant impairment of C's fertility, and

(b) the storage of the gametes is in C's best interests.

(4) Condition C is that, at the time when the gametes are first stored, either—

(a) C has not attained the age of 16 years and is not competent to deal with the issue of consent to the storage of the gametes, or

(b) C has attained that age but, although not lacking capacity to consent to the storage of the gametes, is not competent to deal with the issue of consent to their storage.

(5) Condition D is that C has not, since becoming competent to deal with the issue of consent to the storage of the gametes—

(a) given consent under this Schedule to the storage of the gametes, or

(b) given written notice to the person keeping the gametes that C does not wish them to continue to be stored.

...

10.— (1) The gametes of a person ('P') may be kept in storage without P's consent if the following conditions are met.

(2) Condition A is that the gametes are lawfully taken from or provided by P after P has attained the age of 16 years.

(3) Condition B is that, before the gametes are first stored, a registered medical practitioner certifies in writing that P is expected to undergo medical treatment and that in the opinion of the registered medical practitioner—

(a) the treatment is likely to cause a significant impairment of P's fertility,

(b) P lacks capacity to consent to the storage of the gametes,

(c) P is likely at some time to have that capacity, and

(d) the storage of the gametes is in P's best interests.

(4) Condition C is that, at the time when the gametes are first stored, P lacks capacity to consent to their storage.

(5) Condition D is that P has not subsequently, at a time when P has capacity to give a consent under this Schedule—

(a) given consent to the storage of the gametes, or

(b) given written notice to the person keeping the gametes that P does not wish them to continue to be stored.

...

11. A person's gametes must not be kept in storage by virtue of paragraph 9 or 10 after the person's death.

MAINTENANCE ENFORCEMENT ACT 1991
(1991 c. 17)

The High Court and county courts

1. Maintenance orders in the High Court and county courts: means of payment, attachment of earnings and revocation, variation, etc.

(1) Where the High Court or a county court makes a qualifying periodical maintenance order, it may at the same time exercise either of its powers under subsection (4) below in relation to the order, whether of its own motion or on an application made under this subsection by an interested party.

(1A) Where the family court makes a qualifying periodical maintenance order, it may at the same time exercise any of its powers under subsection (4A) below in relation to the order, whether of its own motion or on an application made under this subsection by an interested party.

(2) For the purposes of this section, a periodical maintenance order is an order—

(a) which requires money to be paid periodically by one person ('the debtor') to another ('the creditor'); and

(b) which is a maintenance order;

and such an order is a 'qualifying periodical maintenance order' if, at the time it is made, the debtor is ordinarily resident in England and Wales.

(3) Where the High Court or the family court has made a qualifying periodical maintenance order, it may at any later time—

(a) on an application made under this subsection by an interested party, or

(b) of its own motion, in the course of any proceedings concerning the order,

exercise either of its powers under subsection (4) below in relation to the order.

(3A) Where the family court has made a qualifying periodical maintenance order, it may at any later time—

(a) on an application made under this subsection by an interested party, or

(b) of its own motion, in the course of any proceedings concerning the order, exercise any of its powers under subsection (4A) below in relation to the order.

(4) The powers mentioned in subsections (1) and (3) above are—

(a) the power to order that payments required to be made by the debtor to the creditor under the qualifying periodical maintenance order in question shall be so made by such a method of payment falling within subsection (5) below as the court may specify in the particular case; or

(b) the power, by virtue of this section, to make an attachment of earnings order under the Attachment of Earnings Act 1971 to secure payments under the qualifying periodical maintenance order in question.

(4A) The powers mentioned in subsections (1A) and (3A) above are—

(a) the power to order that payments under the qualifying periodical maintenance order in question be made to the court;

(b) the power to order that payments under the qualifying periodical maintenance order in question required to be made to the court are to be so made by such method of payment falling within subsection (5) below as the court may specify in the particular case; or

(c) the power to order that payments under the qualifying periodical maintenance order in question be made in accordance with arrangements for their collection made by the Secretary of State under section 30 of the Child Support Act 1991 and regulations made under that section.

(5) The methods of payment mentioned in subsection (4)(a) above are—

(a) payment by standing order; or

(b) payment by any other method which requires the debtor to give his authority for payments of a specific amount to be made from an account of his to an account of the creditor's on specific dates during the period for which the authority is in force and without the need for any further authority from the debtor; or

(c) any method of payment specified in regulations made by the Lord Chancellor.

...

(8) In deciding whether to exercise any of its powers under this section the court in question having (if practicable) given every interested party an opportunity to make representations shall have regard to any representations made by any such party.

(8A) No order made by the family court under subsection (4) or (4A)(a) or (b) above has effect at any time when the Secretary of State is, under section 30 of the Child Support Act 1991 and regulations made under that section, arranging for the collection of payments under the qualifying periodical maintenance order in question.

...

(11) The power of the Lord Chancellor to make regulations under subsection (5)(c) above is exercisable by statutory instrument, and a statutory instrument containing regulations under subsection (5)(c) is subject to annulment in pursuance of a resolution of either House of Parliament.

CHILD SUPPORT ACT 1991
(1991 c. 48)

The basic principles

1. The duty to maintain

(1) For the purposes of this Act, each parent of a qualifying child is responsible for maintaining him.

(2) For the purposes of this Act, a non-resident parent shall be taken to have met his responsibility to maintain any qualifying child of his by making periodical payments of maintenance with respect to the child of such amount, and at such intervals, as may be determined in accordance with the provisions of this Act.

(3) Where a maintenance calculation made under this Act requires the making of periodical payments, it shall be the duty of the non-resident parent with respect to whom the calculation was made to make those payments.

2. Welfare of children: the general principle

Where, in any case which falls to be dealt with under this Act, the Secretary of State is considering the exercise of any discretionary power conferred by this Act, the Secretary of State shall have regard to the welfare of any child likely to be affected by the decision.

3. Meaning of certain terms used in this Act

(1) A child is a 'qualifying child' if—
- (a) one of his parents is, in relation to him, a non-resident parent; or
- (b) both of his parents are, in relation to him, non-resident parents.

(2) The parent of any child is a 'non-resident parent', in relation to him, if—
- (a) that parent is not living in the same household with the child; and
- (b) the child has his home with a person who is, in relation to him, a person with care.

(3) A person is a 'person with care', in relation to any child, if he is a person—
- (a) with whom the child has his home;
- (b) who usually provides day to day care for the child (whether exclusively or in conjunction with any other person); and
- (c) who does not fall within a prescribed category of person.

(4) The Secretary of State shall not, under subsection (3)(c), prescribe as a category—
- (a) parents;
- (b) guardians;
- (c) persons named, in a child arrangements order under section 8 of the Children Act 1989, as persons with whom a child is to live; ...

(5) For the purposes of this Act there may be more than one person with care in relation to the same qualifying child.

(6) Periodical payments which are required to be paid in accordance with a maintenance calculation are referred to in this Act as 'child support maintenance'.

(7) Expressions are defined in this section only for the purposes of this Act.

4. Child support maintenance

(1) A person who is, in relation to any qualifying child or any qualifying children, either the person with care or the non-resident parent may apply to the Secretary of State for a maintenance calculation to be made under this Act with respect to that child, or any of those children.

(2) Where a maintenance calculation has been made in response to an application under this section the Secretary of State may, if the person with care or nonresident parent with respect to whom the calculation was made applies to the Secretary of State under this subsection, arrange for—
- (a) the collection of the child support maintenance payable in accordance with the calculation;
- (b) the enforcement of the obligation to pay child support maintenance in accordance with the calculation.

(2A) The Secretary of State may only make arrangements under subsection (2)(a) if—
(a) the non-resident parent agrees to the arrangements, or
(b) the Secretary of State is satisfied that without the arrangements child support maintenance is unlikely to be paid in accordance with the calculation.
(3) Where an application under subsection (2) for the enforcement of the obligation mentioned in subsection (2)(b) authorises the Secretary of State to take steps to enforce that obligation whenever the Secretary of State considers it necessary to do so, the Secretary of State may act accordingly.
(4) A person who applies to the Secretary of State under this section shall, so far as that person reasonably can, comply with such regulations as may be made by the Secretary of State with a view to the Secretary of State being provided with the information which is required to enable—
(a) the non-resident parent to be identified or traced (where that is necessary);
(b) the amount of child support maintenance payable by the non-resident parent to be calculated; and
(c) that amount to be recovered from the non-resident parent.
(5) Any person who has applied to the Secretary of State under this section may at any time request the Secretary of State to cease acting under this section.
(6) It shall be the duty of the Secretary of State to comply with any request made under subsection (5) (but subject to any regulations made under subsection (8)).
(7) The obligation to provide information which is imposed by subsection (4)—
(a) shall not apply in such circumstances as may be prescribed; and
(b) may, in such circumstances as may be prescribed, be waived by the Secretary of State.
(8) The Secretary of State may by regulations make such incidental, supplemental or transitional provision as he thinks appropriate with respect to cases in which he is requested to cease to act under this section.
(9) No application may be made under this section if there is in force with respect to the person with care and non-resident parent in question a maintenance calculation made in response to an application treated as made under section 6.
(10) No application may be made at any time under this section with respect to a qualifying child or any qualifying children if—
(a) there is in force a written maintenance agreement made before 5th April 1993, or a maintenance order made before a prescribed date, in respect of that child or those children and the person who is, at that time, the non-resident parent; or
(aa) a maintenance order made on or after the date prescribed for the purposes of paragraph (a) is in force in respect of them, but has been so for less than the period of one year beginning with the date on which it was made; or
(b) ...

5. Child support maintenance: supplemental provisions

(1) Where—
(a) there is more than one person with care of a qualifying child; and
(b) one or more, but not all, of them have parental responsibility for the child;
no application may be made for a maintenance calculation with respect to the child by any of those persons who do not have parental responsibility for the child.
(2) Where more than one application for a maintenance calculation is made with respect to the child concerned, only one of them may be proceeded with.
(3) The Secretary of State may by regulations make provision as to which of two or more applications for a maintenance calculation with respect to the same child is to be proceeded with.

8. Role of the courts with respect to maintenance for children

(1) This subsection applies in any case where the Secretary of State would have jurisdiction to make a maintenance calculation with respect to a qualifying child and a non-resident parent of his on an application duly made (or treated as made) by a person entitled to apply for such a calculation with respect to that child.
(2) Subsection (1) applies even though the circumstances of the case are such that the Secretary of State would not make a calculation if it were applied for.
(3) Except as provided in subsection (3A), in any case where subsection (1) applies, no court shall exercise any power which it would otherwise have to make, vary or revive any maintenance order in relation to the child and non-resident parent concerned.
(3A) Unless a maintenance calculation has been made with respect to the child concerned, subsection (3) does not prevent a court from varying a maintenance order in relation to that child and the non-resident parent concerned—
(a) if the maintenance order was made on or after the date prescribed for the purposes of section 4(10)(a) or 7(10)(a); or

(b) where the order was made before then, in any case in which section 4(10) or 7(10) prevents the making of an application for a maintenance calculation with respect to or by that child.

(4) Subsection (3) does not prevent a court from revoking a maintenance order.

(5) The Lord Chancellor or in relation to Scotland the Lord Advocate may by order provide that, in such circumstances as may be specified by the order, this section shall not prevent a court from exercising any power which it has to make a maintenance order in relation to a child if—

(a) a written agreement (whether or not enforceable) provides for the making, or securing, by a non-resident parent of the child of periodical payments to or for the benefit of the child; and

(b) the maintenance order which the court makes is, in all material respects, in the same terms as that agreement.

(5A) The Lord Chancellor may make an order under subsection (5) only with the concurrence of the Lord Chief Justice.

(6) This section shall not prevent a court from exercising any power which it has to make a maintenance order in relation to a child if—

(a) a maintenance calculation is in force with respect to the child;

(b) the non-resident parent's net weekly income exceeds the figure referred to in paragraph 10(3) of Schedule 1 (as it has effect from time to time pursuant to regulations made under paragraph 10A(1)(b)); and

(c) the court is satisfied that the circumstances of the case make it appropriate for the non-resident parent to make or secure the making of periodical payments under a maintenance order in addition to the child support maintenance payable by him in accordance with the maintenance calculation.

(7) This section shall not prevent a court from exercising any power which it has to make a maintenance order in relation to a child if—

(a) the child is, will be or (if the order were to be made) would be receiving instruction at an educational establishment or undergoing training for a trade, profession or vocation (whether or not while in gainful employment); and

(b) the order is made solely for the purposes of requiring the person making or securing the making of periodical payments fixed by the order to meet some or all of the expenses incurred in connection with the provision of the instruction or training.

(8) This section shall not prevent a court from exercising any power which it has to make a maintenance order in relation to a child if—

(a) an allowance under Part IV of the Welfare Reform Act 2012 (personal independence payment) is paid to or in respect of him; or

(b) no such allowance is paid but he is disabled,

and the order is made solely for the purpose of requiring the person making or securing the making of periodical payments fixed by the order to meet some or all of any expenses attributable to the child's disability.

(9) For the purposes of subsection (8), a child is disabled if he is blind, deaf or dumb or is substantially and permanently handicapped by illness, injury, mental disorder or congenital deformity or such other disability as may be prescribed.

(10) This section shall not prevent a court from exercising any power which it has to make a maintenance order in relation to a child if the order is made against a person with care of the child.

(11) In this Act 'maintenance order', in relation to any child, means an order which requires the making or securing of periodical payments to or for the benefit of the child and which is made under—

(a) Part II of the Matrimonial Causes Act 1973;

(b) the Domestic Proceedings and Magistrates' Courts Act 1978;

(c) Part III of the Matrimonial and Family Proceedings Act 1984;

. . .

(e) Schedule 1 to the Children Act 1989;

(ea) Schedule 5, 6 or 7 of the Civil Partnership Act 2004; or

(f) any other prescribed enactment,

and includes any order varying or reviving such an order.

9. Agreements about maintenance

(1) In this section 'maintenance agreement' means any agreement for the making, or for securing the making, of periodical payments by way of maintenance, or in Scotland aliment, to or for the benefit of any child.

(2) Nothing in this Act shall be taken to prevent any person from entering into a maintenance agreement.

(2A) The Secretary of State may, with a view to reducing the need for applications under sections 4 and 7—

(a) take such steps as it considers appropriate to encourage the making and keeping of maintenance agreements, and
(b) in particular, before accepting an application under those sections, invite the applicant to consider with the Secretary of State whether it is possible to make such an agreement.

(3) Subject to section 4(10)(a) and (ab) and section 7(10), the existence of a maintenance agreement shall not prevent any party to the agreement, or any other person, from applying for a maintenance calculation with respect to any child to or for whose benefit periodical payments are to be made or secured under the agreement.

(4) Where any agreement contains a provision which purports to restrict the right of any person to apply for a maintenance calculation, that provision shall be void.

(5) Where section 8 would prevent any court from making a maintenance order in relation to a child and a non-resident parent of his, no court shall exercise any power that it has to vary any agreement so as—
(a) to insert a provision requiring that non-resident parent to make or secure the making of periodical payments by way of maintenance, or in Scotland aliment, to or for the benefit of that child; or
(b) to increase the amount payable under such a provision.

(6) In any case in which section 4(10) or 7(10) prevents the making of an application for a maintenance calculation, subsection 5 shall have effect with omission of paragraph (b).

9A. Maintenance agreements: indicative calculations

(1) A person with care or non-resident parent in relation to any qualifying child or qualifying children may apply to the Secretary of State for an indicative calculation with respect to that child or any of those children.

...

(3) An indicative calculation is a calculation of the amount of child support maintenance which the Secretary of State considers would in accordance with section 11 be fixed by a maintenance calculation if such a calculation were made with respect to the child or children in question.

(4) An indicative calculation does not create any liability on any person to pay child support maintenance.

...

10. Relationship between maintenance calculations and certain court orders and related matters

(1) Where an order of a kind prescribed for the purposes of this subsection is in force with respect to any qualifying child with respect to whom a maintenance calculation is made, the order—
(a) shall, so far as it relates to the making or securing of periodical payments, cease to have effect to such extent as may be determined in accordance with regulations made by the Secretary of State; or
(b) where the regulations so provide, shall, so far as it so relates, have effect subject to such modifications as may be so determined.

(2) Where an agreement of a kind prescribed for the purposes of this subsection is in force with respect to any qualifying child with respect to whom a maintenance calculation is made, the agreement—
(a) shall, so far as it relates to the making or securing of periodical payments, be unenforceable to such extent as may be determined in accordance with regulations made by the Secretary of State; or
(b) where the regulations so provide, shall, so far as it so relates, have effect subject to such modifications as may be so determined.

(3) Any regulations under this section may, in particular, make such provision with respect to—
(a) any case where any person with respect to whom an order or agreement of a kind prescribed for the purposes of subsection (1) or (2) has effect applies to the prescribed court, before the end of the prescribed period, for the order or agreement to be varied in the light of the maintenance calculation and of the provisions of this Act;
(b) the recovery of any arrears under the order or agreement which fell due before the coming into force of the maintenance calculation,

as the Secretary of State considers appropriate and may provide that, in prescribed circumstances, an application to any court which is made with respect to an order of a prescribed kind relating to the making or securing of periodical payments to or for the benefit of a child shall be treated by the court as an application for the order to be revoked.

(4) The Secretary of State may by regulations make provision for—
(a) notification to be given by the Secretary of State to the prescribed person in any case where the Secretary of State considers that the making of a maintenance

calculation has affected, or is likely to affect, any order of a kind prescribed for the purposes of this subsection;

(b) notification to be given by the prescribed person to the Secretary of State in any case where a court makes an order which it considers has affected, or is likely to affect, a maintenance calculation.

(5) Rules of court may require any person who, in prescribed circumstances, makes an application to the family court for a maintenance order to furnish the court with a statement in a prescribed form, and signed by an officer of the Secretary of State, as to whether or not, at the time when the statement is made, there is a maintenance calculation in force with respect to that person or the child concerned.

In this subsection—

'maintenance order' means an order of a prescribed kind for the making or securing of periodical payments to or for the benefit of a child; and

'prescribed' means prescribed by the rules.

Maintenance calculations

11. Maintenance calculations

(1) An application for a maintenance calculation made to the Secretary of State shall be dealt with by the Secretary of State in accordance with the provision made by or under this Act.

(2) The Secretary of State shall (unless the Secretary of State decides not to make a maintenance calculation in response to the application, or makes a decision under section 12) determine the application by making a decision under this section about whether any child support maintenance is payable and, if so, how much.

. . .

(6) The amount of child support maintenance to be fixed by a maintenance calculation shall be determined in accordance with Part I of Schedule I unless an application for a variation has been made and agreed.

(7) If the Secretary of State has agreed to a variation, the amount of child support maintenance to be fixed shall be determined on the basis determined under section 28F(4).

(8) Part II of Schedule I makes further provision with respect to maintenance calculations.

12. Default and interim maintenance decisions

(1) Where the Secretary of State—

(a) is required to make a maintenance calculation; or

(b) is proposing to make a decision under section 16 or 17, and it appears to the Secretary of State that the Secretary of State does not have sufficient information to enable such a decision to be made, the Secretary of State may make a default maintenance decision.

(2) Where an application for a variation has been made under section 28A(1) in connection with an application for a maintenance calculation (or in connection with such an application which is treated as having been made), the Secretary of State may make an interim maintenance decision.

(3) The amount of child support maintenance fixed by an interim maintenance decision shall be determined in accordance with Part I of Schedule 1.

(4) The Secretary of State may by regulations make provision as to default and interim maintenance decisions.

(5) The regulations may, in particular, make provision as to—

(a) the procedure to be followed in making a default or an interim maintenance decision; and

(b) a default rate of child support maintenance to apply where a default maintenance decision is made.

Information

14. Information required by Secretary of State

(1) The Secretary of State may make regulations requiring any information or evidence needed for the determination of any application made or treated as made under this Act, or any question arising in connection with such an application (or application treated as made), or needed for the making of any decision or in connection with the imposition of any condition or requirement under this Act, or needed in connection with the collection or enforcement of child support or other maintenance under this Act, to be furnished—

(a) by such persons as may be determined in accordance with regulations made by the Secretary of State; and

(b) in accordance with the regulations.

(1A) Regulations under subsection (1) may make provision for notifying any person who is required to furnish any information or evidence under the regulations of the possible consequences of failing to do so.

(3) The Secretary of State may by regulations make provision authorising the disclosure by the Secretary of State, in such circumstances as may be prescribed, of such information held by the Secretary of State, for purposes of this Act as may be prescribed.

(4) The provisions of Schedule 2 (which relate to information which is held for purposes other than those of this Act but which is required by the Secretary of State,) shall have effect.

14A. Information offences

(1) This section applies to—

(a) persons who are required to comply with regulations under section 4(4) or 7(5); and

(b) persons specified in regulations under section 14(1)(a).

(2) Such a person is guilty of an offence if, pursuant to a request for information under or by virtue of those regulations—

(a) he makes a statement or representation which he knows to be false; or

(b) he provides, or knowingly causes or knowingly allows to be provided, a document or other information which he knows to be false in a material particular.

(3) Such a person is guilty of an offence if, following such a request, he fails to comply with it.

(3A) In the case of regulations under section 14 which require a person liable to make payments of child support maintenance to notify—

(a) a change of address, or

(b) any other change of circumstances, a person who fails to comply with the requirement is guilty of an offence.

(4) It is a defence for a person charged with an offence under subsection (3) or (3A) to prove that he had a reasonable excuse for failing to comply

(5) A person guilty of an offence under this section is liable on summary conviction to a fine not exceeding level 3 on the standard scale.

. . .

26. Disputes about parentage

(1) Where a person who is alleged to be a parent of the child with respect to whom an application for a maintenance calculation has been made or treated as made ('the alleged parent') denies that he is one of the child's parents, the Secretary of State, shall not make a maintenance calculation on the assumption that the alleged parent is one of the child's parents unless the case falls within one of those set out in subsection (2).

(2) The Cases are—

CASE A1

Where—

(a) the child is habitually resident in England and Wales;

(b) the Secretary of State is satisfied that the alleged parent was married to the child's mother at some time in the period beginning with the conception and ending with the birth of the child; and

(c) the child has not been adopted.

CASE A2

Where—

(a) the child is habitually resident in England and Wales;

(b) the alleged parent has been registered as father of the child under section 10 or 10A of, or regulations made under section 2C, 2D, 2E, 10B or 10C of, the Births and Deaths Registration Act 1953, or in any register kept under section 13 (register of births and still-births) or section 44 (Register of Corrections Etc) of the Registration of Births, Deaths and Marriages (Scotland) Act 1965, or under Article 14 or 18(1)(b)(ii) of the Births and Deaths Registration (Northern Ireland) Order 1976; and

(c) the child has not subsequently been adopted.

CASE A3

Where the result of a scientific test (within the meaning of section 27A) taken by the alleged parent would be relevant to determining the child's parentage, and the alleged parent—

(a) refuses to take such a test; or
(b) has submitted to such a test, and it shows that there is no reasonable doubt that the alleged parent is a parent of the child.

CASE A

Where the alleged parent is a parent of the child in question by virtue of having adopted him.

CASE B

Where the alleged parent is a parent of the child in question by virtue of an order under section 30 of the Human Fertilisation and Embryology Act 1990 (parental orders in favour of gamete donors).

CASE B1

Where the Secretary of State is satisfied that the alleged parent is a parent of the child in question by virtue of section 27 or 28 of the Human Fertilisation and Embryology Act 1990 or any of sections 33 to 46 of the Human Fertilisation and Embryology Act 2008 (which relate to children resulting from human assisted reproduction).

CASE C

Where—

(a) either—
   (i) a declaration that the alleged parent is a parent of the child in question (or a declaration which has that effect) is in force under section 55A or 56 of the Family Law Act 1986 or Article 32 of the Matrimonial and Family Proceedings (Northern Ireland) Order 1989 (declarations of parentage); or
   . . . and
(b) the child has not subsequently been adopted.

. . .

CASE F

Where—

(a) the alleged parent has been found, or adjudged, to be the father of the child in question—
   (i) in proceedings before any court in England and Wales which are relevant proceedings for the purposes of section 12 of the Civil Evidence Act 1968 or in proceedings before any court in Northern Ireland which are relevant proceedings for the purposes of section 8 of the Civil Evidence Act (Northern Ireland) 1971; or
   (ii) in affiliation proceedings before any court in the United Kingdom,
   (whether or not he offered any defence to the allegation of paternity) and that finding or adjudication still subsists; and
(b) the child has not subsequently been adopted.

(3) In this section—
'adopted' means adopted within the meaning of Part IV of the Adoption Act 1976 or Chapter 4 of Part 1 of the Adoption and Children Act 2002.

27. Applications for declaration of parentage under Family Law Act 1986

(1) This section applies where—
   (a) an application for a maintenance calculation has been made or a maintenance calculation is in force, with respect to a person ('the alleged parent') who denies that he is a parent of a child with respect to whom the application or calculation was made or treated as made;
   (b) the Secretary of State is not satisfied that the case falls within one of those set out in section 26(2); and
   (c) the Secretary of State is not satisfied or the person with care makes an application for a declaration under section 55A of the Family Law Act 1986 as to whether or not the alleged parent is one of the child's parents.

(2) Where this section applies—
  (a) if it is the person with care who makes the application, she shall be treated as having a sufficient personal interest for the purposes of subsection (3) of that section; and
  (b) if it is the Secretary of State who makes the application, that subsection shall not apply.

27A. Recovery of fees for scientific tests

(1) This section applies in any case where—
  (a) an application for a maintenance calculation has been made or a maintenance calculation is in force;
  (b) scientific tests have been carried out (otherwise than under a direction or in response to a request) in relation to bodily samples obtained from a person who is alleged to be a parent of a child with respect to whom the application or calculation is made;
  (c) the results of the tests do not exclude the alleged parent from being one of the child's parents; and
  (d) one of the conditions set out in subsection (2) is satisfied.

(2) The conditions are that—
  (a) the alleged parent does not deny that he is one of the child's parents;
  (b) in proceedings under section 55A of the Family Law Act 1986, a court has made a declaration that the alleged parent is a parent of the child in question; or

(3) In any case to which this section applies, any fee paid by the Secretary of State in connection with scientific tests may be recovered by the Secretary of State from the alleged parent as a debt due to the Crown.

...

Variations

28A. Application for variation of usual rules for calculating maintenance

(1) Where an application for a maintenance calculation is made under section 4 or 7, the person with care or the non-resident parent or (in the case of an application under section 7) either of them or the child concerned may apply to the Secretary of State for the rules by which the calculation is made to be varied in accordance with this Act.

(2) Such an application is referred to in this Act as an 'application for a variation'.

(3) An application for a variation may be made at any time before the Secretary of State has reached a decision (under section 11 or 12(1)) on the application for a maintenance calculation (or the application treated as having been made under section 6).

(4) A person who applies for a variation—
  (a) need not make the application in writing unless the Commission directs in any case that he must; and
  (b) must say upon what grounds the application is made.

(5) In other respects an application for a variation is to be made in such manner as may be prescribed.

(6) Schedule 4A has effect in relation to applications for a variation.

28E. Matters to be taken into account

(1) In determining whether to agree to a variation, the Secretary of State shall have regard both to the general principles set out in subsection (2) and to such other considerations as may be prescribed.

(2) The general principles are that—
  (a) parents should be responsible for maintaining their children whenever they can afford to do so;
  (b) where a parent has more than one child, his obligation to maintain any one of them should be no less of an obligation than his obligation to maintain any other of them.

(3) In determining whether to agree to a variation, the Secretary of State shall take into account any representations made to him Secretary of State
  (a) by the person with care or non-resident parent concerned; or
  (b) where the application for the current calculation was made under section 7, by either of them or the child concerned.

(4) In determining whether to agree to a variation, no account shall be taken of the fact that—
  (a) any part of the income of the person with care concerned is, or would be if the Secretary of State agreed to a variation, derived from any benefit; or

(b) some or all of any child support maintenance might be taken into account in any manner in relation to any entitlement to benefit.

(5) In this section 'benefit' has such meaning as may be prescribed.

28F. Agreement to a variation

(1) The Secretary of State may agree to a variation if—

(a) the Secretary of State is satisfied that the case is one which falls within one or more of the cases set out in Part I of Schedule 4B or in regulations made under that Part; and

(b) it is the Secretary of State's opinion that, in all the circumstances of the case, it would be just and equitable to agree to a variation.

(2) In considering whether it would be just and equitable in any case to agree to a variation, the Secretary of State—

(a) must have regard, in particular, to the welfare of any child likely to be affected if Secretary of State— did agree to a variation; and

(b) must, or as the case may be must not, take any prescribed factors into account, or must take them into account (or not) in prescribed circumstances.

(3) The Secretary of State shall not agree to a variation (and shall proceed to make his decision on the application for a maintenance calculation without any variation) if he is satisfied that—

(a) the Secretary of State has insufficient information to make a decision on the application for the maintenance calculation under section 11, and therefore that his decision would be made under section 12(1); or

(b) other prescribed circumstances apply.

(4) Where the Secretary of State agrees to a variation, the Secretary of State shall—

(a) determine the basis on which the amount of child support maintenance is to be calculated in response to the application for a maintenance calculation (including an application treated as having been made); and

(b) make a decision under section 11 on that basis.

(5) If the Secretary of State has made an interim maintenance decision, it is to be treated as having been replaced by the Secretary of State's decision under section 11, and except in prescribed circumstances any appeal connected with it (under section 20) shall lapse.

(6) In determining whether or not to agree to a variation, the Secretary of State shall comply with regulations made under Part II of Schedule 4B.

35 Enforcement of liability orders by taking control of goods

(1) Where a liability order has been made against a person ('the liable person'), the Secretary of State may use the procedure in Schedule 12 to the Tribunals, Courts and Enforcement Act 2007 (taking control of goods) to recover the amount in respect of which the order was made, to the extent that it remains unpaid.

. . .

36. Enforcement in county courts

(1) Where a liability order has been made against a person, the amount in respect of which the order was made, to the extent that it remains unpaid, shall, if a county court so orders, be recoverable by means of garnishee proceedings or a charging order, as if it were payable under a county court order.

(2) In subsection (1) 'charging order' has the same meaning as in section 1 of the Charging Orders Act 1979.

39B. Disqualification for holding or obtaining driving licence or travel authorization

(1) The Secretary of State may make an order under this section (referred to in this section and sections 39C to 39F as a 'disqualification order') against a person where—

(a) the Secretary of State has sought to recover an amount from the person by means of taking enforcement action by virtue of section 35 or 38, or by means of a third party debt order or a charging order by virtue of section 36;

(b) the whole or any part of the amount remains unpaid; and

(c) the Secretary of State is of the opinion that there has been wilful refusal or culpable neglect on the part of the person.

(2) For the purposes of subsection (1)(a), the Secretary of State is to be taken to have sought to recover an amount by means of a charging order if an interim charging order has been made, whether or not any further steps have been taken to recover the amount.

(3) A disqualification order shall provide that the person against whom it is made is disqualified for holding or obtaining—

(a) a driving licence,

(b) a travel authorisation, or

(c) both a driving licence and a travel authorisation,
while the order has effect.

(4) Before making a disqualification order against a person, the Secretary of State shall consider whether the person needs the relevant document in order to earn a living.

(5) A disqualification order shall specify the amount in respect of which it is made.

(6) That amount shall be the aggregate of—

(a) the amount sought to be recovered as mentioned in subsection (1)(a), or so much of it as remains unpaid; and

(b) the amount which the person against whom the order is made is required to pay by the order under section 39DA(1).

(7) The Secretary of State shall serve a copy of the disqualification order (together with a copy of the order under section 39DA(1)) on the person against whom it is made.

(8) In this section—

'driving licence' means a licence to drive a motor vehicle granted under Part 3 of the Road Traffic Act 1988;

'relevant document', in relation to a disqualification order made against a person, means the document (or documents) for the holding or obtaining of which the person is disqualified by the order;

'travel authorisation' means—

(a) a United Kingdom passport (within the meaning of the Immigration Act 1971);

(b) an ID card issued under the Identity Cards Act 2006 that records that the person to whom it has been issued is a British citizen.

39C. Period for which orders are to have effect

(1) A disqualification order shall specify the period for which it is to have effect.

(1A) That period shall not exceed 12 months (subject to any extension under section 39CA or 39CB).

(1B) That period shall begin to run with—

(a) the first day after the end of the period within which an appeal may be brought against the order under section 39CB(1); or

(b) if the running of the period is suspended at that time, the first day when its running is no longer suspended.

(2) On making an order under section 39B, the court may include in the order provision suspending the running of the period for which the order is to have effect until such day and on such conditions (if any) as the court thinks just.

(3) After making such an order the court may by order suspend the running of the period for which it has effect until such day and on such conditions (if any) as the court thinks just.

(4) The powers conferred by subsections (2) and (3) may be exercised by the court only—

(a) if the person against whom the order under section 39B is made agrees to pay the amount specified in the order; or

(b) if the court is satisfied that the suspension in question is justified by exceptional circumstances.

(5) The Secretary of State may make a further application under section 39B if the amount specified in an order under that section has not been paid in full by the end of the period for which the order has effect.

39D. Power to order search

(1) On making an order under section 39B the court may order the person against whom the order is made to be searched.

(2) Any money found on such a search shall, unless the court otherwise directs, be applied towards payment of the amount specified under section 39B(8); and the balance (if any) shall be returned to the person searched.

(3) The court shall not allow the application under subsection (2) of money found on a search under subsection (1) if it is satisfied that the money does not belong to the person searched.

39DA. Recovery of Secretary of State's costs

(1) On making a disqualification order against any person the Secretary of State shall also make an order requiring that person to pay an amount in respect of the costs incurred by the Secretary of State in exercising the functions under section 39B.

. . .

39E. Variation and revocation of orders following payment

(1) If part of the amount specified in an order under section 39B is paid to any person authorised to receive it, the court may, on an application made by the Commission or the person against whom the order is made, by order—

(a) reduce the period for which the order under section 39B is to have effect; or
(b) revoke the order under section 39B.

(1A) The power conferred by subsection (1) shall be exerciseable by the courts instead of by the Secretary of State at any time when an appeal brought under section 39CB against the order has not been determined, withdrawn or discontinued.

(2) If the whole of the amount specified in a disqualification order under section 39B is paid to any person authorised to receive it, the court shall, on an application made by the Commission or the person against whom the order is made, by order revoke the order under section 39B.

. . .

39F. Power to make supplementary provision

The Secretary of State may by regulations—

(a) make provision in relation to orders under section 39B corresponding to the provision that may be made under section 40(11);
(b) make provision for sections 39C to 39E to have effect with prescribed modifications in cases where a person against whom an order under section 39B has effect is outside the United Kingdom.

39H. Applications for curfew orders

(1) The Secretary of State may apply to the court for an order requiring a person to remain, for periods specified in the order, at a place so specified (a 'curfew order') where—
(a) it has sought to recover an amount from the person by means of taking enforcement action by virtue of section 35 or 38, or by means of a third party debt order or a charging order by virtue of section 36;
(b) the whole or any part of the amount remains unpaid; and
(c) the Secretary of State is of the opinion that there has been wilful refusal or culpable neglect on the part of the person.

(2) For the purposes of subsection (1)(a), the Secretary of State is to be taken to have sought to recover an amount by means of a charging order if an interim charging order has been made, whether or not any further steps have been taken to recover the amount.

(3) On an application for a curfew order the court shall (in the presence of the person from whom the Secretary of State has sought to recover the amount) inquire as to—
(a) the person's means; and
(b) whether there has been wilful refusal or culpable neglect on the part of the person.

(4) On an application for a curfew order the court shall not question—
(a) the liability order by reference to which the Secretary of State acted as mentioned in subsection (1)(a); or
(b) the maintenance calculation by reference to which that liability order was made.

(5) If, but only if, the court is of the opinion that there has been wilful refusal or culpable neglect on the part of the person from whom the Secretary of State has sought to recover the amount, it may make a curfew order against the person.

(6) The court may not make a curfew order against a person who is under the age of 18.

(7) In this section and sections 39I to 39O 'the court' means—
(a) in England and Wales, a magistrates' court;
. . .

39I. Curfew orders: duration etc.

(1) The periods and places specified as mentioned in section 39H(1) may include different periods and different places for different days, but shall not include periods which amount to less than 2 hours or more than 12 hours in any one day.

(2) A curfew order shall specify the period for which the requirements imposed by the order shall have effect.

(3) The period so specified—
(a) shall not exceed 6 months; and
(b) shall begin to run with the day on which the order is made unless the order provides (subject to such conditions, if any, as may be specified in the order) for it to begin to run with a later day.

(4) The court shall (so far as practicable) ensure that any requirement imposed by a curfew order is such as to avoid—
(a) any conflict with the religious beliefs of the person against whom the order is made; and
(b) any interference with the times (if any) at which that person normally works or attends any educational establishment.

(5) On making a curfew order—
(a) a magistrates' court may not specify in the order any place outside England and Wales; and
(b) the sheriff may not specify in the order any place outside Scotland.

39L. Power to order search

(1) On making a curfew order, the court may order the person against whom the order is made to be searched.

(2) Any money found on such a search shall, unless the court otherwise directs, be applied towards payment of the amount in respect of which the curfew order is made; and the balance (if any) shall be returned to the person searched.

(3) The court shall not allow the application under subsection (2) of money found on a search under this section if it is satisfied that the money does not belong to the person searched.

(4) The court may exercise the powers conferred on it by section 39K(2) and (5) without the need for an application where money found on a search under this section is applied towards payment of the amount in respect of which a curfew order is made.

39M. Monitoring of curfew orders

(1) A curfew order shall—
 (a) provide for a person's compliance with the requirements imposed by the order to be monitored; and
 (b) make a person specified in the order responsible for that monitoring.

(2) The court may not make a curfew order unless—
 (a) it has been notified by the Secretary of State that arrangements for monitoring compliance with the requirements imposed by such orders are available in the area in which the place proposed to be specified in the order is situated and the notice has not been withdrawn;
 (b) it is satisfied that the necessary provision can be made under those arrangements; and
 (c) it has the consent of any person (other than the person against whom the order is to be made) whose co-operation is necessary to secure the monitoring of compliance with the requirements imposed by the order.

(3) If a curfew order cannot be made because of the absence of any consent required by subsection (2)(c), the court may treat the application for the order as an application under section 40 (or, in the case of an application made to the sheriff, as an application under section 40A).

(4) The Secretary of State may by regulations make provision as to—
 (a) the cases or circumstances in which the person responsible for monitoring a person's compliance with the requirements imposed by a curfew order may allow that person to be absent from the place specified in the curfew order during a period so specified; and
 (b) the requirements which may be imposed in connection with such an absence.

39N. Breaches of curfew orders

(1) The person responsible for monitoring a person's compliance with the requirements imposed by a curfew order, or the Commission, may apply to the court where it appears that the person subject to the requirements in question has failed to comply with—
 (a) any of those requirements; or
 (b) any requirements imposed by virtue of section 39M(4).

(2) On any such application the court shall (in the presence of the person subject to the requirements in question) inquire as to whether the person has failed without reasonable excuse to comply with any of those requirements.

(3) If the court is of the opinion that the person has failed without reasonable excuse to comply with any of those requirements, it may—
 (a) issue a warrant of commitment against that person; or
 (b) by order provide for the requirements imposed by the curfew order to have effect for a specified further period.

(4) A warrant issued under subsection (3)(a) shall order the person against whom it is issued—
 (a) to be imprisoned for a period specified in the warrant; but
 (b) to be released (unless in custody for some other reason) on payment of the amount in respect of which the curfew order in question was made.

(5) A warrant issued under subsection (3)(a) may be directed to such person or persons as the court issuing it thinks fit.

(6) The power conferred by subsection (3)(b) may not be exercised so as to provide for the requirements imposed by the curfew order to have effect for a period exceeding 6 months after the making of the order under that subsection.

(7) Where, following the issue of a warrant under subsection (3)(a), part of the amount specified in the curfew order is paid to any person authorised to receive it, the court may, on an application by the Secretary of State or the person against whom the warrant was issued—

(a) reduce the period specified in the warrant; or
(b) order the release of the person against whom the warrant was issued.

(8) On the hearing of an application made under subsection (7) the Secretary of State may make representations to the court as to which of the powers conferred by that subsection it would be appropriate for the court to exercise, and the person against whom the warrant was issued may reply to those representations.

39O. Effect of custody on curfew orders and power to make curfew orders

(1) The court may not make a curfew order against a person at any time when the person is in custody for any reason.

(2) The running of the period during which the requirements imposed by a curfew order have effect shall be suspended for the whole of any day during any part of which the person against whom the order is made is in custody for any reason.

(3) If the period during which the requirements imposed by a curfew order have effect would have begun to run but for its being suspended by virtue of this section, that period shall instead begin to run with the first day when its running is no longer suspended.

39P. Power to make supplementary provision about curfew orders: England and Wales

(1) The Secretary of State may by regulations make provision for England and Wales with respect to curfew orders.

(2) The regulations may, in particular, make provision—
(a) as to the form and content of a curfew order;
(b) allowing an application for a curfew order to be renewed where no curfew order is made;
(c) that a statement in writing to the effect that wages of any amount have been paid during any period to a person, purporting to be signed by or on behalf of that person's employer, shall be evidence of the facts stated;
(d) that a justice of the peace may issue a summons to a person to appear before a magistrates' court and (if that person does not appear) may issue a warrant for that person's arrest;
(e) that, for the purpose of securing a person's presence before a magistrates' court, a justice of the peace may issue a warrant for that person's arrest without issuing a summons;
(f) as to the execution of a warrant for arrest;
(g) for the amendment or revocation of requirements imposed by a curfew order, on an application made to a magistrates' court by the Commission or the person against whom the order was made;
(h) similar to that made by sections 39J, 39L and 39M(2) and (3), in relation to any amendment of a curfew order;
(i) as to the exercise by a magistrates' court of the powers conferred by sections 39K(2) and (3) and 39N(7).

40. Commitment to prison

. . .

(2A) The Secretary of State may apply to a magistrates' court for the issue of a warrant committing a person to prison where—
(a) the Secretary of State has sought to recover an amount from the person by means of taking enforcement action by virtue of section 35 or 38, or by means of a third party debt order or a charging order by virtue of section 36;
(b) the whole or any part of the amount remains unpaid; and
(c) the Secretary of State is of the opinion that there has been wilful refusal or culpable neglect on the part of the person from whom the Secretary of State has sought to recover the amount ('the liable person').

. . .

51A. Pilot schemes

(1) Any regulations made under this Act may be made so as to have effect for a specified period not exceeding 24 months.

. . .

54. Interpretation

(1) In this Act—
'non-resident parent' has the meaning given in section 3(2);
'application for a variation' means an application under section 28A or 28G;
'benefit Acts' means the Social Security Contributions and Benefits Act 1992 and the Social Security Administration Act 1992;

'charging order' has the same meaning as in section 1 of the Charging Orders Act 1979;
'child benefit' has the same meaning as in the Child Benefit Act 1975;
'child support maintenance' has the meaning given in section 3(6);
'Commission' means the Child Maintenance and Enforcement Commission;
'curfew order' has the meaning given in section 39H(1);
'deduction from earnings order' has the meaning given in section 31(2);
'default maintenance decision' has the meaning given in section 12;
'deposit-taker' means a person who, in the course of business, may lawfully accept deposits in the United Kingdom;
'general qualification' shall be construed in accordance with section 71 of the Courts and Legal Services Act 1990 (qualification for judicial appointments);
'income-based jobseeker's allowance' has the same meaning as in the Jobseekers Act 1995;
'income-related employment and support allowance' means an income-related allowance under Part 1 of the Welfare Reform Act 2007 (employment and support allowance);
'income support' has the same meaning as in the benefit Acts;
'interim maintenance decision' has the meaning given in section 12;
'liability order' has the meaning given in section 32M(2);
'maintenance agreement' has the meaning given in section 9(1);
'maintenance calculation' means a calculation of maintenance made under this Act and, except in prescribed circumstances, includes a default maintenance decision and an interim maintenance decision.
'maintenance order' has the meaning given in section 8(11);
'parent', in relation to any child, means any person who is in law the mother or father of the child;
'parent with care' means a person who is, in relation to a child, both a parent and a person with care.
'parental responsibility', in the application of this Act—
(a) to England and Wales, has the same meaning as in the Children Act 1989;
. . .
'person with care' has the meaning given in section 3(3);
'prescribed' means prescribed by regulations made by the Secretary of State;
'qualifying child' has the meaning given in section 3(1).
'voluntary payment' has the meaning given in section 28J.

(2) The definition of 'deposit-taker' in subsection (1) is to be read with—
(a) section 22 of the Financial Services and Markets Act 2000;
(b) any relevant order under that section; and
(c) Schedule 2 to that Act.

55. Meaning of 'child'

(1) In this Act, 'child' means (subject to subsection (2)) a person who—
(a) has not attained the age of 16, or
(b) has not attained the age of 20 and satisfies such conditions as may be prescribed.

(2) A person who is or has been party to a marriage or civil partnership is not a child for the purposes of this Act.

(3) For the purposes of subsection (2), 'marriage' and 'civil partnership' include a void marriage and a void civil partnership respectively.

SCHEDULES

Section 11

SCHEDULE 1
MAINTENANCE CALCULATIONS

PART I
CALCULATION OF WEEKLY AMOUNT OF CHILD SUPPORT MAINTENANCE

General rule

1.— (1) Subject to paragraph 5A, the weekly rate of child support maintenance is the basic rate unless a reduced rate, a flat rate or the nil rate applies.

(2) Unless the nil rate applies, the amount payable weekly to a person with care is—
(a) the applicable rate, if paragraph 6 does not apply; or
(b) if paragraph 6 does apply, that rate as apportioned between the persons with care in accordance with paragraph 6,

as adjusted, in either case, by applying the rules about shared care in paragraph 7 or 8.

Basic rate

2.— (1) Subject to paragraph 2, the basic rate is the following percentage of the non-resident parent's net weekly income—
12% where he has one qualifying child;
16% where he has two qualifying children;
19% where he has three or more qualifying children.

(2) If the non-resident parent also has one or more relevant other children, the appropriate percentage referred to in sub-paragraph (1) is to be applied instead to his net weekly income less—
9% where he has one relevant other child;
12% where he has two relevant other children;
15% where he has three or more relevant other children.

(3) If the the non-resident parent has one or more relevant other children, gross wealth income shall be treated for the purpose of sub-paragraphs (1) and (2) as reduced by the following percentage—
11% where the non-resident parents has one relevant other child;
14% where the non-resident other parent has two relevant other children;
16% where the non-resident other parent has three or more relevant other children.

Reduced rate

3.— (1) A reduced rate is payable if—
(a) neither a flat rate nor the nil rate applies; and
(b) the non-resident parent's net weekly income is less than £200 but more than £100.

(2) The reduced rate payable shall be prescribed in, or determined in accordance with, regulations.

(3) The regulations may not prescribe, or result in, a rate of less than £7.

Flat rate

4.— (1) Except in a case falling within sub-paragraph (2), a flat rate of £7 is payable if the nil rate does not apply and—
(a) the non-resident parent's net weekly income is £100 or less; or
(b) he receives any benefit, pension or allowance prescribed for the purposes of this paragraph of this sub-paragraph; or
(c) he or his partner (if any) receives any benefit prescribed for the purposes of this paragraph of this sub-paragraph.

(2) A flat rate of a prescribed amount is payable if the nil rate does not apply and—
(a) the non-resident parent has a partner who is also a non-resident parent;
(b) the partner is a person with respect to whom a maintenance calculation is in force; and
(c) the non-resident parent or his partner receives any benefit prescribed under sub-paragraph (1)(c).

(3) The benefits, pensions and allowances which may be prescribed for the purposes of sub-paragraph (1)(b) include ones paid to the non-resident parent under the law of a place outside the United Kingdom.

Nil rate

5. The rate payable is nil if the non-resident parent—
(a) is of a prescribed description; or
(b) has a net weekly income of below £7.

5A.— (1) This paragraph applies where—
(a) the non-resident parent is a party to a qualifying maintenance arrangement with respect to a child of his who is not a qualifying child, and
(b) the weekly rate of child support maintenance apart from this paragraph would be the basic rate or a reduced rate or calculated following agreement to a variation where is rate would otherwise be a flat rate or the nil rate.

(2) The weekly rate of child support maintenance is the greater of £7 and the amount found as follows.

(3) First, calculate the amount which would be payable if the non-resident parent's qualifying children also included every child with respect to whom the non-resident parent is a party to a qualifying maintenance arrangement.

(4) Second, divide the amount so calculated the number of children taken into account for the purposes of the calculation.
(5) Third, multiply the amount the number of children who, for purposes other than the calculation under sub-paragraph (3), are qualifying children of the non-resident parent.
(6) For the purposes of this paragraph, the non-resident parent is a party to a qualifying maintenance arrangement with respect to a child if the non-resident parent is—
(a) liable to pay maintenance or aliment for the child under a maintenance order, or
(b) a party to an agreement of a prescribed description which provides for the non-resident parent to make payments for the benefit of the child,
and the child is habitually resident in the United Kingdom.

Apportionment

6.— (1) If the non-resident parent has more than one qualifying child and in relation to them there is more than one person with care, the amount of child support maintenance payable is (subject to paragraph 7 or 8) to be determined by apportioning the rate between the persons with care.
(2) The rate of maintenance liability is to be divided by the number of qualifying children, and shared among the persons with care according to the number of qualifying children in relation to whom each is a person with care.

Shared care — basic and reduced rate

7.— (1) This paragraph applies only if the rate of child support maintenance payable is the basic rate or a reduced rate, or is determined by paragraph 5A.
(2) If the care of a qualifying child is shared between the non-resident parent and the person with care, so that the non-resident parent from time to time has care of the child overnight, the amount of child support maintenance which he would otherwise have been liable to pay the person with care, as calculated in accordance with the preceding paragraphs of this Part of this Schedule, is to be decreased in accordance with this paragraph.
(3) First, there is to be a decrease according to the number of such nights which the Secretary of State determines there to have been, or expects there to be, or both during a prescribed twelve-month period.
(4) The amount of that decrease for one child is set out in the following Table—

Number of nights	Fraction to subtract
52 to 103	One-seventh
104 to 155	Two-sevenths
156 to 174	Three-sevenths
175 or more	One-half

(5) If the person with care is caring for more than one qualifying child of the non-resident parent, the applicable decrease is the sum of the appropriate fractions in the Table divided by the number of such qualifying children.
(6) If the applicable fraction is one-half in relation to any qualifying child in the care of the person with care, the total amount payable to the person with care is then to be further decreased by £7 for each such child.
(7) If the application of the preceding provisions of this paragraph would decrease the weekly amount of child support maintenance (or the aggregate of all such amounts) payable by the non-resident parent to the person with care (or all of them) to less than £7, he is instead liable to pay child support maintenance at the rate of £7 a week, apportioned (if appropriate) in accordance with paragraph 6.

Shared care — flat rate

8.— (1) This paragraph applies only if—
(a) the rate of child support maintenance payable is a flat rate; and
(b) that rate applies because the non-resident parent falls within paragraph 4(1)(b) or (c) or 4(2).
(2) If the care of a qualifying child is shared as mentioned in paragraph 7(2) for at least 52 nights during a prescribed 12-month period, the amount of child support maintenance payable by the non-resident parent to the person with care of that child is nil.

Regulations about shared care

9. The Secretary of State may by regulations provide—
(a) for which nights are to count for the purposes of shared care under paragraphs 7 and 8, or for how it is to be determined whether a night counts;
(b) for what counts, or does not count, as 'care' for those purposes; and
(ba) for how it is to be determined how many nights count for these purposes; and
. . .

Gross weekly income

10.— (1) For the purposes of this Schedule, gross weekly income is to be determined in such manner as is provided for in regulations.
(2) The regulations may, in particular, provide for the Secretary of State to estimate any income or make an assumption as to any fact where, in Secretary of State view, the information at Secretary of State disposal is unreliable, insufficient, or relates to an atypical period in the life of the non-resident parent.
(3) Any amount of net weekly income (calculated as above) over £3,000 is to be ignored for the purposes of this Schedule.

Regulations about rates, figures, etc.

10A.— (1) The Secretary of State may by regulations provide that—
(a) paragraph 2 is to have effect as if different percentages were substituted for those set out there;
(b) paragraph 3(1) or (3), 4(1), 5, 7(7) or 10(3) is to have effect as if different amounts were substituted for those set out there.
(2) The Secretary of State may by regulations provide that—
(a) the Table in paragraph 7(4) is to have effect as if different numbers of nights were set out in the first column and different fractions were substituted for those set out in the second column;
(b) paragraph 7(6) is to have effect as if a different amount were substituted for that mentioned there, or as if the amount were an aggregate amount and not an amount for each qualifying child, or both.

Regulations about income

10B. The Secretary of State may by regulations provide that, in such circumstances and to such extent as may be prescribed—
(a) where the Secretary of State is satisfied that a person has intentionally deprived himself of a source of income with a view to reducing the amount of his net weekly income, his net weekly income shall be taken to include income from that source of an amount estimated by the Secretary of State;
(b) a person is to be treated as possessing income which he does not possess;
(c) income which a person does possess is to be disregarded.

References to various terms

10C.— (1) References in this Part of this Schedule to 'qualifying children' are to those qualifying children with respect to whom the maintenance calculation falls to be made.
(2) References in this Part of this Schedule to 'relevant other children' are to—
(a) children other than qualifying children in respect of whom the non-resident parent or his partner receives child benefit under Part IX of the Social Security Contributions and Benefits Act 1992; and
(b) such other description of children as may be prescribed.
(3) In this Part of this Schedule, a person 'receives' a benefit, pension, or allowance for any week if it is paid or due to be paid to him in respect of that week.
(4) In this Part of this Schedule, a person's 'partner' is—
(a) if they are a couple, the other member of that couple;
(b) if the person is a husband or wife by virtue of a marriage entered into under a law which permits polygamy, another party to the marriage who is of the opposite sex and is a member of the same household.
(5) In sub-paragraph (4)(a), 'couple' means a man and a woman who are—
(a) married to each other and are members of the same household;
(b) not married to each other but are living together as husband and wife;
(c) two people of the same sex who are civil partners of each other and are members of the same household; or
(d) two people of the same sex who are not civil partners of each other but are living together as if they were civil partners.

(6) For the purposes of this paragraph, two people of the same sex are to be regarded as living together as if they were civil partners if, but only if, they would be regarded as living together as husband and wife were they instead two people of the opposite sex.

PART II
GENERAL PROVISIONS ABOUT MAINTENANCE CALCULATIONS

Effective date of calculation

11.— (1) A maintenance calculation shall take effect on such date as may be determined in accordance with regulations made by the Secretary of State.

(2) That date may be earlier than the date on which the calculation is made.

Form of calculation

12. Every maintenance calculation shall be made in such form and contain such information as the Secretary of State may direct.

Consolidated applications and calculations

14.— (1) The Secretary of State may by regulations provide—

(a) for two or more applications for maintenance calculations to be treated, in prescribed circumstances, as a single application; and

(b) for the replacement, in prescribed circumstances, of a maintenance calculation made on the application of one person by a later maintenance calculation made on the application of that or any other person.

. . .

Separate calculations for different periods

15. Where the Secretary of State is satisfied that the circumstances of a case require different amounts of child support maintenance to be calculated in respect of different periods, the Secretary of State may make separate maintenance calculations each expressed to have effect in relation to a different specified period.

Termination of calculations

16.— (1) A maintenance calculation shall cease to have effect—

(a) on the death of the non-resident parent, or of the person with care, with respect to whom it was made;

(b) on there no longer being any qualifying child with respect to whom it would have effect;

(c) on the non-resident parent with respect to whom it was made ceasing to be a parent of—

(i) the qualifying child with respect to whom it was made; or

(ii) where it was made with respect to more than one qualifying child, all of the qualifying children with respect to whom it was made;

. . .

(10) A person with care with respect to whom a maintenance calculation is in force shall provide the the Secretary of State with such information, in such circumstances, as may be prescribed, with a view to assisting the Secretary of State in determining whether the calculation has ceased to have effect.

(11) The Secretary of State may by regulations make such supplemental, incidental or transitional provision as he thinks necessary or expedient in consequence of the provisions of this paragraph.

SCHEDULE 4A
APPLICATIONS FOR A VARIATION

Interpretation

1. In this Schedule, 'regulations' means regulations made by the Secretary of State.

Applications for a variation

2. Regulations may make provision—

(a) as to the procedure to be followed in considering an application for a variation;

. . .

Completion of preliminary consideration

3. Regulations may provide for determining when the preliminary consideration of an application for a variation is to be taken to have been completed.

Information

4. If any information which is required (by regulations under this Act) to be furnished to the Secretary of State in connection with an application for a variation has not been furnished within such period as may be prescribed, the Secretary of State may nevertheless proceed to consider the application.

Joint consideration of applications for a variation and appeals

5.— (1) Regulations may provide for two or more applications for a variation with respect to the same application for a maintenance calculation to be considered together.

. . .

SCHEDULE 4B

APPLICATIONS FOR A VARIATION: THE CASES AND CONTROLS

PART I

THE CASES

General

1.— (1) The cases in which a variation may be agreed are those set out in this Part of this Schedule or in regulations made under this Part.

(2) In this Schedule 'applicant' means the person whose application for a variation is being considered.

Special expenses

2.— (1) A variation applied for by a non-resident parent may be agreed with respect to his special expenses.

(2) In this paragraph 'special expenses' means the whole, or any amount above a prescribed amount, or any prescribed part, of expenses which fall within a prescribed description of expenses.

(3) In prescribing descriptions of expenses for the purposes of this paragraph, the Secretary of State may, in particular, make provision with respect to—

(a) costs incurred by a non-resident parent in maintaining contact with the child, or with any of the children, with respect to whom the application for a maintenance calculation has been made (or treated as made);

(b) costs attributable to a long-term illness or disability of a relevant other child (within the meaning of paragraph 10C(2) of Schedule 1);

(c) debts of a prescribed description incurred, before the non-resident parent became a non-resident parent in relation to a child with respect to whom the maintenance calculation has been applied for (or treated as having been applied for)—

(i) for the joint benefit of both parents;

(ii) for the benefit of any such child; or

(iii) for the benefit of any other child falling within a prescribed category;

(d) boarding school fees for a child in relation to whom the application for a maintenance calculation has been made (or treated as made);

(e) the cost to the non-resident parent of making payments in relation to a mortgage on the home he and the person with care shared, if he no longer has an interest in it, and she and a child in relation to whom the application for a maintenance calculation has been made (or treated as made) still live there.

(4) For the purposes of sub-paragraph (3)(b)—

(a) 'disability' and 'illness' have such meaning as may be prescribed; and

(b) the question whether an illness or disability is long-term shall be determined in accordance with regulations made by the Secretary of State.

(5) For the purposes of sub-paragraph (3)(d), the Secretary of State may prescribe—

(a) the meaning of 'boarding school fees'; and

(b) components of such fees (whether or not itemised as such) which are, or are not, to be taken into account,

and may provide for estimating any such component.

Property or capital transfers

3.— (1) A variation may be agreed in the circumstances set out in sub-paragraph (2) if before 5th April 1993—

(a) a court order of a prescribed kind was in force with respect to the non-resident parent and either the person with care with respect to the application for the maintenance calculation or the child, or any of the children, with respect to whom that application was made; or

(b) an agreement of a prescribed kind between the non-resident parent and any of those persons was in force.

(2) The circumstances are that in consequence of one or more transfers of property of a prescribed kind and exceeding (singly or in aggregate) a prescribed minimum value—

(a) the amount payable by the non-resident parent by way of maintenance was less than would have been the case had that transfer or those transfers not been made; or

(b) no amount was payable by the non-resident parent by way of maintenance.

(3) For the purposes of sub-paragraph (2), 'maintenance' means periodical payments of maintenance made (otherwise than under this Act) with respect to the child, or any of the children, with respect to whom the application for a maintenance calculation has been made.

Additional cases

4.— (1) The Secretary of State may by regulations prescribe other cases in which a variation may be agreed.

(2) Regulations under this paragraph may, for example, make provision with respect to cases where—

(a) the non-resident parent has assets which exceed a prescribed value;

(b) a person's lifestyle is inconsistent with his income for the purposes of a calculation made under Part I of Schedule 1;

(c) a person has income which is not taken into account in such a calculation;

(d) a person has unreasonably reduced the income which is taken into account in such a calculation.

PART II
REGULATORY CONTROLS

5.— (1) The Secretary of State may by regulations make provision with respect to the variations from the usual rules for calculating maintenance which may be allowed when a variation is agreed.

(2) No variations may be made other than those which are permitted by the regulations.

(3) Regulations under this paragraph may, in particular, make provision for a variation to result in—

(a) a person's being treated as having more, or less, income than would be taken into account without the variation in a calculation under Part I of Schedule 1;

(b) a person's being treated as liable to pay a higher, or a lower, amount of child support maintenance than would result without the variation from a calculation under that Part.

(4) Regulations may provide for the amount of any special expenses to be taken into account in a case falling within paragraph 2, for the purposes of a variation, not to exceed such amount as may be prescribed or as may be determined in accordance with the regulations.

(5) Any regulations under this paragraph may in particular make different provision with respect to different levels of income.

6. The Secretary of State may by regulations provide for the application, in connection with child support maintenance payable following a variation, of paragraph 7(2) to (7) of Schedule 1 (subject to any prescribed modifications).

SOCIAL SECURITY ADMINISTRATION ACT 1992
(1992 c. 5)

PART V
INCOME SUPPORT AND THE DUTY TO MAINTAIN

105. Failure to maintain — general

(1) If—
(a) any person persistently refuses or neglects to maintain himself or any person whom he is liable to maintain; and
(b) in consequence of his refusal or neglect universal credit is paid to or in respect of him or such a person,
he shall be guilty of an offence and liable on summary conviction to a fine of an amount not exceeding level 4 on the standard scale.

. . .

(3) Subject to subsection (4), for the purposes of this Part, a person shall be liable to maintain another person if that other person is—
(a) his or her spouse or civil partner; or
. . .

PENSIONS ACT 1995
(1995 c. 26)

PART IV
MISCELLANEOUS AND GENERAL

Pensions on divorce, etc.

166. Pensions on divorce etc.

. . .

(4) Nothing in the provisions mentioned in subsection (5) applies to a court exercising its powers under section 23 of the Matrimonial Causes Act 1973 (financial provision in connection with divorce proceedings, etc.) in respect of any benefits under a pension arrangement (within the meaning of section 25B(1) of the Matrimonial Causes Act 1973) which a party to the marriage has or is likely to have.
(4A) Subject to the provisions mentioned in subsection (5) applies to a court exercising its powers under Part 6 of Schedule 5 to the Civil Partnership Act 2004 (making Part 1 orders having regard to pension benefits).
(5) The provisions referred to in subsection (4) are—
(a) section 203(1) and (2) of the Army Act 1955, 203(1) and (2) of the Air Force Act 1955, 128G(1) and (2) of the Naval Discipline Act 1957 or 159(4) and (4A) of the Pension Schemes Act 1993 (which prevent assignment, or orders being made restraining a person from receiving anything which he is prevented from assigning),
(b) section 91 of this Act,
(c) any provision of any enactment (whether passed or made before or after this Act is passed) corresponding to any of the enactments mentioned in paragraphs (a) and (b), and
(d) any provision of the arrangement in question corresponding to any of those enactments.
(6) Subsections (3) to (7) of section 25B, and section 25C of the Matrimonial Causes Act 1973, as inserted by this section, do not affect the powers of the court under section 31 of that Act (variation, discharge, etc.) in relation to any order made before the commencement of this section.

CHILD SUPPORT ACT 1995
(1995 c. 34)

Supplemental

26. Regulations and orders

(1) Any power under this Act to make regulations or orders shall be exercisable by statutory instrument.

(2) Any such power may be exercised to make different provision for different cases, including different provision for different areas.

(3) Any such power includes power—

(a) to make such incidental, supplemental, consequential or transitional provision as appears to the Secretary of State to be expedient; and

(b) to provide for a person to exercise a discretion in dealing with any matter.

27. Interpretation

(1) In this Act 'the 1991 Act' means the Child Support Act 1991.

(2) Expressions in this Act which are used in the 1991 Act have the same meaning in this Act as they have in that Act.

FAMILY LAW ACT 1996
(1996 c. 27)

PART I
PRINCIPLES OF PARTS II AND III

1. The general principles underlying Parts II and III

The court and any person, in exercising functions under or in consequence of Parts II and III, shall have regard to the following general principles—

(a) that the institution of marriage is to be supported;

(b) that the parties to a marriage which may have broken down are to be encouraged to take all practicable steps, whether by marriage counselling or otherwise, to save the marriage;

(c) that a marriage which has irretrievably broken down and is being brought to an end should be brought to an end—

(i) with minimum distress to the parties and to the children affected;

(ii) with questions dealt with in a manner designed to promote as good a continuing relationship between the parties and any children affected as is possible in the circumstances; and

(iii) without costs being unreasonably incurred in connection with the procedures to be followed in bringing the marriage to an end; and

(d) that any risk to one of the parties to a marriage, and to any children, of violence from the other party should, so far as reasonably practicable, be removed or diminished.

PART II
DIVORCE AND SEPARATION

Marriage support services

22. Funding for marriage support services

(1) The Secretary of State may, with the approval of the Treasury, make grants in connection with—

(a) the provision of marriage support services;

(b) research into the causes of marital breakdown;

(c) research into ways of preventing marital breakdown.

(2) Any grant under this section may be made subject to such conditions as the Secretary of State considers appropriate.

(3) In exercising his power to make grants in connection with the provision of marriage support services, the Secretary of State is to have regard, in particular, to the desirability of services of that kind being available when they are first needed.

PART IV
FAMILY HOMES AND DOMESTIC VIOLENCE

Rights to occupy matrimonial or civil partnership home

30. Rights concerning home where one spouse or civil partner has no estate, etc.

(1) This section applies if—
(a) one spouse or civil partner ('A') is entitled to occupy a dwelling-house by virtue of—
(i) a beneficial estate or interest or contract; or
(ii) any enactment giving that spouse the right to remain in occupation; and
(b) the other spouse or civil partner ('B') is not so entitled.

(2) Subject to the provisions of this Part, B has the following rights ('home rights')—
(a) if in occupation, a right not to be evicted or excluded from the dwelling-house or any part of it by A except with the leave of the court given by an order under section 33;
(b) if not in occupation, a right with the leave of the court so given to enter into and occupy the dwelling-house.

(3) If B is entitled under this section to occupy a dwelling-house or any part of a dwelling-house, any payment or tender made or other thing done by B in or towards satisfaction of any liability of A in respect of rent, mortgage payments or other outgoings affecting the dwelling-house is, whether or not it is made or done in pursuance of an order under section 40, as good as if made or done by A.

(4) B's occupation by virtue of this section—
(a) is to be treated, for the purposes of the Rent (Agriculture) Act 1976 and the Rent Act 1977 (other than Part V and sections 103 to 106 of that Act), as occupation by A as A's residence, and
(b) if B occupies the dwelling-house as B's only or principal home, is to be treated, for the purposes of the Housing Act 1985, Part I of the Housing Act 1988 and Chapter I of Part V of the Housing Act 1996, as occupation by A as A's only or principal home.

(5) If B—
(a) is entitled under this section to occupy a dwelling-house or any part of a dwelling-house, and
(b) makes any payment in or towards satisfaction of any liability of A in respect of mortgage payments affecting the dwelling-house, the person to whom the payment is made may treat it as having been made by A, but the fact that that person has treated any such payment as having been so made does not affect any claim of B against A to an interest in the dwelling-house by virtue of the payment.

(6) If B is entitled under this section to occupy a dwelling-house or part of a dwelling-house by reason of an interest of A under a trust, all the provisions of subsections (3) to (5) apply in relation to the trustees as they apply in relation to A.

(7) This section does not apply to a dwelling-house which—
(a) in the case of spouses, has at no time been, and which was at the time intended by them to be, a matrimonial home of theirs, and
(b) in the case of civil partners, has at no time been, and was at no time intended to be, a civil partnership home of theirs.

(8) B's home rights continue—
(a) only so long as the marriage or civil partnership subsists, except to the extent that an order under section 33(5) otherwise provides; and
(b) only so long as A is entitled as mentioned in subsection (1) to occupy the dwelling-house, except where provision is made by section 31 for those rights to be a charge on an estate or interest in the dwelling-house.

(9) It is hereby declared that a spouse—
(a) who has an equitable interest in a dwelling-house or in its proceeds of sale, but
(b) is not a spouse in whom there is vested (whether solely or as joint tenant) a legal estate in fee simple or a legal term of years absolute in the dwelling-house,

is to be treated, only for the purpose of determining whether he has matrimonial home rights, as not being entitled to occupy the dwelling-house by virtue of that interest.

31. Effect of home rights as charge on dwelling-house

(1) Subsections (2) and (3) apply if, at any time during a marriage or civil partnership, A is entitled to occupy a dwelling-house by virtue of a beneficial estate or interest.

(2) B's home rights are a charge on the estate or interest.
(3) The charge created by subsection (2) has the same priority as if it were an equitable interest created at whichever is the latest of the following dates—
(a) the date on which A acquires the estate or interest;
(b) the date of the marriage or formation of the civil partnership; and
(c) 1st January 1968 (the commencement date of the Matrimonial Homes Act 1967).
(4) Subsections (5) and (6) apply if, at any time when B's home rights are a charge on an interest of A under a trust, there are, apart from A and B, no persons, living or unborn, who are or could become beneficiaries under the trust.
(5) The rights are a charge also on the estate or interest of the trustees for A.
(6) The charge created by subsection (5) has the same priority as if it were an equitable interest created (under powers overriding the trusts) on the date when it arises.
(7) In determining for the purposes of subsection (4) whether there are any persons who are not, but could become, beneficiaries under the trust, there is to be disregarded any potential exercise of a general power of appointment exercisable by either or both of A or B alone (whether or not the exercise of it requires the consent of another person).
(8) Even though B's home rights are a charge on an estate or interest in the dwelling-house, those rights are brought to an end by—
(a) the death of A, or
(b) the termination (otherwise than by death) of the marriage or civil partnership,
unless the court directs otherwise by an order made under section 33(5).
(9) If—
(a) B's home rights are a charge on an estate or interest in the dwelling-house, and
(b) that estate or interest is surrendered to merge in some other estate or interest expectant on it in such circumstances that, but for the merger, the person taking the estate or interest would be bound by the charge,
the surrender has effect subject to the charge and the persons thereafter entitled to the other estate or interest are, for so long as the estate or interest surrendered would have endured if not so surrendered, to be treated for all purposes of this Part as deriving title to the other estate or interest under A or, as the case may be, under the trustees for A, by virtue of the surrender.
(10) If the title to the legal estate by virtue of which A is entitled to occupy a dwelling-house (including any legal estate held by trustees for A) is registered under the Land Registration Act 2002 or any enactment replaced by that Act—
(a) registration of a land charge affecting the dwelling-house by virtue of this Part is to be effected by registering a notice under that Act; and
(b) B's home rights are not to be capable of falling within paragraph 2 of Schedule 1 or 3 to that Act.
(12) If—
(a) B's home rights are a charge on the estate of A or of trustees of A, and
(b) that estate is the subject of a mortgage,
then if, after the date of the creation of the mortgage ('the first mortgage'), the charge is registered under section 2 of the Land Charges Act 1972, the charge is, for the purposes of section 94 of the Law of Property Act 1925 (which regulates the rights of mortgagees to make further advances ranking in priority to subsequent mortgages), to be deemed to be a mortgage subsequent in date to the first mortgage.
(13) It is hereby declared that a charge under subsection (2) or (5) is not registrable under subsection (10) or under section 2 of the Land Charges Act 1972 unless it is a charge on a legal estate.

32. Further provisions relating to home rights

Schedule 4 (provisions supplementary to sections 30 and 31) has effect.

Occupation orders

33. Occupation orders where applicant has estate or interest etc. or has home rights

(1) If—
(a) a person ('the person entitled')—
(i) is entitled to occupy a dwelling-house by virtue of a beneficial estate or interest or contract or by virtue of any enactment giving him the right to remain in occupation, or
(ii) has matrimonial home rights in relation to a dwelling-house, and
(b) the dwelling-house—
(i) is or at any time has been the home of the person entitled and of another person with whom he is associated, or

(ii) was at any time intended by the person entitled and any such other person to be their home,

the person entitled may apply to the court for an order containing any of the provisions specified in subsections (3), (4) and (5).

(2) If an agreement to marry is terminated, no application under this section may be made by virtue of section 62(3)(e) by reference to that agreement after the end of the period of three years beginning with the day on which it is terminated.

(2A) If a civil partnership agreement (as defined by section 73 of the Civil Partnership Act 2004) is terminated, no application under this section may be made by virtue of section 62(3)(eza) by reference to that agreement after the period of three years beginning with the day on which it is terminated.

(3) An order under this section may—

(a) enforce the applicant's entitlement to remain in occupation as against the other person ('the respondent');

(b) require the respondent to permit the applicant to enter and remain in the dwelling-house or part of the dwelling-house;

(c) regulate the occupation of the dwelling-house by either or both parties;

(d) if the respondent is entitled as mentioned in subsection (1)(a)(i), prohibit, suspend or restrict the exercise by him of his right to occupy the dwelling-house;

(e) if the respondent has home rights in relation to the dwelling-house and the applicant is the other spouse, restrict or terminate those rights;

(f) require the respondent to leave the dwelling-house or part of the dwelling-house; or

(g) exclude the respondent from a defined area in which the dwelling-house is included.

(4) An order under this section may declare that the applicant is entitled as mentioned in subsection (1)(a)(i) or has home rights.

(5) If the applicant has home rights and the respondent is the other spouse or civil partner, an order under this section made during the marriage or civil partnership may provide that those rights are not brought to an end by—

(a) the death of the other spouse or civil partner; or

(b) the termination (otherwise than by death) of the marriage or civil partnership.

(6) In deciding whether to exercise its powers under subsection (3) and (if so) in what manner, the court shall have regard to all the circumstances including—

(a) the housing needs and housing resources of each of the parties and of any relevant child;

(b) the financial resources of each of the parties;

(c) the likely effect of any order, or of any decision by the court not to exercise its powers under subsection (3), on the health, safety or well-being of the parties and of any relevant child; and

(d) the conduct of the parties in relation to each other and otherwise.

(7) If it appears to the court that the applicant or any relevant child is likely to suffer significant harm attributable to conduct of the respondent if an order under this section containing one or more of the provisions mentioned in subsection (3) is not made, the court shall make the order unless it appears to it that—

(a) the respondent or any relevant child is likely to suffer significant harm if the order is made; and

(b) the harm likely to be suffered by the respondent or child in that event is as great as, or greater than, the harm attributable to conduct of the respondent which is likely to be suffered by the applicant or child if the order is not made.

(8) The court may exercise its powers under subsection (5) in any case where it considers that in all the circumstances it is just and reasonable to do so.

(9) An order under this section—

(a) may not be made after the death of either of the parties mentioned in subsection (1); and

(b) except in the case of an order made by virtue of subsection (5)(a), ceases to have effect on the death of either party.

(10) An order under this section may, in so far as it has continuing effect, be made for a specified period, until the occurrence of a specified event or until further order.

34. Effect of order under s. 33 where rights are charge on dwelling-house

(1) If B's home rights are a charge on the estate or interest of A or of trustees for A—

(a) an order under section 33 against A has, except so far as a contrary intention appears, the same effect against persons deriving title under A or under the trustees and affected by the charge, and

(b) sections 33(1), (3), (4) and (10) and 30(3) to (6) apply in relation to any person deriving title under the other spouse or under the trustees and affected by the charge as they apply in relation to A.

(2) The court may make an order under section 33 by virtue of subsection (1)(b) if it considers that in all the circumstances it is just and reasonable to do so.

35. One former spouse or former civil partner with no existing right to occupy

(1) This section applies if—
(a) one former spouse or former civil partner is entitled to occupy a dwelling-house by virtue of a beneficial estate or interest or contract, or by virtue of any enactment giving him the right to remain in occupation;
(b) the other former spouse or former civil partner is not so entitled; and
(c) the dwelling-house—
(i) in the case of former spouses, was at any time their matrimonial home or was at any time intended by them to be their matrimonial home, or
(ii) in the case of former civil partners, was at any time their civil partnership home or was at any time intended by them to be their civil partnership home.

(2) The former spouse or former civil partner not so entitled may apply to the court for an order under this section against the other former spouse or former civil partner ('the respondent').

(3) If the applicant is in occupation, an order under this section must contain provision—
(a) giving the applicant the right not to be evicted or excluded from the dwelling-house or any part of it by the respondent for the period specified in the order; and
(b) prohibiting the respondent from evicting or excluding the applicant during that period.

(4) If the applicant is not in occupation, an order under this section must contain provision—
(a) giving the applicant the right to enter into and occupy the dwelling-house for the period specified in the order; and
(b) requiring the respondent to permit the exercise of that right.

(5) An order under this section may also—
(a) regulate the occupation of the dwelling-house by either or both of the parties;
(b) prohibit, suspend or restrict the exercise by the respondent of his right to occupy the dwelling-house;
(c) require the respondent to leave the dwelling-house or part of the dwelling-house; or
(d) exclude the respondent from a defined area in which the dwelling-house is included.

(6) In deciding whether to make an order under this section containing provision of the kind mentioned in subsection (3) or (4) and (if so) in what manner, the court shall have regard to all the circumstances including—
(a) the housing needs and housing resources of each of the parties and of any relevant child;
(b) the financial resources of each of the parties;
(c) the likely effect of any order, or of any decision by the court not to exercise its powers under subsection (3) or (4), on the health, safety or well-being of the parties and of any relevant child;
(d) the conduct of the parties in relation to each other and otherwise;
(e) the length of time that has elapsed since the parties ceased to live together;
(f) the length of time that has elapsed since the marriage or civil partnership was dissolved or annulled; and
(g) the existence of any pending proceedings between the parties—
(i) for an order under section 23A or 24 of the Matrimonial Causes Act 1973 (property adjustment orders in connection with divorce proceedings etc.);
(ia) for a property adjustment order under Part 2 of Schedule 5 to the Civil Partnership Act 2004;
(ii) for an order under paragraph 1(2)(d) or (e) of Schedule 1 to the Children Act 1989 (orders for financial relief against parents); or
(iii) relating to the legal or beneficial ownership of the dwelling-house.

(7) In deciding whether to exercise its power to include one or more of the provisions referred to in subsection (5) ('a subsection (5) provision') and (if so) in what manner, the court shall have regard to all the circumstances including the matters mentioned in subsection (6)(a) to (e).

(8) If the court decides to make an order under this section and it appears to it that, if the order does not include a subsection (5) provision, the applicant or any relevant child is likely to suffer significant harm attributable to conduct of the respondent, the court shall include the subsection (5) provision in the order unless it appears to the court that—
(a) the respondent or any relevant child is likely to suffer significant harm if the provision is included in the order; and
(b) the harm likely to be suffered by the respondent or child in that event is as great as or greater than the harm attributable to conduct of the respondent which is likely to be suffered by the applicant or child if the provision is not included.

(9) An order under this section—
(a) may not be made after the death of either of the former spouses or former civil partners; and
(b) ceases to have effect on the death of either of them.

(10) An order under this section must be limited so as to have effect for a specified period not exceeding six months, but may be extended on one or more occasions for a further specified period not exceeding six months.

(11) A former spouse or former civil partner who has an equitable interest in the dwelling-house or in the proceeds of sale of the dwelling-house but in whom there is not vested (whether solely or as joint tenant) a legal estate in fee simple or a legal term of years absolute in the dwelling-house is to be treated (but only for the purpose of determining whether he is eligible to apply under this section) as not being entitled to occupy the dwelling-house by virtue of that interest.

(12) Subsection (11) does not prejudice any right of such a former spouse or former civil partner to apply for an order under section 33.

(13) So long as an order under this section remains in force, subsections (3) to (6) of section 30 apply in relation to the applicant—
(a) as if he were B (the person entitled to occupy the dwelling-house by virtue of that section); and
(b) as if the respondent were A (the person entitled as mentioned in subsection (1)(a) of that section).

36. One cohabitant or former cohabitant with no existing right to occupy

(1) This section applies if—
(a) one cohabitant or former cohabitant is entitled to occupy a dwelling-house by virtue of a beneficial estate or interest or contract or by virtue of any enactment giving him the right to remain in occupation;
(b) the other cohabitant or former cohabitant is not so entitled; and
(c) that dwelling-house is the home in which they cohabit or a home in which they at any time cohabited or intended to cohabit.

(2) The cohabitant or former cohabitant not so entitled may apply to the court for an order under this section against the other cohabitant or former cohabitant ('the respondent').

(3) If the applicant is in occupation, an order under this section must contain provision—
(a) giving the applicant the right not to be evicted or excluded from the dwelling-house or any part of it by the respondent for the period specified in the order; and
(b) prohibiting the respondent from evicting or excluding the applicant during that period.

(4) If the applicant is not in occupation, an order under this section must contain provision—
(a) giving the applicant the right to enter into and occupy the dwelling-house for the period specified in the order; and
(b) requiring the respondent to permit the exercise of that right.

(5) An order under this section may also—
(a) regulate the occupation of the dwelling-house by either or both of the parties;
(b) prohibit, suspend or restrict the exercise by the respondent of his right to occupy the dwelling-house;
(c) require the respondent to leave the dwelling-house or part of the dwelling-house; or
(d) exclude the respondent from a defined area in which the dwelling-house is included.

(6) In deciding whether to make an order under this section containing provision of the kind mentioned in subsection (3) or (4) and (if so) in what manner, the court shall have regard to all the circumstances including—
(a) the housing needs and housing resources of each of the parties and of any relevant child;
(b) the financial resources of each of the parties;
(c) the likely effect of any order, or of any decision by the court not to exercise its powers under subsection (3) or (4), on the health, safety or well-being of the parties and of any relevant child;
(d) the conduct of the parties in relation to each other and otherwise;
(e) the length of time that has elapsed since the parties ceased to live together;
(f) the length of time that has elapsed since the marriage or civil partnership was dissolved or annulled; and
(g) the existence of any pending proceedings between the parties—
(i) for an order under section 23A or 24 of the Matrimonial Causes Act 1973 (property adjustment orders in connection with divorce proceedings etc.);
(ia) for a property adjustment order under Part 2 of Schedule 5 to the Civil Partnership Act 2004;

(ii) for an order under paragraph 1(2)(d) or (e) of Schedule 1 to the Children Act 1989 (orders for financial relief against parents); or
(iii) relating to the legal or beneficial ownership of the dwelling-house.

(7) In deciding whether to exercise its powers to include one or more of the provisions referred to in subsection (5) ('a subsection (5) provision') and (if so) in what manner, the court shall have regard to all the circumstances including—
(a) the matters mentioned in subsection (6)(a) to (e);
(b) the questions mentioned in subsection (8).

(8) If the court decides to make an order under this section and it appears to it that, if the order does not include a subsection (5) provision, the applicant or any relevant child is likely to suffer significant harm attributable to conduct of the respondent, the court shall include the subsection (5) provision in the order unless it appears to the court that—
(a) the respondent or any relevant child is likely to suffer significant harm if the provision is included in the order; and
(b) the harm likely to be suffered by the respondent or child in that event is as great as or greater than the harm attributable to conduct of the respondent which is likely to be suffered by the applicant or child if the provision is not included.

(9) An order under this section—
(a) may not be made after the death of either of the former spouses or former civil partners; and
(b) ceases to have effect on the death of either of them.

(10) An order under this section must be limited so as to have effect for a specified period not exceeding six months, but may be extended on one occasion for a further specified period not exceeding six months.

(11) A former spouse or former civil partner who has an equitable interest in the dwelling-house or in the proceeds of sale of the dwelling-house but in whom there is not vested (whether solely or as joint tenant) a legal estate in fee simple or a legal term of years absolute in the dwelling-house is to be treated (but only for the purpose of determining whether he is eligible to apply under this section) as not being entitled to occupy the dwelling-house by virtue of that interest.

(12) Subsection (11) does not prejudice any right of such a person to apply for an order under section 33.

(13) So long as under this section remains in force, subsections (3) to (6) of section 30 apply in relation to the applicant—
(a) as if he were B (the person entitled to occupy the dwelling-house by virtue of that section); and
(b) as if the respondent were A (the person entitled as mentioned in subsection (1)(a) of that section).

37. Neither spouse or civil partner entitled to occupy

(1) This section applies if—
(a) one spouse or former spouse and the other spouse or former spouse occupy a dwelling-house which is or was the matrimonial home; but
(b) neither of them is entitled to remain in occupation—
(i) by virtue of a beneficial estate or interest or contract; or
(ii) by virtue of any enactment giving him the right to remain in occupation.

(1A) This section applies if—
(a) the civil partner or former civil partner and the other civil partner or former civil partner occupy a dwelling-house which is or was the civil partnership home; but
(b) neither of them is entitled to remain in occupation—
(i) by virtue of a beneficial estate or contract; or
(ii) by virtue of any enactment giving him the right to remain in occupation.

(2) Either of the parties may apply to the court for an order against the other under this section.

(3) An order under this section may—
(a) require the respondent to permit the applicant to enter and remain in the dwelling-house or part of the dwelling-house;
(b) regulate the occupation of the dwelling-house by either or both of the parties;
(c) require the respondent to leave the dwelling-house or part of the dwelling-house; or
(d) exclude the respondent from a defined area in which the dwelling-house is included.

(4) Subsections (6) and (7) of section 33 apply to the exercise by the court of its powers under this section as they apply to the exercise by the court of its powers under subsection (3) of that section.

(5) An order under this section must be limited so as to have effect for a specified period not exceeding six months, but may be extended on one or more occasions for a further specified period not exceeding six months.

38. Neither cohabitant or former cohabitant entitled to occupy

(1) This section applies if—
(a) one cohabitant or former cohabitant and the other cohabitant or former cohabitant occupy a dwelling-house which is the home in which they cohabit or cohabited; but
(b) neither of them is entitled to remain in occupation—
(i) by virtue of a beneficial estate or interest or contract; or
(ii) by virtue of any enactment giving him the right to remain in occupation.
(2) Either of the parties may apply to the court for an order against the other under this section.
(3) An order under this section may—
(a) require the respondent to permit the applicant to enter and remain in the dwelling-house or part of the dwelling-house;
(b) regulate the occupation of the dwelling-house by either or both of the parties;
(c) require the respondent to leave the dwelling-house or part of the dwelling-house; or
(d) exclude the respondent from a defined area in which the dwelling-house is included.
(4) In deciding whether to exercise its powers to include one or more of the provisions referred to in subsection (3) ('a subsection (3) provision') and (if so) in what manner, the court shall have regard to all the circumstances including—
(a) the housing needs and housing resources of each of the parties and of any relevant child;
(b) the financial resources of each of the parties;
(c) the likely effect of any order, or of any decision by the court not to exercise its powers under subsection (3), on the health, safety or well-being of the parties and of any relevant child;
(d) the conduct of the parties in relation to each other and otherwise; and
(e) the questions mentioned in subsection (5).
(5) The questions are—
(a) whether the applicant or any relevant child is likely to suffer significant harm attributable to conduct of the respondent if the subsection (3) provision is not included in the order; and
(b) whether the harm likely to be suffered by the respondent or child if the provision is included is as great as or greater than the harm attributable to conduct of the respondent which is likely to be suffered by the applicant or child if the provision is not included.
(6) An order under this section shall be limited so as to have effect for a specified period not exceeding six months, but may be extended on one occasion for a further specified period not exceeding six months.

39. Supplementary provisions

(1) In this Part an 'occupation order' means an order under section 33, 35, 36, 37 or 38.
(2) An application for an occupation order may be made in other family proceedings or without any other family proceedings being instituted.
(3) If—
(a) an application for an occupation order is made under section 33, 35, 36, 37 or 38, and
(b) the court considers that it has no power to make the order under the section concerned, but that it has power to make an order under one of the other sections,

the court may make an order under that other section.
(4) The fact that a person has applied for an occupation order under sections 35 to 38, or that an occupation order has been made, does not affect the right of any person to claim a legal or equitable interest in any property in any subsequent proceedings (including subsequent proceedings under this Part).

40. Additional provisions that may be included in certain occupation orders

(1) The court may on, or at any time after, making an occupation order under section 33, 35 or 36—
(a) impose on either party obligations as to—
(i) the repair and maintenance of the dwelling-house; or
(ii) the discharge of rent, mortgage payments or other outgoings affecting the dwelling-house;
(b) order a party occupying the dwelling-house or any part of it (including a party who is entitled to do so by virtue of a beneficial estate or interest or contract or by virtue of any enactment giving him the right to remain in occupation) to make periodical payments to the other party in respect of the accommodation, if the

other party would (but for the order) be entitled to occupy the dwelling-house by virtue of a beneficial estate or interest or contract or by virtue of any such enactment;
(c) grant either party possession or use of furniture or other contents of the dwelling-house;
(d) order either party to take reasonable care of any furniture or other contents of the dwelling-house;
(e) order either party to take reasonable steps to keep the dwelling-house and any furniture or other contents secure.

(2) In deciding whether and, if so, how to exercise its powers under this section, the court shall have regard to all the circumstances of the case including—
(a) the financial needs and financial resources of the parties; and
(b) the financial obligations which they have, or are likely to have in the foreseeable future, including financial obligations to each other and to any relevant child.

(3) An order under this section ceases to have effect when the occupation order to which it relates ceases to have effect.

Non-molestation orders

42. Non-molestation orders

(1) In this Part a 'non-molestation order' means an order containing either or both of the following provisions—
(a) provision prohibiting a person ('the respondent') from molesting another person who is associated with the respondent;
(b) provision prohibiting the respondent from molesting a relevant child.

(2) The court may make a non-molestation order—
(a) if an application for the order has been made (whether in other family proceedings or without any other family proceedings being instituted) by a person who is associated with the respondent; or
(b) if in any family proceedings to which the respondent is a party the court considers that the order should be made for the benefit of any other party to the proceedings or any relevant child even though no such application has been made.

(3) In subsection (2) 'family proceedings' includes proceedings in which the court has made an emergency protection order under section 44 of the Children Act 1989 which includes an exclusion requirement (as defined in section 44A(3) of that Act).

(4) Where an agreement to marry is terminated, no application under subsection (2)(a) may be made by virtue of section 62(3)(e) by reference to that agreement after the end of the period of three years beginning with the day on which it is terminated.

(4ZA) If a civil partnership agreement (as defined by section 73 of the Civil Partnership Act 2004) is terminated, no application under this section may be made by virtue of section 62(3)(eza) by reference to that agreement after the end of the period of three years beginning with the day on which it is terminated.

(4A) A court considering whether to make an occupation order shall also consider whether to exercise the power conferred by subsection (2)(b).

(4B) In this Part 'the applicant', in relation to a non-molestation order, includes (where the context permits) the person for whose benefit such an order would be or is made in exercise of the power conferred by subsection (2)(b).

(5) In deciding whether to exercise its powers under this section and, if so, in what manner, the court shall have regard to all the circumstances including the need to secure the health, safety and well-being—
(a) of the applicant . . .; and
(b) of any relevant child.

(6) A non-molestation order may be expressed so as to refer to molestation in general, to particular acts of molestation, or to both.

(7) A non-molestation order may be made for a specified period or until further order.

(8) A non-molestation order which is made in other family proceedings ceases to have effect if those proceedings are withdrawn or dismissed.

42A. Offence of breaching non-molestation order

(1) A person who without reasonable excuse does anything he is prohibited from doing by a non-molestation order is guilty of an offence.

(2) In the case of a non-molestation order made by virtue of section 45(1) a person can be guilty of an offence under this section only in respect of conduct engaged in at a time when he was aware of the existence of the order.

(3) Where a person is convicted of an offence under this section in respect of any conduct, that conduct is not punishable as a contempt of court.
(4) A person cannot be convicted of an offence under this section in respect of any conduct which has been punished as a contempt of court.
(5) A person guilty of an offence under this section is liable—
 (a) on conviction on indictment to imprisonment for a term not exceeding 5 years, or a fine, or both;
 (b) on summary conviction, to imprisonment for a term not exceeding 12 months, or a fine not exceeding the statutory maximum, or both.
(6) A reference in any enactment to proceedings under this Part, or to an order under this Part, does not include a reference to proceedings for an offence under this section, or to an order made in such proceedings.
'Enactment' includes an enactment contained in subordinate legislation within the meaning of the Interpretation Act 1978.

Further provisions relating to occupation and non-molestation orders

43. Leave of court required for applications by children under sixteen

(1) A child under the age of sixteen may not apply for an occupation order or a non-molestation order except with the leave of the court.
(2) The court may grant leave for the purposes of subsection (1) only if it is satisfied that the child has sufficient understanding to make the proposed application for the occupation order or non-molestation order.

44. Evidence of agreement to marry or form a civil partnership

(1) Subject to subsection (2), the court shall not make an order under section 33 or 42 by virtue of section 62(3)(e) unless there is produced to it evidence in writing of the existence of the agreement to marry.
(2) Subsection (1) does not apply if the court is satisfied that the agreement to marry was evidenced by—
 (a) the gift of an engagement ring by one party to the agreement to the other in contemplation of their marriage, or
 (b) a ceremony entered into by the parties in the presence of one or more other persons assembled for the purpose of witnessing the ceremony.
(3) Subject to subsection (4), the court shall not make an order under section 33 or 42 by virtue of section 62(3)(eza) unless there is produced to it evidence in writing of the existence of the civil partnership agreement (as defined by section 73 of the Civil Partnership Act 2004).
(4) Subsection (3) does not apply if the court is satisfied that the civil partnership agreement was evidenced by—
 (a) a gift by one party to the agreement to the other as a token of the agreement, or
 (b) a ceremony entered into by the parties in the presence of one or more other persons assembled for the purpose of witnessing the ceremony.

45. Ex parte orders

(1) The court may, in any case where it considers that it is just and convenient to do so, make an occupation order or a non-molestation order even though the respondent has not been given such notice of the proceedings as would otherwise be required by rules of court.
(2) In determining whether to exercise its powers under subsection (1), the court shall have regard to all the circumstances including—
 (a) any risk of significant harm to the applicant or a relevant child, attributable to conduct of the respondent, if the order is not made immediately;
 (b) whether it is likely that the applicant will be deterred or prevented from pursuing the application if an order is not made immediately; and
 (c) whether there is reason to believe that the respondent is aware of the proceedings but is deliberately evading service and that the applicant or a relevant child will be seriously prejudiced by the delay involved in effecting substituted service.
(3) If the court makes an order by virtue of subsection (1) it must afford the respondent an opportunity to make representations relating to the order as soon as just and convenient at a full hearing.
(4) If, at a full hearing, the court makes an occupation order ('the full order'), then—
 (a) for the purposes of calculating the maximum period for which the full order may be made to have effect, the relevant section is to apply as if the period for which the full order will have effect began on the date on which the initial order first had effect; and

(b) the provisions of section 36(10) or 38(6) as to the extension of orders are to apply as if the full order and the initial order were a single order.

(5) In this section—
'full hearing' means a hearing of which notice has been given to all the parties in accordance with rules of court;
'initial order' means an occupation order made by virtue of subsection (1); and
'relevant section' means section 33(10), 35(10), 36(10), 37(5) or 38(6).

46. Undertakings

(1) In any case where the court has power to make an occupation order or non-molestation order, the court may accept an undertaking from any party to the proceedings.

(2) No power of arrest may be attached to any undertaking given under subsection (1).

(3) The court shall not accept an undertaking under subsection (1) instead of making an occupation order in any case where apart from this section a power of arrest would be attached to the order.

(3A) The court shall not accept an undertaking under subsection (1) instead of making a non-molestation order in any case where it appears to the court that—
(a) the respondent has used or threatened violence against the applicant or a relevant child; and
(b) for the protection of the applicant or child it is necessary to make a non-molestation order so that any breach may be punishable under section 42A.

(4) An undertaking given to a court under subsection (1) is enforceable as if the court had made an occupation order or a non-molestation order in terms corresponding to those of the undertaking.

(5) This section has effect without prejudice to the powers of the High Court and the county court apart from this section.

47. Arrest for breach of order

...

(2) If—
(a) the court makes an occupation order; and
(b) it appears to the court that the respondent has used or threatened violence against the applicant or a relevant child,
it shall attach a power of arrest to one or more provisions of the order unless satisfied that in all the circumstances of the case the applicant or child will be adequately protected without such a power of arrest.

(3) Subsection (2) does not apply in any case where the occupation order is made by virtue of section 45(1), but in such a case the court may attach a power of arrest to one or more provisions of the order if it appears to it—
(a) that the respondent has used or threatened violence against the applicant or a relevant child; and
(b) that there is a risk of significant harm to the applicant or child, attributable to conduct of the respondent, if the power of arrest is not attached to those provisions immediately.

(4) If, by virtue of subsection (3), the court attaches a power of arrest to any provisions of an occupation order, it may provide that the power of arrest is to have effect for a shorter period than the other provisions of the order.

(5) Any period specified for the purposes of subsection (4) may be extended by the court (on one or more occasions) on an application to vary or discharge the occupation order.

(6) If, by virtue of subsection (2) or (3), a power of arrest is attached to certain provisions of an order, a constable may arrest without warrant a person whom he has reasonable cause for suspecting to be in breach of any such provision.

(7) If a power of arrest is attached under subsection (2) or (3) to certain provisions of the order and the respondent is arrested under subsection (6)—
(a) he must be brought before the relevant judicial authority within the period of 24 hours beginning at the time of his arrest; and
(b) if the matter is not then disposed of forthwith, the relevant judicial authority before whom he is brought may remand him.
In reckoning for the purposes of this subsection any period of 24 hours, no account is to be taken of Christmas Day, Good Friday or any Sunday.

(8) If the court—
(a) has made a non-molestation order, or
(b) has made an occupation order but has not attached a power of arrest under subsection (2) or (3) to any provision of the order, or has attached that power only to certain provisions of the order,
then, if at any time the applicant considers that the respondent has failed to comply with the order, he may apply to the relevant judicial authority for the issue of a warrant for the arrest of the respondent.

(9) The relevant judicial authority shall not issue a warrant on an application under subsection (8) unless—
(a) the application is substantiated on oath; and
(b) the relevant judicial authority has reasonable grounds for believing that the respondent has failed to comply with the order.

(10) If a person is brought before a court by virtue of a warrant issued under subsection (9) and the court does not dispose of the matter forthwith, the court may remand him.

(11) Schedule 5 (which makes provision corresponding to that applying in magistrates' courts in civil cases under sections 128 and 129 of the Magistrates' Courts Act 1980) has effect in relation to the powers of the High Court and a county court to remand a person by virtue of this section.

(12) If a person remanded under this section is granted bail (whether in the High Court or a county court under Schedule 5 or in a magistrates' court under section 128 or 129 of the Magistrates' Courts Act 1980), he may be required by the relevant judicial authority to comply, before release on bail or later, with such requirements as appear to that authority to be necessary to secure that he does not interfere with witnesses or otherwise obstruct the course of justice.

48. Remand for medical examination and report

(1) If the relevant judicial authority has reason to consider that a medical report will be required, any power to remand a person under section 47(7)(b) or (10) may be exercised for the purpose of enabling a medical examination and report to be made.

(2) If such a power is so exercised, the adjournment must not be for more than 4 weeks at a time unless the relevant judicial authority remands the accused in custody.

(3) If the relevant judicial authority so remands the accused, the adjournment must not be for more than 3 weeks at a time.

(4) If there is reason to suspect that a person who has been arrested—
(a) under section 47(6), or
(b) under a warrant issued on an application made under section 47(8),
is suffering from mental illness or severe mental impairment, the relevant judicial authority has the same power to make an order under section 35 of the Mental Health Act 1983 (remand for report on accused's mental condition) as the Crown Court has under section 35 of the Act of 1983 in the case of an accused person within the meaning of that section.

49. Variation and discharge of orders

(1) An occupation order or non-molestation order may be varied or discharged by the court on an application by—
(a) the respondent, or
(b) the person on whose application the order was made.

(2) In the case of a non-molestation order made by virtue of section 42(2)(b), the order may be varied or discharged by the court even though no such application has been made.

(3) If B's home rights are, under section 31, a charge on the estate or interest of A or of trustees for A, an order under section 33 against A may also be varied or discharged by the court on an application by any person deriving title under A or under the trustees and affected by the charge.

(4) If, by virtue of section 47(3), a power of arrest has been attached to certain provisions of an occupation order . . . the court may vary or discharge the order under subsection (1) in so far as it confers a power of arrest (whether or not any application has been made to vary or discharge any other provision of the order).

Transfer of tenancies

53. Transfer of certain tenancies

Schedule 7 makes provision in relation to the transfer of certain tenancies on divorce etc. or on separation of cohabitants.

Dwelling-house subject to mortgage

54. Dwelling-house subject to mortgage

(1) In determining for the purposes of this Part whether a person is entitled to occupy a dwelling-house by virtue of an estate or interest, any right to possession of the dwelling-house conferred on a mortgagee of the dwelling-house under or by virtue of his mortgage is to be disregarded.

(2) Subsection (1) applies whether or not the mortgagee is in possession.
(3) Where a person ('A') is entitled to occupy a dwelling-house by virtue of an estate or interest, a connected person does not by virtue of—
(a) any home rights conferred by section 30, or
(b) any rights conferred by an order under section 35 or 36,
have any larger right against the mortgagee to occupy the dwelling-house than A has by virtue of his estate or interest and of any contract with the mortgagee.
(4) Subsection (3) does not apply, in the case of matrimonial home rights, if under section 31 those rights are a charge, affecting the mortgagee, on the estate or interest mortgaged.
(5) In this section 'connected person', in relation to any person, means that person's spouse, former spouse, civil partner, former civil partner, cohabitant or former cohabitant.

55. Actions by mortgagees: joining connected persons as parties

(1) This section applies if a mortgagee of land which consists of or includes a dwelling-house brings an action in any court for the enforcement of his security.
(2) A connected person who is not already a party to the action is entitled to be made a party in the circumstances mentioned in subsection (3).
(3) The circumstances are that—
(a) the connected person is enabled by section 30(3) or (6) (or by section 30(3) or (6) as applied by section 35(13) or 36(13)), to meet the mortgagor's liabilities under the mortgage;
(b) he has applied to the court before the action is finally disposed of in that court; and
(c) the court sees no special reason against his being made a party to the action and is satisfied—
(i) that he may be expected to make such payments or do such other things in or towards satisfaction of the mortgagor's liabilities or obligations as might affect the outcome of the proceedings; or
(ii) that the expectation of it should be considered under section 36 of the Administration of Justice Act 1970.
(4) In this section 'connected person' has the same meaning as in section 54.

56. Actions by mortgagees: service of notice on certain persons

(1) This section applies if a mortgagee of land which consists, or substantially consists, of a dwelling-house brings an action for the enforcement of his security, and at the relevant time there is—
(a) in the case of unregistered land, a land charge of Class F registered against the person who is the estate owner at the relevant time or any person who, where the estate owner is a trustee, preceded him as trustee during the subsistence of the mortgage; or
(b) in the case of registered land, a subsisting registration of—
(i) a notice under section 31(10);
(ii) a notice under section 2(8) of the Matrimonial Homes Act 1983; or
(iii) a notice or caution under section 2(7) of the Matrimonial Homes Act 1967.
(2) If the person on whose behalf—
(a) the land charge is registered, or
(b) the notice or caution is entered,
is not a party to the action, the mortgagee must serve notice of the action on him.
(3) If—
(a) an official search has been made on behalf of the mortgagee which would disclose any land charge of Class F, notice or caution within subsection (1)(a) or (b),
(b) a certificate of the result of the search has been issued, and
(c) the action is commenced within the priority period,
the relevant time is the date of the certificate.
(4) In any other case the relevant time is the time when the action is commenced.
(5) The priority period is, for both registered and unregistered land, the period for which, in accordance with section 11(5) and (6) of the Land Charges Act 1972, a certificate on an official search operates in favour of a purchaser.

Jurisdiction and procedure etc.

57. Jurisdiction of courts

(1) For the purposes of this Part 'the court' means the High Court, a county court or a magistrates' court.
(2)–(12) ...

58. Contempt proceedings

The powers of the court in relation to contempt of court arising out of a person's failure to comply with an order under this Part may be exercised by the relevant judicial authority.

60. Provision for third parties to act on behalf of victims of domestic violence

(1) Rules of court may provide for a prescribed person, or any person in a prescribed category, ('a representative') to act on behalf of another in relation to proceedings to which this Part applies.

(2) Rules made under this section may, in particular, authorise a representative to apply for an occupation order or for a non-molestation order for which the person on whose behalf the representative is acting could have applied.

(3) Rules made under this section may prescribe—

(a) conditions to be satisfied before a representative may make an application to the court on behalf of another; and

(b) considerations to be taken into account by the court in determining whether, and if so how, to exercise any of its powers under this Part when a representative is acting on behalf of another.

(4) Any rules made under this section may be made so as to have effect for a specified period and may make consequential or transitional provision with respect to the expiry of the specified period.

(5) Any such rules may be replaced by further rules made under this section.

(6) Except to the extent provided for in any order made under subsection (5), no appeal may be made against any decision of a kind mentioned in that subsection.

General

62. Meaning of 'cohabitants', 'relevant child' and 'associated persons'

(1) For the purposes of this Part—

(a) 'cohabitants' are two persons who are neither married to each other nor civil partners of each other but are living together as husband and wife or as if they were civil partners; and

(b) 'cohabit' and 'former cohabitants' are to be read accordingly, but the latter expression does not include cohabitants who have subsequently married each other or become civil partners of each other.

(2) In this Part, 'relevant child', in relation to any proceedings under this Part, means—

(a) any child who is living with or might reasonably be expected to live with either party to the proceedings;

(b) any child in relation to whom an order under the Adoption Act 1976, the Adoption and Children Act 2002 or the Children Act 1989 is in question in the proceedings; and

(c) any other child whose interests the court considers relevant.

(3) For the purposes of this Part, a person is associated with another person if—

(a) they are or have been married to each other;

(aa) they are or have been civil partners of each other;

(b) they are cohabitants or former cohabitants;

(c) they live or have lived in the same household, otherwise than merely by reason of one of them being the other's employee, tenant, lodger or boarder;

(d) they are relatives;

(e) they have agreed to marry one another (whether or not that agreement has been terminated);

(eza) they have entered into a civil partnership agreement (as defined by section 73 of the Civil Partnership Act 2004) (whether or not that agreement has been terminated);

(ea) they have or have had an intimate personal relationship with each other which is or was of significant duration;

(f) in relation to any child, they are both persons falling within subsection (4); or

(g) they are parties to the same family proceedings (other than proceedings under this Part).

(4) A person falls within this subsection in relation to a child if—

(a) he is a parent of the child; or

(b) he has or has had parental responsibility for the child.

(5) If a child has been adopted or falls within subsection (7), two persons are also associated with each other for the purposes of this Part if—

(a) one is a natural parent of the child or a parent of such a natural parent; and

(b) the other is the child or any person—

(i) who has become a parent of the child by virtue of an adoption order or has applied for an adoption order, or

(ii) with whom the child has at any time been placed for adoption.

(6) A body corporate and another person are not, by virtue of subsection (3)(f) or (g), to be regarded for the purposes of this Part as associated with each other.

(7) A child falls within this section if—

(a) an adoption agency, within the meaning of section 2 of the Adoption and Children Act 2002, has power to place him for adoption under section 19 of that Act (placing children with parental consent) or he has become the subject of an order under section 21 of that Act (placement orders); or

(b) he is freed for adoption by virtue of an order made—

(i) in England and Wales, under section 18 of the Adoption Act 1976,

(ii) in Northern Ireland, under Article 17(1) or 18(1) of the Adoption (Northern Ireland) Order 1987.

63. Interpretation of Part IV

(1) In this Part—

'adoption order' means an adoption order within the meaning of section 72(1) of the Adoption Act 1976 or section 46(1) of the Adoption and Children Act 2002;

'associated', in relation to a person, is to be read with section 62(3) to (6);

'child' means a person under the age of eighteen years;

'cohabit', 'cohabitant' and 'former cohabitant' have the meaning given by section 62(1);

'the court' is to be read with section 57;

'development' means physical, intellectual, emotional, social or behavioural development;

'dwelling-house' includes (subject to subsection (4))—

(a) any building or part of a building which is occupied as a dwelling,

(b) any caravan, house-boat or structure which is occupied as a dwelling,

and any yard, garden, garage or outhouse belonging to it and occupied with it;

'family proceedings' means any proceedings—

(a) under the inherent jurisdiction of the High Court in relation to children; or

(b) under the enactments mentioned in subsection (2);

'harm'—

(a) in relation to a person who has reached the age of eighteen years, means ill-treatment or the impairment of health; and

(b) in relation to a child, means ill-treatment or the impairment of health or development;

'health' includes physical or mental health;

'home rights' has the meaning given by section 30;

'ill-treatment' includes forms of ill-treatment which are not physical and, in relation to a child, includes sexual abuse;

'mortgage', 'mortgagor' and 'mortgagee' have the same meaning as in the Law of Property Act 1925;

'mortgage payments' includes any payments which, under the terms of the mortgage, the mortgagor is required to make to any person;

'non-molestation order' has the meaning given by section 42(1);

'occupation order' has the meaning given by section 39;

'parental responsibility' has the same meaning as in the Children Act 1989;

'relative', in relation to a person, means—

(a) the father, mother, stepfather, stepmother, son, daughter, stepson, stepdaughter, grandmother, grandfather, grandson or granddaughter of that person or of that person's spouse, former spouse, civil partner or former civil partner, or

(b) the brother, sister, uncle, aunt, niece, nephew or first cousin (whether of the full blood or of the half blood or by marriage or civil partnership) of that person or of that person's spouse, former spouse, civil partner or former civil partner,

and includes, in relation to a person who is cohabiting or has cohabited with, any person who would fall within paragraph (a) or (b) if the parties were married to each other;

'relevant child', in relation to any proceedings under this Part, has the meaning given by section 62(2);

'the relevant judicial authority', in relation to any order under this Part, means—

(a) where the order was made by the High Court, a judge of that court;

(aa) where the order was made by the family court, a judge of that court;

(b), (c)...

(2) The enactments referred to in the definition of 'family proceedings' are—

(a) Part II;

(b) this Part;

(ba) Part 4A;

(c) the Matrimonial Causes Act 1973;

(d) the Adoption Act 1976;

(e) the Domestic Proceedings and Magistrates' Courts Act 1978;

(f) Part III of the Matrimonial and Family Proceedings Act 1984;
(g) Parts I, II and IV of the Children Act 1989;
(h) section 54 of the Human Fertilisation and Embryology Act 2008;
(i) the Adoption and Children Act 2002;
(j) Schedules 5 to 7 to the Civil Partnership Act 2004.

(3) Where the question of whether harm suffered by a child is significant turns on the child's health or development, his health or development shall be compared with that which could reasonably be expected of a similar child.

(4) For the purposes of sections 31, 32, 53 and 54 and such other provisions of this Part (if any) as may be prescribed, this Part is to have effect as if paragraph (b) of the definition of 'dwelling-house' were omitted.

(5) It is hereby declared that this Part applies as between the parties to a marriage even though either of them is, or has at any time during the marriage been, married to more than one person.

PART 4A
FORCED MARRIAGE

Forced marriage protection orders

63A. Forced marriage protection orders

(1) The court may make an order for the purposes of protecting—
(a) a person from being forced into a marriage or from any attempt to be forced into a marriage; or
(b) a person who has been forced into a marriage.

(2) In deciding whether to exercise its powers under this section and, if so, in what manner, the court must have regard to all the circumstances including the need to secure the health, safety and well-being of the person to be protected.

(3) In ascertaining that person's well-being, the court must, in particular, have such regard to the person's wishes and feelings (so far as they are reasonably ascertainable) as the court considers appropriate in the light of the person's age and understanding.

(4) For the purposes of this Part a person ('A') is forced into a marriage if another person ('B') forces A to enter into a marriage (whether with B or another person) without A's free and full consent.

(5) For the purposes of subsection (4) it does not matter whether the conduct of B which forces A to enter into a marriage is directed against A, B or another person.

(6) In this Part—
'force' includes coerce by threats or other psychological means (and related expressions are to be read accordingly); and
'forced marriage protection order' means an order under this section.

63B. Contents of orders

(1) A forced marriage protection order may contain—
(a) such prohibitions, restrictions or requirements; and
(b) such other terms;
as the court considers appropriate for the purposes of the order.

(2) The terms of such orders may, in particular, relate to—
(a) conduct outside England and Wales as well as (or instead of) conduct within England and Wales;
(b) respondents who are, or may become, involved in other respects as well as (or instead of) respondents who force or attempt to force, or may force or attempt to force, a person to enter into a marriage;
(c) other persons who are, or may become, involved in other respects as well as respondents of any kind.

(3) For the purposes of subsection (2) examples of involvement in other respects are—
(a) aiding, abetting, counselling, procuring, encouraging or assisting another person to force, or to attempt to force, a person to enter into a marriage; or
(b) conspiring to force, or to attempt to force, a person to enter into a marriage.

63C. Applications and other occasions for making orders

(1) The court may make a forced marriage protection order—
(a) on an application being made to it; or
(b) without an application being made to it but in the circumstances mentioned in subsection (6).

(2) An application may be made by—

(a) the person who is to be protected by the order; or
(b) a relevant third party.

(3) An application may be made by any other person with the leave of the court.

(4) In deciding whether to grant leave, the court must have regard to all the circumstances including—
(a) the applicant's connection with the person to be protected;
(b) the applicant's knowledge of the circumstances of the person to be protected; and
(c) the wishes and feelings of the person to be protected so far as they are reasonably ascertainable and so far as the court considers it appropriate, in the light of the person's age and understanding, to have regard to them.

(5) An application under this section may be made in other family proceedings or without any other family proceedings being instituted.

(6) The circumstances in which the court may make an order without an application being made are where—
(a) any other family proceedings are before the court ('the current proceedings');
(b) the court considers that a forced marriage protection order should be made to protect a person (whether or not a party to the current proceedings); and
(c) a person who would be a respondent to any such proceedings for a forced marriage protection order is a party to the current proceedings.

(7) In this section—
'family proceedings' has the same meaning as in Part 4 (see section 63(1) and (2)) but also includes—
(a) proceedings under the inherent jurisdiction of the High Court in relation to adults;
(b) proceedings in which the court has made an emergency protection order under section 44 of the Children Act 1989 which includes an exclusion requirement (as defined in section 44A(3) of that Act); and
(c) proceedings in which the court has made an order under section 50 of the Act of 1989 (recovery of abducted children etc.); and
'relevant third party' means a person specified, or falling within a description of persons specified, by order of the Lord Chancellor.

(8) An order of the Lord Chancellor under subsection (7) may, in particular, specify the Secretary of State.

63CA Offences of breaching order

(1) A person who without reasonable excuse does anything that the person is prohibited from doing by a forced marriage protection order is guilty of an offence.

(2) In the case of a forced marriage protection order made by virtue of section 63D(1) a person can be guilty of an offence under this section only in respect of conduct engaged in at a time when the person was aware of the existence of the order.

(3) Where a person is convicted under this section in respect of any conduct, the conduct is not punishable as a contempt of court.

(4) A person cannot be convicted of an offence under this section which has been punished as a contempt of court.

...

Further provision about orders

63D. Ex parte orders: Part 4A

(1) The court may, in any case where it considers that it is just and convenient to do so, make a forced marriage protection order even though the respondent has not been given such notice of the proceedings as would otherwise be required by rules of court.

(2) In deciding whether to exercise its powers under subsection (1), the court must have regard to all the circumstances including—
(a) any risk of significant harm to the person to be protected or another person if the order is not made immediately;
(b) whether it is likely that an applicant will be deterred or prevented from pursuing an application if an order is not made immediately; and
(c) whether there is reason to believe that—
(i) the respondent is aware of the proceedings but is deliberately evading service; and
(ii) the delay involved in effecting substituted service will cause serious prejudice to the person to be protected or (if a different person) an applicant.

(3) The court must give the respondent an opportunity to make representations about any order made by virtue of subsection (1).

(4) The opportunity must be—
(a) as soon as just and convenient; and
(b) at a hearing of which notice has been given to all the parties in accordance with rules of court.

63E. Undertakings instead of orders

(1) The court may, subject to subsection (3), accept an undertaking from the respondent to proceedings for a forced marriage protection order if it has power to make such an order.
(2) No power of arrest may be attached to an undertaking given under subsection (1).
(3) The court may not accept an undertaking under subsection (1) instead of making an order if a power of arrest would otherwise have been attached to the order.
(4) An undertaking given to the court under subsection (1) is enforceable as if the court had made the order in terms corresponding to those of the undertaking.
(5) This section is without prejudice to the powers of the court apart from this section.

63F. Duration of orders

A forced marriage protection order may be made for a specified period or until varied or discharged.

63G. Variation of orders and their discharge

(1) The court may vary or discharge a forced marriage protection order on an application by—
(a) any party to the proceedings for the order;
(b) the person being protected by the order (if not a party to the proceedings for the order); or
(c) any person affected by the order.
(2) In addition, the court may vary or discharge a forced marriage protection order made by virtue of section 63C(1)(b) even though no application under subsection (1) above has been made to the court.
(3) Section 63D applies to a variation of a forced marriage protection order as it applies to the making of such an order.
(4) Section 63E applies to proceedings for a variation of a forced marriage protection order as it applies to proceedings for the making of such an order.
(5) Accordingly, references in sections 63D and 63E to making a forced marriage protection order are to be read for the purposes of subsections (3) and (4) above as references to varying such an order.
(6) Subsection (7) applies if a power of arrest has been attached to provisions of a forced marriage protection order by virtue of section 63H.
(7) The court may vary or discharge the order under this section so far as it confers a power of arrest (whether or not there is a variation or discharge of any other provision of the order).

Arrest for breach of orders

63H. Attachment of powers of arrest to orders

(1) Subsection (2) applies if the court—
(a) intends to make a forced marriage protection order otherwise than by virtue of section 63D; and
(b) considers that the respondent has used or threatened violence against the person being protected or otherwise in connection with the matters being dealt with by the order.
(2) The court must attach a power of arrest to one or more provisions of the order unless it considers that, in all the circumstances of the case, there will be adequate protection without such a power.
(3) Subsection (4) applies if the court—
(a) intends to make a forced marriage protection order by virtue of section 63D; and
(b) considers that the respondent has used or threatened violence against the person being protected or otherwise in connection with the matters being dealt with by the order.
(4) The court may attach a power of arrest to one or more provisions of the order if it considers that there is a risk of significant harm to a person, attributable to conduct of the respondent, if the power of arrest is not attached to the provisions immediately.

(5) The court may provide for a power of arrest attached to any provisions of an order under subsection (4) to have effect for a shorter period than the other provisions of the order.
(6) Any period specified for the purposes of subsection (5) may be extended by the court (on one or more occasions) on an application to vary or discharge the order.
(7) In this section 'respondent' includes any person who is not a respondent but to whom an order is directed.

63I. Arrest under attached powers

(1) Subsection (2) applies if a power of arrest is attached to provisions of a forced marriage protection order under section 63H.
(2) A constable may arrest without warrant a person whom the constable has reasonable cause for suspecting to be in breach of any such provision or otherwise in contempt of court in relation to the order.
(3) A person arrested under subsection (2) must be brought before the relevant judge within the period of 24 hours beginning at the time of the person's arrest.
(4) In calculating any period of 24 hours for the purposes of subsection (3), Christmas Day, Good Friday and any Sunday are to be ignored.

63J. Arrest under warrant

(1) Subsection (2) applies if the court has made a forced marriage protection order but—
  (a) no power of arrest is attached to any provision of the order under section 63H;
  (b) such a power is attached only to certain provisions of the order; or
  (c) such a power was attached for a shorter period than other provisions of the order and that period has expired.
(2) An interested party may apply to the relevant judge for the issue of a warrant for the arrest of a person if the interested party considers that the person has failed to comply with the order or is otherwise in contempt of court in relation to the order.
(3) The relevant judge must not issue a warrant on an application under subsection (2) unless—
  (a) the application is substantiated on oath; and
  (b) the relevant judge has reasonable grounds for believing that the person to be arrested has failed to comply with the order or is otherwise in contempt of court in relation to the order.
(4) In this section 'interested party', in relation to a forced marriage protection order, means—
  (a) the person being protected by the order;
  (b) (if a different person) the person who applied for the order; or
  (c) any other person;
  but no application may be made under subsection (2) by a person falling within paragraph (c) without the leave of the relevant judge.

63K. Remand: general

(1) The court before which an arrested person is brought under section 63I(3) or by virtue of a warrant issued under section 63J may, if the matter is not then disposed of immediately, remand the person concerned.
(2) Schedule 5 has effect in relation to the powers of the court to remand a person by virtue of this section but as if the following modifications were made to the Schedule.
(3) The modifications are that—
  (a) in paragraph 2(1) of Schedule 5, the reference to section 47 is to be read as a reference to this section; and
  (b) in paragraph 2(5)(b) of the Schedule, the reference to section 48(1) is to be read as a reference to section 63L(1).
(4) Subsection (5) applies if a person remanded under this section is granted bail under Schedule 5 as modified above.
(5) The person may be required by the relevant judge to comply, before release on bail or later, with such requirements as appear to the relevant judge to be necessary to secure that the person does not interfere with witnesses or otherwise obstruct the course of justice.

63L. Remand: medical examination and report

(1) Any power to remand a person under section 63K(1) may be exercised for the purpose of enabling a medical examination and report to be made if the relevant judge has reason to consider that a medical report will be required.
(2) If such a power is so exercised, the adjournment must not be for more than 4 weeks at a time unless the relevant judge remands the accused in custody.

(3) If the relevant judge remands the accused in custody, the adjournment must not be for more than 3 weeks at a time.
(4) Subsection (5) applies if there is reason to suspect that a person who has been arrested—
...
(a) under section 63I(2); or
(b) under a warrant issued on an application made under section 63J(2);
is suffering from mental illness or severe mental impairment.
(5) The relevant judge has the same power to make an order under section 35 of the Mental Health Act 1983 (remand for report on accused's mental condition) as the Crown Court has under section 35 of that Act in the case of an accused person within the meaning of that section.

Jurisdiction and procedure

63M. Jurisdiction of courts: Part 4A

(1) For the purposes of this Part 'the court' means the High Court or a county court.
...

63O. Contempt proceedings: Part 4A

The powers of the court in relation to contempt of court arising out of a person's failure to comply with a forced marriage protection order or otherwise in connection with such an order may be exercised by the relevant judge.

Supplementary

63Q. Guidance

(1) The Secretary of State may from time to time prepare and publish guidance to such descriptions of persons as the Secretary of State considers appropriate about—
(a) the effect of this Part or any provision of this Part; or
(b) other matters relating to forced marriages.
(2) A person exercising public functions to whom guidance is given under this section must have regard to it in the exercise of those functions.
(3) Nothing in this section permits the Secretary of State to give guidance to any court or tribunal.

63R. Other protection or assistance against forced marriage

(1) This Part does not affect any other protection or assistance available to a person who—
(a) is being, or may be, forced into a marriage or subjected to an attempt to be forced into a marriage; or
(b) has been forced into a marriage.
(2) In particular, it does not affect—
(a) the inherent jurisdiction of the High Court;
(b) any criminal liability;
(c) any civil remedies under the Protection from Harassment Act 1997;
(d) any right to an occupation order or a non-molestation order under Part 4 of this Act;
(e) any protection or assistance under the Children Act 1989;
(f) any claim in tort; or
(g) the law of marriage.

63S. Interpretation of Part 4A

In this Part—
'the court' is to be read with section 63M;
'force'(and related expressions), in relation to a marriage, are to be read in accordance with section 63A(4) to (6);
'forced marriage protection order' has the meaning given by section 63A(6);
'marriage' means any religious or civil ceremony of marriage (whether or not legally binding); and
'the relevant judge', in relation to any order under this Part, means—
(a) where the order was made by the High Court, a judge of that court; and
(b) where the order was made by a family court, a judge of that court.

PART V
SUPPLEMENTAL

64. Provision for separate representation for children

(1) The Lord Chancellor may by regulations provide for the separate representation of children in proceedings in England and Wales which relate to any matter in respect of which a question has arisen, or may arise, under—
  (b) Part IV;
  (c) the 1973 Act;
  (d) the Domestic Proceedings and Magistrates' Courts Act 1978; or
  (e) Schedule 5 or 6 to the Civil Partnership Act 2004.
(2) The regulations may provide for such representation only in specified circumstances.

Section 32

SCHEDULE 4
PROVISIONS SUPPLEMENTARY TO SECTIONS 30 AND 31

Cancellation of registration after termination of marriage or civil partnership, etc.

. . .

4.— (1) Where a spouse's or civil partner's home rights are a charge on an estate in the dwelling-house and the charge is registered under section 31(10) or under section 2 of the Land Charges Act 1972, the Chief Land Registrar shall, subject to sub-paragraph (2), cancel the registration of the charge if he is satisfied—
  (a) in the case of a marriage—
    (i) by the production of a certificate or other sufficient evidence, that either spouse is dead, or
    (ii) by the production of an official copy of a decree or order of a court, that the marriage in question has been terminated otherwise than by death, or
    (iii) by the production of an order of the court, that the spouse's home rights constituting the charge have been terminated by the order.
  (b) in the case of a civil partnership—
    (i) by the production of a certificate, or other sufficient evidence, that either civil partner is dead,
    (ii) by the production of an official copy of an order or decree of a court, that the civil partnership has been terminated otherwise than by death, or
    (iii) by the production of an order of the court, that the civil partner's home rights constituting the change have been terminated by the order.
(2) Where—
  (a) the marriage or civil partnership in question has been terminated by the death of the spouse or civil partner entitled to an estate in the dwelling-house or otherwise than by death, and
  (b) an order affecting the charge of the spouse or civil partner not so entitled had been made under section 33(5),

  then if, after the making of the order, registration of the charge was renewed or the charge registered in pursuance of sub-paragraph (3), the Chief Land Registrar shall not cancel the registration of the charge in accordance with sub-paragraph (1) unless he is also satisfied that the order has ceased to have effect.
(3) Where such an order has been made, then, for the purposes of sub-paragraph (2), the spouse or civil partner entitled to the charge affected by the order may—
  (a) if before the date of the order the charge was registered under section 31(10) or under section 2 of the Land Charges Act 1972, renew the registration of the charge, and
  (b) if before the said date the charge was not so registered, register the charge under section 31(10) or under section 2 of the Land Charges Act 1972.
(4) Renewal of the registration of a charge in pursuance of sub-paragraph (3) shall be effected in such manner as may be prescribed, and an application for such renewal or for registration of a charge in pursuance of that sub-paragraph shall contain such particulars of any order affecting the charge made under section 33(5) as may be prescribed.
(5) The renewal in pursuance of sub-paragraph (3) of the registration of a charge shall not affect the priority of the charge.
(6) In this paragraph 'prescribed' means prescribed by rules made under section 16 of the Land Charges Act 1972 or by land registration rules under the Land Registration Act 2002, as the circumstances of the case require.

Release of home rights

5.— (1) A spouse or civil partner entitled to home rights may by a release in writing release those rights or release them as respects part only of the dwelling-house affected by them.

(2) Where a contract is made for the sale of an estate or interest in a dwelling-house, or for the grant of a lease or underlease of a dwelling-house, being (in either case) a dwelling-house affected by a charge registered under section 31(10) or under section 2 of the Land Charges Act 1972, then, without prejudice to sub-paragraph (1), the home rights constituting the charge shall be deemed to have been released on the happening of whichever of the following events first occurs—

(a) the delivery to the purchaser or lessee, as the case may be, or his solicitor on completion of the contract of an application by the spouse entitled to the charge for the cancellation of the registration of the charge; or

(b) the lodging of such an application at Her Majesty's Land Registry.

Postponement of priority of charge

6. A spouse or civil partner entitled by virtue of section 31 to a charge on an estate or interest may agree in writing that any other charge on, or interest in, that estate or interest shall rank in priority to the charge to which that spouse is so entitled.

Section 47(11)

SCHEDULE 5

POWERS OF HIGH COURT AND COUNTY COURT TO REMAND

Interpretation

1. In this Schedule 'the court' means the High Court or a county court and includes—

(a) in relation to the High Court, a judge of that court, and

(b) in relation to a county court, a judge or district judge of that court.

Remand in custody or on bail

2.— (1) Where a court has power to remand a person under section 47, the court may—

(a) remand him in custody, that is to say, commit him to custody to be brought before the court at the end of the period of remand or at such earlier time as the court may require, or

(b) remand him on bail—

(i) by taking from him a recognizance (with or without sureties) conditioned as provided in sub-paragraph (3), or

(ii) by fixing the amount of the recognizances with a view to their being taken subsequently in accordance with paragraph 4 and in the meantime committing the person to custody in accordance with paragraph (a).

(2) Where a person is brought before the court after remand, the court may further remand him.

(3) Where a person is remanded on bail under sub-paragraph (1), the court may direct that his recognizance be conditioned for his appearance—

(a) before that court at the end of the period of remand, or

(b) at every time and place to which during the course of the proceedings the hearing may from time to time be adjourned.

(4) Where a recognizance is conditioned for a person's appearance in accordance with sub-paragraph (l)(b), the fixing of any time for him next to appear shall be deemed to be a remand; but nothing in this sub-paragraph or sub-paragraph (3) shall deprive the court of power at any subsequent hearing to remand him afresh.

(5) Subject to paragraph 3, the court shall not remand a person under this paragraph for a period exceeding 8 clear days, except that—

(a) if the court remands him on bail, it may remand him for a longer period if he and the other party consent, and

(b) if the court adjourns a case under section 48(1), the court may remand him for the period of the adjournment.

(6) Where the court has power under this paragraph to remand a person in custody it may, if the remand is for a period not exceeding 3 clear days, commit him to the custody of a constable.

Further remand

3.— (1) If the court is satisfied that any person who has been remanded under paragraph 2 is unable by reason of illness or accident to appear or be brought before the court at the expiration of the period for which he was remanded, the court may, in his absence, remand him for a further time; and paragraph 2(5) shall not apply.

(2) Notwithstanding anything in paragraph 2(1), the power of the court under sub-paragraph (1) to remand a person on bail for a further time may be exercised by enlarging his recognizance and those of any sureties for him to a later time.

(3) Where a person remanded on bail under paragraph 2 is bound to appear before the court at any time and the court has no power to remand him under sub-paragraph (1), the court may in his absence enlarge his recognizance and those of any sureties for him to a later time; and the enlargement of his recognizance shall be deemed to be a further remand.

Postponement of taking of recognizance

4. Where under paragraph 2(1)(b)(ii) the court fixes the amount in which the principal and his sureties, if any, are to be bound, the recognizance may thereafter be taken by such person as may be prescribed by rules of court, and the same consequences shall follow as if it had been entered into before the court.

Section 53

SCHEDULE 7
TRANSFER OF CERTAIN TENANCIES ON DIVORCE ETC. OR ON SEPARATION OF COHABITANTS

PART I
GENERAL

Interpretation

1. In this Schedule—

'civil partner', except in paragraph 2, includes (where the context requires) former civil partner;
'cohabitant', except in paragraph 3, includes (where the context requires) former cohabitant;
'the court' does not include a magistrates' court;
'landlord' includes—
(a) any person from time to time deriving title under the original landlord; and
(b) in relation to any dwelling-house, any person other than the tenant who is, or (but for Part VII of the Rent Act 1977 or Part II of the Rent (Agriculture) Act 1976) would be, entitled to possession of the dwelling-house;
'Part II order' means an order under Part II of this Schedule;
'a relevant tenancy' means—
(a) a protected tenancy or statutory tenancy within the meaning of the Rent Act 1977;
(b) a statutory tenancy within the meaning of the Rent (Agriculture) Act 1976;
(c) a secure tenancy within the meaning of section 79 of the Housing Act 1985;
(d) an assured tenancy or assured agricultural occupancy within the meaning of Part I of the Housing Act 1988; or
(e) an introductory tenancy within the meaning of Chapter I of Part V of the Housing Act 1996;
'spouse', except in paragraph 2, includes (where the context requires) former spouse; and
'tenancy' includes sub-tenancy.

Cases in which the court may make an order

2.— (1) This paragraph applies if one spouse or civil partner is entitled, either in his own right or jointly with the other spouse or civil partner, to occupy a dwelling-house by virtue of a relevant tenancy.

(2) The court may make a Part II order—
(a) on granting a decree of divorce, a decree of nullity of marriage or a decree of judicial separation or at any time thereafter (whether, in the case of a decree of divorce or nullity of marriage, before or after the decree is made absolute); or
(b) at any time when it has power to make a property adjustment order under Part 2 of Schedule 5 to the Civil Partnership Act 2004 with respect to the civil partnership.

3.— (1) This paragraph applies if one cohabitant is entitled, either in his own right or jointly with the other cohabitant, to occupy a dwelling-house by virtue of a relevant tenancy.

(2) If the cohabitants cease to cohabit, the court may make a Part II order.

4. The court shall not make a Part II order unless the dwelling-house is or was—
(a) in the case of spouses, a matrimonial home;

(aa) in the case of civil partners, a civil partnership home; or
(b) in the case of cohabitants, a home in which they cohabited.

Matters to which the court must have regard

5. In determining whether to exercise its powers under Part II of this Schedule and, if so, in what manner, the court shall have regard to all the circumstances of the case including—
(a) the circumstances in which the tenancy was granted to either or both of the spouses, civil partners or cohabitants or, as the case requires, the circumstances in which either or both of them became tenant under the tenancy;
(b) the matters mentioned in section 33(6)(a), (b) and (c) and, where the parties are cohabitants and only one of them is entitled to occupy the dwelling-house by virtue of the relevant tenancy, the further matters mentioned in section 36(6)(e), (f), (g) and (h); and
(c) the suitability of the parties as tenants.

PART II
ORDERS THAT MAY BE MADE

References to entitlement to occupy

6. References in this Part of this Schedule to a spouse, a civil partner or a cohabitant being entitled to occupy a dwelling-house by virtue of a relevant tenancy apply whether that entitlement is in his own right or jointly with the other spouse, civil partner or cohabitant.

Protected, secure or assured tenancy or assured agricultural occupancy

7.— (1) If a spouse, civil partner or cohabitant is entitled to occupy the dwelling-house by virtue of a protected tenancy within the meaning of the Rent Act 1977, a secure tenancy within the meaning of the Housing Act 1985, an assured tenancy or assured agricultural occupancy within the meaning of Part I of the Housing Act 1988 or an introductory tenancy within the meaning of Chapter I of Part V of the Housing Act 1996, the court may by order direct that, as from such date as may be specified in the order, there shall, by virtue of the order and without further assurance, be transferred to, and vested in, the other spouse or cohabitant—
(a) the estate or interest which the spouse, civil partner or cohabitant so entitled had in the dwelling-house immediately before that date by virtue of the lease or agreement creating the tenancy and any assignment of that lease or agreement, with all rights, privileges and appurtenances attaching to that estate or interest but subject to all covenants, obligations, liabilities and incumbrances to which it is subject; and
(b) where the spouse, civil partner or cohabitant so entitled is an assignee of such lease or agreement, the liability of that spouse, civil partner or cohabitant under any covenant of indemnity by the assignee express or implied in the assignment of the lease or agreement to that spouse, civil partner or cohabitant.

(2) If an order is made under this paragraph, any liability or obligation to which the spouse, civil partner or cohabitant so entitled is subject under any covenant having reference to the dwelling-house in the lease or agreement, being a liability or obligation falling due to be discharged or performed on or after the date so specified, shall not be enforceable against that spouse, civil partner or cohabitant.

(3) If the spouse, civil partner or cohabitant so entitled is a successor within the meaning of Part 4 of the Housing Act 1985—
(a) his former spouse (or, in the case of judicial separation, his spouse),
(b) his former civil partner (or, if a separation order is in force, his civil partner), or
(c) his former cohabitant,
is to be deemed also to be a successor within the meaning of that Part.

(3A) If the spouse, civil partner or cohabitant so entitled is a successor within the meaning of section 132 of the Housing Act 1996—
(a) his former spouse (or, in the case of a judicial separation, his spouse),
(b) his former civil partner (or if a separation order is in force, his civil partner), or
(c) his former cohabitant,
is to be deemed also to be a successor within the meaning of that section.

(4) If the spouse, civil partner or cohabitant so entitled is for the purposes of section 17 of the Housing Act 1988 a successor in relation to the tenancy or occupation—
(a) his former spouse (or, in the case of a judicial separation, his spouse),
(b) his former civil partner (or, if a separation order is in force, his civil partner), or
(c) his former cohabitant,
is to be deemed to be a successor in relation to the tenancy or occupancy for the purposes of that section.

(5) If the transfer under sub-paragraph (1) is of an assured agricultural occupancy, then, for the purposes of Chapter III of Part I of the Housing Act 1988—
(a) the agricultural worker condition is fulfilled with respect to the dwelling-house while the spouse, civil partner or cohabitant to whom the assured agricultural occupancy is transferred continues to be the occupier under that occupancy, and
(b) that condition is to be treated as so fulfilled by virtue of the same paragraph of Schedule 3 to the Housing Act 1988 as was applicable before the transfer.

Statutory tenancy within the meaning of the Rent Act 1977

8.— (1) This paragraph applies if the spouse, civil partner or cohabitant is entitled to occupy the dwelling-house by virtue of a statutory tenancy within the meaning of the Rent Act 1977.
(2) The court may by order direct that, as from the date specified in the order—
(a) that spouse, civil partner or cohabitant is to cease to be entitled to occupy the dwelling-house; and
(b) the other spouse, civil partner or cohabitant is to be deemed to be the tenant or, as the case may be, the sole tenant under that statutory tenancy.
(3) The question whether the provisions of paragraphs 1 to 3, or (as the case may be) paragraphs 5 to 7 of Schedule 1 to the Rent Act 1977, as to the succession by the surviving spouse or surviving civil partner of a deceased tenant, or by a member of the deceased tenant's family, to the right to retain possession are capable of having effect in the event of the death of the person deemed by an order under this paragraph to be the tenant or sole tenant under the statutory tenancy is to be determined according as those provisions have or have not already had effect in relation to the statutory tenancy.

. . .

PART III
SUPPLEMENTARY PROVISIONS

Compensation

10.— (1) If the court makes a Part II order, it may by the order direct the making of a payment by the spouse, civil partner or cohabitant to whom the tenancy is transferred ('the transferee') to the other spouse, civil partner or cohabitant ('the transferor').
(2) Without prejudice to that, the court may, on making an order by virtue of sub-paragraph (1) for the payment of a sum—
(a) direct that payment of that sum or any part of it is to be deferred until a specified date or until the occurrence of a specified event, or
(b) direct that that sum or any part of it is to be paid by instalments.
(3) Where an order has been made by virtue of sub-paragraph (1), the court may, on the application of the transferee or the transferor—
(a) exercise its powers under sub-paragraph (2), or
(b) vary any direction previously given under that sub-paragraph,
at any time before the sum whose payment is required by the order is paid in full.
(4) In deciding whether to exercise its powers under this paragraph and, if so, in what manner, the court shall have regard to all the circumstances including—
(a) the financial loss that would otherwise be suffered by the transferor as a result of the order;
(b) the financial needs and financial resources of the parties; and
(c) the financial obligations which the parties have, or are likely to have in the foreseeable future, including financial obligations to each other and to any relevant child.
(5) The court shall not give any direction under sub-paragraph (2) unless it appears to it that immediate payment of the sum required by the order would cause the transferee financial hardship which is greater than any financial hardship that would be caused to the transferor if the direction were given.

Liabilities and obligations in respect of the dwelling-house

11.— (1) If the court makes a Part II order, it may by the order direct that both spouses, civil partners or cohabitants are to be jointly and severally liable to discharge or perform any or all of the liabilities and obligations in respect of the dwelling-house (whether arising under the tenancy or otherwise) which—
(a) have at the date of the order fallen due to be discharged or performed by one only of them; or

(b) but for the direction, would before the date specified as the date on which the order is to take effect fall due to be discharged or performed by one only of them.

(2) If the court gives such a direction, it may further direct that either spouse, civil partner or cohabitant is to be liable to indemnify the other in whole or in part against any payment made or expenses incurred by the other in discharging or performing any such liability or obligation.

Date when order made between spouses or civil partners is to take effect

12. The date specified in a Part II order as the date on which the order is to take effect must not be earlier than—

(a) in the case of a marriage in respect of which a decree of divorce or nullity has been granted, the date on which the decree is made absolute;

(b) in the case of a civil partnership in respect of which a dissolution or nullity order has been made, the date on which the order is made final.

Effect of remarriage or subsequent civil partnership

13.— (1) If after the grant of a decree annulling a marriage either spouse remarries or forms a civil partnership, that spouse is not entitled to apply, by reference to the grant of that decree, for a Part II order.

(2) If after the making of a dissolution or nullity order either civil partner forms a subsequent civil partnership or marries, that civil partner is not entitled to apply, by reference to the making of that order, for a Part II order.

(3) In subparagraphs (1) and (2)—

(a) the references to remarrying and marrying include references to cases where the marriage is by law void or voidable; and

(b) the references to forming a civil partnership include references to cases where the civil partnership is by law void or voidable.

Rules of court

14.— (1) Rules of court shall be made requiring the court, before it makes an order under this Schedule, to give the landlord of the dwelling-house to which the order will relate an opportunity of being heard.

(2) Rules of court may provide that an application for a Part II order by reference to an order or decree may not, without the leave of the court by which that order was made or decree was granted, be made after the expiration of such period from the order or grant as may be prescribed by the rules.

Saving for other provisions of Act

15.— (1) If a spouse or civil partner is entitled to occupy a dwelling-house by virtue of a tenancy, this Schedule does not affect the operation of sections 30 and 31 in relation to the other spouse's or civil partner's home rights.

(2) If a spouse, civil partner or cohabitant is entitled to occupy a dwelling-house by virtue of a tenancy, the court's powers to make orders under this Schedule are additional to those conferred by sections 33, 35 and 36.

TRUSTS OF LAND AND APPOINTMENT OF TRUSTEES ACT 1996
(1996 c. 47)

PART I
TRUSTS OF LAND

Introductory

1. Meaning of 'trust of land'

(1) In this Act—

(a) 'trust of land' means (subject to subsection (3)) any trust of property which consists of or includes land, and

(b) 'trustees of land' means trustees of a trust of land.

(2) The reference in subsection (1)(a) to a trust—
(a) is to any description of trust (whether express, implied, resulting or constructive), including a trust for sale and a bare trust, and
(b) includes a trust created, or arising, before the commencement of this Act.

Right of beneficiaries to occupy trust land

12. The right to occupy

(1) A beneficiary who is beneficially entitled to an interest in possession in land subject to a trust of land is entitled by reason of his interest to occupy the land at any time if at that time—
(a) the purposes of the trust include making the land available for his occupation (or for the occupation of beneficiaries of a class of which he is a member or of beneficiaries in general), or
(b) the land is held by the trustees so as to be so available.
(2) Subsection (1) does not confer on a beneficiary a right to occupy land if it is either unavailable or unsuitable for occupation by him.
(3) This section is subject to section 13.

13. Exclusion and restriction of right to occupy

(1) Where two or more beneficiaries are (or apart from this subsection would be) entitled under section 12 to occupy land, the trustees of land may exclude or restrict the entitlement of any one or more (but not all) of them.
(2) Trustees may not under subsection (1)—
(a) unreasonably exclude any beneficiary's entitlement to occupy land, or
(b) restrict any such entitlement to an unreasonable extent.
(3) The trustees of land may from time to time impose reasonable conditions on any beneficiary in relation to his occupation of land by reason of his entitlement under section 12.
(4) The matters to which trustees are to have regard in exercising the powers conferred by this section include—
(a) the intentions of the person or persons (if any) who created the trust,
(b) the purposes for which the land is held, and
(c) the circumstances and wishes of each of the beneficiaries who is (or apart from any previous exercise by the trustees of those powers would be) entitled to occupy the land under section 12.
(5) The conditions which may be imposed on a beneficiary under subsection (3) include, in particular, conditions requiring him—
(a) to pay any outgoings or expenses in respect of the land, or
(b) to assume any other obligation in relation to the land or to any activity which is or is proposed to be conducted there.
(6) Where the entitlement of any beneficiary to occupy land under section 12 has been excluded or restricted, the conditions which may be imposed on any other beneficiary under subsection (3) include, in particular, conditions requiring him to—
(a) make payments by way of compensation to the beneficiary whose entitlement has been excluded or restricted, or
(b) forgo any payment or other benefit to which he would otherwise be entitled under the trust so as to benefit that beneficiary.
(7) The powers conferred on trustees by this section may not be exercised—
(a) so as prevent any person who is in occupation of land (whether or not by reason of an entitlement under section 12) from continuing to occupy the land, or
(b) in a manner likely to result in any such person ceasing to occupy the land,
unless he consents or the court has given approval.
(8) The matters to which the court is to have regard in determining whether to give approval under subsection (7) include the matters mentioned in subsection (4)(a) to (c).

Powers of court

14. Applications for order

(1) Any person who is a trustee of land or has an interest in property subject to a trust of land may make an application to the court for an order under this section.
(2) On an application for an order under this section the court may make any such order—
(a) relating to the exercise by the trustees of any of their functions (including an order relieving them of any obligation to obtain the consent of, or to consult, any person in connection with the exercise of any of their functions), or

(b) declaring the nature or extent of a person's interest in property subject to the trust, as the court thinks fit.

(3) The court may not under this section make any order as to the appointment or removal of trustees.

(4) The powers conferred on the court by this section are exercisable on an application whether it is made before or after the commencement of this Act.

15. Matters relevant in determining applications

(1) The matters to which the court is to have regard in determining an application for an order under section 14 include—

(a) the intentions of the person or persons (if any) who created the trust,

(b) the purposes for which the property subject to the trust is held,

(c) the welfare of any minor who occupies or might reasonably be expected to occupy any land subject to the trust as his home, and

(d) the interests of any secured creditor of any beneficiary.

(2) In the case of an application relating to the exercise in relation to any land of the powers conferred on the trustees by section 13, the matters to which the court is to have regard also include the circumstances and wishes of each of the beneficiaries who is (or apart from any previous exercise by the trustees of those powers would be) entitled to occupy the land under section 12.

(3) In the case of any other application, other than one relating to the exercise of the power mentioned in section 6(2), the matters to which the court is to have regard also include the circumstances and wishes of any beneficiaries of full age and entitled to an interest in possession in property subject to the trust or (in case of dispute) of the majority (according to the value of their combined interests).

(4) This section does not apply to an application if section 335A of the Insolvency Act 1986 (which is inserted by Schedule 3 and relates to applications by a trustee of a bankrupt) applies to it.

PART III

SUPPLEMENTARY

22. Meaning of 'beneficiary'

(1) In this Act 'beneficiary', in relation to a trust, means any person who under the trust has an interest in property subject to the trust (including a person who has such an interest as a trustee or a personal representative).

(2) In this Act references to a beneficiary who is beneficially entitled do not include a beneficiary who has an interest in property subject to the trust only by reason of being a trustee or personal representative.

(3) For the purposes of this Act a person who is a beneficiary only by reason of being an annuitant is not to be regarded as entitled to an interest in possession in land subject to the trust.

SCHEDULES

Section 2

SCHEDULE I

PROVISIONS CONSEQUENTIAL ON SECTION 2

Minors

1.— (1) Where after the commencement of this Act a person purports to convey a legal estate in land to a minor, or two or more minors, alone, the conveyance—

(a) is not effective to pass the legal estate, but

(b) operates as a declaration that the land is held in trust for the minor or minors (or if he purports to convey it to the minor or minors in trust for any persons, for those persons).

(2) Where after the commencement of this Act a person purports to convey a legal estate in land to—

(a) a minor or two or more minors, and

(b) another person who is, or other persons who are, of full age,

the conveyance operates to vest the land in the other person or persons in trust for the minor or minors and the other person or persons (or if he purports to convey it to them in trust for any persons, for those persons).

(3) Where immediately before the commencement of this Act a conveyance is operating (by virtue of section 27 of the Settled Land Act 1925) as an agreement to execute a settlement in favour of a minor or minors—

(a) the agreement ceases to have effect on the commencement of this Act, and

(b) the conveyance subsequently operates instead as a declaration that the land is held in trust for the minor or minors.

2. Where after the commencement of this Act a legal estate in land would, by reason of intestacy or in any other circumstances not dealt with in paragraph 1, vest in a person who is a minor if he were a person of full age, the land is held in trust for the minor.

Family charges

3. Where, by virtue of an instrument coming into operation after the commencement of this Act, land becomes charged voluntarily (or in consideration of marriage) or by way of family arrangement, whether immediately or after an interval, with the payment of—
(a) a rentcharge for the life of a person or a shorter period, or
(b) capital, annual or periodical sums for the benefit of a person,
the instrument operates as a declaration that the land is held in trust for giving effect to the charge.

HOUSING ACT 1996
(1996 c. 52)

PART VII
HOMELESSNESS

Homelessness and threatened homelessness

175. Homelessness and threatened homelessness

(1) A person is homeless if he has no accommodation available for his occupation, in the United Kingdom or elsewhere, which he—
(a) is entitled to occupy by virtue of an interest in it or by virtue of an order of a court,
(b) has an express or implied licence to occupy, or
(c) occupies as a residence by virtue of any enactment or rule of law giving him the right to remain in occupation or restricting the right of another person to recover possession.

(2) A person is also homeless if he has accommodation but—
(a) he cannot secure entry to it, or
(b) it consists of a moveable structure, vehicle or vessel designed or adapted for human habitation and there is no place where he is entitled or permitted both to place it and to reside in it.

(3) A person shall not be treated as having accommodation unless it is accommodation which it would be reasonable for him to continue to occupy.

(4) A person is threatened with homelessness if it is likely that he will become homeless within 28 days.

176. Meaning of accommodation available for occupation

Accommodation shall be regarded as available for a person's occupation only if it is available for occupation by him together with—
(a) any other person who normally resides with him as a member of his family, or
(b) any other person who might reasonably be expected to reside with him.
References in this Part to securing that accommodation is available for a person's occupation shall be construed accordingly.

177. Whether it is reasonable to continue to occupy accommodation

(1) It is not reasonable for a person to continue to occupy accommodation if it is probable that this will lead to domestic violence against him, or against—
(a) a person who normally resides with him as a member of his family, or
(b) any other person who might reasonably be expected to reside with him.
For this purpose 'domestic violence', in relation to a person, means violence from a person with whom he is associated, or threats of violence from such a person which are likely to be carried out.

(2) In determining whether it would be, or would have been, reasonable for a person to continue to occupy accommodation, regard may be had to the general circumstances prevailing in relation to housing in the district of the local housing authority to whom he has applied for accommodation or for assistance in obtaining accommodation.

(3) The Secretary of State may by order specify—
(a) other circumstances in which it is to be regarded as reasonable or not reasonable for a person to continue to occupy accommodation, and

(b) other matters to be taken into account or disregarded in determining whether it would be, or would have been, reasonable for a person to continue to occupy accommodation.

178. Meaning of associated person

(1) For the purposes of this Part, a person is associated with another person if—
(a) they are or have been married to each other;
(aa) they are or have been civil partners of each other;
(b) they are cohabitants or former cohabitants;
(c) they live or have lived in the same household;
(d) they are relatives;
(e) they have agreed to marry one another (whether or not that agreement has been terminated);
(ea) they have entered into a civil partnership agreement between them (whether or not that agreement has been terminated);
(f) in relation to a child, each of them is a parent of the child or has, or has had, parental responsibility for the child.

(2) If a child has been adopted or falls within subsection (2A), two persons are also associated with each other for the purposes of this Part if—
(a) one is a natural parent of the child or a parent of such a natural parent, and
(b) the other is the child or a person—
(i) who has become a parent of the child by virtue of an adoption order or who has applied for an adoption order, or
(ii) with whom the child has at any time been placed for adoption.

(2A) A child falls within this subsection if—
(a) an adoption agency, within the meaning of section 2 of the Adoption and Children Act 2002, is authorised to place him for adoption under section 19 of that Act (placing children with parental consent) or he has become the subject of an order under section 21 of that Act (placement orders), or—
(b) he is freed for adoption by virtue of an order made—
(i) in England and Wales, under section 18 of the Adoption Act 1976,
. . .

(3) In this section—
'adoption order' means an adoption order within the meaning of section 72(1) of the Adoption Act 1976 or section 46(1) of the Adoption and Children Act 2002;
'child' means a person under the age of 18 years;
'civil partnership agreement' has the meaning given by section 73 of the Civil Partnership Act 2004;
'cohabitants' means—
(a) a man and a woman who, although not married to each other, are living together as husband and wife, or
(b) two people of the same sex who, although not civil partners of each other, are living together as if they were civil partners;
and 'former cohabitants' shall be construed accordingly;
'parental responsibility' has the same meaning as in the Children Act 1989; and
'relative', in relation to a person, means—
(a) the father, mother, stepfather, stepmother, son, daughter, stepson, stepdaughter, grandmother, grandfather, grandson or granddaughter of that person or of that person's spouse or former spouse, or
(b) the brother, sister, uncle, aunt, niece or nephew (whether of the full blood or of the half blood or by affinity) of that person or of that person's spouse or former spouse,
and includes, in relation to a person who is living or has lived with another person as husband and wife, a person who would fall within paragraph (a) or (b) if the parties were married to each other.

Interim duty to accommodate

188. Interim duty to accommodate in case of apparent priority need

(1) If the local housing authority have reason to believe that an applicant may be homeless, eligible for assistance and have a priority need, they shall secure that accommodation is available for his occupation pending a decision as to the duty (if any) owed to him under the following provisions of this Part.
(2) The duty under this section arises irrespective of any possibility of the referral of the applicant's case to another local housing authority (see sections 198 to 200).
(3) The duty ceases when the authority's decision is notified to the applicant, even if the applicant requests a review of the decision (see section 202).

The authority may continue to secure that accommodation is available for the applicant's occupation pending a decision on a review.

189. Priority need for accommodation

(1) The following have a priority need for accommodation—

(a) a pregnant woman or a person with whom she resides or might reasonably be expected to reside;

(b) a person with whom dependent children reside or might reasonably be expected to reside;

(c) a person who is vulnerable as a result of old age, mental illness or handicap or physical disability or other special reason, or with whom such a person resides or might reasonably be expected to reside;

(d) a person who is homeless or threatened with homelessness as a result of an emergency such as flood, fire or other disaster.

. . .

Duties to persons found to be homeless or threatened with homelessness

190. Duties to persons becoming homeless intentionally

(1) This section applies where the local housing authority are satisfied that an applicant is homeless and is eligible for assistance but are also satisfied that he became homeless intentionally.

(2) If the authority are satisfied that the applicant has a priority need, they shall—

(a) secure that accommodation is available for his occupation for such period as they consider will give him a reasonable opportunity of securing accommodation for his occupation, and

(b) provide him with advice and such assistance as they consider appropriate in the circumstances in any attempts he may make to secure that accommodation becomes available for his occupation.

(3) If they are not satisfied that he has a priority need, they shall provide him with advice and such assistance as they consider appropriate in the circumstances in any attempts he may make to secure that accommodation becomes available for his occupation.

191. Becoming homeless intentionally

(1) A person becomes homeless intentionally if he deliberately does or fails to do anything in consequence of which he ceases to occupy accommodation which is available for his occupation and which it would have been reasonable for him to continue to occupy.

(2) For the purposes of subsection (1) an act or omission in good faith on the part of a person who was unaware of any relevant fact shall not be treated as deliberate.

(3) A person shall be treated as becoming homeless intentionally if—

(a) he enters into an arrangement under which he is required to cease to occupy accommodation which it would have been reasonable for him to continue to occupy, and

(b) the purpose of the arrangement is to enable him to become entitled to assistance under this Part,

and there is no other good reason why he is homeless.

. . .

192. Duty to persons not in priority need who are not homeless intentionally

(1) This section applies where the local housing authority—

(a) are satisfied that an applicant is homeless and eligible for assistance, and

(b) are not satisfied that he became homeless intentionally,

but are not satisfied that he has a priority need.

(2) The authority shall provide the applicant with advice and such assistance as they consider appropriate in the circumstances in any attempts he may make to secure that accommodation becomes available for his occupation.

193. Duty to persons with priority need who are not homeless intentionally

(1) This section applies where the local housing authority are satisfied that an applicant is homeless, eligible for assistance and has a priority need, and are not satisfied that he became homeless intentionally.

This section has effect subject to section 197 (duty where other suitable accommodation available).

(2) Unless the authority refer the application to another local housing authority (see section 198), they shall secure that accommodation is available for occupation by the applicant.

. . .

195. Duties in case of threatened homelessness

(1) This section applies where the local housing authority are satisfied that an applicant is threatened with homelessness and is eligible for assistance.

(2) If the authority—

(a) are satisfied that he has a priority need, and

(b) are not satisfied that he became threatened with homelessness intentionally,

they shall take reasonable steps to secure that accommodation does not cease to be available for his occupation.

This subsection has effect subject to section 197 (duty where other suitable accommodation available).

(3) Subsection (2) does not affect any right of the authority, whether by virtue of a contract, enactment or rule of law, to secure vacant possession of any accommodation.

. . .

196. Becoming threatened with homelessness intentionally

(1) A person becomes threatened with homelessness intentionally if he deliberately does or fails to do anything the likely result of which is that he will be forced to leave accommodation which is available for his occupation and which it would have been reasonable for him to continue to occupy.

(2) For the purposes of subsection (1) an act or omission in good faith on the part of a person who was unaware of any relevant fact shall not be treated as deliberate.

(3) A person shall be treated as becoming threatened with homelessness intentionally if—

(a) he enters into an arrangement under which he is required to cease to occupy accommodation which it would have been reasonable for him to continue to occupy, and

(b) the purpose of the arrangement is to enable him to become entitled to assistance under this Part,

and there is no other good reason why he is threatened with homelessness.

. . .

Supplementary provisions

213A. Co-operation in certain cases involving children

(1) This section applies where a local housing authority have reason to believe that an applicant with whom a person under the age of 18 normally resides, or might reasonably be expected to reside—

(a) may be ineligible for assistance;

(b) may be homeless and may have become so intentionally; or

(c) may be threatened with homelessness intentionally.

(2) A local housing authority shall make arrangements for ensuring that, where this section applies—

(a) the applicant is invited to consent to the referral of the essential facts of his case to the social services authority for the district of the housing authority (where that is a different authority); and

(b) if the applicant has given that consent, the social services authority are made aware of those facts and of the subsequent decision of the housing authority in respect of his case.

(3) Where the local housing authority and the social services authority for a district are the same authority (a 'unitary authority'), that authority shall make arrangements for ensuring that, where this section applies—

(a) the applicant is invited to consent to the referral to the social services department of the essential facts of his case; and

(b) if the applicant has given that consent, the social services department is made aware of those facts and of the subsequent decision of the authority in respect of his case.

(4) Nothing in subsection (2) or (3) affects any power apart from this section to disclose information relating to the applicant's case to the social services authority or to the social services department (as the case may be) without the consent of the applicant.

(5) Where a social services authority—

(a) are aware of a decision of a local housing authority that the applicant is ineligible for assistance, became homeless intentionally or became threatened with homelessness intentionally, and

(b) request the local housing authority to provide them with advice and assistance in the exercise of their social services functions under Part 3 of the Children Act 1989, the local housing authority shall provide them with such advice and assistance as is reasonable in the circumstances.

(6) A unitary authority shall make arrangements for ensuring that, where they make a decision of a kind mentioned in subsection (5)(a), the housing department provide the social services department with such advice and assistance as the social services department may reasonably request.

(7) In this section, in relation to a unitary authority—
'the housing department' means those persons responsible for the exercise of their housing functions; and
'the social services department' means those persons responsible for the exercise of their social services functions under Part 3 of the Children Act 1989.

EDUCATION ACT 1996
(1996 c. 56)

PART I
GENERAL

CHAPTER I
THE STATUTORY SYSTEM OF EDUCATION

Compulsory education

7. Duty of parents to secure education of children of compulsory school age

The parent of every child of compulsory school age shall cause him to receive efficient full-time education suitable—
(a) to his age, ability and aptitude, and
(b) to any special educational needs he may have, either by regular attendance at school or otherwise.

8. Compulsory school age

(1) Subsections (2) and (3) apply to determine for the purposes of any enactment whether a person is of compulsory school age.
(2) A person begins to be of compulsory school age—
  (a) when he attains the age of five, if he attains that age on a prescribed day, and
  (b) otherwise at the beginning of the prescribed day next following his attaining that age.
(3) A person ceases to be of compulsory school age at the end of the day which is the school leaving date for any calendar year—
  (a) if he attains the age of 16 after that day but before the beginning of the school year next following,
  (b) if he attains that age on that day, or
  (c) (unless paragraph (a) applies) if that day is the school leaving date next following his attaining that age.
(4) The Secretary of State may by order—
  (a) provide that such days in the year as are specified in the order shall be, for each calendar year, prescribed days for the purposes of subsection (2);
  (b) determine the day in any calendar year which is to be the school leaving date for that year.

Education in accordance with parental wishes

9. Pupils to be educated in accordance with parents' wishes

In exercising or performing all their respective powers and duties under the Education Acts, the Secretary of State and local education authorities shall have regard to the general principle that pupils are to be educated in accordance with the wishes of their parents, so far as that is compatible with the provision of efficient instruction and training and the avoidance of unreasonable public expenditure.

PART X
MISCELLANEOUS AND GENERAL

CHAPTER II
PUNISHMENT AND RESTRAINT OF PUPILS

Corporal punishment

548. No right to give corporal punishment

(1) Corporal punishment given by, or on the authority of, a member of staff to a child—
   (a) for whom education is provided at any relevant educational institution, or
   (b) for whom education is provided, otherwise than at a relevant educational institution, under any arrangements made by a local education authority, or
   (c) for whom specified early years education is provided otherwise than at a relevant educational institution, cannot be justified in any proceedings on the ground that it was given in pursuance of a right exercisable by the member of staff by virtue of his position as such.

(2) Subsection (1) applies to corporal punishment so given to a child at any time, whether at the relevant educational institution or other place at which education is provided for the child, or elsewhere.

(3) The following provisions have effect for the purposes of this section.

(4) Any reference to giving corporal punishment to a child is to doing anything for the purpose of punishing that child (whether or not there are other reasons for doing it) which, apart from any justification, would constitute battery.

(5) However, corporal punishment shall not be taken to be given to a child by virtue of anything done for reasons that include averting—
   (a) an immediate danger of personal injury to, or
   (b) an immediate danger to the property of, any person (including the child himself).

(6) 'Member of staff ', in relation to the child concerned, means—
   (a) any person who works as a teacher at the relevant educational institution or other place at which education is provided for the child, or
   (b) any other person who (whether in connection with the provision of education for the child or otherwise)—
      (i) works at that institution or place, or
      (ii) otherwise provides his services there (whether or not for payment),
   and has lawful control or charge of the child.

(7) 'Child' (except in subsection (8)) means a person under the age of 18.

(7A) 'Relevant educational institution' means—
   (a) a school, or
   (b) an independent educational institution in England other than a school.

(7B) In subsection (7A)(b) 'independent educational institution' has the same meaning as in Chapter 1 of Part 4 of the Education and Skills Act 2008 (see section 92 of that Act).

(8) 'Specified early years education' means—
   (a) in relation to England, early years provision as defined by section 20 of the Childcare Act 2006 which is provided under arrangements made by a local authority in England in pursuance of the duty imposed by section 7 of that Act (whether or not the local authority provides the early years provision);
   (b) in relation to Wales, full-time or part-time education suitable for children who have not attained compulsory school age
   which is provided—
      (i) by a local education authority in Wales, or
      (ii) by any other person who is in receipt of financial assistance given by such an authority under arrangements made by them in pursuance of the duty imposed by section 118 of the School Standards and Framework Act 1998.

PROTECTION FROM HARASSMENT ACT 1997
(1997 c. 40)

England and Wales

1. Prohibition of harassment

(1) A person must not pursue a course of conduct—
   (a) which amounts to harassment of another, and
   (b) which he knows or ought to know amounts to harassment of the other.

(1A) A person must not pursue a course of conduct—
(a) which involves harassment of two or more persons, and
(b) which he knows or ought to know involves harassment of those persons, and
(c) by which he intends to persuade any person (whether or not one of those mentioned above)—
(i) not to do something that he is entitled or required to do, or
(ii) to do something that he is not under any obligation to do.
(2) For the purposes of this section or section 2A(2)(c), the person whose course of conduct is in question ought to know that it amounts to harassment of another if a reasonable person in possession of the same information would think the course of conduct amounted to harassment of the other.
(3) Subsection (1) or (1A) does not apply to a course of conduct if the person who pursued it shows—
(a) that it was pursued for the purpose of preventing or detecting crime,
(b) that it was pursued under any enactment or rule of law or to comply with any condition or requirement imposed by any person under any enactment, or
(c) that in the particular circumstances the pursuit of the course of conduct was reasonable.

2. Offence of harassment

(1) A person who pursues a course of conduct in breach of section 1(1) or (1A) is guilty of an offence.
(2) A person guilty of an offence under this section is liable on summary conviction to imprisonment for a term not exceeding six months, or a fine not exceeding level 5 on the standard scale, or both.

2A. Offence of stalking

(1) A person is guilty of an offence if—
(a) the person pursues a course of conduct in breach of section (1), and
(b) the course of conduct amounts to stalking.
(2) For the purposes of subsection (1)(b) (and section 4A(1)(a)) a person's conduct amounts to stalking of another person if—
(a) it amounts to harassment of that person,
(b) the acts or omissions involved are ones association with stalking, and
(c) the person whose course of conduct it is knows or ought to know that the course of conduct amounts to harassment of the other person.

...

3. Civil remedy

(1) An actual or apprehended breach of section 1(1) may be the subject of a claim in civil proceedings by the person who is or may be the victim of the course of conduct in question.
(2) On such a claim, damages may be awarded for (among other things) any anxiety caused by the harassment and any financial loss resulting from the harassment.
(3) Where—
(a) in such proceedings the High Court or a county court grants an injunction for the purpose of restraining the defendant from pursuing any conduct which amounts to harassment, and
(b) the plaintiff considers that the defendant has done anything which he is prohibited from doing by the injunction,

the plaintiff may apply for the issue of a warrant for the arrest of the defendant.
(4) An application under subsection (3) may be made—
(a) where the injunction was granted by the High Court, to a judge of that court, and
(b) where the injunction was granted by a county court, to a judge or district judge of that or any other county court.
(5) The judge or district judge to whom an application under subsection (3) is made may only issue a warrant if—
(a) the application is substantiated on oath, and
(b) the judge or district judge has reasonable grounds for believing that the defendant has done anything which he is prohibited from doing by the injunction.
(6) Where—
(a) the High Court or a county court grants an injunction for the purpose mentioned in subsection (3)(a), and
(b) without reasonable excuse the defendant does anything which he is prohibited from doing by the injunction,

he is guilty of an offence.
(7) Where a person is convicted of an offence under subsection (6) in respect of any conduct, that conduct is not punishable as a contempt of court.

(8) A person cannot be convicted of an offence under subsection (6) in respect of any conduct which has been punished as a contempt of court.

(9) A person guilty of an offence under subsection (6) is liable—

(a) on conviction on indictment, to imprisonment for a term not exceeding five years, or a fine, or both, or

(b) on summary conviction, to imprisonment for a term not exceeding six months, or a fine not exceeding the statutory maximum, or both.

3A. Injunctions to protect persons from harassment within section 1(1A)

(1) This section applies where there is an actual or apprehended breach of section 1(1A) by any person ('the relevant person').

(2) In such a case—

(a) any person who is or may be a victim of the course of conduct in question, or

(b) any person who is or may be a person falling within section 1(1A)(c),

may apply to the High Court or a county court for an injunction restraining the relevant person from pursuing any conduct which amounts to harassment in relation to any person or persons mentioned or described in the injunction.

(3) Section 3(3) to (9) apply in relation to an injunction granted under subsection (2) above as they apply in relation to an injunction granted as mentioned in section 3(3)(a).

4. Putting people in fear of violence

(1) A person whose course of conduct causes another to fear, on at least two occasions, that violence will be used against him is guilty of an offence if he knows or ought to know that his course of conduct will cause the other so to fear on each of those occasions.

(2) For the purposes of this section, the person whose course of conduct is in question ought to know that it will cause another to fear that violence will be used against him on any occasion if a reasonable person in possession of the same information would think the course of conduct would cause the other so to fear on that occasion.

(3) It is a defence for a person charged with an offence under this section to show that—

(a) his course of conduct was pursued for the purpose of preventing or detecting crime,

(b) his course of conduct was pursued under any enactment or rule of law or to comply with any condition or requirement imposed by any person under any enactment, or

(c) the pursuit of his course of conduct was reasonable for the protection of himself or another or for the protection of his or another's property.

(4) A person guilty of an offence under this section is liable—

(a) on conviction on indictment, to imprisonment for a term not exceeding five years, or a fine, or both, or

(b) on summary conviction, to imprisonment for a term not exceeding six months, or a fine not exceeding the statutory maximum, or both.

(5) If on the trial on indictment of a person charged with an offence under this section the jury find him not guilty of the offence charged, they may find him guilty of an offence under section 2 or 2A.

(6) The Crown Court has the same powers and duties in relation to a person who is by virtue of subsection (5) convicted before it of an offence under section 2 or 2A as a magistrates' court would have on convicting him of the offence.

4A Stalking involving fear of violence or distress

(1) A person ('A') whose course of conduct –

(a) amounts to stalking, and

(I) causes another ('B') to fear, on at least two occasions , that violence will be used against B, or

(ii) causes B serious alarm or distress which has a substantial effect on B's usual day-to-day activities,

is guilty of an offence if A knows or ought to know that A's course of conduct will cause B to fear on each of these occasions or (as the case may be) will cause such alarm or distress.

...

5. Restraining orders on conviction

(1) A court sentencing or otherwise dealing with a person ('the defendant') convicted of an offence may (as well as sentencing him or dealing with him in any other way) make an order under this section.

(2) The order may, for the purpose of protecting the victim or victims of the offence, or any other person mentioned in the order, from conduct which—

(a) amounts to harassment, or

(b) will cause a fear of violence,

prohibit the defendant from doing anything described in the order.

(3) The order may have effect for a specified period or until further order.

(3A) In proceedings under this section both the prosecution and the defence may lead, as further evidence, any evidence that would be admissible in proceedings for an injunction under section 3.

(4) The prosecutor, the defendant or any other person mentioned in the order may apply to the court which made the order for it to be varied or discharged by a further order.

(4A) Any person mentioned in the order is entitled to be heard on the hearing of an application under subsection (4).

(5) If without reasonable excuse the defendant does anything which he is prohibited from doing by an order under this section, he is guilty of an offence.

(6) A person guilty of an offence under this section is liable—

(a) on conviction on indictment, to imprisonment for a term not exceeding five years, or a fine, or both, or

(b) on summary conviction, to imprisonment for a term not exceeding six months, or a fine not exceeding the statutory maximum, or both.

(7) A court dealing with a person for an offence under this section may vary or discharge the order in question by a further order.

5A. Restraining orders on acquittal

(1) A court before which a person ('the defendant') is acquitted of an offence may, if it considers it necessary to do so to protect a person from harassment by the defendant, make an order prohibiting the defendant from doing anything described in the order.

(2) Subsections (3) to (7) of section 5 apply to an order under this section as they apply to an order under that one.

...

7. Interpretation of this group of sections

(1) This section applies for the interpretation of sections 1 to 5A.

(2) References to harassing a person include alarming the person or causing the person distress.

(3) A 'course of conduct' must involve—

(a) in the case of conduct in relation to a single person (see section 1(1)), conduct on at least two occasions in relation to that person, or

(b) in the case of conduct in relation to two or more persons (see section 1(1A)), conduct on at least one occasion in relation to each of those persons.

(3A) A person's conduct on any occasion shall be taken, if aided, abetted, counselled or procured by another—

(a) to be conduct on that occasion of the other (as well as conduct of the person whose conduct it is); and

(b) to be conduct in relation to which the other's knowledge and purpose, and what he ought to have known, are the same as they were in relation to what was contemplated or reasonably foreseeable at the time of the aiding, abetting, counselling or procuring.

(4) 'Conduct' includes speech.

(5) References to a person, in the context of the harassment of a person, are references to a person who is an individual.

CRIME AND DISORDER ACT 1998
(1998 c. 37)

PART I
PREVENTION OF CRIME AND DISORDER

CHAPTER I
ENGLAND AND WALES

Youth crime and disorder

8. Parenting orders

(1) This section applies where, in any court proceedings—

(a) a child safety order is made in respect of a child or the court determines on an application under section 12(6) below that a child has failed to comply with any requirement included in such an order;

(aa) a parental compensation order is made in relation to a child's behaviour;
(b) an anti-social behaviour order or sexual offences prevention order is made in respect of a child or young person;
(c) a child or young person is convicted of an offence; or
(d) a person is convicted of an offence under section 443 (failure to comply with school attendance order) or section 444 (failure to secure regular attendance at school of registered pupil) of the Education Act 1996.

(2) Subject to subsection (3) and section 9(1) below, if in the proceedings the court is satisfied that the relevant condition is fulfilled, it may make a parenting order in respect of a person who is a parent or guardian of the child or young person or, as the case may be, the person convicted of the offence under section 443 or 444 ('the parent').

(3) A court shall not make a parenting order unless it has been notified by the Secretary of State that arrangements for implementing such orders are available in the area in which it appears to the court that the parent resides or will reside and the notice has not been withdrawn.

(4) A parenting order is an order which requires the parent—
(a) to comply, for a period not exceeding twelve months, with such requirements as are specified in the order; and
(b) subject to subsection (5) below, to attend, for a concurrent period not exceeding three months and not more than once in any week, such counselling or guidance sessions as may be specified in directions given by the responsible officer;
and in this subsection 'week' means a period of seven days beginning with a Sunday.

(5) A parenting order may, but need not, include such a requirement as is mentioned in subsection (4)(b) above in any case where such an order has been made in respect of the parent on a previous occasion.

(6) The relevant condition is that the parenting order would be desirable in the interests of preventing—
(a) in a case falling within paragraph (a), (aa) or (b) of subsection (1) above, any repetition of the kind of behaviour which led to the child safety order, anti-social behaviour order or sexual offences prevention order being made;
(b) in a case failing within paragraph (c) of that subsection, the commission of any further offence by the child or young person;
(c) in a case falling within paragraph (d) of that subsection, the commission of any further offence under section 443 or 444 of the Education Act 1996.

(7) The requirements that may be specified under subsection (4)(a) above are those which the court considers desirable in the interests of preventing any such repetition or, as the case may be, the commission of any such further offence.

(7A) A counselling or guidance programme which a parent is required to attend by virtue of subsection (4)(b) above may be or include a residential course but only if the court is satisfied—
(a) that the attendance of the parent at a residential course is likely to be more effective than his attendance at a non-residential course in preventing any such repetition or, as the case may be, the commission of any such further offence, and
(b) that any interference with family life which is likely to result from the attendance of the parent at a residential course is proportionate in all the circumstances.

(8) In this section and section 9 below 'responsible officer', in relation to a parenting order, means one of the following who is specified in the order, namely—
(a) an officer of a local probation board;
(b) a social worker of a local authority social services department; and
(bb) a person nominated by a person appointed as director of childrens' services under section 18 of the Children Act 2004 or by a person appointed as chief education officer under section 532 of the Education Act 1996;
(c) a member of a youth offending team.

(9) In this section 'sexual offences prevention order' means an order under section 104 of the Sexual Offences Act 2003 (sexual offences prevention orders).

11. Child safety orders

(1) Subject to subsection (2) below, if the family court, on the application of a local authority, is satisfied that one or more of the conditions specified in subsection (3) below are fulfilled with respect to a child under the age of 10, it may make an order (a 'child safety order') which—
(a) places the child, for a period (not exceeding the permitted maximum) specified in the order, under the supervision of the responsible officer; and
(b) requires the child to comply with such requirements as are so specified.

(2) A court shall not make a child safety order unless it has been notified by the Secretary of State that arrangements for implementing such orders are available in the area in which it appears that the child resides or will reside and the notice has not been withdrawn.

(3) The conditions are—
(a) that the child has committed an act which, if he had been aged 10 or over, would have constituted an offence;
(b) that a child safety order is necessary for the purpose of preventing the commission by the child of such an act as is mentioned in paragraph (a) above;
(c) that the child has contravened a ban imposed by a curfew notice; and
(d) that the child has acted in a manner that caused or was likely to cause harassment, alarm or distress to one or more persons not of the same household as himself.
(4) The maximum period permitted for the purposes of subsection (1)(a) above is three months or, where the court is satisfied that the circumstances of the case are exceptional, 12 months.
(5) The requirements that may be specified under subsection (1)(b) above are those which the court considers desirable in the interests of—
(a) securing that the child receives appropriate care, protection and support and is subject to proper control; or
(b) preventing any repetition of the kind of behaviour which led to the child safety order being made.
(6) Proceedings under this section or section 12 below shall be family proceedings for the purposes of the 1989 Act or section 65 of the Magistrates' Courts Act 1980 ('the 1980 Act'); and the standard of proof applicable to such proceedings shall be that applicable to civil proceedings.
(7) In this section 'local authority' has the same meaning as in the 1989 Act.
(8) In this section and section 12 below, 'responsible officer', in relation to a child safety order, means one of the following who is specified in the order, namely—
(a) a social worker of a local authority social services department; and
(b) a member of a youth offending team.

12. Child safety orders: supplemental

(1) Before making a child safety order, the family court shall obtain and consider information about the child's family circumstances and the likely effect of the order on those circumstances.
(2) Before making a child safety order, the family court shall explain to the parent or guardian of the child in ordinary language—
(a) the effect of the order and of the requirements proposed to be included in it;
(b) the consequences which may follow (under subsection (6) below) if the child fails to comply with any of those requirements; and
(c) that the court has power (under subsection (4) below) to review the order on the application either of the parent or guardian or of the responsible officer.
(3) Requirements included in a child safety order shall, as far as practicable, be such as to avoid—
(a) any conflict with the parent's religious beliefs; and
(b) any interference with the times, if any, at which the child normally attends school.
(4) If while a child safety order is in force in respect of a child it appears to the court which made it, on the application of the responsible officer or a parent or guardian of the child, that it is appropriate to make an order under this subsection, the court may make an order discharging the child safety order or varying it—
(a) by cancelling any provision included in it; or
(b) by inserting in it (either in addition to or in substitution for any of its provisions) any provision that could have been included in the order if the court had then had power to make it and were exercising the power.
(5) Where an application under subsection (4) above for the discharge of a child safety order is dismissed, no further application for its discharge shall be made under that subsection by any person except with the consent of the court which made the order.
(6) Where a child safety order is in force and it is proved to the satisfaction of the court which made it, on the application of the responsible officer, that the child has failed to comply with any requirement included in the order, the court—
(a) . . .
(b) may make an order varying the order—
(i) by cancelling any provision included in it; or
(ii) by inserting in it (either in addition to or in substitution for any of its provisions) any provision that could have been included in the order if the court had then had power to make it and were exercising the power.

HUMAN RIGHTS ACT 1998
(1998 C. 42)

1. The Convention Rights

(1) In this Act 'the Convention rights' means the rights and fundamental freedoms set out in—
  (a) Articles 2 to 12 and 14 of the Convention,
  (b) Articles 1 to 3 of the First Protocol, and
  (c) Article 1 of the Thirteenth Protocol,
  as read with Articles 16 to 18 of the Convention.

(2) Those Articles are to have effect for the purposes of this Act subject to any designated derogation or reservation (as to which see sections 14 and 15).

(3) The Articles are set out in Schedule 1.

(4) The Secretary of State may by order make such amendments to this Act as he considers appropriate to reflect the effect, in relation to the United Kingdom, of a protocol.

(5) In subsection (4) 'protocol' means a protocol to the Convention—
  (a) which the United Kingdom has ratified; or
  (b) which the United Kingdom has signed with a view to ratification.

(6) No amendment may be made by an order under subsection (4) so as to come into force before the protocol concerned is in force in relation to the United Kingdom.

3. Interpretation of legislation

(1) So far as it is possible to do so, primary legislation and subordinate legislation must be read and given effect in a way which is compatible with the Convention rights.

(2) This section—
  (a) applies to primary legislation and subordinate legislation whenever enacted;
  (b) does not affect the validity, continuing operation or enforcement of any incompatible primary legislation; and
  (c) does not affect the validity, continuing operation or enforcement of any incompatible subordinate legislation if (disregarding any possibility of revocation) primary legislation prevents removal of the incompatibility.

4. Declaration of incompatibility

(1) Subsection (2) applies in any proceedings in which a court determines whether a provision of primary legislation is compatible with a Convention right.

(2) If the court is satisfied that the provision is incompatible with a Convention right, it may make a declaration of that incompatibility.

. . .

6. Acts of public authorities

(1) It is unlawful for a public authority to act in a way which is incompatible with a Convention right.

(2) Subsection (1) does not apply to an act if—
  (a) as the result of one or more provisions of primary legislation, the authority could not have acted differently; or
  (b) in the case of one or more provisions of, or made under, primary legislation which cannot be read or given effect in a way which is compatible with the Convention rights, the authority was acting so as to give effect to or enforce those provisions.

(3) In this section 'public authority' includes—
  (a) a court or tribunal, and
  (b) any person certain of whose functions are functions of a public nature,
  but does not include either House of Parliament or a person exercising functions in connection with proceedings in Parliament.

(4) ...

(5) In relation to a particular act, a person is not a public authority by virtue only of subsection (3)(b) if the nature of the act is private.

(6) 'An act' includes a failure to act but does not include a failure to—
  (a) introduce in, or lay before, Parliament a proposal for legislation; or
  (b) make any primary legislation or remedial order.

Section 1(3)

SCHEDULE 1
THE ARTICLES

PART I
THE CONVENTION RIGHTS AND FREEDOMS

Right to life

Article 2

1. Everyone's right to life shall be protected by law. No one shall be deprived of his life intentionally save in the execution of a sentence of a court following his conviction of a crime for which this penalty is provided by law.

. . .

Prohibition of torture

Article 3

No one shall be subjected to torture or to inhuman or degrading treatment or punishment.

Right to respect for private and family life

Article 8

1. Everyone has the right to respect for his private and family life, his home and his correspondence.
2. There shall be no interference by a public authority with the exercise of this right except such as is in accordance with the law and is necessary in a democratic society in the interests of national security, public safety or the economic well-being of the country, for the prevention of disorder or crime, for the protection of health or morals, or for the protection of the rights and freedoms of others.

Right to marry

Article 12

Men and women of marriageable age have the right to marry and to found a family, according to the national laws governing the exercise of this right.

Prohibition of discrimination

Article 14

The enjoyment of the rights and freedoms set forth in this Convention shall be secured without discrimination on any ground such as sex, race, colour, language, religion, political or other opinion, national or social origin, association with a national minority, property, birth or other status.

CRIMINAL JUSTICE AND COURT SERVICES ACT 2000
(2000 c. 43)

PART I
THE NEW SERVICES

CHAPTER II
CHILDREN AND FAMILY COURT ADVISORY AND SUPPORT SERVICE

11. Establishment of the Service

(1) There shall be a body corporate to be known as the Children and Family Court Advisory and Support Service (referred to in this Part as the Service) which is to exercise the functions conferred on it by virtue of this Act and any other enactment.

(2) Schedule 2 (which makes provision about the constitution of the Service, its powers and other matters relating to it) is to have effect.
(3) References in this Act or any other enactment to an officer of the Service are references to—
(a) any member of the staff of the Service appointed under paragraph 5(1)(a) of that Schedule, and
(b) any other individual exercising functions of an officer of the Service by virtue of section 13(2) or (4).

12. Principal functions of the Service

(1) In respect of family proceedings in which the welfare of children is or may be in question, it is a function of the Service to—
(a) safeguard and promote the welfare of the children,
(b) give advice to any court about any application made to it in such proceedings,
(c) make provision for the children to be represented in such proceedings,
(d) provide information, advice and other support for the children and their families.
(2) The Service must also make provision for the performance of any functions conferred on officers of the Service by virtue of this Act or any other enactment (whether or not they are exercisable for the purposes of the functions conferred on the Service by subsection (1)).
(3) Regulations may provide for grants to be paid by the Service to any person for the purpose of furthering the performance of any of the Service's functions.
(4) The regulations may provide for the grants to be paid on conditions, including conditions—
(a) regulating the purposes for which the grant or any part of it may be used,
(b) requiring repayment to the Service in specified circumstances.
(5) In this section, 'family proceedings' has the same meaning as in the Matrimonial and Family Proceedings Act 1984 and also includes any other proceedings which are family proceedings for the purposes of the Children Act 1989, but—
(a) references to family proceedings include (where the context allows) family proceedings which are proposed or have been concluded, and

13. Other powers of the Service

(1) The Service may make arrangements with organisations under which the organisations perform functions of the Service on its behalf.
(2) Arrangements under subsection (1) may provide for the organisations to designate individuals who may perform functions of officers of the Service.
(3) But the Service may only make an arrangement under subsection (1) if it is of the opinion—
(a) that the functions in question will be performed efficiently and to the required standard, and
(b) that the arrangement represents good value for money.
(4) The Service may make arrangements with individuals under which they may perform functions of officers of the Service.
(5) The Service may commission, or assist the conduct of, research by any person into matters concerned with the exercise of its functions.

15. Right to conduct litigation and right of audience

(1) The Service may authorise an officer of the Service of a prescribed description—
(a) to conduct litigation in relation to any proceedings in any court,
(b) to exercise a right of audience in any proceedings before any court,
in the exercise of his functions.

. . .

SCHEDULE 2

CHILDREN AND FAMILY COURT ADVISORY AND SUPPORT SERVICE

Constitution

1. The Service is to consist of a chairman, and not less than nine other members, appointed by the Lord Chancellor.
2. (1) Regulations may provide—
(a) for the appointment of the chairman and other members and for the co-option by the Service for particular purposes of additional members (including the number, or limits on the number, of persons who may be appointed or co-opted and any conditions to be fulfilled for appointment or co-option),
(b) for the tenure of office of the chairman and other members and any co-opted members (including the circumstances in which they cease to hold office or may be removed or suspended from office).

(2) References below in this Schedule to members of the Service do not include co-opted members.

. . .

Delegation

7. The Service may arrange for the chairman or any other member to discharge functions of the Service on its behalf.

. . .

Supervision

9. (1) Functions and other powers of the Service, and functions of any officer of the Service, must be performed in accordance with any directions given by the Lord Chancellor.

(2) In particular, the directions may make provision for the purpose of ensuring that the services provided are of appropriate quality and meet appropriate standards.

. . .

. . .

Complaints

15. The Service must make and publicise a scheme for dealing with complaints made by or on behalf of prescribed persons in relation to the performance by the Service and its officers of their functions.

. . .

ADOPTION AND CHILDREN ACT 2002
(2002 c. 28)

PART 1
ADOPTION

CHAPTER 1
INTRODUCTORY

1. Considerations applying to the exercise of powers

(1) This section applies whenever a court or adoption agency is coming to a decision relating to the adoption of a child.

(2) The paramount consideration of the court or adoption agency must be the child's welfare, throughout his life.

(3) The court or adoption agency must at all times bear in mind that, in general, any delay in coming to the decision is likely to prejudice the child's welfare.

(4) The court or adoption agency must have regard to the following matters (among others)—

(a) the child's ascertainable wishes and feelings regarding the decision (considered in the light of the child's age and understanding),

(b) the child's particular needs,

(c) the likely effect on the child (throughout his life) of having ceased to be a member of the original family and become an adopted person,

(d) the child's age, sex, background and any of the child's characteristics which the court or agency considers relevant,

(e) any harm (within the meaning of the Children Act 1989) which the child has suffered or is at risk of suffering,

(f) the relationship which the child has with relatives, and with any other person in relation to whom the court or agency considers the relationship to be relevant, including—

(i) the likelihood of any such relationship continuing and the value to the child of its doing so,

(ii) the ability and willingness of any of the child's relatives, or of any such person, to provide the child with a secure environment in which the child can develop, and otherwise to meet the child's needs,

(iii) the wishes and feelings of any of the child's relatives, or of any such person, regarding the child.

(5) In placing the child for adoption, the adoption agency must give due consideration to the child's religious persuasion, racial origin and cultural and linguistic background.

(6) The court or adoption agency must always consider the whole range of powers available to it in the child's case (whether under this Act or the Children Act 1989); and the court

must not make any order under this Act unless it considers that making the order would be better for the child than not doing so.

(7) In this section, 'coming to a decision relating to the adoption of a child', in relation to a court, includes—

(a) coming to a decision in any proceedings where the orders that might be made by the court include an adoption order (or the revocation of such an order), a placement order (or the revocation of such an order) or an order under section 26 (or the revocation or variation of such an order),

(b) coming to a decision about granting leave in respect of any action (other than the initiation of proceedings in any court) which may be taken by an adoption agency or individual under this Act, but does not include coming to a decision about granting leave in any other circumstances.

(8) For the purposes of this section—

(a) references to relationships are not confined to legal relationships,

(b) references to a relative, in relation to a child, include the child's mother and father.

CHAPTER 2
THE ADOPTION SERVICE

The Adoption Service

2. Basic definitions

(1) The services maintained by local authorities under section 3(1) may be collectively referred to as 'the Adoption Service', and a local authority or registered adoption society may be referred to as an adoption agency.

(2) In this Act, 'registered adoption society' means a voluntary organisation which is an adoption society registered under Part 2 of the Care Standards Act 2000;...

3. Maintenance of Adoption Service

(1) Each local authority must continue to maintain within their area a service designed to meet the needs, in relation to adoption, of—

(a) children who may be adopted, their parents and guardians,

(b) persons wishing to adopt a child, and

(c) adopted persons, their parents, natural parents and former guardians; and for that purpose must provide the requisite facilities.

(2) Those facilities must include making, and participating in, arrangements—

(a) for the adoption of children, and

(b) for the provision of adoption support services.

(3) As part of the service, the arrangements made for the purposes of subsection (2)(b)—

(a) must extend to the provision of adoption support services to persons who are within a description prescribed by regulations,

(b) may extend to the provision of those services to other persons.

(4) A local authority may provide any of the requisite facilities by securing their provision by—

(a) registered adoption societies, or

(b) other persons who are within a description prescribed by regulations of persons who may provide the facilities in question.

(5) The facilities of the service must be provided in conjunction with the local authority's other social services and with registered adoption societies in their area, so that help may be given in a co-ordinated manner without duplication, omission or avoidable delay.

(6) The social services referred to in subsection (5) are the functions of a local authority which are social services functions within the meaning of the Local Authority Social Services Act 1970 (which include, in particular, those functions in so far as they relate to children).

4. Assessments etc. for adoption support services

(1) A local authority must at the request of—

(a) any of the persons mentioned in paragraphs (a) to (c) of section 3(1), or

(b) any other person who falls within a description prescribed by regulations (subject to subsection (7)(a)), carry out an assessment of that person's needs for adoption support services.

(2) A local authority may, at the request of any person, carry out an assessment of that person's needs for adoption support services.

(3) A local authority may request the help of the persons mentioned in paragraph (a) or (b) of section 3(4) in carrying out an assessment.

(4) Where, as a result of an assessment, a local authority decide that a person has needs for adoption support services, they must then decide whether to provide any such services to that person.

(5) If—

(a) a local authority decide to provide any adoption support services to a person, and

(b) the circumstances fall within a description prescribed by regulations, the local authority must prepare a plan in accordance with which adoption support services are to be provided to the person and keep the plan under review.

(6) Regulations may make provision about assessments, preparing and reviewing plans, the provision of adoption support services in accordance with plans and reviewing the provision of adoption support services.

. . .

(10) Where it appears to a local authority that another local authority could, by taking any specified action, help in the exercise of any of their functions under this section, they may request the help of that other local authority, specifying the action in question.

(11) A local authority whose help is so requested must comply with the request if it is consistent with the exercise of their functions.

5. Local authority plans for adoption services

(1) Each local authority must prepare a plan for the provision of the services maintained under section 3(1) and secure that it is published.

(2) The plan must contain information of a description prescribed by regulations (subject to subsection (4)(b)).

. . .

CHAPTER 3

PLACEMENT FOR ADOPTION AND ADOPTION ORDERS

Placement of children by adoption agency for adoption

18. Placement for adoption by agencies

(1) An adoption agency may—

(a) place a child for adoption with prospective adopters, or

(b) where it has placed a child with any persons (whether under this Part or not), leave the child with them as prospective adopters,

but, except in the case of a child who is less than six weeks old, may only do so under section 19 or a placement order.

(2) An adoption agency may only place a child for adoption with prospective adopters if the agency is satisfied that the child ought to be placed for adoption.

(3) A child who is placed or authorised to be placed for adoption with prospective adopters by a local authority is looked after by the authority.

. . .

19. Placing children with parental consent

(1) Where an adoption agency is satisfied that each parent or guardian of a child has consented to the child—

(a) being placed for adoption with prospective adopters identified in the consent, or

(b) being placed for adoption with any prospective adopters who may be chosen by the agency,

and has not withdrawn the consent, the agency is authorised to place the child for adoption accordingly.

(2) Consent to a child being placed for adoption with prospective adopters identified in the consent may be combined with consent to the child subsequently being placed for adoption with any prospective adopters who may be chosen by the agency in circumstances where the child is removed from or returned by the identified prospective adopters.

(3) Subsection (1) does not apply where–

(a) an application has been made on which a care order might be made and the application has not been disposed of, or

(b) a care order or placement order has been made after the consent was given.

(4) References in this Act to a child placed for adoption under this section include a child who was placed under this section with prospective adopters and continues to be placed with them, whether or not consent to the placement has been withdrawn.

(5) This section is subject to section 52 (parental etc. consent).

20. Advance consent to adoption

(1) A parent or guardian of a child who consents to the child being placed for adoption by an adoption agency under section 19 may, at the same or any subsequent time, consent to the making of a future adoption order.

(2) Consent under this section—

(a) where the parent or guardian has consented to the child being placed for adoption with prospective adopters identified in the consent, may be consent to adoption by them, or

(b) may be consent to adoption by any prospective adopters who may be chosen by the agency.

(3) A person may withdraw any consent given under this section.

(4) A person who gives consent under this section may, at the same or any subsequent time, by notice given to the adoption agency—

(a) state that he does not wish to be informed of any application for an adoption order, or

(b) withdraw such a statement.

(5) A notice under subsection (4) has effect from the time when it is received by the adoption agency but has no effect if the person concerned has withdrawn his consent.

(6) This section is subject to section 52 (parental etc. consent).

21. Placement orders

(1) A placement order is an order made by the court authorising a local authority to place a child for adoption with any prospective adopters who may be chosen by the authority.

(2) The court may not make a placement order in respect of a child unless—

(a) the child is subject to a care order,

(b) the court is satisfied that the conditions in section 31(2) of the 1989 Act (conditions for making a care order) are met, or

(c) the child has no parent or guardian.

(3) The court may only make a placement order if, in the case of each parent or guardian of the child, the court is satisfied—

(a) that the parent or guardian has consented to the child being placed for adoption with any prospective adopters who may be chosen by the local authority and has not withdrawn the consent, or

(b) that the parent's or guardian's consent should be dispensed with.

This subsection is subject to section 52 (parental etc. consent).

(4) A placement order continues in force until—

(a) it is revoked under section 24,

(b) an adoption order is made in respect of the child, or

(c) the child marries, forms a civil partnership or attains the age of 18 years.

'Adoption order' includes a Scottish or Northern Irish adoption order.

22. Applications for placement orders

(1) A local authority must apply to the court for a placement order in respect of a child if—

(a) the child is placed for adoption by them or is being provided with accommodation by them,

(b) no adoption agency is authorised to place the child for adoption,

(c) the child has no parent or guardian or the authority consider that the conditions in section 31(2) of the 1989 Act are met, and

(d) the authority are satisfied that the child ought to be placed for adoption.

(2) If—

(a) an application has been made (and has not been disposed of) on which a care order might be made in respect of a child, or

(b) a child is subject to a care order and the appropriate local authority are not authorised to place the child for adoption,

the appropriate local authority must apply to the court for a placement order if they are satisfied that the child ought to be placed for adoption.

(3) If—

(a) a child is subject to a care order, and

(b) the appropriate local authority are authorised to place the child for adoption under section 19,

the authority may apply to the court for a placement order.

(4) If a local authority—

(a) are under a duty to apply to the court for a placement order in respect of a child, or

(b) have applied for a placement order in respect of a child and the application has not been disposed of,

the child is looked after by the authority.

. . .

23. Varying placement orders

(1) The court may vary a placement order so as to substitute another local authority for the local authority authorised by the order to place the child for adoption.
(2) The variation may only be made on the joint application of both authorities.

24. Revoking placement orders

(1) The court may revoke a placement order on the application of any person.
(2) But an application may not be made by a person other than the child or the local authority authorised by the order to place the child for adoption unless—
  (a) the court has given leave to apply, and
  (b) the child is not placed for adoption by the authority.
(3) The court cannot give leave under subsection (2)(a) unless satisfied that there has been a change in circumstances since the order was made.
(4) If the court determines, on an application for an adoption order, not to make the order, it may revoke any placement order in respect of the child.
(5) Where—
  (a) an application for the revocation of a placement order has been made and has not been disposed of, and
  (b) the child is not placed for adoption by the authority,
the child may not without the court's leave be placed for adoption under the order.

25. Parental responsibility

(1) This section applies while—
  (a) a child is placed for adoption under section 19 or an adoption agency is authorised to place a child for adoption under that section, or
  (b) a placement order is in force in respect of a child.
(2) Parental responsibility for the child is given to the agency concerned.
(3) While the child is placed with prospective adopters, parental responsibility is given to them.
(4) The agency may determine that the parental responsibility of any parent or guardian, or of prospective adopters, is to be restricted to the extent specified in the determination.

26. Contact

(1) On an adoption agency being authorised to place a child for adoption, or placing a child for adoption who is less than six weeks old—
  (a) any contact provision in a child arrangements order under section 8 of the 1989 Act ceases to have effect,
  (b) any order under section 34 of that Act (parental etc contact with children in care) ceases to have effect, and
  (c) any activity direction made in proceedings for the making, variation or discharge of a child arrangements order with respect to the child, or made in other proceedings that relate to the order, is discharged.
(2) While an adoption agency is so authorised or a child is placed for adoption—
  (a) no application may be made for—
    (i) a child arrangements order under section 8 of the 1989 Act containing contact provision, or
    (ii) an order under section 34 of that Act, but
  (b) the court may make an order under this section requiring the person with whom the child lives, or is to live, to allow the child to visit or stay with the person named in the order, or for the person named in the order and the child otherwise to have contact with each other.
(3) An application for an order under this section may be made by—
  (a) the child or the agency,
  (b) any parent, guardian or relative,
  (c) any person in whose favour there was provision which ceased to have effect by virtue of subsection (1)(a) or an order which ceased to have effect by virtue of subsection (1)(b),
  (d) if a child arrangements order was in force immediately before the adoption agency was authorised to place the child for adoption or (as the case may be) placed the child for adoption at a time when he was less than six weeks old, any person named in the order as a person with whom the child was to live,
  (e) if a person had care of the child immediately before that time by virtue of an order made in the exercise of the High Court's inherent jurisdiction with respect to children, that person,
  (f) any person who has obtained the court's leave to make the application.
(4) When making a placement order, the court may on its own initiative make an order under this section.

(5) This section does not prevent an application for a child arrangements order under section 8 of the 1989 Act containing only contact provision being made where the application is to be heard together with an application for an adoption order in respect of the child.

(5A) In this section 'contact provision' means provision which regulates arrangements relating to—

(a) with whom a child is to spend time or otherwise have contact, or

(b) when a child is to spend time of otherwise have contact with any person;

but in paragraphs (a) and (b) a reference to spending time or otherwise having contact with a person is to doing that otherwise than as a result of living with the person.

(6) In this section, 'activity direction' has the meaning given by section 11A of the 1989 Act.

27. Contact: supplementary

(1) An order under section 26—

(a) has effect while the adoption agency is authorised to place the child for adoption or the child is placed for adoption, but

(b) may be varied or revoked by the court on an application by the child, the agency or a person named in the order.

(2) The agency may refuse to allow the contact that would otherwise be required by virtue of an order under that section if—

(a) it is satisfied that it is necessary to do so in order to safeguard or promote the child's welfare, and

(b) the refusal is decided upon as a matter of urgency and does not last for more than seven days.

(3) Regulations may make provision as to—

(a) the steps to be taken by an agency which has exercised its power under subsection (2),

(b) the circumstances in which, and conditions subject to which, the terms of any order under section 26 may be departed from by agreement between the agency and any person for whose contact with the child the order provides,

(c) notification by an agency of any variation or suspension of arrangements made (otherwise than under an order under that section) with a view to allowing any person contact with the child.

(4) Before making a placement order the court must—

(a) consider the arrangements which the adoption agency has made, or proposes to make, for allowing any person contact with the child, and

(b) invite the parties to the proceedings to comment on those arrangements.

(5) An order under section 26 may provide for contact on any conditions the court considers appropriate.

28. Further consequences of placement

(1) Where a child is placed for adoption under section 19 or an adoption agency is authorised to place a child for adoption under that section—

(a) a parent or guardian of the child may not apply for a child arrangements order regulating the child's living arrangements unless an application for an adoption order has been made and the parent or guardian has obtained the court's leave under subsection (3) or (5) of section 47,

(b) if an application has been made for an adoption order, a guardian of the child may not apply for a special guardianship order unless he has obtained the court's leave under subsection (3) or (5) of that section.

(2) Where—

(a) a child is placed for adoption under section 19 or an adoption agency is authorised to place a child for adoption under that section, or

(b) a placement order is in force in respect of a child,

then (whether or not the child is in England and Wales) a person may not do either of the following things, unless the court gives leave or each parent or guardian of the child gives written consent.

(3) Those things are—

(a) causing the child to be known by a new surname, or

(b) removing the child from the United Kingdom.

(4) Subsection (3) does not prevent the removal of a child from the United Kingdom for a period of less than one month by a person who provides the child's home.

(5) For the purposes of subsection (1)(a), a child arrangements order regulates a child's living arrangements if the arrangements regulated by the order consist of, or include, arrangements which relate to either or both of the following—

(a) with whom the child is to live, and

(b) when the child is to live with any person.

29. Further consequences of placement orders

(1) Where a placement order is made in respect of a child and either-
(a) the child is subject to a care order, or
(b) the court at the same time makes a care order in respect of the child,
the care order does not have effect at any time when the placement order is in force.
(2) On the making of a placement order in respect of a child, any order mentioned in section 8(1) of the 1989 Act, and any supervision order in respect of the child, ceases to have effect.
(3) Where a placement order is in force—
(a) no prohibited steps order or specific issue order, and
(b) no supervision order or child assessment order, may be made in respect of the child.
(4) Where a placement order is in force, a child arrangements order may be made with respect to the child's living arrangements only if—
(a) an application for an adoption order has been made in respect of the child, and
(b) the child arrangements order is applied for by a parent or guardian who has obtained the court's leave under subsection (3) or (5) of section 47 or by any other person who has obtained the court's leave under this subsection.
(4A) For the purposes of subsection (4), a child arrangements order is one made with respect to a child's living arrangements if the arrangements regulated by the order consist of, or include, arrangements which relate to either or both of the following—
(a) with whom the child is to live, and
(b) when the child is to live with any person.
(5) Where a placement order is in force, no special guardianship order may be made in respect of the child unless—
(a) an application has been made for an adoption order, and
(b) the person applying for the special guardianship order has obtained the court's leave under this subsection or, if he is a guardian of the child, has obtained the court's leave under section 47(5).

. . .

Removal of children who are or may be placed by adoption agencies

30. General prohibitions on removal

(1) Where—
(a) a child is placed for adoption by an adoption agency under section 19, or
(b) a child is placed for adoption by an adoption agency and either the child is less than six weeks old or the agency has at no time been authorised to place the child for adoption,
a person (other than the agency) must not remove the child from the prospective adopters.
(2) Where—
(a) a child who is not for the time being placed for adoption is being provided with accommodation by a local authority, and
(b) the authority have applied to the court for a placement order and the application has not been disposed of,
only a person who has the court's leave (or the authority) may remove the child from the accommodation.

. . .

31. Recovery by parent etc. where child not placed or is a baby

(1) Subsection (2) applies where—
(a) a child who is not for the time being placed for adoption is being provided with accommodation by an adoption agency, and
(b) the agency would be authorised to place the child for adoption under section 19 if consent to placement under that section had not been withdrawn.
(2) If any parent or guardian of the child informs the agency that he wishes the child to be returned to him, the agency must return the child to him within the period of seven days beginning with the request unless an application is, or has been, made for a placement order and the application has not been disposed of.
(3) Subsection (4) applies where—
(a) a child is placed for adoption by an adoption agency and either the child is less than six weeks old or the agency has at no time been authorised to place the child for adoption, and
(b) any parent or guardian of the child informs the agency that he wishes the child to be returned to him,

unless an application is, or has been, made for a placement order and the application has not been disposed of.

(4) The agency must give notice of the parent's or guardian's wish to the prospective adopters who must return the child to the agency within the period of seven days beginning with the day on which the notice is given.

(5) A prospective adopter who fails to comply with subsection (4) is guilty of an offence and liable on summary conviction to imprisonment for a term not exceeding three months, or a fine not exceeding level 5 on the standard scale, or both.

(6) As soon as a child is returned to an adoption agency under subsection (4), the agency must return the child to the parent or guardian in question.

32. Recovery by parent etc. where child placed and consent withdrawn

(1) This section applies where—
 (a) a child is placed for adoption by an adoption agency under section 19, and
 (b) consent to placement under that section has been withdrawn,
unless an application is, or has been, made for a placement order and the application has not been disposed of.

(2) If a parent or guardian of the child informs the agency that he wishes the child to be returned to him—
 (a) the agency must give notice of the parent's or guardian's wish to the prospective adopters, and
 (b) the prospective adopters must return the child to the agency within the period of 14 days beginning with the day on which the notice is given.

(3) A prospective adopter who fails to comply with subsection (2)(b) is guilty of an offence and liable on summary conviction to imprisonment for a term not exceeding three months, or a fine not exceeding level 5 on the standard scale, or both.

(4) As soon as a child is returned to an adoption agency under this section, the agency must return the child to the parent or guardian in question.

(5) Where a notice under subsection (2) is given, but—
 (a) before the notice was given, an application—
  (i) for an adoption order (including a Scottish or Northern Irish adoption order),
  (ii) for a special guardianship order,
  (iii) for a child arrangements order to which subsection (6) applies, or
  (iv) for permission to apply for an order within paragraph (a) (ii) or (iii),
 was made in respect of the child, and
 (b) the application (and, in a case where permission is given on an application to apply for an order within paragraph (a)(ii) or (iii), the application for the order) has not been disposed of,
the prospective adopters are not required by virtue of the notice to return the child to the agency unless the court so orders.

(6) A child arrangements order is one to which this subsection applies if it is an order regulating arrangements that consist of, or include, arrangements which relate to either or both of the following—
 (a) with whom a child is to live, and
 (b) when the child is to live with any person.

33. Recovery by parent etc. where child placed and placement order refused

(1) This section applies where—
 (a) a child is placed for adoption by a local authority under section 19,
 (b) the authority have applied for a placement order and the application has been refused, and
 (c) any parent or guardian of the child informs the authority that he wishes the child to be returned to him.

(2) The prospective adopters must return the child to the authority on a date determined by the court.

(3) A prospective adopter who fails to comply with subsection (2) is guilty of an offence and liable on summary conviction to imprisonment for a term not exceeding three months, or a fine not exceeding level 5 on the standard scale, or both.

(4) As soon as a child is returned to the authority, they must return the child to the parent or guardian in question.

34. Placement orders: prohibition on removal

(1) Where a placement order in respect of a child—
 (a) is in force, or
 (b) has been revoked, but the child has not been returned by the prospective adopters or remains in any accommodation provided by the local authority,
a person (other than the local authority) may not remove the child from the prospective adopters or from accommodation provided by the authority.

(2) A person who removes a child in contravention of subsection (1) is guilty of an offence.
(3) Where a court revoking a placement order in respect of a child determines that the child is not to remain with any former prospective adopters with whom the child is placed, they must return the child to the local authority within the period determined by the court for the purpose; and a person who fails to do so is guilty of an offence.
(4) Where a court revoking a placement order in respect of a child determines that the child is to be returned to a parent or guardian, the local authority must return the child to the parent or guardian as soon as the child is returned to the authority or, where the child is in accommodation provided by the authority, at once.
(5) A person guilty of an offence under this section is liable on summary conviction to imprisonment for a term not exceeding three months, or a fine not exceeding level 5 on the standard scale, or both.
(6) This section does not affect the exercise by any local authority or other person of a power conferred by any enactment, other than section 20(8) of the 1989 Act.
(7) This section does not prevent the removal of a child who is arrested.
(8) This section applies whether or not the child in question is in England and Wales.

35. Return of child in other cases

(1) Where a child is placed for adoption by an adoption agency and the prospective adopters give notice to the agency of their wish to return the child, the agency must—
(a) receive the child from the prospective adopters before the end of the period of seven days beginning with the giving of the notice, and
(b) give notice to any parent or guardian of the child of the prospective adopters' wish to return the child.
(2) Where a child is placed for adoption by an adoption agency, and the agency—
(a) is of the opinion that the child should not remain with the prospective adopters, and
(b) gives notice to them of its opinion,
the prospective adopters must, not later than the end of the period of seven days beginning with the giving of the notice, return the child to the agency.
(3) If the agency gives notice under subsection (2)(b), it must give notice to any parent or guardian of the child of the obligation to return the child to the agency.
(4) A prospective adopter who fails to comply with subsection (2) is guilty of an offence and liable on summary conviction to imprisonment for a term not exceeding three months, or a fine not exceeding level 5 on the standard scale, or both.
(5) Where—
(a) an adoption agency gives notice under subsection (2) in respect of a child,
(b) before the notice was given, an application—
(i) for an adoption order (including a Scottish or Northern Irish adoption order),
(ii) for an special guardianship order,
(iii) for a child arrangements order to which subsection (5A) applies, or
(iv) for permission to apply for an order within sub-paragraph (ii) or (iii),
was made in respect of the child, and
(c) the application (and, in a case where permission is given on an application to apply for an order within paragraph (b)(ii) or (iii), the application for the order) has not been disposed of,
prospective adopters are not required by virtue of the notice to return the child to the agency unless the court so orders.
(5A) A child arrangements order is one to which this subsection applies if it is an order regulating arrangements that consist of, or include, arrangements which relate to either or both of the following—
(a) with whom a child is to live, and
(b) when a child is to live with any person.
(6) This section applies whether or not the child in question is in England and Wales.

Removal of children in non-agency cases

36. Restrictions on removal

(1) At any time when a child's home is with any persons ('the people concerned') with whom the child is not placed by an adoption agency, but the people concerned—
(a) have applied for an adoption order in respect of the child and the application has not been disposed of,
(b) have given notice of intention to adopt, or
(c) have applied for leave to apply for an adoption order under section 42(6) and the application has not been disposed of,
a person may remove the child only in accordance with the provisions of this group of sections (that is, this section and sections 37 to 40).

The reference to a child placed by an adoption agency includes a child placed by a Scottish or Northern Irish adoption agency.

(2) For the purposes of this group of sections, a notice of intention to adopt is to be disregarded if—
   (a) the period of four months beginning with the giving of the notice has expired without the people concerned applying for an adoption order, or
   (b) the notice is a second or subsequent notice of intention to adopt and was given during the period of five months beginning with the giving of the preceding notice.

(3) For the purposes of this group of sections, if the people concerned apply for leave to apply for an adoption order under section 42(6) and the leave is granted, the application for leave is not to be treated as disposed of until the period of three days beginning with the granting of the leave has expired.

(4) This section does not prevent the removal of a child who is arrested.

(5) Where a parent or guardian may remove a child from the people concerned in accordance with the provisions of this group of sections, the people concerned must at the request of the parent or guardian return the child to the parent or guardian at once.

(6) A person who—
   (a) fails to comply with subsection (5), or
   (b) removes a child in contravention of this section,

is guilty of an offence and liable on summary conviction to imprisonment for a term not exceeding three months, or a fine not exceeding level 5 on the standard scale, or both.

(7) This group of sections applies whether or not the child in question is in England and Wales.

37. Applicants for adoption

If section 36(1)(a) applies, the following persons may remove the child—
(a) a person who has the court's leave,
(b) a local authority or other person in the exercise of a power conferred by any enactment, other than section 20(8) of the 1989 Act.

38. Local authority foster parents

(1) This section applies if the child's home is with local authority foster parents.

(2) If—
   (a) the child has had his home with the foster parents at all times during the period of five years ending with the removal and the foster parents have given notice of intention to adopt, or
   (b) an application has been made for leave under section 42(6) and has not been disposed of,

the following persons may remove the child.

(3) They are—
   (a) a person who has the court's leave,
   (b) a local authority or other person in the exercise of a power conferred by any enactment, other than section 20(8) of the 1989 Act.

(4) If subsection (2) does not apply but—
   (a) the child has had his home with the foster parents at all times during the period of one year ending with the removal, and
   (b) the foster parents have given notice of intention to adopt,

the following persons may remove the child.

(5) They are—
   (a) a person with parental responsibility for the child who is exercising the power in section 20(8) of the 1989 Act,
   (b) a person who has the court's leave,
   (c) a local authority or other person in the exercise of a power conferred by any enactment, other than section 20(8) of the 1989 Act.

39. Partners of parents

(1) This section applies if a child's home is with a partner of a parent and the partner has given notice of intention to adopt.

(2) If the child's home has been with the partner for not less than three years (whether continuous or not) during the period of five years ending with the removal, the following persons may remove the child—
   (a) a person who has the court's leave,
   (b) a local authority or other person in the exercise of a power conferred by any enactment, other than section 20(8) of the 1989 Act.

(3) If subsection (2) does not apply, the following persons may remove the child—
   (a) a parent or guardian,
   (b) a person who has the court's leave,

(c) a local authority or other person in the exercise of a power conferred by any enactment, other than section 20(8) of the 1989 Act.

Preliminaries to adoption

42. Child to live with adopters before application

(1) An application for an adoption order may not be made unless—
(a) if subsection (2) applies, the condition in that subsection is met,
(b) if that subsection does not apply, the condition in whichever is applicable of subsections (3) to (5) applies.
(2) If —
(a) the child was placed for adoption with the applicant or applicants by an adoption agency or in pursuance of an order of the High Court, or
(b) the applicant is a parent of the child,
the condition is that the child must have had his home with the applicant or, in the case of an application by a couple, with one or both of them at all times during the period of ten weeks preceding the application.
(3) If the applicant or one of the applicants is the partner of a parent of the child, the condition is that the child must have had his home with the applicant or, as the case may be, applicants at all times during the period of six months preceding the application.
(4) If the applicants are local authority foster parents, the condition is that the child must have had his home with the applicants at all times during the period of one year preceding the application.
(5) In any other case, the condition is that the child must have had his home with the applicant or, in the case of an application by a couple, with one or both of them for not less than three years (whether continuous or not) during the period of five years preceding the application.
(6) But subsections (4) and (5) do not prevent an application being made if the court gives leave to make it.
(7) An adoption order may not be made unless the court is satisfied that sufficient opportunities to see the child with the applicant or, in the case of an application by a couple, both of them together in the home environment have been given—
(a) where the child was placed for adoption with the applicant or applicants by an adoption agency, to that agency,
(b) in any other case, to the local authority within whose area the home is.

. . .

43. Reports where child placed by agency

Where an application for an adoption order relates to a child placed for adoption by an adoption agency, the agency must—
(a) submit to the court a report on the suitability of the applicants and on any other matters relevant to the operation of section 1, and
(b) assist the court in any manner the court directs.

44. Notice of intention to adopt

(1) This section applies where persons (referred to in this section as 'proposed adopters') wish to adopt a child who is not placed for adoption with them by an adoption agency.
(2) An adoption order may not be made in respect of the child unless the proposed adopters have given notice to the appropriate local authority of their intention to apply for the adoption order (referred to in this Act as a 'notice of intention to adopt').
(3) The notice must be given not more than two years, or less than three months, before the date on which the application for the adoption order is made.
(4) Where—
(a) if a person were seeking to apply for an adoption order, subsection (4) or (5) of section 42 would apply, but
(b) the condition in the subsection in question is not met,
the person may not give notice of intention to adopt unless he has the court's leave to apply for an adoption order.
(5) On receipt of a notice of intention to adopt, the local authority must arrange for the investigation of the matter and submit to the court a report of the investigation.
(6) In particular, the investigation must, so far as practicable, include the suitability of the proposed adopters and any other matters relevant to the operation of section 1 in relation to the application.
(7) If a local authority receive a notice of intention to adopt in respect of a child whom they know was (immediately before the notice was given) looked after by another local

authority, they must, not more than seven days after the receipt of the notice, inform the other local authority in writing that they have received the notice.

(8) Where—
(a) a local authority have placed a child with any persons otherwise than as prospective adopters, and
(b) the persons give notice of intention to adopt,
the authority are not to be treated as leaving the child with them as prospective adopters for the purposes of section 18(1)(b).

(9) In this section, references to the appropriate local authority, in relation to any proposed adopters, are—
(a) in prescribed cases, references to the prescribed local authority,
(b) in any other case, references to the local authority for the area in which, at the time of giving the notice of intention to adopt, they have their home,
and 'prescribed' means prescribed by regulations.

45. Suitability of adopters

(1) Regulations under section 9 may make provision as to the matters to be taken into account by an adoption agency in determining, or making any report in respect of, the suitability of any persons to adopt a child.

(2) In particular, the regulations may make provision for the purpose of securing that, in determining the suitability of a couple to adopt a child, proper regard is had to the need for stability and permanence in their relationship.

46. Adoption orders

(1) An adoption order is an order made by the court on an application under section 50 or 51 giving parental responsibility for a child to the adopters or adopter.

(2) The making of an adoption order operates to extinguish—
(a) the parental responsibility which any person other than the adopters or adopter has for the adopted child immediately before the making of the order,
(b) any order under the 1989 Act or the Children (Northern Ireland) Order 1995,
(c) any order under the Children (Scotland) Act 1995 other than an excepted order, and
(d) any duty arising by virtue of an agreement or an order of a court to make payments, so far as the payments are in respect of the adopted child's maintenance or upbringing for any period after the making of the adoption order.
'Excepted order' means an order under section 9, 11(1)(d) or 13 of the Children (Scotland) Act 1995 or an exclusion order within the meaning of section 76(1) of that Act.

(3) An adoption order—
(a) does not affect parental responsibility so far as it relates to any period before the making of the order, and
(b) in the case of an order made on an application under section 51(2) by the partner of a parent of the adopted child, does not affect the parental responsibility of that parent or any duties of that parent within subsection (2)(d).

(4) Subsection (2)(d) does not apply to a duty arising by virtue of an agreement—
(a) which constitutes a trust, or
(b) which expressly provides that the duty is not to be extinguished by the making of an adoption order.

(5) An adoption order may be made even if the child to be adopted is already an adopted child.

(6) Before making an adoption order, the court must consider whether there should be arrangements for allowing any person contact with the child; and for that purpose the court must consider any existing or proposed arrangements and obtain any views of the parties to the proceedings.

47. Conditions for making adoption orders

(1) An adoption order may not be made if the child has a parent or guardian unless one of the following three conditions is met; but this section is subject to section 52 (parental etc. consent).

(2) The first condition is that, in the case of each parent or guardian of the child, the court is satisfied—
(a) that the parent or guardian consents to the making of the adoption order,
(b) that the parent or guardian has consented under section 20 (and has not withdrawn the consent) and does not oppose the making of the adoption order, or
(c) that the parent's or guardian's consent should be dispensed with.

(3) A parent or guardian may not oppose the making of an adoption order under subsection (2)(b) without the court's leave.

(4) The second condition is that—
(a) the child has been placed for adoption by an adoption agency with the prospective adopters in whose favour the order is proposed to be made,

(b) either–
 (i) the child was placed for adoption with the consent of each parent or guardian and the consent of the mother was given when the child was at least six weeks old, or
 (ii) the child was placed for adoption under a placement order, and
(c) no parent or guardian opposes the making of the adoption order.

(5) A parent or guardian may not oppose the making of an adoption order under the second condition without the court's leave.

(6) The third condition is that the child–
(a) is the subject of a Scottish permanence order which includes provision granting authority for the child to be adopted, or
(b) is free for adoption by virtue of an order made under section 17(1) or 18(1) of the Adoption (Northern Ireland) Order 1987 (S.I.1987/2203 (NI.22)).

(7) The court cannot give leave under subsection (3) or (5) unless satisfied that there has been a change in circumstances since the consent of the parent or guardian was given or, as the case may be, the placement order was made.

(8) An adoption order may not be made in relation to a person who is or has been married.

(8A) An adoption order may not be made in relation to a person who is or has been a civil partner.

(9) An adoption order may not be made in relation to a person who has attained the age of 19 years.

48. Restrictions on making adoption orders

(1) The court may not hear an application for an adoption order in relation to a child, where a previous application to which subsection (2) applies made in relation to the child by the same persons was refused by any court, unless it appears to the court that, because of a change in circumstances or for any other reason, it is proper to hear the application.

(2) This subsection applies to any application–
(a) for an adoption order or a Scottish or Northern Irish adoption order, or
(b) for an order for adoption made in the Isle of Man or any of the Channel Islands.

49. Applications for adoption

(1) An application for an adoption order may be made by–
(a) a couple, or
(b) one person,
but only if it is made under section 50 or 51 and one of the following conditions is met.

(2) The first condition is that at least one of the couple (in the case of an application under section 50) or the applicant (in the case of an application under section 51) is domiciled in a part of the British Islands.

(3) The second condition is that both of the couple (in the case of an application under section 50) or the applicant (in the case of an application under section 51) have been habitually resident in a part of the British Islands for a period of not less than one year ending with the date of the application.

(4) An application for an adoption order may only be made if the person to be adopted has not attained the age of 18 years on the date of the application.

(5) References in this Act to a child, in connection with any proceedings (whether or not concluded) for adoption, (such as 'child to be adopted' or 'adopted child') include a person who has attained the age of 18 years before the proceedings are concluded.

50. Adoption by couple

(1) An adoption order may be made on the application of a couple where both of them have attained the age of 21 years.

(2) An adoption order may be made on the application of a couple where–
(a) one of the couple is the mother or the father of the person to be adopted and has attained the age of 18 years, and
(b) the other has attained the age of 21 years.

51. Adoption by one person

(1) An adoption order may be made on the application of one person who has attained the age of 21 years and is not married or a civil partner.

(2) An adoption order may be made on the application of one person who has attained the age of 21 years if the court is satisfied that the person is the partner of a parent of the person to be adopted.

(3) An adoption order may be made on the application of one person who has attained the age of 21 years and is married if the court is satisfied that–
(a) the person's spouse cannot be found,
(b) the spouses have separated and are living apart, and the separation is likely to be permanent, or

(c) the person's spouse is by reason of ill-health, whether physical or mental, incapable of making an application for an adoption order.

(3A) An adoption order may be made on the application of one person who has attained the age of 21 years and is a civil partner if the court is satisfied that—

(a) the person's civil partner cannot be found,

(b) the civil partners have separated and are living apart, and the separation is likely to be permanent, or

(c) the person's civil partner is by reason of ill health, whether physical or mental, incapable of making an application for an adoption order.

(4) An adoption order may not be made on an application under this section by the mother or the father of the person to be adopted unless the court is satisfied that—

(a) the other natural parent is dead or cannot be found,

(b) by virtue of section 28 of the Human Fertilisation and Embryology Act 1990, there is no other parent, or

(c) there is some other reason justifying the child's being adopted by the applicant alone,

and, where the court makes an adoption order on such an application, the court must record that it is satisfied as to the fact mentioned in paragraph (a) or (b) or, in the case of paragraph (c), record the reason.

(5) The provisions referred to in subsection (4)(b) are—

(a) section 28 of the Human Fertilisation and Embryology Act 1990 (disregarding subsections (5A) to (5I) of that section), or

(b) sections 34 to 47 of the Human Fertilisation and Embryology Act 2008 (disregarding sections 39, 40 and 46 of that Act)

51A Post-adoption contact

(1) This section applies where—

(a) an adoption agency has placed or was authorised to place a child for adoption, and

(b) the court is making or has made an adoption order in respect of the child.

(2) When making the adoption order or at any time afterwards, the court may make an order under this section—

(a) requiring the person in whose favour is or has been made to allow the child to visit or stay with the person named in the order under this section, or for the person named in that order and the child otherwise to have contact with each other, or

(b) prohibiting named in the order under this section from having contact with the child.

...

Placement and adoption: general

52. Parental etc. consent

(1) The court cannot dispense with the consent of any parent or guardian of a child to the child being placed for adoption or to the making of an adoption order in respect of the child unless the court is satisfied that—

(a) the parent or guardian cannot be found or lacks capacity (within the meaning of the Mental Capacity Act 2005) to give consent, or

(b) the welfare of the child requires the consent to be dispensed with.

(2) The following provisions apply to references in this Chapter to any parent or guardian of a child giving or withdrawing—

(a) consent to the placement of a child for adoption, or

(b) consent to the making of an adoption order (including a future adoption order).

(3) Any consent given by the mother to the making of an adoption order is ineffective if it is given less than six weeks after the child's birth.

(4) The withdrawal of any consent to the placement of a child for adoption, or of any consent given under section 20, is ineffective if it is given after an application for an adoption order is made.

(5) 'Consent' means consent given unconditionally and with full understanding of what is involved; but a person may consent to adoption without knowing the identity of the persons in whose favour the order will be made.

(6) 'Parent' (except in subsections (9) and (10) below) means a parent having parental responsibility.

(7) Consent under section 19 or 20 must be given in the form prescribed by rules, and the rules may prescribe forms in which a person giving consent under any other provision of this Part may do so (if he wishes).

(8) Consent given under section 19 or 20 must be withdrawn—

(a) in the form prescribed by rules, or

(b) by notice given to the agency.

(9) Subsection (10) applies if—
(a) an agency has placed a child for adoption under section 19 in pursuance of consent given by a parent of the child, and
(b) at a later time, the other parent of the child acquires parental responsibility for the child.
(10) The other parent is to be treated as having at that time given consent in accordance with this section in the same terms as those in which the first parent gave consent.

54. Disclosing information during adoption process

Regulations under section 9 may require adoption agencies in prescribed circumstances to disclose in accordance with the regulations prescribed information to prospective adopters.

55. Revocation of adoptions on legitimation

(1) Where any child adopted by one natural parent as sole adoptive parent subsequently becomes a legitimated person on the marriage of the natural parents, the court by which the adoption order was made may, on the application of any of the parties concerned, revoke the order.
(2) ...

Disclosure of information in relation to a person's adoption

56. Information to be kept about a person's adoption

(1) In relation to an adopted person, regulations may prescribe—
(a) the information which an adoption agency must keep in relation to his adoption,
(b) the form and manner in which it must keep that information.
(2) Below in this group of sections (that is, this section and sections 57 to 65), any information kept by an adoption agency by virtue of subsection (1)(a) is referred to as section 56 information.
(3) Regulations may provide for the transfer in prescribed circumstances of information held, or previously held, by an adoption agency to another adoption agency.

57. Restrictions on disclosure of protected etc. information

(1) Any section 56 information kept by an adoption agency which—
(a) is about an adopted person or any other person, and
(b) is or includes identifying information about the person in question,
may only be disclosed by the agency to a person (other than the person the information is about) in pursuance of this group of sections.
(2) Any information kept by an adoption agency—
(a) which the agency has obtained from the Registrar General on an application under section 79(5) and any other information which would enable the adopted person to obtain a certified copy of the record of his birth, or
(b) which is information about an entry relating to the adopted person in the Adoption Contact Register,
may only be disclosed to a person by the agency in pursuance of this group of sections.
(3) In this group of sections, information the disclosure of which to a person is restricted by virtue of subsection (1) or (2) is referred to (in relation to him) as protected information.
(4) Identifying information about a person means information which, whether taken on its own or together with other information disclosed by an adoption agency, identifies the person or enables the person to be identified.
(5) This section does not prevent the disclosure of protected information in pursuance of a prescribed agreement to which the adoption agency is a party.
(6) Regulations may authorise or require an adoption agency to disclose protected information to a person who is not an adopted person.

58. Disclosure of other information

(1) This section applies to any section 56 information other than protected information.
(2) An adoption agency may for the purposes of its functions disclose to any person in accordance with prescribed arrangements any information to which this section applies.
(3) An adoption agency must, in prescribed circumstances, disclose prescribed information to a prescribed person.

59. Offence

Regulations may provide that a registered adoption society which discloses any information in contravention of section 57 is to be guilty of an offence and liable on summary conviction to a fine not exceeding level 5 on the standard scale.

60. Disclosing information to adopted adult

(1) This section applies to an adopted person who has attained the age of 18 years.

(2) The adopted person has the right, at his request, to receive from the appropriate adoption agency—

(a) any information which would enable him to obtain a certified copy of the record of his birth, unless the High Court orders otherwise,

(b) any prescribed information disclosed to the adopters by the agency by virtue of section 54.

(3) The High Court or family court may make an order under subsection (2)(a), on an application by the appropriate adoption agency, if satisfied that the circumstances are exceptional.

(4) The adopted person also has the right, at his request, to receive from the court which made the adoption order a copy of any prescribed document or prescribed order relating to the adoption.

(5) Subsection (4) does not apply to a document or order so far as it contains information which is protected information.

61. Disclosing protected information about adults

(1) This section applies where—

(a) a person applies to the appropriate adoption agency for protected information to be disclosed to him, and

(b) none of the information is about a person who is a child at the time of the application.

(2) The agency is not required to proceed with the application unless it considers it appropriate to do so.

(3) If the agency does proceed with the application it must take all reasonable steps to obtain the views of any person the information is about as to the disclosure of the information about him.

(4) The agency may then disclose the information if it considers it appropriate to do so.

(5) In deciding whether it is appropriate to proceed with the application or disclose the information, the agency must consider—

(a) the welfare of the adopted person,

(b) any views obtained under subsection (3),

(c) any prescribed matters,

and all the other circumstances of the case.

(6) This section does not apply to a request for information under section 60(2) or to a request for information which the agency is authorised or required to disclose in pursuance of regulations made by virtue of section 57(6).

62. Disclosing protected information about children

(1) This section applies where—

(a) a person applies to the appropriate adoption agency for protected information to be disclosed to him, and

(b) any of the information is about a person who is a child at the time of the application.

(2) The agency is not required to proceed with the application unless it considers it appropriate to do so.

(3) If the agency does proceed with the application, then, so far as the information is about a person who is at the time a child, the agency must take all reasonable steps to obtain—

(a) the views of any parent or guardian of the child, and

(b) the views of the child, if the agency considers it appropriate to do so having regard to his age and understanding and to all the other circumstances of the case,

as to the disclosure of the information.

(4) And, so far as the information is about a person who has at the time attained the age of 18 years, the agency must take all reasonable steps to obtain his views as to the disclosure of the information.

(5) The agency may then disclose the information if it considers it appropriate to do so.

(6) In deciding whether it is appropriate to proceed with the application, or disclose the information, where any of the information is about a person who is at the time a child—

(a) if the child is an adopted child, the child's welfare must be the paramount consideration,

(b) in the case of any other child, the agency must have particular regard to the child's welfare.

(7) And, in deciding whether it is appropriate to proceed with the application or disclose the information, the agency must consider—

(a) the welfare of the adopted person (where subsection (6)(a) does not apply),

(b) any views obtained under subsection (3) or (4),

(c) any prescribed matters,

and all the other circumstances of the case.

(8) This section does not apply to a request for information under section 60(2) or to a request for information which the agency is authorised or required to disclose in pursuance of regulations made by virtue of section 57(6).

63. Counselling

(1) Regulations may require adoption agencies to give information about the availability of counselling to persons—
 (a) seeking information from them in pursuance of this group of sections,
 (b) considering objecting or consenting to the disclosure of information by the agency in pursuance of this group of sections, or
 (c) considering entering with the agency into an agreement prescribed for the purposes of section 57(5).
(2) Regulations may require adoption agencies to make arrangements to secure the provision of counselling for persons seeking information from them in prescribed circumstances in pursuance of this group of sections.
(3) The regulations may authorise adoption agencies—
 (a) to disclose information which is required for the purposes of such counselling to the persons providing the counselling,
 (b) where the person providing the counselling is outside the United Kingdom, to require a prescribed fee to be paid.
(4) The regulations may require any of the following persons to provide counselling for the purposes of arrangements under subsection (2)—
 (a) a local authority . . .
 (b) a registered adoption society . . .
 (c) an adoption support agency in respect of which a person is registered under Part 2 of the Care Standards Act 2000.

. . .

64. Other provision to be made by regulations

(1) Regulations may make provision for the purposes of this group of sections, including provision as to—
 (a) the performance by adoption agencies of their functions,
 (b) the manner in which information may be received, and
 (c) the matters mentioned below in this section.
(2) Regulations may prescribe—
 (a) the manner in which agreements made by virtue of section 57(5) are to be recorded,
 (b) the information to be provided by any person on an application for the disclosure of information under this group of sections.
(3) Regulations may require adoption agencies—
 (a) to give to prescribed persons prescribed information about the rights or opportunities to obtain information, or to give their views as to its disclosure, given by this group of sections,
 (b) to seek prescribed information from, or give prescribed information to, the Registrar General in prescribed circumstances.
(4) Regulations may require the Registrar General—
 (a) to disclose to any person (including an adopted person) at his request any information which the person requires to assist him to make contact with the adoption agency which is the appropriate adoption agency in the case of an adopted person specified in the request (or, as the case may be, in the applicant's case),
 (b) to disclose to the appropriate adoption agency any information which the agency requires about any entry relating to the adopted person on the Adoption Contact Register.
(5) Regulations may provide for the payment of a prescribed fee in respect of the disclosure in prescribed circumstances of any information in pursuance of section 60, 61 or 62; but an adopted person may not be required to pay any fee in respect of any information disclosed to him in relation to any person who (but for his adoption) would be related to him by blood (including half-blood) or marriage or civil partnership.
(6) Regulations may provide for the payment of a prescribed fee by an adoption agency obtaining information under subsection (4)(b).

65. Sections 56 to 65: interpretation

(1) In this group of sections—
'appropriate adoption agency', in relation to an adopted person or to information relating to his adoption, means—

(a) if the person was placed for adoption by an adoption agency, that agency or (if different) the agency which keeps the information in relation to his adoption,
(b) in any other case,
the local authority to which notice of intention to adopt was given, 'prescribed' means prescribed by subordinate legislation,
'regulations' means regulations under section 9,
'subordinate legislation' means regulations or, in relation to information to be given by a court, rules.

CHAPTER 4
STATUS OF ADOPTED CHILDREN

66. Meaning of adoption in Chapter 4

(1) In this Chapter 'adoption' means—
(a) adoption by an adoption order or a Scottish or Northern Irish adoption order,
(b) adoption by an order made in the Isle of Man or any of the Channel Islands,
(c) an adoption effected under the law of a Convention country outside the British Islands, and certified in pursuance of Article 23(1) of the Convention (referred to in this Act as a 'Convention adoption'),
(d) an overseas adoption, or
(e) an adoption recognised by the law of England and Wales and effected under the law of any other country;
and related expressions are to be interpreted accordingly.
(2) But references in this Chapter to adoption do not include an adoption effected before the day on which this Chapter comes into force (referred to in this Chapter as 'the appointed day').
(3) Any reference in an enactment to an adopted person within the meaning of this Chapter includes a reference to an adopted child within the meaning of Part 4 of the Adoption Act 1976.

67. Status conferred by adoption

(1) An adopted person is to be treated in law as if born as the child of the adopters or adopter.
(2) An adopted person is the legitimate child of the adopters or adopter and, if adopted by—
(a) a couple, or
(b) one of a couple under section 51(2),
is to be treated as the child of the relationship of the couple in question.
(3) An adopted person—
(a) if adopted by one of a couple under section 51(2), is to be treated in law as not being the child of any person other than the adopter and the other one of the couple, and
(b) in any other case, is to be treated in law, subject to subsection (4), as not being the child of any person other than the adopters or adopter;
but this subsection does not affect any reference in this Act to a person's natural parent or to any other natural relationship.
(4) In the case of a person adopted by one of the person's natural parents as sole adoptive parent, subsection (3)(b) has no effect as respects entitlement to property depending on relationship to that parent, or as respects anything else depending on that relationship.
(5) This section has effect from the date of the adoption.
(6) Subject to the provisions of this Chapter and Schedule 4, this section—
(a) applies for the interpretation of enactments or instruments passed or made before as well as after the adoption, and so applies subject to any contrary indication, and
(b) has effect as respects things done, or events occurring, on or after the adoption.

68. Adoptive relatives

(1) A relationship existing by virtue of section 67 may be referred to as an adoptive relationship, and—
(a) an adopter may be referred to as an adoptive parent or (as the case may be) as an adoptive father or adoptive mother,
(b) any other relative of any degree under an adoptive relationship may be referred to as an adoptive relative of that degree.
(2) Subsection (1) does not affect the interpretation of any reference, not qualified by the word 'adoptive', to a relationship.
(3) A reference (however expressed) to the adoptive mother and father of a child adopted by—

(a) a couple of the same sex, or
(b) a partner of the child's parent, where the couple are of the same sex,
is to be read as a reference to the child's adoptive parents.

69. Rules of interpretation for instruments concerning property

(1) The rules of interpretation contained in this section apply (subject to any contrary indication and to Schedule 4) to any instrument so far as it contains a disposition of property.

(2) In applying section 67(1) and (2) to a disposition which depends on the date of birth of a child or children of the adoptive parent or parents, the disposition is to be interpreted as if—
(a) the adopted person had been born on the date of adoption,
(b) two or more people adopted on the same date had been born on that date in the order of their actual births; but this does not affect any reference to a person's age.

(3) Examples of phrases in wills on which subsection (2) can operate are—
1. Children of A 'living at my death or born afterwards'.
2. Children of A 'living at my death or born afterwards before any one of such children for the time being in existence attains a vested interest and who attain the age of 21 years'.
3. As in example 1 or 2, but referring to grandchildren of A instead of children of A.
4. A for life 'until he has a child', and then to his child or children.

Note. Subsection (2) will not affect the reference to the age of 21 years in example 2.

(4) Section 67(3) does not prejudice—
(a) any qualifying interest, or
(b) any interest expectant (whether immediately or not) upon a qualifying interest.
'Qualifying interest' means an interest vested in possession in the adopted person before the adoption.

(5) Where it is necessary to determine for the purposes of a disposition of property effected by an instrument whether a woman can have a child—
(a) it must be presumed that once a woman has attained the age of 55 years she will not adopt a person after execution of the instrument, and
(b) if she does so, then (in spite of section 67) that person is not to be treated as her child or (if she does so as one of a couple) as the child of the other one of the couple for the purposes of the instrument.

(6) In this section, 'instrument' includes a private Act settling property, but not any other enactment.

70. Dispositions depending on date of birth

(1) Where a disposition depends on the date of birth of a person who was born illegitimate and who is adopted by one of the natural parents as sole adoptive parent, section 69(2) does not affect entitlement by virtue of Part 3 of the Family Law Reform Act 1987 (dispositions of property).

(2) Subsection (1) applies for example where—
(a) a testator dies in 2001 bequeathing a legacy to his eldest grandchild living at a specified time,
(b) his unmarried daughter has a child in 2002 who is the first grandchild,
(c) his married son has a child in 2003,
(d) subsequently his unmarried daughter adopts her child as sole adoptive parent.
In that example the status of the daughter's child as the eldest grandchild of the testator is not affected by the events described in paragraphs (c) and (d).

71. Property devolving with peerages etc.

(1) An adoption does not affect the descent of any peerage or dignity or title of honour.

(2) An adoption does not affect the devolution of any property limited (expressly or not) to devolve (as nearly as the law permits) along with any peerage or dignity or title of honour.

(3) Subsection (2) applies only if and so far as a contrary intention is not expressed in the instrument, and has effect subject to the terms of the instrument.

74. Miscellaneous enactments

(1) Section 67 does not apply for the purposes of—
(a) Section 1 of and Schedule 1 to the Marriage Act 1949 or Schedule 1 to the Civil Partnership Act 2004 (prohibited degrees of kindred and affinity),
(b) sections 64 and 65 of the Sexual Offences Act 2003 (sex with an adult relative).

(2) Section 67 does not apply for the purposes of any provision of—
(a) the British Nationality Act 1981,
(b) the Immigration Act 1971,
(c) any instrument having effect under an enactment within paragraph (a) or (b), or

(d) any other provision of the law for the time being in force which determines British citizenship, British overseas territories citizenship, the status of a British National (Overseas) or British Overseas citizenship.

75. Pensions

Section 67(3) does not affect entitlement to a pension which is payable to or for the benefit of a person and is in payment at the time of the person's adoption.

76. Insurance

(1) Where a child is adopted whose natural parent has effected an insurance with a friendly society or a collecting society or an industrial insurance company for the payment on the death of the child of money for funeral expenses, then—
   (a) the rights and liabilities under the policy are by virtue of the adoption transferred to the adoptive parents, and
   (b) for the purposes of the enactments relating to such societies and companies, the adoptive parents are to be treated as the person who took out the policy.

(2) Where the adoption is effected by an order made by virtue of section 51(2), the references in subsection (1) to the adoptive parents are to be read as references to the adopter and the other one of the couple.

CHAPTER 5
THE REGISTERS

Adopted Children Register etc.

77. Adopted Children Register

(1) The Registrar General must continue to maintain in the General Register Office a register, to be called the Adopted Children Register.

(2) The Adopted Children Register is not to be open to public inspection or search.

(3) No entries may be made in the Adopted Children Register other than entries—
   (a) directed to be made in it by adoption orders, or
   (b) required to be made under Schedule 1.

(4) A certified copy of an entry in the Adopted Children Register, if purporting to be sealed or stamped with the seal of the General Register Office, is to be received as evidence of the adoption to which it relates without further or other proof.

(5) Where an entry in the Adopted Children Register contains a record—
   (a) of the date of birth of the adopted person, or
   (b) of the country, or the district and sub-district, of the birth of the adopted person,

a certified copy of the entry is also to be received, without further or other proof, as evidence of that date, or country or district and sub-district, (as the case may be) in all respects as if the copy were a certified copy of an entry in the registers of live-births.

(6) Schedule 1 (registration of adoptions and the amendment of adoption orders) is to have effect.

78. Searches and copies

(1) The Registrar General must continue to maintain at the General Register Office an index of the Adopted Children Register.

(2) Any person may—
   (a) search the index,
   (b) have a certified copy of any entry in the Adopted Children Register.

(3) But a person is not entitled to have a certified copy of an entry in the Adopted Children Register relating to an adopted person who has not attained the age of 18 years unless the applicant has provided the Registrar General with the prescribed particulars.
'Prescribed' means prescribed by regulations made by the Registrar General with the approval of the Chancellor of the Exchequer.

(4) The terms, conditions and regulations as to payment of fees, and otherwise, applicable under the Births and Deaths Registration Act 1953, and the Registration Service Act 1953, in respect of—
   (a) searches in the index kept in the General Register Office of certified copies of entries in the registers of live-births,
   (b) the supply from that office of certified copies of entries in those certified copies, also apply in respect of searches, and supplies of certified copies, under subsection (2).

79. Connections between the register and birth records

(1) The Registrar General must make traceable the connection between any entry in the registers of live-births or other records which has been marked 'Adopted' and any corresponding entry in the Adopted Children Register.

(2) Information kept by the Registrar General for the purposes of subsection (1) is not to be open to public inspection or search.

(3) Any such information, and any other information which would enable an adopted person to obtain a certified copy of the record of his birth, may only be disclosed by the Registrar General in accordance with this section.
(4) In relation to a person adopted before the appointed day the court may, in exceptional circumstances, order the Registrar General to give any information mentioned in subsection (3) to a person.
(5) On an application made in the prescribed manner by the appropriate adoption agency in respect of an adopted person a record of whose birth is kept by the Registrar General, the Registrar General must give the agency any information relating to the adopted person which is mentioned in subsection (3).
'Appropriate adoption agency' has the same meaning as in section 65.
(6) In relation to a person adopted before the appointed day, Schedule 2 applies instead of subsection (5).
(7) On an application made in the prescribed manner by an adopted person a record of whose birth is kept by the Registrar General and who—
(a) is under the age of 18 years, and
(b) intends to be married or form a civil partnership,
the Registrar General must inform the applicant whether or not it appears from information contained in the registers of live-births or other records that the applicant and the intended spouse or civil partner may be within the prohibited degrees of relationship for the purposes of the Marriage Act 1949.
(8) Before the Registrar General gives any information by virtue of this section, any prescribed fee which he has demanded must be paid.
(9) In this section—
'appointed day' means the day appointed for the commencement of sections 56 to 65,
'prescribed' means prescribed by regulations made by the Registrar General with the approval of the Chancellor of the Exchequer.

80. Adoption Contact Register

(1) The Registrar General must continue to maintain at the General Register Office in accordance with regulations a register in two Parts to be called the Adoption Contact Register.
(2) Part 1 of the register is to contain the prescribed information about adopted persons who have given the prescribed notice expressing their wishes as to making contact with their relatives.
(3) The Registrar General may only make an entry in Part 1 of the register for an adopted person—
(a) a record of whose birth is kept by the Registrar General,
(b) who has attained the age of 18 years, and
(c) who the Registrar General is satisfied has such information as is necessary to enable him to obtain a certified copy of the record of his birth.
(4) Part 2 of the register is to contain the prescribed information about persons who have given the prescribed notice expressing their wishes, as relatives of adopted persons, as to making contact with those persons.
(5) The Registrar General may only make an entry in Part 2 of the register for a person—
(a) who has attained the age of 18 years, and
(b) who the Registrar General is satisfied is a relative of an adopted person and has such information as is necessary to enable him to obtain a certified copy of the record of the adopted person's birth.
(6) Regulations may provide for—
(a) the disclosure of information contained in one Part of the register to persons for whom there is an entry in the other Part,
(b) the payment of prescribed fees in respect of the making or alteration of entries in the register and the disclosure of information contained in the register.

81. Adoption Contact Register: supplementary

(1) The Adoption Contact Register is not to be open to public inspection or search.
(2) In section 80, 'relative', in relation to an adopted person, means any person who (but for his adoption) would be related to him by blood (including half-blood), marriage or any civil partnership.
(3) The Registrar General must not give any information entered in the register to any person except in accordance with subsection (6)(a) of that section or regulations made by virtue of section 64(4)(b).
(4) In section 80, 'regulations' means regulations made by the Registrar General with the approval of the Chancellor of the Exchequer, and 'prescribed' means prescribed by such regulations.

General

82. Interpretation

(1) In this Chapter—
'records' includes certified copies kept by the Registrar General of entries in any register of births,
'registers of live-births' means the registers of live-births made under the Births and Deaths Registration Act 1953.

(2) Any register, record or index maintained under this Chapter may be maintained in any form the Registrar General considers appropriate; and references (however expressed) to entries in such a register, or to their amendment, marking or cancellation, are to be read accordingly.

CHAPTER 7
MISCELLANEOUS

Restrictions

92. Restriction on arranging adoptions etc.

(1) A person who is neither an adoption agency nor acting in pursuance of an order of the High Court or family court must not take any of the steps mentioned in subsection (2).

(2) The steps are—
(a) asking a person other than an adoption agency to provide a child for adoption,
(b) asking a person other than an adoption agency to provide prospective adopters for a child,
(c) offering to find a child for adoption,
(d) offering a child for adoption to a person other than an adoption agency,
(e) handing over a child to any person other than an adoption agency with a view to the child's adoption by that or another person,
(f) receiving a child handed over to him in contravention of paragraph (e),
(g) entering into an agreement with any person for the adoption of a child, or for the purpose of facilitating the adoption of a child, where no adoption agency is acting on behalf of the child in the adoption,
(h) initiating or taking part in negotiations of which the purpose is the conclusion of an agreement within paragraph (g),
(i) causing another person to take any of the steps mentioned in paragraphs (a) to (h).

(3) Subsection (1) does not apply to a person taking any of the steps mentioned in paragraphs (d), (e), (g), (h) and (i) of subsection (2) if the following condition is met.

(4) The condition is that—
(a) the prospective adopters are parents, relatives or guardians of the child (or one of them is), or
(b) the prospective adopter is the partner of a parent of the child.

(5) References to an adoption agency in subsection (2) include a prescribed person outside the United Kingdom exercising functions corresponding to those of an adoption agency, if the functions are being exercised in prescribed circumstances in respect of the child in question.

(6) The Secretary of State may, after consultation with the Assembly, by order make any amendments of subsections (1) to (4), and any consequential amendments of this Act, which he considers necessary or expedient.

(7) In this section—
(a) 'agreement' includes an arrangement (whether or not enforceable),
(b) 'prescribed' means prescribed by regulations made by the Secretary of State after consultation with the Assembly.

93. Offence of breaching restrictions under section 92

(1) If a person contravenes section 92(1), he is guilty of an offence; and, if that person is an adoption society, the person who manages the society is also guilty of the offence.

(2) A person is not guilty of an offence under subsection (1) of taking the step mentioned in paragraph (f) of section 92(2) unless it is proved that he knew or had reason to suspect that the child was handed over to him in contravention of paragraph (e) of that subsection.

(3) A person is not guilty of an offence under subsection (1) of causing a person to take any of the steps mentioned in paragraphs (a) to (h) of section 92(2) unless it is proved that he knew or had reason to suspect that the step taken would contravene the paragraph in question.

(4) But subsections (2) and (3) only apply if sufficient evidence is adduced to raise an issue as to whether the person had the knowledge or reason mentioned.

(5) A person guilty of an offence under this section is liable on summary conviction to imprisonment for a term not exceeding six months, or a fine not exceeding £10,000, or both.

94. Restriction on reports

(1) A person who is not within a prescribed description may not, in any prescribed circumstances, prepare a report for any person about the suitability of a child for adoption or of a person to adopt a child or about the adoption, or placement for adoption, of a child. 'Prescribed' means prescribed by regulations made by the Secretary of State after consultation with the Assembly.

(2) If a person—
- (a) contravenes subsection (1), or
- (b) causes a person to prepare a report, or submits to any person a report which has been prepared, in contravention of that subsection,

he is guilty of an offence.

(3) If a person who works for an adoption society—
- (a) contravenes subsection (1), or
- (b) causes a person to prepare a report, or submits to any person a report which has been prepared, in contravention of that subsection,

the person who manages the society is also guilty of the offence.

(4) A person is not guilty of an offence under subsection (2)(b) unless it is proved that he knew or had reason to suspect that the report would be, or had been, prepared in contravention of subsection (1).
But this subsection only applies if sufficient evidence is adduced to raise an issue as to whether the person had the knowledge or reason mentioned.

(5) A person guilty of an offence under this section is liable on summary conviction to imprisonment for a term not exceeding six months, or a fine not exceeding level 5 on the standard scale, or both.

95. Prohibition of certain payments

(1) This section applies to any payment (other than an excepted payment) which is made for or in consideration of—
- (a) the adoption of a child,
- (b) giving any consent required in connection with the adoption of a child,
- (c) removing from the United Kingdom a child who is a Commonwealth citizen, or is habitually resident in the United Kingdom, to a place outside the British Islands for the purpose of adoption,
- (d) a person (who is neither an adoption agency nor acting in pursuance of an order of the High Court or family court) taking any step mentioned in section 92(2),
- (e) preparing, causing to be prepared or submitting a report the preparation of which contravenes section 94(1).

(2) In this section and section 96, removing a child from the United Kingdom has the same meaning as in section 85.

(3) Any person who—
- (a) makes any payment to which this section applies,
- (b) agrees or offers to make any such payment, or
- (c) receives or agrees to receive or attempts to obtain any such payment,

is guilty of an offence.

(4) A person guilty of an offence under this section is liable on summary conviction to imprisonment for a term not exceeding six months, or a fine not exceeding £10,000, or both.

96. Excepted payments

(1) A payment is an excepted payment if it is made by virtue of, or in accordance with provision made by or under, this Act, the Adoption (Scotland) Act 1978 and Children (Scotland) Act 2007 or the Adoption (Northern Ireland) Order 1987.

(2) A payment is an excepted payment if it is made to a registered adoption society by—
- (a) a parent or guardian of a child, or
- (b) a person who adopts or proposes to adopt a child,

in respect of expenses reasonably incurred by the society in connection with the adoption or proposed adoption of the child.

(3) A payment is an excepted payment if it is made in respect of any legal or medical expenses incurred or to be incurred by any person in connection with an application to a court which he has made or proposes to make for an adoption order, a placement order, or an order under section 26, 51A or 84.

. . .

97. Sections 92 to 96: interpretation

In sections 92 to 96—
(a) 'adoption agency' includes a Scottish or Northern Irish adoption agency,
(b) 'payment' includes reward,
(c) references to adoption are to the adoption of persons, wherever they may be habitually resident, effected under the law of any country or territory, whether within or outside the British Islands.

Proceedings

99. Proceedings for offences

Proceedings for an offence by virtue of section 9 or 59 may not, without the written consent of the Attorney General, be taken by any person other than the National Care Standards Commission or the Assembly.

. . .

The Children and Family Court Advisory and Support Service

102 Officers of the Service

(1) For the purpose of—
(a) any relevant application,
(b) the signification by any person of any consent to placement or adoption,
rules must provide for the appointment in prescribed cases of the Children and Family Court Advisory and Support Service ('the Service') or a Welsh family proceedings officer.

. . .

(3) The rules may provide for the officer—
(a) to act on behalf of the child upon he the hearing of any relevant application, with the duty of safeguarding the interests of the child in the prescribed manner,
(b) where the court so requests, to prepare a report on matters relating to the welfare of the child in question,
(c) to witness documents which signify consent to placement or adoption,
(d) to perform prescribed functions.

. . .

PART 3
MISCELLANEOUS AND FINAL PROVISIONS

CHAPTER 1
MISCELLANEOUS

Advertisements in the United Kingdom

123. Restriction on advertisements etc.

(1) A person must not—
(a) publish or distribute an advertisement or information to which this section applies, or
(b) cause such an advertisement or information to be published or distributed.
(2) This section applies to an advertisement indicating that—
(a) the parent or guardian of a child wants the child to be adopted,
(b) a person wants to adopt a child,
(c) a person other than an adoption agency is willing to take any step mentioned in paragraphs (a) to (e), (g) and (h) and (so far as relating to those paragraphs) (i) of section 92(2),
(d) a person other than an adoption agency is willing to receive a child handed over to him with a view to the child's adoption by him or another, or
(e) a person is willing to remove a child from the United Kingdom for the purposes of adoption.
(3) This section applies to—
. . .
(b) information about a particular child as a child available for adoption.
(4) For the purposes of this section and section 124—
(a) publishing or distributing an advertisement or information means publishing it or distributing it to the public and includes doing so by electronic means (for example, by means of the internet),
(b) the public includes selected members of the public as well as the public generally or any section of the public.

(5) Subsection (1) does not apply to publication or distribution by or on behalf of an adoption agency.

(6) The Secretary of State may by order make any amendments of this section which he considers necessary or expedient in consequence of any developments in technology relating to publishing or distributing advertisements or other information by electronic or electro-magnetic means.

. . .

124. Offence of breaching restriction under section 123

(1) A person who contravenes section 123(1) is guilty of an offence.

(2) A person is not guilty of an offence under this section unless it is proved that he knew or had reason to suspect that section 123 applied to the advertisement or information. But this subsection only applies if sufficient evidence is adduced to raise an issue as to whether the person had the knowledge or reason mentioned.

(3) A person guilty of an offence under this section is liable on summary conviction to imprisonment for a term not exceeding three months, or a fine not exceeding level 5 on the standard scale, or both.

Adoption and Children Act Register

125. Adoption and Children Act Register

(1) Her Majesty may by Order in Council make provision for the Secretary of State to establish and maintain a register, to be called the Adoption and Children Act Register, containing—

(a) prescribed information about children who are suitable for adoption and prospective adopters who are suitable to adopt a child,

(b) prescribed information about persons included in the register in pursuance of paragraph (a) in respect of things occurring after their inclusion.

(2) For the purpose of giving assistance in finding persons with whom children may be placed for purposes other than adoption, an Order under this section may—

(a) provide for the register to contain information about such persons and the children who may be placed with them, and

(b) apply any of the other provisions of this group of sections (that is, this section and sections 126 to 131), with or without modifications.

(3) The register is not to be open to public inspection or search.

(4) An Order under this section may make provision about the retention of information in the register.

(5) Information is to be kept in the register in any form the Secretary of State considers appropriate.

126. Use of an organisation to establish the register

(1) The Secretary of State may make an arrangement with an organisation under which any function of his under an Order under section 125 of establishing and maintaining the register, and disclosing information entered in, or compiled from information entered in, the register to any person is performed wholly or partly by the organisation on his behalf.

(2) The arrangement may include provision for payments to be made to the organisation by the Secretary of State.

(3) If the Secretary of State makes an arrangement under this section with an organisation, the organisation is to perform the functions exercisable by virtue of this section in accordance with any directions given by the Secretary of State and the directions may be of general application (or general application in any part of Great Britain) or be special directions.

(4) An exercise of the Secretary of State's powers under subsection (1) or (3) requires the agreement of the Scottish Ministers (if the register applies to Scotland) and of the Assembly (if the register applies to Wales).

(5) References in this group of sections to the registration organisation are to any organisation for the time being performing functions in respect of the register by virtue of arrangements under this section.

127. Use of an organisation as agency for payments

(1) An Order under section 125 may authorise an organisation with which an arrangement is made under section 126 to act as agent for the payment or receipt of sums payable by adoption agencies to other adoption agencies and may require adoption agencies to pay or receive such sums through the organisation.

(2) The organisation is to perform the functions exercisable by virtue of this section in accordance with any directions given by the Secretary of State; and the directions may

be of general application (or general application in any part of Great Britain) or be special directions.

(3) An exercise of the Secretary of State's power to give directions under subsection (2) requires the agreement of the Scottish Ministers (if any payment agency provision applies to Scotland) and of the Assembly (if any payment agency provision applies to Wales).

128. Supply of information for the register

(1) An Order under section 125 may require adoption agencies to give prescribed information to the Secretary of State or the registration organisation for entry in the register.

(2) Information is to be given to the Secretary of State or the registration organisation when required by the Order and in the prescribed form and manner.

(3) An Order under section 125 may require an agency giving information which is entered on the register to pay a prescribed fee to the Secretary of State or the registration organisation.

(4) But an adoption agency is not to disclose any information to the Secretary of State or the registration organisation—

(a) about prospective adopters who are suitable to adopt a child, or persons who were included in the register as such prospective adopters, without their consent,

(b) about children suitable for adoption, or persons who were included in the register as such children, without the consent of the prescribed person.

(5) Consent under subsection (4) is to be given in the prescribed form.

128A. Search and inspection of the register by prospective adopters

(1) Regulations may make provision enabling prospective adopters to search and inspect the register, for the purpose of assisting them to find a child for whom they would be appropriate adopters.

. . .

129. Disclosure of information

(1) Information entered in the register, or compiled from information entered in the register, may only be disclosed under subsection (2), (2A) or (3) or section128A.

(2) Prescribed information entered in the register may be disclosed by the Secretary of State or the registration organisation—

(a) where an adoption agency is acting on behalf of a child who is suitable for adoption, to the agency to assist in finding prospective adopters with whom it would be appropriate for the child to be placed,

(b) where an adoption agency is acting on behalf of prospective adopters who are suitable to adopt a child, to the agency to assist in finding a child appropriate for adoption by them.

(2A) Regulations may make provision permitting disclosure of prescribed information entered in the register or compiled from information entered in the register—

(a) to an adoption agency or to a Welsh, Scottish or Northern Ireland adoption agency for any prescribed purpose, or

(b) for the purpose of enabling the information to be entered in a register which is maintained in respect of Wales, Scotland or Northern Ireland and which contains information about children who are suitable for adoption or prospective adopters who are suitable to adopt a child.

(3) Prescribed information entered in the register, or compiled from information entered in the register, may be disclosed by the Secretary of State or the registration organisation to any prescribed person for use for statistical or research purposes, or for other prescribed purposes.

(4) An Order under section 125 may prescribe the steps to be taken by adoption agencies in respect of information received by them by virtue of subsection (2).

(5) Subsection (1) does not apply —

(a) to a disclosure of information with the authority of the Secretary of State, or

(b) to a disclosure by the registration organisation of prescribed information to the Scottish Ministers (if the register applies to Scotland) or the Assembly (if the register applies to Wales).

(6) Information disclosed to any person under subsection (2) or (3) may be given on any prescribed terms or conditions.

(7) An Order under section 125 may, in prescribed circumstances, require a prescribed fee to be paid to the Secretary of State or the registration organisation—

(a) by a prescribed adoption agency in respect of information disclosed under subsection (2), or

(b) by a person to whom information is disclosed under subsection (3).

(8) If any information entered in the register is disclosed to a person in contravention of subsection (1), the person disclosing it is guilty of an offence.

(9) A person guilty of an offence under subsection (8) is liable on summary conviction to imprisonment for a term not exceeding three months, or a fine not exceeding level 5 on the standard scale, or both.

131. Supplementary

(1) In this group of sections—
(a) 'organisation' includes a public body and a private or voluntary organisation,
(b) 'prescribed' means prescribed by an Order under section 125,
(c) 'the register' means the Adoption and Children Act register,
. . .
(e) 'voluntary organisation providing a registered adoption service' has the same meaning as in section 144(3).

(2) For the purposes of this group of sections—
(a) a child is suitable for adoption if an adoption agency is satisfied that the child ought to be placed for adoption,
(b) prospective adopters are suitable to adopt a child if an adoption agency is satisfied that they are suitable to have a child placed with them for adoption.

(3) Nothing authorised or required to be done by virtue of this group of sections constitutes an offence under section 93, 94 or 95.

(4) No recommendation to make an Order under section 125 is to be made to Her Majesty in Council unless a draft has been laid before and approved by resolution of each House of Parliament.

CHAPTER 2
FINAL PROVISIONS

144. General interpretation etc.

(1) In this Act—
'appropriate Minister' means—
(a) in relation to England, Scotland or Northern Ireland, the Secretary of State,
(b) in relation to Wales, the Assembly,
and in relation to England and Wales means the Secretary of State and the Assembly acting jointly,
'the Assembly' means the National Assembly for Wales,
'body' includes an unincorporated body,
'by virtue of' includes 'by' and 'under',
'child', except where used to express a relationship, means a person who has not attained the age of 18 years,
'the Convention' means the Convention on Protection of Children and Co-operation in respect of Intercountry Adoption, concluded at the Hague on 29th May 1993,
'Convention adoption order' means an adoption order which, by virtue of regulations under section 1 of the Adoption (Intercountry Aspects) Act 1999 (regulations giving effect to the Convention), is made as a Convention adoption order,
'Convention country' means a country or territory in which the Convention is in force,
'court' means, the High Court or the family
'enactment' includes an enactment comprised in subordinate legislation,
'fee' includes expenses,
'guardian' has the same meaning as in the 1989 Act and includes a special guardian within the meaning of that Act,
'information' means information recorded in any form,
'local authority' means any unitary authority, or any county council so far as they are not a unitary authority,
. . .
'notice' means a notice in writing,
'registration authority' (in Part 1) has the same meaning as in the Care Standards Act 2000,
'regulations' means regulations made by the appropriate Minister, unless they are required to be made by the Lord Chancellor, the Secretary of State or the Registrar General,
'relative', in relation to a child, means a grandparent, brother, sister, uncle or aunt, whether of the full blood or half-blood or by marriage or civil partnership,
'rules' means Family Procedure Rules made by virtue of section 141(1),
. . .
'subordinate legislation' has the same meaning as in the Interpretation Act 1978,
'unitary authority' means—

(a) the council of any county so far as they are the council for an area for which there are no district councils,
(b) the council of any district comprised in an area for which there is no county council,
(c) the council of a county borough,
(d) the council of a London borough,
(e) the Common Council of the City of London.

. . .

(4) In this Act, a couple means—
(a) a married couple, or
(aa) two people who are civil partners of each other, or
(b) two people (whether of different sexes or the same sex) living as partners in an enduring family relationship.

(5) Subsection (4)(b) does not include two people one of whom is the other's parent, grandparent, sister, brother, aunt or uncle.

(6) References to relationships in subsection (5)—
(a) are to relationships of the full blood or half blood or, in the case of an adopted person, such of those relationships as would exist but for adoption, and
(b) include the relationship of a child with his adoptive, or former adoptive, parents,
but do not include any other adoptive relationships.

(7) For the purposes of this Act, a person is the partner of a child's parent if the person and the parent are a couple but the person is not the child's parent.

SCHEDULES

Section 77(6)

SCHEDULE 1
REGISTRATION OF ADOPTIONS

Registration of adoption orders

1. (1) Every adoption order must contain a direction to the Registrar General to make in the Adopted Children Register an entry in the form prescribed by regulations made by the Registrar General with the approval of the Chancellor of the Exchequer.

(2) Where, on an application to a court for an adoption order in respect of a child, the identity of the child with a child to whom an entry in the registers of live-births or other records relates is proved to the satisfaction of the court, any adoption order made in pursuance of the application must contain a direction to the Registrar General to secure that the entry in the register or, as the case may be, record in question is marked with the word 'Adopted'.

(3) Where an adoption order is made in respect of a child who has previously been the subject of an adoption order made by a court in England or Wales under Part 1 of this Act or any other enactment—
(a) sub-paragraph (2) does not apply, and
(b) the order must contain a direction to the Registrar General to mark the previous entry in the Adopted Children Register with the word 'Re-adopted'.

(4) Where an adoption order is made, the prescribed officer of the court which made the order must communicate the order to the Registrar General in the prescribed manner; and the Registrar General must then comply with the directions contained in the order. 'Prescribed' means prescribed by rules.

. . .

Amendment of orders and rectification of Registers and other records

4. (1) The court by which an adoption order has been made may, on the application of the adopter or the adopted person, amend the order by the correction of any error in the particulars contained in it.

(2) The court by which an adoption order has been made may, if satisfied on the application of the adopter or the adopted person that within the period of one year beginning with the date of the order any new name—
(a) has been given to the adopted person (whether in baptism or otherwise), or
(b) has been taken by the adopted person, either in place of or in addition to a name specified in the particulars required to be entered in the Adopted Children Register in pursuance of the order, amend the order by substituting or, as the case may be, adding that name in those particulars.

(3) The court by which an adoption order has been made may, if satisfied on the application of any person concerned that a direction for the marking of an entry in the registers of live-births, the Adopted Children Register or other records included in the order in pursuance of paragraph 1(2) or (3) was wrongly so included, revoke that direction.

(4) Where an adoption order is amended or a direction revoked under sub-paragraphs (1) to (3), the prescribed officer of the court must communicate the amendment in the prescribed manner to the Registrar General.
'Prescribed' means prescribed by rules.

(5) The Registrar General must then—
(a) amend the entry in the Adopted Children Register accordingly, or
(b) secure that the marking of the entry in the registers of live-births, the Adopted Children Register or other records is cancelled,
as the case may be.

(6) Where an adoption order is quashed or an appeal against an adoption order allowed by any court, the court must give directions to the Registrar General to secure that—
(a) any entry in the Adopted Children Register, and
(b) any marking of an entry in that Register, the registers of live-births or other records as the case may be, which was effected in pursuance of the order,
is cancelled.

(7) Where an adoption order has been amended, any certified copy of the relevant entry in the Adopted Children Register which may be issued pursuant to section 78(2)(b) must be a copy of the entry as amended, without the reproduction of—
(a) any note or marking relating to the amendment, or
(b) any matter cancelled in pursuance of it.

(8) A copy or extract of an entry in any register or other record, being an entry the marking of which has been cancelled, is not to be treated as an accurate copy unless both the marking and the cancellation are omitted from it.

. . .

Marking of entries on re-registration of birth on legitimation

5. (1) Without prejudice to paragraphs 2(4) and 4(5), where, after an entry in the registers of live-births or other records has been marked in accordance with paragraph 1 or 2, the birth is re-registered under section 14 of the Births and Deaths Registration Act 1953 (re-registration of births of legitimated persons), the entry made on the re-registration must be marked in the like manner.

(2) Without prejudice to paragraph 4(9), where an entry in the registers of live-births or other records is marked in pursuance of paragraph 3 and the birth in question is subsequently re-registered under section 14 of that Act, the entry made on re-registration must be marked in the like manner.

Cancellations in registers on legitimation

6. (1) This paragraph applies where an adoption order is revoked under section 55(1).

(2) The prescribed officer of the court must communicate the revocation in the prescribed manner to the Registrar General who must then cancel or secure the cancellation of—
(a) the entry in the Adopted Children Register relating to the adopted person, and
(b) the marking with the word 'Adopted' of any entry relating to the adopted person in the registers of live-births or other records.
'Prescribed' means prescribed by rules.

(3) A copy or extract of an entry in any register or other record, being an entry the marking of which is cancelled under this paragraph, is not to be treated as an accurate copy unless both the marking and the cancellation are omitted from it.

Section 79(6)

SCHEDULE 2

DISCLOSURE OF BIRTH RECORDS BY REGISTRAR GENERAL

1. On an application made in the prescribed manner by an adopted person-
(a) a record of whose birth is kept by the Registrar General, and
(b) who has attained the age of 18 years,
the Registrar General must give the applicant any information necessary to enable the applicant to obtain a certified copy of the record of his birth.
'Prescribed' means prescribed by regulations made by the Registrar General with the approval of the Chancellor of the Exchequer.

2. (1) Before giving any information to an applicant under paragraph 1, the Registrar General must inform the applicant that counselling services are available to the applicant—
(a) from a registered adoption society, an organisation within section 144(3)(b) or an adoption society which is registered under Article 4 of the Adoption (Northern Ireland) Order 1987,
(b) if the applicant is in England and Wales, at the General Register Office or from any local authority or registered adoption support agency,

. . .

(2) In sub-paragraph (1)(b), 'registered adoption support agency' means an adoption support agency in respect of which a person is registered under Part 2 of the Care Standards Act 2000.

. . .

(4) If the applicant chooses to receive counselling from a person or body within sub-paragraph (1), the Registrar General must send to the person or body the information to which the applicant is entitled under paragraph 1.

. . .

4. (1) Where a person—

(a) was adopted before 12th November 1975, and

(b) applies for information under paragraph 1,

the Registrar General must not give the information to the applicant unless the applicant has attended an interview with a counsellor arranged by a person or body from whom counselling services are available as mentioned in paragraph 2.

(2) Where the Registrar General is prevented by sub-paragraph (1) from giving information to a person who is not living in the United Kingdom, the Registrar General may give the information to any body which-

(a) the Registrar General is satisfied is suitable to provide counselling to that person, and

(b) has notified the Registrar General that it is prepared to provide such counselling.

. . .

Section 147

SCHEDULE 6

GLOSSARY

In this Act, the expressions listed in the left-hand column below have the meaning given by, or are to be interpreted in accordance with, the provisions of this Act or (where stated) of the 1989 Act listed in the right-hand column.

Expression	*Provision*
the 1989 Act	section 2(5)
Adopted Children Register	section 77
Adoption and Children Act Register	section 125
adoption (in relation to Chapter 4 of Part 1)	section 66
adoption agency	section 2(1)
adoption agency placing a child for adoption	section 18(5)
Adoption Contact Register	section 80
adoption order	section 46(1)
Adoption Service	section 2(1)
adoption society	section 2(5)
adoption support agency	section 8
adoption support services	section 2(6)
appointed day (in relation to Chapter 4 of Part 1)	section 66(2)
appropriate Minister	section 144
Assembly	section 144
body	section 144
by virtue of	section 144
care order	section 105(1) of the 1989 Act
child	sections 49(5) and 144
child arrangements order	section 8(1) of the 1989 Act
child assessment order	section 43(2) of the 1989 Act
child in the care of a local authority	section 105(1) of the 1989 Act
child looked after by a local authority	section 22 of the 1989 Act
child placed for adoption by an adoption agency	section 18(5)
child to be adopted, adopted child	section 49(5)
consent (in relation to making adoption orders or placing for adoption)	section 52
the Convention	section 144
Convention adoption	section 66(1)(c)
Convention adoption order	section 144
Convention country	section 144
couple	section 144(4)
court	section 144
disposition (in relation to Chapter 4 of Part 1)	section 73
enactment	section 144
fee	section 144

guardian	section 144
information	section 144
interim care order	section 38 of the 1989 Act
local authority	section 144
local authority foster parent	section 23(3) of the 1989 Act
Northern Irish adoption agency	section 144
Northern Irish adoption order	section 144
notice	section 144
notice of intention to adopt	section 44(2)
overseas adoption	section 87
parental responsibility	section 3 of the 1989 Act
partner, in relation to a parent of a child	section 144(7)
placement order	section 21
placing, or placed, for adoption	sections 18(5) and 19(4)
prohibited steps order	section 8(1) of the 1989 Act
records (in relation to Chapter 5 of Part 1)	section 82
registered adoption society	section 2(2)
registers of live-births (in relation to Chapter 5 of Part 1)	section 82
registration authority (in Part 1)	section 144
regulations	section 144
relative	section 144, read with section 1(8)
residence order	section 8(1) of the 1989 Act
rules	section 144
Scottish adoption agency	section 144(3)
Scottish adoption order	section 144
specific issue order	section 8(1) of the 1989 Act
subordinate legislation	section 144
supervision order	section 31(11) of the 1989 Act
unitary authority	section 144
voluntary organisation	section 2(5)

HUMAN FERTILISATION AND EMBRYOLOGY (DECEASED FATHERS) ACT 2003
(2003 c. 24)

3. Retrospective, transitional and transitory provision

(1) This Act shall (in addition to any case where the sperm or embryo is used on or after the coming into force of section 1) apply to any case where the sperm of a man, or any embryo the creation of which was brought about with the sperm of a man, was used on or after 1st August 1991 and before the coming into force of that section.

(2) Where the child concerned was born before the coming into force of section 1 of this Act, section 28(5A) or (as the case may be) (5B) of the Human Fertilisation and Embryology Act 1990 shall have effect as if for paragraph (e) there were substituted—

'(e) the woman has elected in writing not later than the end of the period of six months beginning with the coming into force of this subsection for the man to be treated for the purpose mentioned in subsection (5I) below as the father of the child,'.

(3) Where the child concerned was born before the coming into force of section 1 of this Act, section 28(5C) of the Act of 1990 shall have effect as if for paragraph (f) there were substituted—

'(f) the woman has elected in writing not later than the end of the period of six months beginning with the coming into force of this subsection for the other party to the marriage to be treated for the purpose mentioned in subsection (5I) below as the father of the child,'.

(4) Where the child concerned was born before the coming into force of section 1 of this Act, section 28(5D) of the Act of 1990 shall have effect as if for paragraph (f) there were substituted—

'(f) the woman has elected in writing not later than the end of the period of six months beginning with the coming into force of this subsection for the man to be treated for the purpose mentioned in subsection (5I) below as the father of the child,'.

(5) Where the child concerned was born before the coming into force of section 1 of this Act, section 28 of the Act of 1990 shall have effect as if—

(a) subsection (5E) were omitted; and
(b) in subsection (5F) for the words from '(which requires' to 'that day)' there were substituted '(which requires an election to be made not later than the end of a period of six months)'.

(6) Where the man who might be treated as the father of the child died before the passing of this Act—
(a) subsections (5A) and (5B) of section 28 of the Act of 1990 shall have effect as if paragraph (d) of each subsection were omitted;
(b) subsections (5C) and (5D) of that section of that Act shall have effect as if paragraph (e) of each subsection were omitted;

. . .

ANTI-SOCIAL BEHAVIOUR ACT 2003
(2003 c. 38)

PART 3
PARENTAL RESPONSIBILITIES

Truancy and misbehaviour at school

19. Parenting contracts in cases of misbehaviour at school or truancy

(1) This section applies where a pupil has been excluded on disciplinary grounds from a relevant school for a fixed period or permanently.

(1A) This section also applies where a local education authority or the governing body of a relevant school have reason to believe that a child who is a registered pupil at a relevant school has engaged in behaviour connected with the school which—
(a) has caused, or is likely to cause—
(i) significant disruption to the education of other pupils, or
(ii) significant detriment to the welfare of the child himself or of other pupils or to the health or safety of any staff, or
(b) forms part of a pattern of behaviour which (if continued) will give rise to a risk of future exclusion from the school on disciplinary grounds.

(1B) For the purposes of subsection (1A) the child's behaviour is connected with the school to the extent that it consists of—
(a) conduct at the school, or
(b) conduct elsewhere in circumstances in which it would be reasonable for the school to regulate his conduct.

(2) This section also applies where a child of compulsory school age has failed to attend regularly at—
(a) a relevant school at which he is a registered pupil,
(b) any place at which education is provided for him in the circumstances mentioned in subsection (1) of section 444ZA of the Education Act 1996, and
(c) any place at which he is required to attend in the circumstances mentioned in subsection (2) of that section.

(3) A local education authority or the governing body of a relevant school may enter into a parenting contract with a parent of the pupil or child.

(4) A parenting contract is a document which contains—
(a) a statement by the parent that he agrees to comply with such requirements as may be specified in the document for such period as may be so specified, and
(b) a statement by the local education authority or governing body that it agrees to provide support to the parent for the purpose of complying with those requirements.

(5) The requirements mentioned in subsection (4) may include (in particular) a requirement to attend a counselling or guidance programme.

(6) The purpose of the requirements mentioned in subsection (4)—
(a) in a case falling within subsection (1) or (1A), is to improve the behaviour of the pupil,
(b) in a case falling within subsection (2), is to ensure that the child attends regularly at the relevant school at which he is a registered pupil.

(7) A parenting contract must be signed by the parent and signed on behalf of the local education authority or governing body.

(8) A parenting contract does not create any obligations in respect of whose breach any liability arises in contract or in tort.

(9) Local education authorities and governing bodies of relevant schools must, in carrying out their functions in relation to parenting contracts, have regard to any guidance which is issued by the appropriate person from time to time for that purpose.

20. Parenting orders in cases of exclusion or potential exclusion from school

(1) Subsection (2) applies where—
(a) a pupil has been excluded on disciplinary grounds from a relevant school for a fixed period or permanently, and
(b) such conditions as may be prescribed in regulations made by the appropriate person are satisfied.

(2) A relevant body may apply to a magistrates' court for a parenting order in respect of a parent of the pupil.

(2A) A relevant body may also apply to a magistrates' court for a parenting order in respect of a pupil at a relevant school if—
(a) it appears to the body making the application that the pupil has engaged in behaviour which would warrant the exclusion of the pupil from the school on disciplinary grounds for a fixed period or permanently, and
(b) such conditions as may be prescribed in regulations made by the appropriate person are satisfied.

(2B) For the purposes of subsection (2A), there are to be disregarded—
(a) any practice restricting the use of exclusion at a particular school, or at schools of a particular description, and
(b) any grounds that might exist for not excluding the pupil, to the extent that those grounds relate to his education or welfare after exclusion.

(3) If an application is made under subsection (2) or (2A), the court may make a parenting order in respect of a pupil if it is satisfied—
(a) in the case of an application under subsection (2A), that the pupil has engaged in behaviour of the kind mentioned in that subsection, and
(b) in any case, that the making of the order would be desirable in the interests of improving the behaviour of the pupil.

(4) A parenting order is an order which requires the parent—
(a) to comply, for a period not exceeding twelve months, with such requirements as are specified in the order, and
(b) subject to subsection (5), to attend, for a concurrent period not exceeding three months, such counselling or guidance programme as may be specified in directions given by the responsible officer.

(5) A parenting order under this section may, but need not, include a requirement mentioned in subsection (4)(b) in any case where a parenting order under this section or any other enactment has been made in respect of the parent on a previous occasion.

(6) A counselling or guidance programme which a parent is required to attend by virtue of subsection (4)(b) may be or include a residential course but only if the court is satisfied that the following two conditions are fulfilled.

(7) The first condition is that the attendance of the parent at a residential course is likely to be more effective than his attendance at a non-residential course in improving the behaviour of the pupil.

(8) The second condition is that any interference with family life which is likely to result from the attendance of the parent at a residential course is proportionate in all the circumstances.

(9) In this section 'a relevant body' means—
(a) a local education authority,
(b) the governing body of any relevant school in England at which the pupil to whom the application relates is a pupil or from which he has been excluded.

21. Parenting orders: supplemental

(1) In deciding whether to make a parenting order under section 20, a court must take into account (amongst other things)—
(a) any refusal by the parent to enter into a parenting contract under section 19 in respect of the pupil in a case falling within subsection (1) or (1A) of that section, or
(b) if the parent has entered into such a parenting contract, any failure by the parent to comply with the requirements specified in the contract.

(1A) In deciding whether to make a parenting order under section 20, a court must also take into account any failure by the parent without reasonable excuse to attend a reintegration interview under section 102 of the Education and Inspections Act 2006 (reintegration interview in case of fixed period exclusion) when requested to do so in accordance with regulations under that section.

(2) Before making a parenting order under section 20 in the case of a pupil under the age of 16, a court must obtain and consider information about the pupil's family circumstances and the likely effect of the order on those circumstances.

(3) Subsections (3) to (7) of section 9 of the Crime and Disorder Act 1998 (supplemental provisions about parenting orders) are to apply in relation to a parenting order under section 20 as they apply in relation to a parenting order under section 8 of that Act.

(4) . . .

(5) Local education authorities, governing bodies, head teachers and responsible officers must, in carrying out their functions in relation to parenting orders, have regard to any guidance which is issued by the appropriate person from time to time for that purpose.

22. Parenting orders: appeals

(1) An appeal lies to the Crown Court against the making of a parenting order under section 20.

(2) Subsections (2) and (3) of section 10 of the Crime and Disorder Act 1998 (appeals against parenting orders) are to apply in relation to an appeal under this section as they apply in relation to an appeal under subsection (1)(b) of that section.

COURTS ACT 2003
(2003 C. 39)

75. Family Procedure Rules

(1) There are to be rules of court (to be called 'Family Procedure Rules') governing the practice and procedure to be followed in family proceedings.

(2) Family Procedure Rules are to be made by a committee known as the Family Procedure Rule Committee.

(3) 'Family proceedings' means—

(a) proceedings in the family court, and

(b) proceedings in the Family Division of the High Court which are business assigned, by or under section 61 of (and Schedule 1 to) the Senior Courts Act 1981, to that Division of the High Court and no other.

(4) The power to make Family Procedure Rules includes power to make different provisions for different cases or different areas, including different provision—

(a) for a specified court or description of courts, or

(b) for specified descriptions of proceedings or a specified jurisdiction.

(5) Any power to make Family Procedure Rules is to be exercised with a view to securing that—

(a) the family justice system is accessible, fair and efficient, and

(b) the rules are both simple and simply expressed.

76. Further provision about scope of Family Procedure Rules

(2) Family Procedure Rules may—

(a) modify or exclude the application of any provision of the County Courts Act 1984, and

(aa) provide subject to any provision that may be made in rules under section 31O(1) of the Matrimonial and Family Proceedings Act 1984 for any functions of a court in family Proceedings to be carried out by officers or other staff of the court.

(2A) Family Procedure Rules may, for the purposes of the law relating to contempt of court, authorise the publication in such circumstances as may be specified of information relating to family proceedings held in private.

(2B) In subsection (2A) 'family proceedings held in private' means family proceedings at which the general public have no right to be present.

(3) Family Procedure Rules may modify the rules of evidence as they may apply to family proceedings.

GENDER RECOGNITION ACT 2004
(2004 c. 7)

Applications for gender recognition certificate

1. Applications

(1) A person of either gender who is aged at least 18 may make an application for a gender recognition certificate on the basis of—

(a) living in the other gender, or

(b) having changed gender under the law of a country or territory outside the United Kingdom.

(2) In this Act 'the acquired gender', in relation to a person by whom an application under subsection (1) is or has been made, means—

(a) in the case of an application under paragraph (a) of that subsection, the gender in which the person is living, or

(b) in the case of an application under paragraph (b) of that subsection, the gender to which the person has changed under the law of the country or territory concerned.

(3) An application under subsection (1) is to be determined by a Gender Recognition Panel.

(4) Schedule 1 (Gender Recognition Panels) has effect.

2. Determination of applications

(1) In the case of an application under section 1(1)(a), the Panel must grant the application if satisfied that the applicant—

(a) has or has had gender dysphoria,

(b) has lived in the acquired gender throughout the period of two years ending with the date on which the application is made,

(c) intends to continue to live in the acquired gender until death, and

(d) complies with the requirements imposed by and under section 3.

(2) In the case of an application under section 1(1)(b), the Panel must grant the application if satisfied—

(a) that the country or territory under the law of which the applicant has changed gender is an approved country or territory, and

(b) that the applicant complies with the requirements imposed by and under section 3.

(3) The Panel must reject an application under section 1(1) if not required by subsection (1) or (2) to grant it.

(3A) This section does not apply to an application under section 1(1)(a) which states that it is an application for a certificate to be granted in accordance with section 3A.

(4) In this Act 'approved country or territory' means a country or territory prescribed by order made by the Secretary of State after consulting the Scottish Ministers and the Department of Finance and Personnel in Northern Ireland.

3. Evidence

(1) An application under section 1(1)(a) must include either—

(a) a report made by a registered medical practitioner practising in the field of gender dysphoria and a report made by another registered medical practitioner (who may, but need not, practise in that field), or

(b) a report made by a chartered psychologist practising in that field and a report made by a registered medical practitioner (who may, but need not, practise in that field).

(2) But subsection (1) is not complied with unless a report required by that subsection and made by—

(a) a registered medical practitioner, or

(b) a chartered psychologist, practising in the field of gender dysphoria includes details of the diagnosis of the applicant's gender dysphoria.

(3) And subsection (1) is not complied with in a case where—

(a) the applicant has undergone or is undergoing treatment for the purpose of modifying sexual characteristics, or

(b) treatment for that purpose has been prescribed or planned for the applicant, unless at least one of the reports required by that subsection includes details of it.

(4) An application under section 1(1)(a) must also include a statutory declaration by the applicant that the applicant meets the conditions in section 2(1)(b) and (c).

(5) An application under section 1(1)(b) must include evidence that the applicant has changed gender under the law of an approved country or territory.

(6) Any application under section 1(1) must include—

(a) a statutory declaration as to whether or not the applicant is married or a civil partner,

(b) any other information or evidence required by an order made by the Secretary of State, and

(c) any other information or evidence which the Panel which is to determine the application may require,

and may include any other information or evidence which the applicant wishes to include.

. . .

(8) If the Panel which is to determine the application requires information or evidence under subsection (6)(c) it must give reasons for doing so.

3A. Alternative grounds for granting applications

(1) This section applies to an application under section 1(1)(a) which states that it is an application for a certificate to be granted in accordance with this section.
(2) The Panel must grant the application if it is satisfied that the applicant complies with the requirements imposed by and under section 3B and meets the conditions in subsections (3) to (6).
(3) The first condition is that the applicant was a party to a protected marriage or a protected civil partnership on or before the date when the application was made.
(4) The second condition is that the applicant—
  (a) was living in the acquired gender for six years before the commencement of section 12 of the Marriage (Same Sex Couples) Act 2013,
  (b) continued to live in the acquired gender until the date the application was made, and
  (c) intends to live in the acquired gender until death.
(5) The third condition is that the applicant—
  (a) has or had had gender dysphoria, or
  (b) has undergone surgical treatment for the purpose of modifying sexual characteristics.
(6) The fourth condition is that the applicant is ordinarily resident in England, Wales or Scotland.
(7) The Panel must reject the application if not required by subsection (2) to grant it.

4. Successful applications

(1) If a Gender Recognition Panel grants an application under section 1(1) it must issue a gender recognition certificate to the applicant.
(2) The certificate is to be a full gender recognition certificate if—
  (a) the applicant is neither a civil partner nor married,
  (b) the applicant is a party to a protected marriage and the applicant's spouse consents to the marriage continuing after the issue of a full gender recognition certificate, or
  (c) the applicant is a party to a protected civil partnership and the Panel has decided to issue a full gender recognition certificate to the other party to the civil partnership.
(3) The certificate is to be an interim gender recognition certificate if—
  (a) the applicant is a party to a protected marriage and the applicant's spouse does not consent to the marriage continuing after the issue of a full gender certificate,
  (b) the applicant is a party to a marriage that is not a protected marriage,
  (c) the applicant is a party to a protected civil partnership and the other party to the civil partnership has not made an application under section 1(1),
  (d) the applicant is a party to a protected civil partnership and the Panel has decided not to issue a full gender recognition certificate to the other party to the civil partnership, or
  (e) the applicant is a party to a civil partnership that is not a protected civil partnership.
(4) Schedule 2 (annulment or dissolution of marriage after issue of interim gender recognition certificate) has effect.

. . .

5. Issue of full certificates where applicant has been married

(1) A court which—
  (a) makes absolute a decree of nullity granted on the ground that an interim gender recognition certificate has been issued to a party to the marriage, or
  (b) . . .
must, on doing so, issue a full gender recognition certificate to that party and send a copy to the Secretary of State.
(2) If an interim gender recognition certificate has been issued to a person and either—
  (a) the person's marriage is dissolved or annulled (otherwise than on the ground mentioned in subsection (1)) in proceedings instituted during the period of six months beginning with the day on which it was issued, or
  (b) the person's spouse dies within that period,
the person may make an application for a full gender recognition certificate at any time within the period specified in subsection (3) (unless the person is neither married nor a civil partner).
(3) That period is the period of six months beginning with the day on which the marriage is dissolved or annulled or the death occurs.
(4) An application under subsection (2) must include evidence of the dissolution or annulment of the marriage and the date on which proceedings for it were instituted, or of the death of the spouse and the date on which it occurred.
(5) An application under subsection (2) is to be determined by a Gender Recognition Panel.

(6) The Panel—
(a) must grant the application if satisfied that the applicant is not married, and
(b) otherwise must reject it.
(7) If the Panel grants the application it must issue a full gender recognition certificate to the applicant.

. . .

5A. Issue of full certificates where applicant has been a civil partner

(1) A court which—
(a) makes final a nullity order made on the ground that an interim gender recognition certificate has been issued to a civil partner, ...

must, on doing so, issue a full gender recognition certificate to that civil partner and send a copy to the Secretary of State.
(2) If an interim gender recognition certificate has been issued to a person and either—
(a) the person's civil partnership is dissolved or annulled (otherwise than on a ground mentioned in subsection (1)) in proceedings instituted during the period of six months beginning with the day on which it was issued, or
(b) the person's civil partner dies within that period,

the person may make an application for a full gender recognition certificate at any time within the period specified in subsection (3) (unless the person is again a civil partner or is married).
(3) That period is the period of six months beginning with the day on which the civil partnership is dissolved or annulled or the death occurs.

. . .

6. Errors in certificates

(1) Where a gender recognition certificate has been issued to a person, the person or the Secretary of State may make an application for—
(a) an interim gender recognition certificate, on the ground that a full gender recognition certificate has been incorrectly issued instead of an interim certificate;
(b) a full recognition certificate, on the ground that an interim gender recognition certificate has been incorrectly issued instead of a full certificate; or
(c) a corrected certificate, on the ground that the certificate which has been issued contains an error.
(2) If the certificate was issued by a court the application is to be determined by the court but in any other case it is to be determined by a Gender Recognition Panel.
(3) The court or Panel—
(a) must grant the application if satisfied that the gender recognition certificate contains an error, and
(b) otherwise must reject it.
(4) If the court or Panel grants the application it must issue a corrected gender recognition certificate to the applicant.

Consequences of issue of gender recognition certificate etc.

9. General

(1) Where a full gender recognition certificate is issued to a person, the person's gender becomes for all purposes the acquired gender (so that, if the acquired gender is the male gender, the person's sex becomes that of a man and, if it is the female gender, the person's sex becomes that of a woman).
(2) Subsection (1) does not affect things done, or events occurring, before the certificate is issued; but it does operate for the interpretation of enactments passed, and instruments and other documents made, before the certificate is issued (as well as those passed or made afterwards).
(3) Subsection (1) is subject to provision made by this Act or any other enactment or any subordinate legislation.

10. Registration

(1) Where there is a UK birth register entry in relation to a person to whom a full gender recognition certificate is issued, the Secretary of State must send a copy of the certificate to the appropriate Registrar General.

. . .

(2) In this Act 'UK birth register entry', in relation to a person to whom a full gender recognition certificate is issued, means—
(a) an entry of which a certified copy is kept by a Registrar General, or
(b) an entry in a register so kept, containing a record of the person's birth or adoption (or, if there would otherwise be more than one, the most recent).

. . .

11A. Change in gender of party to marriage

(1) This section applies in relation to a protected marriage if (by virtue of section 4(2)(b) or 4A) a full gender recognition certificate is issued to a party to the marriage.
(2) The continuity of the marriage is not affected by the relevant change of gender.
(3) If the protected marriage is a foreign marriage—
(a) the continuity of the marriage continues by virtue of subsection (2) notwithstanding any impediment under the proper law of the marriage;
(b) the proper law of the marriage is not affected by its continuation by virtue of subsection (2).

11B. Change in gender of civil partner

The continuity of a civil partnership is not affected by the issuing of full gender recognition certificates (by virtue of section4(2)(c)) to both civil partners.

12. Parenthood

The fact that a person's gender has become the acquired gender under this Act does not affect the status of the person as the father or mother of a child.

13. Social security benefits and pensions

Schedule 5 (entitlement to benefits and pensions) has effect.

15. Succession etc.

The fact that a person's gender has become the acquired gender under this Act does not affect the disposal or devolution of property under a will or other instrument made before the appointed day.

16. Peerages etc.

The fact that a person's gender has become the acquired gender under this Act—
(a) does not affect the descent of any peerage or dignity or title of honour, and
(b) does not affect the devolution of any property limited (expressly or not) by a will or other instrument to devolve (as nearly as the law permits) along with any peerage or dignity or title of honour unless an intention that it should do so is expressed in the will or other instrument.

. . .

SCHEDULE 1 Section 1

GENDER RECOGNITION PANELS

List of persons eligible to sit

1.— (1) Subject to sub-paragraph (1A), the Lord Chancellor must make appointments to a list of persons eligible to sit as members of Gender Recognition Panels.
(1A) The Lord Chancellor may appoint a person under sub-paragraph (1) only with the concurrence of all of the following—
(a) the Lord Chief Justice of England and Wales;
(b) the Lord President of the Court of Session;
(c) the Lord Chief Justice of Northern Ireland.
(2) The only persons who may be appointed to the list are persons who—
(a) have a relevant legal qualification ('legal members'), or
(b) are registered medical practitioners or chartered psychologists ('medical members').
(3) The following have a relevant legal qualification—
(a) a person who has a 7 year general qualification within the meaning of section 71 of the Courts and Legal Services Act 1990,

. . .

President

2.— (1) Subject to sub-paragraph (1A), the Lord Chancellor must—
(a) appoint one of the legal members to be the President of Gender Recognition Panels ('the President'), and
(b) appoint another of the legal members to be the Deputy President of Gender Recognition Panels ('the Deputy President').
(1A) The Lord Chancellor may appoint a person under sub-paragraph (1) only with the concurrence of all of the following—
(a) the Lord Chief Justice of England and Wales;
(b) the Lord President of the Court of Session;
(c) the Lord Chief Justice of Northern Ireland.

(2) The Deputy President has the functions of the President—
(a) if the President is unavailable, and
(b) during any vacancy in the office of President.
. . .

Membership of Panels

4.— (1) The President must make arrangements for determining the membership of Panels.
(2) The arrangements must ensure that a Panel determining an application under section 1(1)(a) includes—
(a) at least one legal member, and
(b) at least one medical member.

5. The arrangements must ensure that a Panel determining an application under section 1(1)(b), 5(2) or 6(1) includes at least one legal member.

Procedure

6.— (1) Where a Panel consists of more than one member, either the President or Deputy President or another legal member nominated by the President must preside.
(2) Decisions of a Panel consisting of more than one member may be taken by majority vote (and, if its members are evenly split, the member presiding has a casting vote).
(3) Panels are to determine applications in private.
(4) A Panel must determine an application without a hearing unless the Panel considers that a hearing is necessary.
(5) The President may, after consulting the Council on Tribunals, give directions about the practice and procedure of Panels.
(6) Panels must give reasons for their decisions.
(7) Where a Panel has determined an application, the Secretary of State must communicate to the applicant the Panel's decision and its reasons for making its decision.

SCHEDULE 3 Section 10

REGISTRATION

PART 1

ENGLAND AND WALES

Introductory

1. In this Part—
'the Registrar General' means the Registrar General for England and Wales, and
'the 1953 Act' means the Births and Deaths Registration Act 1953.

Gender Recognition Register

2.— (1) The Registrar General must maintain, in the General Register Office, a register to be called the Gender Recognition Register.
(2) In this Part 'the Gender Recognition Register' means the register maintained under sub-paragraph (1).
(3) The form in which the Gender Recognition Register is maintained is to be determined by the Registrar General.
(4) The Gender Recognition Register is not to be open to public inspection or search.

Entries in Gender Recognition Register and marking of existing birth register entries

3.— (1) If the Registrar General receives under section 10(1) a copy of a full gender recognition certificate issued to a person, the Registrar General must—
(a) make an entry in the Gender Recognition Register containing such particulars as may be prescribed in relation to the person's birth and any other prescribed matter,
(b) secure that the UK birth register entry is marked in such manner as may be prescribed, and
(c) make traceable the connection between the entry in the Gender Recognition Register and the UK birth register entry.

(2) Sub-paragraph (1) does not apply if the certificate was issued after an application under section 6(1) and that sub-paragraph has already been complied with in relation to the person.

(3) No certified copy of the UK birth register entry and no short certificate of birth compiled from that entry is to include anything marked by virtue of sub-paragraph (1)(b).

(4) Information kept by the Registrar General for the purposes of sub-paragraph (1)(c) is not to be open to public inspection or search.

(5) 'Prescribed' means prescribed by regulations made by the Registrar General with the approval of the Chancellor of the Exchequer.

Indexing of entries in Gender Recognition Register

4.— (1) The Registrar General must make arrangements for each entry made in the Gender Recognition Register to be included in the relevant index kept in the General Register Office.

(2) Any right to search the relevant index includes the right to search entries included in it by virtue of sub-paragraph (1).

(3) Where by virtue of sub-paragraph (1) an index includes entries in the Gender Recognition Register, the index must not disclose that fact.

(4) 'The relevant index', in relation to an entry made in the Gender Recognition Register in relation to a person, means the index of the certified copies of entries in registers, or of entries in registers, which includes the person's UK birth register entry.

Certified copies of entries in Gender Recognition Register

5.— (1) Anyone who may have a certified copy of the UK birth register entry of a person issued with a full gender recognition certificate may have a certified copy of the entry made in relation to the person in the Gender Recognition Register.

(2) Any fee which would be payable for a certified copy of the person's UK birth register entry is payable for a certified copy of the entry made in relation to the person in the Gender Recognition Register.

(3) If the person's UK birth register entry is an entry in the Gender Recognition Register, sub-paragraph (1) applies as if the person's UK birth register entry were the most recent entry within section 10(2)(a) or (b) containing a record of the person's birth or adoption which is not an entry in the Gender Recognition Register.

(4) A certified copy of an entry in the Gender Recognition Register must not disclose the fact that the entry is contained in the Gender Recognition Register.

(5) A certified copy of an entry in the Gender Recognition Register must be sealed or stamped with the seal of the General Register Office.

Short certificates of birth compiled from Gender Recognition Register

6. Where a short certificate of birth under section 33 of the 1953 Act is compiled from the Gender Recognition Register, the certificate must not disclose that fact.

Gender Recognition Register: re-registration

7.— (1) Section 10A of the 1953 Act (re-registration where parents not married) applies where an entry relating to a person's birth has been made in the Gender Recognition Register as where the birth of a child has been registered under that Act.

(2) In its application by virtue of sub-paragraph (1) section 10A has effect—

(a) as if the reference to the registrar in subsection (1) were to the Registrar General, and

(b) with the omission of subsection (2).

(3) Sections 14 and 14A of the 1953 Act (re-registration in cases of legitimation and after declaration of parentage) apply where an entry relating to a person's birth has been made in the Gender Recognition Register as if the references in those sections to the Registrar General authorising re-registration of the person's birth were to the Registrar General's re-registering it.

Correction etc. of Gender Recognition Register

8.— (1) Any power or duty of the Registrar General or any other person to correct, alter, amend, mark or cancel the marking of a person's UK birth register entry is exercisable, or falls to

5. be performed, by the Registrar General in relation to an entry in the Gender Recognition Register which—
(a) relates to that person, and
(b) under paragraph 4(1) is included in the index which includes the person's UK birth register entry.
(2) If the person's UK birth register entry is an entry in the Gender Recognition Register, the references in sub-paragraph (1) to the person's UK birth register entry are to the most recent entry within section 10(2)(a) or (b) containing a record of the person's birth or adoption which is not an entry in the Gender Recognition Register.
(3) The Registrar General may correct the Gender Recognition Register by entry in the margin (without any alteration of the original entry) in consequence of the issue of a full gender recognition certificate after an application under section 6(1).

Revocation of gender recognition certificate etc.

9.— (1) This paragraph applies if, after an entry has been made in the Gender Recognition Register in relation to a person, the High Court or the Court of Session makes an order under section 8(6) quashing the decision to grant the person's application under section 1(1) or 5(2).
(2) The High Court or the Court of Session must inform the Registrar General.
(3) Subject to any appeal, the Registrar General must—
(a) cancel the entry in the Gender Recognition Register, and
(b) cancel, or secure the cancellation, of any marking of an entry relating to the person made by virtue of paragraph 3(1)(b).

Evidence

10.— (1) Section 34(5) of the 1953 Act (certified copy of entry in register under that Act deemed to be true copy) applies in relation to the Gender Recognition Register as if it were a register under that Act.
(2) A certified copy of an entry made in the Gender Recognition Register in relation to a person is to be received, without further or other proof, as evidence—
(a) if the relevant index is the index of the Adopted Children Register, of the matters of which a certified copy of an entry in that Register is evidence,
(b) if the relevant index is the index of the Parental Order Register, of the matters of which a certified copy of an entry in that Register is evidence, and
(c) otherwise, of the person's birth.
(3) And any certified copy which is receivable in evidence of any matter in Northern Ireland by virtue of paragraph 31(2)(a) or (b) of this Schedule is also receivable as evidence of that matter in England and Wales.

Regulatory reform

11. The Chancellor of the Exchequer may by order amend this Part in consequence of any order under section 1 of the Regulatory Reform Act 2001 which includes provision relating to the system of registration of births and adoptions in England and Wales.

. . .

DOMESTIC VIOLENCE, CRIME AND VICTIMS ACT 2004
(2004 c. 28)

Causing or allowing the death of a child or vulnerable adult

5. The offence

(1) A person ('D') is guilty of an offence if—
(a) a child or vulnerable adult ('V') dies as a result of the unlawful act of a person who—
(i) was a member of the same household as V, and
(ii) had frequent contact with him,
(b) D was such a person at the time of that act,

(c) at that time there was a significant risk of serious physical harm being caused to V by the unlawful act of such a person, and
(d) either D was the person whose act caused V's death or—
(i) D was, or ought to have been, aware of the risk mentioned in paragraph (c),
(ii) D failed to take such steps as he could reasonably have been expected to take to protect V from the risk, and
(iii) the act occurred in circumstances of the kind that D foresaw or ought to have foreseen.

(2) The prosecution does not have to prove whether it is the first alternative in subsection (1)(d) or the second (sub-paragraphs (i) to (iii)) that applies.

(3) If D was not the mother or father of V—
(a) D may not be charged with an offence under this section if he was under the age of 16 at the time of the act that caused V's death;
(b) for the purposes of subsection (1)(d)(ii) D could not have been expected to take any such step as is referred to there before attaining that age.

(4) For the purposes of this section—
(a) a person is to be regarded as a 'member' of a particular household, even if he does not live in that household, if he visits it so often and for such periods of time that it is reasonable to regard him as a member of it;
(b) where V lived in different households at different times, 'the same household as V' refers to the household in which V was living at the time of the act that caused V's death.

(5) For the purposes of this section an 'unlawful' act is one that—
(a) constitutes an offence, or
(b) would constitute an offence but for being the act of—
(i) a person under the age of ten, or
(ii) a person entitled to rely on a defence of insanity. Paragraph (b) does not apply to an act of D.

(6) In this section—
'act' includes a course of conduct and also includes omission;
'child' means a person under the age of 16;
'serious' harm means harm that amounts to grievous bodily harm for the purposes of the Offences against the Person Act 1861;
'vulnerable adult' means a person aged 16 or over whose ability to protect himself from violence, abuse or neglect is significantly impaired through physical or mental disability or illness, through old age or otherwise.

(7) A person guilty of an offence under this section is liable on conviction on indictment to imprisonment for a term not exceeding 14 years or to a fine, or to both.

CHILDREN ACT 2004
(2004 c. 31)

PART 1
CHILDREN'S COMMISSIONER

1. Establishment

(1) There is to be an office of Children's Commissioner.
(2) Schedule 1 has effect with respect to the Children's Commissioner.

2. General function

(1) The Children's Commissioner has the function of promoting awareness of the views and interests of children in England.
(2) The primary function includes promoting awareness of the views and interests of children in England.

2A. United Nations Convention on the Rights of the Child

(1) The Children's Commissioner must in particular have regard to the United Nations Convention on the Rights of the Child in considering for the purposes of the primary function what constitutes the rights and interests of children (generally or so far as relates to a particular matter).

...

2B. Involving children in the discharge of the primary function

(1) The Children's Commissioner must take reasonable steps to involve children in the discharge of the primary function.

...

2C. Primary function: reports

(1) This section applies where the Children's Commissioner publishes a report in the discharge of the primary function.

(2) The Commissioner must if and to the extent that he or she considers it appropriate also to publish the report in a version that is suitable for children (or, if the report relates to a particular group of children, for those children).

(3) Where the report contains recommendations about the exercise by a person of functions of a public nature, the Commissioner may require that person to state in writing, within such period as the Commissioner may reasonably require, what action the person has taken or proposes to take in response to the recommendations.

2D. Provision of advice and assistance to certain children in England

(1) The Children's Commissioner may provide advice and assistance to any child who is within section 8A (children living away from home or receiving social care).

...

(3) In the discharge of the primary function, the Children's Commissioner may in particular —
- (a) advise persons exercising functions or engaged in activities affecting children on how to act compatibly with the rights of children;
- (b) encourage such persons to take account of the views and interests of children;
- (c) advise the Secretary of State on the rights, views and interests of children;
- (d) consider the potential effect on the rights of children of government policy and proposals for legislation;
- (e) bring any matter to the attention of either House of Parliament;
- (f) investigate the availability and effectiveness of complaints procedures so far as relating to children;
- (g) investigate the availability and effectiveness of advocacy services for children;
- (h) investigate any other matter relating to the rights or interests of children;
- (i) monitor the implementation in England of the United Nation Convention on the Rights of the Child;
- (j) publish a report on any matter considered or investigated under this section.

(4) In the discharge of the primary function, the Children's Commissioner must have particular regard to the rights of children who are within section 8A (children living away from home or receiving social care) and other groups of children who the Commissioner considers to be at particular risk of having their rights infringed.

...

3. Inquiries initiated by Commissioner

(1) Where the Children's Commissioner considers that the case of an individual child in England raises issues of public policy of relevance to other children, he may hold an inquiry into that case for the purpose of investigating and making recommendations about those issues.

(2) The Children's Commissioner may only conduct an inquiry under this section if he is satisfied that the inquiry would not duplicate work that is the function of another person (having consulted such persons as he considers appropriate).

...

4. Other inquiries held by Commissioner

(1) Where the Secretary of State considers that the case of an individual child in England raises issues of relevance to other children, he may direct the Children's Commissioner to hold an inquiry into that case.

(2) The Children's Commissioner may, if he thinks fit, hold an inquiry under this section, or any part of it, in private.

(3) The Children's Commissioner must, as soon as possible after the completion of an inquiry under this section, make a report in relation to the inquiry and send a copy to the Secretary of State.

(4) The Secretary of State must, subject to subsection (5), publish each report received by him under this section as soon as possible.

(5) Where a report made under this section identifies an individual child and the Secretary of State considers that it would be undesirable for the identity of the child to be made public—
- (a) the Secretary of State may make such amendments to the report as are necessary to protect the identity of the child and publish the amended report only; or
- (b) if he considers that it is not possible to publish the report without identifying the child, he need not publish the report.

(6) The Secretary of State must lay a copy of each report published by him under this section before each House of Parliament.

(7) Subsections (2) to (5) of section 250 of the Local Government Act 1972 apply for the purposes of an inquiry held under this section.

5. Functions of Commissioner in Wales

(1) The Children's Commissioner has the function of promoting awareness of the views and interests of children in Wales, except in so far as relating to any matter falling within the remit of the Children's Commissioner for Wales under section 72B, 73 or 74 of the Care Standards Act 2000.

...

8. Annual reports

(1) As soon as possible after the end of each financial year the Children's Commissioner must make a report on—
   (a) the way in which he has discharged his functions under this Part, other than functions of holding inquiries;
   (b) what he has found in the course of exercising those functions during the year;
   (c) the matters he intends to consider or research in the next financial year.

...

8A. Children in England living away from home or receiving social care

(c) the matters he intends to consider or research in the next financial year.

...

(2) A child is within this subsection if he or she is provided with accommodation by a school or college in England to which section 87(1) of the Chldren Act 1989 applies.

...

PART 2

CHILDREN'S SERVICES IN ENGLAND

General

9A. Targets for safeguarding and promoting the welfare of children

(1) The Secretary of State may, in accordance with regulations, set safeguarding targets for a children's services authority in England.

...

(4) 'Safeguarding targets', in relation to a children's services authority in England, are targets for safeguarding and promoting the welfare of children in the authority's area.

10. Co-operation to improve well-being

(1) Each children's services authority in England must make arrangements to promote co-operation between—
   (a) the authority;
   (b) each of the authority's relevant partners; and
   (c) such other persons or bodies as the authority consider appropriate, being persons or bodies of any nature who exercise functions or are engaged in activities in relation to children in the authority's area.

(2) The arrangements are to be made with a view to improving the well-being of children in the authority's area so far as relating to—
   (a) physical and mental health and emotional well-being;
   (b) protection from harm and neglect;
   (c) education, training and recreation;
   (d) the contribution made by them to society;
   (e) social and economic well-being.

(3) In making arrangements under this section a children's services authority in England must have regard to the importance of parents and other persons caring for children in improving the well-being of children.

...

12. Information databases

(1) The Secretary of State may for the purpose of arrangements under section 10 or 11 above or under section 175 of the Education Act 2002—
   (a) by regulations require children's services authorities in England to establish and operate databases containing information in respect of persons to whom such arrangements relate;
   (b) himself establish and operate, or make arrangements for the operation and establishment of, one or more databases containing such information.

(2) The Secretary of State may for the purposes of arrangements under subsection (1)(b) by regulations establish a body corporate to establish and operate one or more databases.

(3) A database under this section may only include information falling within subsection (4) in relation to a person to whom arrangements specified in subsection (1) relate.

(4) The information referred to in subsection (3) is information of the following descriptions in relation to a person—
(a) his name, address, gender and date of birth;
(b) a number identifying him;
(c) the name and contact details of any person with parental responsibility for him (within the meaning of section 3 of the Children Act 1989) or who has care of him at any time;
(d) details of any education being received by him (including the name and contact details of any educational institution attended by him);
(e) the name and contact details of any person providing primary medical services in relation to him under Part 1 of the National Health Service Act 1977;
(f) the name and contact details of any person providing to him services of such description as the Secretary of State may by regulations specify;
(g) information as to the existence of any cause for concern in relation to him;
(h) information of such other description, not including medical records or other personal records, as the Secretary of State may by regulations specify.

(5) The Secretary of State may by regulations make provision in relation to the establishment and operation of any database or databases under this section.

(6) Regulations under subsection (5) may in particular make provision—
(a) as to the information which must or may be contained in any database under this section (subject to subsection (3));
(b) requiring a person or body specified in subsection (7) to disclose information for inclusion in the database;
(c) permitting a person or body specified in subsection (8) to disclose information for inclusion in the database;
(d) permitting or requiring the disclosure of information included in any such database;
(e) permitting or requiring any person to be given access to any such database for the purpose of adding or reading information;
(f) as to the conditions on which such access must or may be given;
(g) as to the length of time for which information must or may be retained;
(h) as to procedures for ensuring the accuracy of information included in any such database;
(i) in a case where a database is established by virtue of subsection (1)(b), requiring children's services authorities in England to participate in the operation of the database.

(7) The persons and bodies referred to in subsection (6)(b) are—
(a) the persons and bodies specified in section 11(1);
(b) the Learning and Skills Council for England;
(c) the governing body of a maintained school in England (within the meaning of section 175 of the Education Act 2002);
(d) the governing body of an institution in England within the further education sector (within the meaning of that section);
(e) the proprietor of an independent school in England (within the meaning of the Education Act 1996);
(f) a person or body of such other description as the Secretary of State may by regulations specify.

(8) The persons and bodies referred to in subsection (6)(c) are—
(a) a person registered in England for child minding or the provision of day care under Part 10A of the Children Act 1989);
(b) a voluntary organisation exercising functions or engaged in activities in relation to persons to whom arrangements specified in subsection (1) relate;
(c) the Commissioners of Inland Revenue;
(d) a registered social landlord;
(e) a person or body of such other description as the Secretary of State may by regulations specify.

(9) The Secretary of State may provide information for inclusion in a database under this section.

(10) The provision which may be made under subsection (6)(e) includes provision for a person of a description specified in the regulations to determine what must or may be done under the regulations.

(11) Regulations under subsection (5) may also provide that anything which may be done under regulations under subsection (6)(c) to (e) or (9) may be done notwithstanding any rule of common law which prohibits or restricts the disclosure of information.

(12) Any person or body establishing or operating a database under this section must in the establishment or operation of the database have regard to any guidance, and comply with any direction, given to that person or body by the Secretary of State.

(13) Guidance or directions under subsection (12) may in particular relate to—
(a) the management of a database under this section;
(b) the technical specifications for any such database;
(c) the security of any such database;
(d) the transfer and comparison of information between databases under this section;
(e) the giving of advice in relation to rights under the Data Protection Act 1998.

Local Safeguarding Children Boards

13. Establishment of LSCBs

(1) Each local authority in England must establish a Local Safeguarding Children Board for their area.
(2) A Board established under this section must include such representative or representatives of—
(a) the authority by which it is established, and
(b) each Board partner of that authority,
as the Secretary of State may by regulations prescribe.
(3) For the purposes of this section each of the following is a Board partner of a children's services authority in England—
(a) where the authority is a county council for an area for which there is also a district council, the district council;
(b) the chief officer of police for a police area any part of which falls within the area of the authority;
(c) a local probation board for an area any part of which falls within the area of the authority;
(ca) the Secretary of State in relation to his functions under sections 2 and 3 of the Offender Management Act 2007, so far as they are exercisable in relation to England;
(cb) any provider of probation services that is required by arrangements under section 3(2) of the Offender Management Act 2007 to act as a Board partner of the authority;
(d) a youth offending team for an area any part of which falls within the area of the authority;
(da) the National Health Service Commissioning Board;
(db) any clinical commissioning group for an area any part of which falls within the area of the authority;
(e) ...
(f) an NHS trust and an NHS foundation trust all or most of whose hospitals, establishments and facilities are situated in the area of the authority;
(g) a person providing services under section 114 of the Learning and Skills Act 2000 in any part of the area of the authority;
(h) the Children and Family Court Advisory and Support Service;
(i) the governor of any secure training centre in the area of the authority (or, in the case of a contracted out secure training centre, its director);
(j) the governor of any prison in the area of the authority which ordinarily detains children (or, in the case of a contracted out prison, its director).
(4) A local authority in England must take reasonable steps to ensure that the Local Safeguarding Children Board established by them includes representatives of relevant persons and bodies of such descriptions as may be prescribed by the Secretary of State in regulations.
(5) A Local Safeguarding Children Board established under this section may also include representatives of such other relevant persons or bodies as the authority by which it is established consider, after consulting their Board partners, should be represented on it.
(5A) A local authority in England must take reasonable steps to ensure that the Local Safeguarding Children Board established by them also includes two persons who appear to the authority to be representative of persons living in the authority's area.
(5B) An authority may pay remuneration, allowances and expenses to persons who are included by virtue of subsection (5A) in a Local Safeguarding Children Board established by them.
(6) For the purposes of subsections (4) and (5), relevant persons and bodies are persons and bodies of any nature exercising functions or engaged in activities relating to children in the area of the authority in question.
(7) In the establishment and operation of a Local Safeguarding Children Board under this section—
(a) the authority establishing it must co-operate with each of their Board partners; and
(b) each Board partner must co-operate with the authority.

(8) Two or more local authorities in England may discharge their respective duties under subsection (1) by establishing a Local Safeguarding Children Board for their combined area (and where they do so, any reference in this section or sections 14 to 16 to the authority establishing the Board shall be read as a reference to the authorities establishing it).

14. Functions and procedure of LSCBs

(1) The objective of a Local Safeguarding Children Board established under section 13 is—
   (a) to co-ordinate what is done by each person or body represented on the Board for the purposes of safeguarding and promoting the welfare of children in the area of the authority by which it is established; and
   (b) to ensure the effectiveness of what is done by each such person or body for those purposes.

(2) A Local Safeguarding Children Board established under section 13 is to have such functions in relation to its objective as the Secretary of State may by regulations prescribe (which may in particular include functions of review or investigation).

(3) The Secretary of State may by regulations make provision as to the procedures to be followed by a Local Safeguarding Children Board established under section 13.

Local authority administration

18. Director of children's services

(1) A local authority in England may, and with effect from the appointed day must, appoint an officer for the purposes of—
   (a) the functions conferred on or exercisable by the authority which are specified in subsection (2); and
   (b) such other functions conferred on or exercisable by the authority as may be prescribed by the Secretary of State by regulations.

(2) The functions referred to in subsection (1)(a) are—
   (a) functions conferred on or exercisable by the authority in their capacity as a local education authority;
   (b) functions conferred on or exercisable by the authority which are social services functions (within the meaning of the Local Authority Social Services Act 1970), so far as those functions relate to children;
   (c) the functions conferred on the authority under sections 23C to 24D of the Children Act 1989 (so far as not falling within paragraph (b));
   (d) the functions conferred on the authority under sections 10 to 12, 12C, 12D and 17 of this Act; and
   (e) any functions exercisable by the authority under section 75 of the National Health Act 2006 or section 33 of the National Health Service (Wales) Act 2006 on behalf of an NHS body (within the meaning of that section), so far as those functions relate to children.

(3) Subsection (2)(a) does not include—
   (a) functions under section 120(3) of the Education Reform Act 1988 (functions of LEAs with respect to higher and further education);
   (b) functions under section 85(2) and (3) of the Further and Higher Education Act 1992 (finance and government of locally funded further and higher education);
   (c) functions under section 15B of the Education Act 1996 (education for persons who have attained the age of 19);
   (d) functions under section 22 of the Teaching and Higher Education Act 1998 (financial support to students);
   (e) such other functions conferred on or exercisable by a children's services authority in England in their capacity as a local education authority as the Secretary of State may by regulations prescribe.

(4) An officer appointed by a children's services authority in England under this section is to be known as their 'director of children's services'.

(5) The director of children's services appointed by a children's services authority in England may also have responsibilities relating to such functions conferred on or exercisable by the authority, in addition to those specified in subsection (1), as the authority consider appropriate.

(6) The functions in relation to which a director of children's services may have responsibilities by virtue of subsection (5) include those referred to in subsection (3)(a) to (e).

(7) A local authority in England must have regard to any guidance given to them by the Secretary of State for the purposes of this section.

(8) Two or more local authorities in England may for the purposes of this section, if they consider that the same person can efficiently discharge, for both or all of them, the

responsibilities of director of children's services, concur in the appointment of a person as director of children's services for both or all of them.

(9) The amendments in Schedule 2—

(a) have effect, in relation to any authority which appoint a director of children's services before the appointed day, from the day of his appointment; and

(b) on and after the appointed day have effect for all purposes.

(10) In this section, 'the appointed day' means such day as the Secretary of State may by order appoint.

19. Lead member for children's services

(1) A local authority in England must, in making arrangements for the discharge of—

(a) the functions conferred on or exercisable by the authority specified in section 18(1)(a) and (b), and

(b) such other functions conferred on or exercisable by the authority as the authority consider appropriate,

designate one of their members as their 'lead member for children's services'.

(2) A children's services authority in England must have regard to any guidance given to them by the Secretary of State for the purposes of subsection (1).

PART 3

CHILDREN'S SERVICES IN WALES

General

25. Co-operation to improve well-being: Wales

(1) Each children's services authority in Wales must make arrangements to promote co-operation between—

(a) the authority;

(b) each of the authority's relevant partners; and

(c) such other persons or bodies as the authority consider appropriate, being persons or bodies of any nature who exercise functions or are engaged in activities in relation to children in the authority's area.

(2) The arrangements are to be made with a view to improving the well-being of children in the authority's area so far as relating to—

(a) physical and mental health and emotional well-being;

(b) protection from harm and neglect;

(c) education, training and recreation;

(d) the contribution made by them to society;

(e) social and economic well-being.

(3) In making arrangements under this section a children's services authority in Wales must have regard to the importance of parents and other persons caring for children in improving the well-being of children.

...

(8) A local authority in Wales and each of their relevant partners must in exercising their functions under this section have regard to any guidance given to them for the purpose by the Assembly.

...

26. Children and young people's plans: Wales

(1A) A local authority in Wales must, in accordance with regulations made by the Welsh Ministers, prepare and publish a plan setting out the authority's strategy for discharging their functions in relation to children and relevant young persons.

...

Local Safeguarding Children Boards

31. Establishment of LSCBs in Wales

(1) Each local authority in Wales must establish a Local Safeguarding Children Board for their area.

(2) A Board established under this section must include such representative or representatives of—

(a) the authority by which it is established, and

(b) each Board partner of that authority,

as the Assembly may by regulations prescribe.

...

PART 4
ADVISORY AND SUPPORT SERVICES FOR FAMILY PROCEEDINGS

CAFCASS functions in Wales

35. Functions of the Assembly relating to family proceedings

(1) In respect of family proceedings in which the welfare of children ordinarily resident in Wales is or may be in question, it is a function of the Assembly to—
   (a) safeguard and promote the welfare of the children;
   (b) give advice to any court about any application made to it in such proceedings;
   (c) make provision for the children to be represented in such proceedings;
   (d) provide information, advice and other support for the children and their families.

(2) The Assembly must also make provision for the performance of the functions conferred on Welsh family proceedings officers by virtue of any enactment (whether or not they are exercisable for the purposes of subsection (1)).

(3) In subsection (1), 'family proceedings' has the meaning given by section 12 of the Criminal Justice and Court Services Act 2000.

(4) In this Part, 'Welsh family proceedings officer' means—
   (a) any member of the staff of the Assembly appointed to exercise the functions of a Welsh family proceedings officer; and
   (b) any other individual exercising functions of a Welsh family proceedings officer by virtue of section 36(2) or (4).

36. Ancillary powers of the Assembly

(1) The Assembly may make arrangements with organisations under which the organisations perform the functions of the Assembly under section 35 on its behalf.

(2) Arrangements under subsection (1) may provide for the organisations to designate individuals who may perform functions of Welsh family proceedings officers.

(3) The Assembly may only make an arrangement under subsection (1) if it is of the opinion—
   (a) that the functions in question will be performed efficiently and to the required standard; and
   (b) that the arrangement represents good value for money.

(4) The Assembly may make arrangements with individuals under which they may perform functions of Welsh family proceedings officers.

(5) The Assembly may make arrangements with an organisation or individual under which staff of the Assembly engaged in the exercise of its functions under section 35 may work for the organisation or individual.

(6) The Assembly may make arrangements with an organisation or individual under which any services provided by the Assembly's staff to the Assembly in the exercise of its functions under section 35 are also made available to the organisation or individual.

(7) The Assembly may charge for anything done under arrangements under subsection (5) and (6).

(8) In this section, references to organisations include public bodies and private or voluntary organisations.

37. Welsh family proceedings officers

(1) The Assembly may authorise a Welsh family proceedings officer of a description prescribed in regulations made by the Secretary of State—
   (a) to conduct litigation in relation to any proceedings in any court,
   (b) to exercise a right of audience in any proceedings in any court,

   in the exercise of his functions.

(2) A Welsh family proceedings officer exercising a right to conduct litigation by virtue of subsection (1)(a) who would otherwise have such a right by virtue of section 28(2)(a) of the Courts and Legal Services Act 1990 is to be treated as having acquired that right solely by virtue of this section.

(3) A Welsh family proceedings officer exercising a right of audience by virtue of subsection (1)(b) who would otherwise have such a right by virtue of section 27(2)(a) of the Courts and Legal Services Act 1990 is to be treated as having acquired that right solely by virtue of this section.

(4) A Welsh family proceedings officer may, subject to rules of court, be cross-examined in any proceedings to the same extent as any witness.

(5) But a Welsh family proceedings officer may not be cross-examined merely because he is exercising a right to conduct litigation or a right of audience granted in accordance with this section.

(6) In this section, 'right to conduct litigation' and 'right of audience' have the same meanings as in section 119 of the Courts and Legal Services Act 1990.

41. Sharing of information

(1) The Assembly and the Children and Family Court Advisory and Support Service may provide any information to each other for the purposes of their respective functions under this Part and Part 1 of the Criminal Justice and Court Services Act 2000.

(2) A Welsh family proceedings officer and an officer of the Service (within the meaning given by section 11(3) of that Act) may provide any information to each other for the purposes of any of their respective functions.

PART 5
MISCELLANEOUS

Other provisions

58. Reasonable punishment

(1) In relation to any offence specified in subsection (2), battery of a child cannot be justified on the ground that it constituted reasonable punishment.

(2) The offences referred to in subsection (1) are—
  (a) an offence under section 18 or 20 of the Offences against the Person Act 1861 (wounding and causing grievous bodily harm);
  (b) an offence under section 47 of that Act (assault occasioning actual bodily harm);
  (c) an offence under section 1 of the Children and Young Persons Act 1933 (cruelty to persons under 16).

(3) Battery of a child causing actual bodily harm to the child cannot be justified in any civil proceedings on the ground that it constituted reasonable punishment.

(4) For the purposes of subsection (3) 'actual bodily harm' has the same meaning as it has for the purposes of section 47 of the Offences against the Person Act 1861.

...

CIVIL PARTNERSHIP ACT 2004
(2004 c. 33)

PART 1
INTRODUCTION

1. Civil partnership

(1) A civil partnership is a relationship between two people of the same sex ('civil partners')—
  (a) which is formed when they register as civil partners of each other—
    (i) in England or Wales (under Part 2),
    . . .

(2) Subsection (1) is subject to the provisions of this Act under or by virtue of which a civil partnership is void.

(3) A civil partnership ends only—
  (a) on death, dissolution or annulment, or
  (b) in the case of a civil partnership formed as mentioned in subsection (1)(a)(i) or (iv), on the conversion of the civil partnership into a marriage under section 9 of the Marriage (Same Sex Couples) Act 2013.

(4) The references in subsection (3) to dissolution and annulment are to dissolution and annulment having effect under or recognised in accordance with this Act.

...

PART 2
CIVIL PARTNERSHIP: ENGLAND AND WALES

CHAPTER 1
REGISTRATION

Formation, eligibility and parental etc. consent

2. Formation of civil partnership by registration

(1) For the purposes of section 1, two people are to be regarded as having registered as civil partners of each other once each of them has signed the civil partnership document—

(a) at the invitation of, and in the presence of, a civil partnership registrar, and
(b) in the presence of each other and two witnesses.

(2) Subsection (1) applies regardless of whether subsections (3) and (4) are complied with.

(3) After the civil partnership document has been signed under subsection (1), it must also be signed, in the presence of the civil partners and each other, by—
(a) each of the two witnesses, and
(b) the civil partnership registrar.

(4) After the witnesses and the civil partnership registrar have signed the civil partnership document, the relevant registration authority must ensure that—
(a) the fact that the two people have registered as civil partners of each other, and
(b) any other information prescribed by regulations,
is recorded in the register as soon as is practicable.

(5) No religious service is to be used while the civil partnership registrar is officiating at the signing of a civil partnership document.

(6) 'The civil partnership document' has the meaning given by section 7(1).

(7) 'The relevant registration authority' means the registration authority in whose area the registration takes place.

3. Eligibility

(1) Two people are not eligible to register as civil partners of each other if—
(a) they are not of the same sex,
(b) either of them is already a civil partner or lawfully married,
(c) either of them is under 16, or
(d) they are within prohibited degrees of relationship.

(2) Part 1 of Schedule 1 contains provisions for determining when two people are within prohibited degrees of relationship.

4. Parental etc. consent where proposed civil partner under 18

(1) The consent of the appropriate persons is required before a child and another person may register as civil partners of each other.

(2) Part 1 of Schedule 2 contains provisions for determining who are the appropriate persons for the purposes of this section.

(3) The requirement of consent under subsection (1) does not apply if the child is a surviving civil partner or a widower or a widow.

(4) Nothing in this section affects any need to obtain the consent of the High Court before a ward of court and another person may register as civil partners of each other.

(5) In this Part 'child', except where used to express a relationship, means a person who is under 18.

Registration procedure: general

5. Types of pre-registration procedure

(1) Two people may register as civil partners of each other under—
(a) the standard procedure;
(b) the procedure for house-bound persons;
(c) the procedure for detained persons;
(d) the special procedure (which is for cases where a person is seriously ill and not expected to recover).

(2) The procedures referred to in subsection (1)(a) to (c) are subject to—
(a) section 20 (modified procedures for certain non-residents);
(b) Schedule 3 (former spouses one of whom has changed sex).

(3) The procedures referred to in subsection (1) (including the procedures as modified by section 20 and Schedule 3) are subject to—
(a) Part 2 of Schedule 1 (provisions applicable in connection with prohibited degrees of relationship), and
(b) Parts 2 and 3 of Schedule 2 (provisions applicable where proposed civil partner is under 18).

(4) This section is also subject to section 249 and Schedule 23 (immigration control and formation of civil partnerships).

6. Place of registration

(1) The place at which two people may register as civil partners of each other—
(a) must be in England or Wales,
(b) ..., and
(c) must be specified in the notices, or notice, of proposed civil partnership required by this Chapter.

(2) ...
(3) Subsections (3A) and (3B) apply in the case of registration under the standard procedure (including that procedure modified as mentioned in section 5).
(3A) The place must be—
(a) on approved premises, or
(b) in a register office.
(3B) If it is in a register office, the place must be open to any person wishing to attend the registration.
(3C) In this Chapter 'register office' means a register office provided under section 10 of the Registration Service Act 1953.

6A. Power to approve premises

(1) The Secretary of State may by regulations make provision for and in connection with ... the approval by registration authorities of premises for the purposes of section 6(3A).
(2A) Regulations under this section may provide that premises approved for the registration of civil partnerships may differ from those premises approved for the registration of civil marriages.
...
(2C) The power conferred by section 258(2), in its application to the power conferred by this section, includes in particular—
(a) power to make provision in relation to religious premises that differs from provision in relation to other premises;
(b) power to make different provision for different kinds of religious premises.
...
(3A) For the avoidance of doubt, nothing in this Act places an obligation on religious organisations to host civil partnerships if they do not wish to do so.
(3B) 'Civil marriage' means marriage solemnised otherwise than according to the rites of the Church of England or any other religious usages.
(3C) 'Religious premises' means premises which—
(a) are used solely or mainly for religious purposes, or
(b) have been so used and have not subsequently been used solely or mainly for other purposes.

7. The civil partnership document

(1) In this Part 'the civil partnership document' means—
(a) in relation to the special procedure, a Registrar General's licence, and
(b) in relation to any other procedure, a civil partnership schedule.
(2) Before two people are entitled to register as civil partners of each other—
(a) the civil partnership document must be delivered to the civil partnership registrar, and
(b) the civil partnership registrar may then ask them for any information required (under section 2(4)) to be recorded in the register.

The standard procedure

8 Notice of proposed civil partnership and declaration

(1) For two people to register as civil partners of each other under the standard procedure a notice of proposed civil partnership must be given—
(a) if the proposed civil partners have resided in the area of the same registration authority for the period of 7 days immediately before the giving of the notice, by each of them to that registration authority;
(b) if the proposed civil partners have not resided in the area of the same registration authority for that period, by each of them to the registration authority in whose area he or she has resided for that period.
(2) A notice of proposed civil partnership must contain such information as may be prescribed by regulations.
(3) A notice of proposed civil partnership must also include the necessary declaration, made and signed by the person giving the notice—
(a) at the time when the notice is given, and
(b) in the presence of an authorised person; and the authorised person must attest the declaration by adding his name, description and place of residence.
(4) The necessary declaration is a solemn declaration in writing—
(a) that the proposed civil partner believes that there is no impediment of kindred or affinity or other lawful hindrance to the formation of the civil partnership;
(b) that each of the proposed civil partners have for the period of 7 days immediately before the giving of the notice had their usual places of residence in the area of the

registration authority, or in the areas of the registration authorities, to which notice is given.

(5) Where a notice of proposed civil partnership is given to a registration authority in accordance with this section, the registration authority must ensure that the following information is recorded in the register as soon as possible—
 (a) the fact that the notice has been given and the information in it;
 (b) the fact that the authorised person has attested the declaration.

(6) 'Authorised person' means an employee or officer or other person provided by a registration authority who is authorised by that authority to attest notices of proposed civil partnership.

(7) For the purposes of this Chapter, a notice of proposed civil partnership is recorded when subsection (5) is complied with.

CHAPTER 2
DISSOLUTION, NULLITY AND OTHER PROCEEDINGS

Introduction

37. Powers to make orders and effect of orders

(1) The court may, in accordance with this Chapter—
 (a) make an order (a 'dissolution order') which dissolves a civil partnership on the ground that it has broken down irretrievably;
 (b) make an order (a 'nullity order') which annuls a civil partnership which is void or voidable;
 (c) make an order (a 'presumption of death order') which dissolves a civil partnership on the ground that one of the civil partners is presumed to be dead;
 (d) make an order (a 'separation order') which provides for the separation of the civil partners.

(2) Every dissolution, nullity or presumption of death order—
 (a) is, in the first instance, a conditional order, and
 (b) may not be made final before the end of the prescribed period (see section 38);

and any reference in this Chapter to a conditional order is to be read accordingly.

(3) A nullity order made where a civil partnership is voidable annuls the civil partnership only as respects any time after the order has been made final, and the civil partnership is to be treated (despite the order) as if it had existed up to that time.

(4) In this Chapter, other than in sections 58 to 61, 'the court' means—
 (a) the High Court, or
 (b) if a county court has jurisdiction by virtue of Part 5 of the Matrimonial and Family Proceedings Act 1984, a county court.

(5) This Chapter is subject to sections 219 to 224 (jurisdiction of the court).

38. The period before conditional orders may be made final

(1) Subject to subsections (2) to (4), the prescribed period for the purposes of section 37(2)(b) is—
 (a) 6 weeks from the making of the conditional order, or
 (b) if the 6 week period would end on a day on which the office or registry of the court dealing with the case is closed, the period of 6 weeks extended to the end of the first day on which the office or registry is next open.

(2) The Lord Chancellor may by order amend this section so as to substitute a different definition of the prescribed period for the purposes of section 37(2)(b).

(3) But the Lord Chancellor may not under subsection (2) provide for a period longer than 6 months to be the prescribed period.

(4) In a particular case the court dealing with the case may by order shorten the prescribed period.

(5) The power to make an order under subsection (2) is exercisable by statutory instrument.

(6) An instrument containing such an order is subject to annulment in pursuance of a resolution of either House of Parliament.

39. Intervention of the Queen's Proctor

(1) This section applies if an application has been made for a dissolution, nullity or presumption of death order.

(2) The court may, if it thinks fit, direct that all necessary papers in the matter are to be sent to the Queen's Proctor who must under the directions of the Attorney General instruct counsel to argue before the court any question in relation to the matter which the court considers it necessary or expedient to have fully argued.

(3) If any person at any time—

(a) during the progress of the proceedings, or
(b) before the conditional order is made final,

gives information to the Queen's Proctor on any matter material to the due decision of the case, the Queen's Proctor may take such steps as the Attorney General considers necessary or expedient.

(4) If the Queen's Proctor intervenes or shows cause against the making of the conditional order in any proceedings relating to its making, the court may make such order as may be just as to—
(a) the payment by other parties to the proceedings of the costs incurred by him in doing so, or
(b) the payment by the Queen's Proctor of any costs incurred by any of those parties because of his doing so.

(5) The Queen's Proctor is entitled to charge as part of the expenses of his office—
(a) the costs of any proceedings under subsection (2);
(b) if his reasonable costs of intervening or showing cause as mentioned in subsection (4) are not fully satisfied by an order under subsection (4)(a), the amount of the difference;
(c) if the Treasury so directs, any costs which he pays to any parties under an order made under subsection (4)(b).

40. Proceedings before order has been made final

(1) This section applies if—
(a) a conditional order has been made, and
(b) the Queen's Proctor, or any person who has not been a party to proceedings in which the order was made, shows cause why the order should not be made final on the ground that material facts have not been brought before the court.

(2) This section also applies if—
(a) a conditional order has been made,
(b) 3 months have elapsed since the earliest date on which an application could have been made for the order to be made final,
(c) no such application has been made by the civil partner who applied for the conditional order, and
(d) the other civil partner makes an application to the court under this subsection.

(3) The court may—
(a) make the order final,
(b) rescind the order,
(c) require further inquiry, or
(d) otherwise deal with the case as it thinks fit.

(4) Subsection (3)(a)—
(a) applies despite section 37(2) (period before conditional orders may be made final), but
(b) is subject to section 48(4) (protection for respondent in separation cases) and section 63 (restrictions on making of orders affecting children).

41. Time bar on applications for dissolution orders

(1) No application for a dissolution order may be made to the court before the end of the period of 1 year from the date of the formation of the civil partnership.

(2) Nothing in this section prevents the making of an application based on matters which occurred before the end of the 1 year period.

42. Attempts at reconciliation of civil partners

(1) This section applies in relation to cases where an application is made for a dissolution or separation order.

(2) Rules of court must make provision for requiring the solicitor acting for the applicant to certify whether he has—
(a) discussed with the applicant the possibility of a reconciliation with the other civil partner, and
(b) given the applicant the names and addresses of persons qualified to help effect a reconciliation between civil partners who have become estranged.

(3) If at any stage of proceedings for the order it appears to the court that there is a reasonable possibility of a reconciliation between the civil partners, the court may adjourn the proceedings for such period as it thinks fit to enable attempts to be made to effect a reconciliation between them.

(4) The power to adjourn under subsection (3) is additional to any other power of adjournment.

43. Consideration by the court of certain agreements or arrangements

(1) This section applies in relation to cases where—

(a) proceedings for a dissolution or separation order are contemplated or have begun, and
(b) an agreement or arrangement is made or proposed to be made between the civil partners which relates to, arises out of, or is connected with, the proceedings.

(2) Rules of court may make provision for enabling—
(a) the civil partners, or either of them, to refer the agreement or arrangement to the court, and
(b) the court—
(i) to express an opinion, if it thinks it desirable to do so, as to the reasonableness of the agreement or arrangement, and
(ii) to give such directions, if any, in the matter as it thinks fit.

Dissolution of civil partnership

44. Dissolution of civil partnership which has broken down irretrievably

(1) Subject to section 41, an application for a dissolution order may be made to the court by either civil partner on the ground that the civil partnership has broken down irretrievably.

(2) On an application for a dissolution order the court must inquire, so far as it reasonably can, into—
(a) the facts alleged by the applicant, and
(b) any facts alleged by the respondent.

(3) The court hearing an application for a dissolution order must not hold that the civil partnership has broken down irretrievably unless the applicant satisfies the court of one or more of the facts described in subsection (5)(a), (b), (c) or (d).

(4) But if the court is satisfied of any of those facts, it must make a dissolution order unless it is satisfied on all the evidence that the civil partnership has not broken down irretrievably.

(5) The facts referred to in subsections (3) and (4) are—
(a) that the respondent has behaved in such a way that the applicant cannot reasonably be expected to live with the respondent;
(b) that—
(i) the applicant and the respondent have lived apart for a continuous period of at least 2 years immediately preceding the making of the application ('2 years' separation'), and
(ii) the respondent consents to a dissolution order being made;
(c) that the applicant and the respondent have lived apart for a continuous period of at least 5 years immediately preceding the making of the application ('5 years' separation');
(d) that the respondent has deserted the applicant for a continuous period of at least 2 years immediately preceding the making of the application.

45. Supplemental provisions as to facts raising presumption of breakdown

(1) Subsection (2) applies if—
(a) in any proceedings for a dissolution order the applicant alleges, in reliance on section 44(5)(a), that the respondent has behaved in such a way that the applicant cannot reasonably be expected to live with the respondent, but
(b) after the date of the occurrence of the final incident relied on by the applicant and held by the court to support his allegation, the applicant and the respondent have lived together for a period (or periods) which does not, or which taken together do not, exceed 6 months.

(2) The fact that the applicant and respondent have lived together as mentioned in subsection (1)(b) must be disregarded in determining, for the purposes of section 44(5)(a), whether the applicant cannot reasonably be expected to live with the respondent.

(3) Subsection (4) applies in relation to cases where the applicant alleges, in reliance on section 44(5)(b), that the respondent consents to a dissolution order being made.

(4) Rules of court must make provision for the purpose of ensuring that the respondent has been given such information as will enable him to understand—
(a) the consequences to him of consenting to the making of the order, and
(b) the steps which he must take to indicate his consent.

(5) For the purposes of section 44(5)(d) the court may treat a period of desertion as having continued at a time when the deserting civil partner was incapable of continuing the necessary intention, if the evidence before the court is such that, had he not been so incapable, the court would have inferred that the desertion continued at that time.

(6) In considering for the purposes of section 44(5) whether the period for which the civil partners have lived apart or the period for which the respondent has deserted the applicant has been continuous, no account is to be taken of—
(a) any one period not exceeding 6 months, or

(b) any two or more periods not exceeding 6 months in all,

during which the civil partners resumed living with each other.

(7) But no period during which the civil partners have lived with each other counts as part of the period during which the civil partners have lived apart or as part of the period of desertion.

(8) For the purposes of section 44(5)(b) and (c) and this section civil partners are to be treated as living apart unless they are living with each other in the same household, and references in this section to civil partners living with each other are to be read as references to their living with each other in the same household.

46. Dissolution order not precluded by previous separation order etc.

(1) Subsections (2) and (3) apply if any of the following orders has been made in relation to a civil partnership—

(a) a separation order;

(b) an order under Schedule 6 (financial relief in magistrates' courts etc.);

(c) an order under section 33 of the Family Law Act 1996 (occupation orders);

(d) an order under section 37 of the 1996 Act (orders where neither civil partner entitled to occupy the home).

(2) Nothing prevents—

(a) either civil partner from applying for a dissolution order, or

(b) the court from making a dissolution order,

on the same facts, or substantially the same facts, as those proved in support of the making of the order referred to in subsection (1).

(3) On the application for the dissolution order, the court—

(a) may treat the order referred to in subsection (1) as sufficient proof of any desertion or other fact by reference to which it was made, but

(b) must not make the dissolution order without receiving evidence from the applicant.

(4) If—

(a) the application for the dissolution order follows a separation order or any order requiring the civil partners to live apart,

(b) there was a period of desertion immediately preceding the institution of the proceedings for the separation order, and

(c) the civil partners have not resumed living together and the separation order has been continuously in force since it was made,

the period of desertion is to be treated for the purposes of the application for the dissolution order as if it had immediately preceded the making of the application.

(5) For the purposes of section 44(5)(d) the court may treat as a period during which the respondent has deserted the applicant any period during which there is in force—

(a) an injunction granted by the High Court or a county court which excludes the respondent from the civil partnership home, or

(b) an order under section 33 or 37 of the 1996 Act which prohibits the respondent from occupying a dwelling-house in which the applicant and the respondent have, or at any time have had, a civil partnership home.

47. Refusal of dissolution in 5 year separation cases on ground of grave hardship

(1) The respondent to an application for a dissolution order in which the applicant alleges 5 years' separation may oppose the making of an order on the ground that—

(a) the dissolution of the civil partnership will result in grave financial or other hardship to him, and

(b) it would in all the circumstances be wrong to dissolve the civil partnership.

(2) Subsection (3) applies if—

(a) the making of a dissolution order is opposed under this section,

(b) the court finds that the applicant is entitled to rely in support of his application on the fact of 5 years' separation and makes no such finding as to any other fact mentioned in section 44(5), and

(c) apart from this section, the court would make a dissolution order.

(3) The court must—

(a) consider all the circumstances, including the conduct of the civil partners and the interests of the civil partners and of any children or other persons concerned, and

(b) if it is of the opinion that the ground mentioned in subsection (1) is made out, dismiss the application for the dissolution order.

(4) 'Hardship' includes the loss of the chance of acquiring any benefit which the respondent might acquire if the civil partnership were not dissolved.

48. Proceedings before order made final: protection for respondent in separation cases

(1) The court may, on an application made by the respondent, rescind a conditional dissolution order if—

(a) it made the order on the basis of a finding that the applicant was entitled to rely on the fact of 2 years separation coupled with the respondent's consent to a dissolution order being made,
(b) it made no such finding as to any other fact mentioned in section 44(5), and
(c) it is satisfied that the applicant misled the respondent (whether intentionally or unintentionally) about any matter which the respondent took into account in deciding to give his consent.

(2) Subsections (3) to (5) apply if—
(a) the respondent to an application for a dissolution order in which the applicant alleged—
(i) 2 years separation coupled with the respondent's consent to a dissolution order being made, or
(ii) 5 years separation,
has applied to the court for consideration under subsection (3) of his financial position after the dissolution of the civil partnership, and
(b) the court—
(i) has made a conditional dissolution order on the basis of a finding that the applicant was entitled to rely in support of his application on the fact of 2 years or 5 years separation, and
(ii) has made no such finding as to any other fact mentioned in section 44(5).

(3) The court hearing an application by the respondent under subsection (2) must consider all the circumstances, including—
(a) the age, health, conduct, earning capacity, financial resources and financial obligations of each of the parties, and
(b) the financial position of the respondent as, having regard to the dissolution, it is likely to be after the death of the applicant should the applicant die first.

(4) Subject to subsection (5), the court must not make the order final unless it is satisfied that—
(a) the applicant should not be required to make any financial provision for the respondent, or
(b) the financial provision made by the applicant for the respondent is—
(i) reasonable and fair, or
(ii) the best that can be made in the circumstances.

(5) The court may if it thinks fit make the order final if—
(a) it appears that there are circumstances making it desirable that the order should be made final without delay, and
(b) it has obtained a satisfactory undertaking from the applicant that he will make such financial provision for the respondent as it may approve.

Nullity

49. Grounds on which civil partnership is void

Where two people register as civil partners of each other in England and Wales, the civil partnership is void if—
(a) at the time when they do so, they are not eligible to register as civil partners of each other under Chapter 1 (see section 3),
(b) at the time when they do so they both know—
(i) that due notice of proposed civil partnership has not been given,
(ii) that the civil partnership document has not been duly issued,
(iii) that the civil partnership document is void under section 17(3) or 27(2) (registration after end of time allowed for registering),
(iv) that the place of registration is a place other than that specified in the notices (or notice) of proposed civil partnership and the civil partnership document, or
(v) that a civil partnership registrar is not present, or
(c) the civil partnership document is void under paragraph 6(5) of Schedule 2 (civil partnership between child and another person forbidden).

50. Grounds on which civil partnership is voidable

(1) Where two people register as civil partners of each other in England and Wales, the civil partnership is voidable if—
(a) either of them did not validly consent to its formation (whether as a result of duress, mistake, unsoundness of mind or otherwise);
(b) at the time of its formation either of them, though capable of giving a valid consent, was suffering (whether continuously or intermittently) from mental disorder of such a kind or to such an extent as to be unfitted for civil partnership;
(c) at the time of its formation, the respondent was pregnant by some person other than the applicant;

(d) an interim gender recognition certificate under the Gender Recognition Act 2004 has, after the time of its formation, been issued to either civil partner;
(e) the respondent is a person whose gender at the time of its formation had become the acquired gender under the 2004 Act.

(2) In this section and section 51 'mental disorder' has the same meaning as in the Mental Health Act 1983.

51. Bars to relief where civil partnership is voidable

(1) The court must not make a nullity order on the ground that a civil partnership is voidable if the respondent satisfies the court—
(a) that the applicant, with knowledge that it was open to him to obtain a nullity order, conducted himself in relation to the respondent in such a way as to lead the respondent reasonably to believe that he would not seek to do so, and
(b) that it would be unjust to the respondent to make the order.

(2) Without prejudice to subsection (1), the court must not make a nullity order by virtue of section 50(1)(a), (b), (c) or (e) unless—
(a) it is satisfied that proceedings were instituted within 3 years from the date of the formation of the civil partnership, or
(b) leave for the institution of proceedings after the end of that 3 year period has been granted under subsection (3).

(3) A judge of the court may, on an application made to him, grant leave for the institution of proceedings if he—
(a) is satisfied that the applicant has at some time during the 3 year period suffered from mental disorder, and
(b) considers that in all the circumstances of the case it would be just to grant leave for the institution of proceedings.

(4) An application for leave under subsection (3) may be made after the end of the 3 year period.

(5) Without prejudice to subsection (1), the court must not make a nullity order by virtue of section 50(1)(d) unless it is satisfied that proceedings were instituted within the period of 6 months from the date of issue of the interim gender recognition certificate.

(6) Without prejudice to subsections (1) and (2), the court must not make a nullity order by virtue of section 50(1)(c) or (e) unless it is satisfied that the applicant was at the time of the formation of the civil partnership ignorant of the facts alleged.

52. Proof of certain matters not necessary to validity of civil partnership

(1) Where two people have registered as civil partners of each other in England and Wales, it is not necessary in support of the civil partnership to give any proof—
(a) that any person whose consent to the civil partnership was required by section 4 (parental etc. consent) had given his consent, or
(b) that the civil partnership registrar was designated as such by the registration authority in whose area the registration took place;

and no evidence is to be given to prove the contrary in any proceedings touching the validity of the civil partnership.

(2) Subsection (1)(a) is subject to section 49(c) (civil partnership void if forbidden).

53. Power to validate civil partnership

(1) Where two people have registered as civil partners of each other in England and Wales, the Lord Chancellor may by order validate the civil partnership if it appears to him that it is or may be void under section 49(b).

(2) An order under subsection (1) may include provisions for relieving a person from any liability under section 31(2), 32(2) or 33(5) or (7).

(3) The draft of an order under subsection (1) must be advertised, in such manner as the Lord Chancellor thinks fit, not less than one month before the order is made.

(4) The Lord Chancellor must—
(a) consider all objections to the order sent to him in writing during that month, and
(b) if it appears to him necessary, direct a local inquiry into the validity of any such objections.

(5) An order under subsection (1) is subject to special parliamentary procedure.

Presumption of death orders

55. Presumption of death orders

(1) The court may, on an application made by a civil partner, make a presumption of death order if it is satisfied that reasonable grounds exist for supposing that the other civil partner is dead.

(2) In any proceedings under this section the fact that—
(a) for a period of 7 years or more the other civil partner has been continually absent from the applicant, and
(b) the applicant has no reason to believe that the other civil partner has been living within that time,
is evidence that the other civil partner is dead until the contrary is proved.

Separation orders

56. Separation orders

(1) An application for a separation order may be made to the court by either civil partner on the ground that any such fact as is mentioned in section 44(5)(a), (b), (c) or (d) exists.
(2) On an application for a separation order the court must inquire, so far as it reasonably can, into—
(a) the facts alleged by the applicant, and
(b) any facts alleged by the respondent,
but whether the civil partnership has broken down irretrievably is irrelevant.
(3) If the court is satisfied on the evidence of any such fact as is mentioned in section 44(5)(a), (b), (c) or (d) it must, subject to section 63, make a separation order.
(4) Section 45 (supplemental provisions as to facts raising presumption of breakdown) applies for the purposes of an application for a separation order alleging any such fact as it applies in relation to an application for a dissolution order alleging that fact.

57. Effect of separation order

If either civil partner dies intestate as respects all or any of his or her real or personal property while—
(a) a separation order is in force, and
(b) the separation is continuing,
the property as respects which he or she died intestate devolves as if the other civil partner had then been dead.

Declarations

58. Declarations

(1) Any person may apply to the High Court or a county court for one or more of the following declarations in relation to a civil partnership specified in the application—
(a) a declaration that the civil partnership was at its inception a valid civil partnership;
(b) a declaration that the civil partnership subsisted on a date specified in the application;
(c) a declaration that the civil partnership did not subsist on a date so specified;
(d) a declaration that the validity of a dissolution, annulment or legal separation obtained outside England and Wales in respect of the civil partnership is entitled to recognition in England and Wales;
(e) a declaration that the validity of a dissolution, annulment or legal separation so obtained in respect of the civil partnership is not entitled to recognition in England and Wales.
(2) Where an application under subsection (1) is made to a court by a person other than a civil partner in the civil partnership to which the application relates, the court must refuse to hear the application if it considers that the applicant does not have a sufficient interest in the determination of that application.

59. General provisions as to making and effect of declarations

(1) Where on an application for a declaration under section 58 the truth of the proposition to be declared is proved to the satisfaction of the court, the court must make the declaration unless to do so would be manifestly contrary to public policy.
(2) Any declaration under section 58 binds Her Majesty and all other persons.
(3) The court, on the dismissal of an application for a declaration under section 58, may not make any declaration for which an application has not been made.
(4) No declaration which may be applied for under section 58 may be made otherwise than under section 58 by any court.
(5) No declaration may be made by any court, whether under section 58 or otherwise, that a civil partnership was at its inception void.
(6) Nothing in this section affects the powers of any court to make a nullity order in respect of a civil partnership.

60. The Attorney General and proceedings for declarations

(1) On an application for a declaration under section 58 the court may at any stage of the proceedings, of its own motion or on the application of any party to the proceedings, direct that all necessary papers in the matter be sent to the Attorney General.

(2) The Attorney General, whether or not he is sent papers in relation to an application for a declaration under section 58, may—

(a) intervene in the proceedings on that application in such manner as he thinks necessary or expedient, and

(b) argue before the court dealing with the application any question in relation to the application which the court considers it necessary to have fully argued.

(3) Where any costs are incurred by the Attorney General in connection with any application for a declaration under section 58, the court may make such order as it considers just as to the payment of those costs by parties to the proceedings.

61. Supplementary provisions as to declarations

(1) Any declaration made under section 58, and any application for such a declaration, must be in the form prescribed by rules of court.

(2) Rules of court may make provision—

(a) as to the information required to be given by any applicant for a declaration under section 58;

(b) requiring notice of an application under section 58 to be served on the Attorney General and on persons who may be affected by any declaration applied for.

(3) No proceedings under section 58 affect any final judgment or order already pronounced or made by any court of competent jurisdiction.

(4) The court hearing an application under section 58 may direct that the whole or any part of the proceedings must be heard in private.

(5) An application for a direction under subsection (4) must be heard in private unless the court otherwise directs.

General provisions

62. Relief for respondent in dissolution proceedings

(1) If in any proceedings for a dissolution order the respondent alleges and proves any such fact as is mentioned in section 44(5)(a), (b), (c) or (d) the court may give to the respondent the relief to which he would have been entitled if he had made an application seeking that relief.

(2) When applying subsection (1), treat—

(a) the respondent as the applicant, and

(b) the applicant as the respondent,

for the purposes of section 44(5).

64. Parties to proceedings under this Chapter

(1) Rules of court may make provision with respect to—

(a) the joinder as parties to proceedings under sections 37 to 56 of persons involved in allegations of improper conduct made in those proceedings,

(b) the dismissal from such proceedings of any parties so joined, and

(c) the persons who are to be parties to proceedings on an application under section 58.

(2) Rules of court made under this section may make different provision for different cases.

(3) In every case in which the court considers, in the interest of a person not already a party to the proceedings, that the person should be made a party, the court may if it thinks fit allow the person to intervene upon such terms, if any, as the court thinks just.

CHAPTER 3
PROPERTY AND FINANCIAL ARRANGEMENTS

65. Contribution by civil partner to property improvement

(1) This section applies if—

(a) a civil partner contributes in money or money's worth to the improvement of real or personal property in which or in the proceeds of sale of which either or both of the civil partners has or have a beneficial interest, and

(b) the contribution is of a substantial nature.

(2) The contributing partner is to be treated as having acquired by virtue of the contribution a share or an enlarged share (as the case may be) in the beneficial interest of such an extent—

(a) as may have been then agreed, or

(b) in default of such agreement, as may seem in all the circumstances just to any court before which the question of the existence or extent of the beneficial interest of either of the civil partners arises (whether in proceedings between them or in any other proceedings).

(3) Subsection (2) is subject to any agreement (express or implied) between the civil partners to the contrary.

66. Disputes between civil partners about property

(1) In any question between the civil partners in a civil partnership as to title to or possession of property, either civil partner may apply to—
(a) the High Court, or
(b) such county court as may be prescribed by rules of court.

(2) On such an application, the court may make such order with respect to the property as it thinks fit (including an order for the sale of the property).

(3) ...

67. Applications under section 66 where property not in possession etc.

(1) The right of a civil partner ('A') to make an application under section 66 includes the right to make such an application where A claims that the other civil partner ('B') has had in his possession or under his control—
(a) money to which, or to a share of which, A was beneficially entitled, or
(b) property (other than money) to which, or to an interest in which, A was beneficially entitled,
and that either the money or other property has ceased to be in B's possession or under B's control or that A does not know whether it is still in B's possession or under B's control.

(2) For the purposes of subsection (1)(a) it does not matter whether A is beneficially entitled to the money or share—
(a) because it represents the proceeds of property to which, or to an interest in which, A was beneficially entitled, or
(b) for any other reason.

(3) Subsections (4) and (5) apply if, on such an application being made, the court is satisfied that B—
(a) has had in his possession or under his control money or other property as mentioned in subsection (1)(a) or (b), and
(b) has not made to A, in respect of that money or other property, such payment or disposition as would have been appropriate in the circumstances.

(4) The power of the court to make orders under section 66 includes power to order B to pay to A—
(a) in a case falling within subsection (1)(a), such sum in respect of the money to which the application relates, or A's s share of it, as the court considers appropriate, or
(b) in a case falling within subsection (1)(b), such sum in respect of the value of the property to which the application relates, or A's interest in it, as the court considers appropriate.

(5) If it appears to the court that there is any property which—
(a) represents the whole or part of the money or property, and
(b) is property in respect of which an order could (apart from this section) have been made under section 66, the court may (either instead of or as well as making an order in accordance with subsection (4)) make any order which it could (apart from this section) have made under section 66.

(6) Any power of the court which is exercisable on an application under section 66 is exercisable in relation to an application made under that section as extended by this section.

68. Applications under section 66 by former civil partners

(1) This section applies where a civil partnership has been dissolved or annulled.

(2) Subject to subsection (3), an application may be made under section 66 (including that section as extended by section 67) by either former civil partner despite the dissolution or annulment (and references in those sections to a civil partner are to be read accordingly).

(3) The application must be made within the period of 3 years beginning with the date of the dissolution or annulment.

69. Actions in tort between civil partners

(1) This section applies if an action in tort is brought by one civil partner against the other during the subsistence of the civil partnership.

(2) The court may stay the proceedings if it appears—
(a) that no substantial benefit would accrue to either civil partner from the continuation of the proceedings, or

(b) that the question or questions in issue could more conveniently be disposed of on an application under section 66.

(3) Without prejudice to subsection (2)(b), the court may in such an action—
(a) exercise any power which could be exercised on an application under section 66, or
(b) give such directions as it thinks fit for the disposal under that section of any question arising in the proceedings.

70. Assurance policy by civil partner for benefit of other civil partner etc.

Section 11 of the Married Women's Property Act 1882 (money payable under policy of assurance not to form part of the estate of the insured) applies in relation to a policy of assurance—
(a) effected by a civil partner on his own life, and
(b) expressed to be for the benefit of his civil partner, or of his children, or of his civil partner and children, or any of them,
as it applies in relation to a policy of assurance effected by a husband and expressed to be for the benefit of his wife, or of his children, or of his wife and children, or of any of them.

70A. Money and property derived from housekeeping allowance

Section 1 of the Matrimonial Property Act 1964 (money and property derived from housekeeping allowance to be treated as belonging to husband and wife in equal shares) applies in relation to—
(a) money derived from any allowance made by a civil partner for the expenses of the civil partnership home or for similar purposes, and
(b) any property acquired out of such money,
as it applies in relation to money derived from any allowance made by a husband or wife for the expenses of the matrimonial home or for similar purposes, and any property acquired out of such money.

71. Wills, administration of estates and family provision

Schedule 4 amends enactments relating to wills, administration of estates and family provision so that they apply in relation to civil partnerships as they apply in relation to marriage.

72. Financial relief for civil partners and children of family

(1) Schedule 5 makes provision for financial relief in connection with civil partnerships that corresponds to provision made for financial relief in connection with marriages by Part 2 of the Matrimonial Causes Act 1973.
(2) Any rule of law under which any provision of Part 2 of the 1973 Act is interpreted as applying to dissolution of a marriage on the ground of presumed death is to be treated as applying (with any necessary modifications) in relation to the corresponding provision of Schedule 5.
(3) Schedule 6 makes provision for financial relief in connection with civil partnerships that corresponds to provision made for financial relief in connection with marriages by the Domestic Proceedings and Magistrates' Courts Act 1978.
(4) . . .

CHAPTER 4
CIVIL PARTNERSHIP AGREEMENTS

73. Civil partnership agreements unenforceable

(1) A civil partnership agreement does not under the law of England and Wales have effect as a contract giving rise to legal rights.
(2) No action lies in England and Wales for breach of a civil partnership agreement, whatever the law applicable to the agreement.
(3) In this section and section 74 'civil partnership agreement' means an agreement between two people—
(a) to register as civil partners of each other—
(i) in England and Wales (under this Part),
. . .
(4) This section applies in relation to civil partnership agreements whether entered into before or after this section comes into force, but does not affect any action commenced before it comes into force.

74. Property where civil partnership agreement is terminated

(1) This section applies if a civil partnership agreement is terminated.
(2) Section 65 (contributions by civil partner to property improvement) applies, in relation to any property in which either or both of the parties to the agreement had a beneficial

interest while the agreement was in force, as it applies in relation to property in which a civil partner has a beneficial interest.

(3) Sections 66 and 67 (disputes between civil partners about property) apply to any dispute between or claim by one of the parties in relation to property in which either or both had a beneficial interest while the agreement was in force, as if the parties were civil partners of each other.

(4) An application made under section 66 or 67 by virtue of subsection (3) must be made within 3 years of the termination of the agreement.

(5) A party to a civil partnership agreement who makes a gift of property to the other party on the condition (express or implied) that it is to be returned if the agreement is terminated is not prevented from recovering the property merely because of his having terminated the agreement.

PART 6

RELATIONSHIPS ARISING THROUGH CIVIL PARTNERSHIP

246. Interpretation of statutory references to stepchildren etc.

(1) In any provision to which this section applies, references to a stepchild or step-parent of a person (here, 'A'), and cognate expressions, are to be read as follows—

A's stepchild includes a person who is the child of A's civil partner (but is not A's child);

A's step-parent includes a person who is the civil partner of A's parent (but is not A's parent);

A's stepdaughter includes a person who is the daughter of A's civil partner (but is not A's daughter);

A's stepson includes a person who is the son of A's civil partner (but is not A's son);

A's stepfather includes a person who is the civil partner of A's father (but is not A's parent);

A's stepmother includes a person who is the civil partner of A's mother (but is not A's parent);

A's stepbrother includes a person who is the son of the civil partner of A's parent (but is not the son of either of A's parents);

A's stepsister includes a person who is the daughter of the civil partner of A's parent (but is not the daughter of either of A's parents).

(2) For the purposes of any provision to which this section applies—

'brother-in-law' includes civil partner's brother,
'daughter-in-law' includes daughter's civil partner,
'father-in-law' includes civil partner's father,
'mother-in-law' includes civil partner's mother,
'parent-in-law' includes civil partner's parent,
'sister-in-law' includes civil partner's sister, and
'son-in-law' includes son's civil partner.

247. Provisions to which section 246 applies: Acts of Parliament etc.

(1) Section 246 applies to—

(a) any provision listed in Schedule 21 (references to stepchildren, in-laws etc. in existing Acts),

(b) except in so far as otherwise provided, any provision made by a future Act, and

(c) except in so far as otherwise provided, any provision made by future subordinate legislation.

. . .

SCHEDULES

Sections 3(2) and 5(3)

SCHEDULE 1

PROHIBITED DEGREES OF RELATIONSHIP: ENGLAND AND WALES

PART 1

THE PROHIBITIONS

Absolute prohibitions

1. (1) Two people are within prohibited degrees of relationship if one falls within the list below in relation to the other.

Adoptive child
Adoptive parent

Child
Former adoptive child
Former adoptive parent
Grandparent
Grandchild
Parent
Parent's sibling
Sibling
Sibling's child

(2) In the list 'sibling' means a brother, sister, half-brother or half-sister.

Qualified prohibitions

2. (1) Two people are within prohibited degrees of relationship if one of them falls within the list below in relation to the other, unless—

(a) both of them have reached 21 at the time when they register as civil partners of each other, and

(b) the younger has not at any time before reaching 18 been a child of the family in relation to the other.

Child of former civil partner
Child of former spouse
Former civil partner of grandparent
Former civil partner of parent
Former spouse of grandparent
Former spouse of parent
Grandchild of former civil partner
Grandchild of former spouse

(2) 'Child of the family', in relation to another person, means a person who—

(a) has lived in the same household as that other person, and

(b) has been treated by that other person as a child of his family.

3. Two people are within prohibited degrees of relationship if one falls within column 1 of the table below in relation to the other, unless—

(a) both of them have reached 21 at the time when they register as civil partners of each other, and

(b) the persons who fall within column 2 are dead.

Relationship	*Relevant deaths*
Former civil partner of child	The child The child's other parent
Former spouse of child	The child The child's other parent
Parent of former civil partner	The former civil partner The former civil partner's other parent
Parent of former spouse	The former spouse The former spouse's other parent

PART 2
SPECIAL PROVISIONS RELATING TO QUALIFIED PROHIBITIONS

Provisions relating to paragraph 2

4. Paragraphs 5 to 7 apply where two people are subject to paragraph 2 but intend to register as civil partners of each other by signing a civil partnership schedule.

5. (1) The fact that a notice of proposed civil partnership has been given must not be recorded in the register unless the registration authority—

(a) is satisfied by the production of evidence that both the proposed civil partners have reached 21, and

(b) has received a declaration made by each of the proposed civil partners—

(i) specifying their affinal relationship, and

(ii) declaring that the younger of them has not at any time before reaching 18 been a child of the family in relation to the other.

(2) Sub-paragraph (1) does not apply if a declaration is obtained under paragraph 7.

(3) A declaration under sub-paragraph (1)(b) must contain such information and must be signed and attested in such manner as may be prescribed by regulations.

(4) The fact that a registration authority has received a declaration under sub-paragraph (1)(b) must be recorded in the register.

(5) A declaration under sub-paragraph (1)(b) must be filed and kept by the registration authority.

6. (1) Sub-paragraph (2) applies if—

(a) a registration authority receives from a person who is not one of the proposed civil partners a written statement signed by that person which alleges that a declaration made under paragraph 5 is false in a material particular, and

(b) the register shows that such a statement has been received.

(2) The registration authority in whose area it is proposed that the registration take place must not issue a civil partnership schedule unless a High Court declaration is obtained under paragraph 7.

7. (1) Either of the proposed civil partners may apply to the High Court for a declaration that, given that—

(a) both of them have reached 21, and

(b) the younger of those persons has not at any time before reaching 18 been a child of the family in relation to the other,

there is no impediment of affinity to the formation of the civil partnership.

(2) Such an application may be made whether or not any statement has been received by the registration authority under paragraph 6.

8. Section 13 (objection to proposed civil partnership) does not apply in relation to a civil partnership to which paragraphs 5 to 7 apply, except so far as an objection to the issue of a civil partnership schedule is made under that section on a ground other than the affinity between the proposed civil partners.

Provisions relating to paragraph 3

9. (1) This paragraph applies where two people are subject to paragraph 3 but intend to register as civil partners of each other by signing a civil partnership schedule.

(2) The fact that a notice of proposed civil partnership has been given must not be recorded in the register unless the registration authority is satisfied by the production of evidence—

CHILDREN AND ADOPTION ACT 2006
(2006 c. 20)

Transitional provision

8. Transitional provision

(1) This section applies to any contact order under section 8 of the Children Act 1989 made before, and in force on, the relevant date.

(2) For so long as a contact order to which this section applies continues in force on and after the relevant date without being varied, the circumstances in which a notice under section 11I of the Children Act 1989 is to be attached to the contact order include—

(a) where an application for such a notice to be attached to the contact order is made by a person who, as regards the order, falls within any of paragraphs (a) to (d) of section 11J(5) of the Children Act 1989;

(b) where, in any family proceedings, a question arises with respect to the contact order.

(3) Where the person proposing to apply under subsection (2)(a) is the child with respect to whom the contact order was made, subsections (6) and (7) of section 11J have effect in relation to the application under subsection (2)(a) as they have effect in relation to an application under section 11J for an enforcement order.

(4) If a failure to comply with a contact order to which this section applies occurs while the contact order continues in force as described in subsection (2), each of sections 11K(1) and 11P(1) of the Children Act 1989 is to have effect, in relation to the failure, as if for paragraphs (a) and (b) there were substituted 'a notice under section 11I relating to the contact order'.

(5) In this section 'relevant date' means the day on which sections 3 to 5 [of this Act] come into force.

HUMAN FERTILISATION AND EMBRYOLOGY ACT 2008
(2008 c. 22)

PART 2

PARENTHOOD IN CASES INVOLVING ASSISTED REPRODUCTION

Meaning of 'mother'

33. Meaning of 'mother'

(1) The woman who is carrying or has carried a child as a result of the placing in her of an embryo or of sperm and eggs, and no other woman, is to be treated as the mother of the child.

(2) Subsection (1) does not apply to any child to the extent that the child is treated by virtue of adoption as not being the woman's child.

(3) Subsection (1) applies whether the woman was in the United Kingdom or elsewhere at the time of the placing in her of the embryo or the sperm and eggs.

Application of sections 35 to 47

34. Application of sections 35 to 47

(1) Sections 35 to 47 apply, in the case of a child who is being or has been carried by a woman (referred to in those sections as 'W') as a result of the placing in her of an embryo or of sperm and eggs or her artificial insemination, to determine who is to be treated as the other parent of the child.

(2) Subsection (1) has effect subject to the provisions of sections 39, 40 and 46 limiting the purposes for which a person is treated as the child's other parent by virtue of those sections.

Meaning of 'father'

35. Woman married at time of treatment

(1) If—

(a) at the time of the placing in her of the embryo or of the sperm and eggs or of her artificial insemination, W was a party to a marriage, and

(b) the creation of the embryo carried by her was not brought about with the sperm of the other party to the marriage,

then, subject to section 38(2) to (4), the other party to the marriage is to be treated as the father of the child unless it is shown that he did not consent to the placing in her of the embryo or the sperm and eggs or to her artificial insemination (as the case may be).

(2) This section applies whether W was in the United Kingdom or elsewhere at the time mentioned in subsection (1)(a).

36. Treatment provided to woman where agreed fatherhood conditions apply

If no man is treated by virtue of section 35 as the father of the child and no woman is treated by virtue of section 42 as a parent of the child but—

(a) the embryo or the sperm and eggs were placed in W, or W was artificially inseminated, in the course of treatment services provided in the United Kingdom by a person to whom a licence applies,

(b) at the time when the embryo or the sperm and eggs were placed in W, or W was artificially inseminated, the agreed fatherhood conditions (as set out in section 37) were satisfied in relation to a man, in relation to treatment provided to W under the licence,

(c) the man remained alive at that time, and

(d) the creation of the embryo carried by W was not brought about with the man's sperm,

then, subject to section 38(2) to (4), the man is to be treated as the father of the child.

37. The agreed fatherhood conditions

(1) The agreed fatherhood conditions referred to in section 36(b) are met in relation to a man ('M') in relation to treatment provided to W under a licence if, but only if,—

(a) M has given the person responsible a notice stating that he consents to being treated as the father of any child resulting from treatment provided to W under the licence,

(b) W has given the person responsible a notice stating that she consents to M being so treated,

(c) neither M nor W has, since giving notice under paragraph (a) or (b), given the person responsible notice of the withdrawal of M's or W's consent to M being so treated,

(d) W has not, since the giving of the notice under paragraph (b), given the person responsible—
  (i) a further notice under that paragraph stating that she consents to another man being treated as the father of any resulting child, or
  (ii) a notice under section 44(1)(b) stating that she consents to a woman being treated as a parent of any resulting child, and

(e) W and M are not within prohibited degrees of relationship in relation to each other.

(2) A notice under subsection (1)(a), (b) or (c) must be in writing and must be signed by the person giving it.

(3) A notice under subsection (1)(a), (b) or (c) by a person ('S') who is unable to sign because of illness, injury or physical disability is to be taken to comply with the requirement of subsection (2) as to signature if it is signed at the direction of S, in the presence of S and in the presence of at least one witness who attests the signature.

38. Further provision relating to sections 35 and 36

(1) Where a person is to be treated as the father of the child by virtue of section 35 or 36, no other person is to be treated as the father of the child.

(2) In England and Wales and Northern Ireland, sections 35 and 36 do not affect any presumption, applying by virtue of the rules of common law, that a child is the legitimate child of the parties to a marriage.

(3) In Scotland, sections 35 and 36 do not apply in relation to any child who, by virtue of any enactment or other rule of law, is treated as the child of the parties to a marriage.

(4) Sections 35 and 36 do not apply to any child to the extent that the child is treated by virtue of adoption as not being the man's child.

39. Use of sperm, or transfer of embryo, after death of man providing sperm

(1) If—

(a) the child has been carried by W as a result of the placing in her of an embryo or of sperm and eggs or her artificial insemination,

(b) the creation of the embryo carried by W was brought about by using the sperm of a man after his death, or the creation of the embryo was brought about using the sperm of a man before his death but the embryo was placed in W after his death,

(c) the man consented in writing (and did not withdraw the consent)—
  (i) to the use of his sperm after his death which brought about the creation of the embryo carried by W or (as the case may be) to the placing in W after his death of the embryo which was brought about using his sperm before his death, and
  (ii) to being treated for the purpose mentioned in subsection (3) as the father of any resulting child,

(d) W has elected in writing not later than the end of the period of 42 days from the day on which the child was born for the man to be treated for the purpose mentioned in subsection (3) as the father of the child, and

(e) no-one else is to be treated—
  (i) as the father of the child by virtue of section 35 or 36 or by virtue of section 38(2) or (3), or
  (ii) as a parent of the child by virtue of section 42 or 43 or by virtue of adoption,

then the man is to be treated for the purpose mentioned in subsection (3) as the father of the child.

(2) Subsection (1) applies whether W was in the United Kingdom or elsewhere at the time of the placing in her of the embryo or of the sperm and eggs or of her artificial insemination.

(3) The purpose referred to in subsection (1) is the purpose of enabling the man's particulars to be entered as the particulars of the child's father in a relevant register of births.

. . .

40. Embryo transferred after death of husband etc. who did not provide sperm

(1) If—

(a) the child has been carried by W as a result of the placing in her of an embryo,

(b) the embryo was created at a time when W was a party to a marriage,

(c) the creation of the embryo was not brought about with the sperm of the other party to the marriage,

(d) the other party to the marriage died before the placing of the embryo in W,

(e) the other party to the marriage consented in writing (and did not withdraw the consent)—
  (i) to the placing of the embryo in W after his death, and
  (ii) to being treated for the purpose mentioned in subsection (4) as the father of any resulting child,

(f) W has elected in writing not later than the end of the period of 42 days from the day on which the child was born for the man to be treated for the purpose mentioned in subsection (4) as the father of the child, and
(g) no-one else is to be treated—
(i) as the father of the child by virtue of section 35 or 36 or by virtue of section 38(2) or (3), or
(ii) as a parent of the child by virtue of section 42 or 43 or by virtue of adoption,
then the man is to be treated for the purpose mentioned in subsection (4) as the father of the child.

(2) If—
(a) the child has been carried by W as a result of the placing in her of an embryo,
(b) the embryo was not created at a time when W was a party to a marriage or a civil partnership but was created in the course of treatment services provided to W in the United Kingdom by a person to whom a licence applies,
(c) a man consented in writing (and did not withdraw the consent)—
(i) to the placing of the embryo in W after his death, and
(ii) to being treated for the purpose mentioned in subsection (4) as the father of any resulting child,
(d) the creation of the embryo was not brought about with the sperm of that man,
(e) the man died before the placing of the embryo in W,
(f) immediately before the man's death, the agreed fatherhood conditions set out in section 37 were met in relation to the man in relation to treatment proposed to be provided to W in the United Kingdom by a person to whom a licence applies,
(g) W has elected in writing not later than the end of the period of 42 days from the day on which the child was born for the man to be treated for the purpose mentioned in subsection (4) as the father of the child, and
(h) no-one else is to be treated—
(i) as the father of the child by virtue of section 35 or 36 or by virtue of section 38(2) or (3), or
(ii) as a parent of the child by virtue of section 42 or 43 or by virtue of adoption,
then the man is to be treated for the purpose mentioned in subsection (4) as the father of the child.

(3) Subsections (1) and (2) apply whether W was in the United Kingdom or elsewhere at the time of the placing in her of the embryo.

(4) The purpose referred to in subsections (1) and (2) is the purpose of enabling the man's particulars to be entered as the particulars of the child's father in a relevant register of births.

(5) In the application of this section to Scotland, for any reference to a period of 42 days there is substituted a reference to a period of 21 days.

41. Persons not to be treated as father

(1) Where the sperm of a man who had given such consent as is required by paragraph 5 of Schedule 3 to the 1990 Act (consent to use of gametes for purposes of treatment services or non-medical fertility services) was used for a purpose for which such consent was required, he is not to be treated as the father of the child.

(2) Where the sperm of a man, or an embryo the creation of which was brought about with his sperm, was used after his death, he is not, subject to section 39, to be treated as the father of the child.

(3) Subsection (2) applies whether W was in the United Kingdom or elsewhere at the time of the placing in her of the embryo or of the sperm and eggs or of her artificial insemination.

Cases in which woman to be other parent

42. Woman in civil partnership at time of treatment

(1) If at the time of the placing in her of the embryo or the sperm and eggs or of her artificial insemination, W was a party to a civil partnership, then subject to section 45(2) to (4), the other party to the civil partnership is to be treated as a parent of the child unless it is shown that she did not consent to the placing in W of the embryo or the sperm and eggs or to her artificial insemination (as the case may be).

(2) This section applies whether W was in the United Kingdom or elsewhere at the time mentioned in subsection (1).

43. Treatment provided to woman who agrees that second woman to be parent

If no man is treated by virtue of section 35 as the father of the child and no woman is treated by virtue of section 42 as a parent of the child but—

(a) the embryo or the sperm and eggs were placed in W, or W was artificially inseminated, in the course of treatment services provided in the United Kingdom by a person to whom a licence applies,
(b) at the time when the embryo or the sperm and eggs were placed in W, or W was artificially inseminated, the agreed female parenthood conditions (as set out in section 44) were met in relation to another woman, in relation to treatment provided to W under that licence, and
(c) the other woman remained alive at that time,

then, subject to section 45(2) to (4), the other woman is to be treated as a parent of the child.

44. The agreed female parenthood conditions

(1) The agreed female parenthood conditions referred to in section 43(b) are met in relation to another woman ('P') in relation to treatment provided to W under a licence if, but only if,—
  (a) P has given the person responsible a notice stating that P consents to P being treated as a parent of any child resulting from treatment provided to W under the licence,
  (b) W has given the person responsible a notice stating that W agrees to P being so treated,
  (c) neither W nor P has, since giving notice under paragraph (a) or (b), given the person responsible notice of the withdrawal of P's or W's consent to P being so treated,
  (d) W has not, since the giving of the notice under paragraph (b), given the person responsible—
    (i) a further notice under that paragraph stating that W consents to a woman other than P being treated as a parent of any resulting child, or
    (ii) a notice under section 37(1)(b) stating that W consents to a man being treated as the father of any resulting child, and
  (e) W and P are not within prohibited degrees of relationship in relation to each other.

(2) A notice under subsection (1)(a), (b) or (c) must be in writing and must be signed by the person giving it.

(3) A notice under subsection (1)(a), (b) or (c) by a person ('S') who is unable to sign because of illness, injury or physical disability is to be taken to comply with the requirement of subsection (2) as to signature if it is signed at the direction of S, in the presence of S and in the presence of at least one witness who attests the signature.

45. Further provision relating to sections 42 and 43

(1) Where a woman is treated by virtue of section 42 or 43 as a parent of the child, no man is to be treated as the father of the child.

(2) In England and Wales and Northern Ireland, sections 42 and 43 do not affect any presumption, applying by virtue of the rules of common law, that a child is the legitimate child of the parties to a marriage.

(3) ...

(4) Sections 42 and 43 do not apply to any child to the extent that the child is treated by virtue of adoption as not being the woman's child.

46. Embryo transferred after death of civil partner or intended female parent

(1) If—
  (a) the child has been carried by W as the result of the placing in her of an embryo,
  (b) the embryo was created at a time when W was a party to a civil partnership,
  (c) the other party to the civil partnership died before the placing of the embryo in W,
  (d) the other party to the civil partnership consented in writing (and did not withdraw the consent)—
    (i) to the placing of the embryo in W after the death of the other party, and
    (ii) to being treated for the purpose mentioned in subsection (4) as the parent of any resulting child,
  (e) W has elected in writing not later than the end of the period of 42 days from the day on which the child was born for the other party to the civil partnership to be treated for the purpose mentioned in subsection (4) as the parent of the child, and
  (f) no one else is to be treated—
    (i) as the father of the child by virtue of section 35 or 36 or by virtue of section 45(2) or (3), or
    (ii) as a parent of the child by virtue of section 42 or 43 or by virtue of adoption,

  then the other party to the civil partnership is to be treated for the purpose mentioned in subsection (4) as a parent of the child.

(2) If—
(a) the child has been carried by W as the result of the placing in her of an embryo,
(b) the embryo was not created at a time when W was a party to a marriage or a civil partnership, but was created in the course of treatment services provided to W in the United Kingdom by a person to whom a licence applies,
(c) another woman consented in writing (and did not withdraw the consent)—
(i) to the placing of the embryo in W after the death of the other woman, and
(ii) to being treated for the purpose mentioned in subsection (4) as the parent of any resulting child,
(d) the other woman died before the placing of the embryo in W,
(e) immediately before the other woman's death, the agreed female parenthood conditions set out in section 44 were met in relation to the other woman in relation to treatment proposed to be provided to W in the United Kingdom by a person to whom a licence applies,
(f) W has elected in writing not later than the end of the period of 42 days from the day on which the child was born for the other woman to be treated for the purpose mentioned in subsection (4) as the parent of the child, and
(g) no one else is to be treated—
(i) as the father of the child by virtue of section 35 or 36 or by virtue of section 45(2) or (3), or
(ii) as a parent of the child by virtue of section 42 or 43 or by virtue of adoption,
then the other woman is to be treated for the purpose mentioned in subsection (4) as a parent of the child.
(3) Subsections (1) and (2) apply whether W was in the United Kingdom or elsewhere at the time of the placing in her of the embryo.
(4) The purpose referred to in subsections (1) and (2) is the purpose of enabling the deceased woman's particulars to be entered as the particulars of the child's other parent in a relevant register of births.

. . .

47. Woman not to be other parent merely because of egg donation

A woman is not to be treated as the parent of a child whom she is not carrying and has not carried, except where she is so treated—
(a) by virtue of section 42 or 43, or
(b) by virtue of section 46 (for the purpose mentioned in subsection (4) of that section), or
(c) by virtue of adoption.

Effect of sections 33 to 47

48. Effect of sections 33 to 47

(1) Where by virtue of section 33, 35, 36, 42 or 43 a person is to be treated as the mother, father or parent of a child, that person is to be treated in law as the mother, father or parent (as the case may be) of the child for all purposes.
(2) Where by virtue of section 33, 38, 41, 45 or 47 a person is not to be treated as a parent of the child, that person is to be treated in law as not being a parent of the child for any purpose.
(3) Where section 39(1) or 40(1) or (2) applies, the deceased man—
(a) is to be treated in law as the father of the child for the purpose mentioned in section 39(3) or 40(4), but
(b) is to be treated in law as not being the father of the child for any other purpose.
(4) Where section 46(1) or (2) applies, the deceased woman—
(a) is to be treated in law as a parent of the child for the purpose mentioned in section 46(4), but
(b) is to be treated in law as not being a parent of the child for any other purpose.
(5) Where any of subsections (1) to (4) has effect, references to any relationship between two people in any enactment, deed or other instrument or document (whenever passed or made) are to be read accordingly.
(6) In relation to England and Wales and Northern Ireland, a child who—
(a) has a parent by virtue of section 42, or
(b) has a parent by virtue of section 43 who is at any time during the period beginning with the time mentioned in section 43(b) and ending with the time of the child's birth a party to a civil partnership with the child's mother,
is the legitimate child of the child's parents.

(7) In relation to England and Wales and Northern Ireland, nothing in the provisions of section 33(1) or sections 35 to 47, read with this section—
(a) affects the succession to any dignity or title of honour or renders any person capable of succeeding to or transmitting a right to succeed to any such dignity or title, or
(b) affects the devolution of any property limited (expressly or not) to devolve (as nearly as the law permits) along with any dignity or title of honour.

. . .

References to parties to marriage or civil partnership

49. Meaning of references to parties to a marriage

(1) The references in sections 35 to 47 to the parties to a marriage at any time there referred to—
(a) are to the parties to a marriage subsisting at that time, unless a judicial separation was then in force, but
(b) include the parties to a void marriage if either or both of them reasonably believed at that time that the marriage was valid; and for the purposes of those sections it is to be presumed, unless the contrary is shown, that one of them reasonably believed at that time that the marriage was valid.

(2) In subsection (1)(a) 'judicial separation' includes a legal separation obtained in a country outside the British Islands and recognised in the United Kingdom.

50. Meaning of references to parties to a civil partnership

(1) The references in sections 35 to 47 to the parties to a civil partnership at any time there referred to—
(a) are to the parties to a civil partnership subsisting at that time, unless a separation order was then in force, but
(b) include the parties to a void civil partnership if either or both of them reasonably believed at that time that the civil partnership was valid; and for the purposes of those sections it is to be presumed, unless the contrary is shown, that one of them reasonably believed at that time that the civil partnership was valid.

(2) The reference in section 48(6)(b) to a civil partnership includes a reference to a void civil partnership if either or both of the parties reasonably believed at the time when they registered as civil partners of each other that the civil partnership was valid; and for this purpose it is to be presumed, unless the contrary is shown, that one of them reasonably believed at that time that the civil partnership was valid.

(3) In subsection (1)(a), 'separation order' means—
(a) a separation order under section 37(1)(d) or 161(1)(d) of the Civil Partnership Act 2004,
(b) a decree of separation under section 120(2) of that Act, or
(c) a legal separation obtained in a country outside the United Kingdom and recognised in the United Kingdom.

Further provision about registration by virtue of section 39, 40 or 46

51. Meaning of 'relevant register of births'

For the purposes of this Part a 'relevant register of births', in relation to a birth, is whichever of the following is relevant—
(a) a register of live-births or still-births kept under the Births and Deaths Registration Act 1953,

. . .

52. Late election by mother with consent of Registrar General

(1) The requirement under section 39(1), 40(1) or (2) or 46(1) or (2) as to the making of an election (which requires an election to be made either on or before the day on which the child was born or within the period of 42 or, as the case may be, 21 days from that day) is nevertheless to be treated as satisfied if the required election is made after the end of that period but with the consent of the Registrar General under subsection (2).

(2) The Registrar General may at any time consent to the making of an election after the end of the period mentioned in subsection (1) if, on an application made to him in accordance with such requirements as he may specify, he is satisfied that there is a compelling reason for giving his consent to the making of such an election.

. . .

Interpretation of references to father etc. where woman is other parent

53. Interpretation of references to father etc.

(1) Subsections (2) and (3) have effect, subject to subsections (4) and (6), for the interpretation of any enactment, deed or any other instrument or document (whenever passed or made).

(2) Any reference (however expressed) to the father of a child who has a parent by virtue of section 42 or 43 is to be read as a reference to the woman who is a parent of the child by virtue of that section.

(3) Any reference (however expressed) to evidence of paternity is, in relation to a woman who is a parent by virtue of section 42 or 43, to be read as a reference to evidence of parentage.

(4) This section does not affect the interpretation of the enactments specified in subsection (5) (which make express provision for the case where a child has a parent by virtue of section 42 or 43).

(5) Those enactments are—

. . .

(b) the Schedule to the Population (Statistics) Act 1938,

(c) the Births and Deaths Registration Act 1953,

(d) the Registration of Births, Deaths and Marriages (Special Provisions) Act 1957,

. . .

(f) the Congenital Disabilities (Civil Liability) Act 1976,

(g) the Legitimacy Act 1976,

(h) the Births and Deaths Registration (Northern Ireland) Order 1976,

(i) the British Nationality Act 1981,

(j) the Family Law Reform Act 1987,

(k) Parts 1 and 2 of the Children Act,

. . .

(6) This section does not affect the interpretation of references that fall to be read in accordance with section 1(2)(a) or (b) of the Family Law Reform Act 1987 or Article 155(2)(a) or (b) of the Children (Northern Ireland) Order 1995 (references to a person whose father and mother were, or were not, married to each other at the time of the person's birth).

Parental orders

54. Parental orders

(1) On an application made by two people ('the applicants'), the court may make an order providing for a child to be treated in law as the child of the applicants if—

(a) the child has been carried by a woman who is not one of the applicants, as a result of the placing in her of an embryo or sperm and eggs or her artificial insemination,

(b) the gametes of at least one of the applicants were used to bring about the creation of the embryo, and

(c) the conditions in subsections (2) to (8) are satisfied.

(2) The applicants must be—

(a) husband and wife,

(b) civil partners of each other, or

(c) two persons who are living as partners in an enduring family relationship and are not within prohibited degrees of relationship in relation to each other.

(3) Except in a case falling within subsection (11), the applicants must apply for the order during the period of 6 months beginning with the day on which the child is born.

(4) At the time of the application and the making of the order—

(a) the child's home must be with the applicants, and

(b) either or both of the applicants must be domiciled in the United Kingdom or in the Channel Islands or the Isle of Man.

(5) At the time of the making of the order both the applicants must have attained the age of 18.

(6) The court must be satisfied that both—

(a) the woman who carried the child, and

(b) any other person who is a parent of the child but is not one of the applicants (including any man who is the father by virtue of section 35 or 36 or any woman who is a parent by virtue of section 42 or 43),

have freely, and with full understanding of what is involved, agreed unconditionally to the making of the order.

(7) Subsection (6) does not require the agreement of a person who cannot be found or is incapable of giving agreement; and the agreement of the woman who carried the child is ineffective for the purpose of that subsection if given by her less than six weeks after the child's birth.

(8) The court must be satisfied that no money or other benefit (other than for expenses reasonably incurred) has been given or received by either of the applicants for or in consideration of—

(a) the making of the order,

(b) any agreement required by subsection (6),

(c) the handing over of the child to the applicants, or

(d) the making of arrangements with a view to the making of the order,

unless authorised by the court.

(9) For the purposes of an application under this section—

(a) in relation to England and Wales—

(i) 'the court' means the High Court or the family court, and

(ii) proceedings on the application are to be 'family proceedings' for the purposes of the Children Act 1989,

...

(10) Subsection (1)(a) applies whether the woman was in the United Kingdom or elsewhere at the time of the placing in her of the embryo or the sperm and eggs or her artificial insemination.

(11) An application which—

(a) relates to a child born before the coming into force of this section, and

(b) is made by two persons who, throughout the period applicable under subsection (2) of section 30 of the 1990 Act, were not eligible to apply for an order under that section in relation to the child as husband and wife,

may be made within the period of six months beginning with the day on which this section comes into force.

CHILDREN AND YOUNG PERSONS ACT 2008
(2008 c. 23)

7. Well-being of children and young persons

(1) It is the general duty of the Secretary of State to promote the well-being of children in England.

(2) The general duty imposed by subsection (1) has effect subject to any specific duties imposed on the Secretary of State.

(3) The activities which may be undertaken or supported in the discharge of the general duty imposed by subsection (1) include activities in connection with parenting.

...

PENSIONS ACT 2008
(2008 c. 30)

PART 3

PENSION COMPENSATION

CHAPTER 1

PENSION COMPENSATION ON DIVORCE ETC

107. Scope of mechanism

(1) Pension compensation sharing is available under this Chapter in relation to a person's shareable rights to PPF compensation.

(2) For the purposes of this Chapter, a right of a person to PPF compensation is 'shareable' unless it is of a description specified by regulations made by the Secretary of State.

EQUALITY ACT 2010
(2010 C. 15)

PART 2
QUALITY: KEY CONCEPTS

CHAPTER 1
PROTECTED CHARACTERISTICS

4. The protected characteristics

The following characteristics are protected characteristics—

- age;
- disability;
- gender reassignment;
- marriage and civil partnership;
- pregnancy and maternity;
- race;
- religion or belief;
- sex;
- sexual orientation.

5. Age

(1) In relation to the protected characteristic of age—
  (a) a reference to a person who has a particular protected characteristic is a reference to a person of a particular age group;
  (b) a reference to persons who share a protected characteristic is a reference to persons of the same age group.

(2) A reference to an age group is a reference to a group of persons defined by reference to age, whether by reference to a particular age or to a range of ages.

7. Gender reassignment

(1) A person has the protected characteristic of gender reassignment if the person is proposing to undergo, is undergoing or has undergone a process (or part of a process) for the purpose of reassigning the person's sex by changing physiological or other attributes of sex.

(2) A reference to a transsexual person is a reference to a person who has the protected characteristic of gender reassignment.

(3) In relation to the protected characteristic of gender reassignment—
  (a) a reference to a person who has a particular protected characteristic is a reference to a transsexual person;
  (b) a reference to persons who share a protected characteristic is a reference to transsexual persons.

8. Marriage and civil partnership

(1) A person has the protected characteristic of marriage and civil partnership if the person is married or is a civil partner.

(2) In relation to the protected characteristic of marriage and civil partnership—
  (a) a reference to a person who has a particular protected characteristic is a reference to a person who is married or is a civil partner;
  (b) a reference to persons who share a protected characteristic is a reference to persons who are married or are civil partners.

11. Sex

In relation to the protected characteristic of sex—

(a) a reference to a person who has a particular protected characteristic is a reference to a man or to a woman;

(b) a reference to persons who share a protected characteristic is a reference to persons of the same sex.

12. Sexual orientation

(1) Sexual orientation means a person's sexual orientation towards—
  (a) persons of the same sex,
  (b) persons of the opposite sex, or
  (c) persons of either sex.

(2) In relation to the protected characteristic of sexual orientation—
   (a) a reference to a person who has a particular protected characteristic is a reference to a person who is of a particular sexual orientation;
   (b) a reference to persons who share a protected characteristic is a reference to persons who are of the same sexual orientation.

CHAPTER 2
PROHIBITED CONDUCT

Discrimination

13. Direct discrimination

(1) A person (A) discriminates against another (B) if, because of a protected characteristic, A treats B less favourably than A treats or would treat others.
(2) If the protected characteristic is age, A does not discriminate against B if A can show A's treatment of B to be a proportionate means of achieving a legitimate aim.
. . .
(4) If the protected characteristic is marriage and civil partnership, this section applies to a contravention of Part 5 (work) only if the treatment is because it is B who is married or a civil partner.

14. Combined discrimination: dual characteristics

(1) A person (A) discriminates against another (B) if, because of a combination of two relevant protected characteristics, A treats B less favourably than A treats or would treat a person who does not share either of those characteristics.
(2) The relevant protected characteristics are—
   (a) age;
   (b) disability;
   (c) gender reassignment;
   (d) race
   (e) religion or belief;
   (f) sex;
   (g) sexual orientation.
(3) For the purposes of establishing a contravention of this Act by virtue of subsection (1), B need not show that A's treatment of B is direct discrimination because of each of the characteristics in the combination (taken separately).
(4) But B cannot establish a contravention of this Act by virtue of subsection (1) if, in reliance on another provision of this Act or any other enactment, A shows that A's treatment of B is not direct discrimination because of either or both of the characteristics in the combination.
(5) Subsection (1) does not apply to a combination of characteristics that includes disability in circumstances where, if a claim of direct discrimination because of disability were to be brought, it would come within section 116 (special educational needs).
(6) A Minister of the Crown may by order amend this section so as to—
   (a) make further provision about circumstances in which B can, or in which B cannot, establish a contravention of this Act by virtue of subsection (1);
   (b) specify other circumstances in which subsection (1) does not apply.
(7) The references to direct discrimination are to a contravention of this Act by virtue of section 13.

16. Gender reassignment discrimination: cases of absence from work

(1) This section has effect for the purposes of the application of Part 5 (work) to the protected characteristic of gender reassignment.
(2) A person (A) discriminates against a transsexual person (B) if, in relation to an absence of B's that is because of gender reassignment, A treats B less favourably than A would treat B if—
   (a) B's absence was because of sickness or injury, or
   (b) B's absence was for some other reason and it is not reasonable for B to be treated less favourably.
(3) A person's absence is because of gender reassignment if it is because the person is proposing to undergo, is undergoing or has undergone the process (or part of the process) mentioned in section 7(1).

19. Indirect discrimination

(1) A person (A) discriminates against another (B) if A applies to B a provision, criterion or practice which is discriminatory in relation to a relevant protected characteristic of B's.

(2) For the purposes of subsection (1), a provision, criterion or practice is discriminatory in relation to a relevant protected characteristic of B's if—
(a) A applies, or would apply, it to persons with whom B does not share the characteristic,
(b) it puts, or would put, persons with whom B shares the characteristic at a particular disadvantage when compared with persons with whom B does not share it,
(c) it puts, or would put, B at that disadvantage, and
(d) A cannot show it to be a proportionate means of achieving a legitimate aim.
(3) The relevant protected characteristics are—
- age;
- disability;
- gender reassignment;
- marriage and civil partnership;
- race;
- religion or belief;
- sex;
- sexual orientation.

Discrimination: supplementary

23. Comparison by reference to circumstances

(1) On a comparison of cases for the purposes of section 13, 14, or 19 there must be no material difference between the circumstances relating to each case.
. . .
(3) If the protected characteristic is sexual orientation, the fact that one person (whether or not the person referred to as B) is a civil partner while another is married is not a material difference between the circumstances relating to each case.

24. Irrelevance of alleged discriminator's characteristics

(1) For the purpose of establishing a contravention of this Act by virtue of section 13(1), it does not matter whether A has the protected characteristic.
(2) For the purpose of establishing a contravention of this Act by virtue of section 14(1), it does not matter—
(a) whether A has one of the protected characteristics in the combination;
(b) whether A has both.

25. References to particular strands of discrimination

(1) Age discrimination is—
(a) discrimination within section 13 because of age;
(b) discrimination within section 19 where the relevant protected characteristic is age.
. . .
(3) Gender reassignment discrimination is—
(a) discrimination within section 13 because of gender reassignment;
(b) discrimination within section 16;
(c) discrimination within section 19 where the relevant protected characteristic is gender reassignment.
(4) Marriage and civil partnership discrimination is—
(a) discrimination within section 13 because of marriage and civil partnership;
(b) discrimination within section 19 where the relevant protected characteristic is marriage and civil partnership.
. . .
(8) Sex discrimination is—
(a) discrimination within section 13 because of sex;
(b) discrimination within section 19 where the relevant protected characteristic is sex.
(9) Sexual orientation discrimination is—
(a) discrimination within section 13 because of sexual orientation;
(b) discrimination within section 19 where the relevant protected characteristic is sexual orientation.

Other prohibited conduct

26. Harassment

(1) A person (A) harasses another (B) if—
(a) A engages in unwanted conduct related to a relevant protected characteristic, and
(b) the conduct has the purpose or effect of—
(i) violating B's dignity, or
(ii) creating an intimidating, hostile, degrading, humiliating or offensive environment for B.

(2) A also harasses B if—
(a) A engages in unwanted conduct of a sexual nature, and
(b) the conduct has the purpose or effect referred to in subsection (1)(b).
(3) A also harasses B if—
(a) A or another person engages in unwanted conduct of a sexual nature or that is related to gender reassignment or sex,
(b) the conduct has the purpose or effect referred to in subsection (1)(b), and
(c) because of B's rejection of or submission to the conduct, A treats B less favourably than A would treat B if B had not rejected or submitted to the conduct.
(4) In deciding whether conduct has the effect referred to in subsection (1)(b), each of the following must be taken into account—
(a) the perception of B;
(b) the other circumstances of the case;
(c) whether it is reasonable for the conduct to have that effect.
(5) The relevant protected characteristics are—
- age;
- disability;
- gender reassignment;
- race;
- religion or belief;
- sex;
- sexual orientation.

27. Victimisation

(1) A person (A) victimises another person (B) if A subjects B to a detriment because—
(a) B does a protected act, or
(b) A believes that B has done, or may do, a protected act.
(2) Each of the following is a protected act—
(a) bringing proceedings under this Act;
(b) giving evidence or information in connection with proceedings under this Act;
(c) doing any other thing for the purposes of or in connection with this Act;
(d) making an allegation (whether or not express) that A or another person has contravened this Act.
(3) Giving false evidence or information, or making a false allegation, is not a protected act if the evidence or information is given, or the allegation is made, in bad faith.
(4) This section applies only where the person subjected to a detriment is an individual.
(5) The reference to contravening this Act includes a reference to committing a breach of an equality clause or rule.

PART 15
FAMILY PROPERTY

198. Abolition of husband's duty to maintain wife

The rule of common law that a husband must maintain his wife is abolished.

199. Abolition of presumption of advancement

(1) The presumption of advancement (by which, for example, a husband is presumed to be making a gift to his wife if he transfers property to her, or purchases property in her name) is abolished.
(2) The abolition by subsection (1) of the presumption of advancement does not have effect in relation to—
(a) anything done before the commencement of this section, or
(b) anything done pursuant to any obligation incurred before the commencement of this section.

CRIME AND SECURITY ACT 2010
(2010 c. 17)

Domestic violence

24. Power to issue a domestic violence protection notice

(1) A member of a police force not below the rank of superintendent ('the authorising officer') may issue a domestic violence protection notice ('a DVPN') under this section.

(2) A DVPN may be issued to a person ('P') aged 18 years or over if the authorising officer has reasonable grounds for believing that—
(a) P has been violent towards, or has threatened violence towards, an associated person, and
(b) the issue of the DVPN is necessary to protect that person from violence or a threat of violence by P.
(3) Before issuing a DVPN, the authorising officer must, in particular, consider—
(a) the welfare of any person under the age of 18 whose interests the officer considers relevant to the issuing of the DVPN (whether or not that person is an associated person),
(b) the opinion of the person for whose protection the DVPN would be issued as to the issuing of the DVPN,
(c) any representations made by P as to the issuing of the DVPN, and
(d) in the case of provision included by virtue of subsection (8), the opinion of any other associated person who lives in the premises to which the provision would relate.
(4) The authorising officer must take reasonable steps to discover the opinions mentioned in subsection (3).
(5) But the authorising officer may issue a DVPN in circumstances where the person for whose protection it is issued does not consent to the issuing of the DVPN.
(6) A DVPN must contain provision to prohibit P from molesting the person for whose protection it is issued.
(7) Provision required to be included by virtue of subsection (6) may be expressed so as to refer to molestation in general, to particular acts of molestation, or to both.
(8) If P lives in premises which are also lived in by a person for whose protection the DVPN is issued, the DVPN may also contain provision—
(a) to prohibit P from evicting or excluding from the premises the person for whose protection the DVPN is issued,
(b) to prohibit P from entering the premises,
(c) to require P to leave the premises, or
(d) to prohibit P from coming within such distance of the premises as may be specified in the DVPN.
(9) An 'associated person' means a person who is associated with P within the meaning of section 62 of the Family Law Act 1996.
(10) Subsection (11) applies where a DVPN includes provision in relation to premises by virtue of subsection (8)(b) or (8)(c) and the authorising officer believes that—
(a) P is a person subject to service law in accordance with sections 367 to 369 of the Armed Forces Act 2006, and
(b) the premises fall within paragraph (a) of the definition of 'service living accommodation' in section 96(1) of that Act.
(11) The authorising officer must make reasonable efforts to inform P's commanding officer (within the meaning of section 360 of the Armed Forces Act 2006) of the issuing of the notice.

25. Contents and service of a domestic violence protection notice

(1) A DVPN must state—
(a) the grounds on which it has been issued,
(b) that a constable may arrest P without warrant if the constable has reasonable grounds for believing that P is in breach of the DVPN,
(c) that an application for a domestic violence protection order under section 27 will be heard within 48 hours of the time of service of the DVPN and a notice of the hearing will be given to P,
(d) that the DVPN continues in effect until that application has been determined, and
(e) the provision that a magistrates' court may include in a domestic violence protection order.
(2) A DVPN must be in writing and must be served on P personally by a constable.
(3) On serving P with a DVPN, the constable must ask P for an address for the purposes of being given the notice of the hearing of the application for the domestic violence protection order.

26. Breach of a domestic violence protection notice

(1) A person arrested by virtue of section 25(1)(b) for a breach of a DVPN must be held in custody and brought before the magistrates' court which will hear the application for the DVPO under section 27—
(a) before the end of the period of 24 hours beginning with the time of the arrest, or
(b) if earlier, at the hearing of that application.
(2) If the person is brought before the court by virtue of subsection (1)(a), the court may remand the person.

(3) If the court adjourns the hearing of the application by virtue of section 27(8), the court may remand the person.

(4) In calculating when the period of 24 hours mentioned in subsection (1)(a) ends, Christmas Day, Good Friday, any Sunday and any day which is a bank holiday in England and Wales under the Banking and Financial Dealings Act 1971 are to be disregarded.

27. Application for a domestic violence protection order

(1) If a DVPN has been issued, a constable must apply for a domestic violence protection order ('a DVPO').

(2) The application must be made by complaint to a magistrates' court.

(3) The application must be heard by the magistrates' court not later than 48 hours after the DVPN was served pursuant to section 25(2).

(4) In calculating when the period of 48 hours mentioned in subsection (3) ends, Christmas Day, Good Friday, any Sunday and any day which is a bank holiday in England and Wales under the Banking and Financial Dealings Act 1971 are to be disregarded.

(5) A notice of the hearing of the application must be given to P.

(6) The notice is deemed given if it has been left at the address given by P under section 25(3).

(7) But if the notice has not been given because no address was given by P under section 25(3), the court may hear the application for the DVPO if the court is satisfied that the constable applying for the DVPO has made reasonable efforts to give P the notice.

(8) The magistrates' court may adjourn the hearing of the application.

(9) If the court adjourns the hearing, the DVPN continues in effect until the application has been determined.

(10) On the hearing of an application for a DVPO, section 97 of the Magistrates' Courts Act 1980 (summons to witness and warrant for his arrest) does not apply in relation to a person for whose protection the DVPO would be made, except where the person has given oral or written evidence at the hearing.

28. Conditions for and contents of a domestic violence protection order

(1) The court may make a DVPO if two conditions are met.

(2) The first condition is that the court is satisfied on the balance of probabilities that P has been violent towards, or has threatened violence towards, an associated person.

(3) The second condition is that the court thinks that making the DVPO is necessary to protect that person from violence or a threat of violence by P.

(4) Before making a DVPO, the court must, in particular, consider—
   (a) the welfare of any person under the age of 18 whose interests the court considers relevant to the making of the DVPO (whether or not that person is an associated person), and
   (b) any opinion of which the court is made aware—
      (i) of the person for whose protection the DVPO would be made, and
      (ii) in the case of provision included by virtue of subsection (8), of any other associated person who lives in the premises to which the provision would relate.

(5) But the court may make a DVPO in circumstances where the person for whose protection it is made does not consent to the making of the DVPO.

(6) A DVPO must contain provision to prohibit P from molesting the person for whose protection it is made.

(7) Provision required to be included by virtue of subsection (6) may be expressed so as to refer to molestation in general, to particular acts of molestation, or to both.

(8) If P lives in premises which are also lived in by a person for whose protection the DVPO is made, the DVPO may also contain provision—
   (a) to prohibit P from evicting or excluding from the premises the person for whose protection the DVPO is made,
   (b) to prohibit P from entering the premises,
   (c) to require P to leave the premises, or
   (d) to prohibit P from coming within such distance of the premises as may be specified in the DVPO.

(9) A DVPO must state that a constable may arrest P without warrant if the constable has reasonable grounds for believing that P is in breach of the DVPO.

(10) A DVPO may be in force for—
   (a) no fewer than 14 days beginning with the day on which it is made, and
   (b) no more than 28 days beginning with that day.

(11) A DVPO must state the period for which it is to be in force.

29. Breach of a domestic violence protection order

(1) A person arrested by virtue of section 28(9) for a breach of a DVPO must be held in custody and brought before a magistrates' court within the period of 24 hours beginning with the time of the arrest.

(2) If the matter is not disposed of when the person is brought before the court, the court may remand the person.
(3) In calculating when the period of 24 hours mentioned in subsection (1) ends, Christmas Day, Good Friday, any Sunday and any day which is a bank holiday in England and Wales under the Banking and Financial Dealings Act 1971 are to be disregarded.

33. Pilot schemes

(1) The Secretary of State may by order made by statutory instrument provide for any provision of sections 24 to 32 to come into force for a period of time to be specified in or under the order for the purpose of assessing the effectiveness of the provision.
(2) Such an order may make different provision for different areas.
(3) More than one order may be made under this section.
(4) Provision included in an order under this section does not affect the provision that may be included in relation to sections 24 to 32 in an order under section 59 (commencement).

CHILDREN, SCHOOLS AND FAMILIES ACT 2010
(2010 c. 26)

PART 2
FAMILY PROCEEDINGS

11. Restriction on publication of information relating to family proceedings

(1) This section applies in relation to any relevant family proceedings at which the public are not (or, in the case of proceedings which have already taken place, were not) entitled to be present.
(2) The publication of information relating to the proceedings is a contempt of court committed by the publisher unless the publication of the information is—
   (a) an authorised publication of the text, or a summary, of the whole or part of an order made or judgment given by the court in the proceedings (see section 12),
   (b) an authorised news publication (see section 13), or
   (c) authorised by rules of court.
(3) Nothing in this section makes it a contempt of court to publish information with the permission of the court.
(4) 'Family proceedings' means family proceedings within the meaning of—
   (a) section 65 of the Magistrates' Courts Act 1980, or
   (b) section 32 of the Matrimonial and Family Proceedings Act 1984.
(5) Where proceedings are family proceedings at the time they are commenced and, but for this subsection, would later cease to be family proceedings, for the purposes of this section they continue to be family proceedings.
(6) 'Relevant family proceedings' means family proceedings other than—
   (a) matrimonial causes and matters;
   (b) applications under Part 3 of the Family Law Act 1986 (declarations of status);
   (c) applications under section 27 of the Matrimonial Causes Act 1973 (financial provision where failure to maintain);
   (d) civil partnership causes and matters;
   (e) applications under section 58 of the Civil Partnership Act 2004 (declarations relating to civil partnerships);
   (f) applications under Part 9 of Schedule 5 to that Act (financial provision where failure to maintain);
   (g) causes and matters relating to non-contentious or common form probate business (within the meaning of section 128 of the Senior Courts Act 1981).
(7) The Lord Chancellor may, by order made by statutory instrument, amend the definition of 'relevant family proceedings' in subsection (6).
(8) An order under subsection (7) may make transitional provision or savings.
(9) A statutory instrument containing an order under subsection (7) may not be made unless a draft of the instrument containing the order has been laid before, and approved by a resolution of, each House of Parliament.

12. Authorised publication of court orders and judgments

(1) A publication of the text, or a summary, of the whole or part of an order made by a court in the proceedings is an authorised publication—
   (a) in a case where the proceedings are adoption proceedings or parental order proceedings or a case where the publication of the text or summary contains identification information relating to an individual involved in the proceedings, to

the extent that the publication of the text or summary is permitted by the court for the purposes of this section, and
(b) in any other case, to the extent that the publication of the text or summary is not prohibited by, and does not breach any restriction imposed by, the court for the purposes of this section.

(2) A publication of the text, or a summary, of the whole or part of a judgment given by a court in the proceedings is an authorised publication to the extent that the publication of the text or summary is permitted by the court for the purposes of this section.

(3) The court may permit, prohibit or restrict publication for the purposes of this section on its own initiative or on the application of any interested person.

(4) The court may permit publication for the purposes of this section subject to conditions specified by the court.

(5) In this section—
'adoption proceedings' means proceedings under the Adoption and Children Act 2002 (other than proceedings on an application for a placement order under section 22 of that Act);
'parental order proceedings' means proceedings for parental orders under section 30 of the Human Fertilisation and Embryology Act 1990 or section 54 of the Human Fertilisation and Embryology Act 2008.

13. Authorised news publications

(1) A publication of information is an authorised news publication if the following conditions are met.

(2) Condition 1 is that the information was obtained by an accredited news representative by observing or listening to the proceedings when attending them in exercise of a right conferred on accredited news representatives by rules of court.

(3) Condition 2 is that the publisher of the information—
(a) is the accredited news representative,
(b) publishes the information with the consent of, or pursuant to a contract or other agreement entered into with, that representative, or
(c) has obtained the information from a publication of information which is an authorised news publication.

(4) Condition 3 is that—
(a) the information is not—
(i) identification information relating to an individual involved in the proceedings,
(ii) sensitive personal information relating to the proceedings, or
(iii) restricted adoption information or restricted parental order information,
(b) the information is information within paragraphs (i) to (iii) of paragraph (a) and the publication is permitted by the court for the purposes of this Condition, or
(c) the information is identification information relating to an individual involved in the proceedings (but not restricted adoption information or restricted parental order information) and the individual is a professional witness in the proceedings.

(5) Condition 4 is that if the publication is—
(a) a publication of the text, or a summary, of an order made by a court in adoption proceedings or parental order proceedings, or
(b) a publication of the text, or a summary, of a judgment given by a court in relevant family proceedings,
the publication is permitted by the court for the purposes of section 12.

(6) Condition 5 is that the publication is not prohibited by, and does not breach any restriction imposed by, the court for the purposes of this condition or section 12.

(7) The court may permit the publication of information for the purposes of Condition 3 or prohibit or restrict the publication of information for the purposes of Condition 5 on its own initiative or on the application of any interested person.

14. Permitting publication for purposes of section 13: general

(1) This section applies where the court is determining whether to permit the publication of information for the purposes of Condition 3 in section 13 (except where section 15 applies).

(2) The court may not permit the publication of the information unless it is satisfied of one or more of the following matters.

(3) The matters are—
(a) that it is in the public interest to give the permission;
(b) that it is appropriate to give the permission so as to avoid injustice to a person involved in, referred to in or otherwise connected with the proceedings;
(c) that it is necessary to give the permission in the interests of the welfare of a child or vulnerable adult involved in, referred to in or otherwise connected with the proceedings;

(d) that an application for permission has been made by a party to the proceedings, or on behalf of a child who is the subject of the proceedings, and granting the permission is appropriate in all the circumstances.

(4) The court must have regard to any risk which publication of the information would pose to the safety or welfare of any individual involved in, referred to in or otherwise connected with the proceedings.

(5) The court may permit the publication subject to conditions specified by the court.

15. Permitting publication for purposes of section 13: adoption etc

(1) This section applies where the court is determining whether to permit the publication of restricted adoption information or restricted parental order information for the purposes of Condition 3 in section 13.

(2) 'Restricted adoption information' means information the publication of which is likely to lead one or more persons—

(a) to identify a person as—

(i) a prospective adopter of a child,

(ii) a person who has adopted a child, or

(iii) a person who has been, or may be, adopted, or

(b) to identify the whereabouts of a person identified as a person within sub-paragraph (i), (ii) or (iii) of paragraph (a).

(3) 'Restricted parental order information' means information the publication of which is likely to lead one or more persons—

(a) to identify a person as—

(i) a person who has applied for a parental order,

(ii) a person in respect of whom a parental order has been made, or

(iii) a child in relation to whom a parental order has been, or may be, made, or

(b) to identify the whereabouts of a person identified as a person within sub-paragraph (i), (ii) or (iii) of paragraph (a).

(4) If the person who has been or may be adopted or in relation to whom a parental order has been or may be made ('the affected person')—

(a) is a child,

(b) lacks capacity to consent to the publication, or

(c) cannot be found,

the court may not permit the publication of the information unless it is satisfied that publication of the information would not prejudice the safety or welfare of the affected person.

(5) In any other case where the affected person is alive, the court may not permit the publication except with the consent of the affected person.

(6) The court must have regard to whether consent to the publication has been given by—

(a) in the case of restricted adoption information, any prospective adopter of, or person who has adopted, the child in question, and

(b) in the case of restricted parental order information, any person who applied for the parental order or in respect of whom the parental order has been made.

(7) The court must have regard to any risk which publication of the information would pose to the safety or welfare of any individual involved in, referred to in or otherwise connected with the proceedings.

(8) The court may permit the publication subject to conditions specified by the court.

(9) For the purposes of this section—

'adoption' means adoption under the Adoption Act 1976 or the Adoption and Children Act 2002 (and related terms are to be construed accordingly);

'parental order' means a parental order under section 30 of the Human Fertilisation and Embryology Act 1990 or section 54 of the Human Fertilisation and Embryology Act 2008.

16. Prohibiting or restricting publication for purposes of section 13

(1) The court may not prohibit or restrict the publication of information for the purposes of Condition 5 in section 13 unless subsection (2) or (3) applies (or both subsections apply).

(2) This subsection applies if the court is satisfied that in the absence of the prohibition or restriction there is a real risk that the publication would prejudice—

(a) the safety of any person,

(b) the welfare of a child or vulnerable adult, or

(c) the interests of justice in the proceedings in question.

(3) This subsection applies if the information is identification information relating to a professional witness in the proceedings and—

(a) the information is also identification information relating to—

(i) another individual involved in the proceedings (other than a professional witness in the proceedings), or

(ii) an individual otherwise connected with the proceedings,

(b) the information is also sensitive personal information relating to the proceedings, or
(c) the court is satisfied that the professional witness is, has been or will be involved in the care or treatment of an individual involved in, or otherwise connected with, the proceedings, otherwise than for the purpose of being a professional witness in the proceedings.

17. Defences to contempt of court

(1) A person is not guilty of a contempt of court under section 11 by reason of the publication of information relating to relevant family proceedings if subsection (2), (3) or (4) applies.
(2) This subsection applies if the person proves that at the time of the publication the person did not know and had no reason to suspect that the information was information relating to the proceedings.
(3) This subsection applies if the person proves that—
(a) the person obtained the information from a previous publication, and
(b) at the time of the person's publication the person did not know and had no reason to suspect that the previous publication was not an authorised news publication.
(4) This subsection applies if the person proves that—
(a) the publication of the information would be an authorised news publication but for the failure to meet Condition 3 in section 13, and
(b) at the time of the publication the person did not know and had no reason to suspect that the information was—
(i) identification information relating to an individual involved in the proceedings,
(ii) sensitive personal information relating to the proceedings, or
(iii) restricted adoption information or restricted parental order information.

18. Appeals against decisions under section 12 or 13

(1) Rules of court—
(a) may make provision about appeals against decisions within subsection (2) (including provision which modifies provision made by or under any Act as it applies to such appeals), and
(b) to the extent that provision is not made by or under any Act for appeals against such decisions, must make such provision (including provision about the route of such appeals).
(2) Those decisions are—
(a) decisions to permit, or refuse to permit, publication of information for the purposes of section 12 or Condition 3 in section 13,
(b) decisions to impose, or refuse to impose, conditions on permission granted for those purposes, and
(c) decisions to prohibit or restrict, or refuse to prohibit or restrict, publication of information for the purposes of section 12 or Condition 5 in section 13.

19. Power to alter treatment of sensitive personal information

(1) Schedule 1 (which contains amendments which alter the treatment under this Part of sensitive personal information) has effect.
(2) In this section 'the Part 2 amending provisions' means the provisions of that Schedule and any related repeal in Schedule 4.
(3) The Lord Chancellor may not make an order under section 29(4) bringing into force any of the Part 2 amending provisions unless—
(a) an independent person appointed by the Lord Chancellor has carried out a review of the operation of this Part,
(b) in carrying out the review the independent person consulted the public about the operation of this Part, and
(c) the conclusions of the review have been set out in a report which has been laid before Parliament.
(4) No review for the purposes of subsection (3)(a) may be commenced before the end of the period of 18 months beginning with the time section 11 comes into force.
(5) Where section 11 is initially brought into force for one or more specified purposes only, the reference in subsection (4) to the time that section comes into force is to the earliest time it comes into force for any purpose.
(6) A statutory instrument containing an order under section 29(4) bringing into force any of the Part 2 amending provisions may not be made unless a draft of the instrument containing the order has been laid before, and approved by a resolution of, each House of Parliament.

21. Interpretation of Part 2, etc

(1) In this Part—
'accredited news representative', in relation to any proceedings, means a representative of one or more news organisations who is a member of a class of representatives of news organisations on which rules of court confer a right to attend the proceedings;

'child' means a person under the age of 18;
'court' includes a judge and any person exercising the functions of a court or a judge;
'identification information', in relation to an individual involved in or otherwise connected with proceedings, means—
(a) information, including in particular information as to any of the matters set out in subsection (2), the publication of which is likely to lead members of the public to identify the individual as someone who is or has been involved in or otherwise connected with the proceedings, and
(b) in a case where the individual is a child, information the publication of which is likely to lead members of the public to identify the address or school of the individual as being that of an individual who is or has been involved in or otherwise connected with the proceedings;
'judgment' includes a record produced by the court of its reasons for a decision;
'news organisation' means a news gathering or reporting organisation;
'professional witness', in any proceedings, means a person-
(a) who has given, or whom it is proposed will give, written or oral evidence in the proceedings in exchange for a fee, and
(b) whose instruction by a party to the proceedings has been authorised by the court for the purposes of the proceedings;
'publication' includes disclosure or communication in any form to any person or persons;
'publisher' means—
(a) where the information is published in a newspaper or periodical, any proprietor, any editor and any publisher of the newspaper or periodical;
(b) where the information is published in a relevant programme—
(i) any body corporate or Scottish partnership engaged in providing the programme service in which the programme is included, and
(ii) any person having functions in relation to the programme corresponding to those of an editor of a newspaper;
(c) in the case of any other publication of information, any person publishing it;
'relevant family proceedings' has the meaning given by section 11;
'relevant programme' means a programme included in a programme service, within the meaning of the Broadcasting Act 1990;
'restricted adoption information' has the meaning given by section 15;
'restricted parental order information' has the meaning given by section 15;
'sensitive personal information', in relation to any proceedings, means information listed in Schedule 2.

(2) The matters referred to in the definition of 'identification information' in subsection (1) are—
(a) the name of the individual or any title, pseudonym or alias of the individual;
(b) the address or locality of any place where the individual lives or works or is educated or taken care of;
(c) the individual's appearance or style of dress;
(d) any employment or other occupation of, or position held by, the individual;
(e) the individual's relationship to particular relatives, or association with particular friends or acquaintances, of the individual;
(f) the individual's recreational interests;
(g) the individual's political, philosophical or religious beliefs or interests;
(h) any property (whether real or personal) in which the individual has an interest or with which the individual is otherwise associated.

(3) For the purposes of this Part an individual is 'involved' in proceedings if the individual—
(a) is or was a party to the proceedings or the subject of the proceedings,
(b) is a person called, or whom it is proposed to call, as a witness in the proceedings, or
(c) is a person who has given written evidence in connection with the proceedings.

(4) The Lord Chancellor may, by order made by statutory instrument, amend—
(a) the definition of 'professional witness' in subsection (1);
(b) Schedule 2 (list of sensitive personal information).

(5) An order under subsection (4) may make transitional provision or savings.

(6) A statutory instrument containing an order under subsection (4) may not be made unless a draft of the statutory instrument containing the order has been laid before, and approved by a resolution of, each House of Parliament.

(7) Nothing in this Part prejudices any other power a court may have to prevent or restrict the publication of information relating to relevant family proceedings.

(8) No provision of this Part (or of Part 2 of Schedule 3 or Part 2 of Schedule 4) applies in relation to relevant family proceedings concluded before the coming into force of the provision in question.

...

RIGHTS OF CHILDREN AND YOUNG PERSONS (WALES) MEASURE 2011
(2011 nawm 2)

1. Duty to have due regard to Convention on the Rights of the Child

(1) From the beginning of May 2014, the Welsh Ministers must, when exercising any of their functions, have due regard to the requirements of—
(a) Part I of the Convention,
(b) articles 1 to 7 of the Optional Protocol to the Convention on the Rights of the Child on the involvement of children in armed conflict, except article 6(2), and
(c) articles 1 to 10 of the Optional Protocol to the Convention on the Rights of the Child on the sale of children, child prostitution and child pornography.
(2) From the beginning of May 2012 until the end of April 2014, the Welsh Ministers must, in making any decision which falls within subsection (3), have due regard to the requirements of Part I of the Convention and the Protocols.
(3) A decision falls within this subsection if it is a decision about any of the following—
(a) provision proposed to be included in an enactment;
(b) formulation of a new policy;
(c) a review of or change to an existing policy.
(4) References in this Measure to the Welsh Ministers' duty under this section are—
(a) from the beginning of May 2012 until the end of April 2014, to the duty in subsection (2); and
(b) from the beginning of May 2014, to the duty in subsection (1).
(5) This section applies to the First Minister as to the Welsh Ministers (and any reference in this Measure to the duty under this section is to be read accordingly).

LEGAL AID, SENTENCING AND PUNISHMENT OF OFFENDERS ACT 2012
(2012, c. 10)

PART 1
LEGAL AID

Provision of legal aid

1. Lord Chancellor's functions

(1) The Lord Chancellor must secure that legal aid is made available in accordance with this Part.
(2) In this Part 'legal aid' means—
(a) civil legal services required to be made available under section 9 or 10 or paragraph 3 of Schedule 3 (civil legal aid), and
(b) services consisting of advice, assistance and representation required to be made available under section 13, 15 or 16 or paragraph 4 or 5 of Schedule 3 (criminal legal aid).
(3) The Lord Chancellor may secure the provision of—
(a) general information about the law and the legal system, and
(b) information about the availability of advice about, and assistance in connection with, the law and the legal system.
(4) The Lord Chancellor may do anything which is calculated to facilitate, or is incidental or conducive to, the carrying out of the Lord Chancellor's functions under this Part.
(5) Nothing in this Part affects the powers that the Lord Chancellor has otherwise than under this Part.

2. Arrangements

(1) The Lord Chancellor may make such arrangements as the Lord Chancellor considers appropriate for the purposes of carrying out the Lord Chancellor's functions under this Part.
(2) The Lord Chancellor may, in particular, make arrangements by—
(a) making grants or loans to enable persons to provide services or facilitate the provision of services,
(b) making grants or loans to individuals to enable them to obtain services, and
(c) establishing and maintaining a body to provide services or facilitate the provision of services.

(3) The Lord Chancellor may by regulations make provision about the payment of remuneration by the Lord Chancellor to persons who provide services under arrangements made for the purposes of this Part.

(4) If the Lord Chancellor makes arrangements for the purposes of this Part that provide for a court, tribunal or other person to assess remuneration payable by the Lord Chancellor, the court, tribunal or person must assess the remuneration in accordance with the arrangements and, if relevant, with regulations under subsection (3).

. . .

4. Director of Legal Aid Casework

(1) The Lord Chancellor must designate a civil servant as the Director of Legal Aid Casework ('the Director').

Civil legal aid

8. Civil legal services

(1) In this Part 'legal services' means the following types of services—
 (a) providing advice as to how the law applies in particular circumstances,
 (b) providing advice and assistance in relation to legal proceedings,
 (c) providing other advice and assistance in relation to the prevention of disputes about legal rights or duties ('legal disputes') or the settlement or other resolution of legal disputes, and
 (d) providing advice and assistance in relation to the enforcement of decisions in legal proceedings or other decisions by which legal disputes are resolved.

(2) The services described in subsection (1) include, in particular, advice and assistance in the form of—
 (a) representation, and
 (b) mediation and other forms of dispute resolution.

(3) In this Part 'civil legal services' means any legal services other than the types of advice, assistance and representation that are required to be made available under sections 13, 15 and 16 (criminal legal aid).

9. General cases

(1) Civil legal services are to be available to an individual under this Part if—
 (a) they are civil legal services described in Part 1 of Schedule 1, and
 (b) the Director has determined that the individual qualifies for the services in accordance with this Part (and has not withdrawn the determination).

(2) The Lord Chancellor may by order—
 (a) add services to Part 1 of Schedule 1, or
 (b) vary or omit services described in that Part,(whether by modifying that Part or Part 2, 3 or 4 of the Schedule).

10. Exceptional cases

(1) Civil legal services other than services described in Part 1 of Schedule 1 are to be available to an individual under this Part if subsection (2) or (4) is satisfied.

(2) This subsection is satisfied where the Director—
 (a) has made an exceptional case determination in relation to the individual and the services, and
 (b) has determined that the individual qualifies for the services in accordance with this Part,(and has not withdrawn either determination).

(3) For the purposes of subsection (2), an exceptional case determination is a determination—
 (a) that it is necessary to make the services available to the individual under this Part because failure to do so would be a breach of—
  (i) the individual's Convention rights (within the meaning of the Human Rights Act 1998), or
  (ii) any rights of the individual to the provision of legal services that are enforceable EU rights, or
 (b) that it is appropriate to do so, in the particular circumstances of the case, having regard to any risk that failure to do so would be such a breach.

(4) This subsection is satisfied where—
 (a) the services consist of advocacy in proceedings at an inquest under the Coroners Act 1988 into the death of a member of the individual's family,
 (b) the Director has made a wider public interest determination in relation to the individual and the inquest, and
 (c) the Director has determined that the individual qualifies for the services in accordance with this Part,

(and neither determination has been withdrawn).

(5) For the purposes of subsection (4), a wider public interest determination is a determination that, in the particular circumstances of the case, the provision of advocacy under this Part for the individual for the purposes of the inquest is likely to produce significant benefits for a class of person, other than the individual and the members of the individual's family.

(6) For the purposes of this section an individual is a member of another individual's family if—

(a) they are relatives (whether of the full blood or half blood or by marriage or civil partnership),

(b) they are cohabitants (as defined in Part 4 of the Family Law Act 1996), or

(c) one has parental responsibility for the other.

Contributions and costs

25. Charges on property in connection with civil legal services

(1) Where civil legal services are made available to an individual under this Part, the amounts described in subsection (2) are to constitute a first charge on—

(a) any property recovered or preserved by the individual in proceedings, or in any compromise or settlement of a dispute, in connection with which the services were provided (whether the property is recovered or preserved for the individual or another person), and

(b) any costs payable to the individual by another person in connection with such proceedings or such a dispute.

(2) Those amounts are—

(a) amounts expended by the Lord Chancellor in securing the provision of the services (except to the extent that they are recovered by other means), and

(b) other amounts payable by the individual in connection with the services under section 23 or 24.

(3) Regulations may make provision for exceptions from subsection (1).

. . .

Providers of services etc

27. Choice of provider of services etc

(1) The Lord Chancellor's duty under section 1(1) does not include a duty to secure that, where services are made available to an individual under this Part, they are made available by the means selected by the individual.

(2) The Lord Chancellor may discharge that duty, in particular, by arranging for the services to be provided by telephone or by other electronic means.

(3) The Lord Chancellor's duty under section 1(1) does not include a duty to secure that, where services are made available to an individual under this Part, they are made available by a person selected by the individual, subject to subsections (4) to (10).

Supplementary

38. Abolition of Legal Services Commission

(1) The Legal Services Commission ceases to exist.

(2) Schedule 4 (transfer of employees and property etc of Legal Services Commission) has effect.

. . .

SCHEDULES

SCHEDULE 1
CIVIL LEGAL SERVICES

PART 1
SERVICES

Care, supervision and protection of children

1. (1) Civil legal services provided in relation to—
(a) orders under section 25 of the Children Act 1989 ('the 1989 Act') (secure accommodation);
(b) orders under Part 4 of the 1989 Act (care and supervision);
(c) orders under Part 5 of the 1989 Act (protection of children);
(d) approval by a court under paragraph 19 of Schedule 2 to the 1989 Act (arrangements to assist children to live abroad);
(e) parenting orders under section 8 of the Crime and Disorder Act 1998 ('the 1998 Act');
(f) child safety orders under section 11 of the 1998 Act;
(g) orders for contact under section 26 of the Adoption and Children Act 2002 ('the 2002 Act');
(h) applications for leave of the court to remove a child from a person's custody under section 36 of the 2002 Act;
(i) placement orders, recovery orders or adoption orders under Chapter 3 of Part 1 of the 2002 Act (see sections 21, 41 and 46 of that Act);
(j) orders under section 84 of the 2002 Act (parental responsibility prior to adoption abroad).

(2) Civil legal services provided in relation to an order under an enactment made—
(a) as an alternative to an order mentioned in sub-paragraph (1), or
(b) in proceedings heard together with proceedings relating to such an order.

Exclusions

(3) Sub-paragraphs (1) and (2) are subject to the exclusions in Parts 2 and 3 of this Schedule.

Definitions

(4) In this paragraph 'children' means persons under the age of 18.

Inherent jurisdiction of High Court in relation to children and vulnerable adults

9. (1) Civil legal services provided in relation to the inherent jurisdiction of the High Court in relation to children and vulnerable adults.

Exclusions

(2) Sub-paragraph (1) is subject to the exclusions in Parts 2 and 3 of this Schedule.

Definitions

(3) In this paragraph—
'adults' means persons aged 18 or over;
'children' means persons under the age of 18.

Unlawful removal of children

10. (1) Civil legal services provided to an individual in relation to the following orders and requirements where the individual is seeking to prevent the unlawful removal of a related child from the United Kingdom or to secure the return of a related child who has been unlawfully removed from the United Kingdom—
(a) a prohibited steps order or specific issue order (as defined in section 8(1) of the Children Act 1989);

(b) an order under section 33 of the Family Law Act 1986 for disclosure of the child's whereabouts;
(c) an order under section 34 of that Act for the child's return;
(d) a requirement under section 37 of that Act to surrender a passport issued to, or containing particulars of, the child.

(2) Civil legal services provided to an individual in relation to the following orders and applications where the individual is seeking to secure the return of a related child who has been unlawfully removed to a place in the United Kingdom—
(a) a prohibited steps order or specific issue order (as defined in section 8(1) of the Children Act 1989);
(b) an application under section 27 of the Family Law Act 1986 for registration of an order relating to the child;
(c) an order under section 33 of that Act for disclosure of the child's whereabouts;
(d) an order under section 34 of that Act for the child's return.

Exclusions

(3) Sub-paragraphs (1) and (2) are subject to the exclusions in Parts 2 and 3 of this Schedule.

Definitions

(4) For the purposes of this paragraph, a child is related to an individual if the individual is the child's parent or has parental responsibility for the child.
(5) In this paragraph 'child' means a person under the age of 18.

Family homes and domestic violence

11. (1) Civil legal services provided in relation to home rights, occupation orders and non molestation orders under Part 4 of the Family Law Act 1996.
(2) Civil legal services provided in relation to the following in circumstances arising out of a family relationship—
(a) an injunction following assault, battery or false imprisonment;
(b) the inherent jurisdiction of the High Court to protect an adult.

Exclusions

(3) Sub-paragraphs (1) and (2) are subject to—
(a) the exclusions in Part 2 of this Schedule, with the exception of paragraphs 3 and 11 of that Part, and
(b) the exclusion in Part 3 of this Schedule.

Definitions

(4) For the purposes of this paragraph—
(a) there is a family relationship between two people if they are associated with each other, and
(b) 'associated' has the same meaning as in Part 4 of the Family Law Act 1996 (see section 62 of that Act).
(5) For the purposes of this paragraph, the Lord Chancellor may by regulations make provision about when circumstances arise out of a family relationship.

Victims of domestic violence and family matters

12. (1) Civil legal services provided to an adult ('A') in relation to a matter arising out of a family relationship between A and another individual ('B') where—
(a) there has been, or is a risk of, domestic violence between A and B, and
(b) A was, or is at risk of being, the victim of that domestic violence.

General exclusions

(2) Sub-paragraph (1) is subject to the exclusions in Part 2 of this Schedule, with the exception of paragraph 11 of that Part.
(3) But the exclusions described in sub-paragraph (2) are subject to the exception in subparagraph (4).
(4) The services described in sub-paragraph (1) include services provided in relation to conveyancing, but only where—
(a) the services in relation to conveyancing are provided in the course of giving effect to a court order made in proceedings, and

(b) services described in that sub-paragraph (other than services in relation to conveyancing) are being or have been provided in relation to those proceedings under arrangements made for the purposes of this Part of this Act.

(5) Sub-paragraph (1) is subject to the exclusion in Part 3 of this Schedule.

Specific exclusion

(6) The services described in sub-paragraph (1) do not include services provided in relation to a claim in tort in respect of the domestic violence.

Definitions

(7) For the purposes of this paragraph—

(a) there is a family relationship between two people if they are associated with each other, and

(b) 'associated' has the same meaning as in Part 4 of the Family Law Act 1996 (see section 62 of that Act).

(8) For the purposes of this paragraph—

(a) matters arising out of a family relationship include matters arising under a family enactment, and

(b) (subject to paragraph (a)) the Lord Chancellor may by regulations make provision about when matters arise out of a family relationship.

(9) In this paragraph—

'adult' means a person aged 18 or over;

'domestic violence' means any incident of threatening behaviour, violence or abuse (whether psychological, physical, sexual, financial or emotional) between individuals who are associated with each other;

'family enactment' means—

(a) section 17 of the Married Women's Property Act 1882 (questions between husband and wife as to property);

(b) the Maintenance Orders (Facilities for Enforcement) Act 1920;

(c) the Maintenance Orders Act 1950;

(d) the Maintenance Orders Act 1958;

(e) the Maintenance Orders (Reciprocal Enforcement) Act 1972;

(f) Schedule 1 to the Domicile and Matrimonial Proceedings Act 1973 (staying of matrimonial proceedings) and corresponding provision in relation to civil partnerships made by rules of court under section 223 of the Civil Partnership Act 2004;

(g) the Matrimonial Causes Act 1973;

(h) the Inheritance (Provision for Family Dependants) Act 1975;

(i) the Domestic Proceedings and Magistrates' Courts Act 1978;

(j) Part 3 of the Matrimonial and Family Proceedings Act 1984 (financial relief after overseas divorce etc);

(k) Parts 1 and 3 of the Family Law Act 1986 (child custody and declarations of status);

(l) Parts 1 and 2 of the Children Act 1989 (orders with respect to children in family proceedings);

(m) section 53 of, and Schedule 7 to, the Family Law Act 1996 (transfer of tenancies on divorce etc or separation of cohabitants);

(n) Chapters 2 and 3 of Part 2 of the Civil Partnership Act 2004 (dissolution, nullity and other proceedings and property and financial arrangements);

(o) section 54 of the Human Fertilisation and Embryology Act 2008 (applications for parental orders).

Protection of children and family matters

13. (1) Civil legal services provided to an adult (lA') in relation to the following orders and procedures where the child who is or would be the subject of the order is at risk of abuse from an individual other than A—

(a) orders under section 4(2A) of the Children Act 1989 ('the 1989 Act') (removal of father's parental responsibility);

(b) orders under section 6(7) of the 1989 Act (termination of appointment of guardian);

(c) orders mentioned in section 8(1) of the 1989 Act (residence, contact and other orders);

(d) special guardianship orders under Part 2 of the 1989 Act;

(e) orders under section 33 of the Family Law Act 1986 ('the 1986 Act') (disclosure of child's whereabouts);

(f) orders under section 34 of the 1986 Act (return of child).

Exclusions

(2) Sub-paragraph (1) is subject to the exclusions in Parts 2 and 3 of this Schedule.

Definitions

(3) In this paragraph—
'abuse' means physical or mental abuse, including—
(a) sexual abuse, and
(b) abuse in the form of violence, neglect, maltreatment and exploitation;
'adult' means a person aged 18 or over;
'child' means a person under the age of 18.

Mediation in family disputes

14. (1) Mediation provided in relation to family disputes.
(2) Civil legal services provided in connection with the mediation of family disputes.

Exclusions

(3) Sub-paragraphs (1) and (2) are subject to the exclusions in Part 2 of this Schedule, with the exception of paragraph 11 of that Part.
(4) But the exclusions described in sub-paragraph (3) are subject to the exception in subparagraph (5).
(5) The services described in sub-paragraph (2) include services provided in relation to conveyancing, but only where—
(a) the services in relation to conveyancing are provided in the course of giving effect to arrangements for the resolution of a family dispute, and
(b) services described in that sub-paragraph or sub-paragraph (1) (other than services in relation to conveyancing) are being or have been provided in relation to the dispute under arrangements made for the purposes of this Part of this Act.
(6) Sub-paragraphs (1) and (2) are subject to the exclusion in Part 3 of this Schedule.

Definitions

(7) For the purposes of this paragraph—
(a) a dispute is a family dispute if it is a dispute between individuals about a matter arising out of a family relationship between the individuals,
(b) there is a family relationship between two individuals if they are associated with each other, and
(c) 'associated' has the same meaning as in Part 4 of the Family Law Act 1996 (see section 62 of that Act).
(8) For the purposes of this paragraph—
(a) matters arising out of a family relationship include matters arising under a family enactment, and
(b) (subject to paragraph (a)) the Lord Chancellor may by regulations make provision about when matters arise out of a family relationship.
(9) In this paragraph—
'child' means a person under the age of 18;
'family enactment' has the meaning given in paragraph 12.
Children who are parties to family proceedings

15. (1) Civil legal services provided to a child in relation to family proceedings—
(a) where the child is, or proposes to be, the applicant or respondent;
(b) where the child is made a party to the proceedings by a court under rule 16.2 of the Family Procedure Rules;
(c) where the child is a party to the proceedings and is conducting, or proposes to conduct, the proceedings without a children's guardian or litigation friend in accordance with rule 16.6 of the Family Procedure Rules.

Exclusions

(2) Sub-paragraph (1) is subject to the exclusions in Parts 2 and 3 of this Schedule.

Definitions

(3) For the purposes of this paragraph—
(a) proceedings are family proceedings if they relate to a matter arising out of a family relationship,

(b) there is a family relationship between two individuals if they are associated with each other, and
(c) 'associated' has the same meaning as in Part 4 of the Family Law Act 1996 (see section 62 of that Act).

(4) For the purposes of this paragraph—
(a) matters arising out of a family relationship include matters arising under a family enactment, and
(b) (subject to paragraph (a)) the Lord Chancellor may by regulations make provision about when matters arise out of a family relationship.

(5) In this paragraph—
'child' means a person under the age of 18;
'family enactment' has the meaning given in paragraph 12.

Forced marriage

16. (1) Civil legal services provided in relation to forced marriage protection orders under Part 4A of the Family Law Act 1996.

Exclusions

(2) Sub-paragraph (1) is subject to the exclusions in Parts 2 and 3 of this Schedule.

EU and international agreements concerning children

17. (1) Civil legal services provided in relation to—
(a) an application made to the Lord Chancellor under the 1980 European Convention on Child Custody for the recognition or enforcement in England and Wales of a decision relating to the custody of a child;
(b) an application made to the Lord Chancellor under the 1980 Hague Convention in respect of a child who is, or is believed to be, in England and Wales;
(c) the recognition or enforcement of a judgment in England and Wales in accordance with Article 21,28, 41,42 or 48 of the 2003 Brussels Regulation.

Exclusions

(2) Sub-paragraph (1) is subject to the exclusions in Parts 2 and 3 of this Schedule.

Definitions

(3) In this paragraph—
'the 1980 European Convention on Child Custody' means the European Convention on Recognition and Enforcement of Decisions concerning Custody of Children and on the Restoration of Custody of Children which was signed in Luxembourg on 20 May 1980;
'the 1980 Hague Convention' means the Convention on the Civil Aspects of International Child Abduction which was signed at The Hague on 25 October 1980;
'the 2003 Brussels Regulation' means Council Regulation (EC) No. 2001/2003 of 27 November 2003 concerning jurisdiction and the recognition and enforcement of judgments in matrimonial matters and the matters of parental responsibility.

(4) For the purposes of this paragraph, an application is made to the Lord Chancellor if it is addressed to the Lord Chancellor or transmitted to the Lord Chancellor in accordance with section 3 or 14 of the Child Abduction and Custody Act 1985.

EU and international agreements concerning maintenance

18. (1) Civil legal services provided in relation to an application under the following for the recognition or enforcement in England and Wales of a maintenance order—
(a) the 1968 Brussels Convention;
(b) the 1973 Hague Convention;
(c) the 1989 Lugano Convention;
(d) the 2000 Brussels Regulation;
(e) the 2007 Lugano Convention.

(2) Civil legal services provided in relation to an application under Article 56 of the EU Maintenance Regulation (applications relating to maintenance decisions).

(3) Civil legal services provided to an individual in relation to proceedings in England and Wales relating to the recognition, enforceability or enforcement of a maintenance

decision in circumstances in which the individual falls within Article 47(2) or (3) of the EU Maintenance Regulation (parties who benefited from free legal aid etc in Member State of origin).

Exclusions

(4) Sub-paragraphs (1) to (3) are subject to—
 (a) the exclusions in Part 2 of this Schedule, with the exception of paragraph 11 of that Part, and
 (b) the exclusion in Part 3 of this Schedule.

Definitions

(5) In this paragraph—
'the 1968 Brussels Convention' means the Convention on jurisdiction and the enforcement of judgments in civil and commercial matters (including the Protocol annexed to that Convention) signed at Brussels on 27 September 1968;
'the 1973 Hague Convention' means the Convention on the recognition and enforcement of decisions relating to maintenance obligations concluded at The Hague on 2 October 1973;
'the 1989 Lugano Convention' means the Convention on jurisdiction and the enforcement of judgments in civil and commercial matters (including the Protocols annexed to that Convention) opened for signature at Lugano on 16 September 1988 and signed by the United Kingdom on 18 September 1989;
'the 2000 Brussels Regulation' means Council Regulation (EC) No. 44/2001 of 22 December 2000 on jurisdiction and the recognition and enforcement of judgments in civil and commercial matters;
'the 2007 Lugano Convention' means the Convention on jurisdiction and enforcement of judgments in civil and commercial matters, between the European Community and the Republic of Iceland, the Kingdom of Norway, the Swiss Confederation and the Kingdom of Denmark signed on behalf of the European Community on 30 October 2007;
'the EU Maintenance Regulation' means Council Regulation (EC) No. 4/2009 of 18 December 2008 on jurisdiction, applicable law, recognition and enforcement of decisions and co-operation in matters relating to maintenance obligations;
'maintenance order', in relation to a convention or regulation listed in this paragraph, means a maintenance judgment within the meaning of that convention or regulation.

Judicial review

19. (1) Civil legal services provided in relation to judicial review of an enactment, decision, act or omission.

General exclusions

(2) Sub-paragraph (1) is subject to—
 (a) the exclusions in Part 2 of this Schedule, with the exception of paragraphs 1,2, 3, 4, 5, 6, 8, 12, 15 and 16 of that Part, and
 (b) the exclusion in Part 3 of this Schedule.

Specific exclusion: benefit to individual

(3) The services described in sub-paragraph (1) do not include services provided to an individual in relation to judicial review that does not have the potential to produce a benefit for the individual, a member of the individual's family or the environment.
(4) Sub-paragraph (3) does not exclude services provided in relation to a judicial review where the judicial review ceases to have the potential to produce such a benefit after civil legal services have been provided in relation to the judicial review under arrangements made for the purposes of this Part of this Act.

Specific exclusions: immigration cases

(5) The services described in sub-paragraph (1) do not include services provided in relation to judicial review in respect of an issue relating to immigration where—
 (a) the same issue, or substantially the same issue, was the subject of a previous judicial review or an appeal to a court or tribunal,
 (b) on the determination of the previous judicial review or appeal (or, if there was more than one, the latest one), the court, tribunal or other person hearing the case found against the applicant or appellant on that issue, and

(c) the services in relation to the new judicial review are provided before the end of the period of 1 year beginning with the day of that determination.

(6) The services described in sub-paragraph (1) do not include services provided in relation to judicial review of removal directions in respect of an individual where the directions were given not more than 1 year after the latest of the following—

(a) the making of the decision (or, if there was more than one, the latest decision) to remove the individual from the United Kingdom by way of removal directions;

(b) the refusal of leave to appeal against that decision;

(c) the determination or withdrawal of an appeal against that decision.

(7) Sub-paragraphs (5) and (6) do not exclude services provided to an individual in relation to—

(a) judicial review of a negative decision in relation to an asylum application (within the meaning of the EU Procedures Directive) where there is no right of appeal to the First-tier Tribunal against the decision;

(b) judicial review of certification under section 94 or 96 of the Nationality, Immigration and Asylum Act 2002 (certificate preventing or restricting appeal of immigration decision).

(8) Sub-paragraphs (5) and (6) do not exclude services provided in relation to judicial review of removal directions in respect of an individual where prescribed conditions relating to either or both of the following are met—

(a) the period between the individual being given notice of the removal directions and the proposed time for his or her removal;

(b) the reasons for proposing that period.

Definitions

(9) For the purposes of this paragraph an individual is a member of another individual's family if—

(a) they are relatives (whether of the full blood or half blood or by marriage or civil partnership),

(b) they are cohabitants (as defined in Part 4 of the Family Law Act 1996), or

(c) one has parental responsibility for the other.

(10) In this paragraph—

'EU Procedures Directive' means Council Directive 2005/85/EC of 1 December 2005 on minimum standards on procedures in Member States for granting and withdrawing refugee status;

'an issue relating to immigration' includes an issue relating to rights described in paragraph 30 of this Part of this Schedule;

'judicial review' means—

(a) the procedure on an application for judicial review (see section 31 of the Senior Courts Act 1981), but not including the procedure after the application is treated under rules of court as if it were not such an application, and

(b) any procedure in which a court, tribunal or other person mentioned in Part 3 of this Schedule is required by an enactment to make a decision applying the principles that are applied by the court on an application for judicial review;

'removal directions' means directions under—

(a) paragraphs 8 to 10A of Schedule 2 to the Immigration Act 1971 (removal of persons refused leave to enter and illegal entrants);

(b) paragraphs 12 to 14 of Schedule 2 to that Act (removal of seamen and aircrew);

(c) paragraph 1 of Schedule 3 to that Act (removal of persons liable to deportation);

(d) section 10 of the Immigration and Asylum Act 1999 (removal of certain persons unlawfully in the United Kingdom);

(e) section 47 of the Immigration, Asylum and Nationality Act 2006 (removal of persons with statutorily extended leave).

MARRIAGE (SAME SEX COUPLES ACT) 2013 (2013 C. 30)

1. Extension of marriage to same sex couples

(1) Marriage of same sex couples is lawful.

(2) The marriage of a same sex couple may only be solemnized in accordance with—

(a) Part 3 of the Marriage Act 1949,

(b) Part 5 of the Marriage Act 1949,

(c) the Marriage (Registrar General's Licence) Act 1970, or
(d) an Order in Council made under Part 1 or 3 of Schedule 6.

(3) No Canon of the Church of England is contrary to section 3 of the Submission of the Clergy Act 1533 (which provides that no Canons shall be contrary to the Royal Prerogative or the customs, laws or statutes of this realm) by virtue of its making provision about marriage being the union of one man with one woman.

(4) Any duty of a member of the clergy to solemnize marriages (and any corresponding right of persons to have their marriages solemnized by members of the clergy) is not extended by this Act to marriages of same sex couples.

(5) A 'member of the clergy' is—
(a) a clerk in Holy Orders of the Church of England, or
(b) a clerk in Holy Orders of the Church in Wales.

2. Marriage according to religious rites: no compulsion to solemnize etc

(1) A person may not be compelled by any means (including by the enforcement of a contract or a statutory or other legal requirement) to—
(a) undertake an opt-in activity, or
(b) refrain from undertaking an opt-out activity.

(2) A person may not be compelled by any means (including by the enforcement of a contract or a statutory or other legal requirement)—
(a) to conduct a relevant marriage,
(b) to be present at, carry out, or otherwise participate in, a relevant marriage, or
(c) to consent to a relevant marriage being conducted,
where the reason for the person not doing that thing is that the relevant marriage concerns a same sex couple.

(3) In this section—
"opt-in activity" means an activity of the kind specified in an entry in the first column of the following table which falls to be undertaken for the purposes of any enactment specified in the corresponding entry in the second column;
"opt-out activity" means an activity which reverses, or otherwise modifies, the effect of an opt-in activity.

Activity	*Enactment*
Giving consent	Any of these provisions of the 1949 Act: (a) section 26A(3); (b) section 26B(2), (4) or (6); (c) section 44A(6); (d) section 46(1C)
	Regulations under section 70A(5) of the 1949 Act (as mentioned in section 70A(6)(c) of that Act) relating to an application for registration
	Section 1(3) of the Marriage (Registrar General's Licence) Act 1970
	An armed forces overseas marriage Order in its application to marriages of same sex couples (as mentioned in paragraph 9(5) of Schedule 6)
Applying for the registration of a building	Section 43A of the 1949 Act
Authorising a person to be present at the solemnization of marriages of same sex couples in a building registered under section 43A of the 1949 Act	Section 43B of the 1949 Act
Being authorised to be present at the solemnization of marriages of same sex couples in a building registered under section 43A of the 1949 Act	Section 43B of the 1949 Act
Giving a certificate, giving a copy of a consent, or certifying any matter	Any of these provisions of the 1949 Act: (a) section 43A(3); (b) section 43B(2); (c) section 44A(7)

(4) In this section—
"1949 Act" means the Marriage Act 1949;
"armed forces overseas marriage Order" means an Order in Council under Part 3 of Schedule 6;
"person"—
(a) includes a religious organisation;
(b) does not include a registrar, a superintendent registrar or the Registrar General;
"relevant marriage" means—
(a) a marriage of a same sex couple solemnized in accordance with—
(i) section 26A or 26B of the 1949 Act (marriage in a place of worship or in another place according to religious rites or usages),
(ii) Part 5 of the 1949 Act (marriage in a naval, military or air force chapel),
(iii) section 1 of the Marriage (Registrar General's Licence) Act 1970 (deathbed marriage), where the marriage is according to religious rites or usages, or
(iv) an armed forces overseas marriage Order, where the marriage is according to religious rites or usages,
including any ceremony forming part of, or connected with, the solemnization of such a marriage; and
(b) a marriage ceremony read or celebrated in accordance with section 46 of the 1949 Act in respect of a same sex couple (religious ceremony after registrar's marriage of same sex couple);
and a reference to conducting a relevant marriage is to be read accordingly.

9. Conversion of civil partnership into marriage

(1) The parties to an England and Wales civil partnership may convert their civil partnership into a marriage under a procedure established by regulations made by the Secretary of State.
(2) The parties to a civil partnership within subsection (3) may convert their civil partnership into a marriage under a procedure established by regulations made by the Secretary of State.
(3) A civil partnership is within this subsection if—
(a) it was formed outside the United Kingdom under an Order in Council made under Chapter 1 of Part 5 of the Civil Partnership Act 2004 (registration at British consulates etc or by armed forces personnel), and
(b) the part of the United Kingdom that was relevant for the purposes of section 210(2)(b) or (as the case may be) section 211(2)(b) of that Act was England and Wales.
(4) Regulations under this section may in particular make—
(a) provision about the making by the parties to a civil partnership of an application to convert their civil partnership into a marriage;
(b) provision about the information to be provided in support of an application to convert;
(c) provision about the making of declarations in support of an application to convert;
(d) provision for persons who have made an application to convert to appear before any person or attend at any place;
(e) provision conferring functions in connection with applications to convert on relevant officials, relevant armed forces personnel, the Secretary of State, or any other persons;
(f) provision for fees, of such amounts as are specified in or determined in accordance with the regulations, to be payable in respect of—
(i) the making of an application to convert;
(ii) the exercise of any function conferred by virtue of paragraph (e).
(5) Functions conferred by virtue of paragraph (e) of subsection (4) may include functions relating to—
(a) the recording of information on the conversion of civil partnerships;
(b) the issuing of certified copies of any information recorded;
(c) the conducting of services or ceremonies (other than religious services or ceremonies) following the conversion of a civil partnership.
(6) Where a civil partnership is converted into a marriage under this section—
(a) the civil partnership ends on the conversion, and
(b) the resulting marriage is to be treated as having subsisted since the date the civil partnership was formed.
(7) In this section—
"England and Wales civil partnership" means a civil partnership which is formed by two people registering as civil partners of each other in England or Wales (see Part 2 of the Civil Partnership Act 2004);

"relevant armed forces personnel" means—
(a) a member of Her Majesty's forces;
(b) a civilian subject to service discipline (within the meaning of the Armed Forces Act 2006);
and for this purpose "Her Majesty's forces" has the same meaning as in the Armed Forces Act 2006;
"relevant official" means—
(a) the Registrar General;
(b) a superintendent registrar;
(c) a registrar;
(d) a consular officer in the service of Her Majesty's government in the United Kingdom;
(e) a person authorised by the Secretary of State in respect of the solemnization of marriages or formation of civil partnerships in a country or territory in which Her Majesty's government in the United Kingdom has for the time being no consular representative.

10. Extra-territorial matters

(1) A marriage under—
(a) the law of any part of the United Kingdom (other than England and Wales), or
(b) the law of any country or territory outside the United Kingdom,
is not prevented from being recognised under the law of England and Wales only because it is the marriage of a same sex couple.
(2) For the purposes of this section it is irrelevant whether the law of a particular part of the United Kingdom, or a particular country or territory outside the United Kingdom—
(a) already provides for marriage of same sex couples at the time when this section comes into force, or
(b) provides for marriage of same sex couples from a later time.
(3) Schedule 2 (extra-territorial matters) has effect.

13. Marriage overseas

(1) Schedule 6 (marriage overseas) has effect.
(2) The Foreign Marriage Act 1892 is repealed.

CHILDREN AND FAMILIES ACT 2014 (2014 c. 6)

10. Family mediation information and assessment meetings

(1) Before making a relevant family application, a person must attend a family mediation information and assessment meeting.
(2) Family Procedure Rules—
(a) may provide for subsection (1) not to apply in circumstances specified in the Rules,
(b) may make provision about convening a family mediation information and assessment meeting, or about the conduct of such a meeting,
(c) may make provision for the court not to issue, or otherwise deal with, an application if, in contravention of subsection (1), the applicant has not attended a family mediation information and assessment meeting, and
(d) may provide for a determination as to whether an applicant has contravened subsection (1) to be made after considering only evidence of a description specified in the Rules.
(3) In this section—
'the court' means the High Court or the family court;
'family mediation information and assessment meeting', in relation to a relevant family application, means a meeting held for the purpose of enabling information to be provided about—
(a) mediation of disputes of the kinds to which relevant family applications relate,
(b) ways in which disputes of those kinds may be resolved otherwise than by the court, and
(c) the suitability of mediation, or of any such other way of resolving disputes, for trying to resolve any dispute to which the particular application relates;
'family proceedings' has the same meaning as in section 75 of the Courts Act 2003;
'relevant family application' means an application that—

(a) is made to the court in, or to initiate, family proceedings, and
(b) is of a description specified in Family Procedure Rules.

(4) This section is without prejudice to sections 75 and 76 of the Courts Act 2003 (power to make Family Procedure Rules).

11 Welfare of the child: parental involvement

(1) Section 1 of the Children Act 1989 (welfare of the child) is amended as follows.

(2) –

(2A) A court, in the circumstances mentioned in subsection (4)(a) or (7), is as respects each parent within subsection (6)(a) to presume, unless the contrary is shown, that involvement of that parent in the life of the child concerned will further the child's welfare.

(2B) In subsection (2A) "involvement" means involvement of some kind, either direct or indirect, but not any particular division of a child's time."

(6) In subsection (2A) "parent" means parent of the child concerned; and, for the purposes of that subsection, a parent of the child concerned—
(a) is within this paragraph if that parent can be involved in the child's life in a way that does not put the child at risk of suffering harm; and
(b) is to be treated as being within paragraph (a) unless there is some evidence before the court in the particular proceedings to suggest that involvement of that parent in the child's life would put the child at risk of suffering harm whatever the form of the involvement.

(7) The circumstances referred to are that the court is considering whether to make an order under section 4(1)(c) or (2A) or 4ZA(1)(c) or (5) (parental responsibility of parent other than mother)."

ANTI-SOCIAL BEHAVIOUR, CRIME AND POLICING ACT 2014 (2014 c. 12)

121 Offence of forced marriage: England and Wales

(1) A person commits an offence under the law of England and Wales if he or she—
(a) uses violence, threats or any other form of coercion for the purpose of causing another person to enter into a marriage, and
(b) believes, or ought reasonably to believe, that the conduct may cause the other person to enter into the marriage without free and full consent.

(2) In relation to a victim who lacks capacity to consent to marriage, the offence under subsection (1) is capable of being committed by any conduct carried out for the purpose of causing the victim to enter into a marriage (whether or not the conduct amounts to violence, threats or any other form coercion).

(3) A person commits an offence under the law of England and Wales if he or she—
(a) practises any form of deception with the intention of causing another person to leave the United Kingdom, and
(b) intends the other person to be subjected to conduct outside the United Kingdom that is an offence under subsection (1) or would be an offence under that subsection if the victim were in England or Wales.

(4) 'Marriage' means any religious or civil ceremony of marriage (whether or not legally binding).

(5) 'Lacks capacity' means lacks capacity within the meaning of the Mental Capacity Act 2005.

(6) It is irrelevant whether the conduct mentioned in paragraph (a) of subsection (1) is directed at the victim of the offence under that subsection or another person.

(7) A person commits an offence under subsection (1) or (3) only if, at the time of the conduct or deception—
(a) the person or the victim or both of them are in England or Wales,
(b) neither the person nor the victim is in England or Wales but at least one of them is habitually resident in England and Wales, or
(c) neither the person nor the victim is in the United Kingdom but at least one of them is a UK national.

(8) "UK national" means an individual who is—
(a) a British citizen, a British overseas territories citizen, a British National (Overseas) or a British Overseas citizen;
(b) a person who under the British Nationality Act 1981 is a British subject; or
(c) a British protected person within the meaning of that Act.

(9) A person guilty of an offence under this section is liable—
 (a) on summary conviction, to imprisonment for a term not exceeding 12 months or to a fine or both;
 (b) on conviction on indictment, to imprisonment for a term not exceeding 7 years.

(10) In relation to an offence committed before the commencement of section 154(1) of the Criminal Justice Act 2003, the reference to 12 months in subsection (9)(a) is to be read as a reference to six months.

SOME FURTHER EXTRACTS FROM THE CONVENTION FOR THE PROTECTION OF HUMAN RIGHTS AND FUNDAMENTAL FREEDOMS (1950)

Right to a fair trial

Article 6

1. In the determination of his civil rights and obligations or of any criminal charge against him, everyone is entitled to a fair and public hearing within a reasonable time by an independent and impartial tribunal established by law. Judgment shall be pronounced publicly but the press and public may be excluded from all or part of the trial in the interests of morals, public order or national security in a democratic society, where the interests of juveniles or the protection of the private life of the parties so require, or to the extent strictly necessary in the opinion of the court in special circumstances where publicity would prejudice the interests of justice.
2. Everyone charged with a criminal offence shall be presumed innocent until proved guilty according to law.
3. Everyone charged with a criminal offence has the following minimum rights:
 (a) to be informed promptly, in a language which he understands and in detail, of the nature and cause of the accusation against him;
 (b) to have adequate time and facilities for the preparation of his defence;
 (c) to defend himself in person or through legal assistance of his own choosing or, if he has not sufficient means to pay for legal assistance, to be given it free when the interests of justice so require;
 (d) to examine or have examined witnesses against him and to obtain the attendance and examination of witnesses on his behalf under the same conditions as witnesses against him;
 (e) to have the free assistance of an interpreter if he cannot understand or speak the language used in court.

THE FIRST PROTOCOL

Protection of property

Article 1

Every natural or legal person is entitled to the peaceful enjoyment of his possessions. No one shall be deprived of his possessions except in the public interest and subject to the conditions provided for by law and by the general principles of international law.

The preceding provisions shall not, however, in any way impair the right of a State to enforce such laws as it deems necessary to control the use of property in accordance with the general interest or to secure the payment of taxes or other contributions or penalties.

Right to education

Article 2

No person shall be denied the right to education. In the exercise of any functions which it assumes in relation to education and to teaching, the State shall respect the right of parents to ensure such education and teaching in conformity with their own religious and philosophical convictions.

EUROPEAN CONVENTION ON RECOGNITION AND ENFORCEMENT OF DECISIONS CONCERNING CUSTODY OF CHILDREN (1980)

The Member States of the Council of Europe, signatory hereto,

Recognising that in the Member States of the Council of Europe the welfare of the child is of overriding importance in reaching decisions concerning his custody;

Considering that the making of arrangements to ensure that decisions concerning the custody of a child can be more widely recognised and enforced will provide greater protection of the welfare of children;

Considering it desirable, with this end in view, to emphasise that the right of access of parents is a normal corollary to the right of custody;

Noting the increasing number of cases where children have been improperly removed across an international frontier and the difficulties of securing adequate solutions to the problems caused by such cases;

Desirous of making suitable provision to enable the custody of children which has been arbitrarily interrupted to be restored;

Convinced of the desirability of making arrangements for this purpose answering to different needs and different circumstances;

Desiring to establish legal co-operation between their authorities, Have agreed as follows:—

Article 1

For the purposes of this Convention:—

(a) 'child' means a person of any nationality, so long as he is under sixteen years of age and has not the right to decide on his own place of residence under the law of his habitual residence, the law of his nationality or the internal law of the State addressed;

(b) 'authority' means a judicial or administrative authority;

(c) 'decision relating to custody' means a decision of an authority in so far as it relates to the care of the person of the child, including the right to decide on the place of his residence, or to the right of access to him;

(d) 'improper removal' means the removal of a child across an international frontier in breach of a decision relating to his custody which has been given in a Contracting State and which is enforceable in such a State; 'improper removal' also includes:

  (i) the failure to return a child across an international frontier at the end of a period of the exercise of the right of access to this child or at the end of any other temporary stay in a territory other than that where the custody is exercised;

  (ii) a removal which is subsequently declared unlawful within the meaning of Article 12.

PART 1

CENTRAL AUTHORITIES

Article 2

(1) Each Contracting State shall appoint a central authority to carry out the functions provided for by this Convention.

(2) Federal States and States with more than one legal system shall be free to appoint more than one central authority and shall determine the extent of their competence.

(3) The Secretary General of the Council of Europe shall be notified of any appointment under this Article.

Article 3

(1) The central authorities of the Contracting States shall co-operate with each other and promote co-operation between the competent authorities in their respective countries. They shall act with all necessary despatch.

(2) With a view to facilitating the operation of this Convention, the central authorities of the Contracting States:—

  (a) shall secure the transmission of requests for information coming from competent authorities and relating to legal or factual matters concerning pending proceedings;

  (b) shall provide each other on request with information about their law relating to the custody of children and any changes in that law;

  (c) shall keep each other informed of any difficulties likely to arise in applying the Convention and, as far as possible, eliminate obstacles to its application.

Article 4

(1) Any person who has obtained in a Contracting State a decision relating to the custody of a child and who wishes to have that decision recognised or enforced in another Contracting State may submit an application for this purpose to the central authority in any Contracting State.

(2) The application shall be accompanied by the documents mentioned in Article 13.

(3) The central authority receiving the application, if it is not the central authority in the State addressed, shall send the documents directly and without delay to that central authority.

(4) The central authority receiving the application may refuse to intervene where it is manifestly clear that the conditions laid down by this Convention are not satisfied.

(5) The central authority receiving the application shall keep the applicant informed without delay of the progress of his application.

Article 5

(1) The central authority in the State addressed shall take or cause to be taken without delay all steps which it considers to be appropriate, if necessary by instituting proceedings before its competent authorities, in order:—

- (a) to discover the whereabouts of the child.
- (b) to avoid, in particular by any necessary provisional measures, prejudice to the interests of the child or of the applicant;
- (c) to secure the recognition or enforcement of the decision;
- (d) to secure the delivery of the child to the applicant where enforcement is granted;
- (e) to inform the requesting authority of the measures taken and their results.

(2) Where the central authority in the State addressed has reason to believe that the child is in the territory of another Contracting State it shall send the documents directly and without delay to the central authority of that State.

(3) With the exception of the cost of repatriation, each Contracting State undertakes not to claim any payment from an applicant in respect of any measures taken under paragraph 1 of this Article by the central authority of that State on the applicant's behalf, including the costs of proceedings and, where applicable, the costs incurred by the assistance of a lawyer.

(4) If recognition or enforcement is refused, and if the central authority of the State addressed considers that it should comply with a request by the applicant to bring in that State proceedings concerning the substance of the case, that authority shall use its best endeavours to secure the representation of the applicant in the proceedings under conditions no less favourable than those available to a person who is resident in and a national of that State and for this purpose it may, in particular, institute proceedings before its competent authorities.

Article 6

(1) Subject to any special agreements made between the central authorities concerned and to the provisions of paragraph 3 of this Article:—

- (a) communications to the central authority of the State addressed shall be made in the official language or in one of the official languages of that State or be accompanied by a translation into that language;
- (b) the central authority of the State addressed shall nevertheless accept communications made in English or in French or accompanied by a translation into one of these languages.

(2) Communications coming from the central authority of the State addressed, including the results of enquiries carried out, may be made in the official language or one of the official languages of that State or in English or French.

(3) A Contracting State may exclude wholly or partly the provision of paragraph 1(b) of this Article. When a Contracting State has made this reservation any other Contracting State may also apply the reservation in respect of that State.

PART II

RECOGNITION AND ENFORCEMENT OF DECISIONS AND RESTORATION OF CUSTODY OF CHILDREN

Article 7

A decision relating to custody given in a Contracting State shall be recognised and, where it is enforceable in the State of origin, made enforceable in every other Contracting State.

Article 8

(1) In the case of an improper removal, the central authority of the State addressed shall cause steps to be taken forthwith to restore the custody of the child where:—

(a) At the time of the institution of the proceedings in the State where the decision was given or at the time of the improper removal, if earlier, the child and his parents had as their sole nationality the nationality of that State and the child had his habitual residence in the territory of that State, and

(b) a request for the restoration was made to a central authority within a period of six months from the date of the improper removal.

(2) If, in accordance with the law of the State addressed, the requirements of paragraph 1 of this Article cannot be complied with without recourse to a judicial authority, none of the grounds of refusal specified in this Convention shall apply to the judicial proceedings.

(3) Where there is an agreement officially confirmed by a competent authority between the person having the custody of the child and another person to allow the other person a right of access, and the child, having been taken abroad, has not been restored at the end of the agreed period to the person having the custody, custody of the child shall be restored in accordance with paragraphs 1(b) and 2 of this Article. The same shall apply in the case of a decision of the competent authority granting such a right to a person who has not the custody of the child.

Article 9

(1) In cases of improper removal, other than those dealt with in Article 8, in which an application has been made to a central authority within a period of six months from the date of the removal, recognition and enforcement may be refused only if:—

(a) in the case of a decision given in the absence of the defendant or his legal representative, the defendant was not duly served with the document which instituted the proceedings or an equivalent document in sufficient time to enable him to arrange his defence; but such a failure to effect service cannot constitute a ground for refusing recognition or enforcement where service was not effected because the defendant had concealed his whereabouts from the person who instituted the proceedings in the State of origin;

(b) in the case of a decision given in the absence of the defendant or his legal representative, the competence of the authority giving the decision was not founded:—

(i) on the habitual residence of the defendant; or

(ii) on the last common habitual residence of the child's parents, at least one parent being still habitually resident there, or

(iii) on the habitual residence of the child;

(c) the decision is incompatible with a decision relating to custody which became enforceable in the State addressed before the removal of the child, unless the child has had his habitual residence in the territory of the requesting State for one year before his removal.

(2) Where no application has been made to a central authority, the provisions of paragraph 1 of this Article shall apply equally, if recognition and enforcement are requested within six months from the date of the improper removal.

(3) In no circumstances may the foreign decision be reviewed as to its substance.

Article 10

(1) In cases other than those covered by Articles 8 and 9, recognition and enforcement may be refused not only on the grounds provided for in Article 9 but also on any of the following grounds:

(a) if it is found that the effects of the decision are manifestly incompatible with the fundamental principles of the law relating to the family and children in the State addressed;

(b) if it is found that by reason of a change in the circumstances including the passage of time but not including a mere change in the residence of the child after an improper removal, the effects of the original decision are manifestly no longer in accordance with the welfare of the child;

(c) if at the time when the proceedings were instituted in the State of origin;

(i) the child was a national of the State addressed or was habitually resident there and no such connection existed with the State of origin;

(ii) the child was a national both of the State of origin and of the State addressed and was habitually resident in the State addressed;

(d) if the decision is incompatible with a decision given in the State addressed or enforceable in that State after being given in a third State, pursuant to proceedings begun before the submission of the request for recognition or enforcement, and if the refusal is in accordance with the welfare of the child.

(2) Proceedings for recognition or enforcement may be adjourned on any of the following grounds:—

(a) if an ordinary form of review of the original decision has been commenced;

(b) if proceedings relating to the custody of the child, commenced before the proceedings in the State of origin were instituted, are pending in the State addressed;

(c) if another decision concerning the custody of the child is the subject of proceedings for enforcement or of any other proceedings concerning the recognition of the decision.

Article 11

(1) Decisions on rights of access and provisions of decisions relating to custody which deal with the right of access shall be recognised and enforced subject to the same conditions as other decisions relating to custody.

(2) However, the competent authority of the State addressed may fix the conditions for the implementation and exercise of the right of access taking into account, in particular, undertakings given by the parties on this matter.

(3) Where no decision on the right of access has been taken or where recognition or enforcement of the decision relating to custody is refused, the central authority of the State addressed may apply to its competent authorities for a decision on the right of access if the person claiming a right of access so requests.

Article 12

Where, at the time of the removal of a child across an international frontier, there is no enforceable decision given in a Contracting State relating to his custody, the provisions of this Convention shall apply to any subsequent decision, relating to the custody of that child and declaring the removal to be unlawful, given in a Contracting State at the request of any interested person.

PART III
PROCEDURE

Article 13

(1) A request for recognition or enforcement in another Contracting State of a decision relating to custody shall be accompanied by:—

(a) a document authorising the central authority of the State addressed to act on behalf of the applicant or to designate another representative for that purpose;

(b) a copy of the decision which satisfies the necessary conditions of authenticity;

(c) in the case of a decision given in the absence of the defendant or his legal representative, a document which establishes that the defendant was duly served with the document which instituted the proceedings or an equivalent document;

(d) if applicable, any document which establishes that, in accordance with the law of the State of origin, the decision is enforceable;

(e) if possible, a statement indicating the whereabouts or likely whereabouts of the child in the State addressed;

(f) proposals as to how the custody of the child should be restored.

(2) The documents mentioned above shall, where necessary, be accompanied by a translation according to the provisions laid down in Article 6.

Article 14

Each Contracting State shall apply a simple and expeditious procedure for recognition and enforcement of decisions relating to the custody of a child. To that end it shall ensure that a request for enforcement may be lodged by simple application.

Article 15

(1) Before reaching a decision under paragraph (1)(b) of Article 10, the authority concerned in the State addressed:—

(a) shall ascertain the child's views unless this is impracticable having regard in particular to his age and understanding; and

(b) may request that any appropriate inquiries be carried out.

(2) The cost of inquiries in any Contracting State shall be met by the authorities of the State where they are carried out.
Requests for inquiries and the results of inquiries may be sent to the authority concerned through the central authorities.

Article 16

For the purposes of this Convention, no legalisation or any like formality may be required.

PART IV
RESERVATIONS

Article 17

(1) A Contracting State may make a reservation that, in cases covered by Articles 8 and 9 or either of these Articles, recognition and enforcement of decisions relating to custody may be refused on such of the grounds provided under Article 10 as may be specified in the reservation.

(2) Recognition and enforcement of decisions given in a Contracting State which has made the reservation provided for in paragraph 1 of this Article may be refused in any other Contracting State on any of the additional grounds referred to in that reservation.

Article 18

A Contracting State may make a reservation that it shall not be bound by the provisions of Article 12. The provisions of this Convention shall not apply to decisions referred to in Article 12 which have been given in a Contracting State which has made such a reservation.

PART V
OTHER INSTRUMENTS

Article 19

This Convention shall not exclude the possibility of relying on any other international instrument in force between the State of origin and the State addressed or on any other law of the State addressed not derived from an international agreement for the purpose of obtaining recognition or enforcement of a decision.

Article 20

(1) This Convention shall not affect any obligations which a Contracting State may have towards a non-contracting State under an international instrument dealing with matters governed by this Convention.

(2) When two or more Contracting States have enacted uniform laws in relation to custody of children or created a special system of recognition or enforcement of decisions in this field, or if they should do so in the future, they shall be free to apply, between themselves, those laws or that system in place of this Convention or any part of it. In order to avail themselves of this provision the States shall notify their decision to the Secretary General of the Council of Europe. Any alteration or revocation of this decision must also be notified.

PART VI
FINAL CLAUSES

Article 21

This Convention shall be open for signature by the Member States of the Council of Europe. It is subject to ratification, acceptance or approval. Instruments of ratification, acceptance or approval shall be deposited with the Secretary General of the Council of Europe.

Article 22

(1) This Convention shall enter into force on the first day of the month following the expiration of a period of three months after the date on which three Member States of the Council of Europe have expressed their consent to be bound by the Convention in accordance with the provisions of Article 21.

(2) In respect of any Member State which subsequently expresses its consent to be bound by it, the Convention shall enter into force on the first day of the month following the expiration

of a period of three months after the date of the deposit of the instrument of ratification, acceptance or approval.

Article 23

(1) After the entry into force of this Convention, the Committee of Ministers of the Council of Europe may invite any State not a member of the Council to accede to this Convention, by a decision taken by the majority provided for by Article 20(d) of the Statute and by the unanimous vote of the representatives of the Contracting States entitled to sit on the Committee.

(2) In respect of any acceding State, the Convention shall enter into force on the first day of the month following the expiration of a period of three months after the date of deposit of the instrument of accession with the Secretary General of the Council of Europe.

Article 24

(1) any State may at the time of signature or when depositing its instrument of ratification, acceptance, approval or accession, specify the territory or territories to which this Convention shall apply.

(2) Any State may at any later date, by a declaration addressed to the Secretary General of the Council of Europe, extend the application of this Convention to any other territory specified in the declaration. In respect of such territory, the Convention shall enter into force on the first day of the month following the expiration of a period of three months after the date of receipt by the Secretary General of such declaration.

(3) Any declaration made under the two preceding paragraphs may, in respect of any territory specified in such declaration, be withdrawn by a notification addressed to the Secretary General. The withdrawal shall become effective on the first day of the month following the expiration of a period of six months after the date of receipt of such notification by the Secretary General.

Article 25

(1) A State which has two or more territorial units in which different systems of law apply in matters of custody of children and of recognition and enforcement of decisions relating to custody may, at the time of signature or when depositing its instrument of ratification, acceptance, approval or accession, declare that this Convention shall apply to all its territorial units or to one or more of them.

(2) Such a State may at any later date, by a declaration addressed to the Secretary General of the Council of Europe, extend the application of this Convention to any other territorial unit specified in the declaration. In respect of such territorial unit the Convention shall enter into force on the first day of the month following the expiration of a period of three months after the date of receipt by the Secretary General of such declaration.

(3) Any declaration made under the two preceding paragraphs may, in respect of any territorial unit specified in such declaration, be withdrawn by notification addressed to the Secretary General. The withdrawal shall become effective on the first day of the month following the expiration of a period of six months after the date of receipt of such notification by the Secretary General.

Article 26

(1) In relation to a State which has in matters of custody two or more systems of law of territorial application:—

- (a) reference to the law of a person's habitual residence or to the law of a person's nationality shall be construed as referring to the system of law determined by the rules in force in that State or, if there are no such rules, to the system of law with which the person concerned is most closely connected;
- (b) reference to the State of origin or to the State addressed shall be construed as referring, as the case may be, to the territorial unit where the decision was given or to the territorial unit where recognition or enforcement of the decision or restoration of custody is requested.

(2) Paragraph 1(a) of this Article also applies mutatis mutandis to States which have in matters of custody two or more systems of law of personal application.

Article 27

(1) Any State may, at the time of signature or when depositing its instrument of ratification, acceptance, approval or accession, declare that it avails itself of one or more of the reservations provided for in paragraph 3 of Article 6, Article 17 and Article 18 of this Convention. No other reservation may be made.

(2) Any Contracting State which has made a reservation under the preceding paragraph may wholly or partly withdraw it by means of a notification addressed to the Secretary General of the Council of Europe. The withdrawal shall take effect on the date of receipt of such notification by the Secretary General.

Article 28

At the end of the third year following the date of entry into force of this Convention and, on his own initiative, at any time after this date, the Secretary General of the Council of Europe shall invite the representatives of the central authorities appointed by the Contracting States to meet in order to study and to facilitate the functioning of the Convention. Any Member State of the Council of Europe not being a party to the Convention may be represented by an observer. A report shall be prepared on the work of each of these meetings and forwarded to the Committee of Ministers of the Council of Europe for information.

Article 29

(1) Any party may at any time denounce this Convention by means of a notification addressed to the Secretary General of the Council of Europe.

(2) Such denunciation shall become effective on the first day of the month following the expiration of a period of six months after the date of receipt of the notification by the Secretary General.

Article 30

The Secretary General of the Council of Europe shall notify the Member States of the Council and any State which has acceded to this Convention, of:—

(a) any signature;

(b) the deposit of any instrument of ratification, acceptance, approval or accession;

(c) any date of entry into force of this Convention in accordance with Articles 22, 23, 24 and 25;

(d) any other act, notification or communication relating to this Convention.

In witness whereof the undersigned, being duly authorised thereto, have signed this Convention.
Done at Luxembourg, this 20th day of May 1980, in English and French, both texts being equally authentic, in a single copy which shall be deposited in the archives of the Council of Europe. The Secretary General of the Council of Europe shall transmit certified copies to each Member State of the Council of Europe and to any State invited to accede to this Convention.

HAGUE CONVENTION ON THE CIVIL ASPECTS OF INTERNATIONAL CHILD ABDUCTION (1980)

CHAPTER 1—SCOPE OF THE CONVENTION

Article 1

The objects of the present Convention are—

(a) to secure the prompt return of children wrongfully removed to or retained in any Contracting State; and

(b) to ensure that rights of custody and of access under the law of one Contracting State are effectively respected in other Contracting States.

Article 2

Contracting States shall take all appropriate measures to secure within their territories the implementation of the objects of the Convention. For this purpose they shall use the most expeditious procedures available.

Article 3

The removal or the retention of a child is to be considered wrongful where—

(a) it is in breach of rights of custody attributed to a person, an institution or any other body, either jointly or alone, under the law of the State in which the child was habitually resident immediately before the removal or retention; and

(b) at the time of removal or retention those rights were actually exercised, either jointly or alone, or would have been so exercised but for the removal or retention.

The rights of custody mentioned in sub-paragraph a above, may arise in particular by operation of law or by reason of a judicial or administrative decision, or by reason of an agreement having legal effect under the law of that State.

Article 4

The Convention shall apply to any child who was habitually resident in a Contracting State immediately before any breach of custody or access rights. The Convention shall cease to apply when the child attaint the age of 16 years.

Article 5

For the purposes of this Convention—

(a) 'rights of custody' shall include rights relating to the care of the person of the child and, in particular, the right to determine the child's place of residence;

(b) 'rights of access' shall include the right to take a child for a limited period of time to a place other than the child's habitual residence.

CHAPTER II—CENTRAL AUTHORITIES

Article 6

A Contracting State shall designate a Central Authority to discharge the duties which are imposed by the Convention upon such authorities.

Federal States, States with more than one system of law or States having autonomous territorial organisations shall be free to appoint more than one Central Authority and to specify the territorial extent of their powers. Where a State has appointed more than one Central Authority, it shall designate the Central Authority to which applications may be addressed for transmission to the appropriate Central Authority within that State.

Article 7

Central Authorities shall co-operate with each other and promote co-operation amongst the competent authorities in their respective States to secure the prompt return of children and to achieve the other objects of this Convention.

In particular, either directly or through any intermediary, they shall take all appropriate measures—

(a) to discover the whereabouts of a child who has been wrongfully removed or retained;

(b) to prevent further harm to the child or prejudice to interested parties by taking or causing to be taken provisional measures;

(c) to secure the voluntary return of the child or to bring about an amicable resolution of the issues;

(d) to exchange, where desirable, information relating to the social background of the child;

(e) to provide information of a general character as to the law of their State in connection with the application of the Convention;

(f) to initiate or facilitate the institution of judicial or administrative proceedings with a view to obtaining the return of the child and, in a proper case, to make arrangements for organizing or securing the effective exercise of rights of access;

(g) where the circumstances so require, to provide or facilitate the provision of legal aid and advice, including the participation of legal counsel and advisers;

(h) to provide such administrative arrangements as may be necessary and appropriate to secure the safe return of the child;

(i) to keep other each other informed with respect to the operation of this Convention and, as far as possible, to eliminate any obstacles to its application.

CHAPTER III—RETURN OF CHILDREN

Article 8

Any person, institution or other body claiming that a child has been removed or retained in breach of custody rights may apply either to the Central Authority of the child's habitual residence or to the Central Authority of any other Contracting State for assistance in securing the return of the child.

The application shall contain—

(a) information concerning the identity of the applicant, of the child and of the person alleged to have removed or retained the child;

(b) where available, the date of birth of the child;

(c) the grounds on which the applicant's claim for return of the child is based;

(d) all available information relating to the whereabouts of the child and the identity of the person with whom the child is presumed to be.

The application may be accompanied or supplemented by—

(e) an authenticated copy of any relevant decision or agreement;

(f) a certificate or an affidavit emanating from a Central Authority, or other competent authority of the State of the child's habitual residence, or from a qualified person, concerning the relevant law of that State;

(g) any other relevant document.

Article 9

If the Central Authority which receives an application referred to in Article 8 has reason to believe that the child is in another Contracting State, it shall directly and without delay transmit the application to the Central Authority of that Contracting State and inform the requesting Central Authority, or the applicant, as the case may be.

Article 10

The Central Authority of the State where the child is shall take or cause to be taken all appropriate measures in order to obtain the voluntary return of the child.

Article 11

The judicial or administrative authorities of Contracting States shall act expeditiously in proceedings for the return of children.

If the judicial or administrative authority concerned has not reached a decision within six weeks from the date of commencement of the proceedings, the applicant or the Central Authority of the requested State, on its own initiative or if asked by the Central Authority of the requesting State, shall have the right to request a statement of the reasons for the delay. If a reply is received by the Central Authority of the requested State, that Authority shall transmit the reply to the Central Authority of the requesting State, or to the applicant, as the case may be.

Article 12

Where a child has been wrongfully removed or retained in terms of Article 3 and, at the date of the commencement of the proceedings before the judicial or administrative authority of the Contracting State where the child is, a period of less than one year has elapsed from the date of the wrongful removal or retention, the authority concerned shall order the return of the child forthwith.

The judicial or administrative authority, even where the proceedings have been commenced after the expiration of the period of one year referred to in the preceding paragraph, shall also order the return of the child, unless it is demonstrated that the child is now settled in its new environment.

Where the judicial or administrative authority in the requested State has reason to believe that the child has been taken to another State, it may stay the proceedings or dismiss the application for the return of the child.

Article 13

Notwithstanding the provisions of the preceding Article, the judicial or administrative authority of the requested State is not bound to order the return of the child if the person, institution or other body which opposes its return establishes that—

(a) the person, institution or other body having the care of the person of the child was not actually exercising the custody rights at the time of removal or retention, or had consented to or subsequently acquiesced in the removal of retention; or

(b) there is a grave risk that his or her return would expose the child to physical or psychological harm or otherwise place the child in an intolerable situation.

The judicial or administrative authority may also refuse to order the return of the child if it finds that the child objects to being returned and has attained an age and degree of maturity at which it is appropriate to take account of its views.

In considering the circumstances referred to in this Article, the judicial and administrative authorites shall take into account the information relating to the social background of the child provided by the Central Authority or other competent authority of the child's habitual residence.

Article 14

In ascertaining whether there has been a wrongful removal of retention within the meaning of Article 3, the judicial or administrative authorities of the requested State may take notice directly of the law of, and of judicial or administrative decisions, formally recognized or not in the State of the habitual residence of the child, without recourse to the specific procedures for the proof of that law or for the recognition of foreign decisions which would otherwise be applicable.

Article 15

The judicial or administrative authorities of a Contracting State may, prior to the making of an order for the return of the child, request that the applicant obtain from the authorities of the State of the habitual residence of the child a decision or other determination that the removal or retention was wrongful within the meaning of Article 3 of the Convention, where sucha decision or determination may be obtained in that State. The Central Authorities of the Contracting States shall so far as practicable assist applicants to obtain such a decision or determination.

Article 16

After receiving notice of a wrongful removal or retention of a child in the sense of Article 3, the judicial or administrative authorities of the Contracting State to which the child has been removed or in which it has been retained shall not decide on the merits of rights of custody until it has been determined that the child is not to be returned under this Convention or unless an application under the Convention is not lodged within a reasonable time following receipt of the notice.

Article 17

The sole fact that a decision relating to custody has been given in or is entitled to recognition in the requested State shall not be a ground for refusing to return a child under this Convention, but the judicial or administrative authorities of the requested State may take account of the reasons for that decision in applying this Convention.

Article 18

The provisions of this Chapter do not limit the power of a judicial or administrative authority to order the return of the child at any time.

Article 19

A decision under this Convention concerning the return of the child shall not be taken to be determination on the merits of any custody issue.

CHAPTER IV—RIGHTS OF ACCESS

Article 21

An application to make arrangements for organizing or securing the effective exercise of rights of access may be presented to the Central Authorities of the Contracting States in the same way as an application for the return of a child.

The Central Authorities are bound by the obligations of co-operation which are set forth in Article 7 to promote the peaceful enjoyment of access rights and the fulfillment of any conditions to which the exercise of such rights may be subject. The central Authorities shall take steps to remove, as far as possible, all obstacles to the exercise of such rights. The Central Authorities, either directly or through intermediaries, may initiate or assist in the institution of proceedings with a view to organizing or protecting these rights and securing respect for the conditions to which the exercise of these rights may be subject.

CHAPTER V—GENERAL PROVISIONS

Article 22

No security, bond or deposit, however described, shall be required to guarantee the payment of costs and expenses in the judicial or administrative proceedings falling within the scope of this Convention.

Article 23

No legalisation or similar formality may be required in the context of this Convention.

Article 24

Any application, communication or other document sent to the Central Authority of the requested State shall be in the original language, and shall be accompanied by a translation into the official language or one of the official languages of the requested State or, where that is not feasible, a translation into French or English.

Article 25

Nationals of the Contracting States and persons who are habitually resident within those States shall be entitled in matters concerned with the application of this Convention to legal aid and advice in any other Contracting State on the same conditions as if they themselves were nationals of and habitually resident in that State.

Article 26

Each Central Authority shall bear its own costs in applying this Convention.

Central Authorities and other public services of Contracting States shall not impose any charges in relation to applications submitted under this Convention. In particular, they may not require any payment from the applicant towards the costs and expenses of the proceedings or, where applicable, those arising from the participation of legal counsel or advisers. However, they may require the payment of the expenses incurred or to be incurred in implementing the return of the child.

However, a Contracting State may, by making a reservation in accordance with Article 42, declare that it shall not be bound to assume any costs referred to in the preceding paragraph resulting from the participation of legal counsel or advisers or from court proceedings, except insofar as those costs may be covered by its system of legal aid and advice.
Upon ordering the return of a child or issuing an order concerning rights of access under this Convention, the judicial or administrative authorities may, where appropriate, direct the person who removed or retained the child, or who prevented the exercise of rights of access, to pay necessary expenses incurred by or on behalf of the applicant, including travel expenses, any costs incurred or payments made for locating the child, the costs of legal representation of the applicant, and those of returning the child.

Article 27

When it is manifest that the requirements of this Convention are not fulfilled or that the application is otherwise not well founded, a Central Authority is not bound to accept the application. In that case, the Central Authority shall forthwith inform the applicant or the Central Authority through which the application was submitted, as the case may be, of its reasons.

Article 28

A Central Authority may require that the application be accompanied by a written authorization empowering it to act on behalf of the applicant, or to designate a representative so to act.

Article 29

This Convention shall not preclude any person, institution or body who claims that there has been a breach of custody or access rights within the meaning of Article 3 or 21 from applying directly to the judicial or administrative authorities of a Contracting State, whether or not under the provisions of this Convention.

Article 30

Any application submitted to the Central Authorities or directly to the judicial or administrative authorities of a Contracting State in accordance with the terms of this Convention, together with documents and any other information appended thereto or provided by a Central Authority, shall be admissible in the courts or administrative authorities of the Contracting States.

Article 31

In relation to a State which in matters of custody of children has two or more systems of law applicable in different territorial units—

(a) any reference to habitual residence in that State shall be construed as referring to habitual residence in a territorial unit of that State;
(b) any reference to the law of the State of habitual residence shall be construed as referring to the law of the territorial unit in that State where the child habitually resides.

Article 32

In relation to a State which in matters of custody of children has two or more systems of law applicable to different categories of persons, any reference to the law of that State shall be construed as referring to the legal system specified by the law of that State.

UNITED NATIONS CONVENTION ON THE RIGHTS OF THE CHILD (1989)

PART I

Article 1

For the purposes of the present Convention, a child means every human being below the age of eighteen years unless, under the law applicable to the child, majority is attained earlier.

Article 2

1. States Parties shall respect and ensure the rights set forth in the present Convention to each child within their jurisdiction without discrimination of any kind, irrespective of the child's or his or her parent's or legal guardian's race, colour, sex, language, religion, political or other opinion, national, ethnic or social origin, property, disability, birth or other status.
2. States Parties shall take all appropriate measures to ensure that the child is protected against all forms of discrimination or punishment on the basis of the status, activities, expressed opinions, or beliefs of the child's parents, legal guardians, or family members.

Article 3

1. In all actions concerning children, whether undertaken by public or private social welfare institutions, courts of law, administrative authorities or legislative bodies, the best interests of the child shall be a primary consideration.
2. States Parties undertake to ensure the child such protection and care as is necessary for his or her well-being, taking into account the rights and duties of his or her parents, legal guardians, or other individuals legally responsible for him or her, and to this end, shall take all appropriate legislative and administrative measures.
3. States Parties shall ensure that the institutions, services and facilities responsible for the care or protection of children shall conform with the standards established by competent authorities, particularly in the areas of safety, health, in the number and suitability of their staff, as well as competent supervision.

Article 6

1. States Parties recognise that every child has the inherent right to life.
2. States Parties shall ensure to the maximum extent possible the survival and development of the child.

Article 7

1. The child shall be registered immediately after birth and shall have the right from birth to a name, the right to acquire a nationality and, as far as possible, the right to know and be cared for by his or her parents.
2. States Parties shall ensure the implementation of these rights in accordance with their national law and their obligations under the relevant international instruments in this field, in particular where the child would otherwise be stateless.

Article 8

1. States Parties undertake to respect the right of the child to preserve his or her identity, including nationality, name and family relations as recognized by law without unlawful interference.
2. Where a child is illegally deprived of some or all of the elements of his or her identity, States Parties shall provide appropriate assistance and protection, with a view to re-establishing speedily his or her identity.

Article 9

1. States Parties shall ensure that a child shall not be separated from his or her parents against their will, except when competent authorities subject to judicial review determine, in accordance with applicable law and procedures, that such separation is necessary for the best interests of the child. Such determination may be necessary in a particular case such as one involving abuse or neglect of the child by the parents, or one where the parents are living separately and a decision must be made as to the child's place of residence.
2. In any proceedings pursuant to paragraph 1 of the present article, all interested parties shall be given the opportunity to participate in the proceedings and make their views known.
3. States Parties shall respect the right of the child who is separated from one or both parents to maintain personal relations and direct contact with both parents on a regular basis, except if it is contrary to the child's best interests.
4. Where such separation results from any action initiated by a State Party, such as the detention, imprisonment, exile, deportation or death (including death arising from any cause while the person is in the custody of the State) of one or both parents or of the child, that State Party shall, upon request, provide the parents, the child or, if appropriate, another member of the family with the essential information concerning the whereabouts of the absent member(s) of the family unless the provision of the information would be detrimental to the well-being of the child. States Parties shall further ensure that the submission of such a request shall of itself entail no adverse consequences for the person(s) concerned.

Article 10

1. In accordance with the obligation of States Parties under article 9, paragraph 1, applications by a child or his or her parents to enter or leave a State Party for the purposes of family reunification shall be dealt with by States Parties in a positive, humane and expeditious manner. States Parties shall further ensure that the submission of such a request shall entail no adverse consequences for the applicants and for the members of their family.
2. A child whose parents reside in different States shall have the right to maintain on a regular basis, save in exceptional circumstances, personal relations and direct contacts with both parents. Towards that end and in accordance with the obligation of States Parties under article 9, paragraph 1, States Parties shall respect the right of the child and his or her parents to leave any country, including their own, and to enter their own country. The right to leave any country shall be subject only to such restrictions as are prescribed by law and which are

necessary to protect the national security, public order (*ordre public*), public health or morals or the rights and freedoms of others and are consistent with the other rights recognised in the present Convention.

Article 11

1. States Parties shall take measures to combat the illicit transfer and non-return of children abroad.
2. To this end, States Parties shall promote the conclusion of bilateral or multilateral agreements or accession to existing agreements.

Article 12

1. States Parties shall assure to the child who is capable of forming his or her own views the right to express those views freely in all matters affecting the child, the views of the child being given due weight in accordance with the age and maturity of the child.
2. For this purpose, the child shall in particular be provided the opportunity to be heard in any judicial and administrative proceedings affecting the child, either directly, or through a representative or an appropriate body, in a manner consistent with the procedural rules of national law.

Article 13

1. The child shall have the right to freedom of expression; this right shall include freedom to seek, receive and impart information and ideas of all kinds, regardless of frontiers, either orally, in writing or in print, in the form of art, or through any other media of the child's choice.
2. The exercise of this right may be subject to certain restrictions, but these shall only be such as are provided by law and are necessary:
   (a) For respect of the rights or reputations of others; or
   (b) For the protection of national security or of public order (ordre public), or of public health or morals.

Article 14

1. States Parties shall respect the right of the child to freedom of thought, conscience and religion.
2. States Parties shall respect the rights and duties of the parents and, when applicable, legal guardians, to provide direction to the child in the exercise of his or her right in a manner consistent with the evolving capacities of the child.
3. Freedom to manifest one's religion or beliefs may be subject only to such limitations as are prescribed by law and are necessary to protect public safety, order, health or morals, or the fundamental rights and freedoms of others.

Article 15

1. States Parties recognize the rights of the child to freedom of association and to freedom of peaceful assembly.
2. No restrictions may be placed on the exercise of these rights other than those imposed in conformity with the law and which are necessary in a democratic society in the interests of national security or public safety, public order (ordre public), the protection of public health or morals or the protection of the rights and freedoms of others.

Article 16

1. No child shall be subjected to arbitrary or unlawful interference with his or her privacy, family, or correspondence, nor to unlawful attacks on his or her honour and reputation.
2. The child has the right to the protection of the law against such interference or attacks.

Article 17

States Parties recognize the important function performed by the mass media and shall ensure that the child has access to information and material from a diversity of national and international sources, especially those aimed at the promotion of his or her social, spiritual and moral well-being and physical and mental health.
To this end, States Parties shall:

(a) Encourage the mass media to disseminate information and material of social and cultural benefit to the child and in accordance with the spirit of article 29;
(b) Encourage international co-operation in the production, exchange and dissemination of such information and material from a diversity of cultural, national and international sources;
(c) Encourage the production and dissemination of children's books;
(d) Encourage the mass media to have particular regard to the linguistic needs of the child who belongs to a minority group or who is indigenous;
(e) Encourage the development of appropriate guidelines for the protection of the child from information and material injurious to his or her well-being, bearing in mind the provisions of articles 13 and 18.

Article 18

1. States Parties shall use their best efforts to ensure recognition of the principle that both parents have common responsibilities for the upbringing and development of the child. Parents or, as the case may be, legal guardians, have the primary responsibility for the upbringing and development of the child. The best interests of the child will be their basic concern.
2. For the purpose of guaranteeing and promoting the rights set forth in the present Convention, States Parties shall render appropriate assistance to parents and legal guardians in the performance of their child-rearing responsibilities and shall ensure the development of institutions, facilities and services for the care of children.
3. States Parties shall take all appropriate measures to ensure that children of working parents have the right to benefit from child-care services and facilities for which they are eligible.

Article 19

1. States Parties shall take all appropriate legislative, administrative, social and educational measures to protect the child from all forms of physical or mental violence, injury or abuse, neglect or negligent treatment, maltreatment or exploitation, including sexual abuse, while in the care of parent(s), legal guardian(s) or any other person who has the care of the child.
2. Such protective measures should, as appropriate, include effective procedures for the establishment of social programmes to provide necessary support for the child and for those who have the care of the child, as well as for other forms of prevention and for identification, reporting, referral, investigation, treatment and follow-up of instances of child maltreatment described heretofore, and, as appropriate, for judicial involvement.

Article 20

1. A child temporarily or permanently deprived of his or her family environment, or in whose own best interests cannot be allowed to remain in that environment, shall be entitled to special protection and assistance provided by the State.
2. States Parties shall in accordance with their national laws ensure alternative care for such a child.
3. Such care could include, inter alia, foster placement, kafalah of Islamic law, adoption or if necessary placement in suitable institutions for the care of children. When considering solutions, due regard shall be paid to the desirability of continuity in a child's upbringing and to the child's ethnic, religious, cultural and linguistic background.

Article 21

States Parties that recognize and/or permit the system of adoption shall ensure that the best interests of the child shall be the paramount consideration and they shall:

(a) Ensure that the adoption of a child is authorized only by competent authorities who determine, in accordance with applicable law and procedures and on the basis of all pertinent and reliable information, that the adoption is permissible in view of the child's status concerning parents, relatives and legal guardians and that, if required, the persons concerned have given their informed consent to the adoption on the basis of such counselling as may be necessary;

(b) Recognize that inter-country adoption may be considered as an alternative means of child's care, if the child cannot be placed in a foster or an adoptive family or cannot in any suitable manner be cared for in the child's country of origin;

(c) Ensure that the child concerned by inter-country adoption enjoys safeguards and standards equivalent to those existing in the case of national adoption;

(d) Take all appropriate measures to ensure that, in inter-country adoption, the placement does not result in improper financial gain for those involved in it;

(e) Promote, where appropriate, the objectives of the present article by concluding bilateral or multilateral arrangements or agreements, and endeavour, within this framework, to ensure that the placement of the child in another country is carried out by competent authorities or organs.

Article 22

1. States Parties shall take appropriate measures to ensure that a child who is seeking refugee status or who is considered a refugee in accordance with applicable international or domestic law and procedures shall, whether unaccompanied or accompanied by his or her parents or by any other person, receive appropriate protection and humanitarian assistance in the enjoyment of applicable rights set forth in the present convention and in other international human rights or humanitarian instruments to which the said States are Parties.
2. For this purpose, States Parties shall provide, as they consider appropriate, co-operation in any efforts by the United Nations and other competent intergovernmental organisations or non-governmental organisations co-operating with the United Nations to protect and assist such a child and to trace the parents or other members of the family of any refugee child in order to obtain information necessary for reunification with his or her family. In cases where

no parents or other members of the family can be found, the child shall be accorded the same protection as any other child permanently or temporarily deprived of his or her family environment for any reason, as set forth in the present Convention.

Article 23

1. States Parties recognize that a mentally or physically disabled child should enjoy a full and decent life, in conditions which ensure dignity, promote self-reliance and facilitate the child's active participation in the community.
2. States Parties recognize the right of the disabled child to special care and shall encourage and ensure the extension, subject to available resources, to the eligible child and those responsible for his or her care, of assistance for which application is made and which is appropriate to the child's condition and to the circumstances of the parents or others caring for the child.
3. Recognizing the special needs of a disabled child, assistance extended in accordance with paragraph 2 of the present article shall be provided free of charge, whenever possible, taking into account the financial resources of the parents or others caring for the child, and shall be designed to ensure that the disabled child has effective access to and receives education, training, health care services, rehabilitation services, preparation for employment and recreation opportunities in a manner conducive to the child's achieving the fullest possible social integration and individual development, including his or her cultural and spiritual development
4. States Parties shall promote, in the spirit of international cooperation, the exchange of appropriate information in the field of preventive health care and of medical, psychological and functional treatment of disabled children, including dissemination of and access to information concerning methods of rehabilitation, education and vocational services, with the aim of enabling States Parties to improve their capabilities and skills and to widen their experience in these areas. In this regard, particular account shall be taken of the needs of developing countries.

Article 24

1. States Parties recognize the right of the child to the enjoyment of the highest attainable standard of health and to facilities for the treatment of illness and rehabilitation of health. States Parties shall strive to ensure that no child is deprived of his or her right of access to such health care services.
2. States Parties shall pursue full implementation of this right and, in particular, shall take appropriate measures:
   (a) To diminish infant and child mortality;
   (b) To ensure the provision of necessary medical assistance and health care to all children with emphasis on the development of primary health care;
   (c) To combat disease and malnutrition, including within the framework of primary health care, through, inter alia, the application of readily available technology and through the provision of adequate nutritious foods and clean drinking-water, taking into consideration the dangers and risks of environmental pollution;
   (d) To ensure appropriate pre-natal and post-natal health care for mothers;
   (e) To ensure that all segments of society, in particular parents and children, are informed, have access to education and are supported in the use of basic knowledge of child health and nutrition, the advantages of breastfeeding, hygiene and environmental sanitation and the prevention of accidents;
   (f) To develop preventive health care, guidance for parents and family planning education and services.
3. States Parties shall take all effective and appropriate measures with a view to abolishing traditional practices prejudicial to the health of children.
4. States Parties undertake to promote and encourage international co-operation with a view to achieving progressively the full realization of the right recognized in the present article. In this regard, particular account shall be taken of the needs of developing countries.

Article 25

States Parties recognize the right of a child who has been placed by the competent authorities for the purposes of care, protection or treatment of his or her physical or mental health, to a periodic review of the treatment provided to the child and all other circumstances relevant to his or her placement.

Article 26

1. States Parties shall recognize for every child the right to benefit from social security, including social insurance, and shall take the necessary measures to achieve the full realization of this right in accordance with their national law.
2. The benefits should, where appropriate, be granted, taking into account the resources and the circumstances of the child and persons having responsibility for the maintenance of the

child, as well as any other consideration relevant to an application for benefits made by or on behalf of the child.

Article 27

1. States Parties recognize the right of every child to a standard of living adequate for the child's physical, mental, spiritual, moral and social development.
2. The parent(s) or others responsible for the child have the primary responsibility to secure, within their abilities and financial capacities, the conditions of living necessary for the child's development.
3. States Parties, in accordance with national conditions and within their means, shall take appropriate measures to assist parents and others responsible for the child to implement this right and shall in case of need provide material assistance and support programmes, particularly with regard to nutrition, clothing and housing.
4. States Parties shall take all appropriate measures to secure the recovery of maintenance for the child from the parents or other persons having financial responsibility for the child, both within the State Party and from abroad. In particular, where the person having financial responsibility for the child lives in a State different from that of the child, States Parties shall promote the accession to international agreements or the conclusion of such agreements, as well as the making of other appropriate arrangements.

Article 28

1. States Parties recognize the right of the child to education, and with a view to achieving this right progressively and on the basis of equal opportunity, they shall, in particular:
    (a) Make primary education compulsory and available free to all;
    (b) Encourage the development of different forms of secondary education, including general and vocational education, make them available and accessible to every child, and take appropriate measures such as the introduction of free education and offering financial assistance in case of need;
    (c) Make higher education accessible to all on the basis of capacity by every appropriate means;
    (d) Make educational and vocational information and guidance available and accessible to all children;
    (e) Take measures to encourage regular attendance at schools and the reduction of drop-out rates.
2. States Parties shall take all appropriate measures to ensure that school discipline is administered in a manner consistent with the child's human dignity and in conformity with the present Convention.
3. States Parties shall promote and encourage international cooperation in matters relating to education, in particular with a view to contributing to the elimination of ignorance and illiteracy throughout the world and facilitating access to scientific and technical knowledge and modern teaching methods. In this regard, particular account shall be taken of the needs of developing countries.

Article 29

1. States Parties agree that the education of the child shall be directed to:
    (a) The development of the child's personality, talents and mental and physical abilities to their fullest potential;
    (b) The development of respect for human rights and fundamental freedoms, and for the principles enshrined in the Charter of the United Nations;
    (c) The development of respect for the child's parents, his or her own cultural identity, language and values, for the national values of the country in which the child is living, the country from which he or she may originate, and for civilizations different from his or her own;
    (d) The preparation of the child for responsible life in a free society, in the spirit of understanding, peace, tolerance, equality of sexes, and friendship among all peoples, ethnic, national and religious groups and persons of indigenous origin;
    (e) The development of respect for the natural environment.
2. No part of the present article or article 28 shall be construed so as to interfere with the liberty of individuals and bodies to establish and direct educational institutions, subject always to the observance of the principle set forth in paragraph 1 of the present article and to the requirements that the education given in such institutions shall conform to such minimum standards as may be laid down by the State.

Article 30

In those States in which ethnic, religious or linguistic minorities or persons of indigenous origin exist, a child belonging to such a minority or who is indigenous shall not be denied the right, in community with other members of his or her group, to enjoy his or her own culture, to profess and practise his or her own religion, or to use his or her own language.

Article 31

1. States Parties recognize the right of the child to rest and leisure, to engage in play and recreational activities appropriate to the age of the child and to participate freely in cultural life and the arts.
2. States Parties shall respect and promote the right of the child to participate fully in cultural and artistic life and shall encourage the provision of appropriate and equal opportunities for cultural, artistic, recreational and leisure activity.

Article 32

1. States Parties recognize the right of the child to be protected from economic exploitation and from performing any work that is likely to be hazardous or to interfere with the child's education, or to be harmful to the child's health or physical, mental, spiritual, moral or social development.
2. States Parties shall take legislative, administrative, social and educational measures to ensure the implementation of the present article. To this end, and having regard to the relevant provisions of other international instruments, States Parties shall in particular:
   (a) Provide for a minimum age or minimum ages for admission to employment;
   (b) Provide for appropriate regulation of the hours and conditions of employment;
   (c) Provide for appropriate penalties or other sanctions to ensure the effective enforcement of the present article.

Article 33

States Parties shall take all appropriate measures, including legislative, administrative, social and educational measures, to protect children from the illicit use of narcotic drugs and psychotropic substances as defined in the relevant international treaties, and to prevent the use of children in the illicit production and trafficking of such substances.

Article 34

States Parties undertake to protect the child from all forms of sexual exploitation and sexual abuse. For these purposes, States Parties shall in particular take all appropriate national, bilateral and multilateral measures to prevent:

(a) The inducement or coercion of a child to engage in any unlawful sexual activity;
(b) The exploitative use of children in prostitution or other unlawful sexual practices;
(c) The exploitative use of children in pornographic performances and materials.

Article 35

States Parties shall take all appropriate national, bilateral and multilateral measures to prevent the abduction of, the sale of or traffic in children for any purpose or in any form.

Article 36

States Parties shall protect the child against all other forms of exploitation prejudicial to any aspects of the child's welfare.

Article 37

States Parties shall ensure that:

(a) No child shall be subjected to torture or other cruel, inhuman or degrading treatment or punishment. Neither capital punishment nor life imprisonment without possibility of release shall be imposed for offences committed by persons below eighteen years of age;
(b) No child shall be deprived of his or her liberty unlawfully or arbitrarily. The arrest, detention or imprisonment of a child shall be in conformity with the law and shall be used only as a measure of last resort and for the shortest appropriate period of time;
(c) Every child deprived of liberty shall be treated with humanity and respect for the inherent dignity of the human person, and in a manner which takes into account the needs of persons of his or her age. In particular, every child deprived of liberty shall be separated from adults unless it is considered in the child's best interest not to do so and shall have the right to maintain contact with his or her family through correspondence and visits, save in exceptional circumstances;
(d) Every child deprived of his or her liberty shall have the right to prompt access to legal and other appropriate assistance, as well as the right to challenge the legality of the deprivation of his or her liberty before a court or other competent, independent and impartial authority, and to a prompt decision on any such action.

Article 38

1. States Parties undertake to respect and to ensure respect for rules of international humanitarian law applicable to them in armed conflicts which are relevant to the child.
2. States Parties shall take all feasible measures to ensure that persons who have not attained the age of fifteen years do not take a direct part in hostilities.

3. States Parties shall refrain from recruiting any person who has not attained the age of fifteen years into their armed forces. In recruiting among those persons who have attained the age of fifteen years but who have not attained the age of eighteen years, States Parties shall endeavour to give priority to those who are oldest.
4. In accordance with their obligations under international humanitarian law to protect the civilian population in armed conflicts, States Parties shall take all feasible measures to ensure protection and care of children who are affected by an armed conflict.

Article 39

States Parties shall take all appropriate measures to promote physical and psychological recovery and social reintegration of a child victim of: any form of neglect, exploitation, or abuse; torture or any other form of cruel, inhuman or degrading treatment or punishment; or armed conflicts. Such recovery and reintegration shall take place in an environment which fosters the health, self-respect and dignity of the child.

Article 40

1. States Parties recognise the right of every child alleged as, accused of, or recognised as having infringed the penal law to be treated in a manner consistent with the promotion of the child's sense of dignity and worth, which reinforces the child's respect for the human rights and fundamental freedoms of others and which takes into account the child's age and the desirability of promoting the child's reintegration and the child's assuming a constructive role in society.
2. To this end, and having regard to the relevant provisions of international instruments, States Parties shall, in particular, ensure that:
   (a) No child shall be alleged as, be accused of, or recognised as having infringed the penal law by reason of acts or omissions that were not prohibited by national or international law at the time they were committed;
   (b) Every child alleged as or accused of having infringed the penal law has at least the following guarantees:
      (i) To be presumed innocent until proven guilty according to law;
      (ii) To be informed promptly and directly of the charges against him or her, and, if appropriate, through his or her parents or legal guardians, and to have legal or other appropriate assistance in the preparation and presentation of his or her defence;
      (iii) To have the matter determined without delay by a competent, independent and impartial authority or judicial body in a fair hearing according to law, in the presence of legal or other appropriate assistance and, unless it is considered not to be in the best interest of the child, in particular, taking into account his or her age or situation, his or her parents or legal guardians;
      (iv) Not to be compelled to give testimony or to confess guilt; to examine or have examined adverse witnesses and to obtain the participation and examination of witnesses on his or her behalf under conditions of equality;
      (v) If considered to have infringed the penal law, to have this decision and any measures imposed in consequence thereof reviewed by a higher competent, independent and impartial authority or judicial body according to law;
      (vi) To have the free assistance of an interpreter if the child cannot understand or speak the language used;
      (vii) To have his or her privacy fully respected at all stages of the proceedings.
3. States Parties shall seek to promote the establishment of laws, procedures, authorities and institutions specifically applicable to children alleged as, accused of, or recognised as having infringed the penal law, and, in particular:
   (a) The establishment of a minimum age below which children shall be presumed not to have the capacity to infringe the penal law;
   (b) Whenever appropriate and desirable, measures for dealing with such children without resorting to judicial proceedings, providing that human rights and legal safeguards are fully respected.
4. A variety of dispositions, such as care, guidance and supervision orders; counselling; probation; foster care; education and vocational training programmes and other alternatives to institutional care shall be available to ensure that children are dealt with in a manner appropriate to their well-being and proportionate both to their circumstances and the offence.

Article 41

Nothing in the present Convention shall affect any provisions which are more conducive to the realization of the rights of the child and which may be contained in:

(a) The law of a State party; or

(b) International law in force for that State.

PART II

Article 42

States Parties undertake to make the principles and provisions of the Convention widely known, by appropriate and active means, to adults and children alike.

Article 43

1. For the purpose of examining the progress made by States Parties in achieving the realization of the obligations undertaken in the present Convention, there shall be established a Committee on the Rights of the Child, which shall carry out the functions hereinafter provided.
2. The Committee shall consist of eighteen experts of high moral standing and recognized competence in the field covered by this Convention. The members of the Committee shall be elected by States Parties from among their nationals and shall serve in their personal capacity, consideration being given to equitable geographical distribution, as well as to the principal legal systems.
3. The members of the Committee shall be elected by secret ballot from a list of persons nominated by States Parties. Each State Party may nominate one person from among its own nationals.
4. The initial election to the Committee shall be held no later than six months after the date of the entry into force of the present Convention and thereafter every second year. At least four months before the date of each election, the Secretary-General of the United Nations shall address a letter to States Parties inviting them to submit their nominations within two months. The Secretary-General shall subsequently prepare a list in alphabetical order of all persons thus nominated, indicating States Parties which have nominated them, and shall submit it to the States Parties to the present Convention.
5. The elections shall be held at meetings of States Parties convened by the Secretary-General at United Nations Headquarters. At those meetings, for which two thirds of States Parties shall constitute a quorum, the persons elected to the Committee shall be those who obtain the largest number of votes and an absolute majority of the votes of the representatives of States Parties present and voting.
6. The members of the Committee shall be elected for a term of four years. They shall be eligible for re-election if renominated. The term of five of the members elected at the first election shall expire at the end of two years; immediately after the first election, the names of these five members shall be chosen by lot by the Chairman of the meeting.
7. If a member of the Committee dies or resigns or declares that for any other cause he or she can no longer perform the duties of the Committee, the State Party which nominated the member shall appoint another expert from among its nationals to serve for the remainder of the term, subject to the approval of the Committee.
8. The Committee shall establish its own rules of procedure.
9. The Committee shall elect its officers for a period of two years.
10. The meetings of the Committee shall normally be held at United Nations Headquarters or at any other convenient place as determined by the Committee. The Committee shall normally meet annually. The duration of the meetings of the Committee shall be determined, and reviewed, if necessary, by a meeting of the States Parties to the present Convention, subject to the approval of the General Assembly.
11. The Secretary-General of the United Nations shall provide the necessary staff and facilities for the effective performance of the functions of the Committee under the present Convention.
12. With the approval of the General Assembly, the members of the Committee established under the present Convention shall receive emoluments from United Nations resources on such terms and conditions as the Assembly may decide.

Article 44

1. States Parties undertake to submit to the Committee, through the Secretary-General of the United Nations, reports on the measures they have adopted which give effect to the rights recognized herein and on the progress made on the enjoyment of those rights
   (a) Within two years of the entry into force of the Convention for the State Party concerned;
   (b) Thereafter every five years.
2. Reports made under the present article shall indicate factors and difficulties, if any, affecting the degree of fulfilment of the obligations under the present Convention. Reports shall also contain sufficient information to provide the Committee with a comprehensive understanding of the implementation of the Convention in the country concerned.
3. A State Party which has submitted a comprehensive initial report to the Committee need not, in its subsequent reports submitted in accordance with paragraph 1 (b) of the present article, repeat basic information previously provided.
4. The Committee may request from States Parties further information relevant to the implementation of the Convention.
5. The Committee shall submit to the General Assembly, through the Economic and Social Council, every two years, reports on its activities.
6. States Parties shall make their reports widely available to the public in their own countries.

HAGUE CONVENTION ON JURISDICTION, APPLICABLE LAW, RECOGNITION, ENFORCEMENT AND CO-OPERATION IN RESPECT OF PARENTAL RESPONSIBILITY AND MEASURES FOR THE PROTECTION OF CHILDREN (1996)

The States signatory to the present Convention,
Considering the need to improve the protection of children in international situations,
Wishing to avoid conflicts between their legal systems in respect of jurisdiction, applicable law, recognition and enforcement of measures for the protection of children,
Recalling the importance of international co-operation for the protection of children,
Confirming that the best interests of the child are to be a primary consideration,
Noting that the *Convention of 5 October 1961 concerning the powers of authorities and the law applicable in respect of the protection of minors* is in need of revision,
Desiring to establish common provisions to this effect, taking into account the *United Nations Convention on the Rights of the Child* of 20 November 1989,
Have agreed on the following provisions —

CHAPTER I - SCOPE OF THE CONVENTION

Article 1

(1) The objects of the present Convention are —
- (a) to determine the State whose authorities have jurisdiction to take measures directed to the protection of the person or property of the child;
- (b) to determine which law is to be applied by such authorities in exercising their jurisdiction;
- (c) to determine the law applicable to parental responsibility;
- (d) to provide for the recognition and enforcement of such measures of protection in all Contracting States;
- (e) to establish such co-operation between the authorities of the Contracting States as may be necessary in order to achieve the purposes of this Convention.

(2) For the purposes of this Convention, the term 'parental responsibility' includes parental authority, or any analogous relationship of authority determining the rights, powers and responsibilities of parents, guardians or other legal representatives in relation to the person or the property of the child.

Article 2

The Convention applies to children from the moment of their birth until they reach the age of 18 years.

Article 3

The measures referred to in Article 1 may deal in particular with -
- (a) the attribution, exercise, termination or restriction of parental responsibility, as well as its delegation;
- (b) rights of custody, including rights relating to the care of the person of the child and, in particular, the right to determine the child's place of residence, as well as rights of access including the right to take a child for a limited period of time to a place other than the child's habitual residence;
- (c) guardianship, curatorship and analogous institutions;
- (d) the designation and functions of any person or body having charge of the child's person or property, representing or assisting the child;
- (e) the placement of the child in a foster family or in institutional care, or the provision of care by kafala or an analogous institution;
- (f) the supervision by a public authority of the care of a child by any person having charge of the child;
- (g) the administration, conservation or disposal of the child's property.

Article 4

The Convention does not apply to -
- (a) the establishment or contesting of a parent-child relationship;
- (b) decisions on adoption, measures preparatory to adoption, or the annulment or revocation of adoption;
- (c) the name and forenames of the child;
- (d) emancipation;
- (e) maintenance obligations;
- (f) trusts or succession;

(g) social security;
(h) public measures of a general nature in matters of education or health;
(i) measures taken as a result of penal offences committed by children;
(j) decisions on the right of asylum and on immigration.

CHAPTER II - JURISDICTION

Article 5

(1) The judicial or administrative authorities of the Contracting State of the habitual residence of the child have jurisdiction to take measures directed to the protection of the child's person or property.
(2) Subject to Article 7, in case of a change of the child's habitual residence to another Contracting State, the authorities of the State of the new habitual residence have jurisdiction.

Article 6

(1) For refugee children and children who, due to disturbances occurring in their country, are internationally displaced, the authorities of the Contracting State on the territory of which these children are present as a result of their displacement have the jurisdiction provided for in paragraph 1 of Article 5.
(2) The provisions of the preceding paragraph also apply to children whose habitual residence cannot be established.

Article 7

(1) In case of wrongful removal or retention of the child, the authorities of the Contracting State in which the child was habitually resident immediately before the removal or retention keep their jurisdiction until the child has acquired a habitual residence in another State, and
  (a) each person, institution or other body having rights of custody has acquiesced in the removal or retention; or
  (b) the child has resided in that other State for a period of at least one year after the person, institution or other body having rights of custody has or should have had knowledge of the whereabouts of the child, no request for return lodged within that period is still pending, and the child is settled in his or her new environment.
(2) The removal or the retention of a child is to be considered wrongful where -
  (a) it is in breach of rights of custody attributed to a person, an institution or any other body, either jointly or alone, under the law of the State in which the child was habitually resident immediately before the removal or retention; and
  (b) at the time of removal or retention those rights were actually exercised, either jointly or alone, or would have been so exercised but for the removal or retention.

  The rights of custody mentioned in sub-paragraph a above, may arise in particular by operation of law or by reason of a judicial or administrative decision, or by reason of an agreement having legal effect under the law of that State.
(3) So long as the authorities first mentioned in paragraph 1 keep their jurisdiction, the authorities of the Contracting State to which the child has been removed or in which he or she has been retained can take only such urgent measures under Article 11 as are necessary for the protection of the person or property of the child.

Article 8

(1) By way of exception, the authority of a Contracting State having jurisdiction under Article 5 or 6, if it considers that the authority of another Contracting State would be better placed in the particular case to assess the best interests of the child, may either
  — request that other authority, directly or with the assistance of the Central Authority of its State, to assume jurisdiction to take such measures of protection as it considers to be necessary, or
  — suspend consideration of the case and invite the parties to introduce such a request before the authority of that other State.
(2) The Contracting States whose authorities may be addressed as provided in the preceding paragraph are
  (a) a State of which the child is a national,
  (b) a State in which property of the child is located,
  (c) a State whose authorities are seised of an application for divorce or legal separation of the child's parents, or for annulment of their marriage,
  (d) a State with which the child has a substantial connection.
(3) The authorities concerned may proceed to an exchange of views.

(4) The authority addressed as provided in paragraph 1 may assume jurisdiction, in place of the authority having jurisdiction under Article 5 or 6, if it considers that this is in the child's best interests.

Article 9

(1) If the authorities of a Contracting State referred to in Article 8, paragraph 2, consider that they are better placed in the particular case to assess the child's best interests, they may either

— request the competent authority of the Contracting State of the habitual residence of the child, directly or with the assistance of the Central Authority of that State, that they be authorised to exercise jurisdiction to take the measures of protection which they consider to be necessary, or

— invite the parties to introduce such a request before the authority of the Contracting State of the habitual residence of the child.

(2) The authorities concerned may proceed to an exchange of views.

(3) The authority initiating the request may exercise jurisdiction in place of the authority of the Contracting State of the habitual residence of the child only if the latter authority has accepted the request.

Article 10

(1) Without prejudice to Articles 5 to 9, the authorities of a Contracting State exercising jurisdiction to decide upon an application for divorce or legal separation of the parents of a child habitually resident in another Contracting State, or for annulment of their marriage, may, if the law of their State so provides, take measures directed to the protection of the person or property of such child if

(a) at the time of commencement of the proceedings, one of his or her parents habitually resides in that State and one of them has parental responsibility in relation to the child, and

(b) the jurisdiction of these authorities to take such measures has been accepted by the parents, as well as by any other person who has parental responsibility in relation to the child, and is in the best interests of the child.

(2) The jurisdiction provided for by paragraph 1 to take measures for the protection of the child ceases as soon as the decision allowing or refusing the application for divorce, legal separation or annulment of the marriage has become final, or the proceedings have come to an end for another reason.

Article 11

(1) In all cases of urgency, the authorities of any Contracting State in whose territory the child or property belonging to the child is present have jurisdiction to take any necessary measures of protection.

(2) The measures taken under the preceding paragraph with regard to a child habitually resident in a Contracting State shall lapse as soon as the authorities which have jurisdiction under Articles 5 to 10 have taken the measures required by the situation.

(3) The measures taken under paragraph 1 with regard to a child who is habitually resident in a non-Contracting State shall lapse in each Contracting State as soon as measures required by the situation and taken by the authorities of another State are recognised in the Contracting State in question.

Article 12

(1) Subject to Article 7, the authorities of a Contracting State in whose territory the child or property belonging to the child is present have jurisdiction to take measures of a provisional character for the protection of the person or property of the child which have a territorial effect limited to the State in question, in so far as such measures are not incompatible with measures already taken by authorities which have jurisdiction under Articles 5 to 10.

(2) The measures taken under the preceding paragraph with regard to a child habitually resident in a Contracting State shall lapse as soon as the authorities which have jurisdiction under Articles 5 to 10 have taken a decision in respect of the measures of protection which may be required by the situation.

(3) The measures taken under paragraph 1 with regard to a child who is habitually resident in a non-Contracting State shall lapse in the Contracting State where the measures were taken as soon as measures required by the situation and taken by the authorities of another State are recognised in the Contracting State in question.

Article 13

(1) The authorities of a Contracting State which have jurisdiction under Articles 5 to 10 to take measures for the protection of the person or property of the child must abstain from exercising

this jurisdiction if, at the time of the commencement of the proceedings, corresponding measures have been requested from the authorities of another Contracting State having jurisdiction under Articles 5 to 10 at the time of the request and are still under consideration.

(2) The provisions of the preceding paragraph shall not apply if the authorities before whom the request for measures was initially introduced have declined jurisdiction.

Article 14

The measures taken in application of Articles 5 to 10 remain in force according to their terms, even if a change of circumstances has eliminated the basis upon which jurisdiction was founded, so long as the authorities which have jurisdiction under the Convention have not modified, replaced or terminated such measures.

CHAPTER III - APPLICABLE LAW

Article 15

(1) In exercising their jurisdiction under the provisions of Chapter II, the authorities of the Contracting States shall apply their own law.

(2) However, in so far as the protection of the person or the property of the child requires, they may exceptionally apply or take into consideration the law of another State with which the situation has a substantial connection.

(3) If the child's habitual residence changes to another Contracting State, the law of that other State governs, from the time of the change, the conditions of application of the measures taken in the State of the former habitual residence.

Article 16

(1) The attribution or extinction of parental responsibility by operation of law, without the intervention of a judicial or administrative authority, is governed by the law of the State of the habitual residence of the child.

(2) The attribution or extinction of parental responsibility by an agreement or a unilateral act, without intervention of a judicial or administrative authority, is governed by the law of the State of the child's habitual residence at the time when the agreement or unilateral act takes effect.

(3) Parental responsibility which exists under the law of the State of the child's habitual residence subsists after a change of that habitual residence to another State.

(4) If the child's habitual residence changes, the attribution of parental responsibility by operation of law to a person who does not already have such responsibility is governed by the law of the State of the new habitual residence.

Article 17

The exercise of parental responsibility is governed by the law of the State of the child's habitual residence. If the child's habitual residence changes, it is governed by the law of the State of the new habitual residence.

Article 18

The parental responsibility referred to in Article 16 may be terminated, or the conditions of its exercise modified, by measures taken under this Convention.

Article 19

(1) The validity of a transaction entered into between a third party and another person who would be entitled to act as the child's legal representative under the law of the State where the transaction was concluded cannot be contested, and the third party cannot be held liable, on the sole ground that the other person was not entitled to act as the child's legal representative under the law designated by the provisions of this Chapter, unless the third party knew or should have known that the parental responsibility was governed by the latter law.

(2) The preceding paragraph applies only if the transaction was entered into between persons present on the territory of the same State.

Article 20

The provisions of this Chapter apply even if the law designated by them is the law of a non-Contracting State.

Article 21

(1) In this Chapter the term "law" means the law in force in a State other than its choice of law rules.

(2) However, if the law applicable according to Article 16 is that of a non-Contracting State and if the choice of law rules of that State designate the law of another non-Contracting State which

would apply its own law, the law of the latter State applies. If that other non-Contracting State would not apply its own law, the applicable law is that designated by Article 16.

Article 22

The application of the law designated by the provisions of this Chapter can be refused only if this application would be manifestly contrary to public policy, taking into account the best interests of the child.

CHAPTER IV - RECOGNITION AND ENFORCEMENT

Article 23

(1) The measures taken by the authorities of a Contracting State shall be recognised by operation of law in all other Contracting States.

(2) Recognition may however be refused -

- (a) if the measure was taken by an authority whose jurisdiction was not based on one of the grounds provided for in Chapter II;
- (b) if the measure was taken, except in a case of urgency, in the context of a judicial or administrative proceeding, without the child having been provided the opportunity to be heard, in violation of fundamental principles of procedure of the requested State;
- (c) on the request of any person claiming that the measure infringes his or her parental responsibility, if such measure was taken, except in a case of urgency, without such person having been given an opportunity to be heard;
- (d) if such recognition is manifestly contrary to public policy of the requested State, taking into account the best interests of the child;
- (e) if the measure is incompatible with a later measure taken in the non-Contracting State of the habitual residence of the child, where this later measure fulfils the requirements for recognition in the requested State;
- (f) if the procedure provided in Article 33 has not been complied with.

Article 24

Without prejudice to Article 23, paragraph 1, any interested person may request from the competent authorities of a Contracting State that they decide on the recognition or non-recognition of a measure taken in another Contracting State. The procedure is governed by the law of the requested State.

Article 25

The authority of the requested State is bound by the findings of fact on which the authority of the State where the measure was taken based its jurisdiction.

Article 26

(1) If measures taken in one Contracting State and enforceable there require enforcement in another Contracting State, they shall, upon request by an interested party, be declared enforceable or registered for the purpose of enforcement in that other State according to the procedure provided in the law of the latter State.

(2) Each Contracting State shall apply to the declaration of enforceability or registration a simple and rapid procedure.

(3) The declaration of enforceability or registration may be refused only for one of the reasons set out in Article 23, paragraph 2.

Article 27

Without prejudice to such review as is necessary in the application of the preceding Articles, there shall be no review of the merits of the measure taken.

Article 28

Measures taken in one Contracting State and declared enforceable, or registered for the purpose of enforcement, in another Contracting State shall be enforced in the latter State as if they had been taken by the authorities of that State. Enforcement takes place in accordance with the law of the requested State to the extent provided by such law, taking into consideration the best interests of the child.

CHAPTER V - CO-OPERATION

Article 29

(1) A Contracting State shall designate a Central Authority to discharge the duties which are imposed by the Convention on such authorities.

(2) Federal States, States with more than one system of law or States having autonomous territorial units shall be free to appoint more than one Central Authority and to specify the territorial or personal extent of their functions. Where a State has appointed more than one Central Authority, it shall designate the Central Authority to which any communication may be addressed for transmission to the appropriate Central Authority within that State.

Article 30

(1) Central Authorities shall co-operate with each other and promote co-operation amongst the competent authorities in their States to achieve the purposes of the Convention.

(2) They shall, in connection with the application of the Convention, take appropriate steps to provide information as to the laws of, and services available in, their States relating to the protection of children.

Article 31

The Central Authority of a Contracting State, either directly or through public authorities or other bodies, shall take all appropriate steps to -

(a) facilitate the communications and offer the assistance provided for in Articles 8 and 9 and in this Chapter;

(b) facilitate, by mediation, conciliation or similar means, agreed solutions for the protection of the person or property of the child in situations to which the Convention applies;

(c) provide, on the request of a competent authority of another Contracting State, assistance in discovering the whereabouts of a child where it appears that the child may be present and in need of protection within the territory of the requested State.

Article 32

On a request made with supporting reasons by the Central Authority or other competent authority of any Contracting State with which the child has a substantial connection, the Central Authority of the Contracting State in which the child is habitually resident and present may, directly or through public authorities or other bodies,

(a) provide a report on the situation of the child;

(b) request the competent authority of its State to consider the need to take measures for the protection of the person or property of the child.

Article 33

(1) If an authority having jurisdiction under Articles 5 to 10 contemplates the placement of the child in a foster family or institutional care, or the provision of care by kafala or an analogous institution, and if such placement or such provision of care is to take place in another Contracting State, it shall first consult with the Central Authority or other competent authority of the latter State. To that effect it shall transmit a report on the child together with the reasons for the proposed placement or provision of care.

(2) The decision on the placement or provision of care may be made in the requesting State only if the Central Authority or other competent authority of the requested State has consented to the placement or provision of care, taking into account the child's best interests.

Article 34

(1) Where a measure of protection is contemplated, the competent authorities under the Convention, if the situation of the child so requires, may request any authority of another Contracting State which has information relevant to the protection of the child to communicate such information.

(2) A Contracting State may declare that requests under paragraph 1 shall be communicated to its authorities only through its Central Authority.

Article 35

(1) The competent authorities of a Contracting State may request the authorities of another Contracting State to assist in the implementation of measures of protection taken under this Convention, especially in securing the effective exercise of rights of access as well as of the right to maintain direct contacts on a regular basis.

(2) The authorities of a Contracting State in which the child does not habitually reside may, on the request of a parent residing in that State who is seeking to obtain or to maintain access to the child, gather information or evidence and may make a finding on the suitability of that parent to exercise access and on the conditions under which access is to be exercised. An authority exercising jurisdiction under Articles 5 to 10 to determine an application concerning access to the child, shall admit and consider such information, evidence and finding before reaching its decision.

(3) An authority having jurisdiction under Articles 5 to 10 to decide on access may adjourn a proceeding pending the outcome of a request made under paragraph 2, in particular, when it is considering an application to restrict or terminate access rights granted in the State of the child's former habitual residence.

(4) Nothing in this Article shall prevent an authority having jurisdiction under Articles 5 to 10 from taking provisional measures pending the outcome of the request made under paragraph 2.

Article 36

In any case where the child is exposed to a serious danger, the competent authorities of the Contracting State where measures for the protection of the child have been taken or are under consideration, if they are informed that the child's residence has changed to, or that the child is present in another State, shall inform the authorities of that other State about the danger involved and the measures taken or under consideration.

Article 37

An authority shall not request or transmit any information under this Chapter if to do so would, in its opinion, be likely to place the child's person or property in danger, or constitute a serious threat to the liberty or life of a member of the child's family.

Article 38

(1) Without prejudice to the possibility of imposing reasonable charges for the provision of services, Central Authorities and other public authorities of Contracting States shall bear their own costs in applying the provisions of this Chapter.

(2) Any Contracting State may enter into agreements with one or more other Contracting States concerning the allocation of charges.

Article 39

Any Contracting State may enter into agreements with one or more other Contracting States with a view to improving the application of this Chapter in their mutual relations. The States which have concluded such an agreement shall transmit a copy to the depositary of the Convention.

CHAPTER VI - GENERAL PROVISIONS

Article 40

(1) The authorities of the Contracting State of the child's habitual residence, or of the Contracting State where a measure of protection has been taken, may deliver to the person having parental responsibility or to the person entrusted with protection of the child's person or property, at his or her request, a certificate indicating the capacity in which that person is entitled to act and the powers conferred upon him or her.

(2) The capacity and powers indicated in the certificate are presumed to be vested in that person, in the absence of proof to the contrary.

(3) Each Contracting State shall designate the authorities competent to draw up the certificate.

IFLA FAMILY LAW ARBITRATION SCHEME RULES (4TH EDITION, 2015)

Article 1 - Introductory

1.1 The Family Law Arbitration Scheme ('the Scheme') is a scheme under which financial or property disputes with a family background may be resolved by arbitration.

1.2 The Scheme is administered and run by the Institute of Family Law Arbitrators Limited ('IFLA'), a company limited by guarantee whose members are the Chartered Institute of Arbitrators ('CIArb'), Resolution and the Family Law Bar Association ('FLBA').

1.3 Disputes referred to the Scheme will be arbitrated in accordance with:

(a) the provisions of the Arbitration Act 1996 ('the Act'),both mandatory and non-mandatory;

(b) these Rules, to the extent that they exclude, replace or modify the non-mandatory provisions of the Act; and

(c) the agreement of the parties, to the extent that that excludes, replaces or modifies the non-mandatory provisions of the Act or these Rules; except that the parties may not agree to exclude, replace or modify Art.3 (Applicable Law).

1.4 The parties may not amend or modify these Rules or any procedure under them after the appointment of an arbitrator unless the arbitrator agrees to such amendment or modification; and may not amend or modify Art.3 (Applicable Law) in any event.

1.5 Expressions used in these Rules which are also used in the Act have the same meaning as they do in the Act and any reference to a section number means the section of the Act so numbered, unless otherwise indicated.

Article 2 - Scope of the Scheme

2.1 The Scheme covers financial and property disputes arising from:
(a) marriage and its breakdown (including financial provision on divorce, judicial separation or nullity);
(b) civil partnership and its breakdown;
(c) co-habitation and the ending of co-habitation;
(d) parenting or those sharing parental responsibility;
(e) provision for dependants from the estate of the deceased.

2.2 The Scheme covers (but is not limited to) claims which would come within the following statutes:
(a) the Married Women's Property Act 1882, s.17;
(b) the Matrimonial Causes Act 1973, Part II;
(c) the Inheritance (Provision for Family and Dependants) Act 1975;
(d) the Matrimonial and Family Proceedings Act 1984, s.12 (financial relief after overseas divorce);
(e) the Children Act 1989, Sched.1;
(f) the Trusts of Land and Appointment of Trustees Act 1996;
(g) the Civil Partnership Act 2004 Sched.5, or Sched.7, Part 1, para.2 (financial relief after overseas dissolution).

2.3 The Scheme does not apply to disputes directly concerning:
(a) the liberty of individuals;
(b) the status either of individuals or of their relationship;
(c) the care or parenting of children;
(d) bankruptcy or insolvency;
(e) any person or organisation which is not a party to the arbitration.

Article 3 - Applicable law

3. The arbitrator will decide the substance of the dispute only in accordance with the law of England and Wales. The arbitrator may have regard to, and admit evidence of, the law of another country insofar as, and in the same way as, a Judge exercising the jurisdiction of the High Court would do so.

Article 4 - Starting the arbitration

4.1 The parties may refer a dispute to arbitration under the Scheme by making an agreement to arbitrate in Form ARB1, signed by both parties or their legal representatives, and submitting it to IFLA.

4.2 IFLA has set up a Panel of arbitrators who are experienced family law professionals, are Members of the Chartered Institute of Arbitrators and have received specific training in arbitrating family disputes ('the Panel').

4.3.1 The parties may agree to nominate a particular arbitrator from the Panel; and may, if they are agreed, approach a particular arbitrator directly. Any arbitrator directly approached must refer the approach to IFLA before accepting appointment in order to facilitate the completion of Form ARB1 before the arbitration commences. IFLA will offer the appointment to the agreed arbitrator. If the appointment is not accepted by their first choice of arbitrator the parties may, if they agree, make a second or subsequent choice. Otherwise it will be offered to another member of the Panel chosen by IFLA in accordance with paragraph 4.3.3 below.

4.3.2 Alternatively, the parties may agree on a shortlist of arbitrators from the Panel any one of whom would be acceptable to them, and may ask IFLA to select one of the arbitrators on the shortlist without reference to any criteria. In this case, IFLA will offer the appointment to one of the shortlisted arbitrators chosen at random. If the appointment is not accepted by the first choice of arbitrator, IFLA will offer the appointment to a second or subsequent shortlisted arbitrator, similarly chosen at random. If none of the shortlisted arbitrators accepts the appointment, IFLA will inform the parties and invite them to submit further agreed names.

4.3.3 In all other cases (including if so requested by the parties) IFLA will offer the appointment to a sole arbitrator from the Panel whom it considers appropriate having regard to the nature of the dispute; any preferences expressed by the parties as to the qualifications, areas of experience, expertise or other attributes of the arbitrator; and preference expressed by the parties as to the geographical location of the arbitration; and any other relevant circumstances.

4.4 If, after considering Form ARB 1 and any representations from the parties, either IFLA or the arbitrator considers that the dispute is not suitable for arbitration under the Scheme, then the parties will be so advised and their reference of the matter to the Scheme will be treated as withdrawn.

4.5 The arbitration will be regarded as commenced when the arbitrator communicates to the parties his or her acceptance of the appointment.

4.6 Except as provided in Art 47, a party to an arbitration under this Scheme may be represented in the proceedings by a lawyer or other person chosen by him; or if he is acting in person, may receive the advice of a McKenzie Friend.

4.7 If at any time the arbitrator forms the view that the participation of a non-lawyer representative or the assistance of a McKenzie Friend unreasonably impedes or is likely to impede the conduct of the arbitral proceedings or the administration of justice, he may direct that the relevant party should not continue to be so represented or assisted, as the case may be, and will state his reasons in writing.

Article 5 - Arbitrator's appointment

5.1 Before accepting the appointment or as soon as the relevant facts are known, the arbitrator will disclose to the parties any actual or potential conflict of interest or any matter that might give rise to justifiable doubts as to his or her impartiality.

5.2 In the event of such disclosure, the parties, or either of them (as appropriate), may waive any objection to the arbitrator continuing to act, in which case the arbitrator may commence or continue with the arbitration. If an objection is maintained, the arbitrator will decide whether to continue to act, subject to any agreement by the parties to revoke his or her authority or intervention by the court.

5.3 After accepting appointment, the arbitrator may not subsequently act in relation to the same dispute in a different capacity.

5.4 If the arbitrator ceases to hold office through revocation of his or her authority, removal by the court, resignation or death, or is otherwise unable, or refuses, to act, and either party or the existing arbitrator so requests, IFLA may appoint a replacement arbitrator from the Panel.

5.5 The replacement arbitrator may determine whether and if so to what extent the previous proceedings should stand.

Article 6 - Communications between parties, the arbitrator and IFLA

6.1 Any communication between the arbitrator and either party will be copied to the other party.

6.2 Unless agreed by the parties, the arbitrator will designate one party as the lead party. For the purposes of the Act, the lead party will equate to a claimant, but will be formally referred to in the arbitration as the 'Applicant'. The other party will equate to a respondent, and will be formally referred to in the arbitration as the 'Respondent'.

6.3 The arbitrator will not discuss any aspect of the dispute or of the arbitration with either party or their legal representatives in the absence of the other party or their legal representatives, unless such communication is solely for the purpose of making administrative arrangements.

6.4 Neither IFLA, the CIArb, Resolution nor the FLBA will be required to enter into any correspondence concerning the arbitration or its outcome.

Article 7- Powers of the arbitrator

7.1 The arbitrator will have all the powers given to an arbitrator by the Act including those contained in section 35 (consolidation of proceedings and concurrent hearings); and section 39 (provisional orders), but limited as provided by Art.7.2.

7.2 In relation to substantive relief of an interim or final character, the arbitrator will have the power to make orders or awards to the same extent and in the same or similar form as would a Judge exercising the jurisdiction of the High Court. (For the avoidance of doubt, the arbitrator's power does not extend to interim injunctions; committal; or jurisdiction over non-parties without their agreement.)

7.3 The arbitrator will have the power to award interest in accordance with section 49 (interest) whether or not it is specifically claimed.

7.4 If the arbitrator considers that the dispute is not suitable for arbitration under the Scheme the arbitrator will have the power to terminate the proceedings.

Article 8 - Powers of the arbitrator concerning procedure

8.1 The arbitrator will decide all procedural and evidential matters (including, but not limited to, those referred to in section 34(2)), subject to the right of the parties to agree any matter (if necessary, with the concurrence of the arbitrator (see Art. 1.4)).

8.2 In accordance with section 37 (power to appoint experts), the arbitrator may appoint experts to report on specific issues or prepare valuations.

8.3 The arbitrator may limit the number of expert witnesses to be called by any party or may direct that no expert be called on any issue or issues or that expert evidence may be called only with the permission of the arbitrator.

8.4 Further, and/or in particular, the arbitrator will have the power to:

(a) direct a party to produce information, documents or other materials in a specified manner and/or within a specified time;

(b) give directions in relation to any property which is the subject of the proceedings or as to which any question arises in the proceedings, and which is owned by or is in the possession or control of a party to the proceedings for the inspection, photographing, valuation, preservation, custody or detention of the property by the tribunal, an expert or a party.

8.5 If, without showing sufficient cause, a party fails to comply with its obligations under section 40 (general duty of parties) or with these Rules, or is in default as set out in section 41(4) (failure to attend a hearing or make submissions), then, after giving that party due notice, the arbitrator may continue the proceedings in the absence of that party or without any written evidence or submissions on their behalf and may make an award on the basis of the evidence before him or her.

8.6 The parties agree that if one of them fails to comply with a peremptory order made by the arbitrator and another party wishes to apply to the court for an order requiring compliance under s.42 (enforcement of peremptory orders of tribunal), the powers of the court under that section are available.

Article 9 - Form of procedure

9.1 The parties are free to agree as to the form of procedure (if necessary, with the concurrence of the arbitrator (see Art.1.4)) and, in particular, to adopt a documents-only procedure or some other simplified or expedited procedure.

9.2 If there is no such agreement, the arbitrator will have the widest possible discretion to adopt procedures suitable to the circumstances of the particular case in accordance with section 33 (general duty of the tribunal).

Article 10 - General procedure

10.1 Generally, on commencement of the arbitration, the arbitrator will invite the parties to make submissions setting out briefly their respective views as to the nature of the dispute, the issues, what form of procedure should be adopted, the timetable and any other relevant matters.

10.2 If appropriate, the arbitrator may convene a preliminary meeting, telephone conference or other suitable forum for exchange of views.

10.3 Within a reasonable time of ascertaining the parties' views, the arbitrator will give directions and set a timetable for the procedural steps in the arbitration, including (but not limited to) the following:

(a) written statements of case;
(b) disclosure and production of documents as between the parties;
(c) the exchange of witness statements;
(d) the number and type of expert witnesses, exchange of their reports and meetings between them;
(e) arrangements for any meeting or hearing and the procedures to be adopted at these events;
(f) time limits to be imposed on oral submissions or the examination of witnesses, or any other procedure for controlling the length of hearings.

10.4 The arbitrator may at any time direct any of the following to be delivered in writing:

(a) submissions on behalf of any party;
(b) questions to be put to any witness;
(c) answers by any witness to specific questions.

Article 11 - Applications for directions as to procedural or evidential matters

11.1 The arbitrator may direct a time limit for making or responding to applications for directions as to procedural or evidential matters.

11.2 Any application by a party for directions as to procedural or evidential matters will be accompanied by such evidence and/or submissions as the applicant may consider appropriate or as the arbitrator may direct.

11.3 A party responding to such an application will, if feasible, have a reasonable opportunity to consider and agree the order or directions proposed.

11.4 Any agreement will be communicated to the arbitrator promptly and will be subject to the arbitrator's concurrence, if necessary (see Art. 1.4).

11.5 Unless the arbitrator convenes a meeting, telephone conference or other forum for exchange of views, any response to the application will be followed by an opportunity for the party applying to comment on that response; and the arbitrator will give directions within a reasonable time after receiving the applicant's comments.

Article 12 - Alternative procedure

12.1 In any case where it is appropriate, the parties may agree or the arbitrator may decide to adopt the procedure set out in this Article.

12.2 The parties may at any stage agree (with the concurrence of the arbitrator) or the arbitrator may direct any variation or addition to the following steps and/or timetable. In particular, the arbitrator may at any stage allow time for the parties to consider their positions and pursue negotiations with a view to arriving at an amicable settlement (see, also, Arts.17.1 and 17.2).

12.3 Within 56 days of the arbitrator communicating to the parties his or her acceptance of the appointment, each party will complete and send to the arbitrator and to the other party a sworn statement as to their financial situation (in the form of the 'Form E' or 'Form E1' Financial Statement in accordance with the Family Procedure Rules 2010, as appropriate) together with such further evidence or information as the arbitrator may direct.

12.4 Within 28 days of receipt of the other party's financial statement, each party may send to the arbitrator and to the other party a questionnaire raising questions and/or requesting information and/or documents.

12.5 Within 14 days of receipt of a questionnaire, a party may send to the arbitrator and to the other party reasoned objections to answering any of the questions or meeting any of the requests, together with a submission as to whether a preliminary meeting is required.

12.6 Within 14 days of receipt of objections or, if there is a preliminary meeting, within a reasonable time after that meeting, the arbitrator will direct in respect of each party:

(a) which questions are to be answered and which requests are to be met, together with the time within which these things are to be done;

(b) which property is to be valued, who is to undertake the valuation, how they are to be appointed and the time within which the valuation is to be carried out; and

(c) any other steps for providing information, dealing with enquiries or clarifying issues as may be appropriate.

12.7 Within a reasonable time of receipt from both parties of replies to questionnaires, valuations and any other information as may have been required, the arbitrator may convene a further meeting to review progress, address outstanding issues and consider what further directions are necessary.

12.8 The arbitrator will give detailed directions for all further procedural steps in the arbitration including (but not limited to) the following:

(a) the drawing up of lists of issues and schedules of assets;

(b) written submissions;

(c) arrangements for any meeting or hearing and the procedures to be adopted at these events;

(d) time limits to be imposed on oral submissions or the examination of witnesses, or any other procedure for controlling the length of hearings.

Article 13 - Awards

13.1 The arbitrator will deliver an award within a reasonable time after the conclusion of the proceedings or the relevant part of the proceedings.

13.2 Any award will be in writing, will state the seat of the arbitration, will be dated and signed by the arbitrator, and will contain sufficient reasons to show why the arbitrator has reached the decisions contained in it, unless the parties agree otherwise or the award is by consent.

13.3 Once an award has been made, it will be final and binding on the parties, subject to the following:

(a) any challenge to the award by any available arbitral process of appeal or review or in accordance with the provisions of Part 1 of the Act;

(b) insofar as the subject matter of the award requires it to be embodied in a court order (see Art. 13.4), any changes which the court making that order may require;

(c) insofar as the award provides for continuing payments to be made by one party to another, or to a child or children, a subsequent award or court order reviewing and varying or revoking the provision for continuing payments, and which supersedes an existing award.

13.4 If and so far as the subject matter of the award makes it necessary, the parties will apply to an appropriate court for an order in the same or similar terms as the award or the relevant part of the award and will take all reasonably necessary steps to see that such an order is made. In this context, 'an appropriate court' means a court which has jurisdiction to make a substantive order in the same or similar terms as the award, whether on primary application or on transfer from another division of the court.

13.5 The arbitrator may refuse to deliver an award to the parties except upon full payment of his or her fees or expenses. Subject to this entitlement, the arbitrator will send a copy of the award to each party or its legal representatives.

Article 14 - Costs

14.1 In this Article any reference to costs is a reference to the costs of the arbitration as defined in section 59 (costs of the arbitration) including the fees and expenses of IFLA, unless otherwise indicated.

14.2 The arbitrator may require the parties to pay his or her fees and expenses accrued during the course of the arbitration at such interim stages as may be agreed with the parties, and in the absence of agreement, at reasonable intervals.

14.3 The arbitrator may order either party to provide security for the arbitrator's fees and expenses and the fees and expenses of IFLA.

14.4 Unless otherwise agreed by the parties, the arbitrator will make an award allocating costs as between the parties in accordance with the following general principle:

(a) the parties will bear the arbitrator's fees and expenses and the fees and expenses of IFLA in equal shares;

(b) there will be no order or award requiring one party to pay the legal or other costs of another party.

This principle is subject to the arbitrator's overriding discretion set out in Art. 14.5.

14.5 Where it is appropriate to do so because of the conduct of a party in relation to the arbitration (whether before or during it), the arbitrator may at any stage order that party:

(a) to bear a larger than equal share, and up to the full amount, of the arbitrator's fees and expenses and the fees and expenses of IFLA;

(b) to pay the legal or other costs of another party; and may make an award accordingly.

14.6 In deciding whether, and if so, how to exercise the discretion set out in Art.14.5, the arbitrator will have regard to the following:

(a) any failure by a party to comply with these Rules or any order or directions which the arbitrator considers relevant;

(b) any open offer to settle made by a party;

(c) whether it was reasonable for a party to raise, pursue or contest a particular allegation or issue;

(d) the manner in which a party has pursued or responded to a claim or a particular allegation or issue;

(e) any other aspect of a party's conduct in relation to the arbitration which the arbitrator considers relevant; and

(f) the financial effect on the parties of any costs order or award.

14.7 Unless the parties agree otherwise, no offer to settle which is not an open offer to settle shall be admissible at any stage of the arbitration.

14.8 These rules as to costs will not apply to applications made to the court where costs fall to be determined by the court.

Article 15 - Conclusion of the arbitration

15.1 The agreement to arbitrate will be discharged (and any current arbitration will terminate) if:

(a) a party to the arbitration agreement dies; or

(b) a party to the arbitration agreement lacks, or loses, capacity (within the meaning of the Mental Capacity Act 2005); except that:

(i) if the party is represented by an attorney who has the power so to act, the attorney may, in his or her discretion, continue with the arbitration or terminate it;

(ii) if a Deputy is appointed by the Court of Protection in relation to that party and has the power so to act, the Deputy may, in his or her discretion, continue with the arbitration or terminate it.

15.2 The arbitration will be terminated:

(a) If the arbitrator considers that the dispute is not suitable for arbitration under the Scheme and terminates the proceedings;

(b) If and insofar as a court entertains concurrent legal proceedings and declines to stay them in favour of arbitration;

(c) If the parties settle the dispute and, in accordance with section 51 (settlement), the arbitrator terminates the proceedings;

(d) If the parties agree in writing to discontinue the arbitration and notify the arbitrator accordingly;

(e) On the arbitrator making a final award dealing with all the issues, subject to any entitlement of the parties to challenge the award by any available arbitral process of appeal or review or in accordance with the provisions of Part 1 of the Act.

Article 16 - Confidentiality

16.1 The general principle is that the arbitration and its outcome are confidential, except insofar as disclosure may be necessary to challenge, implement, enforce or vary an award (see Art. 13.3(c)), in relation to applications to the court or as may be compelled by law.

16.2 All documents, statements, information and other materials disclosed by a party will be held by any other party and their legal representatives in confidence and used solely for the purpose of the arbitration, unless otherwise agreed by the disclosing party or compelled by law.

16.3 Any transcript of the proceedings will be provided to all parties and to the arbitrator. It will similarly be confidential and used solely for the purpose of the arbitration, implementation or enforcement of any award or applications to the court, unless otherwise agreed by the parties or compelled by law.

16.4 The arbitrator will not be called as a witness by any party either to testify or to produce any documents or materials received or generated during the course of the proceedings in relation to any aspect of the arbitration, unless with the agreement of the arbitrator or compelled by law.

Article 17- General

17.1 At relevant stages of the arbitration, the arbitrator may encourage the parties to consider using an alternative dispute resolution procedure other than arbitration, such as mediation or negotiation, in relation to the dispute or a particular aspect of the dispute.

17.2 If the parties agree to use an alternative dispute resolution procedure such as mediation or negotiation, then the arbitrator will facilitate its use and may, if appropriate, stay the arbitration or a particular aspect of the arbitration for an appropriate period of time for that purpose.

17.3 In the event that the dispute is settled (following a mediation or otherwise), the parties will inform the arbitrator promptly and section 51 (settlement) will apply. Fees and expenses accrued due to arbitrator by that stage will remain payable.

17.4 The parties will inform the arbitrator promptly of any proposed application to the court and will provide him or her with copies of all documentation intended to be used in any such application.

17.5 IFLA, the CIArb, Resolution, the FLBA, their employees and agents will not be liable:

(a) for anything done or omitted in the actual or purported appointment or nomination of an arbitrator, unless the act or omission is shown to have been in bad faith;

(b) by reason of having appointed or nominated an arbitrator, for anything done or omitted by the arbitrator (or his employees or agents) in the discharge or purported discharge of his functions as an arbitrator;

(c) for any consequences if, for whatever reason, the arbitral process does not result in an award or, where necessary, a court order embodying an award by which the matters to be determined are resolved.

INDEX